This Day in Baptist History

E. Wayne Thompson
and David L. Cummins

366 daily devotions

drawn from the Baptist heritage

BOB JONES UNIVERSITY PRESS
GREENVILLE, SOUTH CAROLINA 29614

Library of Congress Cataloging-in-Publication Data

Thompson, E. Wayne (Edmond Wayne), 1926-
This day in Baptist history : 366 daily devotions drawn from the Baptist heritage / E. Wayne Thompson and David L. Cummins.
p. cm.
Includes bibliographical references (pp. 553-63) and index.
ISBN 0-89084-709-6
1. Devotional calendars—Baptists. 2. Baptists—Prayer-books and devotions—English. 3. Baptists—History. I. Cummins, David L., 1929- . II. Title.
BV4810.T46 1993
286.1' 09—dc20 93-32398
CIP

NOTE:
The fact that materials produced by other publishers are referred to in this volume does not constitute an endorsement by Bob Jones University Press of the content or theological position of materials produced by such publishers. The position of Bob Jones University Press, and the University itself, is well known. Any references and ancillary materials are listed as an aid to the reader and in an attempt to maintain the accepted academic standards of the publishing industry.

This Day in Baptist History
by E. Wayne Thompson and David L. Cummins

Edited by Manda Cooper
Cover designed by Dan VanLeeuwen
Cover photos by George R. Collins

Greenville, South Carolina 29614

Printed in the United States of America

ISBN 0-89084-709-6

15 14 13 12 11 10 9 8 7 6 5

Contents

Preface

Every book, ministry, project, or enterprise begins with a vision. ''Where there is no vision, the people perish'' (Prov. 29:18). After many years of ministry, the authors of this book have concluded that in our affluent, self-sufficient society there is a great need for real, experiential knowledge of God and for a revival of a more intimate relationship with the Almighty. Today's pragmatic approach to the ministry has caused Christians to rely more on methodologies than on the power of the Holy Spirit. Because of this viewpoint, Baptists also have not valued their heritage enough to explore in depth their roots.

We have found much ignorance among Baptists concerning our distinctives; some even count Baptists among the Protestants, believing our roots go back with the reformers into Rome. Present-day Baptists have little understanding that our spiritual forefathers were sanctified and denominated by certain distinctives that involved convictions concerning their knowledge of God and their faithfulness to the teachings of His Holy Word.

As a result of our individual and combined research, we have concluded that there have been and continue to be individuals and local churches who have held, and continue to hold in succession, *principles* for which Bible-believing Baptists are distinguished and which have been notable from the beginning of the New Testament churches. These individuals and churches never yielded allegiance to or were identified with Rome or any other church/state hierarchy. Because of their zealous resistance to these religio-political powers and their opposition to these pseudo-doctrines, countless Christians were persecuted in the severest manner. Many, after suffering, forfeited their lives for the principles set forth in the Scriptures they held so dear.

These saints were designated in different ways and with varying names: some after their outstanding leaders, others after their locations, and yet others for those principles peculiarly different than that of the established religion. They were *among* those called Paulicians, Montenses, Donatists, Novations, Waldenses, Petrobrussians, Albigenses, Lollards, Anabaptists, and other ancient sects. We emphasize *among* because not all Waldenses or Anabaptists, and so on, were Baptists. For example, some Waldenses had enough Romish characteristics and lack of conviction that under the pressure of persecution they recanted and yielded to Rome. There were those among the Anabaptists who went to great unbiblical and fanatical extremes, repudiating true Baptist principles. The enemies of the Baptists have always pointed to these heretical groups in an effort to destroy Baptist testimony and influence. Not all Anabaptists held to Baptist beliefs, and at times those holding to distinctive Baptist principles were not denominated Baptists. Others, usually enemies, give names merely to reproach a people who hold tenaciously to certain biblical principles. When "the disciples were called Christians first in Antioch" (Acts 11:26), the title was one of reproach in the eyes of the world, but one of great honor and responsibility in the hearts of the disciples because it involved the name and character of their Lord. The name *Baptist* relates one with that blessed ordinance that publicly identifies one with that same name and character of the same Lord and His finished work of redemption. Even in our day we can accurately say, "Not all who are called Baptists truly hold to Baptist distinctives, and many who hold to Baptist distinctives are not called Baptists."

Because "true Baptists" have held firmly to biblical principles, the fires of persecution have raged about them, often obliterating entire communities and vast libraries of records concerning their history and principles. Often there was enough written by their enemies who desired to wipe their memory from the face of the earth to establish the existence of this people and their principles. Most of the persecution was brought upon the Baptists by their antipedobaptist position. Truly we can say that from the most ancient time, the Baptists have traveled a road of persecution from Jerusalem to Asia, to Africa, to Europe, and to America. While Bunyan and many others were experiencing the burning stakes, pillories, and prisons of England, John Clarke, Obadiah Holmes, and others were experiencing similar persecution as they planted the standard of truth and freedom of conscience in the wilds of New England.

The spirit of the episcopacy was ever present in England, even during the republic under Cromwell, for whom the Baptists fought valiantly. Cromwell's army was filled with Baptists whose hope was liberty of conscience. Never before had the world seen such an army. Many of the officers preached, and the privates were constantly busy searching the Scriptures. These same Baptists were valiant for truth, and on the battlefields in the republic's army, they continued to be persecuted by a Protestant establishment. This same establishment was continued in the New World by the Congregationalists in New England and the Anglicans in the southern colonies, particularly Virginia, where dunking chairs, whipping posts, pillories, and prisons were familiar places of suffering for our Baptist forefathers. Over forty Baptist preachers were arrested and imprisoned for vagrancy and disturbing the peace because they preached the gospel of the grace of God without church/state licensure or state/church ordination. One can find in the pages of this volume documented evidence that those statesmen who had the greatest part in bringing forth the documents of freedom and liberty in this nation were largely influenced by the principles, sufferings, and petitions of the humble people called Baptists.

One can trace Baptist history and testimony from ancient times to America, through its wilderness, and on to the uttermost parts of the earth. Although these great, but humble, people have suffered severe persecution, not one instance of persecuting others can be traced to them. While religious establishments bring forth the mechanism of persecution, the very nature of Baptist principles are repulsed by such actions. In more recent years, Baptists have endured the fires of persecution in lands dominated by communism, Romanism, and Islam. Preaching the gospel of the grace of God and planting churches continues as our mandate.

This volume has unfolded purposely as a literary hybrid. We desire it to be challenging and inspirational, as a devotional, and at the same time informative, as a history. We desire to provide the reader with truth that will motivate him to investigate further our great spiritual heritage. The footnotes and selected bibliography provide the investigator with over two hundred valuable sources of available material. We believe this volume is a must for the libraries of pastors, churches, colleges, and Christian day schools. It can be used as a source of good, factual sermon illustrations and a treasure trove for preparing devotionals. All teachers of Baptist history should have this book on their required reading list. Pastors should encourage their members to make it a part of their personal and family devotions. *This Day in Baptist History* provides a knowledge of great men of God after which to pattern lives.

Because historical records previous to the sixteenth century listed years and months but not the day, the vast majority of information is from the sixteenth century onward. We want to convey the message of what happened in history on the very day the person is reading. Thus we have written *This Day in Baptist History* and make the volume available to the public with the prayer that it will inform them of "The People Called Baptists," challenge them to cherish such a great spiritual heritage, and motivate them to preserve this witness and testimony for future generations by propagating the gospel of the grace of God in Christ Jesus and by memorializing Baptist principles. This book is our attempt to speak the truth in love.

In the Beloved One,
David L. Cummins
E. Wayne Thompson

Acknowledgments

This is to express our sincere appreciation to *Faith Baptist Church* of Warren, Michigan, which has assisted in so many ways in the publication of this volume. The membership has listened to many of the recorded events in sermons presented by Pastor Cummins and has sheltered their pastor by granting him the necessary time to read and do research from Baptist history, with their complete cooperation.

Mrs. Judy Pittman, church secretary, and her daughter, Davette Pittman, have carefully read the manuscript, given most helpful criticism, and typed many corrections into the computer.

Mrs. Sue Ward, assisted by Mrs. Jerry Braschayko, has spent a multitude of hours typing and retyping the manuscripts.

The following members of the congregation have volunteered much of their time in proofreading the manuscripts and have offered effective suggestions: Jean Allam, Flossie Battishill, Wayne Bradley, Jerry Braschayko, Paul Braschayko, Marilyn Bugay, Sue Hermes, Dr. Mary Kraus, Dan McKnight, Davette Pittman, Denise Scally, the Reverend Richard St. Amand, Sue Ward, Joanna Weishan, Marilyn Wipf, and Jim Wright.

The Reverend Marvin L. Summers of Dearborn, Michigan, has graciously provided fine service in seeking and obtaining used volumes of Baptist history to aid the authors in their research.

The authors also wish to thank Mr. James R. Lynch, archivist of the American Baptist Historical Society in Rochester, New York, for assisting Pastor Cummins during a diligent week of research in that amazing treasure trove of history.

To all of these, we, the authors, are greatly indebted and wish to acknowledge their valuable service in making this publication possible. But especially we wish to thank our wives—two magnificent women, both named "Mary"—for their patience and forbearance during the long period of research and production. Without them, this effort could never have been successful.

January

January 1—The Baptist Witness Is Introduced in Georgia

Scripture: Acts 18:1-11

The history of the "Separate Baptists" has been an ignored subject of our Baptist history, and yet we cannot account for the rapid growth of Baptists in the South and the proliferation of the Southern Baptist Convention without considering the influence of this group. Though our primary purpose is not to deal with the Separates, we will read much of their work in these pages.

The Separates were led primarily by Shubal Stearns (North Carolina), Daniel Marshall (Georgia), and Samuel Harriss (Virginia). Everywhere these men went churches were established and a mighty moving of the Holy Spirit was experienced. Our subject now is Daniel Marshall who, after having ministered in South Carolina, began incursions into Georgia. Though there was a trace of Baptists in Georgia prior to his efforts, Marshall planted at Kiokee the first Baptist church in the province. The story of that ministry is amazing!

On January 1, 1771, Marshall moved to Georgia, and by the spring of 1772, he had led a small congregation in the formation of the First Baptist Church of Kiokee and served as pastor until his death in 1784.[1] The inspiring account of that ministry will be shared on several pages of this volume, but just now we are interested in the narrative of the beginning of the Kiokee church.

A Georgia law of 1757 prohibited any worship not "according to the rites and ceremonies of the Church of England," but Marshall led a "brush arbor" service. As he bowed in prayer, he was interrupted by a heavy hand on his shoulder and the declaration, "You are my prisoner!" The sixty-five-year-old preacher stood to his feet only to hear the young constable inform him that he had "preached in the parish of St. Paul." Before Marshall could assure the constable that he would appear in court the next day, Mrs. Marshall addressed the officer of the law and quoted Scripture which the Lord ultimately used to bring about the official's conviction and conversion.

When he appeared in court the next day, Marshall was ordered to leave Georgia. His son, Abraham, quoted the elder Marshall as responding, "Whether it be right to obey God or man, judge ye," and he went on his way preaching with great power. This incident was not without its spiritual fruit, however, because the twenty-one-year-old constable, Samuel Cartledge, was gloriously saved and in 1777 was baptized. After serving as a deacon, in 1789 Cartledge was ordained to preach, and he ministered in Georgia and South Carolina until his death at age ninety-three. One of Cartledge's descendants who has continued the gospel ministry has referred to his forebear as the "Colonial 'Saul of Tarsus,' "[2] and we rejoice in this spectacular introduction of Baptist labors in the province of Georgia.

DLC

---

[1]Joe M. King, *A History of South Carolina Baptists* (n.p.: South Carolina Baptist Convention, 1964), p. 340.

[2]Tony W. Cartledge, "Samuel Cartledge: Colonial 'Saul of Tarsus,' " *Viewpoints—Georgia Baptist History* (Georgia Baptist Historical Society), 8 (1982):13-31.

January 2—Taking the Baptist Message to Germany

Scripture: Acts 8:26-40

As a teen-ager Johann Gerhard Oncken left his native Germany for England where the young Lutheran served an apprenticeship under a devout Scottish Presbyterian tradesman. He treasured his Bible and read regularly, but it was only following a serious accident that the young man became sensitive to his personal spiritual needs. After recovering from his near encounter with death, Oncken accepted Christ upon hearing a rousing sermon in a Methodist church, and immediately he thought of becoming a missionary. He later wrote, "From that day I became a witness, albeit a weak one, of God's love to sinners and His all-powerful grace."[1]

Presenting himself for German missionary service, Oncken was sent out by the British Continental Society. The Lutheran faith lacked evangelistic fervor; so Oncken united with the English Reformed Church and set out for Hamburg. His ministry was disapproved by the German state church, and he was forbidden to preach. Thus he resorted to distributing Bibles and became an agent of the Edinburgh Bible Society. During the course of his lifetime, Oncken distributed over two million copies of the Scriptures!

When his wife gave birth to their first child, he began to wonder about having the infant christened. As he studied God's Word, Oncken became convinced that there was no authority in Scripture for infant baptism; and accepting believer's immersion as the true New Testament teaching, Johann longed to be immersed. For five years he could find no one to perform the New Testament ordinance, but in the course of time the Reverend Barnas Sears, an American studying in Germany, met Oncken and six others who desired to be faithful to God's Word. On April 22, 1834, these seven believers became the first fruits of thousands in Germany as they were immersed at night in the river Elbe near Hamburg. The next day these seven were constituted a church, the first Baptist church of modern time in Germany, and Oncken was chosen pastor.

Oncken's life from that time on is an amazing narrative, for within little more than four years, churches were begun in Berlin, Oldenburg, and Stuttgart. Oncken was soon summoned before the magistrates, and the Senate of Hamburg attempted to suppress these Baptists. Finally, in May of 1840, he was arrested and cast in prison for the first of what became numerous imprisonments. This opposition merely caused spiritual advance! Oncken's witness was not limited to Germany, for he carried the work into Denmark and the Netherlands and preached as well in Lithuania, Switzerland, Poland, and Russia.

In 1860 a law was passed giving religious freedom, and on April 17, 1867, the First Baptist Church of Hamburg dedicated a new building seating 1,400 people. On January 2, 1884, "the soul of Mr. Oncken stretched its wings for the land of unfading day, at Zurich, Switzerland,"[2] and the "Apostle of the German Baptists"[3] was ushered home.

DLC

---

[1]Frank T. Hoadley and Benjamin P. Browne, *Baptists Who Dared* (Valley Forge, Pa.: Judson Press, 1980), p. 63.

[2]Rev. G. Winfred Hervey, *The Story of Baptist Missions in Foreign Lands* (St. Louis: C. R. Barnes Publishing Co., 1892), p. 798.

[3]William Cathcart, *The Baptist Encyclopedia,* ed. Louis H. Everts (Philadelphia: Louis H. Everts, 1881), 2:869.

January 3—When God Reached Out to the Delaware Indians

Scripture: Isaiah 55

"Rev. Charles Journeycake. Born December 16, 1817. Died January 3, 1894. A kind and loving father and a friend to the needy; he died as he lived, a pure and upright man, after many years' faithful service in the ministry and as chief adviser for his people, the Delawares."[1] So, in part, reads the inscription upon the white marble monument in the old cemetery at Lightning Creek that marks the burial spot of our subject.

Charles Journeycake was the son of a full-blooded Delaware Indian father, and his mother was Mrs. Sally Journeycake, a Caucasian who spoke English and several Indian dialects. Because of her ability she became an expert interpreter, and when a Methodist mission was started among the Wyandottes on the reservation adjacent to that of the Delawares, Sally became the interpreter. At that time there was not a Christian Delaware in the settlement.

Late in 1827 Mrs. Journeycake became gravely ill, and her husband went to find help for her. During his absence it was supposed that Mrs. Journeycake was dying, but she awoke out of her comatose condition and began praising God. The Word of God that she had heard had registered by the Holy Spirit's power, and she was gloriously saved. She immediately began living for the Lord, and it was in that environment that young Charles was then raised. The testimony of his mother made a marked impression on his young life, and he was saved in 1833 and became the first Delaware Indian to be baptized. Soon thereafter both of his parents were baptized, and so was formed the nucleus of a Baptist church among the Delawares.

In a few short years, Journeycake began to preach in his own language as well as in the Shawnee, Wyandotte, Seneca, and Ottawa dialects. His status among his people continued to grow, and ultimately Journeycake was elected the principal chief of his tribe and became an influential negotiator with the United States Government for his people. In all, he made twenty-four visits to Washington, D.C., as he represented the Delawares.

Though Journeycake was doubtless "the outstanding Native American Baptist clergyman among the Indian tribes,"[2] he was not ordained until he was fifty-five years of age—and then only at the demand of his people. He had been serving as pastor of the Delaware Baptist Church, and a new building had been constructed to serve the more than one hundred members. The new building was dedicated on September 22, 1872, and the following day his ordination took place. Journeycake continued to preach in area revivals and baptized 266 among the various Indian tribes from 1871 through 1880. Following the death of his wife on January 13, 1893, the Reverend Mr. Journeycake's health declined rapidly, and in less than a year, he too was called to his eternal home to be forever with the Lord.

DLC

---

[1]Rev. S. H. Mitchell, *The Indian Chief, Journeycake* (Philadelphia: American Baptist Publication Society, 1895), p. 7.

[2]William Henry Brackney, *The Baptists* (New York: Greenwood Press, 1988), p. 203.

January 4—For Christ Imprisoned, They Preached Through the Grates

Scripture: Ephesians 3

As Paul the Apostle was familiar with the inside of crude prisons, so were William Webber and Joseph Anthony of Virginia. Few men in Virginia suffered more persecution than Webber. He was seized in Chesterfield County, December 7, 1770, and imprisoned in the county jail until March 7, 1771.[1]

When William Webber and Joseph Anthony went from Goochland County across the James River into Chesterfield County, there was not a Baptist in the entire county. These men, being church planters, met with severe treatment. The magistrates, finding that many were turning to righteousness (to madness, as they would state it), and that these young laborers were likely to do them much harm, issued warrants and had them apprehended and cast into prison.[2]

The order book of Chesterfield County, No. 4, page 489, January 4, 1771, records the charges as follows:

> Joseph Anthony and William Webber being brought into court on a warrant issued against them for misbehavior by itinerant preaching in this county being of that sect of dissenters from the Church of England commonly called Anabaptists, and on hearing they acknowledged that

> they had preached in the upper end of this county at a meeting of sundry people there whereupon it is ordered that the said Joseph and William be committed until they enter into recognizance touching the premises themselves in the penalty of one hundred pounds and two Sureties in penalty of fifty pounds each or their respective goods, &c. to be levied &c. for their being of good behavior for the space of one year ensuing.

In Chesterfield County seven Baptist preachers were confined in its jail, which still stands. Some were brutally whipped and several fined.

While in prison Webber and Anthony made regular preaching appointments twice a week, and, as they could not go to the congregations, the congregations came to them. The space around the jail was the meeting place, and the sill of the jail window was the desk upon which their Bibles lay along with their hymnals, while the iron grating was but slight interruption to their earnest utterance of God's truth. The strong bars could confine their bodies but could not confine their voices nor their souls. There were precious revival scenes and scores of conversions to Jesus Christ under those windows.

Baptist principles were largely advertised in Chesterfield County at the expense of the state, and ever since, these principles have molded the sentiments, controlled the consciences, and comforted the hearts of masses of people.

EWT

---

[1]Robert B. Semple, *A History of the Rise and Progress of the Baptists in Virginia* (Richmond: Published by the author, 1810), pp. 422-25.

[2]Lewis Peyton Little, *Imprisoned Preachers and Religious Liberty in Virginia* (Lynchburg, Va.: J. P. Bell Co., 1938), pp. 209-13.

January 5—Being Faithful unto Death

Scripture: Revelation 12:11

Believing, as we do, in the perpetuity of truth, we are delighted to include in this volume several accounts of Anabaptist martyrs of the sixteenth century. The Anabaptists believed in a "free church" composed of regenerate members who had experienced believer's baptism. As Felix Manz expressed it, their ambition was "to bring together those who were willing to accept Christ, obey the Word, and follow in His footsteps, to unite with these by baptism, and to leave the rest in their present conviction."[1]

Felix Manz was born an illegitimate son of a Roman Catholic priest who served as Canon in Zurich. It is apparent that the young Manz was given the education of the privileged classes, for he was well trained in Latin, Greek, and Hebrew. As a young Greek scholar, he joined with others in studying the New Testament with the reformer Ulrich Zwingli and was converted under the reformer's teaching. As the young student continued his study, he became dissatisfied with Zwingli's program of reform, and others joined Manz as they met regularly at his home. It was from these studies in Felix Manz's home that the first believer's baptism among the Brethren was administered in 1525.

These young believers began to follow the New Testament plan in a house-to-house visitation in Zurich, and many others soon followed in "believer's baptism." The reformers looked upon these Anabaptists as a threat, and on October 8, 1525, several of the Anabaptists were arrested and imprisoned. Manz escaped that arrest but was soon apprehended and incarcerated with Conrad Grebel and George Blaurock in the castle at Gruningen. The three were later moved to the Witch's Tower in Zurich and made a successful escape from that facility. However, Manz was rearrested on several occasions and reminds us of the Apostle Paul with his constantly repeated imprisonments.

On January 5, 1587, Felix Manz was sentenced to death "because contrary to Christian order and custom he had become involved in Anabaptism . . . because he confessed to having said that he wanted to gather those who wanted to accept Christ and follow Him, and unite himself with them through baptism." The reformers had demanded the death penalty for rebaptizing in March of 1526, but Felix Manz would be the first victim!

> Manz, according to the sentence, was taken bound from the Wellenberg prison past the fish market to the boat. All along the way he witnessed to the members of the dismal procession and to those standing on the banks of the Limmat River. His mother's voice was heard above the ripple of the water, entreating him to remain true to Christ in the hour of temptation. Quietly the boat slipped out into the lake. As his arms and legs were being bound, he sang out with a loud voice, *in manus tuas, Domine, commendo spiritum meum* ("into thy hands, O Lord, I commend my spirit"). A few moments later the cold waters of Lake Zurich closed over the head of Felix Manz."[2]

However, the cause of Christ did not die, and we thank God that we stand in such a strong spiritual heritage!

DLC

---

[1]Leonard Verduin, *The Reformers and Their Stepchildren* (Grand Rapids: Eerdmans Publishing Co., 1961), p. 74.

[2]W. R. Estep, *The Anabaptist Story* (Nashville: Broadman Press, 1963), p. 30.

January 6—The Writing of a Great Hymn

Scripture: Acts 20:17-38

Born January 6, 1740,[1] the young, gifted pastor of the Baptist church in Wainsgate, England, had been converted at age sixteen under the powerful preaching of George Whitefield. At age nineteen, John Fawcett had been baptized into the fellowship of the Baptist church at Bradford. His ordination had taken place in 1765 as he assumed the pastorate at Wainsgate. Fawcett's extensive culture and talents became known far and wide through his published works in poetry and prose and through the flourishing academy he conducted.

Six years after Fawcett had assumed the Wainsgate pastorate, the well-known Dr. John Gill passed away, leaving the famed Baptist congregation in Southwark, London, without a pastor. In the course of time, Pastor John Fawcett was offered the position and accepted the call to London. His rural church was small, and the young man of God felt the call to the larger congregation would give him greater opportunities and would increase his small stipend and thus relieve him of anxiety. The news came to the Wainsgate congregation that their beloved pastor had accepted the invitation and would be leaving them. The parishioners were filled with grief. In those days rarely did a pastor move. The ideal was for a man of God to live and die in the midst of his people whom he served in the gospel. It seemed impossible to the good people of Wainsgate that this could happen!

But the fateful day arrived. The van came that had been ordered to remove Fawcett's belongings to London, and the good man watched his things as they were taken from the house and loaded for the trip. Men and women who had been brought to a saving knowledge of Christ under the pastor's ministry stood in little groups with tearful faces, looking on in silence. Mrs. Fawcett went into the house for one last look around the old home, and she came out weeping. "John," she said to her husband, "I know not how to go." "Neither do I," he replied. Then turning to the operator of the van, he said, "Put the furniture back." [2] As soon as the men who were watching understood what was being done, they offered their assistance as well. When the room had been prepared, Pastor Fawcett sat down and wrote:

Blest be the tie that binds
Our hearts in Christian love;
The fellowship of kindred minds
Is like to that above.

In later years Fawcett became a Doctor of Divinity and was invited to the principalship of Bristol College, but he died as he had lived, among his own people.

At one time a quotation from Dr. Fawcett's work was recited before King George III, and, being attracted to the small volume from which the quotation was made, the King contacted Dr. Fawcett and offered to render him some service. The pastor declined the favor for himself but afterward accepted it by saving one man from being executed and several others from heavy legal penalties.

The next time you sing that great hymn of parting, think of Pastor and Mrs. Fawcett and the dear people at Wainsgate.

DLC

---

[1]William Cathcart, *The Baptist Encyclopedia,* ed. Louis H. Everts (Philadelphia: Louis H. Everts, 1881), 1:211-12.

[2]John C. Carlile, *The Story of the English Baptists* (London: James Clarke and Co., 1905), p. 390.

January 7—"Pray Ye Therefore the Lord of the Harvest"

Scripture: Matthew 9:35-38

Though the Baptist Missionary Society was in its early years, great strides were being made for Christ in India. As William Carey, "the Father of Modern Missions," led the way on the field, godly pastors, such as John Ryland, were upholding the cause of worldwide evangelism back in England. An incident concerning Carey's son Jabez is worthy of mention. After the conversion of two of his sons, Dr. Carey became very anxious about the soul of Jabez, who had just begun practicing law; and he wrote his support team, requesting prayer for his son.

On the Society's twentieth anniversary, Dr. Ryland addressed two thousand "of the Mission's friends in London (in the Dutch Church, Austin Friars) on 'The zeal of the Lord of hosts shall perform this.' "[1] As he preached he spoke of Carey's joy in his sons Felix and William in their work for the Lord. "But he has a third son," said Ryland, "giving him pain; because, though dutiful, he is unconverted." At this point, Dr. Ryland began to cry, and he urged the audience to join in a fervent prayer for the conversion of Jabez Carey. Nearly two thousand joined before the throne of God's grace,[2] and God wonderfully answered.

In the very next Indian mail, William Carey received a letter that told of the conversion of Jabez. His regeneration had been synchronous with the united prayer meeting. Jabez had been "articled to an attorney," but in a short time he became interested in missionary service. In the providence of God, an invitation was received by William Carey on January 7, 1814, to send a missionary to Amboyna where twenty thousand national believers had no missionary to minister to them. Jabez immediately offered himself; and, though he was not yet twenty years of age, he crowded his marriage, ordination, and farewell into a short time and then left for his new assignment.

At Jabez's ordination, where his father and two brothers laid hands upon him, Dr. Carey lifted his voice in praise to God and said, "I trust this will be a matter of everlasting praise. O praise the Lord with me, and let us exalt his name together! To me the Lord has been very, very gracious. I trust all my children love the Lord, and three out of the four are actually engaged in the important work of publishing His Gospel among the heathen; two of them in new countries."[3]

We cannot all go to a foreign mission field, but oh, may we learn the vital part that prayer plays in the missionary enterprise! In those early days in the ministry of William Carey, some Baptist pastors in the Northamptonshire Association of England called upon the churches to appoint a day each month for prayer. Paul assured the Corinthians that they were "helping together by prayer." May we pray forth our own children to the harvest fields of the world!

DLC

---

[1]S. Pearce Carey, *William Carey* (London: Hodder and Stoughton, 1924), p. 300.

[2]John Brown Myers, ed., *The Centenary Volume of the Baptist Missionary Society, 1792-1892* (London: Baptist Missionary Society, 1892), p. 5.

[3]F. A. Cox, *History of the Baptist Missionary Society* (London: T. Ward and G. J. Dyer, 1842), 1:242.

January 8—Illinois's Initial Icy Immersion

Scripture: Romans 6:1-6

Our Baptist forefathers were a hardy breed, and they were determined to obey the Lord regardless of the cost. I wonder if our suave sophistication does not oftentimes hinder our willing sacrifice to follow the Lord.

Can you imagine gathering at an ice-covered creek in February and then cutting a hole in the ice and descending into the icy water to observe the ordinance of baptism? And yet that is exactly what took place on that February day in 1794 when James Lemen, his wife Catherine, and two others were "buried in the likeness of His death" in Fountaine Creek, in Monroe County, Illinois.[1]

James Lemen had been saved during one of the visits of the first evangelical minister to sojourn in Illinois in 1787. The Reverend James Smith of Kentucky brought the gospel to the area. However, Lemen delayed his baptism until Elder Josiah Dodge from Kentucky decided to preach in the area. On inquiry, Elder Dodge discovered that Mr. and Mrs. Lemen, along with two others, John Gibbons and Isaac Enochs, were desirous of receiving baptism, and the date was set for the occasion. On the appointed day a great multitude gathered from all parts to witness the first baptism in Illinois. At the water's edge a hymn was sung, the Scripture authority for the ordinance was read and explained by the preacher, and prayer was offered. As the newly immersed followers of Christ came up out of the water, another stanza was sung, the benediction was pronounced, and the multitude dispersed. One shivers just thinking about those hardy candidates! What about Elder Dodge who remained in the waters throughout?

Two years later the Lemens, along with a few others, united in forming the first Baptist church in Illinois, and their pastor was the Reverend Mr. David Badgley.[2]

Even before his conversion, Lemen had been in a small company who met together on the Lord's Day to read the Bible with a sermon whenever they could secure the services of a preacher. After Lemen was baptized, he grew rapidly in the Word of God, and in 1808 he was licensed to preach. Though already fifty years old, he was an active, zealous minister until his death on January 8, 1823.

In our days of heated baptisteries in air-conditioned auditoriums, we do well to consider the privations of the early Baptists of America whose faith overcame many obstacles. The next time some modern-day convert calls to postpone baptism because of a slight cold, I am going to insist that he consider the Lemens, John Gibbons, and Isaac Enochs! Thank God for our heritage in this great land!

DLC

---

[1]Edward P. Brand, *Illinois Baptists: A History* (Bloomington, Ill.: Pantagraph Printing Co., 1930), p. 24.

[2]William Cathcart, *The Baptist Encyclopedia,* ed. Louis H. Everts (Philadelphia: Louis H. Everts, 1881), 2:683-84.

January 9—The Father of American Religious Freedom

Scripture: Matthew 22:21

Strange as it may seem, religious freedom was unknown in America in the days of the early settlers! One had to conform to the institutional church (and yet later, to the state church) or be banished from the settlement. Indeed, this is what happened to Roger Williams in October 1635 when he was tried by the General Court and found guilty of "newe and dangerous opinions against the authorities," according to Governor John Winthrop's account; and he escaped just ahead of Massachusetts soldiers who had been sent to arrest and deport him to England.

Removing to what is now called Providence, Rhode Island, Williams and his followers were presented land as a gift by his friends, the two Narraganset chiefs, Canonicus and Miantunomi. It was there that the great American dream of religious freedom was born! He led in the formation of Rhode Island and obtained a charter from England which called for liberty of conscience. When attempts were made to rescind the charter of 1644, Williams, along with Dr. John Clarke of Newport, returned to England; and in 1663 King Charles II granted Rhode Island a favorable new charter "to hold forth a lively experiment that a most flourishing civil state may stand and best be maintained with full liberty of religious concernments."

Baptist historians have long debated the question of which Baptist church has the honor of being the first real Baptist church in America, but in March 1638 "in the chilly waters of a nearby stream, Roger Williams had himself immersed by Ezekiel Holliman, who had been a member of the Salem church; then Williams baptized Holliman and the others. Thus was organized the Providence Baptist Church . . . ." [1] Surely this church was the first in the new land to offer separation of church and state, soul liberty, and complete religious freedom. For this, Roger Williams is to be greatly revered in our history.

On January 9, 1872, a monument was unveiled in the National Capitol honoring Roger Williams. The dedicatory speech was delivered by Senator Henry Bowen Anthony of the state of Rhode Island, and the senator said:

> Religious freedom, which now by general consent underlies the foundation principle of civilized government, was at that time looked upon as a wilder theory than any proposition, moral, political, or religious, that has since engaged the serious attention of mankind. It was regarded as impracticable, disorganizing, impious, and if not utterly subversive of social order, it was not so only because its manifest absurdity would prevent any serious effort to enforce it.[2]

The monument, a sculpture of Roger Williams, had been done by Franklin Simmons in 1872 and may be seen today on the first floor of the House Wing in the Hall of Columns in Washington, D.C.

In 1965 our National Congress authorized a National Memorial for Roger Williams, and four and one-half acres were purchased by the National Park Service in 1974 in downtown Providence for this purpose. Though Roger Williams died in 1683, his Baptist conviction of religious freedom has lived on in America, and we owe an incalculable debt to his vision of freedom.

DLC

---

[1]O. K. Armstrong and Marjorie Armstrong, *The Baptists in America* (New York: Doubleday and Co., 1979), p. 55.

[2]Rev. R. C. Mosher, *The Baptist in History* (Albert Lea, Minn.: Simonson and Whitcomb, 1900), p. 139.

January 10—A Black Doctor Who Died Reaching Africans

Scripture: Romans 9:1-3

Early in her youth, Louise (''Lulu'') Celestia Fleming had heard the story of her grandfather's capture in Africa and enslavement in Florida. She was brought to saving faith in the Lord Jesus Christ in her teens and baptized in January of 1877. As a child Miss Fleming dreamed of returning to ''her people,''[1] but she began now to plan her life with that very reality in mind. She pursued an education at Shaw University in Raleigh, North Carolina. Then with the encouragement of Dr. Kellsey of the Sixth Avenue Church in Brooklyn, New York, and the financial assistance of the ''Young Ladies Home Mission Society,'' Miss Fleming enrolled in the Estey Seminary Course, graduating as the class valedictorian in 1885.

A great revival had broken out in the Congo, and a call had been made for single women to assist in training new converts. Miss Fleming responded to the call and was appointed by the Woman's American Baptist Foreign Missionary Society of the West on January 10, 1886.[2] She set sail for the Congo in March of 1887 and arrived on the field in May. She served in Palabala as a matron for the station girls and a teacher in the schools. In a letter dated January 10, 1891, Miss Fleming had written: "The work at Palabala has known its hardest trial this past year and also its greatest blessing. More people have been reached and some have turned from sin and darkness into light."

Her physical strength having failed, Miss Fleming returned to the States in 1891. As she recovered, she determined to study medicine before going back to Africa. She enrolled in the full medical course of the Woman's Medical College of Pennsylvania and graduated in 1895. Having affiliated with the Grace Baptist Church of Philadelphia, she returned to the Congo in 1895, fully supported by her home church. Serving now as a medical missionary, Dr. Fleming literally gave herself to her "own people" and contracted the dreaded African Sleeping Sickness from which she died.

Dr. Fleming was buried in Philadelphia on June 14, 1899, and an editorial following her death reads as follows: "Dr. Fleming was a woman of strong characteristics and fitted to overcome the many obstacles encountered in missionary work and had the promise of large usefulness in winning the hearts of the Congo people, putting herself in close touch and sympathy with them."

How we could wish that the spirit of Miss Fleming could be multiplied in our day, for the answer to the injustices of the human race is still the age-old gospel of our Lord Jesus Christ.

DLC

---

[1]William Henry Brackney, *The Baptists* (New York: Greenwood Press, 1988), p. 166.

[2]*Biographical Digest of Lulu Celestia Fleming* (Valley Forge, Pa.: International Ministries of the American Baptist Churches, U.S.A., n.d.), p. 1.

January 11—When Church and State Marry, Justice Will Miscarry!

Scripture: Matthew 10:16-23

It is difficult for modern-day Americans to realize that our nation has not always experienced religious freedom. "On January 11, 1758, the General Assembly, meeting at Savannah (Georgia), passed a law making the Church of England the church of the province.''[1]

Though it is not our purpose to catalogue all of the state churches' efforts in the colonies, the following examples will suffice. ''In early Virginia, Massachusetts, and several other colonies, laws were enacted to support an established church by taxes, to compel church attendance, and to forbid the worshipping of dissenting sects.'' ''Some type of state church was to be found in all five southern colonies, as well as in three New England provinces: Massachusetts, Connecticut, and New Hampshire.''[2]

In South Carolina as early as 1706, ''the Board of Trade approved a new law establishing the Church of England with support from the public funds.'' In North Carolina in 1732, ''a law (was passed) establishing the Church of England.''[3]

The Puritans had established a theocracy in Massachusetts, New Hampshire, and Connecticut. In time, the Puritan churches were called Congregational churches, and they persecuted those of different religious beliefs.[4]

We ought to thank God for our Constitution and Bill of Rights. I thrill to the words of the First Amendment, knowing it is the product of the Baptist input of James Madison. ''Congress shall make no law respecting an establishment of religion, or prohibiting the free exercise thereof; or abridging the freedom of speech, or of the press; or the right of the people peaceably to assemble, and to petition the Government for a redress of grievances.'' Read those words carefully! No constitutional restriction was placed on the church. Rather, limitations were imposed on the role of government. Some years later, Thomas Jefferson spoke of the ''wall of separation,'' but we hasten to point out that he was referring to a wall that kept government out of the church—not church people out of the government!

How the pendulum has swung! Baptists opposed the concept of a state church, for we have always believed in religious freedom for all people, but today many liberals are attempting to falsely interpret the First Amendment to remove all religion and morals from our public life. It is true that ''when church and state marry, justice will miscarry,'' but may we also perceive that ''Blessed is the nation whose God is the Lord'' (Ps. 33:12).

The true understanding of the separation of church and state has made America the great republic that it is to this day.

DLC

---

[1]Thomas Armitage, *The History of the Baptists* (1890; reprint ed., Watertown, Wis.: Maranatha Baptist Press, 1976), 2:771.

[2]Oscar Theodore Barck, Jr., and Hugh Talmadge Lefler, *Colonial America* (New York: Macmillan Co., 1968), p. 391.

[3]Louis B. Wright, *The Cultural Life of the American Colonies* (New York: Harper and Row, 1962), p. 87.

[4]Arthur E. Soderlind, *Colonial Connecticut* (New York: Thomas Nelson Inc., 1976), p. 75.

January 12—From a Virginia Militia Colonel to a Virginia Baptist Apostle

Scripture: Matthew 8:5-13

Samuel Harriss was born to respectable parents in Hanover County, Virginia, January 12, 1724. While he was still a youth, the Harriss family moved to the county of Pittsylvania where Samuel received the favor of men who appointed him church warden, sheriff, a justice of the peace, burgess for the county, colonel of the militia, captain of Fort Mayo, and commissary for the fort and the army. All this notoriety did not fulfill the need of his soul, and Samuel Harriss came under deep conviction.

Harriss ventured to attend the meetings of the sect called Baptists, that at that time was everywhere spoken against. On one of his routes to visit some of the forts in his military dress, Harriss stopped at a small house where he heard Joseph and William Murphy (at that time called the "Murphy Boys") preach the gospel. He seated himself behind a loom. God found him out and brought him under such deep conviction that he left his sword and other parts of his uniform scattered in various places. At one place after prayer, Harriss was prostrated over a pew and, when aroused, with ecstasy of joy on his face, exclaimed, "Glory! glory! glory!"

His conversion took place sometime in 1758, and Harriss immediately began his ministerial labors. In his early ministry he traveled often with Daniel Marshall, who greatly influenced him. Harriss became so effectual that he acquired the name "Virginia Apostle."

At the invitation of Allen Wyley, Harriss traveled to the area of Culpeper. On subsequent visits along with others, such as James Read from North Carolina, they became almost constant travelers into the area between the James and Rappahannock rivers and venturing as far as the Shenandoah Valley.

Although a man of some means at the time of his conversion experience, Harriss forsook all and provided for his family in a very frugal manner in order to propagate the gospel far and wide. His preaching talents lay chiefly in addressing the heart. Semple tells us "perhaps even Whitefield did not surpass him in this." Some described him, when exhorting at great meetings, as pouring forth streams of celestial lightning from his eyes, which, whithersoever he turned his face, would strike down hundreds at once.

Like Daniel Marshall, Harris possessed a spirit incapable of being discouraged by any difficulty. While preaching in Orange County, Harriss was pulled down, dragged about sometimes by his hair and sometimes by his leg. On another occasion he was knocked down by a rude fellow. He went to preach to the prisoners in the town of Hillsborough, where they locked him up for a considerable time.

A man owed Harriss a sum of money and refused to pay him unless sued in court. After meditation he sued at the Court of Heaven, saying, "O blessed Jesus! Thou eternal God. Thou knowest that I need the money which this man owes me to supply the wants of my family; but he will not pay me without a lawsuit. Dear Jesus, shall I quit Thy cause, and leave the souls of men to perish? Or wilt Thou in mercy open some other way of relief?"

Elder Harriss received such assurance that God would secure his debt that he wrote a receipt for the discharge of the debt, much to the amazement of the debtor, who ultimately paid him in full.[1]

God grant us men of conviction, integrity, and courage in our day who will know how to appeal to the Court of Heaven and not be distracted by the trivial things of life.

EWT

---

[1]Robert B. Semple, *A History of the Rise and Progress of Baptists in Virginia* (Richmond: Published by the author, 1810), pp. 377-85.

January 13—When the Atheist Left Town Early

Scripture: Matthew 27:11-22

There was a time in the history of America when public debating was used forcefully by Bible believers to sound forth their message. Elder J. N. Hall, gifted with keen logic, personal magnetism, and unusual oratory has been referred to as "the peerless defender of the Baptist faith."[1] Elder Hall was born in 1849 and was ordained to the ministry on January 13, 1872.[2] An indefatigable laborer, Hall preached an average of a sermon a day and entered as well into the work of editing several Baptist journals of his time, but whenever he was called upon to defend the Baptist position, he excelled in debating.

An infidel club in Trigg County, Kentucky, had made great strides, and the atheist members continually challenged the Christians to debate. The Baptist pastor in the area realized that his disregarding of the demand was interpreted by the general population as weakness; and, therefore, something had to be done. Asking the infidels to obtain the services of the noted agnostic, Robert Ingersoll, the pastor set out to obtain the services of Elder J. N. Hall. Ingersoll refused but recommended the President of the Free Thought Association of America, a certain Mr. Putman. Putman accepted, the time of the debate was set, and the terms were accepted by both parties.

As the hour of 7:00 P.M. approached, the auditorium was full, and Putman was present; however, Elder Hall could not be found. The Christian people were in despair, but Putman rose to speak and stated that it was apparent that Hall was afraid to meet him, and since he had already been paid, he was prepared to set forth the issues of the day, "Hall or no Hall." He spoke two hours, and being eloquent, the effect on the congregation was overwhelming. The infidels were delighted, but a young lad came into the auditorium just at the conclusion of Putman's speech, slipped over to the Baptist preacher, and whispered something to him. At the conclusion of Putman's oration, the preacher announced that Elder Hall had been detained but he would be present the next morning.

Arriving early, Hall took Putman aside and asked for the arguments he had made the previous night. Then Hall spoke for two hours and totally decimated his opposition. Putman never rallied again, and at the end of the second day, the atheist debater announced that he had "pressing business in New York" and left. Elder Hall now turned to preaching the gospel, and his closing presentation was "What Think Ye of Christ?" At the conclusion he invited infidels and skeptics to trust Christ, and forty-seven came forward! The backbone of infidelity in the area was broken, and the gospel had free course.

DLC

---

[1]W. M. Barker, *Memoirs of Elder J. N. Hall* (Fulton, Ky.: Baptist Flag Print, 1907), title page.

[2]Ben M. Bogard, *Pillars of Orthodoxy; or, Defenders of the Faith* (Louisville: Baptist Book Concern, 1900), p. 441.

January 14—From the Dance Floor to the Pulpit to the Prison

Scripture: Hebrews 13:1-6

John Picket was born on this date in the year 1744. When he was grown to maturity, he had a strong propensity to gaming and sports of every kind. He followed the business of dancing master which took him to Pee Dee, North Carolina, from his home in King George County, Virginia, about the year 1764.

While under the preaching of Josiah Murphy in North Carolina in 1766, Picket was converted to Christ and baptized in 1766. He then began to loathe the sports and pleasures to which he had been devoted. He also wrote to his parents, who were then in Fauquier County, Virginia, informing them of his marvelous change. They thought it strange indeed that this son they considered lost should become so fervently pious.

Upon the death of his father in 1767, Picket returned to Fauquier. Finding his friends and neighbors in spiritual darkness, he began to exhort them in private conversation, then to hold family worship, and ultimately to preach in public. The work spread far and near. Josiah Murphy came and baptized a few, and later, Samuel Harriss and James Read came and baptized thirty-seven and organized them into a church. John Picket, being ordained May 27, 1772, took the care of the church known as Carter's Run.[1]

The planting of this church was not without violent opposition. A mob broke into the meetinghouse, disrupted the service, and split to pieces the pulpit and communion table while the magistrates issued their warrant. Seizing John Picket, they thrust him into Fauquier prison. He continued there for about three months, preaching through the grates and admonishing as many as came to him to repent and turn to God. The Word of God was not bound. Great numbers were awakened to their need of Christ under Picket's prison labors. One of his flock wrote, "He stood sound in the faith, calling on sinners to repent; not sparing his own but gave his labors to the Lord and to his fellow men; and went on with zeal and courage."[2]

EWT

---

[1]Robert B. Semple, *A History of the Rise and Progress of the Baptists in Virginia,* (Richmond: Published by the author, 1810), pp. 412-14.

[2]Lewis Peyton Little, *Imprisoned Preachers and Religious Liberty in Virginia* (Lynchburg, Va.: J. P. Bell Co., 1938), pp. 192-97.

January 15—The National Sin of Slavery

Scripture: Romans 2:1-4

The practice of slavery had been introduced into Virginia in 1619 and was, at first, resisted by the southern colonies. However, in time, the tragedy of slavery became the most divisive issue ever to face our nation. Baptist leaders divided severely on the matter, but brethren of the British Baptist Union wrote to the ministers and messengers of the Baptist churches in the United States on January 15, 1838, urging them to use their influence to bring about full emancipation.

After opening the letter with words of esteem, J. H. Hinton, chairman, wrote: "We have not been ignorant that slavery existed in the States; entailed, we are humbled and ashamed to acknowledge, by British influence, authority and example. But we had, until of late, no conception of the extent to which multitudes of professing Christians in your land, by indifference, by connivance, by apology, or by actual participation are implicated in it."[1]

In this volume we shall mention several little-known facts concerning the dread practice of slavery. However, let me point out that Isaac Backus, who became famous for his work as a Baptist pastor-historian, was raised as a member of the Standing Order of New England, an order in which the Congregational churches had assumed the privileged position of an official state church. Yet "the family owned a slave and an Indian girl apprenticed as a servant."[2] Thus we learn that in the first half of the eighteenth century, slaves were held in Connecticut. And the famed *Diary* of Isaac Backus reports the death of a slave who was owned by one of the members of Backus' church in Middleborough, Massachusetts.[3]

To be sure, slavery was practiced in the North as well as in the southern states, but two things were involved in shifting the "slave" population to the South. The cold northern winters made the adjustment from Africa very difficult, and slavery therefore became unprofitable. However, the biggest factor was doubtless the invention of the cotton gin, which in 1793 contributed "to the resuscitation of the institution of slavery which now could be profitably utilized." "The south had at first rejected slavery, then protested against it, and after 1793, began to embrace it.''[4]

Make no mistake about it, slavery was a calamity, but it was a national and not merely a regional sin! Let us thank God for the freedom that the gospel brings!

DLC

---

[1]*The Baptist Quarterly of the Baptist Historical Society* (London: Baptist Union Publication Department, 1924-25), 2:332.

[2]William G. McLoughlin, ed., *Isaac Backus and the American Pietistic Tradition* (Boston: Little, Brown and Co., 1967), p. 4.

[3]William G. McLoughlin, ed., *The Diary of Isaac Backus* (Providence: Brown University Press, 1979), 2:771.

[4]Robert A. Baker, *The Southern Baptist Convention and Its People, 1607-1972* (Nashville: Broadman Press, 1974), pp. 118-19.

January 16—Felistis Jans Resinx, a Burnt Offering

Scripture: Proverbs 31:10-31

The testimony and execution of Felistis are recorded from the criminal records deposited with the secretary of the city of Amsterdam, Holland. A brief extract from her sentence of death reveals her witness for Jesus Christ.

Felistis Jans Resinx had assembled with a sect of Anabaptists and thus doing had separated from the obedience and beliefs of the (so-called) holy (that is, Roman) church. She judged erroneously the sacrament of the altar and had entertained and shown hospitality to Anabaptists. She seduced certain people from obedience to the Romish church and was unwilling to forsake her aforesaid errors. All of these things were opposed to the ordinances of the state church and the proclamations of his imperial majesty.

The sentence was that Felistis should be executed by fire and that all her worldly goods should be confiscated to the use of the emperor.

During the time of her imprisonment, Felistis was condemned to the torture of the rack, which she bore faithfully. She also demonstrated her kind servant spirit by assisting the jailer's wife in the household.

On January 16, 1553, Felistis was seen approaching the scaffold on which she was to be burned, adorned in a clean dress and white apron as if to show by her outward dress how purely and uprightly a

Christian maiden ought internally to be adorned in order to please her heavenly bridegroom, Jesus Christ.

We must also remember another faithful martyr of Christ, Herman Janson, who, on the same occasion, at the same place, and for the same reason was burned alive and was added to the great number who gave their lives for the truth of God's Word.

May our Lord grant us the same love, faithfulness, and resolution in the hour of our trial.[1]

EWT

---

[1]T. J. Van Braght, trans., and Edward Bean Underhill, ed., *A Martyrology of the Churches of Christ Commonly Called Baptists,* (London: Hanserd Knollys Society, 1853), pp. 29-31.

January 17—The Light of the Gospel in Switzerland

Scripture: Acts 5:29

The term *Anabaptist* has been contemptuously given to all those who opposed the union of church and state and conscientiously remained outside the state churches. Modern research has vindicated many of these men, and the present authors are pleased to look upon them as familial prototypes of current-day Baptists. Henry S. Burrage has pointed out some of the distinctives of those godly men, and we gladly embrace these truths as trademarks of Baptists today. Burrage lists the following:

1. That the Scriptures are the only authority in matters of faith and practice.
2. That only personal faith in Christ secures salvation; therefore, infant baptism is to be rejected.
3. That a church is composed of believers only who have been baptized on a personal confession of faith in Jesus Christ.
4. That each church has the entire control of its affairs, without interference on the part of any external power.
5. That while the State may demand obedience in all things not contrary to the law of God, it has no right to set aside the dictates of conscience.[1]

Conrad Grebel was from a prominent and wealthy Swiss family. His father served as magistrate in Gruningen, just east of Zurich, and Conrad enjoyed educational advantages. Soon after his marriage, young Grebel was saved, and by 1522 he publicly defended the gospel and expressed a desire to become a minister. Falling in with the teachings of Ulrich Zwingli, Grebel gave himself to the Scriptures. Grebel and other young so-called Anabaptists owed much to Zwingli, but they owed more to the Bible. These two loyalties soon came to a head, and it was Grebel who initiated believer's baptism on that historic night in January 1525. As such, young Grebel emerged as a champion of the Anabaptist reformation.[2]

Early in 1525 a child was born to the Grebel household. Conrad Grebel did not baptize his baby because he had become convinced that christening finds no support in the New Testament. This development soon caused a stir in Zurich, and the city council moved against the heretic by arranging a confrontation which had all the earmarks of a trial. The session was held on January 17, 1525, and resulted in an edict ordering all parents who had unbaptized infants to present them for baptism within eight days or face expulsion from the city.[3]

As men measure success, it is tragic that Grebel had only one year and eight months to proclaim the gospel, for in spite of numerous imprisonments and increasingly poor health, the accomplishments of those months were little short of phenomenal. He preached, visited from door-to-door, baptized those who were saved, and was again arrested and imprisoned in Gruningen Castle. Being brought to trial, Grebel, Blaurock, and Manz were sentenced to an indefinite term of internment in November 1525. They were allowed no visitors and were given only a diet of bread and water. Again Grebel was able to escape, but his freedom was short-lived, for he died in the summer of 1526, probably a victim of the plague, but a hero of the faith that lives on even today!

DLC

---

[1]Henry S. Burrage, *A History of the Anabaptists in Switzerland* (Philadelphia: American Baptist Publication Society, 1882), pp. 222-23.

[2]William R. Estep, *The Anabaptist Story* (Nashville: Broadman Press, 1963), pp. 21-28.

[3]Leonard Verduin, *The Anatomy of a Hybrid* (Grand Rapids: Eerdmans Publishing Co., 1976), pp. 155-57.

January 18—God Has Children but No Grandchildren

Scripture: John 1:11-14

One of the most treasured Baptist distinctives is the tenet of "soul liberty," and it was a major teaching of Roger Williams, founder of

Rhode Island. But some today ask, "What is it?" Dr. George Truett, speaking from the steps of our National Capitol in 1917, said:

> The individual is segregated from family, from church, from state and from society, from dearest friends or institutions, and brought into direct personal dealings with God. Everyone must give account of himself to God. There can be no sponsors or deputies or proxies in such a vital matter. Each one must repent for himself and believe for himself, and be baptized for himself, both in time and in eternity.

Where in England could Roger Williams have learned this principle? Dr. William Cathcart suggests, "It is probable that Roger Williams learned 'soul liberty' from Samuel Howe, whose church believed that 'the king was only to be obeyed in civil matters;' that 'no prince had power to make laws to bind the consciences of men.' "[1]

Samuel Howe pastored the church that met in "Deadman's Place," London, for seven years and made no small stir in the religious circle of his day. His followers admitted that "they owned no other head of the church but Jesus Christ." Howe was bitterly persecuted and then imprisoned where he died on January 18, 1641.

Roger Williams in *The Hireling Ministry* speaks in such glowing terms of Samuel Howe that we do well to quote a few sentences to reveal the godly influence that Howe had upon him. Williams wrote: "I cannot but with honorable testimony remember that eminently Christian witness and prophet of Christ, even that despised and yet beloved Samuel Howe, who, being by calling a cobbler . . . yet . . . by searching the Holy Scriptures, grew so excellent a textuary, or Scripture-learned man, that few of those high rabbies . . . could apply or readily from the Holy Scriptures outgo him."

At Samuel Howe's death, the state church officials refused his burial in the "consecrated ground" and even posted a guard at the parish cemetery at Shoreditch to ensure that his remains would not be interred there. The dear man of God was buried at Agnes-la-Clair and according to Roger Williams, "hundreds of God's people" attended the service.

It is possible that Samuel Howe was not well educated (though he authored a small volume entitled *The Sufficiency of the Spirit's Teaching*), but it is likely that he worked as a cobbler to provide for his needs. Many Baptist pastors supported themselves as they ministered to small, persecuted flocks. Howe's testimony reminds us of another "cobbler," Dr. William Carey, the "Father of Modern-Day Missions." Thank God for these wonderful men who had their feet on the ground but their hearts in heaven! As we think of America's greatest and finest principles, we rejoice in the memories of these humble men—Samuel Howe and Roger Williams—who insisted on separation of church and state and "soul-liberty" because they dared to take God's Word at face value!

DLC

---

[1]William Cathcart, *The Baptist Encyclopedia,* ed. Louis H. Everts (Philadelphia: Louis H. Everts, 1881), 1:550.

January 19—Religious Liberty and Virginia Baptists

Scripture: Leviticus 25:1-23

The first recorded imprisonment of Baptist preachers in Virginia occurred on June 4, 1768, in Fredericksburg.[1] On October 16, 1777, in a back room in that same city, Thomas Jefferson, George Mason, Edmund Pendleton, George Wythe, and Thomas Ludwell Lee, deliberated for many hours and then emerged from that room with the first draft of the Virginia Statute of Religious Liberty.

These men knew of the convictions of Baptists concerning liberty of conscience and their willingness to suffer persecution because of exercising these convictions. Jefferson had attended some of their small churches in Albemarle and Orange Counties, and Mason's law office was located right across the street from where Jeremiah Moore was imprisoned in Alexandria for preaching without state licensure or state church ordination.

The struggle was so intense that it took nearly ten years of lobbying and petitioning the legislature (the Baptists had three representing them at one time) before the statute was passed on January 19, 1776. Jefferson stated that it was the most fiercely contested piece of legislation of his entire political career.[2] During the same period there was great contention relating to taxation for the support of state church clergy. At one point Jeremiah Moore, Jeremiah Walker, and John Young delivered, in a wheelbarrow, to the Virginia legislature meeting in a warehouse in Richmond, a petition signed by ten thousand Virginians opposing the general assessment plan for the support of religious teachers. It was the defeat of this legislation that finally paved the way for Jefferson's statute.

William Warren Sweet, in his *Story of Religion in America,* is justified in saying,

> Religious freedom had triumphed in Virginia and was soon to spread throughout the nation and a few years later, in the form of the First

> Amendment to the Federal Constitution, was to become a part of the fundamental law of the land. At the time of the passage of the measure, Jefferson, its author, was in France, but so proud was he of his part in the memorable struggle that he asked that it be recorded on his gravestone: "Thomas Jefferson, Author of the Declaration of Independence, of the Statute of Virginia for Religious Freedom, and Father of the University of Virginia.
>
> But justice compels the admission that Jefferson's part in this accomplishment was not so great as that of James Madison, nor were the contributions of either or both as important as was that of the humble people called Baptists.[3]

The statesmen spoke and wrote with eloquence; the Baptists preached, petitioned, and suffered persecution. God used these humble people to have religious liberty as a fundamental principle of our society set forth in two great documents: *The Virginia Declaration of Rights* and *The Statute of Virginia for Religious Freedom.* From these were drawn the opening words of the Federal Bill of Rights, which states, "Congress shall make no law respecting an establishment of religion, or prohibiting the free exercise thereof." May we "stand fast therefore in the liberty wherewith Christ hath made us free" (Gal. 5:1) and "proclaim liberty throughout all the land unto all the inhabitants thereof" (Lev. 25:10).

EWT

---

[1]Lewis Peyton Little, *Imprisoned Preachers and Religious Liberty in Virginia* (Lynchburg, Va.: J. P. Bell Co., 1938), pp. 93-98, 510-15.

[2]Charles F. James, *A Documentary History of the Struggle for Religious Liberty in Virginia* (1900; reprint ed., New York: Da Capo Press, 1971), pp. 137-41.

[3]William Warren Sweet, *The Story of Religion in America* (1950; reprint ed., Grand Rapids: Baker Book House, 1973), p. 193.

January 20—America's First Missionary—A Black Man

Scripture: John 1:35-51

The first missionary to leave the shores of America for foreign service was George Leile, a former slave. When it became apparent to Deacon Henry Sharp of the First Baptist Church of Savannah, Georgia, that his slave George Leile was called of God, he "emancipated the stirring preacher so he might give himself wholly to the preaching of the Gospel (to) the people of color.'' Ordained on May 20, 1775, Leile labored in and around Savannah with great success before leaving as a missionary for Jamaica in 1779. Thus Leile predated the service of William Carey, ''the founder of modern Baptist missions.''[1]

One of Leile's converts in the Savannah area was Andrew Bryan, who became an outstanding preacher among his people. In his early ministry, Bryan was persecuted for his efforts, but he grew greatly in public acclaim, and his master, Jonathan Bryan, allowed him to construct a building on land at Yamacraw in the suburbs of Savannah. This was the first black Baptist church in America, and it grew to over eight hundred members and ultimately mothered two other such churches.

The birth of the church that Bryan pastored provides another interesting story. ''The greatest achievement of Abraham Marshall in founding churches . . . is a story which reads more strangely than fiction. His father (Daniel) founded the first Baptist church in Georgia, but to Abraham goes the honor of constituting the first Negro Baptist church in Georgia.''[2] As Abraham Marshall traveled in the Savannah area, one day he baptized forty-five black believers, and along with the others who had been previously baptized, he formed them into a church and ordained Andrew Bryan as their pastor. The certificate of ordination read:

> This is to certify that the Ethiopian Church of Jesus Christ of Savannah, have called their beloved brother Andrew Bryan to the work of the ministry. We have examined into his qualifications, and believing it to be the will of the great head of the Church, we have appointed him to preach the Gospel, and administer the ordinances as God, in His providence may call. January 20, 1788. A. Marshall.[3]

The ministry of Andrew Bryan was surely blessed of God, and at his death the following resolution was passed by the Savannah Association in 1812:

> The Association is sensibly affected by the death of the Rev. Andrew Bryan, a man of color, and pastor of the First Colored Church in Savannah. This son of Africa, after suffering inexpressible persecutions in the cause of his divine Master, was at length permitted to discharge the duties of the ministry among his colored friends in peace and quiet, hundreds of whom, through his instrumentality, were brought to a knowledge of the truth as it is in Jesus. He closed his extensively useful and amazingly luminous course in lively exercise of faith, and in the joyful hope of a happy immortality.[4]

DLC

---

[1]Jesse L. Boyd, *A History of Baptists in America Prior to 1845* (New York: American Press, 1957), p. 146.

[2]James Donovan Mosteller, *A History of the Kiokee Baptist Church in Georgia* (Ann Arbor: Edwards Brothers, 1952), p. 149.

[3]Leroy Fitts, *A History of Black Baptists* (Nashville: Broadman Press, 1985), p. 37.

[4]Albert Henry Newman, *A History of the Baptist Churches in the United States* (Philadelphia: American Baptist Publication Society, 1915), p. 331.

January 21—The Preacher Who Confounded the Court

Scripture: Acts 22:1-3

We often think of our early Baptist forefathers as being poorly educated and primarily men of fervor but with few academic achievements. However, God raised up some unique men with great mental abilities among our progenitors. Surely John Bunyan was such a man, but the truth is that many men in the Bedford Church in England were outstanding.

On January 21, 1672, at the meeting in which John Bunyan was called to the pastorate of the Bedford Church, seven other men were examined and set apart to the work of the ministry. Among these men was Nehemiah Coxe, who is described as "a very excellent, learned, and judicious divine."[1] Coxe was a native of Bedford and had been received into the membership of the church in June 1669, and it is believed that he had been immersed by John Bunyan. Coxe proved to be an able author and wrote several published treatises that were used of God. He refused a call to a nearby Baptist church in Hitchin, and in the course of time he is said to have been imprisoned at Bedford for preaching the gospel.

An interesting development took place on the day Coxe was haled into court. In earlier days Coxe had been a shoemaker, and thus he was known in court as a "cordwainer." The Reverend Mr. Coxe presented his own case before the court in the Greek language, and he further confounded the prosecution by responding to their charges in Hebrew. "The judge expressed his surprise, remarking that none there could answer him. Coxe claimed the right to plead in what language he pleased. The judge dismissed him, saying to the bar, 'Well, the cordwainer has wound us all up, Gentlemen.' "[2]

Later Coxe moved to London and supported himself in the medical profession,[3] for the persecuted churches were small, and most pastors had to labor on the side. Ultimately, he accepted a call to the joint-pastorate of a well-known Baptist church in London, that of Petty-France. It is also of interest that in 1678 the Petty-France Baptist Church united with the Particular Baptist Association. Coxe attended as a messenger to the associational meetings and reported to his congregation.[4]

In 1682 a great storm of persecution came down upon the Petty-France Church, but Dr. Coxe served the congregation faithfully with his co-pastor, William Collins, for at least twenty years.

DLC

---

[1]Thomas Crosby, *The History of the English Baptists* (1738-40; reprint ed., Lafayette, Tenn.: Church History Research and Archives, 1979), 4:265.

[2]Thomas Armitage, *The History of the Baptists* (1890; reprint ed., Watertown, Wis.: Maranatha Baptist Press, 1976), 2:524.

[3]W. T. Whitley, *A History of British Baptists* (London: Charles Griffin and Co., 1923), pp. 131-32.

[4]J. Jackson Goadby, *Bye-Paths in Baptist History* (New York: Bible Publishing Co., n.d.), p. 191.

January 22—A Many-Gifted Servant of Christ

Scripture: John 12:24

One of the most versatile Baptist leaders of early America was Dr. Hezekiah Smith. He was born in April 1737 at Long Island, New York, but his family soon moved to New Jersey. Being influenced early in his life by the ministry of John Gano, the young man was saved and then trained in the first Baptist educational institution established by Baptists, the Hopewell Academy. He then attended Princeton College where he graduated in 1762.

Having been called of God to preach, Hezekiah Smith went immediately into the field of evangelism and traveled into the South. In fifteen months he traversed 4,235 miles and preached 173 sermons. He returned to the North and learned that the Philadelphia Association had resolved to establish an institute of higher learning for the Baptists, and Smith threw himself into the project. The result was the formation of the Rhode Island College, which later became Brown University.

Smith had been ordained in Charleston, South Carolina, but he continued in the ministry of evangelism. In 1765 he was urged by converts and constrained by the Holy Spirit to establish a Baptist church in Haverhill, Massachusetts. He was publicly recognized as pastor on November 12, 1766, and he served that congregation faithfully for forty years until his death on January 22, 1805.

At the outbreak of the Revolution, the Reverend Mr. Smith offered his service and was appointed brigade-chaplain for General Washington's army. At least six of the twenty-one chaplains of the Revolutionary War were known to have been Baptists.[1] Smith served with the army of Horatio Gates during the Burgoyne campaign and continued later along the Hudson with the army of Washington. President Washington himself said that the Baptists were "throughout America, uniformly and almost unanimously, the firm friends to civil liberty, and the persevering promoters of our glorious Revolution."

Returning to Haverhill, he continued faithfully as a pastor with vision. Under the direction of the church, Dr. Smith would take one or two of his members on evangelistic tours into New Hampshire and Maine. In the course of time he helped to establish thirteen churches in those areas. He was instrumental in forming the first missionary society in America, the Massachusetts Baptist Missionary Society, and he was a deciding factor in the formation of the Warren Association as well.

Late in his labors, this man of God spoke from John 12:24 concerning a corn of wheat falling and dying that it might bring forth much fruit, and revival followed in his church. But on the following Thursday, Dr. Hezekiah Smith was seized with paralysis and never spoke again on earth.[2] He lay in that condition for a week and then awakened in the likeness of the Lord with His praise again filling his mouth.

DLC

---

[1]Henry C. Vedder, *A Short History of the Baptists* (Philadelphia: American Baptist Publication Society, 1897), p. 312.

[2]William Cathcart, *The Baptist Encyclopedia,* ed. Louis H. Everts (Philadelphia: Louis H. Everts, 1881), 2:1065-66.

January 23—John Weatherford and Martyr Marks of God's Hero

Scripture: Galatians 6:11-17

A small boy clasped tightly his father's hand as they filed past the coffin that held the remains of John Weatherford, the last of the old veteran Baptist preachers, who had gone to his eternal reward on

January 23, 1833. As he gazed upon the body of this old soldier of the cross, the boy noticed the stiff, bloodless hands that lay folded across his breast. The peculiar white, rigid seams on the hands made an indelible impression upon his young mind.[1]

In his latter years as an eminent physician, he learned that Pastor Weatherford had been imprisoned in the Chesterfield County jail of the colony of Virginia for five months in the year 1773. The iron bars of the prison did not limit the preaching of this servant of God. He proclaimed the message of salvation to the waiting congregation with great demonstration, extending his hands through the grates. Men of a baser sort were instigated to stand on either side of the window and slash his hands with knives until the blood would stream down and sprinkle those who listened to the message of redemption.

Dr. White had wondered for more than sixty years what those white, rigid seams were. When he discovered the cause, he called them "the marks of the Lord Jesus—martyr marks of God's hero. Honor to his noble memory and to all who have suffered for the kingdom of God."

After being held in close prison for some time, Weatherford was allowed the privilege of the prison bounds. Sometime later an order for his release was secured. The jailer refused to free Weatherford until the jail fees (room and board) were paid, which amounted to a considerable sum because of the length of his imprisonment. Not long afterward, this fee was paid by someone whose name was concealed, and Weatherford was set at liberty. More than twenty years later, upon removal of Patrick Henry to Charlotte County, Henry became a neighbor of John Weatherford, who was the pastor of a nearby Baptist church. On recounting their early experiences in the struggle for civil and religious liberty, Pastor Weatherford learned for the first time that Patrick Henry had paid his fine and secured his release to the prison bounds. He always afterwards spoke of Patrick Henry with a glow of affection.

In his later years Weatherford became too infirm to travel far from home but frequently preached in his own neighborhood. During his last illness, he often referred to the astonishing love of God to poor sinners. Every day he requested the beautiful lines of Newton's "Amazing Grace" to be sung. Those present would be called to his bedside that he might speak to them of the loving-kindness of the Lord. With shouts of praises and unwavering faith, Weatherford went into the presence of his Lord, being more than ninety years of age.

EWT

---

[1]Lewis Peyton Little, *Imprisoned Preachers and Religious Liberty in Virginia* (Lynchburg, Va.: J. P. Bell Co., 1938), pp. 338-58.

January 24—James Madison, a Frustrated Virginian Gentleman

Scripture: Acts 5:26-42

Some leaders of the former established state church desired to erase the stain of religious persecution from official records and from the memory of their posterity. But official records in Orange County, Virginia, contain much evidence that Virginia Baptists were held in close jail for preaching the gospel of Jesus Christ.[1]

James Madison was aware of these persecutions in his county as well as adjacent counties. Concerning one of these counties, Semple records, "They sent the sheriff and posse after him [Elijah Craig], when at his plough. He was taken and carried before three magistrates of Culpeper. They, without hearing arguments pro or con, ordered him to jail. At court, he, with others, was arraigned. One of the lawyers told the court they had better discharge them; for that oppressing them would rather advance than retard them. He said that they were like a bed of camomile; the more they were trod, the more they would spread. The court thought otherwise, and determined to imprison them."[2]

As a citizen of Orange County, James Madison was deeply disturbed by the general moral and spiritual degeneration of the clergy and laity alike. The Baptists boldly cried out against wickedness and only brought down upon themselves a greater degree of wrath from the state establishment. Madison's observation and frustrations were expressed in a letter to his friend Bradford, of Philadelphia, dated January 24, 1774. He writes:

> Union of religious sentiments begets a surprising confidence and ecclesiastical establishments tend to great ignorance and corruption, all of which facilitates the execution of mischievous projects. . . . I want again to breathe your free air. I expect it will mend my constitution and confirm my principles. I have, indeed, as good an atmosphere at home as the climate will allow, but have nothing to brag of as to the state and liberty of my country. Poverty and luxury prevail among all sorts; pride, ignorance and knavery among the priesthood, and vice and wickedness among the laity. This is bad enough; but it is not the worst I have to tell you. That diabolical, hell-conceived principle of persecution rages among some, and, to their eternal infamy the clergy can furnish their quota of imps for such purposes. This vexes me the worst of anything whatever. There are at this time in the adjacent

> country not less than five or six well-meaning men in close jail for publishing their religious sentiments, which, in the main, are very orthodox. I have neither patience to hear, talk, or think anything relative to this matter; for I have squabbled and scolded, abused and ridiculed so long about it, to little purpose, that I am without common patience. So I must beg you to pity me, and pray for liberty of conscience to all.[3]

Often God raises up wise and prudent men to places of great influence to plead the cause of the weak and despised, and He opens their understanding to biblical principles that deliver men from the oppressor. May we pray for this provision in our day when we see so few with understanding of the true relationship between the church and state.

EWT

---

[1]Lewis Peyton Little, *Imprisoned Preachers and Religious Liberty in Virginia* (Lynchburg, Va.: J. P. Bell Co., 1938), pp. 128-36.

[2]Robert B. Semple, *A History of the Rise and Progress of the Baptists in Virginia* (Richmond: Published by the author, 1810), pp. 415-16.

[3]Charles F. James, *A Documentary History of the Struggle for Religious Liberty in Virginia* (1900; reprint ed. New York: Da Capo Press, 1971), p. 36.

January 25—When the Righteous Suffer as Evil Doers

Scripture: Proverbs 29:2; Psalm 12:1

The history of the Baptists in England following the Commonwealth from 1660 to 1688 is a sad recital of a search for survival rather than of expansion. In November of 1660, John Bunyan began his twelve-year jail term in Bedford, England. Others of the principal Baptist ministers were also imprisoned. On October 19, 1661, John James, a Sabbatarian Baptist minister, was dragged from his pulpit in Bulstrake Alley, Whitechapel in London, and committed to the Newgate jail. On November 26, 1661, he was taken to Tyburn to be hanged. Through all of this abuse King Charles II was unmoved.

The Baptists had no recourse but to seek favorable public relations through publications of their plight. Two publications were issued in 1661 in this cause. The first, written by "John Sturgion, a member of the baptized people," was entitled, *A Plea for Toleration of Opinions and Persuasions in Matters of Religion, differing from the Church of England.* This, along with the second, was an attempt to show the wickedness of persecutions and claim religious freedom. It also declared the willingness of Baptists, as loyal subjects, to obey the king and his officers in civil matters. The second piece of literature was entitled, *Sion's Groans for Her Distressed; or, Sober Endeavours to Prevent Innocent Blood.* Seven Baptist ministers affixed their names to the document. They included Joseph Wright, Thomas Monck, George Hammon, William Jeffrey, Francis Stanley, William Reynolds, and Francis Smith. Joseph Wright spent no less than twenty years in prison for the sake of truth!

Throughout all England the Baptists were pursued with wrath. But still the Baptists appealed to the king. A petition had been presented to King Charles II in July 1660 in which the supplicants mentioned that Baptists were even being threatened for praying in their own homes. On January 25, 1661, another petition entitled "The humble petition and presentation of the sufferings of several peaceable subjects, called by the name of Anabaptists, inhabitants in the county of Kent, and now prisoners in the jail at Maidstone, for the testimony of a good conscience" was presented.[1]

In time, the monarchy attempted to stifle the nonconforming Baptists by the Conventicle Act (1664), which limited the size of religious gatherings to no more than four, other than in the church buildings of the state church, and the Five Mile Act which would keep the Baptist preachers from towns and cities. But though the Government imposed severe penalties, the Baptists determined to obey God rather than man. Prisons were crowded with the godly, but our forefathers would not bow to the pressures. The full story cannot be given in such a short space, but Baptists today in America owe a great appreciation to their spiritual predecessors who believed that coercion has no place in spiritual reality.

May we determine to provide future generations with a similar heritage!

DLC

---

[1]J. M. Cramp, *Baptist History* (London: Elliott Stock, 1870), p. 285.

January 26—"Every Baptist a Missionary"

Scripture: Proverbs 3:5-10

The entry for January 2 refers to Johann Gerhard Oncken as the "Apostle of the German Baptists." Oncken's life was spiritually rich and proves challenging to Baptists today. This date in 1800 marks his birth, and for fifty years he served the Lord tirelessly! Thus, he also became known as the "Father of Continental Baptists."

> Oncken served as a one-man mission society, theological seminary, and literature distribution center. Seldom has one person contributed so much to the development of a denomination nor left his stamp more indelibly upon it. Not only in Germany but also throughout Europe much of the Baptist work stems either directly from Oncken or from others whom he trained and sent out. He served in an almost apostolic role, making extensive missionary tours of his own, writing letters to win new converts and to confirm others in the faith, and sending out missionaries and ministers to sustain the work thus begun.[1]

Oncken's motto was *Jeder Baptist ein Missionar* ("every Baptist a missionary"), and by 1850 the First Baptist Church of Hamburg supported three missionaries and assisted in raising funds to erect more than twenty Baptist church buildings in Europe.

But Johann Oncken was himself a missionary! In 1847 he went to Switzerland, and gaining converts, he baptized them and formed a church. Again in 1847 he traveled to Austria and baptized several. Eighteen fifty-five found our hero in Latvia preaching the gospel. In one of his tours, Oncken baptized a Rumanian convert who began work in Bucharest in 1858 as a colporteur, and in time, a church was formed there as well. Some Hungarians in Germany came into contact with Oncken and, after being converted, went back as missionaries to their own people.[2]

Believing in the power of the printed page, Johann Oncken distributed gospel literature everywhere he went. He organized the laymen of his church in Hamburg to distribute tracts from house to house, and he assisted in establishing the first regularly published Baptist paper in Europe, *Das Missionblatt* ("The Mission Paper"). In hopes of distributing the gospel message far and wide, Oncken would visit ships in port, distributing tracts and Bibles, for he believed the Word of God was living and could produce spiritual life.

In every way Oncken was a unique man who bought up every opportunity to share the message of redemption, and with indefatigable effort, he made an enduring impression for Christ. Cathcart has written, "Mr. Oncken . . . could not be intimidated nor silenced; he paid no heed to the prohibitions of the authorities; he dreaded not the dungeon, and yielded not, even when incarcerated."[3] Surely his life is an inspiration and calls for us to be faithful as well to our blessed Lord.

DLC

---

[1]H. Leon McBeth, *The Baptist Heritage* (Nashville: Broadman Press, 1987), p. 470.

[2]Henry C. Vedder, *A Short History of Baptist Missions* (1907; reprint ed., Philadelphia: Judson Press, 1927), pp. 387-88, 412, 429-30.

[3]William Cathcart, *The Baptist Encyclopedia,* ed. Louis H. Everts (Philadelphia: Louis H. Everts, 1881), 2:869.

January 27—Baptist Life Behind the Iron Curtain

Scripture: Psalm 11:3; I Corinthians 4:2

Born in 1928 to godly parents in Russia, Georgi P. Vins learned early the Communist opposition to the gospel. Georgi's father, the Reverend Peter I. Vins, had studied theology in America and returned to the USSR in 1922 where he ministered in pioneer work in Siberia. That ministry was fruitful but brief, for in 1930 he was arrested and sentenced to three years in concentration camps. In 1936 Peter Vins was arrested for the second time and incarcerated in prison, where he was held without trial for nine months and then released. However, in 1937, Georgi's father was arrested for the third time while pastoring the Baptist church in Omsk, Siberia. That church had one thousand members but was forcibly closed after Pastor Vins's arrest.

Young Georgi's life was indelibly stamped by such experiences, and years later he wrote of going to the prison with his mother to encourage his father. They were not allowed to "visit" per se, but they discovered that his father's fourth floor window had not been screened, and they sat on a bench on the adjacent street for hours and periodically Peter Vins waved his hand to his wife and son. And why was the Baptist preacher jailed? For preaching the gospel of the Lord Jesus Christ! The day came when the elder Vins was moved from the prison, never to be seen again by his wife and son, for he died in a concentration camp in Siberia in 1943.

Young Georgi matured and completed his education with two degrees in Kiev, but the godly influence of his home had deeply planted within him the need of remaining true to the Lord and preaching the gospel. His mother, Mrs. Lidia Vins, who had led the Council of Prisoners' Relatives, was arrested, and on February 8, 1970, she was sentenced to three years of imprisonment for her activities.

Meanwhile, Georgi Vins had become a leading voice among the Baptists. When the Russian government passed a law which forced all churches to register with the government, Brother Vins was one of the leaders of the Baptists who refused to comply and allow governmental control of local churches. His resistance led to his arrest and trial in

November 1966 and a sentence for three years in concentration camps. After his release in May 1969, he was sentenced again for a year of forced labor in Kiev. Being released, he was unable to pursue his ministry openly, and thus Vins hid for nearly four years. During that time he traveled in the Soviet Union without authorization, preaching and encouraging saints as the opportunities arose. However, in March 1974 Vins was rearrested, and at his trial on January 27, 1975, he was sentenced to five years in concentration camps, followed by five years of exile in Siberia and the confiscation of all his property.[1]

For the Lord's undertaking in this matter, you will want to read the entry for March 30. How we in America should thank God for the religious liberty that our Baptist forefathers championed on these shores!

DLC

---

[1]Alexander de Chalandeau, *The Christians in the USSR* (Chicago: Harper and Row, 1978), pp. 20-22.

January 28—Shubal Stearns, "The Old Father" of the Separates

Scripture: II Timothy 2:1-4

There is no doubt that Baptists in America owe a great debt to the evangelism of George Whitefield and his preaching tours of our land. Everywhere he preached souls were saved, and often his converts, driven to the Bible as they were, became ardent Baptists. In New England many Congregationalists accepted Christ through Whitefield's ministry and were set aflame with the gospel. These men were termed "New Lights," and they almost immediately advocated a regenerate church membership, a tenet that was unacceptable to the General Association of Congregational Churches in Connecticut.[1] As these "New Lights" continued in the Word of God, many embraced the biblical teaching of believer's immersion. Three such men were Isaac Backus, who became known as the "Apostle of Liberty"; Shubal Stearns, who became the outstanding leader of the Separate Baptists; and Daniel Marshall, who became the progenitor of the Baptist cause in Georgia.

Shubal Stearns was born on January 28, 1706. In 1745 he joined the "New Lights" and preached as a "New Light Congregationalist" until 1751, when he became convinced of believer's immersion and was baptized. On May 20, 1751, he was ordained into the Baptist ministry.

Being led of the Spirit, Stearns moved south to Opeckon Creek, Virginia, and preached in that area. Stearns was disappointed with the spiritual results of his ministry, for he had been impressed that God had a great work for him to do. Thus, on June 13, 1755, upon receiving a letter from some New England friends who had gone to North Carolina, he took it as the call of God and removed, with his relatives, to Sandy Creek, North Carolina. Upon his arrival there, a Baptist church was constituted with sixteen members. His brother-in-law, Daniel Marshall, had accompanied him and was of great assistance. A mighty outpouring of the Holy Spirit's power fell on the preaching of Shubal Stearns, and with Daniel Marshall and Joseph Breed as his assistants, in a short time the church had over six hundred members.

Shubal Stearns and the others traveled extensively, and the Spirit of God attended their ministry, not only calling the lost to salvation but also calling a host of young men to the ministry. John Dillahunty, Philip Mulkey, Joseph and William Murphy, James Read, Nathaniel Power, and James Turner were all called to preach. Soon Baptist churches flourished, and the Sandy Creek Association was formed to serve all the Separate Baptist churches in Virginia and the Carolinas. Shubal Stearns was lovingly revered as the "Old Father."

In time, the Association divided into three parts as the brethren from Virginia and South Carolina found the growth of the Baptist cause in their states sufficient to warrant closer attention. Daniel Harris had baptized Samuel Harriss, who was to become the so-called Apostle of Virginia. Stearns in North Carolina, Harriss in Virginia, and Marshall in the state of Georgia were mightily used in evangelizing the South, but Shubal Stearns must be considered the father of the movement. He died on November 20, 1771, and was buried near the Sandy Creek church. Cathcart opined:

> Few men ever enjoyed more of the Spirit's presence in the closet and in preaching the Gospel. Had he been a Romish priest, with as flattering a record of service to the church of the popes, long since he would have been canonized, and declared the 'Patron Saint' of North Carolina . . . and stately churches would have been dedicated to the holy and blessed St. Shubal Stearns, the apostle of North Carolina and the adjacent states.[2]

DLC

---

[1]William L. Lumpkin, *Baptist Foundations in the South* (Nashville: Broadman Press, 1961), p. 13.

[2]William Cathcart, *The Baptist Encyclopedia,* ed. Louis H. Everts (Philadelphia: Louis H. Everts, 1881), 2:1100.

January 29—When Royalty Embraced Immersion

Scripture: I Corinthians 1:25-31

Born in an affluent Christian home in old England, Lucy Hutchinson was given a superior education and witnessed early the blessedness of a holy life. Lucy was born on January 29, 1620,[1] in the Tower of London, where her father, Sir Allen Apsley, was governor.

Lucy developed a great fondness for reading, and when she reached womanhood, she was as well informed as any lady in the land. Before the years of maturity, she embraced Jesus Christ as her Savior and proved her love for Him with a life of wholehearted service. After Lucy married Colonel John Hutchinson, he was appointed governor of Nottingham and its castle. The couple exerted immense influence for English liberty and became great favorites among their countrymen. Colonel John Hutchinson, born in 1616, was the son of a baronet and had been educated at Cambridge.[2] The couple had an ample estate to allow them to live a quiet, peaceable life, but when the civil war broke out, Colonel Hutchinson devoted himself to the cause of his people with great fervor. When five of her husband's soldiers were wounded and carried to the castle, Lucy devoted herself to the task of binding up the bleeding limbs and bodies of the sufferers. Throughout her life she ever showed a strong faith that revealed itself with courage and benevolence. However, her experience with the wounded stamped her life in an unusual way.

The Hutchinsons were Presbyterians, and Lucy tells the interesting story of their conversion to Baptist principles. Before the birth of their first child, the Hutchinsons began to examine the Scriptures concerning infant baptism. They consulted with several Presbyterian divines at their home but concluded that the Word of God gave no warrant for infant baptism. While assisting the wounded in the castle, Lucy had been in the room of the cannoneers and had found some notes that had been used by Baptist soldiers when they had held a Bible study and prayer meeting. She carefully examined those notes, comparing them with Scripture, and ultimately she confessed her faith in believer's baptism. Colonel Hutchinson followed suit, professing Baptist principles as well. The colonel was a firm defender of religious liberty, and

George Fox, who established the Friends Society, found him his chief protector when Fox was a prisoner at Nottingham.

Lucy lived long enough to write her husband's "Memoirs," and she did so in a style that has been spoken of as prose excelled in the seventeenth century only by *Pilgrim's Progress.* Thank God that His Word has said, "Not *many* noble are called," rather than "Not *any* noble are called"! May we be willing, regardless of our station in life, to stand for the truth once for all delivered to the saints.

DLC

---

[1]William Cathcart, *The Baptist Encyclopedia,* ed. Louis H. Everts (Philadelphia: Louis H. Everts, 1881), 1:565-66.

[2]Thomas Armitage, *The History of the Baptists* (1890; reprint ed., Watertown, Wis.: Maranatha Baptist Press, 1976), 1:466.

January 30—When a "Lane" Became a "Highway" for Righteousness

Scripture: Romans 15:20

Tidence Lane was born near Baltimore, Maryland, on August 31, 1724. At that time, the chances of his ever becoming a Baptist preacher seemed most remote. His Anglican father, Richard Lane, was an ardent opponent of the Baptists. In time, the Lane family moved to North Carolina, and it was not long until the message of the Separate Baptists had a marked impression on the family.

Soon after his marriage to Esther Bibber in May 1743, Tidence heard the gospel through the preaching of Shubal Stearns, and he fell under conviction which led to his glorious salvation. Soon after his conversion, Tidence surrendered to preach the gospel. This must have been quite a blow to his father, for in 1758 Tidence's young brother Dutton was saved and called to preach, and his father was so irate that he pursued the young Dutton with the intention of killing him.[1] The story of the marvelous conversion of the father will be related later in this volume.

To Tidence and Esther Lane were born seven sons and two daughters. As political pressures were brought to bear upon the Baptists in North Carolina by the British governor, William Tryon, Tidence's desire to preach the gospel where it had never been declared caused him to turn his face toward Tennessee. Thus it was that Tidence Lane earned the honor of being "the first pastor of the first permanent church organization of any denomination in the state of Tennessee . . . in 1779." He also has the distinction of being "the first Moderator of the first association of any denomination in the state, the old Holston, organized at 'Cherokee meeting house,' in Washington County," on Saturday, October 21, 1786. This was ten years before the territory of Tennessee was admitted into the Union.[2]

Tennessee was but a wilderness, and it is believed that the early records of the church at Buffalo Ridge were destroyed during the Indian wars of 1774. David Benedict's description of Tidence Lane as being a preacher of "reputation and success" is surely borne out by the fact that by 1790 Tennessee had one association: 18 churches, 21 preachers, and 889 members.[3] Surely Tidence Lane was gifted with fine organizational skills along with pulpit ability.

Continuing in the work of the pastorate until his death on January 30, 1806, Lane labored in the ministry for over sixty years, and he lived to see growth as many were saved and churches were established in the westward thrust of the gospel. Surely those days called for men with a pioneering spirit who were willing to "spend and be spent" for Christ, and we honor on this day the memory of this true servant of Christ.

DLC

---

[1]Morgan Edwards, *Materials Toward a History of the Baptists* (Danielsville, Ga.: Heritage Papers, 1984), 2:45.

[2]Norman Wade Cox, ed., *Encyclopedia of Southern Baptists* (Nashville: Broadman Press, 1958), 2:758-59.

[3]Robert Baker, *The Southern Baptist Convention and Its People, 1607-1972* (Nashville: Broadman Press, 1974), pp. 90-91.

January 31—A Testimony of Baptists from Without

Scripture: II Corinthians 13:1

For years, students of Baptist history in America have alluded to a quotation from two Dutch scholars who were commissioned by the king of the Netherlands to investigate the claim of Dutch Baptists to an apostolic origin. The two Dutch scholars were Dr. Anne Ypeij, Professor of Theology in Gronigen, and Isaac Johannes Dermout, chaplain to the king. In fact, Baptists ascribe this material to this date, for the Reverend Mr. Dermout was born on January 31, 1777. Having discovered references to this material through the years, I was most pleased to discover a copy of the very volume in the Dutch language in the Western Theological Seminary in Holland, Michigan. The book is entitled, *Geschiedenis der Nederlandsche Hervormde Kerk.* A translation of the material into English reads as follows:

> We have now seen that the Baptists who were formerly called Anabaptists, and in later times Mennonites, were the original Waldenses, and who have long in the history of the church received the honor of that origin. On this account the Baptists may be considered as the only Christian community which has stood since the days of the apostles, and as a Christian society which has preserved pure the doctrines of the Gospel through all ages. The perfectly correct external and internal economy of the Baptist denomination tends to confirm the truth, disputed by the Romish Church, that the Reformation brought about in the sixteenth century was in the highest degree necessary, and at the same time goes to refute the erroneous notion of the Catholics, that their denomination is the most ancient.[1]

Baptists have espoused various theories concerning Baptist origins from the position of unbroken succession from the apostles, held by most Baptist historians of the nineteenth century, to the belief that Baptists descended from certain English Separatists who were congregational in their polity, held by the majority of historians in this century. This issue stirred Southern Baptists late in the nineteenth century, when Dr. William Whitsitt, then president of the Southern Baptist Seminary, published an article claiming that "believer's baptism" by immersion was restored by English Baptists in 1641. A relentless debate was waged by some Baptist newspaper editors against Dr. Whitsitt and the Seminary, bringing about his resignation in 1899.

The authors of this volume consider themselves "students" and not "accomplished scholars" in the area of Baptist history, but we maintain a position of "Principles Successionism," for we believe there has been a continuation of Baptist principles from apostolic days to the present. In any case, statements such as the above-mentioned declaration force us to realize that our forebears surely preceded the Reformation, and though they may not have been known by the name "Baptists," to paraphrase the well-known statement, "A Baptist by any other name is still a Baptist!" We thank God for our history and rejoice in the honesty of these two Dutch scholars.

DLC

---

[1]Anne Ypeij and Isaac Johannes Dermout, *Geschiedenis der Nederlandsche Hervormde Kerk* (Te Breda: W. Van Bergen en Comp., 1819), p. 148.

February

February 1—Prompt Obedience: The Will of God

Scripture: Isaiah 1:19

Time and again in our reading of Baptist history, we come upon the names of men such as Adoniram Judson, Luther Rice, Shubal Stearns, and Isaac Backus, who were involved in the ministry before coming to the point of being immersed with believer's baptism. But perhaps no such decision was as trying as that of Dr. Arthur T. Pierson.

Dr. A. T. Pierson, after fine academic training, entered the pastorate of a Congregational church in New York at age twenty-four. His first pastoral experience met with much blessing, and he learned many important lessons of self-discipline and seemed destined for a brilliant pastoral career. In 1863 he was called to a church of his boyhood denomination, Presbyterian, and he pursued the work as a Presbyterian minister for the next thirty-three years, becoming one of the best-known pastors in America. With a systematic schedule of Bible study and a love of the Lord, Pierson became one of the nation's leading expositors and became known for several very important theological volumes. During his pastorates in four Presbyterian churches, he adopted and perfected philosophies of growth that made him a leader in evangelism, Sunday school, and worldwide missions. Pierson counted as his personal friends men such as D. L. Moody, Charles H. Spurgeon, George Müller, and A. J. Gordon. In time, his ability in the Word of God and the pulpit caused him to receive many invitations to conferences of both missionary and prophetical import. Thus, he resigned his last pastorate in 1889 and began missionary crusades.

In 1891 Pierson was invited to serve the Metropolitan Tabernacle in the pastor's absence for "three, four, five or six months" until Spurgeon should recover. However, on January 31, 1892, the Lord called Spurgeon home. Pierson continued in the pulpit ministry while James Spurgeon, Charles's brother, carried on the pastoral responsibilities. Pierson had been considering the subject of baptism, and although he was slowly adopting Baptist views, he feared that some might misunderstand any action at that time, for they might think he was attempting to gain support to become permanent pastor. Thus he postponed all action, and the Tabernacle called Spurgeon's son, Thomas Spurgeon, to the pastorate.

Pierson continued in his conference ministry, but the Holy Spirit was burdening his heart about obedience. Pierson had planned to ask A. J. Gordon to immerse him, but Dr. Gordon, after a brief illness, passed away. So it was that having been invited by Dr. James A. Spurgeon to preach at West Croydon Chapel, London, arrangements were made for Pierson's immersion by Dr. Spurgeon on February 1, 1896. As Pierson had feared, his motives even then were questioned. On April 6, 1896, the Philadelphia Presbytery requested his resignation.

With peace of heart produced by obedience, Pierson wrote the presbytery, "Had I this action to take again I would only do it more promptly, for in the nature of the case . . . my only motive could be a desire 'to fulfill all righteousness.' "[1] Thank God for the testimony of Dr. A. T. Pierson, even in the face of misunderstanding!

DLC

---

[1]Delavan L. Pierson, *Arthur T. Pierson* (New York: Fleming H. Revell Co., 1912), p. 270.

February 2—An American Patriot

Scripture: Hebrews 12:1-2

Samuel Francis Smith was born in Boston, Massachusetts, on October 21, 1808, and became an excellent student. He was prepared for college in the Latin School of Boston and graduated from Harvard in 1829, immediately entering Andover Theological Institute. It was there in 1832, as a twenty-three-year-old Baptist seminary student, that he penned the words to the patriotic hymn "America." The date was February 2 as he sat at his desk translating from an old German hymnbook.[1] The music of one of the songs attracted his eye, and he hurriedly translated the words from German and realized as he did so that it was a lovely patriotic hymn. He began to think of his own great land, and as he did, he began to write, "Our fathers' God, to Thee, / Author of liberty, / To Thee we sing; / Long may our land be bright / With Freedom's holy light; / Protect us by Thy might, / Great God, our King.'' It was dark before he finished penning these words of the fourth stanza of what has become a favorite American hymn of patriotism.

Following his graduation from seminary, Smith became the editor of *The Baptist Magazine,* and though he pastored successfully, he became a great advocate of the new interest of Baptists in the work of foreign missions. He wrote the great missionary hymn of that day, ''The Morning Light is Breaking,'' and he served for seven years as the editor of *Christian Review* and then became the editor and translator for fifteen years of the *Missionary Union*. The busy pen of Smith stirred the hearts of men to the needs of the fields of the world, and he visited and ministered to missionaries in Burma, India, Ceylon, France, Germany, Denmark, Sweden, Austria, Turkey, Greece, Italy, and Spain. To Samuel Smith, missions was not merely a subject of interest but a commitment of heart. His son, the Reverend Dr. D. A. W. Smith, went to serve the Lord in Burma in 1863. Dr. Samuel Smith married the granddaughter of Dr. Hezekiah Smith, of great renown in Baptist history in America. We would surely expect then that his son would follow in such a fine tradition and also serve the Lord, but his willingness to go to Burma in that day was a tribute to his father's world vision.

Today when we think of Samuel Francis Smith, our minds return to the campus at Andover, and we envision the young student huddled in his meagerly furnished room when the love of country swept over his soul. The nation was young, and many could still give personal accounts of the battle to secure our liberty. The young theologian knew and acknowledged that our freedom had come from the ''Author of liberty.'' At our National Centenary, it was said, ''Mr. Rev. Dr. S. F. Smith's National Hymn, 'My Country, 'Tis of Thee,' set by Dr. Mason to the air of the English national anthem, though it has endured some severe criticism, has a popularity that no criticism seems able to shake.''[2] Thank God for the patriotism of our early Baptist leaders of America. May that spirit of love of country be reborn in our hearts in these days!

DLC

---

[1]William D. Blake, *An Almanac of the Christian Church* (Minneapolis: Bethany House Publishers, 1987), p. 41.

[2]Lemuel Moss, ed., *The Baptists and the National Centenary* (Philadelphia: American Baptist Publication Society 1876), p. 283.

February 3—A Businessman with a Song in His Heart

Scripture: Psalm 40:1-3

Christian businessmen have always played an important role in the expansion of Baptist causes, but William Howard Doane was a unique individual. Born on February 3, 1831, William Doane trusted Christ as his Savior while only sixteen, and he was baptized into the fellowship of the Central Baptist Church of Norwich, Connecticut, in 1851. Upon completing his education, Doane was hired as an accountant in a company that manufactured woodworking tools, and ultimately he became a partner in the firm. He spent most of his adult life in Cincinnati, Ohio, with the same corporation.

Early in life, Doane developed a taste for good music and became a serious student of music. He served as conductor of the Norwich Harmonic Society and became known for his musical productions. However, when he was thirty-one years of age, Doane suffered a serious heart disease, and he made a covenant with the Lord to use his talents to promote the gospel. From that time, Doane turned his attention to Christian music and composed many songs, particularly for Sunday school and evangelistic use. He published a number of hymnbooks which became popular in American Sunday schools. He is also credited with popularizing Christmas cantatas for use in local churches.

Doane's business flourished, and in 1878 he furnished a gift to the Denison University (Baptist institution) to construct a library building. His greatest contribution, however, was not financial gifts, but rather inspirational music. Doane wrote much of the music for the poetry of Fanny Crosby. On one occasion, during the summer of 1868, he knocked at Fanny Crosby's door. Upon being admitted, he rushed to Miss Crosby and said, "Miss Fanny, I have exactly forty minutes before my train leaves for Cincinnati, and I must make that train." When she asked the reason for his call in view of his schedule, he told her that there was a statewide Sunday school convention in his hometown the next month. He had written a melody and wanted her to write the words for a hymn that would be meaningful to the young people and children that would attend. Just that day Fanny Crosby had been reflecting upon the words of Scripture, "Underneath are the everlasting arms." Thus, as Doane played the melody, Miss Crosby wrote the wonderful words to the hymn "Safe in the Arms of Jesus." Completing the writing, she folded the sheet of paper, and putting it in an envelope, she urged him to hurry to his train and to read the lines there. Doane thanked her, and on the train read for the first time the words that have been such a blessing for so long to so many.[1] Doane and Miss Crosby collaborated in writing some of our most meaningful hymns: "Pass Me Not, O Gentle Savior," "To God be the Glory," "I Am Thine, O Lord," "Near the Cross," and many more.

In 1888, Doane edited the *Baptist Hymnal,* published by the American Baptist Publication Society.[2] This hymnal became perhaps the most widely used hymnal in Baptist churches throughout America. It was on Christmas Eve in 1915 that William Doane entered into the glories of the presence of our Lord and heard the heavenly music. The benevolent businessman blessed and benefited our churches with lovely melodies that are still enjoyed today.

DLC

---

[1]Ernest K. Emurian, *Living Stories of Famous Hymns* (Grand Rapids: Baker Book House, 1955), p. 112.

[2]William Henry Brackney, *The Baptists* (New York: Greenwood Press, 1988), p. 156.

February 4—Prayer Connects the Impotence of Man with the Omnipotence of God

Scripture: Acts 12:1-17

According to the Order Book of Chesterfield County, Virginia, Number 5, page 400, David Tinsley was arrested on February 4, 1774. The charges were as follows:

> David Tinsley being committed, charged with having assembled and preached to the people at sundry times and places in this county as a Baptist preacher, and the said David acknowledging in court that he has done so. On consideration thereof the court being of opinion that the same is the breach of the peace and good behavior, It is ordered that he give surety for keeping the peace & of being of good behavior for one year next ensuing himself in the penalty of 50 pounds & two sureties in penalty of 25 pounds each.[1]

The statement of the court on this occasion indicates that it was a crime to be a Baptist and to preach the gospel of Jesus Christ. On

March 4 of this same year, Archibald W. Roberts was indicted for using hymns and poems instead of the psalms of David following Communion and the sermon. The state and its church were using every avenue to stifle the voices of these Baptist evangelists who were heralding the message of the grace of God.

Tinsley was confined for four months and sixteen days, during which time he, with others of his fellow prisoners, preached to the assembled crowds through the grates of the prison. The Chesterfield officials were debating what really constituted the law in these cases while Tinsley languished in prison. He appealed by letter to his brethren in association assembled at Hall's Meeting House in Halifax County, on the second Saturday in May 1774. The associational record has this to say about Tinsley's appeal in part: "The hearts of their brethren were affected at their sufferings, in consequence of which it was agreed to raise contributions for their aid. A resolution was entered into to set apart for second and third Saturdays in June as public fast days to pray for the 'poor blind persecutors, and for the releasement of our brethren.' "[2]

The money raised was sent, wrapped in a handkerchief, to Patrick Henry for his employment in behalf of the preachers' release. It was returned that way by that noble patriot even though he interceded in their behalf. When a wall was erected about the jail to prevent the preachers from exhorting the people, a handkerchief was displayed on a pole as a signal that the people were ready to hear. This fellowship, formed between all those involved, became known as the "bandana brigade." Historic handkerchief! Never did a standard give signal in a worthier cause or float before a nobler beleaguered band.

The fasting and praying were effectual. The date of Tinsley's release was close to, if not on, the second public fast day. Prayer is the link that connects earth and heaven, the impotence of man with the omnipotence of God. Not only was David Tinsley released about that time, but the series of imprisonments was drawing to a close. Only two more arrests are known to have been made throughout the colony and Commonwealth of Virginia—one in 1775 and another in 1778.

During the course of these imprisonments, many a curious person went to the jail to hear and ridicule these preachers, only to fall under deep conviction of sin by their messages of truth. Great numbers were saved and became Baptists, and some became Baptist preachers.

EWT

---

[1]Lewis Peyton Little, *Imprisoned Preachers and Religious Liberty in Virginia* (Lynchburg, Va.: J. P. Bell Co., 1938), pp. 441-46.

[2]Ibid.

February 5—America's First Baptist Chaplain

Scripture: Nehemiah 4

The first Baptist pastor ever to become a chaplain in the American military was the Reverend David Jones, who in 1776 was appointed to serve Colonel St. Clair's regiment. He also served under General Horatio Gates and General Anthony Wayne. He was highly trusted by General George Washington and preached to the troops at Valley Forge.

The life of David Jones was filled with learning and adventure. He was reared in a hearty Welsh Baptist family, was saved early in life, and trained for three years.in the Hopewell Academy (America's first Baptist academic facility) in New Jersey. He studied medicine but doubtless was influenced by the life and ministry of David Brainerd among the Indians, for while pastoring the Freehold Baptist Church in Monmouth County, New Jersey, Jones actually became the first Baptist missionary to the Indians in Ohio on two extended tours that consumed over a year.

Upon returning to the pastorate in Freehold, the firmness of Jones's expression concerning a desire for American freedom rendered him unpopular. Thus in April 1775, he accepted the call to become pastor of the Great Valley Baptist Church in Chester County, Pennsylvania. The Continental Congress called for a day of fasting and prayer (July 20, 1775), and Jones preached to an army regiment on the subject "Defensive War in a Just Cause Sinless." The die was cast, and in 1776 he left his flock to serve the first of three tours of duty with the American forces. There were few major events in the war that Jones missed, for he was at Ticonderoga, Morristown, and Brandywine. He narrowly escaped being killed at the Paoli Massacre, and he spent the winter with the troops at Valley Forge. So valuable was he considered by the English that General Howe offered a reward for his capture. When victory came at Yorktown in 1781, he was present for the surrender of Lord Cornwallis.

Chaplain Jones was called upon to use his medical skills as well and removed bullets and even performed amputations, although he lacked the benefit of anesthetic. It might amaze some to realize that Chaplain Jones carried a pistol or a musket and was not unwilling to use it in battle.

After American independence had been secured, Jones returned to the pastoral ministry, but when General Wayne requested that he serve as chaplain to the troops during the Indian War in the Northwest Territory, he responded and served from 1794-96 and was present at the signing of the treaty at Greenville. Again, the Reverend Mr. Jones returned to his pastoral duties.

Incredible as it may sound, David Jones at age seventy-six was appointed chaplain once again in the War of 1812, and he served America faithfully. One of his last public addresses was delivered at the dedication of the monument commemorating the Paoli Massacre, where he had been so close to death. Jones died on February 5, 1820, at age 84. He had served as an author, pastor, missionary, medical doctor, and chaplain. "In danger he knew no fear, in fervent patriotism he had no superiors and few equals, in the Revolutionary struggle he was a tower of strength. . . . He was a Christian without reproach."[1] We do well to pray for Bible-believing chaplains to serve in our military forces today.

DLC

---

[1]William Cathcart, *The Baptist Encyclopedia,* ed. Louis H. Everts (Philadelphia: Louis H. Everts, 1881), 1:611.

February 6—He Was Defended by Giants

Scripture: Psalm 91

A stately brick home stands near Chantilly, Virginia, which was the residence of Richard Major, an early colonial Baptist preacher. His grave, a few hundred feet behind the house, is marked by a weathered stone. The house remains one of a few structures of its kind, standing as a landmark to our early Baptist history in America.

Richard Major was born near Pennsbury, Pennsylvania, February 6, 1722, into a Presbyterian household.[1] During his early years, he was brought occasionally under terrible conviction of sin, which he would endeavor to shake off by resorting to wild company. He continued to pursue the most horrid temptations until in the years of maturity grace prevailed, and he became a most zealous Christian. He embraced Baptist principles in 1764 and moved to Loudon County, Virginia, in 1766.

Though he was not a man of much schooling, Major had a vigorous mind; and devoting himself to the study of the Scripture, he became well taught in the school of Christ. He was ordained by and became the pastor of the Little River Church, out of which it is reputed that he planted six or eight churches.[2]

For many years after Major began preaching, he met a great deal of opposition. Warrants were issued for his arrest, but the officers always failed to take him. At Bull Run a mob armed with clubs rose to assist in the execution of a warrant, but the Davis brothers, giants of men who had been enlisted to oppose him, after hearing him preach, became well affected toward him and threatened to chastise anyone who disturbed him.

A certain man whose wife had been baptized by Major determined to kill him on sight and went to a meeting for that purpose. He hoped to catch him in some obnoxious expression and use it as a pretense to attack him. The Lord intervened, and the man became so convicted that he could not stay on his feet and was afterwards baptized by the man he intended to murder.

On another occasion, a man violently attacked him with a club. Richard Major turned to him and said, "Satan, I command thee to come out of the man." The club immediately fell to the ground, and the lion became as quiet as a lamb. These were just a few of many similar incidents during his ministry.

Major began to suffer from a malady called "gravel." Someone recommended a remedy: one gill of the juice of a red onion, mixed with the juice of horsemint, taken each morning. This he did and found some relief for several years and was able to continue his ministry.

Major was highly esteemed in his latter years. This caused him some alarm because he remembered that the Lord warned to beware when all men speak well of you. This uneasiness was calmed when he accidentally overheard someone laying to his charge a most abominable crime.

May our Lord once again permit us to have our ministries interrupted by His intervention and give us the discernment to understand it.

EWT

---

[1]David Benedict, *A General History of the Baptist Denomination in America* (Boston: Manning and Loring, 1813), 2:349-50.

[2]Robert B. Semple, *A History of the Rise and Progress of the Baptists in Virginia* (Richmond: Published by the author, 1810), pp. 432-33.

February 7—The Hercules of the Anabaptists

Scripture: I Corinthians 4:11-13

The entries for January 5 and January 17 describe the strong convictions that faith in the Word of God had produced in the lives of the Swiss Anabaptists Felix Manz and Conrad Grebel, but we would be remiss in failing to mention George Blaurock. Born in Bonaduz, a village in Grisons, Switzerland, in 1491, George Blaurock was destined to become a leader among the Anabaptists. We know little of his early life, but he was educated in the University of Leipzig, was a married man before becoming involved with the Anabaptists, and had been a Roman Catholic priest. He has been alluded to as "the Hercules of the Anabaptists," but the name "Blaurock" was given to him because of the "blue coat" that he wore.[1] He has also been referred to as "the second Paul" because of his oratorical gifts.[2]

Blaurock was primarily known for his boldness and zeal rather than his intellectual ability, but his debates with Zwingli evidenced that he had a keen mind too. In personal appearance he was described as being "a tall, powerful figure with fiery eyes, black hair and a small bald spot."[3]

His record of imprisonment and suffering is amazing. Blaurock was arrested on February 7, 1525, along with Manz and twenty-four parents who had refused to have their children baptized, and for a week he was incarcerated in the Augustinian cloister. At the end of the week, he was released. On November 6, 1525, he was rearrested and placed in chains. On the eighteenth of the month, he was sentenced to imprisonment in the New Tower, to be kept on a diet of bread and water. On January 5, 1527, the day of Felix Manz's glorious martyrdom,

> Blaurock's hands were bound, his body was stripped to the waist, and as he passed along the street from the Fishmarket to the Niederdorf Gate, he was beaten with rods until the blood flowed from the wounds thus made. Blaurock endured his sufferings not less heroically than Manz. At the gate an oath that he would not return was demanded of him by the officers who had conducted him thither; but he refused, saying that to take an oath is forbidden by God. On this account, he was taken back to the Wellenberg to await the further decision of the Council. Blaurock soon concluded to take the oath, it is said; but as he left Zurich he shook the dust from his blue coat and his shoes as a testimony against his persecuting adversaries.[4]

But Blaurock was a man of conviction and could not be silenced. He continued for two years to carry on the work of the Anabaptists in Switzerland. "On September 6, 1529, when he was the pastor of a small church of believers in Tyrol, George was burned at the stake. That little group of believers was once more without a pastor; its previous one had been burned there a mere three months earlier."[5]

Thank God, truth cannot be drowned or burned! As we read the accounts of such men of God, may we resolve within our hearts as well to be witnesses of the Lord Jesus Christ, either by life or by death!

DLC

---

[1]William R. Estep, *The Anabaptist Story* (Nashville: Broadman Press, 1963), p. 31.

[2]Henry S. Burrage, *A History of the Anabaptists in Switzerland* (Philadelphia: American Baptist Publication Society, 1882), p. 96.

[3]Estep, p. 31.

[4]Burrage, p. 175.

[5]Leonard Verduin, *The Anatomy of a Hybrid* (Grand Rapids: Eerdmans Publishing Company, 1976), p. 171.

February 8—The Man for Whom Death Held No Fear

Scripture: Luke 14:25-27

"In the days of the long ago, Roman Catholic and Protestant leaders harbored a strong dislike for one another, but they harmonized in persecuting the people of the Baptist faith and practice."[1] This quotation from Joseph Meyer is surely confirmed by the history of the early days of the Reformation. The Anabaptists of Germany knew the hatred of both groups.

George Wagner of Emmerick was taken into custody at Munich in Bavaria because of four articles of faith. "First, that the priests cannot forgive men their sins; secondly, he did not believe that a man can bring God from heaven; thirdly, he did not believe that God, or Christ, is bodily in the bread that the priest places upon the altar, but that it is the bread of the Lord; and fourthly, he held not the belief that the baptism of water saves men."[2]

The sad story of the martyrdom of George Wagner is told us graphically in the history of the period. Being unwilling to renounce his position and recant, he was inhumanely tortured. Inasmuch as the torture was so severe, the prince had compassion upon him and personally visited him, requesting that Wagner recant. Failing in this, the prince sent his tutor to attempt to reason with the suffering Anabaptist, but this too failed. Wagner's wife and child were then brought to the prison and placed before him, but Wagner said that though his wife and child were indeed so valuable to him that all the wealth of the kingdom could not be compared, yet he could not forsake the Lord his God! Priests were paraded into his cell to persuade him, but he was unmovable. Thus he was condemned to die in the flames. Finally, Conrad Schaider, the master of St. Peter's school in Munich, made his effort to detour Wagner from his course. He asked, "George, what thinkest thou that holdest baptism to be nothing, and yet thou knowest that Christ was baptized in Jordan.'' Wagner answered, showing the true design of baptism, and then reaffirmed that it was necessary for Christ to die on the cross in order to redeem sinners. Then he said, ''Even that Christ is my Savior: for faith in Whom I today yield up my self, and whom today with a good confession before all, I will glorify.''

Being committed into the hands of the executioner, he was led to the middle of the city and cried, ''Today I will confess my God before all the world.'' He experienced such joy in the Lord that he showed no fear but went smiling to the fire! When thrown into the flames, he cried with a loud voice, ''Jesus! Jesus!'' And thus he died on February 8, 1527, bearing witness of the truth as it is in Christ Jesus.

This sequel too is of interest: ''The sheriff, however, surnamed Eisenreich von Landsberg, while returning home from the place of execution, traveling on horseback; purposing to apprehend others of the brethren, died suddenly in the night, and was found dead in his bed in the morning, having thus been removed through the wrath of God.''[3]

Thank God for a faith worth living or dying for!

DLC

---

[1]Joseph Meyer, ed., *Baptist Establishers of Religious Liberty* (Chicago: Privately printed, 1923), p. 98.

[2]J. Newton Brown, *Memorials of Baptist Martyrs* (Philadelphia: American Baptist Publication Society, 1854), p. 55.

[3]Thieleman J. van Braght, Jr., *The Bloody Theater* (Scottsdale, Pa.: Herald Press, 1950), p. 416.

February 9—The Making of a Great Preacher

Scripture: Romans 8:28

One of the most famous Baptist preachers that America ever knew was Dr. George W. Truett of the First Baptist Church of Dallas, Texas. His sermons are still treasured, and his voice, once heard, could never be forgotten! His voice, full of pathos and almost sorrow, was used of God to call countless to repentance of sin and faith in the Lord Jesus Christ. But few people in our generation know the experience that transformed the ministry of that great man of God.

On the fourth of February, 1898, Pastor Truett, along with Captain J. C. Arnold, Chief of the Dallas Police Department, went quail hunting with the Reverend George W. Baines, pastor of the First Baptist Church of Cleburne, Texas. The trio greatly enjoyed the fellowship together as they hunted east of Cleburne. But as they prepared to return to Baines's home, Dr. Truett shifted his hammerless shotgun from one arm to the other, and it accidentally discharged. The blast struck Captain Arnold in the right leg, causing a terrible wound. Thinking that the wound was not serious, the Captain tried to reassure his pastor, but almost with a foreboding from the Lord, the thirty-year-old pastor was in unspeakable agony of heart. Captain Arnold was taken to Dallas for treatment, but he continued with great suffering, and on the evening of February 5, he passed away into the presence of the Lord.

The Reverend Mr. Baines conducted the funeral from the First Baptist Church of Dallas on Wednesday, February 9, and young George Truett was filled with the agony of self-condemnation for his carelessness. He vowed to his wife that he would never be able to preach again, and he continually paced the floor. When it was announced that the cause of death was the formation of a blood clot in the heart, George Truett was totally crushed. The attempts of Mrs. Truett to console her husband seemed futile.

As the Lord's Day approached, Truett could not rest, and as he paced the floor, he continually said, "My times are in thy hands." With complete exhaustion the man of God finally fell asleep. It was that night that his entire life and ministry were transformed! Only with great reluctance did he allow the details to be told, but that night he had a most vivid, three-fold dream. The man of God saw our Lord Jesus Christ standing by his bedside, and three times over our Lord said, "Be not afraid. You are my man from now on."[1] Many have found that account difficult to believe, but on the morrow, with drawn face and sad eyes, he entered the pulpit to preach. Things were different, and the results cannot be disputed. During his forty-seven-year pastorate at First Baptist Church, more than twenty thousand members were added. By the time of his death in 1944, perhaps no other preacher in America was better known, for he had become the Lord's man through a bitter experience that allowed him to reach into the very hearts of his hearers—whether they sat in the pew or sought his counsel in the hour of their sorrow—for none had experienced a greater sorrow than had that great man of God, and the Lord had sustained him.

DLC

---

[1]H. Leon McBeth, *The First Baptist Church of Dallas* (Grand Rapids: Zondervan Publishing House, 1968), pp. 135-37.

February 10—A Man Greatly Mourned

Scripture: Psalm 77:11-14

Ancient Baptist history has been difficult to discover for two primary reasons. First, the books and writing of many of the Baptist martyrs were cast into the flames in which the martyrs were burned to death, and second, much that has been preserved has been written by opponents of the Baptists and has portrayed them in a very distorted light. The persecution of Baptists in England was severe, but one of the oldest Baptist churches known in Great Britain is the Baptist church at Hill Cliffe in the County of Chester.

The earliest evidence of the existence of that assembly of believers is found on a gravestone bearing the date 1357, located near the ancient chapel. Surely the members at Hill Cliffe suffered intensely during the reign of the bloody Queen Mary, for on June 27, 1558, Roger Holland suffered martyrdom for the testimony of his faith. Apparently, it was at that time that an excavation, about four yards long and three yards wide, was made in the sandstone beneath the chapel, providing a haven for those fleeing their persecutors.

The church had employed an outdoor baptistery of stone work in the ground which was uncovered when the chapel was rebuilt in 1800. Of course, the stone baptistery reveals that immersion had long been practiced by the members of the chapel and thus designates it as a long-established Baptist congregation.

The earliest minister that can be identified, according to some deeds discovered years ago, is a Mr. Weyerburton, who served the church until his death in 1594. However, to reveal the growth and permanence of this witness for Christ, our interest at this time is to mention the death of one of the pastors, James Bradford, who died on February 10, 1830. The Hill Cliffe Church had prospered under the beloved Pastor Bradford, and his funeral was preached by Mr. Moses Fisher of Liverpool. According to the "Baptist Magazine" of July 1880, more than 1,600 persons attended the funeral, which of necessity had to be conducted in the open air between the chapel and the burying grounds at Hill Cliffe. The fact that 1,600 persons attended the funeral confirms the growth of the influence of the church and the testimony of the faithful pastor who has been described as a humble Christian with ardent piety. The tombstone in the burial ground bears the following inscription:

> IN MEMORY OF JAMES BRADFORD THE FAITHFUL AND LABORIOUS PASTOR OF THIS CHURCH, WAS ORDAINED OCT. 12th, 1820, AND WAS CALLED TO HIS REST ON THE 10th FEBRUARY, 1830. AGED 44 YEARS. HIS LIFE WAS EXEMPLARY; HIS MINISTRY USEFUL; HIS DEATH HAPPY.[1]

The history of the Hill Cliffe Church was first written in 1882, has recently been reprinted, and it serves as yet another link in our present-day Baptist pedigree investigation as we seek our spiritual "roots."

DLC

---

[1]James Kenworthy, *History of the Baptist Church at Hill Cliffe* (1882; reprint ed., Gallatin, Tenn.: Church History Research and Archives, 1987), p. 81.

February 11—A Living Sacrifice for the Indians

Scripture: II Corinthians 12:14-15

The inscription over the tomb of the Reverend Isaac McCoy reads as follows: "For nearly thirty years his entire time and energies were devoted to the civil and religious improvement of the aborigines of this country. He projected and founded the plan of their colonization, their only hope, and the imperishable monument of his wisdom and benevolence."[1]

Isaac McCoy has justly been called "The apostle of the Indians of the West,"[2] for his sacrificial life of privation was consumed in the interest of the Indians.

McCoy was born in Pennsylvania on June 13, 1784, but six years later his family moved to Kentucky. There he trusted Christ Jesus as Savior, was baptized, and united with the Buck Creek Baptist Church. He married in 1803, and the next year he and his wife moved to Indiana. He soon evidenced spiritual leadership and was licensed to preach. He was then ordained by the Maria Creek Baptist Church and served as pastor. The church grew as the pastor, "with the Bible in one hand and rifle in the other, went everywhere preaching, 'the Lord working with him.' "[3]

In 1817 the McCoys were appointed missionaries to the Indians of Indiana and Illinois, and his lifework began. McCoy founded a mission just west of what is now Niles, Michigan, and named it "Carey" after the great missionary. McCoy rode hundreds of miles on horseback through the wilderness, swam swollen streams, and slept on the wet ground at night that he might tell the Indians of the Savior. One of his greatest sorrows came when, while he was away preaching, sickness and death visited his family. Five of his six children died at different times while he was absent from home, but the McCoys were dedicated to God's call, and no sacrifice was too great. Not only did McCoy ride horseback to preach the gospel, but he made numerous trips to Washington, D.C., to set before Congress the needs of the Indians. In 1826 he gave up the superintendence of the Carey Mission for the purpose of surveying and selecting lands for the Indians further west. Upon returning in 1833 from such a trip, which had been filled with the hardship of winter as the temperature fell from 20° to 30° below zero and the marauding bands of Indians had proven troublesome, McCoy found a summons to go to Washington again. Thus, on February 11, 1834, he left home for the national capital and was overjoyed to discover that the secretary of war had submitted his plan for the organization of Indian affairs.

In his many labors and much travel, Isaac McCoy composed hymns which were used by the Indians in their worship of the true God. He secured a printing press, and on March 1, 1835, he printed in the Shawnee tongue the first newspaper ever published in an Indian language. In his journeys he preached the first English sermon delivered in Chicago or near its site. In 1842 he was appointed the Secretary of the American Indian Association of the Triennial Baptist Convention.

At age sixty-three, returning home from preaching, Isaac McCoy was caught in a rainstorm and became sick, and in a few days, on June 21, 1846, he entered his eternal home with the Lord Jesus Christ.

DLC

---

[1]Walter Sinclair Stewart, *Early Baptist Missionaries and Pioneers* (Philadelphia: Judson Press, 1925), p. 228.

[2]William Cathcart, *The Baptist Encyclopedia,* ed. Louis H. Everts (Philadelphia: Louis H. Everts, 1881), 2:767.

[3]William T. Stott, *Indiana Baptist History* (n.p., 1908), p. 53.

February 12—The Bohemian Judson

Scripture: Acts 20:20-24

Resetov, Czechoslovakia, was an important center of the religious movement during the Reformation, and many clandestine Protestant meetings were held in the vicinity. By the middle of the seventeenth century, the Roman Catholic church was strongly entrenched, but there was still a residue of the opposition, and secret meetings were being held. Into such an environment Henry Novotny was born on July 12, 1846. Henry's mother died when he was only seven years old, but his father cared well for the family.

While still a youth, Henry visited a secret meeting of the Protestants and was so impressed that he asked permission to attend regularly. He began to enjoy reading the forbidden Bible and other literature. In the course of time, one of the little group died, and, not wanting a Catholic priest to conduct the funeral, they asked young Henry to do so. Still belonging to the Catholic church, Henry questioned whether he should, but he finally consented, and his message stirred the little flock. From that time on, Henry was the preacher of the group.

Then young Novotny faced an important decision. It was not proper for him to belong to the Roman Catholic church and serve as a Protestant preacher. However, if he left the Catholic church openly, it would lead to suspicion and persecution. Finally he announced to the little flock, "I resolve that with God's help I shall leave the Roman Catholic Church and become a Protestant."[1] The congregation was moved by his courage.

Henry's gift for preaching convinced him that God was calling him into the ministry, and in November, 1870, he left for Switzerland and entered a theological institute. From there he received a scholarship in Edinburgh, Scotland, and upon completing the course, he became a Congregational church missionary in Prague.

While in Prague, Novotny met August Meereis, a Baptist from Bavaria. The two became friends and exchanged literature as they studied the Scriptures, and Novotny came to the position of accepting believer's immersion. He was immersed on February 12, 1885, in Lodz, Russian-Poland. Shortly thereafter, he was ordained into the Baptist ministry at Zyradow. He spent the remainder of his life in Bohemia in the service of the Lord. He trained his converts to be missionaries and to assist him in the work in his absence. The Baptists were hated and despised, persecuted and imprisoned, and could not even own property as a church. Novotny faced the challenges, and with wisdom he led his people to overcome the obstacles and to expand their influence. "Henry Novotny was not only a good theologian, pastor and preacher, but also a good father, whom God blessed with . . . three sons and three daughters. . . . All the children engaged in some sort of missionary work." We honor on this day the memory of Henry Novotny, "The Bohemian Judson," and remember his obedience to the Lord in his baptism.

DLC

---

[1]Vaclav Vojta, *Czechoslovak Baptists* (Minneapolis: Czechoslovak Baptist Convention, 1941), pp. 43-44.

February 13—Every Obstacle Became an Opportunity

Scripture: II Corinthians 12:10

John Dagg's life is a complete and thrilling saga of a man overcoming trials and limitations. Born in Virginia on February 13, 1794, young Dagg pursued his early studies by candlelight and mastered Latin, Greek, and Hebrew. However, he permanently impaired his eyesight, and in later years he had to be assisted, both in reading and writing because of that handicap.[1]

According to his personal testimony, John Dagg "obtained a joyful sense of acceptance with God" on his fifteenth birthday. The young man was baptized in 1813, began to preach in 1816, and was ordained to the gospel ministry in 1817. For several years he pastored small Baptist churches in Virginia, but because these churches were unable to support him fully, he was compelled to serve in the field of education as well, as a teacher.

In 1825 the Reverend Mr. Dagg accepted the call to the pastorate of the prestigious Sansom Street Baptist Church in Philadelphia, where he succeeded the well-loved Dr. William Staughton. The amazing thing is that Dagg should be called to such a prominent church, for he had been severely injured by a fall in his twenties. At times the dear man of God was so infirm that he was housebound and unavailable to minister to his people. With an indomitable spirit, John Dagg persevered. He had overcome the lack of formal education, damage to his sight, and a crippling injury, and yet he continued in the work of God. His trials were not complete, however, for when throat problems developed and he could speak only in a whisper, he was forced to resign from a preaching ministry. Thus he left Philadelphia after nine years in the pastorate there.[2]

With an invincible attitude he moved to Tuscaloosa, Alabama, and took charge of the Alabama Female Atheneum, and finally in 1844, although he had never received a formal college education, he was appointed president of Mercer University in Macon, Georgia. The twelve years of his presidency witnessed tremendous strides in the theological department, where he also taught. However, with advancing age, he resigned in 1856. His work was still not done. Retiring to Alabama, Dr. Dagg accomplished perhaps his greatest success in life. In 1857 he published his *Manual of Theology*. This volume became most influential in directing the theology of Southern Baptists in those days. Dagg's theology was biblical rather than philosophical. He wrote, "We yield everything which is not required by the Word of God; but in what this word requires, we have no compromise to make."[3] Dr. Dagg overcame a multitude of problems to become a leading Christian educator, inspirational missions leader, encourager of the Baptist Publication Society, pastor, and author. The Lord called His servant home on June 11, 1884, after a full life of usefulness in the work of God.

DLC

---

[1]Norman Wade Cox, ed., *Encyclopedia of Southern Baptists* (Nashville: Broadman Press, 1958), 1:345.

[2]William Cathcart, *The Baptist Encyclopedia*, ed. Louis H. Everts (Philadelphia: Louis H. Everts, 1881), 1:306.

[3]William Henry Brackney, *The Baptists* (New York: Greenwood Press, 1988), p. 155.

February 14—Adversity Could Not Dissuade Him

Scripture: Philippians 3:13-17

It is generally agreed that Baptist principles were known in Wales at a very early period. We can say as well that early in our American history, the Welsh Baptists influenced the Baptist effort in America. In 1663 "an immigrant church which was organized in Wales in 1649 . . . came to this country in a body, 'bringing their church records with them,' and settled on a grant of land near the Rhode Island frontier. . . . John Miles was the pastor, leading this group of Baptists from the Old to the New World."[1]

The Welsh Baptists brought an emphasis on church associations, Bible-based Sunday schools, and joyous congregational singing. "From the earliest days Welsh Baptists have exerted a very positive influence upon the denominational life of English-speaking America. There can be little doubt that the type of American Baptist life was struck in a Welsh mold."[2]

With our modern-day travel, we find it difficult to appreciate the privations of early seekers of religious freedom. Unfortunately, John

Miles and his flock fled persecution only to meet it again at the hands of the Plymouth Court. However, another Welsh Baptist preacher, Abel Morgan, felt the constraining hand of God to move from Wales to America, and the story of his persistence should prove a blessing. On August 23, 1711, the church in Blaenaugwent held a special service of honor for their pastor who had served them for fifteen years, and with broken hearts they said their farewells. To part with such a celebrated minister whom they loved so dearly seemed more than they could bear, but Pastor Morgan was answering the direction of the Spirit of God. His last address to his flock was recorded in their church for the benefit of those generations that would follow.

Soon thereafter the Morgans went to Bristol, and on September 28 they sailed for America. However, the winds were contrary, and the ship had to turn into a haven, and they were detained for three weeks. When again they sailed, they were driven by turbulent winds to Cork in Ireland, and again they were delayed for five additional weeks in harsh circumstances due to the illness of many of the passengers. However, on November 19 they finally were able to begin the arduous trip. On December 14 Abel Morgan's son died, and three days later his dearly beloved wife breathed her last, and both had to be buried at sea. Surely this was a severe trial, but in complete confidence upon the Lord, God's servant would persevere and not complain! Finally, on February 14, 1711, they arrived in America, and Morgan took up the work of the ministry in Penepeck near Philadelphia, and he labored there until the time of his death on December 16, 1722.[3]

The old Welsh preachers were known for their vigorous declaration of truth. Preaching was preeminent among the Welsh Baptists, and doubtless the biblical foundation laid by such virile preaching laid the groundwork for the Welsh revival. May God give us preachers in our day who preach with power, passion, and persuasion under the Holy Spirit!

DLC

---

[1]Jesse L. Boyd, *A History of Baptists in America Prior to 1845* (New York: American Press, 1957), pp. 31-32.

[2]Albert Henry Newman, *A Century of Baptist Achievement* (Philadelphia: American Baptist Publication Society, 1901), p. 60.

[3]J. Davis, *History of the Welsh Baptists* (Pittsburgh: J. M. Hogan, 1835), pp. 68-69.

February 15—Thou Hast a Little Strength and Hast Kept My Word

Scripture: Revelation 3:7-12

In the middle 1600s there was a great ferment in the Massachusetts Bay Colony. The colonists were facing the problem of children born to parents who had been baptized in infancy but had not confirmed their faith since becoming adults. The result of the debates over this issue was the Half-Way Covenant, a compromise by which parents, through intellectual assent to the tenets of the faith and obedience to the discipline of the church, could transmit the same degree of church membership to their offspring, that is, baptism, but not the right to the Lord's Supper or voting privileges. By 1677 many ministers were advocating the extension of full church privileges to the Half-Way members. This filled the churches with unconverted people, deadened preaching, and contributed to a reliance upon man's works to get people into the "kingdom."[1]

John Eliot, a devout man from Roxbury, had begun teaching Christianity among some of the Indians around 1646. A society was incorporated to promote the work. Eliot became proficient in their language and translated the Bible into it. With the help of some others, he formed twelve praying societies among the Indians. These were scattered during the bloody King Philip's War. In spite of their persecutions, the Baptists fought valiantly during that war with the Indians to protect the settlements. One company, made up mostly of Baptists, was led by William Turner and distinguished itself in combat.[2]

The Baptists were increasing enough to alarm the ministers of the state church. They had their law to banish Baptists reprinted in 1672 and often fined and imprisoned Baptist violators. One of their ministers, William Hubbard, in a sermon said, "It is made, by learned and judicious writers that one of the undoubted rights of sovereignty is to determine what religion shall be publicly professed and exercised within their dominions." He also said that it was morally impossible to rivet the Christian religion into the body of a nation without infant baptism. By proportion, he proclaimed, it will necessarily follow that the neglect or disuse thereof will directly tend to root it out.

Greater numbers were coming out of this religious system and joining with the Baptists in and around Boston. In February 1678 the

Baptists decided to build a meetinghouse in Boston. They carried this out very quietly and cautiously because they did not want to attract the attention of their adversaries. The general populace did not know what the building was designed for until the Baptists moved into it February 15, 1679, John Russell becoming the pastor.

Today government is establishing licensing and zoning laws that will enable officials to have at their disposal the same legal tools that determined the future of the little church pastored by John Russell. God help us to oppose strongly such legislation that would take away the heritage of liberty of conscience from our posterity.

EWT

---

[1]James Donovan Mosteller, *A History of the Kiokee Baptist Church in Georgia* (Ann Arbor: Edwards Brothers, 1952), p. 3.

[2]Isaac Backus, *Your Baptist Heritage, 1620–1804,* (1844; reprint ed., Little Rock: Challenge Press, 1976), pp. 87-88.

February 16—Would You Walk 120 Miles to Be Immersed?

Scripture: Psalm 100

When only five years old, Dan Taylor began to work in the coal mines of England with his father. The lad learned to read at an early age and often descended into the mines with a book to enjoy during any leisure time. He grew into a sturdy young man, "rather under size, strongly built, and with a frame that exhausting labor in a coal mine had rather more firmly knit than wasted."[1] Later in life he "blamed his shortness of stature on being too much deprived of sunshine in the bowels of the earth during his growing years."[2]

His family was not exceedingly religious, but they claimed to be of the Church of England, and young Dan was confirmed when sixteen. However, a few years later he became a Methodist and was made a lay preacher. He delivered his first sermon in 1761, but his study of the Bible led him to request immersion from a Baptist minister. He was refused believer's immersion by several because of his belief in the unlimited atonement of our Lord, but he continued his search and ultimately heard of a society of General Baptists in Lincolnshire. Dan set out on foot in the winter and walked the 120 miles that he might obey the Lord's command. He was baptized on February 16, 1763, and by the next autumn he had become a General Baptist pastor in Wadsworth.

Soon Taylor found that the General Baptist Churches were primarily cold, and with his passion for souls, he felt out of place. Withdrawing from the Association, Taylor, along with nine other ministers, formed the Assembly of Free Grace General Baptists, and they were generally called the "New Connection." The group affirmed their belief in the natural depravity of man, the obligation of the moral law, the deity of Christ, the universal design of the atonement, the promise of salvation for all who believe, the necessity of regeneration by the Holy Spirit, and the obligation upon repentance of immersion.

Dan Taylor's life was filled with service. He traveled twenty-five thousand miles, mostly by foot, on preaching tours. At such times he would average nine sermons a week, and he did not preach the same sermons over and over. It is said that he believed any day in which he did not preach was a failure. Fearing his sight was failing, he memorized a great portion of the New Testament. His efforts resulted in the establishment of an academy, which in time became a college to train men for the ministry. He authored forty-five publications, from brief tracts to sizable volumes. He established the *General Baptist Magazine* in 1798 and served as its first editor. Many Baptists of Taylor's day had embraced the Arian teaching, but he insisted upon the full deity as well as the humanity of our Savior.

Dan Taylor died on November 26, 1816, at the age of seventy-eight.[3] Without his leadership, the movement waned, and in 1891 a merger was effected between the "New Connection" and the Baptist Union in England. Thank God for the memory of another great Baptist!

DLC

---

[1]John C. Carlile, *The Story of the English Baptists* (London: James Clarke and Co., 1905), p. 169.

[2]H. Leon McBeth, *The Baptist Heritage* (Nashville: Broadman Press, 1987), p. 160.

[3]Ollie Latch, *History of the General Baptists* (Poplar Bluff, Mo.: General Baptist Press, 1954), p. 95.

February 17—The President, the Baptist, and the Original Big Cheese

Scripture: Psalm 47

Thomas Jefferson was elected the third president of the United States of America by the House of Representatives on the thirty-sixth ballot on February 17, 1801. Aaron Burr, who finished second in the balloting, automatically became the vice president.[1]

Elder John Leland had come to Virginia from Massachusetts to preach the gospel and to work hard for religious liberty. He was a neighbor of James Madison and Thomas Jefferson. Being very active in the political arena, he not only expressed Baptist views of liberty of conscience but he rallied the Baptists in support of James Madison as a delegate to the Virginia Constitutional Convention and later in his election to the House of Representatives. Madison had promised the Baptists that if elected, he would introduce a Bill of Rights early in the first session of Congress.

Upon Leland's return to Cheshire, Massachusetts, in 1792, he continued as a political activist and led voter drives for his former neighbor, Thomas Jefferson, prior to the presidential election of February 1801, and celebrated with his congregation when the Republican candidate was elected.[2]

In Leland's view, America at last had a "people's president" who understood the common man. To further celebrate this event, one day all of the milk from nine hundred local, loyal Republican cows was collected and brought into Cheshire, where the population gathered to sing hymns, socialize, and make cheese. The product of this effort was a mammoth cheese wheel four feet, four and one-half inches in diameter, fifteen inches thick, and weighing 1,235 pounds.

Leland and Darius Brown loaded up the cheese and set off for Washington, District of Columbia. They transported it by sleigh and by horse and wagon and boarded a sloop at the Hudson River where they embarked for Baltimore. Leland took advantage of the crowds that gathered to see the big cheese and preached the gospel to them. Upon arrival Jefferson warmly welcomed the Baptists to the executive mansion. Leland said that the great cheese "was not made . . . with a view to gain (us) dignified titles or lucrative offices, but by the personal labor of freeborn farmers, without a single slave to assist, for an elective president of the free people."

Leland remained in Washington for several days. Having arrived Friday, January 1, 1802, he preached on Sunday, January 3, at a religious service that was held weekly in the Capitol during Jefferson's administration. Federalist congressman Manessah Cutler, also a minister, complained that he had to sit and listen to such a "poor, ignorant, illiterate cheesemonger" and later wrote that Leland's sermon was "a farrago bawled with stunning voice, horrid tone, frightful grimaces and extravagant gestures."

The cheese graced White House parties for many months. One source says it lasted until a presidential reception in 1805. Another rumor has it that whatever remained of it that year was dumped into the Potomac River.

Though the Cheshire Cheese is small compared to the modern record of the 34,591 pound cheddar displayed at the New York World's Fair for the Wisconsin Cheese Foundation, it will always remain as the Original Big Cheese that coined the phrase. It is memorialized in concrete near the post office on Church Street in Cheshire, Massachusetts.

May we always remember that Baptists influenced statesmen to stand against state-established religion, but never did they favor a wall of separation between the state and the influence of biblical principles.

EWT

---

[1]*World Book Encyclopedia* (1968), 2:64.

[2]Richard Sassaman, ''The Original 'Big Cheese,' '' *American History Illustrated,* January 1989, pp. 34-35.

February 18—Blacks and Whites Before the Civil War

Scripture: Psalm 29

Can you imagine the problems that a white pastor might have faced in 1836, upon accepting the call to a southern church that had 1,384 black members and 333 white members? Are you surprised that a southern church even had black members? Unfortunately, many distortions are maintained due to a lack of the knowledge of Baptist history. For instance, in 1827 the First Baptist Church of Charleston, South Carolina, had 862 members, 697 of whom were black and only 165 white.[1] Jeremiah Bell Jeter became the pastor of the First Baptist Church of Richmond, Virginia, in 1836, and he immediately observed that the segregated space for the 1,384 black members was insufficient. After a careful two-year study, Pastor Jeter concluded that neither the blacks nor the whites could best be served in one facility, and thus he proposed that the congregation build a new building and give the existing facility to a newly created First African Baptist Church. Furthermore, the pastor prevailed upon Robert Ryland, president of Richmond College, to become the first pastor of that church.

Jeremiah Bell Jeter was born on July 18, 1802, and was saved in an old-fashioned camp meeting. He was baptized while still a teenager in December 1821. After being baptized, he stood on the banks of the stream and made his first public address. Within a matter of weeks, he preached his first sermon, and on May 4, 1824, he was ordained to the work of the ministry. Though J. B. Jeter was not an outstanding pulpit orator, his ministry was greatly successful, for he baptized over one thousand people in about nine years. The records further reveal that in fourteen years as pastor of First Baptist Church of Richmond, he baptized almost a thousand more converts. Having been saved in a revival meeting, the pastor knew the benefits of such efforts, and he encouraged protracted meetings throughout his ministry. In 1842 an evangelistic campaign continued for five months, and during that time, one hundred and sixty-seven members were added to the church by baptism.

Pastor Jeter was a very missions-minded leader. In 1846 Adoniram Judson visited in Richmond, and the welcoming address delivered by Dr. Jeter to the venerable missionary to Burma made such an impact that it has been quoted in almost every biography written concerning Dr. Judson.[2] Because of his love of missions, Dr. Jeter served as president of the Virginia Baptist Foreign Mission Society and served on the Board of Managers of the Triennial Convention of American Baptists. When the division between the Baptists of the North and the South took place, Dr. Jeter served as president of the southern Foreign Mission Board as well.

At the close of the Civil War, Dr. J. B. Jeter became the editor of *The Religious Herald* and sought to be a reconciling agent between the Baptists of the North and South. He served in that capacity until his death on February 18, 1880. Without malice or hatred, his life was a successful one, and we look back with respect on the memory of this dear man of God.

DLC

---

[1]Robert A. Baker and Paul J. Craven, Jr., *Adventure in Faith* (Nashville: Broadman Press, 1982), p. 213.

[2]Blanche Sydnor White, *First Baptist Church—Richmond, 1780–1955* (Richmond: Whittet and Shepperson, 1955), p. 60.

February 19—Baptists of America Are Confronted with Missions

Scripture: Psalm 119:89, 105, 130

The year was 1808, and though still unconverted, Adoniram Judson applied for entrance into Andover Theological Seminary. Judson was happily saved in the month of September and consecrated himself to the work of the Christian ministry. Before the first year of his training was completed, Judson read a sermon entitled "The Star in the East," and in February 1809, he resolved to become a missionary. Events then moved quickly, for in June 1809 he met Ann Hasseltine, who was to become his wife. In September 1811 he was commissioned as a missionary; on February 5, 1812, he and Ann were married; on February 6 he was ordained as a Congregational minister; and on the 19th, the couple embarked on the brig *Caravan* for Calcutta, India. Their honeymoon was spent on the long voyage that ended on June 17 with their arrival after a very pleasant journey.

However, tremendous changes took place for the young couple aboard the ship, for Judson expected to be located in the vicinity of William Carey and other English Baptist missionaries. The thought occurred to him that he might have to defend his position on the subject of baptism, and thus he began a thorough investigation on that subject in the New Testament in the original text. He was amazed at what he discovered, and only after a long struggle, he adopted the Baptist position. Thus it was on September 6 Adoniram and Ann were immersed in the Baptist chapel in Calcutta. Later Ann wrote a friend saying, "Thus, my dear Nancy, we are confirmed Baptists, not because we wished to be, but because truth compelled us to be. . . . We feel that we are alone in the world, with no real friend but each other, no one on whom we can depend but God."[1]

But let me quote from the letter of explanation sent by Adoniram Judson to the Third (Congregational) Church in Plymouth:

> I knew that I had been sprinkled in infancy, and that this had been deemed baptism. But throughout the whole New Testament I could find nothing that looked like sprinkling, in connection with the ordinance of Baptism. It appeared to me, that if a plain person should, without any previous information on the subject, read through the

> New Testament, he would never get the idea, that baptism consisted in sprinkling. He would find that baptism, in all the cases particularly described, was administered in rivers, and the parties are represented as going down into the water, and coming up out of the water, which they would not have been so foolish as to do for the purpose of sprinkling.
>
> In regard to the word itself which is translated baptism, a very little search convinced me that its plain, appropriate meaning was immersion or dipping; and though I read extensively on the subject, I could not find that any learned Pedobaptist had ever been able to produce an instance, from any Greek writer, in which it meant sprinkling, or any thing but immersion, except in some figurative applications, which could not be fairly brought into the question.[2]

Out of this experience, Baptists in America organized in 1814 to support the cause of worldwide missions. What a thrilling day then is February 19 in our story of Baptist history!

DLC

---

[1]Jesse L. Boyd, *A History of Baptists in America Prior to 1845* (New York: American Press, 1957), p. 96.

[2]Francis Wayland, *A History of the Life and Labors of the Rev. Adoniram Judson* (New York: Sheldon and Co., 1860), 1:102-3.

February 20—Two Hundred Pastors Attended the Funeral!

Scripture: Isaiah 38:17

Andrew Gifford was born into a godly home in Bristol, England, on August 17, 1700. His father, Emmanuel Gifford, had endured much suffering because of his dissenting principles, and his grandfather had been imprisoned four times because of his scriptural beliefs. It does not surprise us then that early in life Andrew Gifford trusted Jesus Christ as his Savior, and he was immersed when he was fifteen.

Following his training, Andrew Gifford served as an assistant pastor in both Nottingham and Bristol before becoming pastor of the Little Wild Street Church in London on February 5, 1729. Difficulty arose in the Little Wild Street Church, and in 1736 Gifford and the majority of the members left and erected a new facility in Eagle Street, Red Lion Square. The new church was dedicated on February 20, 1737; and for almost half a century, Pastor Gifford served that flock of God.

Twice the building had to be enlarged in order to accommodate the ever-increasing congregation.

Gifford was early recognized for his knowledge of ancient manuscripts and coins. His own collection of rare coins was the most valuable in Great Britain, and in time, King George II purchased it for his own display.

In 1754 Gifford received the Doctor of Divinity degree from the Marischal College, Aberdeen, and in 1757 he was appointed assistant librarian of the British Museum. However, he was first and foremost a pastor and did not allow his duties in the museum to interfere with his pastoral labors. Dr. Gifford was a warm friend of George Whitefield and preached for Whitefield on several occasions.

On June 6, 1784, near the end of his life, Pastor Gifford told his people, "With my soul have I desired to eat this passover with you before I suffer." After the Communion service, he spoke with much power on the words, "Thou hast, in love to my soul, cast all my sins behind Thy back." The following evening he preached his last sermon in his beloved chapel from Hebrews 13:1, "Let brotherly love continue." He said farewell with a cheerful voice but later returned to take one last look at his Meeting House, repeating with emphasis his "Farewell."

Three days before he died, he said, "I am in great pain, but, bless God, this is not hell! O, blessed be God for Jesus Christ!" When the end was close at hand, he whispered, "O, what should I do now, if it were not for Jesus Christ? What should I do now, but for an interest in Jesus?"[1]

His death took place on Saturday morning, June 19, 1784, and he was buried in Bunhill on Friday, July 2, at 6:00 A.M. He had wanted an early morning funeral to reaffirm his faith in the resurrection of the Savior. The funeral message was delivered by John Ryland in the presence of two hundred ministers and a vast crowd who had come to pay their tribute to a man who walked with God and served his generation faithfully. Dr. Gifford bequeathed his library and manuscripts to the Bristol Baptist College.

DLC

---

[1]Alfred W. Light, *Bunhill Fields* (London: C. J. Farncombe and Sons, 1915), pp. 65-66.

February 21—But Leave Our Consciences to God

Scripture: Psalm 17

Governments that were accustomed to supporting an established religion by taxing their people felt obligated to continue such a practice, even after the disestablishment of the state religion. The misconception was the idea that the teachers of religion could not survive without the support of Caesar.

The Baptists, who had been taxed for the support of a religious system that was repugnant to them and that they considered antichrist, had stood solidly together against any general assessment for the support of any religion, including their own.

When, on February 21, 1785, an act by the Georgia legislature was passed for the support of religion, prorated by the number in each denomination, and providing that any "thirty heads of families" in any community might choose a minister "to explain and inculcate the duties of religion," and "four pence on every hundred pounds valuation of property" should be taken out of the public tax for any such minister, the Baptists rose up and united in sending a remonstrance to the legislature by the hands of Silas Mercer and Peter Smith the following May.[1] They insisted that the obnoxious law should be repealed on the grounds that the state had nothing to do with the support of religion by public tax, and it was repealed.

In Virginia this same issue was debated for a decade. The Virginia capital was moved from Williamsburg to Richmond in the 1780s, and for eight years the state legislators met in two wooden warehouses near the James River. During this time a General Assessment for Religious Teachers was proposed. The Virginia Baptists strongly opposed the Bill and obtained ten thousand signatures against its passage.[2]

Elder David Thomas, the church planter and spiritual father of many Baptist preachers in northern Virginia at that time, wrote the following poem concerning the proposed legislation:

> Tax all things; water, air and light
> If need there be; yea, tax the night:
> But let our brave heroic minds
> Move freely as celestial winds.
> Make vice and folly feel your rod,
> But leave our consciences to God.[3]

The Baptist General Committee meeting at Dupuy's Meeting House in Powahatan, Virginia, August 13, 1785, resolved:

> that it is believed to be repugnant to the spirit of the Gospel for the Legislature thus to proceed in the matters of religion; that no human laws ought to be established for this purpose, but that every person ought to be left entirely free in respect to matters of religion; that the Holy Author of our religion needs no such compulsive measure for the promotion of His cause; that the Gospel wants not the feeble arm of man for its support, that it has made, and will again through divine

> power make, its way against all opposition; and that, should the Legislature assume the right of taxing the people for the support of the Gospel, it will be destructive to religious liberty.[4]

Baptists in Georgia and Virginia stood firm on conviction and principle, even when it appeared they could have benefited by compromising those convictions and principles. Religious liberty was of greater value than material gain. God grant that we uphold those values to our posterity.

EWT

---

[1]Thomas Armitage, *The History of the Baptists* (1890; reprint ed., Watertown, Wis.: Maranatha Baptist Press, 1976), 2:774.

[2]*Historical Records,* Commonwealth of Virginia Archives, Richmond.

[3]Robert Allen Rutland, *The Birth of the Bill of Rights, 1776-1791* (Chapel Hill, N.C.: Universtiy of North Carolina Press, 1955), p. 86.

[4]Charles F. James, D.D., *A Documentary History of the Struggle for Religious Liberty in Virginia* (1900, reprint ed., New York: Da Capo Press, 1971), p. 138.

February 22—A Royal Lady with a Loyal Love

Scripture: II John

Lady Deborah Moody was the widow of Sir Henry of Garsden in Wiltshire, England, but she came to the American colonies because of the religious persecution in her homeland. It is difficult for our current generation to understand that the early Baptists of America suffered opposition, endured injustice, and underwent widespread persecution. The Puritans, who came that they might freely worship God in what they thought to be the scriptural manner, did not allow others on our shores to worship God as they saw fit.

Lady Moody settled in Lynn, Massachusetts, where she purchased the estate of Mr. Humphrey, one of the magistrates. She had intended to become a permanent resident, but soon after settling in, she embraced the principles of the Baptists. In December 1642 Lady Moody, Mrs. King of Swampscott, and the wife of John Tillton were all tried at the Quarterly Court "for houldinge that the baptizing of infants is noe ordinance of God." Perhaps because of her position in society, she was not banished from Massachusetts. However, she revolted and determined to seek shelter among strangers. Thus, in 1643 she removed to New Amsterdam (New York). A settlement was formed on Long

Island, and Lady Moody took a patent, which, among other things, guaranteed "the free libertie of conscience according to the costome of Holland, without molestation or disturbance from any madgistrate or madgistrates, or any other ecclesiastical minister that may pretend jurisdiction over them."

Governor John Winthrop stated that she left "against the advice of all her friends. Many others affected with Anabaptism removed thither also." She was after "excommunicated" from the Salem Church. In a letter written by John Endicott to Governor Winthrop, dated February 22, 1644, from Salem, he says that Mr. Norrice had informed him that she intended to return, and he advises against it, "unless shee will acknowledge her ewill [evil] in opposing the Churches & leave her opinions behinde her, ffor she is a dangerous woeman. My brother Ludlow writt to mee that, by meanes of a booke she sent to Mrs. Eaton, shee questions her owne baptisme, it is verie doubtefull whether shee will be reclaymed, shee is so far ingaged."[1]

On her way from Massachusetts, Lady Moody stopped for a time in New Haven and made several converts to believer's baptism and experienced anew the religious opposition. Mrs. Eaton, wife of the first governor of the New Haven Colony, was one of the converts, and she too suffered at the hands of the Congregational church at New Haven. The records show that she firmly denied that "baptism [had] come in the place of circumcision, and [was] to be administered unto infants."

To the credit of the Dutch, when Long Island was invaded by the Indians, forty Dutchmen defended the house of Lady Moody at the peril of their own lives. Lady Moody, it is believed, died on Long Island about 1659.

How we ought to thank the Lord for what America has become, for Baptists have been allied from the beginning with the cause of religious liberty.

DLC

---

[1]Thomas Armitage, *The History of the Baptists* (1890; reprint ed., Watertown, Wis.: Maranatha Baptist Press, 1976), 2:747.

February 23—The "Old War Horse" from Kentucky

Scripture: Psalm 146

Elder James Smith Coleman was known as the "Old War Horse" in his native Kentucky for good reason. He refused calls to large city churches, wishing to remain in the hill country doing the work of a pastor-evangelist. His great-grandparents had come to Baptist convictions upon coming to America, for they read Luther's translation of the Greek *baptizō* with the German "taufen," and, being German, they knew that meant immersion! James Smith Coleman was born on February 23, 1827, and was saved early in life, uniting with the Beaver Dam Baptist Church when he was eleven. In adulthood he set aside the call to preach and was elected sheriff of his county, but one evening as he attended a revival service in a neighboring church, the Holy Spirit burdened his heart, and he resigned his office as sheriff and began preaching with great power. From his first efforts there were conversions every time he preached!

We have alluded previously to the use of debates in getting the gospel out in earlier days of our history, and Coleman was gifted with a lucid mind and an orator's tongue. He was asked to debate the subject of believer's immersion with the Reverend William L. Caskey, a Methodist, at Calhoun, Kentucky. Knowing the age-old argument of "household baptism" used by pedobaptist scholars and that the whole basis is inference, Coleman determined to meet the problem with the same approach.

The debate began and Caskey argued as expected that since households were baptized by the apostles, it is only reasonable to infer that infants were included and thus infant baptism is scriptural. Elder Coleman spoke as follows:

> I am surprised at Brother Caskey's limited information concerning Lydia's household. He has inferred that Lydia had children, under the age of accountability, and that, therefore these children were baptized. I am surprised, Sir, that you do not know that Lydia was a widow, and a traveling cloth merchant, and that she never had but one child, and that was a daughter, who married a red-headed, one-eyed shoemaker, and had moved off to Damascus, and had not been at home for years, and that her household at that time consisted of herself and servants, who assisted her in her business. I am surprised, Sir, that you did not know this.

Caskey, in his confusion, spoke out and said, "Dr. Coleman, how do you know what you have just said?" In a lionlike voice the reply came, "I inferred it, Sir, just like you inferred that there were children in the household."[1]

The audience broke into a roar of laughter, and for all intents and purposes, the debate was over. Who won the debate? Shortly thereafter, Mr. W. Pope Yeaman, Methodist class leader, became a Baptist and ultimately served the Lord in Baptist churches in Missouri and the West.

EWT

---

[1]Ben M. Bogard, *Pillars of Orthodoxy; or, Defenders of the Faith* (Louisville: Baptist Book Concern, 1900), pp. 333-45.

February 24—"Congo's Pioneer and Explorer"

Scripture: Exodus 14:14-15

George Grenfell, who must rank in history "among the great missionaries who have also been great explorers, was born at Sancreed (in England), a sequestered village lying on the uplands behind Penzance."[1] In 1852 the Grenfell family moved to Birmingham, England, but George returned to Sancreed whenever possible, for he enjoyed life in the country much more than city living. The Grenfell home was a religious environment associated with the Church of England. However, George in his youth was attracted to the Sunday school of the Heneage Street Baptist Church and was soon involved with a group of young men in Christian service. During this time he read *Livingstone's Travels* and dedicated his life to service in Africa.

Grenfell entered the Bristol Baptist College in 1873, but before completing his training, he discovered that Alfred Saker (one of his missionary heroes) was in England on what proved to be Saker's last furlough. Grenfell wrote to Saker concerning missionary service in Africa, and Saker responded immediately to the correspondence. It was determined that Grenfell would accompany Saker upon his return to the Cameroons. Thus, when he was little past twenty-five years of age, Grenfell began his lifework in Africa.

It soon became apparent that Alfred Saker could not long endure the rigors of continued service, and when Saker left for England, Grenfell escorted him. On February 11, 1876, Grenfell married his fiancee, and on February 24, 1876, the two sailed for Africa where Grenfell was to become known as "Congo's Pioneer and Explorer."[2] Before a year had passed, his bride succumbed to dysentery, and Grenfell was a widower. In the course of time, Grenfell remarried, and his wife, Rose Grenfell, traveled with him on many of his most adventurous journeys.

In August 1877 Henry M. Stanley, the man who had been sent to find David Livingstone, appeared at the mouth of the Congo River. The world was electrified by his exploit, for Stanley had entered Africa from the east coast, and almost three years later he had emerged on the west coast to give his findings to the world. The Congo River was six hundred miles south of the work in the Cameroons, but Grenfell was immediately attracted to the challenge of planting the message of the cross of Christ through the use of the immense waterway. God also moved in the heart of a Christian benefactor in England who envisioned a ship that could be used to penetrate central Africa with the gospel. Grenfell, through the remainder of his life, with untold sacrifices and privations, gave himself to the work that resulted in opening the vast continent to the gospel. He buried his children in Africa and grieved continually over the deaths of his fellow missionaries, but he wrote, "God's finger points ONWARD! FORWARD!" That which caused him the most pain in life was the indifference of the home churches to sending missionaries. When his mission agency considered receding, he wrote, "It is either advance or retreat; but if it is retreat, you must not count on me. I will be no party to it, and you will have to do it without me."

Grenfell died on July 1, 1906, but what would he think of our meager missionary efforts today in the face of a world in such great need of our message?

DLC

---

[1]George Hawker, *The Life of George Grenfell* (London: Religious Tract Society, 1909), p. 1.

[2]Walter Sinclair Stewart, *Later Baptist Missionaries and Pioneers* (Philadelphia: Judson Press, 1928), p. 150.

February 25—The Pen Is Mightier Than the Sword

Scripture: Deuteronomy 6:3-9

Christian literature has long played a vital role in the dissemination of the message of God's love. Early in America, Christian people had united to prepare and print materials to evangelize and educate. "The Evangelical Tract Society" was formed in Boston in 1811; the Philadelphia Sunday School and Adult School Union was organized in 1817, and then in 1824 Baptists joined with other denominations in organizing the American Sunday School Union. However, an agitation arose among Baptist leaders in favor of "the desirableness and feasibility of having a Baptist Sunday School Union for the United States," for the purpose of preparing and publishing their own Sunday school literature.[1] It was argued that distinctive and important Baptist doctrines were excluded from materials provided by interdenominational groups.

On February 25, 1824, a meeting was held in Washington, D.C., and the "Baptist General Tract Society" was born. The names of the officers are not vital to us now, but it is interesting to observe that Luther Rice was elected treasurer. We shall meet Luther Rice again and again in this volume, but let us be reminded that he was the partner with Adoniram Judson who had also become a Baptist and returned to America to raise support among the Baptists for the Judsons. Rice envisioned making "Washington a Baptist center of influence,"[2] but plates for the tracts had to be made in Philadelphia and then shipped to Washington for printing. Half of the finished product had to be returned to Philadelphia for shipment to southern distribution points. This was costly and time consuming, and over the protests of Rice, the society voted to relocate in Philadelphia in 1826.

In the 1830s the society sent out printed matter for general use, and the Triennial Convention in 1835 called upon the Baptist General Tract Society to expand into the publication of books that could be used in homes and Sunday schools. The request was finally heeded. "On April 30, 1840, in New York City, [the] representatives from fifteen states, from New Hampshire to Louisiana, voted to change the complexion and name of the tract society to 'The American Baptist Publication and Sunday School Society.'"[3] From that time Baptists have been able to obtain distinctive Baptist literature to train members in those areas of belief in which other evangelicals do not agree. Throughout the years, Baptists have revealed little of the sectarian exclusiveness that has characterized some denominations, but it became apparent that strong traditions cannot be maintained unless they are based upon a viable memory bank. Thus, the "Manual" was published early and consisted of a Doctrinal Series, Historical Series, and a Biographical Series.[4]

In our day the printed page is vital! Communism, along with every heretical cult, has made great strides by the use of the press. It is time again for Baptists to rediscover the faithful use of Baptist gospel tracts and to make every member of our churches a courier of the truth!

DLC

---

[1]Jesse L. Boyd, *A History of Baptists in America Prior to 1845* (New York: American Press, 1957), p. 112.

[2]Daniel Gurden Stevens, *The First Hundred Years of the American Baptist Publication Society* (Philadelphia: American Baptist Publication Society, n.d.), p. 10.

[3]Boyd, p. 113.

[4]Lemuel Call Barnes, Mark Clark Barnes, and Edward M. Stephenson, *Pioneers of Light* (Philadelphia: American Baptist Publication Society, 1924), p. 36.

February 26—Preaching, Confrontation, and Incarceration

Scripture: Jeremiah 38:1-13

The opposition that John Picket met was fierce, varied, and sometimes unexpected as he heralded forth the gospel of the grace of God. There were times when he would go to an appointment to preach in the open air, such as a grove of trees in the Culpeper area, when the state church parson would suddenly appear with some of his supporters, place a chair on which he would seat himself three or four yards from Mr. Picket, and take out a pen, paper, and ink with which to take down notes of what he considered to be false doctrine. While Picket would endeavor to deliver his message, the parson's friends would stand smugly and leer at him.[1] This, of course, was very distracting and impeded his delivery but had no effect upon the truth of his message.

Following his sermon, the parson would call him a schismatic, a broacher of false doctrines, and one that held up damnable errors. Of course, this was done to discredit him among the citizenry, much to the elation of the parson's supporters. Actually, it had the opposite effect in that many turned a sympathetic ear toward the preacher who was being treated so rudely. At that time, many were disgusted with the state hirelings, among whom there were those of disrepute. There were those being attracted by the prospect of a confrontation and debate who came under the sound of the gospel and were converted.

The three-month imprisonment of John Picket, mentioned in the entry for January 14, began February 26, 1770, in a log building described in the Fauquier County, Virginia Order Book for 1766, pages 242 and 243, as a building eighteen feet long and sixteen feet wide, constructed of hewed logs twelve inches square, laid close, the whole to be dovetailed, having a layer of good mortar between each log. The building was divided into two rooms by a brick wall with a provision for a fireplace in each room, secured with grates above and below to prevent the prisoners from escaping up the chimney. The corners of the house were to be pinned and braced, and the entire building undergirded with brick at least eighteen inches thick. The only ventilation was a window twelve inches square in each room. These colonial prisons were not at all the "country clubs" of our day. They were like ovens in summer and like freezers in winter, with most of the heat going up the chimney. Many of those early preachers lost their good health from these harsh conditions and never recovered their strength.

John Picket's zeal was not quenched by this experience. After his release, he extended his labors around the Culpeper area and over the Blue Ridge. He was so successful that on the first baptizing that was supposed to have taken place in the Shenandoah, there were as many as fifty who followed their Lord in this ordinance.[2]

God grant us men in our day who will demonstrate the same zeal and perseverance when confronted with opposition to God's truth. I am sure that the tempter would come often to John Picket as he languished in that bare room to draw him away from his determination to be faithful to the truth of God. So often today we see the compromise of biblical principles for some sensual gratification. God grant us power to face the enemy's onslaught with the same grace and courage that our forefathers demonstrated.

EWT

---

[1]Lewis Peyton Little, *Imprisoned Preachers and Religious Liberty in Virginia* (Lynchburg, Va.: J. P. Bell Co., 1938), pp. 154, 194.

[2]Robert B. Semple, *A History of the Rise and Progress of the Baptists in Virginia* (Richmond: Published by the author, 1810), p. 414.

February 27—College President Fired Because of His Faith

Scripture: Micah 6:8

Henry Dunster was born in England about 1612 and early came to know our Savior. He testified by saying, "The Lord gave me an attentive ear and heart to understand preaching. . . . The Lord showed me my sins and reconciliation by Christ . . . and this word was more sweet to me than anything else in the world."[1] He graduated from Cambridge University with a bachelor's degree in 1630 and then took his master's degree there as well in 1634. He was apparently ordained as a minister in the Church of England, but his heart was grieved with corruptions in the church. He thus left England and sailed to America.

Soon after arriving in Boston, Dunster was unanimously elected to serve as the first president of Harvard College in August of 1640. His leadership was appreciated, and the college grew during his early years of administration.

We must point out that some in the Church of England in those days still practiced immersion, and Dunster was among them. He united with the Cambridge church, and his only doctrinal difference was on the point of immersion. In 1641 Dunster married a widow of a minister and assumed the responsibility of rearing her five children. Two years later he became a widower, and in 1644 he remarried. To this marriage were born five children.

During the period of 1648 and 1653, President Dunster reached the settled conviction that "visible believers only should be baptized." It is believed that the matter came to a head in 1653 when Dunster withheld a newly born infant from being sprinkled. The Reverend Mr. Mitchell was pastor of the Cambridge church at that time, and he met with the college president and sought to dissuade him. However, the logic of Dunster was so strong that the young pastor left with fear, lest he be overtaken with thoughts that "infant baptism [was] an invention of men." President Dunster continued to preach against infant baptism, and on February 2 and 3, 1654, a special Boston area minister's conference was called and President Dunster was summoned to appear. He gave a creditable defense of his position, but the ministers were not impressed. *The History of Harvard University* gives the following account: "Indicted by the grand jury for disturbing the ordinance of infant baptism in the Cambridge church, convicted by the court, sentenced to a public admonition on lecture day, and laid under bonds for good behaviour, Dunster's martyrdom was consummated by being compelled, in October 1654, to resign his office of President."[2]

President Dunster petitioned the court that because of the hardship of changing his residence at that time of year and on so short notice, he should be granted a short extension. Ultimately the court yielded, and he was permitted to remain until the following spring.

Because of his firm convictions, Dunster left Cambridge. Can you imagine such persecution of early Baptists? Can you reaffirm such conviction in your own life? May God make us people of conviction rather than of convenience. Henry Dunster died on February 27, 1659, in Scituate, Massachusetts, and awoke where the weary are at rest.

DLC

---

[1]Albert Henry Newman, *A History of the Baptist Churches in the United States* (Philadelphia: American Baptist Publication Society, 1915), p. 139.

[2]Josiah Quincy, *The History of Harvard University* (Cambridge: John Owen, 1840), 1:18.

February 28—An Aged and Infirm Sufferer

Scripture: Psalm 73:14-18

The early days in the colony of Massachusetts were most difficult for our forefathers who held to Baptist convictions. William Witter was such a man, and he was arraigned before the Salem Court on February 28, 1644. The records of the case are most enlightening. We are told that "For entertaining that the baptism of infants was sinful," Witter was sentenced "to acknowledge his fault . . . and enjoined to be here next Court at Salem."[1]

William Witter was a man of conviction, however, and later Court records read: "At the Court of Salem, held the 18th day of the 12th month, 1645, William Witter of Lynn, was presented by the grand jury for saying that they who stayed whiles a child is baptized do worship the devil."

Witter was sentenced to answer at yet another session of the Court. Once again the Court records of June 24, 1651, find him accused of "absenting himself from the public ordinances nine months or more, and for being re-baptized."

In time William Witter united with the Baptist church in Newport, Rhode Island, that was pastored by Dr. John Clarke. However, Witter was advanced in age and had become blind, and therefore it became impossible for him to travel often from Lynn, Massachusetts, to Newport, Rhode Island, to fellowship with his church family. Therefore, on July 19, 1651, Pastor Clarke, Obadiah Holmes, and John Crandall, "being representatives of the Baptist church in Newport, upon the request of William Witter, of Lynn, arrived there."[2] The men had walked for two days making the eighty mile trip and arrived at Witter's home on Saturday night.[3]

The authorities in Boston were made aware that the Baptists had come into the jurisdiction of Massachusetts, and deputies of the marshal were sent to spy upon the trio. Being weary from their trip, Clarke, Holmes, and Crandall determined to spend the night at Witter's home and then encourage him with a private worship service on the Lord's Day. But the heinous crime of conducting divine services without the consent of the established Congregational church of the Massachusetts Bay Colony caused the three men to be arrested and hurried away to a tavern. Then to cleanse their souls of such wickedness as worshiping in an unauthorized manner, they were forced to attend an afternoon worship service in the established church. Finally, they were imprisoned in the Boston jail, and a great miscarriage of justice followed, but that incident will be addressed in a later entry.

Come again with me to consider William Witter. He surely had an indomitable spirit, but it is evident that he was aged and infirm, else he too would have been taken to jail and tried for complicity in the crime of unauthorized worship, for he had invited the gentlemen and had lodged them in his home.

I fear that we take our freedom of worship far too lightly in America today. In fact, for many, freedom of worship has come to mean freedom from worship. Let us treasure every opportunity to gather for worship without fear and determine thus to keep America free!

DLC

---

[1]John T. Christian, *A History of the Baptists* (1922; reprint ed., Nashville: Broadman Press, 1926), 1:52-53, 2:379.

[2]Ibid.

[3]O. K. and Marjorie Armstrong, *The Baptists in America* (New York: Doubleday and Co., 1979), pp. 66-67.

February 29—To Sing or Not to Sing, That Was the Question

Scripture: Ephesians 5:1-21

Benjamin Keach was born into the humble home of John Keach of Stokehamon, Buckinghamshire, England, February 29, 1640.[1]

By applying himself to the study of the Scriptures at a very early age, Benjamin became fully persuaded of believer's baptism. He submitted himself to the ordinance on the profession of his faith in Christ at the age of fifteen. Though having a very limited formal education, he became very proficient in the Word of God, and at the age of eighteen, the society of believers with whom he fellowshiped saw fit to set him apart to the gospel ministry. At age twenty-eight, he became pastor of the Baptist church in Horsleydown, London. At first meeting in homes because of persecution, they ultimately built a meetinghouse when the persecutions eased. This building they enlarged several times until it could hold nearly a thousand.

He wrote many treatises and apologies relating to the issues of his day, including his antipedobaptism convictions. Because of these published works and his preaching, he found himself in court on any number of occasions, some of which will be mentioned later in this volume.

There were not only controversies with the state church officials, but also differences of opinions among the Baptists relating to doctrine and practice. (Of course, the freedom to differ on noncardinal issues always has been and will be a Baptist distinctive.) One controversy had to do with the question of whether or not to have congregational singing in public worship. The presses groaned with pamphlets and books on the subject. Keach was among those who were drawn into the dispute, and in 1691 he published a book on the topic. He decided to introduce congregational singing into his church, come what may, and great opposition came. His was probably the first Baptist church to introduce singing, being first used only at the Lord's Supper around 1673 and confined to the Communion services for about six years. The practice was extended to days of public thanksgiving, which practice continued about fourteen years. After about twenty years the church, with some dissent, was persuaded to sing every Lord's Day, but only after the sermon and prayer. Some of the dissenters would leave the building and stand in the yard because they could not conscientiously stay and hear the singing. Even though they were not censured for leaving, the anti-singing people separated themselves and established another body exactly like the old church except without singing. When they had left, Keach and his church resolved to "let their songs abound" and voted "that they who are for singing may sing as above said."[2] The new anti-singing church remained songless until 1793.

Because of persecution, secret worship had made it necessary to avoid singing until around 1680. The whole question turned on one point, whether there was precept or example for the whole congregation, converted and unconverted, to join in the singing as a part of divine worship. Yet they believed that those whom God had gifted to sing might do so, one by one, but only as the heart dictated the melody and not by use of rhyme or written note.

Thanks to Benjamin Keach and others of his persuasion, we have the blessing of congregational singing in our Baptist churches.

EWT

---

[1]Thomas Crosby, *The History of the English Baptists* (1738-40; reprint ed., Lafayette, Tenn.: Church History Research and Archives, 1979), 2:143-44, 4:269-82.

[2]Thomas Armitage, *The History of the Baptists* (1890; reprint ed., Watertown, Wis.: Maranatha Baptist Press, 1976), 2:547-51.

March

March 1—A Humble Preacher Honored for His Godliness

Scripture: Luke 6:26-28; 14:1

Given the evangelistic fervor of Baptists, one would hardly expect to find a group in Baptist history that was characterized by monastic living, but such were the Seventy-Day Baptists in Ephrata, Pennsylvania. Conrad Beissel was born in Germany on March 1, 1691, and was reared as a Presbyterian. He arrived in Boston in 1720 and settled in Lancaster County, Pennsylvania. He embraced the principles of the Baptists in 1724, and on November 12, 1724, with six others, he was immersed, and the seven incorporated into a church. Conrad Beissel was chosen to be their minister.[1] The group entered into a communal lifestyle and soon adopted celibacy as the preferred manner of living. Beissel organized the group, but in 1733 he left them, traveled alone, and actually lived for a time as a hermit, planting crops for his own subsistence. However, his followers soon found him and moved there as well.

Life was austere as the members sought to mortify the flesh. They slept at first on board benches with blocks of wood for pillows, but ultimately they adopted the use of beds. The doors to the rooms were low, causing the inhabitants continually to bow humbly. Their diet was very simple and often limited, for they existed solely on the products of the land. The brethren farmed and operated a printing office, a paper mill, and a grist mill while the sisters were active in spinning, weaving, and sewing. Primarily they were interested in pleasing the Lord, and they worshiped morning and evening and sometimes in the night. "From the uncouth dress, the recluse and ascetic life . . . sour aspects and rough manners might be expected; but on the contrary, a smiling innocence and meekness grace their countenances, and a softness of tone and accent adorn their conversation, and make their deportment gentle and obliging. Their singing is charming; partly owing to the pleasantness of their voices, the variety of parts . . . and the devout manner of performance.''[2]

Beissel passed away on July 6, 1768, and was succeeded by Peter Miller as pastor. An interesting story is related concerning Miller during the Revolutionary War. Near Ephrata lived a man who abused the pastor in every way. The man became involved in treason, was arrested, and was sentenced to be hanged. Miller walked on foot the seventy miles to Philadelphia to plead for the man's life. General Washington heard his plea, but he said, ''No, your plea for your friend cannot be granted.'' ''My friend!'' said the pastor, ''He is the worst enemy I have!'' ''What,'' said Washington, ''you have walked nearly seventy miles to save the life of an enemy? That puts the matter in a different light. I will grant the pardon.''

As would be expected, Ephrata died out in 1813 through the practice of celibacy, but the state of Pennsylvania has preserved the facility, and it is a fascinating tour for a family. One can still ''get the feel'' for this ancient Baptist monastic lifestyle in early Ephrata.

DLC

---

[1]Morgan Edwards, *Materials Toward a History of the Baptists* (Danielsville, Ga.: Heritage Papers, 1984), 1:37.

[2]Ibid.

March 2—A Famed Texan Who Loved the Lord

Scripture: Acts 2:41-47

The name Sam Houston should be known by every school child in America. Samuel Houston arrived in Texas from Virginia late in 1832, and in 1835 he was elected major general of the Texas troops. When the rising storm of opposition to Mexico brought on a war, he dealt a crushing blow to Santa Anna and procured the independence of the Republic.[1] He became a delegate to the 1836 Convention in Texas and assisted in securing the recognition of the Republic by the United States. He was elected governor of Texas in 1859.

Samuel Houston was born on March 2, 1793. Apparently, during his youth, he had little interest in spiritual matters. His educational background was limited, but he obviously had a good intellect, for after enlisting in the United States Army, he became a lieutenant, lawyer, district attorney, adjutant general, congressman, and the governor of Tennessee. He accomplished all of this before moving to Texas.

> Houston's . . . conversion . . . was doubtless due primarily to the remarkable influence of his devout wife, who was Maggie Lea, prior to their marriage in 1840. . . . He did not make a public profession of faith until 1854, when he united with the Baptist church at Independence and was baptized by Dr. R. C. Burleson November 19 of that year. . . . He then became a regular attendant upon preaching and prayer meeting service. . . . He led in public prayer, and when he lay dying at his home in Huntsville, he expressed to his family and friends his implicit faith in the Savior.[2]

After Texas was admitted into the Union, Houston served in the United States Senate for fourteen years. He was inaugurated governor of Texas on December 21, 1859, and these became the most trying days of his life, for there was a great ferment just prior to the Civil War.

> For more than a generation, sectional passion had run riot. . . . In the intense sectional passion which swayed the masses, Texas shared with the other states of the South. During the year 1860, little else than politics was discussed. . . . Extravagant predictions, born of heated passion, were made concerning the results of the war, which was now inevitable. . . . There moved a few cool spirits who would have averted the disaster, if possible, but it was folly to interpose. Among those who shared in the desire to settle the sectional differences was Governor Houston. Of his patriotism there was no doubt . . . of his loyalty and devotion to the South, there could be no question . . . of his familiarity with the pending discussion, no one could gainsay, for he had shared it on the floor of the Senate. He regarded the secession movement with more than doubt; it was with a feeling akin to dismay.[3]

However, Governor Sam Houston was in the minority, for on February 23, 1861, the people of Texas voted to secede from the United States, and because he stood by his convictions, Houston's office was declared vacant. Thus deposed, Houston relinquished his office and retired to his farm in Huntsville, Texas, where he died on July 26, 1863.

Thankfully, history has a way of vindicating fallen heroes. Texans today revere the memory of Samuel Houston, but Christians rejoice in his personal testimony in our Savior.

DLC

---

[1]B. F. Riley, *History of the Baptists in Texas* (Dallas: Published by the author, 1907), p. 26.

[2]L. R. Elliott, ed., *Centennial Story of Texas Baptists* (Dallas: Baptist General Convention of Texas, 1936), pp. 247-48.

[3]Ibid., p. 148.

March 3—Reports of Additional Missionary Heroes

Scripture: Romans 11:29

Elisha Litchfield Abbott was born in Cazenovia, New York, in 1809, and his ministry among the Karens of Bassein, Burma, was a highlight of early Baptist missionary activity. After his training, Abbott went to the field in 1836 and remained until after the death of his wife in 1845. At that time, with symptoms of consumption, he returned to the States, bringing his children for their safety. It was apparent to Abbott that he had to have an assistant if he were to return to the field, and during his time in America, he sought such a man. Perhaps the Lord was preparing the Reverend Mr. Abbott to accept the fact that his time of service would be limited, for he was forced by poor health to return from the field in 1852 and died on December 3, 1854. To Elisha Abbott is due the credit for establishing the principle of the indigenous policy in the fifty churches he established among the Karens, for they supported their own pastors.

However, at the time of Abbott's first return to the States, a young man was pursuing his studies at Hamilton Theological Seminary in Hamilton, New York. John Sidney Beecher fully intended to give his life as a missionary in the western territories of our nation. Abbott visited the seminary in quest for an associate and approached young Beecher. The veteran missionary asked Beecher to consider the matter and pray about it until Saturday before giving his answer. His classmate reports, "Brother Beecher came to my room in great perplexity. 'I have never,' said he, 'thought of going to the Eastern field. I cannot decide to go without consulting Miss Martha Foote and I have not the slightest idea of her views on the subject.' I suggested writing to her, but she was in Chicago, and it would take more than a week to get her answer."

With great concern Beecher left the room, but in a short time he returned and showed his classmate a letter he had just received from his fiancée, and in it she had written, "I think we ought always to go where duty calls; and if any time you should come to think it your duty to go to an Eastern field, I should lay no obstacle in your way.''[1] God had answered wonderfully.

That very evening Beecher consented to go, and in 1846 he was ordained, and he and Miss Foote were united in marriage and left for the mission field. The Lord attended the efforts of Abbott and Beecher with great success, but as Mrs. Beecher was returning to America, she died unexpectedly and was buried at sea on March 3, 1854. Though Beecher's heart was grieved, the man of God believed the call of God upon his life was without repentance, and he continued on in his labors of grace, even though he was forced to change mission agencies. With failing health, he was compelled to journey to England for recuperation in September of 1866, and though it was thought he was improving, on October 21, 1866, his spirit went home to be with the Lord, even before his friends were aware of his departure. A marble plaque to Beecher's memory in a school hall in Burma was dedicated in 1878 in which he is accorded ''the distinguished honor of establishing the first Christian school in Burma on the basis of the indigenous support.'' Let us not forget to pray for our faithful missionaries in our day!

DLC

---

[1]G. Winfred Hervey, *The Story of Baptist Missions in Foreign Lands* (St. Louis: C. R. Barnes Publishing Co., 1892), pp. 430-32.

March 4—Life with Fickle-Minded Legislators

Scripture: Psalm 57:5-6

Early in the seventeenth century in England, Samuel Oates, ''a very popular preacher and great disputant, taking a journey into Essex, preached in several parts of that, and one of the adjoining countries, and baptized great numbers of people.''

> ''It happened that among the hundreds whom Mr. Oates had baptized, a young woman, named Anne Martin, died a few weeks after; and this they attributed to her being dipped in cold water. They accordingly prevailed on the magistrates to send him [Oates] to prison, and put him in irons as a murderer, in order to his trial at the next assizes. He was tried at Chelmsford . . . many credible witnesses were produced, and . . . the mother of the young woman . . . testified that the said Anne Martin was in better health for several days after her baptism than she had been for several years before. The jury . . . pronounced

a verdict of not guilty. . . ." However, "so great was the enmity against Mr. Oates, that on his going to Dunmow in Essex not long after this, some of the town's people dragged him out of the house where he was and threw him into a river, boasting that they had thoroughly dipped him."[1]

"Mr. Henry Denne [another controversial preacher] was apprehended again in June . . . and committed to prison at Spalding in Lincolnshire, for preaching and baptizing by immersion."[2]

Thus the Baptists must have thrilled when on March 4, 1647, the Lords and Commons published a declaration that, in essence, provided for some religious freedom. It read:

> The name of Anabaptism hath indeed contracted much odium by reason of the extravagant opinions of some of that name in Germany, tending to the disturbance of the government, and the peace of all states, which opinions and practices we abhor and detest. But for their opinion against the baptism of infants, it is only a difference about a circumstance of time in the administration of an ordinance, wherein in former ages, as well as in this, learned men have differed both in opinion and practice. And though we could wish that all men would satisfy themselves, and join with us in our judgment and practice in this point; yet herein we hold it fit that men should be convinced by the word of God, with great gentleness and reason, and not beaten out of it by force and violence.[3]

The peace of the Baptists was short-lived, however; for on May 2, 1648, an ordinance of the Lords and Commons, assembled in Parliament, for the punishment of blasphemies and heresies was issued. One article stated: "Whosoever shall say that the baptism of infants is unlawful, or that such baptism is void, and that such persons ought to be baptized again, and in pursuance thereof shall baptize any person formerly baptized . . . (shall) be ordered to renounce his said error in public congregation of the parish where the offence was committed, and in case of refusal, he shall be committed to prison till he find sureties that he shall not publish or maintain the said error any more."[4]

We take so lightly our freedoms in our day! The religious pluralism of America is not embraced freely around the world. Let us thank God for religious freedom and determine ever to defend it, regardless of the price.

DLC

---

[1]Joseph Ivimey, *History of the English Baptists* (London: Bruditt and Morris, 1811), pp. 197-98.

[2]Ibid., p. 198.

[3]Ibid., p. 200.

[4]Ibid., pp. 200-201.

March 5—He Forsook All to Follow Christ

Scripture: Matthew 14:1-13

At Cologne on the Rhine there was a printer, Thomas van Imbroek, a God-fearing man who was apprehended for the sake of the truth of the gospel in the year of 1557. As he was confined in a tower, he was interrogated concerning his opinions relating to baptism and marriage. He answered the objections to his doctrine so skillfully with the Scriptures that they ceased the interrogations and moved him to another tower.[1]

While confined in this manner, his wife, a pious woman, wrote a letter to him, exhorting him to contend in a godly manner and to remain steadfast in the truth. He heartily thanked her for her comfort and exhortation and showed by many Scriptures that the righteous have always suffered. He was persuaded that his conscience was void of offense before God by forsaking wife, child, and all earthly things to follow Christ, rejoicing that God had counted him worthy to suffer for His name.

Two priests debated with him concerning infant baptism. They did not agree with each other; the one would have infants who died unbaptized to be lost, and the other admitted that they would be saved. They would urge him vehemently to repent and asked why he did not have his children baptized. He answered, "The Scriptures teach nothing of infant baptism; and they who will be baptized according to God's Word must first be believers." The priests proclaimed him a heretic and brought him to the rack, where he was closely questioned but not tortured, although the executioner had all things ready, because the magistrates were not agreed among themselves. This occurred three times successively. After this he was brought to the landgrave's house (a count of superior authority). The landgrave would willingly have set him at liberty had he not been fearful of the emperor's proclamation and the bishop's displeasure. Thomas, undaunted and full of comfort, was prepared to lay down his life for the name of Christ and to remain steadfast in the truth and love of God so that neither fire, water, sword, nor any other thing should move him from his convictions.

Being brought to the landgrave's house again, the landgrave's people endeavored to instruct him for the purpose of persuading him to recant. To cause someone to recant was of greater value to the opposers of God's truth than the martyrdom of one of His saints. This is why much time and torture were given to persuade someone to deny his Lord, instead of putting him to an immediate death. There were always those within whom dwelt a sadistic spirit and who were prepared to use the instruments of cruel torture upon those of great piety and purity. True Christians always represent that which the satanic, immoral forces of the world hate and bring forth from them the most violent and cruel conduct.

Ultimately, Thomas was brought before the high court of justice, where he was condemned to death in the presence of the landgrave, who then, for the first time, administered the law and dyed his staff of authority in Christian blood by having Thomas van Imbroek beheaded on the fifth day of March in the year of his Lord 1558.

He was a faithful, persevering witness of Christ and sealed his testimony with his blood at the tender age of twenty-five years. The letters he had sent from prison to his wife and brethren, along with other things, contained a confession of his faith and his beliefs about baptism. A small volume was published from these writings.

EWT

---

[1]T. J. Van Braght, trans., and Edward Bean Underhill, ed., *A Martyrology of the Churches of Christ Commonly Called Baptists* (London: J. Haddon and Son, 1853), 2:138-40.

March 6—A Steadfast Servant

Scripture: I Timothy 3:1-7

The Reverend Caleb Blood was born in Charlton, Massachusetts, on August 18, 1754. We know little concerning his youth, but when he was attending a dance at the age of twenty, he was struck with a deep sense of his sinfulness and was gloriously converted. Within a year and a half, he had progressed so in the knowledge of the Word of God that he was licensed to preach by the Baptist church in Charlton and in 1776 began preaching as an itinerant.

Late in 1777 an ordination council was convened, and Caleb Blood was ordained in Marlow, New Hampshire, and for four years he served as pastor in the newly formed Baptist church there. In 1781 he accepted a call to minister in Newton, Massachusetts. For seven years he played an active part in the Warren Association and was successful in combating the doctrines of Universalism. However, unable to support his family on the salary that he received, in 1788 he accepted a call to the Fourth Baptist Church of Shaftsbury, Vermont, and ministered with great blessing there for twenty years. In the winter of 1798-99, a great revival broke out, and during that season, approximately 175 people were added to the church. Along with his pastoral responsibilities, the Reverend Mr. Blood traveled in missionary expansion into the northwest sections of New York and Canada as well.

> His preaching was attended with powerful revivals, but he always discouraged an excess of mere . . . feeling and knew well the difference between the genuine operations of the Holy Spirit and mere human excitement. We are told that "in the earlier part of his ministry, attending a meeting marked with excitement and zeal, but, as he thought, 'not according to knowledge,' a good woman, at the close, came to him, with uplifted hands, exclaiming, 'Oh, Mr. Blood, did you ever see such a meeting before?' 'No,' he promptly replied, 'and I hope I never shall again.' "[1]
>
> From . . . its founding in 1791, Blood served the University of Vermont as a trustee until he left the state in 1807 to assume the pastorate of the Third Baptist Church in Boston. Tragedy struck when the pastor suffered a blow on the face "that . . . seemed trifling . . . [yet] often occasioned him great pain. . . . At one time, in consequence of taking cold in the part affected, a fever ensued, which . . . well-nigh proved fatal."[2]

Being depressed in spirit, Blood resigned but soon accepted the pastorate of the First Baptist Church in Portland, Maine, where he served for the remainder of his life. Though he suffered great physical pain, he continued to preach. His exhorting took on a fuller earnestness during that period. His last sickness lasted from February 19, 1814 to the date of his death on March 6. He had perfect peace and expressed one great desire that ministers might be faithful, souls saved, and his Master glorified.

The Reverend Caleb Blood has been called "one of the leading Baptist ministers in Massachusetts and Vermont."[3] He authored several tracts on the differences between Baptists and pedobaptists and a pamphlet for youth and another on marriage. During his ministry, Baptists were grappling with the propriety of their members' being allied with secret societies such as the Freemasons. Blood was one of the first of the early Baptist leaders to speak out against the participation of Baptists in the Freemasons and all other secret societies.

DLC

---

[1]William Cathcart, *The Baptist Encyclopedia,* ed. Louis H. Everts (Philadelphia: Louis H. Everts, 1881), 1:108.

[2]William B. Sprague, *Annuals of the American Pulpit* (New York: Robert Carter and Bros., 1865), 6:194.

[3]William G. McLoughlin, ed., *The Diary of Isaac Backus* (Providence: Brown University Press, 1979), 2:1032.

March 7—Freedom Removed in the Name of Freedom

Scripture: Luke 20:9-18

Conditions in the Massachusetts Bay Colony had become intolerable for any who held views that tended toward liberty of conscience or baptism for believers only. Isaac Backus records that the Massachusetts court ruled,

> This court doth not nor will hereafter approve any such companies of men, as shall henceforth join in any way of church fellowship without they shall first acquaint the magistrates, and the elders of the greater part of the churches of this jurisdiction, and have their approbation herein. And further it is ordered, that no person being an elder of any church which shall hereafter be gathered without the approbation of the magistrates and greater part of the said churches shall be admitted to the *freedom* of this Commonwealth.[1] [emphasis added]

Where is there freedom when freedom is taken away? When liberty of conscience is taken away, all liberty is lost.

Great controversy resulted. The House of Deputies was dissolved and reappointed to suit the ministers; men and women were banished from the colony and others put to death as heretics. Ultimately, Massachusetts made a law to compel all the inhabitants in each town to pay an equal proportion towards the support of religious ministers, although many had no vote in choosing them.

It was under these influences that John Clarke, his brother Joseph, and others moved away. On March 7, 1638, they entered into the following covenant:

	We whose names are underwritten do here solemnly in the presence of JEHOVAH, incorporate
EXODUS 34:3, 4	ourselves into a body politic, and as He shall help, will submit our persons, lives and estates
I CHRON. 11:3	unto our Lord Jesus Christ, the King of kings, and Lord of lords, and to all those perfect and
II KINGS 11:17	most absolute laws of His, given us in His Holy Word of truth, to be guided and judged thereby.

Backus relates that when "they could not find laws to govern such a body in the New Testament, they went back to the laws of Moses, and elected a judge and three elders to rule them." An assembly of their freemen said on January 2, 1639, " 'that the judge, together with the elders, shall rule and govern according to the general rules of the Word of God, when they have no particular rule from God's Word, by the body prescribed as a direction unto them in the case.' On March 12, 1640, they changed their plan of government and elected a governor and four assistants, until they came under a charter from England at a later time."[2]

It becomes very clear that any government of men is as fallible as the men who govern and that the trials and errors of the colonies, endeavoring to set up systems of government to guarantee order and yet give the people governed liberty of conscience, resulted in a Constitution and a Bill of Rights that brought the leaders as well as the people under law. Our Constitution was not thrown together but was born after much travail by millions of people over hundreds of years of suffering. God bless America!

EWT

---

[1]Isaac Backus, *Your Baptist Heritage, 1620–1804* (1844; reprint ed., Little Rock: Challenge Press, 1976), p. 37.

[2]Ibid., pp. 39-40.

March 8—A Nailed Door Mysteriously Opened

Scripture: I Corinthians 16:1-9

The Baptists had quietly and cautiously built their meetinghouse in Boston, but it soon came to the attention of the authorities when they began to assemble therein February 15, 1679. A law was made the following May to take it from them if they continued to meet in it. Under the threat of this law, the Baptists ceased to occupy their own building of assembly until King Charles II required all authorities to allow liberty of conscience to all non-Catholics with the following words:

> We shall henceforth expect that there be suitable obedience in respect of freedom and liberty of conscience, so as those that desire to serve God in the way of the Church of England, be not thereby made obnoxious or discountenanced from sharing in government, much less that any other of our good subjects (not being Papists) who do not

> agree in the Congregational way, be by law subjected to fines or forfeitures, or other incapacities, for the same; which is a severity the more to be wondered at, whereas liberty of conscience was made one principle motive for your transportation into those parts.[1]

Being informed by some friends in London of the king's decree, the Baptists met in their building again. The spiritual leadership of the church was called before the Court of Assistants, and because they would not promise not to meet there again, the court sent an officer who nailed up the doors of the building March 8, 1680, and forbad them to meet there with the following order posted on the door: "All persons are to take notice that, by order of the court, the doors of this house are shut up, and that they are inhibited to hold any meetings therein, or to open the doors thereof, without license from authority, till the court take further order, as they will answer the contrary to their peril."[2]

The Baptists held their services in the yard for several Sundays until one Sunday, upon their arrival, they found the doors of the building open, much to their surprise. Not knowing whether man or angel had opened them, they entered and conducted services, saying, "The court had not done it legally, and that we were denied a copy of the constable's order and Marshall's warrant, we concluded to go into our house, it being our own, having a civil right to it."[3]

Dr. Increase Mather published a pamphlet against the Baptists, and John Russell wrote an answer to what Mather had said against their character. It was printed in London with a preface by some noted Baptist Ministers of England. They said,

> It seems most strange that our Congregational brethren in New England, who with liberal estates, chose rather to depart from their native soil into a wilderness, than to be under the lash of those who upon religious pretenses took delight to smite their fellow servants, should exercise towards others the like severity that themselves at so great hazard and hardship sought to avoid; especially considering that it is against their brethren, who profess and appeal to the same rule with themselves for guidance in the worship of God, and the ordering of their whole conversation.[4]

EWT

---

[1]Isaac Backus, *Your Baptist Heritage, 1620–1804* (1844; reprint ed., Little Rock: Challenge Press, 1976), pp. 90-91.

[2]Thomas Armitage, *The History of the Baptists* (1890; reprint ed., Watertown, Wis.: Maranatha Baptist Press, 1976), 2:703.

[3]Ibid.

[4]Backus, p. 91.

March 9—A Question That Could Not Be Ignored

Scripture: Genesis 3:9

Born in England in 1745, Edmund Botsford at the age of seven lost both his parents in death. The lad's aunt became his guardian, and he was sent to board with a Baptist lady who had been an intimate friend of his mother. He attended Baptist services with the lady and early was subjected to strong religious impressions which were caused by his reading of Bunyan's works. However, as he grew older, he lost interest in spiritual matters and became careless in his living. In time he enlisted in the army, and finally at age twenty, he sailed to Charleston, South Carolina, arriving in 1766 to begin a new life.

His early religious impressions were renewed, and he went to hear the Reverend Oliver Hart, pastor of the First Baptist Church in Charleston. In the course of time, Botsford was converted, and on March 13, 1767, he was baptized.

As he grew in grace, Botsford was called of God to devote himself to the gospel ministry and was licensed to preach by the Charleston church in February 1771. Pastor Hart trained Botsford, and in a matter of months his friends equipped him with clothing, a horse, and a saddle, and he left to continue his training under the Reverend Mr. Pelot at Eutaw. However, the Reverend Benjamin Stirk of Tuckaseeking, Georgia, had died, and the church there invited Botsford to lead them. He remained there for a year and preached extensively in the area, both in Georgia and South Carolina. In 1772 his ministry was primarily that of an evangelist as he preached on the frontiers of expansion. Though a "Regular Baptist," Botsford preached at the Kiokee Church (in Georgia) and became a dear friend of both Daniel and Abraham Marshall. On one such trip, Botsford stopped at the home of Loveless Savage for instructions to Kiokee, and Savage said, "I suppose you are the Baptist minister, who is to preach today at the Kiokee." "Yes, Sir; will you go?" "No, I am not fond of the Baptists; they think nobody is baptized but themselves." "Have you been baptized?" "Yes, to be sure." "How do you know?" "How do I know, why, my parents have told me I was." "Then you do not know, only by information." On this, Botsford left him, but "How do you know?" haunted Savage till he became convinced of his duty. Savage was baptized by Daniel Marshall and began to preach the same day.[1]

Botsford was ordained by the First Baptist Church of Charleston on March 14, 1773, but prior to his ordination, Daniel Marshall baptized many of Botsford's converts, including Botford's first wife, Susanna Nun. In 1774, Botsford received an inheritance from the estate of his brother in England, and this allowed Edmund and Susanna to live quite comfortably even though his ministerial compensation was small. To this union God granted six children, but in the spring of 1779, they were driven from their home by the horrors of the Revolutionary War. Edmund, being English, and Susanna, being Irish, were in danger of being taken by the English troops. Thus they left for Virginia with only two horses and a cart and the little they could carry. Botsford's home was ruined during the war and his library completely destroyed.

Mrs. Botsford passed away on March 9, 1790, though only thirty-nine years old.[2] Botsford's life was a benediction, but we shall see him again in this volume.

DLC

---

[1]James Donovan Mosteller, *A History of the Kiokee Baptist Church in Georgia* (Ann Arbor: Edwards Brothers, 1952), p. 232.

[2]William B. Sprague, *Annals of the American Pulpit* (New York: Robert Carter and Bros., 1865), 6:141.

March 10—From a Close Friend to a Bitter Persecutor

Scripture: Galatians 2:11-21

Balthazar Hubmaer (Hubmeyer) was born at Friedburg, Bavaria, in 1480. Even though he studied philosophy and theology under Eck, the great antagonist of Martin Luther, he embraced Luther's views in 1522.[1] He was in full communication with Zwingli and assisted him in the great debate at Zurich with the Catholics in 1523, after which they became the closest and warmest of friends.

Hubmaer, being a biblical scholar and preacher of power, soon discovered that the Reformation in Zurich had not gone back to the apostolic model. Gradually and deliberately, he embraced Anabaptist principles, which caused a severe rupture in his relationship with Zwingli. He formed an Anabaptist church and baptized more than three hundred of his former hearers. He would preach in the open air, and soon the population became largely Baptist.

The popularity of the preacher and the effectiveness of his preaching soon attracted the attention of the Reformers and Catholics alike. He was soon arrested and cast into a dungeon, where he lay four months appealing to his old friend Zwingli, to the emperor, and to the Confederation and Council, but in vain. His health broke, his wife was in prison, and he lay in a dungeon with more than twenty others. There was no light of the sun nor moon; bread and water were his only nourishment, and these could not be eaten for days on end because of the sickening odors of the place where the living were shut up with the dead. The only hope of escape was in death or recantation. The Zurich inquisition used all methods to persuade him to recant. Zwingli and others visited him in prison for the purpose of getting him to recant, and by the use of the rack and because of his weakened condition, he agreed to do so on some points. In his words, "They compelled, or sought to compel, me, a sick man, just risen from a bed of death; hunted, exiled, and having lost all that I had, to teach another faith." In the presence of a large congregation, after Zwingli had preached against the Anabaptist heretics, the broken and meek Hubmaer climbed to the pulpit, where he began to read his recantation in a weak and quavering voice. As he swayed to and fro in weakness, suddenly, being strengthened by the power of God, he raised himself to his full height and filled the great cathedral with the shout, "Infant baptism is not of God, and men must be baptized by faith in Christ." The crowd surged, some seized with horror, and others shouted approval till the cathedral rang, as Hubmaer was dragged from the pulpit and through the mass of people, being hustled back to his dungeon. There he once again wrote his confession of faith.

On March 10, 1528, he was led forth to his death with his heart fixed on the truth which he found in Christ Jesus and His Word. With his wife exhorting him to be strong and faithful, he was led to the place of execution which was a pile of fagots, where he was stripped of his clothing. His executioners then rubbed sulfur and gunpowder into his long beard. During this procedure, he was exhorting others, praying to God and asking forgiveness, and commending his spirit to his Lord. The fagots were ignited, and when his beard and hair caught fire, he cried out, "O Jesus, Jesus." Suffocating from the smoke of the burning sulfur and gun powder, he died.[2] Three days later his wife joined him in the presence of their Lord, being executed by drowning in the Danube River.

Once again a church state had stained its garments with the blood of the saints of God.

EWT

[1]Thomas Armitage, *The History of the Baptists* (1890; reprint ed., Watertown, Wis.: Maranatha Baptist Press, 1976), 1:336-39.

[2]William R. Estep, *The Anabaptist Story* (Nashville: Broadman Press, 1963), p. 63.

March 11—The Sacred Desk or the Legislative Desk

Scripture: Mark 10:38-42

Many of God's choicest servants were called upon to go through the crucible of suffering early in life. Thus it was in the experience of Joseph Crandall, whose mother died when he was thirteen, and not many years later his father also died. It would appear that his mother was a godly woman; for when she was about to depart this life, she summoned her son to her bedside, took him by the hand, and said, "Joseph, the Lord has a great work for you to do when I am gone."[1] These words, uttered with all the pathos of a mother's dying love, made an impression that never left him.

And a great work he did. His parents, having moved to Nova Scotia the year before the Revolution, had also in the providence of God made every needful provision for his support. Under the ministry of Harris Harding and Joseph Dimock, Crandall saw himself condemned justly to endless misery. He said, "I saw mercy so connected with the justice of God, that they were both one; that what God had done in the person of Christ was alone sufficient to save all that would come to God for mercy through Jesus Christ, and I felt as though the whole creation ought to know what I felt and saw; for indeed it appeared of more importance to me than the whole world."[2]

Soon after he had tasted of the Savior's love, he was engaged in a painful struggle relative to preaching the gospel. How could he embark on so great a venture with no education and no means of obtaining it? The two ministers, Dimock and Harding, recognized that he had a special call to preach and afforded him opportunity to exercise his gifts. The humble beginning of his ministry was accomplished with a manifestation of God's power and continued as he evangelized throughout the Maritime provinces, where multitudes gladly received the Word and were baptized.

In middle life he was persuaded to accept a seat in the provincial legislature of New Brunswick. At that time the government of the country was entirely in the hands of those who believed in the doctrine of "vested rights" and in the right of the "selected few" to govern the many. To dissent from the church/state notions of that day was, in the judgment of some, treason against the laws of the land. Crandall stood as the bold and uncompromising advocate of equal rights. He preached frequently at Fredericton, New Brunswick. On March 11, 1818, the legislature of New Brunswick passed an act stating that no avowed preacher of the gospel should have a seat in the legislature.[3] The question was whether he should pursue politics or God's calling. He was given to understand that if he were in the pulpit of Fredericton as usual on Sunday morning, he would be dismissed from the legislative seat early in the week. The Lord's day found him behind the sacred desk, as he had chosen to forsake the legislative desk. His influence in the provinces did not diminish but rather increased. He had chosen the reproach of Christ of greater value than the riches and fame of this world.

God help us to set our affection on things above.

EWT

---

[1]I. E. Bill, *Fifty Years with the Baptist Ministers and Churches of the Maritime Provinces of Canada* (Saint John, N.B.: Barnes and Co., 1880), p. 205.

[2]Ibid.

[3]Ibid., p. 212.

March 12—Holy of Life, Eloquent of Speech, Patriotic of Spirit

Scripture: Acts 18:18-28

Samuel Stillman was born in Philadelphia February 27, 1737. At the age of eleven he, along with his parents, moved to South Carolina. Under the preaching of Oliver Hart, he was converted to Jesus Christ. Stillman was baptized by Hart and studied theology under his tutelage. In later years Hart founded a Baptist Education Society in Charleston, South Carolina. When Samuel was twenty-one, he began to preach on James Island near Charleston.

Because of ill health, he moved to New Jersey, where he spent two years until he was called to become the assistant pastor of the Second Baptist Church of Boston. He served in this capacity for only one year and then became the pastor of the First Baptist Church of that city on

January 9, 1765. He ministered there until his death forty-two years later on March 12, 1807.

The Baptists, with very few exceptions, stood solidly behind the Revolution, and Samuel Stillman was no exception. Armitage says,

> Samuel Stillman was as noble a man and as holy a patriot as ever trod American soil. He read the signs of the times with a true eye, and stood his lot to breast the Revolutionary storm as long as it was possible. He was ever delicate in health, but earnest and fearless. He was deeply stirred by the outrages inflicted upon the Baptists of Massachusetts, and especially upon those of Ashfield, and signed a powerful petition, of which he was evidently the author, to the General Court for redress.[1]

This petition had to do with a general assessment for the support of a state church.

In 1766, ten years before the Declaration of Independence, Stillman denounced the Stamp Act from his pulpit. He again supported the colonial cause in a sermon on the general election in 1770 and did not leave his post until the British troops occupied Boston in 1775. His church was scattered for a short time until he returned in 1776. He regathered his flock and kept his church open throughout the war, even during periods when all others were closed.

Stillman was an eloquent pulpit orator. People would walk great distances to hear him preach and find standing room only. He would on no account swerve from the biblical principles of the gospel, even when the elite of Boston attended his meetings. Regularly John Adams, John Hancock, General Knox, and other dignitaries mingled with the crowd to hear his expositions on depravity, sovereignty, retribution, and redemption. On one occasion his denunciation of sin was so scathing and awful that a refined gentleman remarked, " 'The doctor makes us all out a set of rascals, but he does it so gracefully and eloquently that I am not disposed to find fault.' "[2] The forty-two years he spent in Boston covered the great debates that led to the Revolution, the war itself, the birth of the nation, the Federal Constitution, and the presidencies of Washington, Adams, and Jefferson. His ministry brought many to our Lord. Marked revivals crowned his efforts, and he always looked for opportunities to answer the question, "What must I do to be saved?"

Samuel Stillman lived in momentous times. He had the courage to stand true to the principles of God's Word, became involved in the political issues of his day, and still maintained a balance in his ministry by faithfully feeding his flock and winning precious souls to Jesus Christ. God help us in our momentous times to keep our spiritual balance.

EWT

---

[1]Thomas Armitage, *The History of the Baptists* (1890; reprint ed., Watertown, Wis.: Maranatha Baptist Press, 1976), 2:781-82.

[2]Ibid., p. 782.

March 13—A Courthouse Converted to a Church House

Scripture: Isaiah 61

This day was very significant in 1774 for several reasons. The Piscataway Baptist Church, located seven miles southwest of Tappahannock, Virginia, was constituted, and on the same day a warrant was issued to apprehend all the Baptist preachers at the meeting.

John Waller, John Shackleford, Robert Ware, and Ivison Lewis were taken before a magistrate. Ivison Lewis was released because it was not established that he had preached within the bounds of the county, but the others were sent to prison. They, however, from the beginning to the end of their imprisonment, preached twice during the week, gave godly advice to those who visited them, read the Scriptures a great deal, and prayed almost without ceasing. During this time they seemed to lack the sweet comfort and consolation which generally attended such experiences. John Waller in his journal wrote that they passed through various fiery trials, their minds being harassed by the enemy of souls.[1]

The court record of Essex County, Virginia, records the proceedings of the twenty-first day of March, in the year of our Lord 1774.

> John Waller, Robert Ware, and John Shackleford, Anabaptist preachers being brought before this court by a warrant from under the hand of Archibald Ritchie, Gent., for preaching and expounding the Scriptures contrary to law, and confessing the fact, it is ordered that they and each of them do give security in the sum of twenty pounds with two good and sufficient securities in the sum of ten pounds each for their behavior twelve months: And it is also ordered that they be forthwith committed to the gaol of this county there to remain the aforesaid term, unless they give such security.[2]

Robert Ware and John Shackleford both gave security and were released. This had been the second imprisonment for Robert Ware, who had been in prison at Urbana in Middlesex County jail with John Waller for forty-six days. This was John Shackleford's only imprisonment to our knowledge.

Waller was always doubtful about the propriety of giving any bond whatever and was determined to go back to jail. He felt deserted by his brethren and scoffed and persecuted by his enemies, and he was locked up with a set of drunken and profane rowdies. After remaining in jail for fourteen days, he gave consent for bond and went home. This was his fourth and last imprisonment.

The old brick courthouse building where these men were arraigned as lawbreakers is still standing on U.S. Route 17 in the town of Tappahannock. It is now a Baptist church. The walls of the building that resounded with the condemnation of Baptist preachers for preaching the gospel of Jesus Christ have reverberated for many years now with the proclamation of that gospel and the songs of praise to its Author, Jesus Christ. Soon after the organization of the Centennial Baptist Church, the members bought the old courthouse and used it as a house of worship. The church changed its name to Beal's Memorial Baptist Church in 1908 after Pastor Frank B. Beal, who faithfully served for a total of twenty-eight years.

This building is one of the few standing memorials that remind us of the great sacrifices our forefathers made to sow the gospel seed throughout the land and plant local churches in multitudes of communities. Many of the early buildings were of log and have since deteriorated, and others have burned, particularly during the Civil War. The forefathers also stood firmly for soul freedom and liberty of conscience. May we make every effort to preserve these landmarks and pass on to generations to come the importance of the principles for which our forefathers were willing to be imprisoned.

EWT

---

[1]Lewis Peyton Little, *Imprisoned Preachers and Religious Liberty in Virginia* (Lynchburg, Va.: J. P. Bell Co., 1938), pp. 399-407.

[2]Ibid.

March 14—Living with Eternity in View

Scripture: Job 14:14

On March 14, 1773, Edmund Botsford was ordained into the gospel ministry by his old mentor, the Reverend Oliver Hart, pastor of the First Baptist Church of Charleston, South Carolina. The ordination took place in Savannah, Georgia, and in the ordination sermon, taken from I Timothy 4:16, Pastor Hart said, "A plain and simple stile, seems best to comport with the simplicity of the Gospel, but let it not be low, or groveling—however plain, it ought to be manly & striking."[1]

As we search the record of Botsford's life, we are informed,

> In the parts of Georgia where Mr. Botsford labored, the inhabitants were a mixed multitude, of emigrants from many different places; most of them were destitute of any form of religion, and the few who paid any regard to it were zealous churchmen and Lutherans and violently opposed to the Baptists. In the same journey in which he fell in with Mr. Savidge, [Mr. Savage—March 9], he preached at the court-house in Burk county. The assembly at the first paid a decent attention: but, towards the close of the sermon, one of them bawled out with a great oath, "The rum is come." Out he rushed, others followed, the assembly was soon left small, and by the time Mr. Botsford got out to his horse, he had the unhappiness to find many of his hearers intoxicated and fighting. An old gentleman came up to him, took his horse by the bridle, and in his profane dialect most highly extolled him and his discourse, swore he must drink with him, and come and preach in his neighborhood. It was now no time to reason or reprove; and as preaching was Mr. Botsford's business, he accepted the old man's invitation, and made an appointment. His first sermon was blessed to the awakening of his wife; one of his sons also became religious, and others in the settlement, to the number of fifteen were in a short time hopefully brought to the knowledge of the truth, and the old man himself became sober and attentive to religion, although he never made a public profession of it.[2]

During the last fifteen or sixteen years of his life, Botsford suffered from a disease of the nerves in one side of his head. Oftentimes while preaching, his whole frame would be subject to the most distressing paroxysms, and they would last from a half minute to several minutes. In whatever position he was in when the seizure struck, he became fixed as a statue and remained until it passed off. Amazingly, he became so accustomed to the agony that it did not disturb his train of thought, and he would resume his message where he had stopped. In a letter to a Christian friend, Botsford alluded to one of his attacks. He wrote: "Last Lord's day, in the midst of my discourse, I was struck so violently that I was obliged to desist from speaking, and could not, for some minutes, dismiss the congregation, who were all attentive. Who knows but some sudden stroke may unawares send me to Heaven! Surely I ought to live each day looking for my change."[3]

Oh, that we too might live each day with eternity in view!

DLC

---

[1]Robert A. Baker and Paul J. Craven, Jr., *Adventure in Faith* (Nashville: Broadman Press, 1982), p. 140.

[2]Charles G. Sommers, William R. Williams, and Levi L. Hill, *The Baptist Library* (New York: Lewis Colby and Co., 1846), 1:40.

[3]William B. Sprague, *Annals of the American Pulpit* (New York: Robert Carter and Bros., 1865), 6:140-41.

March 15—He Forsook All to Follow Christ

Scripture: Matthew 19:29

The young man had not planned to remain unmarried, and during his college days he met a lovely young lady, and a mutual attachment grew. But when the young man announced his plans to serve the Lord across the seas, the two dissolved their association, and the young man resolved to forsake all and follow the Lord's leading, wherever it may take him. That young man was Luther Rice. He was born in March of 1783, was converted during his days as an academy student, became a student at Williams College, and then attended Andover Seminary. Young Rice was ordained in 1812, and along with Gordon Hall, Adoniram Judson, Samuel Newell, and Samuel Nott, he petitioned the American Board of Commissioners for Foreign Missions (Congregational) for service in India. Two of these men were bachelors.

The Judsons and Newells sailed aboard the "Caravan," and Rice, Hall, and the Notts were passengers on the "Harmony" in 1812, as they sailed for India. The story has often been told of the Judsons' conversion to Baptist doctrine, but Rice, too, confronted the matter of immersion as he sailed, and the foundation was laid for his adoption of immersion. William Johns, an English Baptist missionary, was a passenger as well, and he and Rice discussed the matter thoroughly. Four months after arriving in India, Rice "was baptized at Calcutta, November first."[1]

Adoniram and Ann Judson then met with Luther Rice to determine their course of action. "The threesome reasoned that the Board of Commissioners needed to hear firsthand about their change to Baptist sentiments. . . . Also important, the Baptist churches in America (should) be fully [apprised] of the distant mission and their support could be more directly enlisted."[2] It was concluded that Rice would return to America. Though the two men exchanged letters in the future, they would never meet again on earth. "As (Rice) bade farewell to his beloved associates on March 15, 1813, he reviewed his commitment to foreign missions: 'I renewedly give myself to the Lord; renewedly devote myself to the cause of missions, and beg of God to accept me as his, and particularly as devoted to the missionary service.' "[3]

Rice returned to the States, and his life of sacrifice can hardly be exaggerated. With what seemed to be inexhaustible energy, he devoted his life to raising support for Baptist missions. Rice envisioned and promoted a united missionary effort among Baptists, and when, in May of 1814, "The General Missions" was organized, Rice was appointed the Agent of the Convention. He had expected to return to Burma as a foreign missionary, but now he was challenged to travel extensively to raise support for the missionary cause. By horseback Rice traveled thousands of miles a year, preaching and representing missions. He had no home, no wardrobe but what he could carry, no bank account, and when he died on September 25, 1836, he bequeathed his whole earthly estate—a worn-out horse and rickety old sulky—to Columbian College in Washington, D.C., which he had founded. Today, when we think of missions, we ought to pause and give thanks for Luther Rice, a real Baptist builder!

DLC

---

[1]G. Winfred Hervey, *The Story of Baptist Missions In Foreign Lands* (St. Louis: C. R. Barnes Publishing Co., 1892), p. 174.

[2]William H. Brackney, *Dispensations of Providence* (Rochester, N.Y.: American Baptist Historical Society, 1984), p. 43.

[3]Ibid., p. 44.

March 16—The First White Woman to See Japan

Scripture: Psalm 46

The members of the congregation surely never gave much thought to one of their number gaining any renown, for the First Baptist Church of Napoleon, Michigan, was housed in a little, unpretentious white frame building. In 1834, when the church had been organized, most of the members were transplants from the East. Lucy Ann St. John was the daughter of one of the deacons of the Napoleon church, and in 1853 she married the Reverend Miles J. Knowlton, and the two sailed on December 10 for Ningpo, China.

Knowlton, upon graduation from Madison University, had been desirous of being appointed to labor in Burma, but the Board of the

Missionary Union had great need for missionaries in China. Though the field was very unattractive, Knowlton responded to the challenge, and thus the Knowltons began their nine-month journey. They traveled from New York around Cape Horn and stopped at Japan before reaching their destination. Mrs. Lucy Ann Knowlton "was the first white woman to visit the Sunrise Kingdom."[1] How unlikely that a young lady from a rural setting in Michigan should be so privileged, but God's servants are always honored of Him!

The Knowltons arrived in China as civil war was raging, and the war did not abate for many years. Mr. Knowlton launched into the work of evangelism and was very successful during his twenty-one years of ministry there. In 1861 the civil war swept into their area of service at Ningpo, and Mrs. Lucy experienced such a shock that she was returned to America for restoration of her health. In two years she was enabled to return, and the Knowltons had a blessed spiritual harvest. At the conclusion of fifteen exhausting years of labor and with Lucy's health again becoming a problem, the Knowltons took a two-year furlough back home. This was Knowlton's only return to America, and during that time as he lectured in several colleges and seminaries, he was granted a Doctor of Divinity degree.

Dr. Knowlton was originally from Vermont, and during his furlough, he preached as an evangelist in his home state and his own native town and had the joy of baptizing converts into the fellowship of the little church of his youth.

In 1872 the Knowltons sailed again for Ningpo, China, but this time they left from San Francisco and arrived back on the field in about four weeks. However, after two years of renewed efforts, Dr. Knowlton died unexpectedly. His medical doctor reported: "He undertook to perform the labors of two well-conditioned men, and thereby prematurely expended the large stock of force with which he was endowed."[2] Dr. Knowlton died in his forty-ninth year. Mrs. Knowlton returned to America not long after her husband's death and survived him by more than twenty years. During those years she was invited often to speak to ladies' groups concerning the challenge of China. Lucy A. Knowlton passed away on March 16, 1907, in Chicago at the home of their only child. The work of the Knowltons is rightly classed as pioneer missionary service and was of a very high character.

DLC

---

[1]M.E.D. Trowbridge, *History of Baptists in Michigan* (n.p.: Michigan Baptist State Convention, 1909), p. 190.

[2]G. Winfred Hervey, *The Story of Baptist Missions in Foreign Lands* (St. Louis: C. R. Barnes Publishing Co., 1892), p. 528.

March 17—When Strangulation Was an Act of Mercy

Scripture: Psalm 16

Some of the most meaningful prayers, sincere exhortations, and fervent defenses of the faith have come from the lips of little-known soldiers of the cross who sealed their testimony with their own blood as they endured the most horrible executions. Literally thousands of Anabaptists were put to death in Holland for their witness for Christ during the sixteenth century. The inquisitors had no respect for age nor sex. The blood of the aged was mingled with the blood of the youth. Women were tortured with the same ferocity as men. The desire for violence in the name of Christianity equaled that of the Roman arena.[1] The experience of Jacob Dirks and two of his sons, Andrew and Jan, is typical of literally millions who lived in that era. Jacob was a tailor who resided with his family in the city of Utrecht. Upon hearing that the magistrates wished to arrest him and fearing their tyranny, he fled to Antwerp. His wife, not sharing his doctrinal views, remained behind, but the constables seized her goods and kept possession of half of them. She died in Utrecht before she could be reunited with her family.

Afterwards, the authorities at Antwerp arrested Jacob and two of his sons to be condemned for their Anabaptist views. On their way to the place of the great trial by fire that was more precious than gold, they were met by Jacob's youngest son, Peter, who, upon hearing of the fate of his father and brothers, threw himself upon his father's neck in deep sorrow. The executioner with great cruelty tore him from his father's embrace and threw him to the ground to be trampled by the crowd that followed them. This, of course, added much to the distress of his father and brothers.

Upon arrival at the place of execution and being secured at the stake, Jacob said to his sons, ''How is it with you, my dear sons?'' They answered, ''Dear father, all is well.'' Andrew was at the time a bridegroom; his bride and his sister beheld the sacrifice at a distance with weeping and broken hearts. They witnessed how the bridegroom and brother, forsaking the dearest earthly ties and affection, had chosen above all the heavenly Bridegroom, Jesus Christ.

These courageous men were each strangled by the executioner, which was considered an act of mercy, before the fire was kindled at the stake, and the smoke of their sacrifice arose unto God as the sweet incense of their faithfulness unto death. They had testified to God's truth and sealed their faith with their own blood and by fire.

These executions which have taken place down through the centuries by the millions have given testimony to the authority and validity of the gospel as well as to the sustaining grace of God under the most trying circumstances. On some occasions the martyr would raise his hands toward heaven as a prearranged signal to the observers that God truly provided supernatural strength to bear the flames. Others would sing anthems of praise and adoration until the smoke and flames would extinguish their voices. The most terrible trials occurred when the wood was inadequate to bring a quick death or the wind blew the flames away from the victim, prolonging the agony.

These acts of persecution demonstrate the utter depravity of man, who is capable with all his intellectual abilities to commit such atrocious acts, as well as the power of God to strengthen His saints through any trial and to comfort those who sometimes must observe their sufferings. May we never forget God's suffering saints in our prayers.

EWT

---

[1]T. J. Van Braght, trans., and Edward Bean Underhill, ed., *A Martyrology of the Churches of Christ Commonly Called Baptists* (London: J. Haddon and Son, 1853), 2:449-50.

March 18—Forty-Two Years with Only Two Furloughs

Scripture: Galatians 6:8-10

How shocking will be the disclosure at the Judgment Seat of Christ when unsung heroes of whom we have never heard are honored by our blessed Lord. Surely Edward Payson Scott was such a man. "With his Bible and violin he went into the head-hunting territory of the Nagas in Assam. The first twelve Nagas who approached him changed their menacing attitude to one of joy when he played and sang 'Am I a Soldier of the Cross?' and thus he won entry into the land of the music-loving Nagas. It was not a spear but cholera which killed Scott later that same year."[1]

Another unsung hero, however, was being groomed by the Lord to follow up that advance. Edward W. Clark had been born in New York on February 25, 1830. Being introduced early to salvation, though just a farm boy, he looked forward to Christian service. He graduated from Brown University in 1857 and entered seminary in Rochester, New York. He married Mary Mead and served a short pastorate in Logansport, Indiana. He then became the editor of a Christian periodical and became acquainted with the potential of the printed page. In 1868 he was asked to take charge of the mission printing press in Sibsagor, the ancient capital of Assam, India; and following a difficult voyage of 136 days, Mr. and Mrs. Clark arrived in Calcutta. In Sibsagor, the Reverend Dr. Clark was challenged as never before with the great needs of the heathen world. The year was 1869 when the Reverend Edward Payson Scott had gone into the Nagas territory, dying that same year. Now Clark learned of the wider fields toward the south hills of Assam, where savagery existed in its worst form. He determined to go, and he did not rest until he had penetrated those hills.

Surely the accomplishments of the Reverend Dr. Clark and his wife deserve to rank among those of the great missionary pioneers! It was some time before they could settle at Molung where they were surrounded by savage head-hunters, the Ao-Nagas. The Clarks were the first whites to be seen by many of the nationals. For seventeen years they remained, without furlough, laboring among their adopted people. In spite of all of his responsibilities in introducing the gospel, Dr. Clark found time to do a great deal of literary work. "He reduced the language to writing, translated some of the Gospels, and printed many books for use in the schools. His last work was the Ao-Naga-English Dictionary, upon which he worked more or less steadily for the last seven years of his life. In May, 1911, he returned to his home in America, after forty-two years' service in India, with only two furloughs."[2]

The Reverend Edward W. Clark was honored three times with the degree of Doctor of Divinity, but he considered his greatest honor in being a servant of the Lord Jesus Christ. He was energetic and brave, yet simple and unassuming and was characterized by great faith in God and His Word! Dr. Edward W. Clark "passed away on March 18, 1913, in St. Augustine, Florida, at the age of eighty-three years."[3] Doubtless the story of Dr. and Mrs. Clark will be duplicated over and again when we gather at the Judgment Seat of Christ and hear our Savior intone those glorious words to so many unsung heroes, "Well done, thou good and faithful servant."

DLC

---

[1]Davis Collier Woolley, ed., *Baptist Advance* (Nashville: Broadman Press, 1964), pp. 77-78.

[2]*Indiana Baptist Annual* (Indiana Baptist Convention, Printed by Order of the Convention, Proceedings of the Eighty-First Anniversary, Oct. 14-17, 1913), p. 86.

[3]Ibid., p. 85.

March 19—Out of the Ashes They Continued to Build

Scripture: Ezra 3

The motive for Timothy Gilbert, S. H. Shipley, Thomas Gould, and William S. Donwell to purchase the Tremont Theater in 1843 for $55,000 and completely remodel it at the cost of $24,284 was a very unusual one. They desired to secure a place of meeting for the Tremont Street Baptist Church and also to provide "free seats" for the poor and strangers coming into the city to seek employment whose means would not permit them to rent pews, which was the common practice of that period in Boston, Massachusetts.

The main assembly room, a 90' x 80' structure capable of seating two thousand persons, provided ample room for such people. This met the needs of the ministry until March 31, 1852, when it was totally destroyed by fire. Although this was a great setback, it did not keep those dedicated to the ministry from pressing on. On May 25, 1853, they were laying the foundation of a new building, and on Christmas Day of the same year, they held their first public meeting in the new auditorium, which was fully furnished with new pews and an organ.

The owners transferred the new building to the newly formed Evangelical Baptist Benevolent and Missionary Society. The Society granted a lease to the Tremont Baptist Church for the use of the building as a place of worship and teaching of God's Word as long as they supported a good and sufficient pastor and all the pews remained free of charge.

On the night of August 14, 1879, the comparatively new building was razed by fire, but the directors took immediate steps to rebuild and go on with the ministry. The objectives of the Tremont Baptist Temple were to maintain evangelistic preaching, to support and provide colporteur and missionary laborers in Boston and the surrounding areas, as well as to provide in a special way for the spiritual needs of the destitute.[1]

The enemy of the gospel and of the souls of men would not give up testing this church and ministry with fire. On March 19, 1893,

Tremont Temple burned once again. Not only was the meeting place destroyed but also its valuable library. Along with that, a museum with portraits and other objects of great significance and value was burned. The insurance could rebuild and restore the material structure, but there were many articles that could never be replaced. The people once again devoted themselves to the task of rebuilding.[2]

Baptists always have had to be a hardy people. When they commit themselves to an enterprise for the purpose of propagating the gospel, God has always granted the will to rise above the circumstances and to rebuild out of the ashes of great loss to become a stronger, more dedicated people. Some have been consumed bodily in the fire, and others have seen all their earthly belongings go up in smoke. The destructive fires Tremont Baptist Temple experienced could have caused men of lesser character and dedication to surrender the cause and quit. Fires of the magnitude that destroyed Tremont Temple are awesome, but the people of this great church were held in greater awe by the prospects of men and women suffering in the fires of hell. Men can recover from material loss, but the loss of a soul is eternal. Jesus reminds us of this when he says, "What is a man profited, if he shall gain the whole world, and lose his own soul? or what shall a man give in exchange for his soul?" (Matthew 16:26). What shall we be willing to give for the souls of others?

Tremont Baptist Temple was an early great example of what an inner-city ministry should be and reached thousands with the gospel. It also was an example of a people who persevered in the face of tremendous difficulties. May God grant us the same perseverance and strength to reach the people of our inner cities today. Jesus Christ is the true panacea for our urban ills.

EWT

---

[1]William Cathcart, *The Baptist Encyclopedia,* ed. Louis H. Everts (Philadelphia: Louis H. Everts, 1881), 2:1162-64.

[2]Henry S. Burrage, *A History of the Baptists in New England* (Philadelphia: American Baptist Publication Society, 1894), p. 168.

March 20—A Man Mighty in the Scriptures

Scripture: Acts 17:10-12

As one reads the early history of our Baptist forefathers, one of the continual similarities that is observed is their lack of formal education.

How could men of such little academic accomplishment achieve so much? A case in point is the life of Samuel L. Straughan of Virginia. Born in July of 1783, Straughan assisted his father on the farm and had only two or three years of formal education. At the age of eleven, he became gainfully employed, and formative years in a classroom were unavailable to him. We are assured that "during his childhood, he exhibited a sobriety and manliness of character much beyond his years; and so fond was he of reading and hearing upon religious subjects, that his father used playfully to call him his preacher."[1]

For several months in 1802, Straughan grappled with the matter of his personal salvation, and it was in the fall of that year when assurance of eternal life became his. He was baptized in April of 1803, and shortly after that he began to preach occasionally. His friends recognized the call of God upon his life, but it was not until March 20, 1806, that he was ordained. On that very day he received a unanimous call to the Wicomico Baptist Church, which was a small flock of perhaps two dozen people. Straughan, however, was soon to rank among the leading Baptist preachers in Virginia, for the church quickly increased to nearly three hundred members. The next year he was called also to pastor the Morattico Baptist Church. He accepted this call and again experienced great growth under his ministry. The spirit of revival invaded the congregations, and the man of God with little formal training was pastoring two prospering churches. In 1814 the Missionary Society of Richmond appointed Pastor Straughan to travel into Maryland to preach the gospel. Wondering what the Lord had planned for him in this new invitation, the pastor requested both churches to have a day of fasting and prayer to assist him in knowing the mind of the Lord. This was done, and the result was a determination to accept the appointment while continuing to pastor both churches. His schedule now seemed almost impossible, but he was accompanied with great success in all that he undertook, both in his pastoral labors and his missionary trips for evangelism. Pastor Straughan was overtaken with a pulmonary disease that ultimately caused his death in his thirty-eighth year on June 9, 1821, but our interest is how he and others in those early years were able, without benefit of great formal education, to become such outstanding leaders.

Our purpose is not to depreciate the benefits of academic training. Surely the Lord is pleased to use sharpened tools, but the secret of Straughan's success seems to have been his insatiable love of the Word of God. He spoke extemporaneously, and he possessed a rich, sonorous voice. He majored on the theme of the atonement of Christ, but his messages were saturated with the Scriptures. "He committed large portions of the Bible to memory, and so much of it did he quote in the pulpit, that it was not uncommon . . . [for hearers] to count the passages in a single sermon, and they would often reach nearly a hundred.''[2] Pastor Straughan was ''mighty in the Scriptures,'' and we believe such a renewed emphasis would be blessed today, for education can never replace the illumination of God's Word!

DLC

---

[1]William B. Sprague, *Annals of the American Pulpit* (New York: Robert Carter and Bros., 1865), 6:514.

[2]Ibid, 6:516.

March 21—"Write This for a Memorial in a Book"

Scripture: Exodus 17:8-16

For varied reasons, Baptists in the past have been remiss in recording history. We surely concur with the familiar statement, ''Those who cannot remember the past are condemned to repeat it.''[1] One's heritage cannot be sustained without a viable memory bank. The faithful account of past events, heroes, and tenets is essential so that future generations maintain convictions of merit.

Thomas Crosby was born on March 21, 1683.[2] The smoke of the martyr fires had just dissipated, and the sounds of the clanging chains had just faded away. After his conversion, Crosby united with the Goat Street Baptist Church (England), where the pastor was the Reverend Benjamin Stinton, Crosby's brother-in-law. Stinton had compiled historical materials and planned to write a Baptist history of England, but he died an untimely death. In time, the papers came into the possession of Crosby, and as he devoured the substance, he added information that he had obtained. Crosby had no training as a historian and felt an inadequacy to undertake the actual writing of such a history. In time, Crosby approached Daniel Neal, a Puritan historian who was preparing his *History of the Puritans,* and asked him to include a section on the Baptists. After several years the work was published and Crosby wrote: ''I was surprised to see the ill use Mr. Neal made of these materials; and that the rise and progress of the English Baptist . . . were contained in less than five pages of his third volume; and that too with very great partiality.''[3]

Disappointed with the application that Neal had made of the information and with a desire for redress of the Baptist cause, Crosby wrote a four-volume work which he published as *The History of the English Baptists, from the Reformation to the Beginning of the Reign of King George I.* The work appeared from 1738 to 1740 and formed the first attempt at a complete history of the Baptists.

We have alluded to the fact that Crosby was not a historian in the true sense of the term, but inasmuch as his pastor, Benjamin Stinton, was also the son-in-law of the Reverend Benjamin Keach, Crosby had a wealth of data. A great amount of valuable biographical material concerning many of the earlier Baptist ministers is made available in Crosby's book.[4] Doubtless, Crosby's effort to correct the misrepresentations of Neal may have caused him to overcompensate, yet the pages provide invaluable information to twentieth-century Baptists. Of course, the set appeared in the difficult-to-read seventeenth-century typeface, and when it was reprinted in 1978, the old pages were photographed and copied. The modern reader will therefore find an added challenge in the reading, but the effort is well rewarded.

May we learn the essential lesson of saturating the minds of our Baptist youth with our history so that they might learn of the outstanding personalities, principles, and polity that have merged to provide us with such a great heritage.

DLC

---

[1]George Santayana, *The Life of Reason* (New York: Charles Scribner's Sons, 1953), p. 82.

[2]William Henry Brackney, *The Baptists* (New York: Greenwood Press, 1988), p. 151.

[3]Thomas Crosby, *The History of the English Baptists* (1738-40; reprint ed., Lafayette, Tenn.: Church History Research and Archives, 1978), p. 2.

[4]W. T. Whitley, *A History of British Baptists* (London: Charles Griffin and Co., 1923), p. 180.

March 22—A Baptist Martin Luther

Scripture: Ezekiel 22:30

William Bell Riley could have been accurately described as a tall, strikingly handsome man possessing a commanding presence with charming charisma. His resonant voice was compelling, and he had an excellent sense of humor. Such was the man that many called the most important fundamentalist of his generation. At his funeral on December

9, 1947, Dr. Richard V. Clearwaters referred to him as "the Martin Luther of Protestantism."[1]

W. B. Riley had been born in Green County, Indiana, on March 22, 1861, just prior to the Civil War. His father was sympathetic to the South, and thus the family moved to Kentucky, where young Riley was reared. He was converted at seventeen years of age and received his college training at Hanover College in Indiana, graduating in 1885. Young Riley considered a legal profession, for he had an astute mind and enjoyed debating, but he surrendered to the call to preach and entered Southern Baptist Theological Seminary for his training, graduating in 1888.

After pastoring several smaller churches, Riley was called by the First Baptist Church in Minneapolis, Minnesota, and pastored there for forty-five years until his retirement in 1942. During his ministry, the congregation grew from 585 to over 3,500 members. Riley was a preacher, pastor, author, evangelist, administrator, debater, civic leader, and social critic, and First Baptist Church knew continual growth. In 1902 he founded the Northwestern Bible and Missionary Training School, and the student body grew to over 800. In 1938 he added the Northwestern Evangelical Seminary. In 1944 he established the Northwestern College. Doubtless his early association with D. L. Moody, while Riley was still a seminary student, made a deep impression on his life. The church allowed him four months a year for evangelism, and he served as an evangelist in every section of the nation.

Riley authored sixty books including a forty-volume set known as *The Bible of the Expositor and Evangelist,* which was the compilation of ten years of his morning messages.

Unafraid of controversy, Riley put his debating ability to use as he attacked liberal theology, evolution, and the cults across America. Riley envisioned purging liberalism from the Northern Baptist Convention and rallied forces to assist in the battle. Thus he became a leader in the Fundamentalism/Modernism battles from 1920 through the 1940s. With unbounded energy, Riley participated in the formation of the World Christian Fundamentals Association in 1919 and served as president. He spoke in the formational meeting of the Fundamental Baptist Fellowship in Buffalo in 1920. In 1923 he shared in the constituting of the Baptist Bible Union. Riley wrested the Minnesota Baptist Convention from the Northern Baptist Convention while serving as president of the state body in 1944-45.

True to his convictions and unable to alter the course of the Northern Convention and failing during his tenure as pastor to lead his congregation out, W. B. Riley personally resigned his membership in the Northern Baptist Convention in May of 1947, just seven months before his death on December 5, 1947. "Both friend and foe could agree with the tribute of Harry A. Ironside, pastor of the Moody Memorial Church, in Chicago, at the time of Riley's death: . . . God never repeats Himself. . . . He will raise up others to carry on, but there will never be a second man of Dr. Riley's stamp."[2]

DLC

---

[1]Dr. R. V. Clearwaters, "The Passing of Dr. W. B. Riley." *Central Baptist Quarterly,* Spring 1961, p. 11.

[2]C. Allyn Russell, *Voices of American Fundamentalism* (Philadelphia: Westminster Press, 1976), p. 80.

March 23—Vestry Laws Abolished, Disestablishment Accomplished

Scripture: I Corinthians 1:12-24

The Vestry Law adopted March 23, 1660 or 1661, in the colony of Virginia stated,

> "That twelve of the most able men of each parish, be by the major part of each parish, chosen to be a vestry; out of which number, the minister and vestry, to make choice of two church wardens yearly; as also in the case of any vestryman, or his departure from the parish, that the minster and said vestry, make choice of another in his room." To qualify them for this office they were required to take the oath of supremacy to the British Sovereign, and "Subscribe the doctrine and discipline of the Church of England." Among their most prominent duties, they were "to lay the parish levy and collect, and pay over the amount to the minister."[1]

Various laws were passed from 1655 to 1748 involving the provision of glebes for the minister at the expense of the citizenry through taxation. The glebes were rather elaborate and extensive properties consisting of at least two hundred acres of land and a mansion with a kitchen, a barn, stables, a dairy, a meat house, a corn house, and a fenced-in garden. Every parish was to be provided with a glebe through money provided by the "tithable persons" regardless of sect.

As we have previously observed, the Baptists strongly resisted such taxation in several of the colonies where they were levied.

There were those who desired to carry over an established church and these vestry laws into the laws of the Commonwealth of Virginia after the Declaration of Independence. Disestablishment came only after a long and bitter struggle. Even those who had befriended the Baptists in the past, such as Patrick Henry, desired to maintain some form of religious establishment. The Baptists, convinced that true religion did not need to be propped up by government and remembering their persecutions under a religious state, kept the pressure on the legislature by sending commissioners with petitions to repeal certain acts that tended to re-establish a state church. Finally, in response to this pressure, the Virginia Legislature passed an act in 1799 whose preamble states in part "the power of reviving any species of ecclesiastical or church government, in lieu of that so dissolved, by referring the subject of religion to the conscience." All religious matters were referred to the individual conscience of each person. The incorporation of any religious society was in violation of the principles of religious freedom. Churches are not incorporated in Virginia to this day.

This act prepared for, but did not provide for, the sale of the glebes. There was great debate concerning the sale and the disposition of the proceeds. The Baptists contended that it was the people's money that purchased these extensive plantations and that they should be sold and the proceeds returned to the people. Finally, they saw victory by a law passed January 12, 1802. The final nail was driven into the coffin of the established church. A long, bitter war had ended, and the position of Baptists who suffered under religious establishment was vindicated. We should thank God for the perseverance of our forefathers whose courage and willingness to suffer purchased our liberty to pursue and propagate the truth as our consciences dictate. May we carry out this great tradition and not think that one battle won means the war is over.

EWT

---

[1]Robert Boyte and C. Howell, *The Early Baptists of Virginia* (Philadelphia: American Baptist Publication Society, 1857), pp. 96-99.

March 24—Roger Williams Prepares the Way

Scripture: Hebrews 6

Roger Williams, along with a few others among the Puritans, had a genuine spiritual concern for the Indians. He went out among the Massasoits, made friends, learned their language, and taught them the Christian gospel. The Indians were delighted that a white man met them as equals. Williams drafted a treaty of friendship with this tribe, which paved the way for the establishment of future colonies.

Later when the Boston authorities were planning to seize Williams and put him on a ship bound for England, he decided to escape and continue the fight for liberty of conscience. He bundled himself in his greatcoat, stuffed some food into his pockets, kissed his wife and baby good-bye, and stole out into the darkness.

A severe winter storm was brewing, and by midnight it had turned into a blizzard. Williams pushed through drifting snow, over fields, and through forests as the bitterly cold wind shrieked about him. The next day he reached a camp of the Narraganset Indians. Greeting him as a friend, they took him, fed him, thawed him out, and insisted that he remain in hiding with them. During his winter stay, he became a mediator and helped to reconcile problems that had developed between two chieftains. War was averted, and Chief Massasoit in gratitude gave him a tract of land. Also during this exile, Williams decided to establish his own independent colony, one that would be open to all who desired to enjoy religious freedom.[1]

This later benefited not only Williams but also John Clarke, who became disenchanted with the Puritans and Pilgrims. He formed a company of nineteen people, and in the winter of 1637-38 they went forth to discover a new home. They went first to what is now New Hampshire, but finding the climate so harsh, they turned south toward Long Island and Delaware. Stopping on the way at Providence, they stayed with Roger Williams, who persuaded them to go to the island of Aquidnet. They first went to Plymouth to make sure that no claim had been made to it.[2] Finding that the land was available, Roger Williams, acting as their agent, procured from the Narraganset sachems a deed for Aquidnet Island for them on March 24, 1638, and another for himself for Providence on the same day.[3]

At a time when some in the Massachusetts colony had a belligerent spirit and often exploited the Indians, the Spirit of God worked through Roger Williams to prepare the way for the establishment of a place where religious liberty could prosper, where those who loved it could settle, and from which the freedom of conscience could be proclaimed as a witness to the world.

EWT

---

[1]O. K. and Marjorie Armstrong, *Baptists Who Shaped a Nation* (Nashville: Broadman Press, 1975), pp. 39-43.

[2]Robert C. Newman, *Baptists and the American Tradition* (Des Plaines, Ill.: Regular Baptist Press, 1976), p. 15.

[3]Isaac Backus, *Your Baptist Heritage, 1620–1804* (1844; reprint ed., Little Rock: Challenge Press, 1976), p. 40.

March 25—A Missionary Statesman Was Born

Scripture: Acts 9:1-19

Although there was some missionary activity in the colonies in the efforts to reach the Indians and the settlers as they migrated westward, it was not until the early 1800s that the Baptists seriously considered the commission of our Lord to include the great masses of people on other continents of the world. This took place in a very unusual manner and as the result of revival fires burning in the hearts of some college students who were at that time Congregationalists, not Baptists.

At the Congregationalist Williams College in Massachusetts, a fellowship of students became vitally interested in world evangelism and began meeting regularly for prayer. Out of this group was formed the missionary fellowship known as the "Brethren." They continued in their prayer for the peoples of the world who lived in spiritual darkness. They often met in the open air, and one hot, humid day as they continued their intercession, a thunderstorm swept through, driving them to take refuge under the sheaves of a nearby haystack. Some believe that this "Haystack Prayer Meeting" marked the birth of the foreign missions movement in America because it was there that these students resolved to put their prayers and talk into action.[1]

Luther Rice, who was a part of the "Brethren" fellowship but was not at that particular "Haystack Prayer Meeting," later made the commitment, "I have deliberately made up my mind to preach the Gospel to the heathen, and I do not know but it may be Asia."

Being a Congregationalist and a student in their schools of higher learning, little did Rice know that he would be at the very heart of the Baptist missionary movement for years to come. Born into a pedobaptist home March 25, 1783, he was committed to that system until he, along with Adoniram Judson, sailing on different ships to India, reexamined the New Testament teaching concerning baptism. They came to the same conclusion that the Baptist views were correct on the subject and were baptized by immersion. This decision changed the entire course of their lives because they felt compelled to sever relationships with their former sending agency and to identify themselves with the Baptists in America.[2]

Rice returned to America to stir up the Baptists for world evangelism, which he surely did. This missionary zeal also stirred up some controversy relating to missionary methods as well. Thus began the split between the Baptists of the South, who favored conventionism, and the Baptists of the North, who favored societies. The Baptists of the South also split over missions methods into the New School and Old School Baptists, and ultimately, the Southern Baptist Convention was born.

Though Luther Rice had fully intended to return to Burma, he became so involved in raising interest and support for missions and Christian education that his desire to return never became a reality. The endless travel was very difficult. At first he used the stagecoach or other public conveyance. Later he rode horseback. One day he rode ninety-three miles, breaking John Wesley's record of ninety miles. Later he acquired a one-horse sulky to make his long trips. He swam rivers, braved blizzards, endured heat, was in jeopardy of wild Indians and bandits, and lodged under the open sky. When he did find lodging in a home, whether in a crude log cabin or a fine mansion, he would read the Bible, sing a hymn, pray, and usually give a testimony concerning missions.[3]

One cannot measure the impact of this man's life and witness upon the thousands throughout the world who heard the gospel because of his missionary zeal. Missionary societies were formed, publications begun, colleges founded, and churches planted, as well as hundreds of missionaries being thrust out into the harvest field. That seed that was willing to die still bears much fruit. O Lord, please give us more Luther Rices.

EWT

---

[1]H. Leon McBeth, *The Baptist Heritage* (Nashville: Broadman Press, 1987), pp. 344-45.

[2]Thomas Armitage, *The History of the Baptists* (1890; reprint ed., Watertown, Wis.: Maranatha Baptist Press, 1976), 2:814.

[3]McBeth, p. 351.

March 26—"There Arose No Small Stir About That Way"

Scripture: Acts 19:23-41

The Chappawamsic Baptist Church was planted by David Thomas, who was probably the most learned and scholarly of the early Baptist preachers in Virginia. He was a Regular Baptist from Pennsylvania. After having visited Virginia on some preaching missions, he finally settled in the northern part of the colony. He was constantly threatened by ruffians with clubs and guns as were so many of our early preachers.[1]

Chappawamsic Baptist Church was the mother church of the Potomack Baptist Church, which was constituted in Stafford County, March 26, 1771. Under the leadership of David Thomas, the Chappawamsic Church produced some of the great and useful preachers of that day. Among these were church planters like Jeremiah Moore, Daniel Fristoe, and his brother William. William Fristoe wrote an early history of the Ketocton Baptist Association and planted the Potomack Baptist Church.

William Fristoe walked in the footsteps of his spiritual father, and became the object of the same violence of those opposers of the gospel. The planting of these churches was resisted by large gangs of men with clubs and rocks as they attempted to break up the meetings and beat the preacher. One remarkable example of this involved a gang of around forty men led by Robert Ashby, who entered the meetinghouse with the purpose of disrupting the meeting. Some stout fellows at the door took Ashby by the neck and heels and threw him out. This resulted in a melee involving the whole multitude in a knockdown-dragout battle. Soon after this incident, Ashby cut his knee, which became badly infected so that the joint opened and his leg hung only by the hamstrings. On his sickbed he would not let anyone touch him, and he desired preaching, but when the preacher began preaching, he would stop his ears and desire the preacher to stop because he could not stand to hear it. He died a horrible death of great suffering. So strongly did this impress the people that God had intervened that it put a damper on the mischievous designs of others to disrupt the Baptist meetings. The early preachers often had faithful laymen to help them such as Allen Wyley who assisted William Fristoe in his pastorate. Also being baptized by David Thomas in Fauquier County, Wyley was of great value to the ministry. He was the first to invite Samuel Harriss, the Separate Baptist in the South, to come and preach at his own house in Culpeper County. The second day of the meetings, Captain Ball and his gang came and said, "You shall not preach here." One Jeremiah Minor replied, "But we shall." Sharp words and blows followed. To escape the mob, Colonel Harriss was then taken to a house, where Lewis Craig was left to guard the door. Ball's gang came and battered the door down after driving the guard away only to be confronted by the people within. The day ended with confusion.

Though not an ordained minister, Wyley probably was an exhorter. In my early years in the ministry, I preached among some old Regular

Baptist churches in Kentucky which still hold to the traditional order of service that the early Baptists in Virginia followed which included an exhorter. Without hymnals or accompaniment, the music was led by one who chanted a line followed by the congregation's singing that line. Following the singing, there would be one who would introduce the sermon with a brief message followed by a long, loud prayer. Another would preach the message, after which an exhorter would admonish the hearers to act upon the truth which they had heard. Singing would begin as the exhorter continued with his exhortation. Those making profession of faith would approach the preacher, who would stop the singing and give the professor the opportunity to testify to his experience with Christ. Also, if during one's discourse, the congregation thought that the speaker was too long or not Spirit-filled, they would sing him down. In some instances where certain practices were expedient because of the circumstances of the times, they evolved into doctrine, and those who discontinued the practices were considered unspiritual.

EWT

---

[1]Lewis Peyton Little, *Imprisoned Preachers and Religious Liberty in Virginia* (Lynchburg, Va.: J. P. Bell Co., 1938), pp. 60-72, 227-28.

March 27—Baptism Ridiculed

Scripture: Psalm 56:1-4

Many present-day Americans are unaware of the heroic struggles that early Baptists waged in the formative days of our republic to ensure religious freedom for all. We do well to remind ourselves that we are responsible to assure the continuation of our liberty for yet another generation.

Isaiah Parker and Samuel Fletcher, two young Baptist itinerant preachers, were invited to Pepperell, Massachusetts, by the local Baptists and asked to preach. Attempting outdoor evangelism on March 27, 1778, they personally witnessed the local bigotry as threats were made against them. Being unwilling to surrender to such pressures, the two young men visited Pepperell several times during the spring and summer. Samuel Fletcher's father lived in the town, and doubtless his visits were personal as well as evangelistic.

During a visit to Pepperell on June 26, however, a real disorder erupted. Six converts presented themselves for baptism, and arrangements were made to obey the commandment of the Lord. In his *Diary,* Isaac Backus makes an entry on September 9, 1778, concerning a letter from the Baptists at Pepperell which was discussed by the Warren Association.

> They met in a field by a river side, where prayers were made, and a sermon begun, when the chief officers of the town, with many followers, came and interrupted their worship. The owner of the field warned them [the town rowdies] to depart out of it, if they would not be peaceable; but they refused to go. One of the Baptist ministers desired them to act like men, if they would not [act] like Christians; and reminded them of the liberty of conscience which is generally allowed, and even by the powers we were at war with; and began to open the divine warrant therefore; upon which an officer said, "Don't quote scripture here!" . . . A dog was carried into the river and plunged, in evident contempt of our sentiments. A gentleman of the town then invited the Baptists to go and hold their meeting at his house, which was near another river. They accepted of it, and so went through with their worship. At the close of which a man was hired with a bowl of liquor to go into the river, and dip another two or three times over; where also two or three dogs were plunged. After which three officers of the town came into the house where the Baptist ministers were, and advised them immediately to depart out of that town for their own safety. . . . Seeing their temper (i.e., the temper of the ruffians), the Baptists agreed to disperse, and to meet at a distant place of water; which was done, and those six persons were decently baptized, though further abuse was offered at the close of it.[1]

Elsewhere in his *Diary,* Backus tells of rioting mobs who did all in their power to disturb and disrupt the Baptist ministry in New England. The result of this opposition only strengthened the resolve of our forefathers. Baptists never attempted to coerce others in spiritual matters, for the spirit of voluntarism characterizes true biblical Christianity. Knowing that man must, of his own volition "seek the Lord," Baptists have always been willing to grant full religious freedom to others, but they demand it as well for themselves.

DLC

---

[1]William G. McLoughlin, ed., *The Diary of Isaac Backus* (Providence: Brown University Press, 1979), 2:1001.

March 28—The Onesimus of Colonial America

Scripture: Philemon

John Jasper was a black man, born into slavery on July 4, 1812, and was never privileged to attend school, but he used his native eloquence as few others have. In the process of time, Jasper became one of the greatest preachers of his day! Literally thousands were swayed by his oratory, and many who had come to ridicule stood at the close of his sermons openly weeping. It is impossible in such a limited sketch to present his story as one could wish, but the brief panorama of his amazing life might still prove inspirational.

Before John was born, his father, who had been a slave Baptist preacher, died and his mother, Tina, dedicated John to the Lord. Her prayers continually were, "Lord, if dis chile you's sendin' me is a boy, doan' let him do nuthin' else but sing de praises of Jesus!"[1] At his birth she insisted on naming him "John" after John the Baptist!

John was just another wayward youth, but his mother persisted in prayer. The Jaspers were owned by Widow Mary Belle Peachy until her death and then by her son, John Peachy. At the time of Peachy's death, John Jasper was purchased by Samuel Hardgrove, a deacon in the First Baptist Church of Richmond. Hardgrove used John in his tobacco stemmery. John's mother continued praying for him, and the Lord brought conviction in John's life. His testimony is graphic: "I was seekin' God six weeks—jes' cause I was sich a fool I couldn't see de way."[2] On July 25, 1839, John was wonderfully saved at the tobacco stemmery and began to shout for joy. His overseer came in to see what the shouts were about and threatened John. Simultaneously, Hardgrove entered upon the scene and took John to his office. Hearing John's testimony, Hardgrove gave John the remainder of the day off to share his testimony with friends and neighbors.

John began to preach the funerals of slaves almost immediately, and God's power was very evident. Folks would flock to hear him comfort the grieving and lift them into the very presence of God with his descriptive oratory, and before long, the whites were also enthralled with his funeral orations. John prayed that he might be enabled to learn to read, and for seven months another slave, William Johnson, labored with him from a tattered copy of the *New York Speller*. Soon John became an earnest Bible reader. He sought opportunities to hear other men preach and cultivated a close friendship with Dr. William Hatcher, a local Baptist pastor. John's love for "Mars Sam" (Sam Hardgrove) and Dr. Hatcher became most apparent in his preaching.

Hardgrove gave John his freedom to preach and preach he did! John founded the Sixth Mount Zion Baptist Church. He "began with nine members, and it was reported that there were over 2,000 at the time of his death."[3] Whites flocked to hear him, and his humor sparkled. When the Virginia state legislature was present in a body at this church, John cried out, "Pharaoh was an awful liar. Just like they tell me most politicians are."[4] We thank God for the memory of John Jasper, who died on March 28, 1901, the "Onesimus of Colonial America."

DLC

---

[1]Richard Ellsworth Day, *Rhapsody in Black* (Valley Forge, Pa.: Judson Press, 1953), p. 40.

[2]Ibid., p. 55.

[3]William E. Hatcher, *John Jasper* (New York: Fleming H. Revell Co., 1908), p. 105.

[4]Day, p. 116.

March 29—Like Father, Like Son

Scripture: Revelation 5:9-14

Someone has well observed that "if there are no successors, there is no success!" If that proverb is true, the Marshall family of the early Separate Baptists knew real blessing as grandfather Daniel Marshall, father Abraham Marshall, and grandson Jabez Marshall pastored the Kiokee Baptist Church in Georgia from 1772 to 1832. We have considered the beginning of that church and shall come back to that subject, but Jabez Marshall is our consideration now.

Jabez was the eldest son of Abraham and Ann Marshall, but his early life gave no promise of spiritual fruitfulness, for he evidenced little regard for the faith of his parents. His father was concerned that he have an adequate education, and thus Jabez was sent off to college, but he had little interest in academic life. After graduation, Jabez returned home where he soon became convicted of his sin, repented, was baptized, and united with the Kiokee Church. Soon he was preaching and exhorting, and after proving the reality of his faith, he was licensed to preach and then ordained into the gospel ministry.

Abraham Marshall passed away in the summer of 1819, and his son served first as the interim pastor and then was called officially to the pastorate at Kiokee in November of 1821. Jabez proved himself to be the same caliber of leader as his grandfather and father, for he was tireless in his labors. He was diligent in sermon preparation, and his messages were profound. He was persuasive in his preaching, and his messages never lacked doctrinal undergirding.

Jabez Marshall was weariless in his activities to extend the work of God. Though many of the records have been lost, it is apparent that he not only served the Kiokee Church but pastored the Sharon Baptist Church simultaneously. In 1827 he led in constituting the Salem Baptist Church, and it was there that he preached his last sermon. Jabez was active in the local association of churches and served as well as clerk at the formation of the state convention in 1822.

In 1830, Jabez performed the marriage for Issachar J. Roberts and his bride near Augusta, Georgia. Roberts was the Baptist missionary who pioneered in missions to lepers in China and finally died there of leprosy himself in 1866. Jabez Marshall was a zealous advocate of every possible missionary activity to fulfill the command of our Lord.

On March 29, 1832, Jabez died and thus ended the pastoral ministry of the Marshall family in Kiokee after sixty years of service.[1] Pastor Jabez Marshall "apparently died of measles, but there were complications, and an over-worked body gave way to these ravages."[2] At his own request, Jabez was buried at the church rather than in the family cemetery. He was not yet forty years of age, and it is beyond our reckoning to know what he might have accomplished with a longer life. One thing is sure: Daniel, Abraham, and Jabez closed out an illustrious ministry here but began a ministry of praise on that day in March as they worshiped together around the throne of the Lamb.

DLC

---

[1]Norman Wade Cox, ed., *Encyclopedia of Southern Baptists* (Nashville: Broadman Press, 1958), 2:824.

[2]James Donovan Mosteller, *A History of Kiokee Baptist Church in Georgia* (Ann Arbor: Edwards Brothers, 1952), p. 161.

March 30—Fifteen Years a Russian Prisoner

Scripture: Psalm 57

"On April 27 [1980] in New York City, Russia exchanged five Russian dissidents detained or sentenced in jail as opponents of the government for two Russian citizens convicted of spying in the United States.'' So reads *The World Book Encyclopedia Year Book* for 1980, page 470. The same volume reports, ''The release in April of Georgi P. Vins, 50, a Baptist who resisted the Communist regime, was a major event. For his resistance, he spent 15 years in Siberian prisons. Vins's group is a secessionist 'Reform Baptist' assembly that is more militant about religious rights than is the mainline Baptist group in Russia.''[1] Georgi Vins, like many of his counterparts in the USSR, was desirous of maintaining the age-old principle of religious liberty.

Vins refused to have the local churches and their pastors controlled by the government. His strong position in resisting state control led to his arrest and trial in November of 1966, and he was sentenced to three years in concentration camps. Following his release, Vins was intransigent, and thus in 1970, he was sentenced to a year of forced labor. Upon his next release from incarceration, being unable to minister without being under constant surveillance, Vins hid from public view; but he carried on his ministry covertly, traveling without authorization.

During the time that Pastor Vins was underground, his mother was arrested, tried, and sentenced to three years of imprisonment. The entry for January 27 mentions that Georgi P. Vins's father, the Reverend Peter I. Vins, also a Baptist pastor, had died in a Siberian concentration camp in 1943. ''On March 30, 1974, Rev. G. P. Vins was arrested and on January 27, 1975, at a trial which lasted five days, he was sentenced to five years in concentration camps, followed by five years of exile in Siberia and the confiscation of all his property.''[2]

Why would anyone be so determined to dogmatically stand for the principle of religious liberty when the cost of conviction would be so great? When our Lord said, ''Render unto Caesar the things which are Caesar's; and unto God the things that are God's,'' He forever pronounced the separate roles of church and state. Until the time of Constantine the Great, emperor of Rome, that practice was observed! From Constantine's time until the days of Roger Williams in New England, many Bible believers either worshipped underground or compromised their convictions as they were controlled by the state. Today there are four church-state arrangements practiced in the world. There is the concept that places the church *above* the state, a theory that makes the ecclesiastical head also the political leader. Another arrangement puts the church *alongside* the state. This is the theory practiced by ''state churches.'' Then there is the theory practiced by totalitarian governments where the state is *above* the church. Under this type of regime, Georgi Vins paid the necessary price for his convictions. In America we have seen established the principle that the church is *separate* from the state.

Thank God that Georgi Vins was freed! Let us continue to stand for this vital Baptist principle that grants religious freedom to all.

DLC

---

[1]*The 1980 World Book Year Book* (Chicago: Doubleday and Co., 1980), pp. 454, 470.

[2]Alexander de Chalandeau, *The Christians in the USSR* (Chicago: Harper and Row, 1978), p. 22.

March 31—A Whirlwind Romance

Scripture: Genesis 2:18-25

After serving the Kiokee Baptist Church (Georgia) for eight years as a bachelor-pastor, Abraham Marshall determined that the Lord would surely be pleased to provide him a wife "to divide the sorrows and double the joys of life."[1] Abraham concluded that he would travel the 2,200 miles to New England (the place of his birth) and trust the Lord to enable him somewhere along the way to meet a life-partner who would enhance his ministry. He prayed for a good horse and for Divine guidance for such a venture. He set out from Kiokee in 1792, and soon after, his first request was answered. A gentleman, knowing of his journey, exchanged horses with the preacher. With confidence from this experience, Pastor Marshall continued his journey in quest for the answer to his second petition.

His diary does not tell us how he happened to stop at the home of John Waller, the famed Separate Baptist preacher in Spottsylvania, Virginia, but he did. It was there that he met Miss Ann Waller, who was to become his wife, and they were greatly attracted to each other. He was so bold as to explain the purpose of his trip and then continued onward to New England. He returned as soon as possible, and the forty-four-year-old preacher and thirty-one-year-old maiden had a breathtaking, six-day romance. On March 31, 1792, three days after his arrival back from New England, he spoke again of his intention of marriage. On Tuesday, April 3, 1792, the emboldened, romantic preacher proposed, and at 7 o'clock that evening, the couple were married before a group of friends.

A six-day courtship seems rather short, but Abraham Marshall was an intense personality who consolidated every effort to accomplish as much as possible in the briefest period of time possible! Mrs. Ann Marshall proved to be of the same hardy stock, and the couple set out on the "horseback honeymoon," which covered approximately five hundred and fifty miles. Again in his diary, Marshall summarized the trip and spoke of "having a river or creek to swim, horses loose, lying out of doors, rainy days and dark nights, and ever and anon meeting with excellent friends . . . until three months absence to a day, found us at home amid the tears, joys and congratulations of friends, on Big Kiokee."[2]

With great faithfulness to her husband's ministry, Mrs. Marshall proved a decided blessing. The couple had four sons, and their son Jabez, who succeeded his father as pastor at Kiokee, wrote tenderly of his mother, "Through the whole of her life she was exemplarily pious. . . . Often, when her husband was traveling and preaching the glad tidings of great joy to perishing sinners, would she collect her little family at home, her children and servants, and teach them and instruct them in the ways of truth. . . . Often would she sing with them, and collect them around her upon her knees, and supplicate the God in whom she had trusted, to bless her rising family."[3]

Ann Marshall died in the fall of 1815 in her fifty-fourth year, and Abraham was united with her in the presence of the Lord in the summer of 1819 in his seventy-second year of life and in his fiftieth year of ministry in the gospel.

DLC

---

[1]James Donovan Mosteller, *A History of the Kiokee Baptist Church in Georgia* (Ann Arbor: Edwards Brothers, 1952), p. 146.

[2]Jabez P. Marshall, *Memoirs of the Late Rev. Abraham Marshall* (Mount Zion, Ga.: Published by the author, 1824), p. 71.

[3]Ibid., p. 73.

April

April 1—The Baptist Invasion of Kentucky

Scripture: Psalm 90

William Hickman was born in Virginia on February 4, 1747. While he was still a lad, both of his parents died, and he became the ward of his grandmother. The boy's educational possibilities were limited, but his grandmother gave him a Bible and insisted that he read it. When fourteen years of age, he was apprenticed to learn a trade, and in nine years he was secure enough to marry his master's daughter, Sarah Sanderson. Soon after being married, he learned that the Baptists (then called New Lights) were in the area, and against his wife's wishes, he went to hear the preaching. He discovered that the next day they would be "dipping" the converts, and he determined to go even though his wife disapproved. Hickman was not saved at that time, but he began to experience conviction and even cried at seeing the ordinance of baptism administered.

The next fall the Hickmans moved to Cumberland County, Kentucky, and William threw off the conviction, but the Lord sent His servants to that area, and Mrs. Hickman was converted along with other neighbors. Hickman kept his wife "from being baptized several months. He persuaded her to attend the Episcopal church, and strove to convince her of the validity of infant baptism. For this purpose, he studied the New Testament closely. This investigation led him to the conclusion that infant baptism was not taught in the Bible. He finally consented to his wife's being baptized."[1]

Under the preaching of David Tinsley, an oft-imprisoned Baptist preacher of Virginia, Hickman became overwhelmed with a sense of his guilt. On February 21, 1773, while he was seeking the Lord, the peace of God flooded his heart, and he knew blessed contentment. Two months later Hickman was baptized.

Having no pastor in their church, several of the young converts took on the task of preaching, and five young men from that group, William Hickman included, were among the early Baptist preachers who made spiritual inroads into Kentucky. Hickman and several companions arrived in Harrodsburg on April 1, 1776, and the first recorded Baptist preaching done in Kentucky was by Thomas Tinsley and William Hickman. It was Hickman's first sermon other than in his home church, and it was evident that the hand of God was upon him. Two years later he was ordained in Virginia and spent eight years of active service there. Though he was not imprisoned during that time, he received his share of rude persecution.

In the summer of 1784, the Hickman family moved permanently to Kentucky, and for the next four years Hickman ministered at every opportunity. On January 17, 1788, Elder Hickman moved to Forks of Elkhorn, and his soulwinning preaching resulted in the establishing of the Forks of Elkhorn Church, where he pastored until his death in 1834. He served that church for a period of forty-five years, with the exception of two years, during which period "he was out of fellowship with the church because of his opposition to slavery 'as being tolerated by the members of a Baptist society.' "[2] During the great revival period of 1800-1803, Pastor Hickman baptized over five hundred converts. Thus, the poorly educated orphan lad became a faithful servant of our Lord Jesus Christ.

DLC

---

[1]J. H. Spencer, *A History of Kentucky Baptists from 1769 to 1885* (Cincinnati: J. R. Baumes, 1886), 1:154.

[2]Norman Wade Cox, ed., *Encyclopedia of Southern Baptists* (Nashville: Broadman Press, 1958), 1:606-7.

April 2—Spurgeon's Convictions of Baptist Beginnings

Scripture: I Corinthians 3:10-11

The famed "Metropolitan Tabernacle," known to many as "Spurgeon's Tabernacle," was opened in London on March 18, 1861, and dedicatory services extended into April as church members and London residents united in praising God for His blessings! On April 2 a public meeting was held for the Baptist brethren of London, and on April 3 Spurgeon greeted the general public of the various denominations from the city as they attended a service to rejoice in the goodness of God to the church pastored by Spurgeon. This is surely evidence that Baptists have never claimed a monopoly on truth. Tragically, however, in the twentieth century, Baptists have seemingly lost their realization of historical continuity, and we do well to ask the question, "Who are the Baptists?"

Consider the words of greeting of Spurgeon on April 2, 1861, as he welcomed the area Baptist brethren to the new building. He said:

> We believe that the Baptists are the original Christians. We did not commence our existence at the reformation, we were reformers before Luther and Calvin were born; we never came from the Church of Rome, for we were never in it, but we have an unbroken line up to the apostles themselves. We have always existed from the very days of Christ, and our principles, sometimes veiled and forgotten, like a river which may travel under ground for a little season, have always had honest and holy adherents. Persecuted alike by Romanists and Protestants of almost every sect, yet there has never existed a Government holding Baptist principles which persecuted others; nor, I believe, any body of Baptists ever held it to be right to put the consciences of others under the control of man. We have ever been ready to suffer, as our martyrologies will prove, but we are not ready to accept any help from the State, to prostitute the purity of the Bride of Christ to any alliance with Government, and we will never make the Church, although the Queen, the despot over the consciences of men.[1]

Baptist historians vary widely in their views on Baptist beginnings. Martyr flames have consumed volumes of priceless diaries and records that would be a great treasure in our day. Religious suppression caused many ancients of Baptist views either to desist from writing or to make notes in such an abbreviated way that they alone could decipher the meaning. It seems to the present authors that confident identification is not possible in tracing the name "Baptist" all the way back to our Lord, but we concur with Spurgeon's statement that Baptist principles, though traveling underground for a period, are clearly seen, and our derivations come not from some comparatively modern-day movement, but are rooted principally in the imperishable church which has Jesus Christ for its foundation. We do not claim exclusivity of truth, but we do acknowledge with joy the continuity of biblical principles among us to this good day.

DLC

---

[1]C. H. Spurgeon, *Metropolitan Tabernacle Pulpit* (1861; reprint ed., Pasadena, Tex.: Pilgrim Publications, 1969), 7:225.

April 3—Fleeing Dutchmen Were Persecuted in England

Scripture: Matthew 10:22-42

There was extensive persecution of those who stood firm on Anabaptist principles in the Netherlands during the reign of Philip II, who was a chief ally of the pope and Jesuits in their efforts to check Protestantism in the latter half of the sixteenth century. Philip II resorted to great cruelty in his efforts to bring back his possessions in the Netherlands to what he believed to be the true faith. He dispatched the remorseless Duke of Alva, whose conduct made the Duke's name synonymous with blind, unmeasured cruelty.[1]

Alva brought with him a fine army of Spanish soldiers, ten thousand in number and superbly equipped. He established a special court for the speedy trial and condemnation of all those whose fidelity to Philip was suspected. This was popularly known as the Council of Blood and the Duke of Alva as the Butcher General of Europe and England. The persecuted felt that in England they would surely be safe. Many groups of Protestants found a refuge, but the persecution raged even there against the Anabaptists.

On April 3, 1575, a small congregation of Dutch Anabaptists convened in a private house outside the city of London. While they were at worship, a constable interrupted the service and took twenty-five people before a magistrate, who committed them to prison. They remained there for two days when, upon posting bond, they were released on giving promise to appear before the court when summoned.

Information was given to the Queen (Elizabeth I), and a Royal Commission was issued to Sandys, Bishop of London, and some others to interrogate the parties and proceed accordingly. The Anabaptists appeared before the commissioners, where their confession of faith was rejected, and they were required to subscribe to four articles that condemned their own principles. Of course, these involved pedobaptism. These staunch believers refused to subscribe to the articles presented to them.

Sandys said "that [their] misdeeds therein were so great that [they] could not enjoy the favor of God. . . . He then said to [them] all, that [they] should be imprisoned in the Marshalsea." The prison was later called the "Queen's Bench." There were many efforts made by the ministers of the Dutch church and others to persuade them to submit and recant. The Anabaptists said, "Master Joris came to us and said that if we would join the Dutch Church, our chains should be struck off and our bonds loosed. The bishop had given him authority to do so. But we remained steadfast to the truth of Jesus Christ. He indeed is our Captain and no other; yea! in Him is all our trust."[2]

It is interesting to note that William of Orange, called the Silent, liberated the Northern Provinces of the Netherlands from Philip II and Rome. Later dissenters in England found refuge from persecution in Holland. Jesus instructed His disciples, "But when they persecute you in this city, flee into another." This often has been God's method of spreading the gospel. Baptists have been a fleeing people and an evangelizing people. Seeing God's sovereign hand through all their tribulations, the believers rejoiced and seized the occasion as an opportunity instead of retreating in self-pity.

EWT

---

[1]J. H. Breasted and J. H. Robinson, *History of Europe, Ancient and Medieval* (New York: Ginn and Co., 1914), pp. 538-39.

[2]J. M. Cramp, *Baptist History* (London: Elliott Stock, 1870), pp. 270-71.

April 4—The Beloved Physician Who Led Dr. Carey to India

Scripture: I Corinthians 3:6; Colossians 4:14

The name of Dr. John Thomas is practically unknown among Baptists today, but Dr. Thomas was greatly used of God in opening the door of the modern-day missionary movement. Reared in the home of a Baptist deacon in England, John Thomas was early subjected to the gospel. He was not saved, however, until after his completion of medical training and his marriage. "Turning eagerly to the Scriptures, he accepted Christ as his Saviour. 'And then,' he says, 'my assurance of pardon and everlasting happiness ran high and strong.' "[1]

Dr. Thomas had been assigned as the assistant surgeon on one of His Majesty's ships and sailed several times to India. The British East

India Company had begun as a commercial organization and later became a branch of the English government. The company was greatly opposed to the thought of "missions," for they sought only financial gain. However, a few of the employees who served in India were Christians and built a small building in Calcutta in 1715 for their own worship. Still, they were not primarily interested in the salvation of the heathen that surrounded them. On one of his trips, Dr. Thomas ministered the Word of God and was asked to remain in India to preach. At great expense to himself, Dr. Thomas overcame the obstacles and accepted the invitation.

In a short time, Dr. Thomas discovered that his Baptist doctrines were unacceptable to the Anglican Christians stationed in India. He was threatened with the loss of financial support if he insisted on teaching immersion. Facing monetary collapse, Dr. Thomas in 1790 began to plan a return to England. The Lord had been moving in the hearts of several of His servants, and while Thomas was toiling in India, William Carey, the shoemaker-preacher, was having his eyes opened to the needs of the heathen world. When Carey brought his famed sermon that actually moved the hearts of men toward missions, Thomas was homeward-bound to England. On October 2, 1792, the "Particular Baptist Missionary Society for Propagating the Gospel amongst the Heathen" was born, but what field should they enter? Carey thought of Tahiti or Western Africa. Samuel Pearce proposed the Pelew Islands. But then Dr. Thomas arrived, and our Lord drew the attention of the newly-formed society to India.

Funds were raised, and Carey and Thomas were commissioned on March 20, 1793. Mrs. Carey could not go just then, but Carey was determined that this was God's direction, and thus on April 4, 1793, Carey and Thomas boarded the "Earl of Oxford" for Calcutta.[2] However, when the ship's captain was informed that he would forfeit his commission if he took the missionaries, the two men were put ashore. Through Thomas's hard work, arrangements were made with a Danish ship, and despair was transformed to joy as Mrs. Carey and the Carey children were able to travel as well. They sailed on June 13, and God's purpose would be fulfilled! Dr. John Thomas suffered many tragedies and died on October 13, 1801, but to this servant of Christ, we are indebted, for he it was who led Carey to India.

DLC

---

[1]Arthur C. Chute, *John Thomas, First Baptist Missionary to Bengal* (Halifax, N.S.: Baptist Book and Tract Society, 1893), p. 13.

[2]Austen Kennedy de Blois, *Fighters for Freedom* (Philadelphia: Judson Press, 1929), p. 264.

April 5—The Aristocrat, by Christ Apprehended, Served Humbly

Scripture: I Corinthians 1:23-31

The Apostle Paul, writing to the Corinthians about the "calling" of a Christian, said that "after the flesh not many mighty, not many noble are called." "Thank God for the letter 'M'," a lady of nobility in England is quoted as saying. Her reasoning was that without it, "many" would become "any," and she would have no hope of eternal life. Dr. William H. Brisbane, who was born into aristocracy near Charleston, South Carolina, was also called out, by the grace of God, among the "not many." He fell heir to great wealth and position in this life and, by the mercy of God, became an heir and joint-heir with Jesus Christ.

Brisbane's early education was entrusted to Bishop England of the Roman Catholic church and subsequently to the Reverend William T. Brantly, then president of Beaufort College. At age fifteen he was sent to a military school at Middletown, Connecticut, from which he graduated with honors at the age of nineteen. Shortly after graduating, he was converted to Christ, and immediately he felt it his duty to preach the gospel. His fine culture and attainments and his dedication to the work placed him in the front ranks of the Baptist ministry of the South.

Brisbane became familiar with public affairs and current political matters, and his culture and wealth gave him access to influential people like Jackson, Calhoun, Clay, Webster, and Benton. Living in a momentous period from the forming of the nation on through the great convulsion of civil strife that nearly rent the nation asunder, Brisbane spent much time at the state and national capitals. He became deeply involved in the questions that were agitating the nation. Because he was a large slaveholder, the subject of slavery had taken a deep and absorbing hold upon his mind early in his life. He struggled with this question honestly and prayerfully over a period of years, and he finally concluded that slavery was morally and spiritually wrong. Because he was a man of principle, Brisbane wanted to rectify his wrongdoing as a slaveholder justly and with compassion. He expended some of his wealth and purchased some land in Ohio, and after purchasing back some former slaves that he had sold, he went to Ohio and settled them in their new homes, supplying them abundantly with their immediate needs. Dr.

Brisbane then became a resident of Cincinnati, where he labored with renewed vigor in the work of the ministry.

Brisbane later moved to Wisconsin where he preached the gospel for twenty-five years. In declining age, he was known widely as a friend and champion of every good cause. Dr. Brisbane truly was the salt of the earth in that he influenced the society in which he lived by humbly and conscientiously dedicating himself to the cause of truth and righteousness until his death April 5, 1878.[1]

EWT

---

[1]William Cathcart, *The Baptist Encyclopedia,* ed. Louis H. Everts (Philadelphia: Louis H. Everts, 1881), 1:135.

April 6—Doctrinal Disaster

Scripture: Ephesians 4:14-15

Liberty of conscience and freedom from all authority apart from the Word of God have assured that Baptists would exhibit more diversity than any other denomination. A case in point is Daniel Parker, antimissionary leader among a small group of Baptists. Parker was born in Culpeper County, Virginia, on April 6, 1781. In his youth his family moved to Georgia, where Parker was reared in extreme poverty and without benefit of formal academic training. Parker possessed a keen mind and eventually developed into a skilled debater. He was licensed to preach by the Nails Creek Church in Franklin, Georgia, and then he moved to Tennessee and was soon ordained. Parker served a pastorate in Tennessee, and there he was introduced to a form of predestination that would color the remainder of his life. Parker moved to Illinois in 1817.

By 1815, while serving as moderator of a local association, Parker had condemned missions, seminaries, and Bible societies, and in 1820 he published a pamphlet presenting these views as he became a leader in an antimissionary movement. His work extended through North Carolina, Tennessee, Kentucky, Illinois, Indiana, and Texas. By 1926 Parker's borrowed "two-seed" doctrine concerning predestination was developed fully in his mind, and he wrote two books which professed that everyone was born with the "seed," good or evil, and this alone determined one's destiny. Of course, if that were true, missionary activity would be useless and even presumptuous. The "elect" belonged to God and needed no missionaries, and the "non-elect" were without hope of redemption! Parker infiltrated many churches with his doctrine and made life much more difficult for missionary leaders such as Luther Rice and John Mason Peck.

The *Baptist Encyclopedia* presents Parker as being uncouth in manners, slovenly in dress, and unimpressive in appearance. His enthusiasm bordered on insanity. It is interesting to note that he condemned religious newspapers, tracts, and books, yet for two years he wrote and published a monthly paper, the *Church Advocate,* in which he set forth his distorted view of predestination and opposition to missions!

Daniel Parker possessed a shrewd and surely brilliant mind despite his lack of formal training. This fact may be seen in his response to the passing of a law prohibiting the organization of non-Catholic churches in Texas.

> At least one Baptist discovered a way to introduce non-Catholic faith into the territory. . . . This singular, astute person was Elder Daniel Parker, founder of the 'Two-Seed' sect of Baptists, lately come from Illinois. There might be a law against organizing a non-Catholic church he said, but not against immigrating one into the state. Accordingly, he returned to Crawford County, Illinois, and on July 26, 1833, there organized "The Pilgrim Church of Predestinarian Regular Baptists," with seven members, who set out for Texas. Under the leadership of Pastor Parker, the Church en route acquired eleven more members, and in due time, January 20, 1834, Pilgrim Church held its first conference within the bounds of Austin's colony.[1]

Daniel Parker died in Elkhart, Texas, December 3, 1844, and doubtless was surprised in heaven to find that all who responded to "whosoever will" were there.

DLC

---

[1]L. R. Elliott, ed., *Centennial Story of Texas Baptists* (Dallas: Baptist General Convention of Texas, 1936), p. 21.

April 7—A Patient Sowing and Enduring Bringeth Forth Fruit

Scripture: James 5:1-7

Seeds must be sown and a patient waiting and laboring for maturing must occur before the harvest can be realized. So it was with the planting of the Baptist churches in the Massachusetts Bay Colony. The seeds of biblical truth and religious liberty were sown in the heat of religious persecution. It takes hearty plants to endure the rigors of burning sun and violent storms.

It was upon the persecution of Obadiah Holmes and others who had taken a strong stand for believers' baptism that Henry Dunster, President of Cambridge College (now Harvard), was so stirred in his mind that he turned his attention to the subject of infant baptism and soon rejected it altogether. The faithfulness of Holmes, the publicity his enemies gave to his convictions, his willingness to suffer for convictions, and the beastliness of a church-state that denied its citizens religious freedom all magnified the truth he propagated.

Dunster's success in promoting Harvard by furthering its interests, collecting large sums of money in its behalf, and even giving one hundred acres to it, was marvelous and testified to his commitment to the institution. But he had a higher commitment to the truth of God and began to preach against infant baptism in the church at Cambridge in 1653, to the great alarm of the entire community. Armitage quotes Prince in pronouncing Dunster " 'one of the greatest masters of the Oriental languages that hath been known in these ends of the earth', but he laid aside all his honors and positions in obedience to his convictions."[1]

Dunster was forced to resign his presidency of Harvard College, April 7, 1657, after which he was arraigned before the Middlesex court for refusing to have his child baptized. The court records indicate that Dunster had been forbidden to speak but stated Dunster's position as follows: "The subjects of baptism were visible penitent believers and they only." Also, after protesting the christening of a child in the congregation, Dunster said, "There is an action now to be done which is not according to the institution of Christ. That the exposition as it had been set forth was not the mind of Christ. That the covenant of Abraham is not a ground of baptism, no not after the institution thereof. That there were such corruptions stealing into the Church which every faithful Christian ought to bear witness against."[2]

Now the influential Dunster had planted in the heart of the Puritan Commonwealth seed which was indestructible. Cambridge and the adjoining town of Charlestown had been filled with these principles, and out of the center of that influence came the First Baptist Church of Massachusetts Bay proper.

God grant to us in this day of compromise and "instant everything" (including a pseudo-success complex) a willingness to endure the affliction that comes with planting the seed and the patience to wait upon its germination and fruit-bearing.

EWT

---

[1]Thomas Armitage, *The History of the Baptists* (1890; reprint ed., Watertown, Wis.: Maranatha Baptist Press, 1976), 2:498-99.

[2]Ibid., p. 498.

April 8—The Humility of a Great Man of God

Scripture: I Thessalonians 5:12-13

One could never do justice, in a volume of this nature, to some of the outstanding personalities of Baptist history. You will find no apology, therefore, for the fact that numerous references are made to William Carey. Justly called "the Father of Modern Missions," Carey was involved in an amazing amount of activity. William Carey was not a genius, so we are told, and yet his accomplishments are astounding. He spoke at least seventeen languages,[1] "mastered numerous Indian languages, preached in the vernacular, labored constantly for the conversion of individuals, and led in establishing twenty churches and mission stations in India by 1814."[2] Furthermore, he

> superintended the translation of the Bible in forty-two Oriental tongues and thus made the Word of God accessible to a third of the world. In speaking to his Nephew late in life, he said, "Eustace, if, after my removal, any one should think it worth his while to write my life, I will give you a criterion by which you may judge of its correctness. If he gives me credit for being a plodder, he will describe me justly. Anything beyond this will be too much. I can plod. I can persevere in any definite pursuit. To this I owe everything."

What humility! Surely he did plod, and on one occasion, he told the Reverend Mr. Swan, pastor of the Cannon Street Baptist Church, Birmingham, England, "I never could say—'No.' I began to preach in Moulton, because I could not say 'No.' I went to Leicester, because I could not say 'No.' I became a missionary, because I could not say 'No.' "[3]

It comes as no surprise, then, to read of Carey's reaction when he had been informed that he was to be proposed as Professor of Bengali in the English Government's Fort William College. Joshua Marshman, Carey's close associate, recorded the following in his diary:

> Wednesday, April 8, 1801. This morning Carey came to me in great haste, almost before I was awake. He had received a note from our good friend, Rev. David Brown concerning a matter of great moment, to which an immediate answer must be given. "He wishes to propose

> him as Professor of Bengali in the new College. Would he give consent?'' Going over to Carey's room, I found (William) Ward summoned in the same earnest manner. . . . After discussing the subject pretty liberally, we agreed that, as it came unsought, and might in easily-imagined circumstances be of essential service to the Mission, we would consent, leaving it to God to fulfil or frustrate, as was best—there being yet much uncertainty in the business.[4]

Since William Carey had never attended college, he questioned his ability to produce in a classroom. Surely Carey was a modest, meek, unassuming man, but twenty-one of his first forty-five students rose to be judges and others held leading positions in the government. Of course, the Lord had planned the position in the college to provide standing and stability for the work of the mission. Carey continued as missionary/educator and produced grammars and lexicons in six different languages. William Carey died on June 9, 1834, ''the greatest missionary since the Apostle Paul.''[5]

DLC

---

[1]S. Pearce Carey, *William Carey* (London: Hodder and Stoughton, 1924), p. 260.

[2]Norman Wade Cox, ed., *Encyclopedia of Southern Baptists* (Nashville: Broadman Press, 1958), 1:231.

[3]Eustace Carey, *Memoirs of William Carey* (Boston: Gould, Kendall and Lincoln, 1836), p. 417.

[4]S. Pearce Carey, p. 205.

[5]Thomas Armitage, *The History of the Baptists* (1890; reprint ed., Watertown, Wis.: Maranatha Baptist Press, 1976), 2:583.

April 9—A Great Evangelistic Couple

Scripture: II Corinthians 2:14-15

Justus H. Vinton was born on February 17, 1806, in Willington, Connecticut. He was saved at the age of ten and called to preach when only fourteen. In 1826 he entered the Institute at Hamilton, New York, and during college years Vinton preached in all the surrounding area. Calista Holman was born in Union, Connecticut, on April 9, 1807. In her sixteenth year she contracted an illness that was feared could cause her death. Having been saved, she requested baptism before death, and so, on a cold day in March, she was transported by sleigh to the water's edge, and supported by Pastor Grow and a deacon, she was immersed.

The service seemed to her friends like a funeral, but from that day, her recovery began, and she was restored to health. Miss Holman wanted to spend her life in the Lord's service, and she, too, entered the Institute at Hamilton. Justus and Calista met in a class where the Karen language was being taught by Professor Wade, assisted by a national convert, and the young couple turned their thoughts toward Burma.

On April 9, 1834, Justus and Calista were united in marriage, and they sailed for Burma in July of that year, arriving in Maulmain in December. Vinton, ever a soulwinner, conducted religious services aboard ship, and his preaching resulted in the salvation of the ship's captain, the steward, and a number of sailors as well.

Being familiar with the language, the Vintons were able within a week to begin their work among the Karens, and soon they received so many invitations from distant villages that they determined to separate to cover twice the territory that would otherwise be possible. Each took a group of national Christians and went from village to village. It was primarily this plan that the Vintons used for twenty-five years.

With the return of physical problems on the part of Mrs. Vinton and an urgent need in America for Mr. Vinton's return to stimulate again a vision for missions, the Vintons furloughed to the States in 1848. In two years Mrs. Vinton's health was renewed, and Mr. Vinton had stirred anew the flame for missions. The couple returned to the field of God's appointment. Soon war broke out, and Dr. Eugenio Kincaid, Burmese evangelist in Rangoon, called for the Vintons to assist there. The Vinton's fellow missionaries in Maulmain urged them to go, believing it was the Lord's will. The Vintons plunged into the work of preaching and caring for the physical needs of many injured. Unfortunately, the mission directors in America did not understand this action, and the Vintons were forced to resign from the mission as a result. That did not stop them for they ministered with all their resources and even purchased rice at greatly inflated prices on credit to feed the starving. During one period of twenty months, Vinton baptized 441 converts. In 1858 Vinton contacted a jungle fever, and he died in March. Mrs. Vinton continued the work with unabated zeal until 1862, when sickness demanded that she return to the States. With renewed health, she later returned to Burma, but becoming sick again, she passed away on December 18, 1864.

"Dr. Vinton was mighty in prayer, firm in will to do what was right, untiring in effort, generous to a fault, and wholly consecrated to God."[1] One of the greatest tributes to the Vintons is the fact that their son and daughter both followed in the footsteps of service to our Lord.

DLC

---

[1]William Cathcart, *The Baptist Encyclopedia,* ed. Louis H. Everts (Philadelphia: Louis H. Everts, 1881), 2:1310.

April 10—Ten Shillings or Ten Lashes

Scripture: Psalm 91

Joshua Morse's father was not a professing believer, but his grandfather, who came from the west of England to Rhode Island in the early days of the settlement of that colony, was a Baptist. The grandfather served as a chaplain in the first war between the English colonies and the French.

Young Joshua at the age of sixteen was attracted by the "New Light Stir," and motivated by curiosity and a desire to mock and reproach those who were involved, he attended their meetings. He did not hesitate to conclude that they all were deluded, but he came away from the first meeting under fearful apprehensions of being made miserable forever. It was not long until he surrendered to God's truth and became a zealous exhorter.

When Morse was eighteen, he began his ministerial labors at a time when every man who opened his door for a dissenter to preach was fined five pounds, the preacher ten shillings, and the hearer five shillings. The very first time that Morse preached at Stoningham, he was apprehended, and the magistrate sentenced him to be fined ten shillings or to receive ten lashes at the whipping post. The fine he could not pay, and the lashes he was prepared to receive.

It is recorded in the *Biographical Sketches of the Standard Baptist Works* that,

> he was taken to the post by the order of the magistrate, but the constable instead of inflicting the lashes, pled the cause of the innocent sufferer, remonstrated against the wickedness of the law, the cruelty of the court, and utterly refused performing the barbarous duty which had been assigned him. After spending sometime in this awkward position, the constable rendered the magistrate from his own pocket the fine which had been exacted. The magistrate probably ashamed of his conduct, offered it to Mr. Morse, and bid him receive it and peaceably go on his way. But as he would pay no money, so he would receive none, and his persecutors finding him rather unmanageable, went off and left him to take his own course. For a number of years after this he was often opposed, sometimes by law, but more frequently by mobs.[1]

Morse was knocked down often by blows while praying and preaching as well as being dragged around by the hair of his head. He carried some of the scars on his head and face to his grave. On one occasion a man struck Morse in his temple with such violence that it brought him to the floor from which he arose with emotion and pity and said, "If you die a natural death, the Lord hath not spoken by me." This man, not long after, went to sea, fell from the ship, and was drowned.

In the midst of all these persecutions, Morse's labors were attended with great success. Many were quickened to salvation under his preaching, and churches were planted through his efforts. He was early acquainted with George Whitefield and caught much of his zeal.

Having been born April 10, 1726, Morse's life spanned many eventful years during the establishment of our nation. About a month before his death in July of 1795, after a long ministry, he called his church together and gave them his last advice and benediction. He had composed a hymn to be sung at his funeral and chose a passage to be preached from, which was, "This is a faithful saying, and worthy of all acceptation, that Christ Jesus came into the world to save sinners, of whom I am chief."

May we, who have been fellow-partakers of God's grace, acknowledge that we also are the chief of sinners saved by a wonderful Savior.

EWT

---

[1]Charles G. Sommers, William R. Williams, and Levi L. Hill, eds., *The Baptist Library* (New York: Lewis Colby and Co., n.d.), 1:312-14.

April 11—The Last Baptist Martyr in England

Scripture: Psalm 56:7-11

The last execution for "heresy" in England took place by the burning alive at Lichfield of a dissenter who was guilty of the wicked doctrines of "Ebion, Cerinthus, Valentinus, Arius, Macedonius, Simon Magus, of Manes, Photinus, and of the Anabaptists, and other arch-heretics."[1] The martyr in the flames was Edward Wightman, the date was April 11, 1612, and the English King upon the throne was none other than King James I, just a year after his "Authorized Version" of the Scriptures became public!

Was Wightman guilty of the charges? Probably not! Dr. Cramp points out that Bishop Neile of Lichfield and his coadjutors, who acted as Royal Commissioners on the occasion, were manifestly "forgers of lies." And Thomas Crosby mentions that "many of the heresies they charge upon him are as foolish and inconsistent, that it very much discredits what they say." What was the real cause of his martyrdom? "Among other charges brought against him were these: 'That the baptizing of infants is an abominable custom; that the Lord's supper and baptism are not to be celebrated as they are now practiced in the church of England; and that Christianity is not wholly professed and preached in the church of England, but only in part.' "[2]

That was the crux of the matter, but the general English public was becoming weary of the martyr fires against the dissenters, and it was needful to make the victim look as hideous and dangerous as possible so that the death penalty would seem the only option available! After mentioning that "one of the counts in the indictment was that he declared 'the use of baptism to be administered in water only to converts of sufficient age and understanding,' " Carlile opines as follows: "They found him guilty of many heresies, some of which were probably unknown to him, even by name."[3]

What kind of man was Edward Wightman? I am sure that the answer to that question would be given by his progeny. If you had asked the Baptists in Connecticut in the early days of America, they could have told you, for Valentine Wightman (1681-1747) was a descendant of the English martyr, and it was Valentine who formed the first Baptist church in the colony of Connecticut under the terms of the Toleration Act of 1689. Valentine was probably a great-grandson of Edward Wightman, and he was a Baptist. Valentine and his wife established the First Baptist Church of Groton in 1705. When Valentine passed away, the Groton Church was pastored by his son, Timothy Wightman, and when the Lord called Timothy home, the church was pastored by his son, John Gano Wightman. We shall examine these men in greater detail later in this volume; however, it is clear that the last English martyr to surrender his life in the flames was a Baptist by conviction.

We do well to bear in mind that though we treasure the King James Version of the Scriptures, the king was no friend of Baptists! Thank the Lord for the memory of Edward Wightman, who sealed his testimony for Christ, even with his death. May our offspring be as faithful and fruitful as his!

DLC

---

[1]J. M. Cramp, *Baptist History* (London: Elliott Stock, 1870), p. 258.

[2]J. Newton Brown, *Memorials of Baptist Martyrs* (Philadelphia: American Baptist Publication Society, 1854), p. 240.

[3]John C. Carlile, *The Story of the English Baptists* (London: James Clarke and Co., 1905), p. 80.

April 12—They Sought a Place of Refuge

Scripture: II Peter 2:11-17

William Screven emigrated to Boston from Somerton, England, about the year 1668. He became a successful merchant of the city. Desiring to form a dissenters' church in Boston, he was informed that he would be violating the laws of Massachusetts Bay Colony. He moved to Kittery in the Province of Maine. After Massachusetts acquired the area of Maine, the authorities began to watch Screven closely because of his Baptist views.

Ultimately, Screven was charged first with not attending meetings on the Lord's Day, from which he was exonerated. Later he was charged with making blasphemous speeches against the ''holy order of pedobaptism.'' After spending some time in jail for refusing to pay a bond of £100,

> on April 12, 1682 he was brought before the court at York and the examination resulted as follows: ''This court having considered the offensive speeches of William Screven, Viz.' his rash inconsiderate words tending to blasphemy, do judge the delinquent for his offense to pay ten pounds into the treasury of the county or province. And further the court doth further discharge the said Screven under any pretence to keep any private exercise at his own house or elsewhere, upon the Lord's Days, either in Kittery or any other place within the limits of this province, and is for the future enjoined to observe the public worship of God in our public assemblies upon the Lord's Days according to the laws here established in this Province, upon such penalties as the law requires upon his neglect of the premises.''[1]

Screven seemed to have paid no attention to that order and was brought before the entire General Assembly of the Province of Maine, where he ultimately promised to stop holding services or leave the colony.[2] Evidently, he had become weary of the persecution, and not being able to find liberty of conscience nor freedom to worship God in Maine, Screven and his associates determined to seek freedom elsewhere.

After forming a church out of the Baptist church in Boston, most of Screven's congregation took ship for the Carolinas. They settled on the Cooper River not far from the present city of Charleston. Armitage tells us that "some of the early colonists of South Carolina were Baptists from the west of England, and it is very likely that these two bands from New and Old England formed a new church."[3] The move to Charleston took place by 1693. This was the first Baptist church of the South.

No Baptist church was traceable in Kittery after Screven and his company departed. In fact, nearly a century passed before one could find another Baptist church within the bounds of what is now the state of Maine. Persecution through bigotry withheld the blessing of the gospel of the grace of God, as the Baptists proclaimed it, from a people for nearly one hundred years. God's people should always consider themselves pilgrims and sojourners in this world. As we therefore go, let us preach.

EWT

---

[1]Henry S. Burrage, *History of the Baptists in Maine* (Portland, Maine: Marks Printing House, 1904), pp. 18-19.

[2]O.K. and Marjorie Armstrong, *Baptists Who Shaped a Nation* (Nashville: Broadman Press, 1975), p. 73.

[3]Thomas Armitage, *The History of the Baptists* (1890; reprint ed., Watertown, Wis.: Maranatha Baptist Press, 1976) 2:704.

April 13—She Saw That He Was a Proper Child

Scripture: I Samuel 1:9-18

Spencer H. Cone was born at Princeton, New Jersey, April 13, 1785, to parents of outstanding gifts. His father was a high-spirited, fearless gentleman who fought with great bravery in the Revolutionary War. His mother possessed a vigorous intellect and indomitable moral courage. They both were members of the Hopewell Baptist Church. Armitage quotes from one of Dr. Cone's sermons: "My mother was baptized when I was a few months old, and soon after her baptism, as I was sleeping on her lap, she was much drawn out in prayer for her babe and supposed she received an answer, with the assurance that the child should live to preach the Gospel of Christ. This assurance never left her."[1]

At the age of twelve, the precocious youngster entered the freshman class at Princeton College, whose president predicted for him a brilliant future as an orator. But because his father developed a serious mental illness, Cone was forced to leave school at the age of fourteen to support the family. He taught Latin, worked as an actor on stage, was a bookkeeper in newspaper offices, published a paper in Philadelphia, and was devoted to the politics of Jefferson and Madison.[2]

While Cone was in a bookstore, he discovered the works of John Newton, and he purchased the volume. Upon reading the *Life of Newton,* Cone was moved to the great agony of the conviction of sin. Armitage quotes him as saying, "I felt that as a sinner I was condemned and justly exposed to immediate and everlasting destruction. I saw distinctly that in Christ alone I must be saved, if saved at all; and the view I had at that moment of Christ's method of saving sinners, I do still most heartily entertain after thirty years experience of His love."[3]

Cone fought bravely in the War of 1812 as the captain of artillery at the battles of Northpoint, Bladensburg, and Baltimore. Not long after the war, he went to preach in Washington, D.C., and became so popular that he was elected as chaplain of the Congress. For a time Cone was a pastor in Alexandria, Virginia, and he ultimately accepted the pastorate of the First Baptist Church of New York City.

For about forty years, he was a leader in home and foreign mission work and in the great modern movement for a purely translated Bible. He firmly believed that the word "baptize" in the Bible meant to immerse, that it was his duty to God to preach it, and that it was as clearly his duty to print it; therefore, he had many enemies. There was a great stir when a revision of the word "baptize" should be rendered "immerse" and "baptism" should be rendered "immersion." It was claimed by the pedobaptists that such renderings were interpretations, not translations. Of course, *baptizō* should be rendered immersion, if rightly translated, instead of being transliterated. Dr. Cone stood on solid ground.

In the prime of his life, Cone was said to have been the most active Baptist minister in the United States and the most popular clergyman in America. Though he valued education, he was mostly concerned with the purity of the Word that men might truly know the mind of Christ in the Scriptures, translated faithfully into the languages of all men. God help us to be as concerned with the purity of God's truth and as faithful in walking in obedience to its precepts.

EWT

---

[1]Thomas Armitage, *The History of the Baptists* (1890; reprint ed., Watertown, Wis.: Maranatha Baptist Press, 1976), 2:904.

[2]Jesse L. Boyd, *A History of Baptists in America Prior to 1845* (New York: American Press, 1957), p. 165.

[3]Armitage, p. 905.

April 14—An Outstanding Early Black Pastor

Scripture: II Corinthians 4:1-2

Thomas Paul was a "free black" from New Hampshire. He had been born in September of 1773, and when he was sixteen years of age, he was born the second time. Without the opportunity of an expanded education, he must have disciplined himself, for on May 1, 1805, he was ordained at Nottingham West, New Hampshire. Black Baptists were numerous by the beginning of the nineteenth century, but there were very few black churches, and those that existed were primarily in the South. Black Baptists were members of white churches, and even in the North, they were segregated in the galleries or sometimes as a group in the auditoriums. It is estimated that by the close of the Civil War, there were four hundred thousand black Baptists in America.

The Reverend Mr. Paul formed the African Baptist Church in Boston (later known as the Joy Street Baptist Church) and served as pastor for more than twenty years.[1] His preaching was fervent and attractive, the church grew, and his fame reached throughout the area. Spiritual revivals occurred under his ministry, and he was greatly respected wherever he was known.

> He was not an ordinary man. . . . His understanding was vigorous, his imagination was vivid, his personal appearance was interesting, and his elocution was graceful. We have heard him preach to an audience of more than one thousand persons, when he seemed to have command of their feelings of an hour together. On baptismal occasions he was truly eloquent. His arguments were unanswerable, and his appeals to the heart were powerful. The slow and gentle manner in which he placed candidates under the water and raised them up again produced an indelible impression upon the spectators, that they had indeed seen "a burial with Christ in baptism."[2]

Paul's renown passed to New York, and some of the black members of the Gold Street Baptist Church there invited him to come to New York to help them. Paul assisted them in separating from the Gold Street Church and establishing the Abyssinian Baptist Church. In 1809 the new congregation purchased a vacant church building, and with four men, twelve women, and three new converts, Paul led them as their pastor.

About that time, Baptists were awakening to the challenge of missions worldwide. William Carey and Dr. John Thomas had gone to India, and in 1802, the Massachusetts Baptist Missionary Society was formed. In 1815, the African Baptist Missionary Society was formed by black Baptists in Richmond, Virginia. Thomas Paul's heart was moved concerning the need of preaching the gospel in regions beyond, and in 1823 he applied to the Massachusetts Baptist Missionary Society to serve in the field of Haiti. The fifty-year-old pastor was accepted, and he gave himself with earnestness to the work on the island. However, not knowing the French language, he could not function as he desired, and in time, he returned home. Thomas Paul, by force of character, piety, and gifts, commanded the recognition of the good hand of God upon his life. Thomas Paul passed into the presence of his Lord on April 14, 1831, and today we honor the memory of this man of God.

DLC

---

[1]H. Leon McBeth, *The Baptist Heritage* (Nashville: Broadman Press, 1987), p. 780.

[2]William Cathcart, *The Baptist Encyclopedia,* ed. Louis H. Everts (Philadelphia: Louis H. Everts, 1881), 2:889.

April 15—Life on Earth Is the Time to Serve the Lord

Scripture: Ecclesiastes 9:10-18

James Greenwood was known for his consistent life of piety and good character. He fulfilled the scriptural qualifications of a bishop and steward in being blameless and faithful until his death April 15, 1815. These qualities will enable a man with few talents to do much good, while those with greater gifts and strong intellects who lack these qualities can be a curse to the cause of the gospel.

Notwithstanding the excellent character sustained by this servant of God, he did not escape the rage of those who, in his day, persecuted the church of God and wasted it. Semple tells us that "in August 1772, James Greenwood and William Loval were preaching not far from the place where Bruington Meeting House now stands, in the county of King and Queen, when they were seized and, by virtue of a warrant, immediately conveyed to prison."[1] Bruington was the home church of Dr. Charles H. Ryland, who founded the Virginia Baptist Historical

Society and acted as its secretary for thirty-three years. From an unknown source, Dr. Ryland jotted down the following account in the flyleaf of his Bible:

> Previous to the constitution of Bruington Church the Baptists of the neighborhood worshipped in Ware's barn "across the swamp" from my father's residence where Wiley and subsequently Don Brown lived. Then an arbor was erected where Dentist T. M. Henley now lives and almost in sight of the present house of worship. Here James Greenwood and William Loval were seized while preaching and conveyed to the King and Queen jail singing, "Life is the time to serve the Lord" and they gave notice that they would preach the next Lord's Day from the jail windows.[2]

Although Greenwood and Loval did reside in prison sixteen days, they probably did not preach through the grates, because the jailer, a Mr. Harwood, and his wife treated them very kindly and gave them the bounds of the jail. This enabled them to preach regularly, which they did without hindrance. This kindness was not the rule but the exception. John Bunyan, while in prison in England, experienced kind treatment as well. Bunyan was even permitted by the jailer to leave the prison to visit friends and to be with his family.

The hymn Grenwood and Loval sang challenges the Christian today to use the time he has in this life to accomplish the work of Christ, regardless of his treatment or surroundings:

> Life is the time to serve the Lord,
> The time to insure the great reward;
> And while the lamp holds out to burn,
> The vilest sinner may return!
> Then what my thoughts design to do,
> My hands, with all your might pursue;
> Since no device or work is found,
> Nor faith, nor hope beneath the ground.[3]

EWT

---

[1]Robert B. Semple, *A History of the Rise and Progress of the Baptists in Virginia* (Richmond: Published by the author, 1810), p. 22.

[2]Lewis Peyton Little, *Imprisoned Preachers and Religious Liberty in Virginia* (Lynchburg, Va.: J. P. Bell Co., 1938), p. 315.

[3]W. Howard Doane and E. H. Johnson, eds., *The Baptist Hymnal* (Philadelphia: American Baptist Publication Society, 1883), hymn 252, stanzas 1 and 4.

April 16—The Preacher's Fire That Produced Smoke

Scripture: Psalm 64

John Young lived a long and useful life in the service of his Lord and Savior, Jesus Christ. He was instrumental not only in the salvation of hundreds of precious souls but also in bringing forth some of the most fruitful preachers in Virginia. This ministry continued into his old age until he went to his eternal home April 16, 1817.

In 1908 Lewis Peyton Little located a granddaughter of John Young who gave the following interesting information:

> He was converted and began preaching. He, with others, was imprisoned for preaching what he believed to be the truth. His mother, who had care of his motherless children, visited him regularly once a week taking the children with her. Each preacher was in a room to himself. Each room had one small window, placed so high up in the wall that only a patch of sky could be seen, nothing on the earth. The congregations of the different ministers learned, each, which was his pastor's window. Once a week John Young's congregation (and I suppose the other's too), would assemble under his window, and run up a flag, to let him know they were there and he would preach to them. In this way a great many people were converted. The authorities said, "These heretics make more converts in jail than they do out", so when the congregation assembled, that pastor was smoked out by burning pepper to prevent his preaching.[1]

Young had been arrested on June 13, 1771, ostensibly for preaching without a license. He was incarcerated for approximately six months in the jail in Caroline County, Virginia. He appealed to the general court and by a writ of habeas corpus was transported to the state capital, then Williamsburg, for trial. The six-month imprisonment was a great burden upon the man of God because of the separation from his children, whose mother had died.

Two years after his imprisonment, Young was ordained and became pastor of the "Reeds Church" in lower Caroline County. He continued to be active in the cause of the gospel and defended the principles of God's Word as set forth by the Baptists. During his pastorate there,

Young was the first to sign a petition of 143 signatories against establishing a tax to provide for teachers of the Christian religion. This group recognized the importance of the separation of church and state.

About 1798 John Young moved to what is now Amherst County and a year later became pastor of what is now known as the Mt. Moriah Church. His body rests on property he once owned, awaiting the resurrection at the coming of our Lord Jesus Christ. May we be as faithful in our lives so that we shall not be ashamed at our Lord's return.

EWT

---

[1]Lewis Peyton Little, *Imprisoned Preachers and Religious Liberty in Virginia* (Lynchburg, Va.: J. P. Bell Co., 1938), pp. 236-39.

April 17—Missionary Heroics During World War II

Scripture: Acts 27:1-25

The missionary movement that began with William Carey has continued among Baptists to this very day! Throughout the years, believers have cried out, "Here am I, Lord, send me," and through trials and tribulation men and women have continued to "go into all the world." Florence Almen had gone from America in 1936 and had served for a term in French Equatorial Africa. After returning to her homeland for a year of furlough, Florence said her farewells to family and friends and boarded the *Zam Zam* on March 21, 1941, for her return to her labors. The *Zam Zam* had at one time been in the British fleet, but now it was a rickety old Egyptian ship bound for Alexandria, via Recife, Brazil, and the Cape of Good Hope. Miss Almen hoped to disembark at Cape Town, to catch a steamer to Matadi, and from there, to take a river boat back to Bangui.

The ship carried 201 passengers, including 144 missionaries.[1] They made their way to Baltimore and picked up additional crew and then continued on to Brazil. Leaving Brazil for Cape Town on April 9, they traveled without lights and maintained radio silence, for the German U-boats were very active. All seemed to go well until April 17, just two days from the arrival in Cape Town. A terrible vibration rocked the ship, and the screaming crash of shells awakened passengers and crew. The old ship was under attack.

Miss Almen and her two roommates hurriedly dressed and put on their money belts, which contained their passports and documents, and donned the life preservers. The shells were flying everywhere as they scurried to the deck. They found that their lifeboat had been hit, but they finally discovered another. As the lifeboat pulled away from the listing *Zam,* they found that it, too, had been riddled with gun fire and was filling with water. Florence Almen did not know how to swim, but heroically to lighten the load, she jumped overboard. As she did so, she cried out to the Lord, "I'll be seeing your face today, Lord Jesus." She further testified, "I wasn't alone. God was there. Underneath were the everlasting arms. I felt His Presence—really real."[2] After a time in the water, she was able to draw near the lifeboat again and place a hand on its side to keep her head above water.

In a short time, they heard a motor and discovered that the German captain of the raider (the *Tamesis*) had sent a launch to pick up those in the water. The Lord had moved upon his heart, and thinking of his own wife and children back in Germany, he had gone back and forth picking up survivors, even at his own risk. The next day, the passengers were transferred to the *Dresden,* where they lived for a month as prisoners of war. For thirty-three days they experienced many privations along with a flu epidemic, seasickness, and dysentery, but on May 19, after a zigzagging course in their attempt to avert British vessels, the *Dresden* entered the territorial waters of Spain. The next day, the ship was run aground on the sandy beaches in German-occupied France. In time, the United States citizens, through the intervention of the American ambassador to Spain, were returned to New York.

The Lord had graciously protected all aboard, and there were absolutely no casualties.

DLC

---

[1]William Blake, *An Almanac of the Christian Church* (Minneapolis: Bethany House Publishers, 1987), p. 113.

[2]Polly Strong, *Burning Wicks* (Cleveland: Baptist Mid-Missions, 1984), p. 201.

April 18—Abel Morgan, an Evangelical Apologist

Scripture: Colossians 1:9-14

The Welsh Tract Church was one of the five original churches that constituted the Philadelphia Association in 1707. Prior to the association's existence, the churches had participated in semiannual meetings dating back to 1688. Actually, this church was constituted in South

Wales in 1701 when the first members were about to come to Pennsylvania. Along with their pastor, Thomas Griffith, they arrived in this country and ultimately settled at Welsh Tract. Out of this church several able and gifted ministers were raised.[1] Baptist churches in the middle and southern colonies drew heavily from the Welsh migration in the eighteenth century. The Welsh not only provided members and ministers for the Baptist churches but also shaped their spirit, doctrines, worship patterns, and organizational practices.[2] The New England Baptists had some of the conservatism of the Congregationalists from which many dissented, but the Welsh churches had a vigorous and aggressive missionary spirit. Armitage tells us, "As from a central fortress they sent out their little bands, here a missionary and there a handful of colonists, who penetrated farther into the wilderness, and extended the frontiers of the denomination."[3]

Abel Morgan was born at Welsh Tract on April 18, 1713. He was from a line of Welsh Baptist preachers. His father Enoch was born in Wales in 1673 and came to this country where he became pastor of the Welsh Tract Church. He died in 1740. His Uncle Abel, for whom he was named, pastored in South Wales before he came to America, where he supplied the Lower Dublin and Philadelphia churches, besides visiting many other places. He wrote and published the first Welsh concordance of the Holy Scriptures that was ever published in that language.

Abel Morgan, the nephew, one of the leading minds of his day, was ordained at the Welsh Tract Church in 1734. Five years later he became pastor of Middletown Baptist Church, New Jersey, where he served until his death in 1785.

The Reverend Samuel Finley, who became president of Princeton College, challenged Pastor Morgan to a discussion relating to baptism. Finley wrote a pro-pedobaptist treatise, *A Charitable Plea for the Speechless,* and Abel Morgan replied with his *Anti-Paedo Rantism; or, Mr. Samuel Finley's Charitable Plea for the Speechless Examined and Refuted, the Baptism of Believers Maintained and the Mode of It by Immersion Vindicated.* This treatise was printed in Philadelphia by Benjamin Franklin in 1747.

Morgan was a careful scholar and was the first to receive the honorary degree of M.A. from Brown University. His great life work was in preaching the gospel. During the forty years of his pastorate in a sparsely settled area, Morgan received three hundred persons into the fellowship of his church on the confession of their faith. He held regular services at other meeting places and churches. Morgan was a burning and shining lamp with a very fruitful ministry.

EWT

---

[1]A. D. Gillette, ed., *Minutes of the Philadelphia Baptist Association from A.D. 1707 to A.D. 1807* (1851; reprint ed., Minneapolis: James Publishing Co., n.d.), p. 15.

[2]H. Leon McBeth, *The Baptist Heritage* (Nashville: Broadman Press, 1987), p. 211.

[3]Thomas Armitage, *The History of the Baptists* (1890; reprint ed., Watertown, Wis.: Maranatha Baptist Press, 1976), p. 713.

April 19—He Lived Up to His Name

Scripture: Proverbs 22

Dr. A. J. Gordon's father was named after John Calvin, the theological systematist, but Gordon, at his birth in New Hampshire, April 19, 1836, was named for the first American Baptist Missionary to Burma, Adoniram Judson. At the age of fifteen, he came into vital union with Jesus Christ as his Savior. Upon completing his education and theological training, he was ordained and became the pastor at Jamaica Plain, Massachusetts. From 1867 he was sought for the pastorate of Clarendon Street Baptist Church, Boston, but did not accept the position until late in 1869. The only stipulation in accepting the call to this church was the replacement of the paid choir by congregational singing. He was a hymn writer, a composer of hymn tunes, and a compiler of hymnals.

Dr. Gordon was well named, and certainly his naming was bathed in much prayer. His most influential work was related to world evangelism. Over one-half of his travels were related to missions. He served for over twenty years as a member of the board or as executive chairman of the American Baptist Missionary Union. Although he favored sound financial support, he also emphasized the faith element in missions.

Dr. Gordon was dominated by the conviction that nothing is practical except the spiritual, and nothing is spiritual unless it is practical. He became greatly persuaded through his own experience and study of the Bible that the new birth by the Holy Spirit which effects the union of a believer with Jesus Christ is essential. He participated in Dwight L. Moody's evangelistic meetings and was a consistent soul-winner and evangelistic preacher himself. Gordon understood the absolute necessity of the power of the Holy Spirit in carrying on the work of world evangelism and soulwinning. He understood that all teaching and ministering of the Word was futile apart from the power of the Holy Spirit. He had many lectures published on this subject including *The Holy Spirit in Missions.*

Gordon was an apologist for biblical Christianity against Darwinism, agnosticism, Unitarianism, transcendentalism, Christian Science, baptismal regeneration, and the influence of materialism in the evangelical churches of his day.

Dr. Gordon was a fundamentalist before fundamentalism. He held that the Bible was inerrant and infallible, the presence of the Holy Spirit in the believer was continual, the second coming of Jesus Christ was imminent and premillennial. Dr. Gordon's gravestone reflects his blessed hope: "Pastor A. J. Gordon: 1836-1895, 'Until He Come.' "[1]

EWT

---

[1]Norman Wade Cox, ed., *Encyclopedia of Southern Baptists* (Nashville: Broadman Press, 1958), 1:570-71.

April 20—John Clarke, Persevering for Liberty of Conscience

Scripture: Nehemiah 1–2:8

In establishing Rhode Island as a haven of religious freedom among the American colonies, the name of John Clarke must be written beside that of Roger Williams. This well-educated Englishman was born in London in 1609. Apprenticed to a doctor, he became a skilled physician. He also was an earnest student of law and theology and an ardent advocate of liberty of conscience until his death, April 20, 1676.[1]

Clarke, upon becoming a dissenter, moved to Leyden, Holland, to avoid persecution. There he came in contact with some Baptists but did not join their fellowship in that city. Armitage tells us, "A long train of circumstances indicate that his steps had led in the same path with those of Williams in the main; through Puritanism, love of religious liberty, disgust at the intolerance of Massachusetts, and so into full Baptist position."[2]

Probably Clarke's greatest accomplishment was the securing of a permanent charter for all the Rhode Island communities. The Baptist minister returned to London, supposing that the Protestant military genius, Oliver Cromwell, who was installed at the head of the military and civil regime, would be sympathetic to the cause of religious liberty and speedily grant the request for a Rhode Island charter. The Baptists, after all, had been solidly behind Cromwell. Clarke's expectation was not to become a reality. Cromwell's attention was directed elsewhere.

It was only after the monarchy was restored and Charles II was crowned king that anything was accomplished. After twelve years in England, Clarke returned to a jubilant people with a charter that declared:

> Our royal will and pleasure is, that no person within said Colony, at any time hereafter, shall be in any wise molested, punished, disquieted, or called in question for differences of opinion in matters of religion, that do not actually disturb the civil peace of said Colony; but that all and any persons may, from time to time, and at all times hereafter, freely and fully have and enjoy his and their own judgments and consciences in matters of religious concernments throughout the tract of land hereafter mentioned, they behaving themselves peacefully and quietly, not using this liberty to licentiousness and profaneness, not to civil injury or outward disturbance of others, any law, statute or clause therein contained, usage or custom of this realm to the contrary thereof in any wise not withstanding.

The following words of Charles II were added and later engraved upon the state house in Providence, Rhode Island, as a memorial for future generations: "It is much on their hearts (if they may be permitted) to hold a lively experiment that a most flourishing civil state may stand and best be maintained, and that among our English subjects, with full liberty in religious concernments."[3]

The experiment has stood for nearly three hundred and fifty years. Amen!

EWT

---

[1]O. K. and Marjorie Armstrong, *Baptists Who Shaped a Nation* (Nashville: Broadman Press, 1975), pp. 61-63.

[2]Thomas Armitage, *The History of the Baptists* (1890; reprint ed., Watertown, Wis.: Maranatha Baptist Press, 1976), 2:671.

[3]Armstrong, pp. 61-63

April 21—Race Relationship Among Early Baptists in America

Scripture: Acts 10:23-48

The relationship among the races in Baptist churches, both before and after the Civil War in America, is rarely considered in our day. In 1639 John Clarke organized the Baptist church in Newport, Rhode Island, and in 1652, America's first black Baptist, "Jack, a colored man,'' was baptized and added to the church's membership.[1] Living in Rhode Island, ''Jack'' was doubtless a free man, but many slaves in the South came to a saving knowledge of the Lord Jesus Christ, and ''as far as membership was concerned, the Negroes were received and dismissed, as well as excommunicated, in the same way as whites'' in Kiokee, Georgia.[2] It is surprising, yet true, that in the South the blacks usually outnumbered the whites in the membership of Baptist churches by a six-to-one ratio![3]

The history of the First Baptist Church of Richmond, Virginia, records the fact that ''colored deacons were elected, whose duty it was to watch over slave and free Negro members. According to custom, the church licensed certain colored men who, by consecration and aptitude, seemed best fitted to 'exercise their spiritual gifts in public.' ''[4] At least fifteen years prior to William Carey's sailing for India, George Lisle, the ''first ordained Baptist Negro in America,''[5] went to Jamaica as a missionary. Lott Carey, member of the First Baptist Church of Richmond, purchased his and his children's freedom for eight hundred and fifty dollars in 1813. Carey, along with Collin Teague, sailed in 1821 for Liberia and established the First Baptist Church in Monrovia. Prior to the Civil War, Abraham Marshall, pastor at Kiokee, ordained Andrew Bryan in Savannah. It was prior to the Civil War that John Jasper was saved and sent by his ''master'' to preach the gospel. However, the church minutes prior to the Civil War always alluded to blacks as ''belonging to . . .'' and the name of the ''master'' followed. After the Civil War, the minutes named the black and then stated, ''formerly the property of. . . .'' Following the Civil War, as before, blacks were still ordained into the gospel ministry. On April 21, 1867, we read from the Kiokee minutes: ''The Baptist Church of Christ at Kiokee met and proceeded to the ordination of Brother Billy Harriss, colored, to preach the Gospel.''[6]

Soon after the War Between the States, the blacks in the South desired their own places of worship. It is to the credit of the Baptists that the races separated amiably into black and white Baptist churches, for other denominations opposed such separation. On many occasions, the white Baptist congregations helped their black brethren to organize, ordained their pastors, and, in some instances, provided them a building in which to meet. It is noteworthy that prior to the Civil War, some of the white Baptist pastors had undertaken in personal, supervised study to train some of their black members for the ministry. This explains why, at least in part, Baptists made such tremendous historical inroads among the black race in the South.

DLC

---

[1]Edwin S. Gaustad, *Baptist Piety* (Grand Rapids: Christian University Press, 1978), p. 42.

[2]James Donovan Mosteller, *A History of the Kiokee Baptist Church in Georgia* (Ann Arbor: Edwards Brothers, 1952), p. 180.

[3]Ibid.

[4]Blanch Sydnor White, *First Baptist Church—Richmond, 1780-1955* (Richmond: Whittet and Shepperson, 1955), p. 95.

[5]Robert G. Torbet, *A History of the Baptists* (Philadelphia: Judson Press, 1950), p. 369.

[6]Mosteller, p. 182.

April 22—Prayer and a Biblical Educator

Scripture: Acts 11:19-30

James Petigru Boyce was a fine scholar and very popular in his ways. He received his college education when it was not unusual for students and faculty to meet for prayer every evening. The spiritual welfare of Boyce became of great concern to some of his fellow students, and he became the object of special prayer that his gifts and graces might all be consecrated to Christ.[1]

Shortly after one of these times of special prayer and fasting, Boyce took a ship from New York to Charleston, South Carolina. During this long journey, it was observed that he spent a great deal of time in his stateroom. A friend discovered that he was reading his Bible, and after much discourse together, Boyce came under deep conviction. Upon reaching the city, he found that his sister was also concerned with her spiritual welfare and that a close friend had just made his profession of faith.

Dr. Richard Fuller was preaching in the city with great effect, and a spiritual awakening was under way. Boyce's conviction of sin increased, and he felt himself a ruined sinner and looked to the merits of Jesus Christ alone for his salvation. On April 22, 1846, he was baptized on that profession of faith.[2]

Boyce graduated from Brown University in 1847 and studied theology at Princeton from 1848 to 1851. He became pastor of the church at Columbia, South Carolina, in 1851. In 1855 Boyce accepted the chair of theology at Furman University. He accepted a professorship in the Theological Seminary at Greenville, South Carolina, in 1858. The seminary was located there until 1873. Louisville, Kentucky, offered three hundred thousand dollars for the permanent establishment of the seminary there if two hundred thousand dollars could be provided from other sources. When financial ruin faced the institution, Dr. Boyce, by his patience, financial talents, and resources, saw the seminary through seven years of great difficulty. His enthusiasm sparked anew the energies of his brethren and led the movement to success.[3]

In his 1856 inaugural address as professor of theology at Furman University, Boyce set the direction for future theological education among Baptists of the South. "He suggested three principles: (1) that Baptist schools of theology provide a suitable course of study for students who had not completed college, (2) that the schools provide on another track the very highest academic theological educations, and (3) that the faculty sign a statement of Baptist faith."[4]

The seminary charter of April 30, 1858, provided that "every professor of the institution shall be a member of a regular Baptist Church; and all persons accepting Professorships in this Seminary, shall be considered by such acceptance, as engaging to teach in accordance with, and not contrary to, the Abstract of Principles hereinafter laid down."[5]

Dr. Wayland, then president of Brown University, in commending Boyce for requiring an affirmation from the faculty, said that such seminaries "have . . . proved to be after a generation or two, schools of heresy."[6] Since their day many such institutions have become "schools of heresy," because words spoken by the lips have not been the conviction of the heart. God help us to make frequent recurrence to fundamental principles.

EWT

---

[1]John A. Broadus, *Memoir of James Petigru Boyce* (New York: A. C. Armstrong, 1893), p. 44.

[2]Ibid., p. 45.

[2]Thomas Armitage, *The History of the Baptists* (1890; reprint ed., Watertown, Wis.: Maranatha Baptist Press, 1976), 2:876.

[4]H. Leon McBeth, *The Baptist Heritage* (Nashville: Broadman Press, 1987), p. 445.

[5]Ibid.

[6]Ibid.

April 23—A Great Pastor/Evangelist of Power

Scripture: II Timothy 4:1-2

This volume may seem to have an excessive concern with the Separate Baptists and the work of God in Kiokee, Georgia, but this author confesses an attraction to the ministry of Abraham Marshall. He had little education, yet others, too, witnessed in him an unusual spiritual power. For instance, Dr. James D. Mosteller has said that "in many respects the son was a greater pastor than his father, and certainly as willing to travel as an evangelist."[1] In his preaching in New England, Marshall was likened to George Whitefield "in the fervor and power of his eloquence."[2] These accolades might be thought to be exaggerations unless one examines the actual results of his traveling ministry.

Abraham Marshall was born on April 23, 1748. He was twenty-two when he was converted and twenty-seven when he was ordained. Soon after the death of his father, Daniel Marshall, Abraham Marshall assumed the pastorate of the Kiokee Church. The business affairs of his father necessitated Abraham's first trip to New England, and at age thirty-eight, he mounted his horse and became an amazing evangelist, preaching almost every day on the journey coming and going. Conversions were numerous and estimated in the hundreds.[3] Vast crowds came to hear him, and we merely note some of the accounts recorded in his journal as he preached 197 times in seven states.[4]

One hot Sunday in August in the state of Connecticut, Marshall preached to 1,300 in the morning and then, after a brief rest, addressed 1,500 at 2 P.M. On another August Sunday he preached in Poquonock in Windsor, Connecticut, to 1,500, and in the same place on September 10, he addressed 3,500, which was the largest religious rally ever held in that vicinity. On a Sunday afternoon on Broad Street in Windsor, Marshall spoke to 2,000 in a building from which Baptists had been barred for thirty years. In the State House in Hartford, he addressed 1,500. The next Lord's Day in Simsbury, he spoke in the Presbyterian meetinghouse to 1,200 in the morning, and when 2,400 crowded in to hear him in the afternoon, the galleries actually collapsed.

Abraham's diary gives us great insight to the dear man of God. Not only did he preach with power to large audiences, but he also graciously spoke to small clusters of sinners and saints as well. His entries reveal his expressions of despair when little moving of the Holy Spirit seemed evident. He spoke glowingly of his Savior and revealed a humility of character when estimating his own personal worthiness. He rejoiced in the good fellowship of the spiritual leaders whom he met—men such as the Reverend Thomas Ustick; the Reverend Oliver Hart; the Reverend William Van Horn; Dr. James Manning, president of Brown University; and the Reverend John Gano, pastor of the First Baptist Church in New York City.

During his travels, Marshall grew weary and became discouraged and even sick, but still he preached, for Abraham was a great pastor/evangelist. We mark the day of his birth with thanksgiving to God and cry out, "Lord, do it again. Lord, do it again! Give America such preachers."

DLC

---

[1]James Donovan Mosteller, *A History of the Kiokee Baptist Church in Georgia* (Ann Arbor: Edwards Brothers, 1952), p. 132.

[2]Jesse L. Boyd, *A History of Baptists in America Prior to 1845* (New York: American Press, 1957), p. 45.

[3]Mosteller, p. 137.

[4]Ibid.

April 24—Adoniram Judson, Alone in Burma

Scripture: Psalm 27

We cannot anticipate what one year may bring forth in our experiences as we sojourn through this world. In fact, some of our worst fears as well as some of our best laid plans for pleasant relationships with those dearest on earth to us may never become a reality. God, in His mercy, shields us from the dread of anticipating horrible experiences and provides us with His grace when the fiery trials come.

We often fail to realize the agony and suffering some of God's choice servants have gone through to take the gospel of Jesus Christ to those who were chained in the dungeons of spiritual darkness. Such were the experiences of Adoniram Judson, who lost his wives and children to the ravages of disease in Burma. We receive some insight into the anguish of soul on the part of this missionary statesman on the occasion of the death of his young daughter Maria, who died a few months after her mother Ann in Burma. He wrote to his first wife's mother, Rebecca Hasseltine, in a letter dated April 26, 1827:

> My sweet little Maria lies by the side of her fond mother. The complaint, to which she was subject several months, (an affection of the bowels,) proved incurable. She had the best medical advice; and the kind care of Mrs. Wade could not have been, in any respect, exceeded by that of her own mother. But all our efforts, and prayers, and tears, could not propitiate the cruel disease. The work of death went forward; and after the usual process, excruciating to a parent's feelings, she ceased to breathe, on the 24th inst., at three o'clock P.M. aged two years and three months. We then closed her faded eyes, and bound up her discolored lips, where the dark touch of death first appeared, and

folded her little hands—the exact pattern of her mother's on her cold breast. The next morning, we made her last bed, in the small closure which surrounds her mother's grave. Together they rest in hope, under the hope tree, (Hopia) which stands at the head of the graves; and together, I trust, their spirits are rejoicing, after a short separation of precisely six months.

Thus I am left alone in this wide world. My father's family and all my relatives, have been, for many years, separated from me, by seas that I shall never pass. They are the same to me as if buried. My own dear family I have actually buried: one in Rangoon, and two in Amherst. What remains for me, but to hold myself in readiness to follow the dear departed to that blessed world, "Where my best friends, my kindred dwell, Where God, my Savior, reigns."[1]

One can sense the anguish and loneliness expressed in this correspondence, as well as the dedication to continue in his ministry, to give the Bible in the Burmese language and win perishing souls to Jesus Christ. Thus today such choice servants follow in Judson's footsteps. May God help us to sustain these missionaries of the cross through their lonely hours and days of anguish and toil by our intercession at the throne of grace.

EWT

---

[1]James D. Knowles, *Memoir of Ann H. Judson* (Philadelphia: American Baptist Publication Society, 1835), pp. 339-40.

April 25—A Neglected Grave on a Lonely Hill

Scripture: Deuteronomy 34

Some years ago my attention was called to a hill not far from the Shenandoah River where a small family graveyard was located. Upon investigation, I discovered it overgrown with weeds and saplings and overrun with cattle. Not only was it sad that a family burying place should be so neglected, but the crude stone hand-chiseled memorial to the life and final resting place of the body of John Koontz was gone. This pioneer colonial Baptist preacher's mortal remains were laid to rest here after he went to his eternal reward April 25, 1832. Places such as this should be sacred memorials instead of neglected, forgotten, overrun briar patches.

John Koontz was the first Baptist preacher to proclaim the gospel message of salvation by grace through faith in the area of Page County, which was then Shenandoah County, Virginia. His ministry was blessed with much success, which aroused not only perishing souls from their spiritual deadness but also the enemies of the truth which he proclaimed. Koontz's zeal for the pure gospel message was not quenched by the violence perpetuated upon him.

On one occasion, Koontz attended a meeting near Smith's Creek where he was met by a gang of ruffians who forbad his preaching. A respected man, Captain Learhorn, insisted that he should preach and prevailed. The persecutors threatened Koontz with a beating if he ever came that way again. Not being one deterred by threats, he returned to preach and found that his enemies had paid money to a "son of Belial" to beat him. The hooligan proceeded to beat him with the butt end of a large cane, requiring Koontz to promise never to return. This Koontz refused to do, and the man continued the beating until he almost disabled the preacher.[1]

Sometime later, while he and a companion, Martin Kaufman, were sitting in a house awaiting the time to preach, Koontz heard a man asking about him. Suspecting some mischief, he got up and stepped out of sight into an adjoining room. The man, supposing Martin Kaufman to be John Koontz, fell upon Kaufman and beat him severely with a stick. Kaufman received many blows before he could convince the man that he was not Koontz.[2]

On another occasion, Koontz was taken to be imprisoned. Just a short distance away, a man coming to hear him preach attempted to rescue him but was beaten off. After continuing a ways further, Koontz warned them to take heed what they did, because if he were a man of God, they would be fighting against God. Immediately one of the men was alarmed and relented, soon to be followed by the others. The man who became alarmed first and two or three of the others afterwards became Baptists.[3]

West of Luray, Virginia, on U.S. Route 211 is the "White House Bridge." It is named for a white house which can be seen a few hundred yards downriver. John Koontz and the early Baptists met in this house and ultimately planted the Mill Creek Baptist Church in 1772. In a nearby gravesite beside the highway lies the body of John Koontz's companion in the gospel, Martin Kaufman.

May the memory of these faithful men of God challenge, encourage, and sustain us in the day of our adversity.

EWT

---

[1]Lewis Peyton Little, *Imprisoned Preachers and Religious Liberty in Virginia* (Lynchburg, Va.: J. P. Bell Co., 1938), p. 220.

[2]Ibid., p. 221.

[3]Ibid., pp. 221-22.

April 26—He Left the Prison to Enter the Palace

Scripture: II Timothy 3:10-12

We read a great deal about Pastor Thomas Ewins in the *Broadmead Records,* the minutes of the "Baptized Congregation" in Broadmead, Bristol, England. Edward Terrill, clerk of the church, has enriched our understanding of the sufferings that Baptists endured during the reign of Charles II. In the providence of God, Edward Terrill, born at Almondsbury, Gloucestershire, was taken to Bristol, England, in 1640 by his mother and apprenticed as a scrivener. He worked as a writing schoolmaster and became involved in the sugar trade that developed between Bristol and the West Indies. In time "he . . . inherited wealth by his marriage . . . in 1668."[1] As Terrill served as clerk in Broadmead, he used materials of others for the years 1640-54 to supplement his own work and ultimately produced the historically valuable *Broadmead Records.*

The Broadmead Church was founded in 1640, and the members met regularly for worship from that time. In 1651 Thomas Ewins, who had been formerly an Episcopalian minister and had converted to Baptist views, was called as pastor. The work grew under his leadership; however, problems began in 1661, as the pastor was apprehended even as he preached on July 27 and was jailed. After being imprisoned for two months, he was released and began his ministering again immediately. On October 4, 1663, Pastor Ewins and several others were arrested, and this time he languished in the jail for almost a year. During this imprisonment, the people would gather around the prison and Ewins would preach to them through his open window from his fourth-floor cell.

The suffering of the congregation is well set forth in the records of the church as they met many times in the out-of-doors or from house to house or wherever they could find peace from their governmental tormentors. It is interesting to note that when meeting on a second-floor level, the ladies would often sit on the stairs and begin to sing when the constable would arrive, thus warning the folk in the meeting room of impending danger.

> They were compelled for a time to worship in private houses. The constables frequently disturbed them, and many were imprisoned and fined. Sometimes, when they learnt that the officers were coming, they evaded them by taking refuge in a cellar, and sometimes by climbing

> into a garret. Still they resolutely kept up their assemblies. . . . Their firmness was remarkably shown by a resolution passed to the effect, that those who absented themselves from worship through fear should be dealt with as disorderly members.[2]

Pastor Ewins had been physically weakened by his imprisonments. Edward Terrill gives this tragic yet triumphant report:

> Anno 1670. Our Pastor, Br. Ewins, having layen a greate while weake, he Departed this life . . . (April 26, 1670) in ye worke of ye Ministry; Preaching ye Gospell clearly of Free Grace by faith in Christ Jesus. Wherein he laboured aboundantly, in ye Publick, and in his particular charge ye Congregation. . . . He was a man full of selfe-denyall, and subdueing his Natural Temper; soe that he walked very lovely and holy in his Conversation, shewing patience where it required, and meekness toward all men; Visiting all his members Carefully, and searching into ye State of their Soules. . . He was interred in James's Yeard. . . . Accompanied with many hundreds to ye Grave, ye like funerall not seen long before in Bristoll. He left soe good a Savour behind for faithfulness to Gode, and humility towards men, That his very chief Persecutor, (Sr. Jo Knight), said, he did believe he was gone to heaven.[3]

Would that our testimony should be so meaningful!

DLC

---

[1]Norman S. Moon, *Education for Ministry—Bristol Baptist College, 1679-1979* (Bristol, Eng.: Bristol Baptist College, n.d.), p. 105.

[2]J. M. Cramp, *Baptist History* (London: Elliott Stock, 1870), p. 305.

[3]Edward Terrill, *The Records of a Church of Christ Meeting in Broadmead, Bristol*, ed. Nathaniel Haycroft (London: J. Heaton and Son, 1865), pp. 64-66.

April 27—A Golden Chain of Christian Workers

Scripture: Romans 1:16-17

The succession of the faith will never be fully appreciated by us until in glory we bow before the Divine Clerk and observe the passing of the truth from "faith to faith." The Reverend Hezekiah Smith, versatile leader of early American Baptists, was led to personal faith in Christ by the Reverend John Gano in New York City early in the 1740s. On June 14, 1770, the Reverend Hezekiah Smith was called upon to immerse the Reverend Eliaphalet Smith, former Presbyterian pastor. The Reverend Eliaphalet Smith had become convinced that believer's baptism by immersion only is a divine institution. He and a portion of his former Presbyterian members followed the Lord in obedience, and he formed them into a Baptist church.

In the course of time, the Reverend Eliaphalet Smith was invited to Livermore, Maine, to preach, and as there was no church building available for the meeting, Mr. Otis Robinson was asked to open his home for the occasion. Robinson was not at home when the service was held, but upon his return, he asked his wife the minister's subject. She answered that his text was, "Who hath warned you to flee from the wrath to come?" These words refreshed the conviction that Robinson had experienced in bygone days, and he sought out Smith to discuss his sense of guilt. Immediate relief did not come, but after several weeks of great conviction, Robinson obtained the peace of salvation and described his experience thus: "A view of the glorious bleeding Savior on the cross, was presented to my mind, as groaning and dying for such a guilty sinful wretch as I had been. O the streams of love that flowed into my soul, no mortal tongue can describe: my cup was full, my joy was great, my peace like a river."[1]

On April 27, 1793, Robinson was baptized by Smith and united with others in forming a Baptist church in Livermore. His growth in grace was rapid, and soon he experienced the call of God upon his heart to preach. Being licensed by the church, he visited the town of Sanford and preached several Lord's Days in a Baptist church there. Robinson was called to become their pastor and was ordained on June 7, 1798, the day of his 34th birthday. His ministry was blessed of the Lord in revival, and the work grew as he baptized one hundred and sixty-five there and many others in his itinerant work throughout the area.

Having a heart burdened for missions, Robinson resigned in the fall of 1809 and moved to Salisbury, New Hampshire, to establish a church. In the spring of 1810, he had gathered enough converts to begin a church and was settled as pastor. His labors were continued for sixteen years, and he finally resigned the pastorate in 1826. The church had grown to one hundred and thirty members and many more were in attendance.

Though he resigned as pastor, the Reverend Mr. Robinson remained in the membership of the church and preached in the destitute areas at hand. In December of 1834 he became ill and came to believe that his work was completed and he would soon be called to his eternal home. After setting his business in order, Robinson awaited with joy the hour of his departure and died on March 1, 1835, in the seventy-first year of his age and thirty-seventh year of ministry.

The old records do not inform us of others who were called to preach through Robinson's ministry, but eternity will reveal the continuing chain of service. How wonderful to realize that our spiritual forebears have not "gone to their reward," for their premiums continue to grow, and they being dead yet speak.

DLC

---

[1]"Memoir of the Rev. Otis Robinson, of Salisbury N. H.," *American Baptist Magazine,* (Boston: John Putnam, 1835), pp. 462-64.

April 28—Tragic Consequences of the Sin of Slavery

Scripture: Galatians 2:11-12

The slavery-abolition controversy in America was a deep-seated problem for a number of years. The Virginia colonial government had protested the introduction of slavery by the British in 1619, but their complaints were ignored. We must ever remind ourselves that slavery was not entirely a sectional issue in America, for "the North and South were equally guilty in this sin. . . . A geographic and climatic determinism shuttled practically all of the slaves from northern ports, to which they were brought from Africa, into various parts of the south."[1] It is shocking to many to realize that there were "white slaves" from Scotland sent to America as well—slaves because of their faith rather than because of their race![2]

When William Wilberforce was successful in leading the abolitionists in England to end slavery in the British West Indies, pressures began to mount from Baptists in Great Britain against their American counterparts to conclude the wicked practice. As early as 1833, correspondence was sent to the Baptist Board of Foreign Missions urging that the Baptists take action against slavery in America. During this same period of history, our nation was experiencing a polarization of sectional loyalty which was strengthened by cultural differences which had grown out of historic, geographic, and climatic factors. Ultimately these divergences tore the Baptists of America apart, and in 1845, with the organization of the Southern Baptist Convention, the rift was permanent.

The real cleavage began in the 1830s. Feelings ran high as a literary debate between two leaders, President Wayland of Brown University and Richard Fuller of South Carolina, was conducted.[3] The abusive language of others deepened the split. William Brisbane, editor of the magazine *Southern Baptist,* a slaveholder and defender of the right to hold slaves, became convinced of the need for abolition, resigned his post, moved to the North, and spent the last twenty years of his life preaching in small Baptist churches in Wisconsin.

Before the break of the southern brethren to begin their own convention, some of the northern brethren met on May 11, 1839, and formed the American Baptist Anti-Slavery Convention. Holding its first session in New York City, on April 28, 29, and 30, 1840, the northern Baptists addressed their southern equivalents as follows: "It is our firm conviction that the whole system of American slavery, in theory and practice, is a violation of the instincts of nature,—a perversion of the first principle of justice,—and a positive transgression of the revealed will of God. . . . Thus we behold, in all the Scriptures a virtual and total condemnation of American slavery."[4]

After much maneuvering on the part of brethren from North and South to affect some compromise, a test case was presented the Home Society when a slaveholder was presented as a missionary candidate. The candidate was rejected, and this brought about the formation of the Southern Baptist Convention in 1845. The schism would prove permanent, but even then fraternal relations were continued by some, and the phenomenon can only be explained by the commonality of faith.

DLC

---

[1]Davis Collier Woolley, ed., *Baptist Advance* (Nashville: Broadman Press, 1964), p. 262.

[2]Alexander Smellie, *Men of the Covenant* (Edinburgh, Scot.: Banner of Truth Trust, 1975), pp. 394-95.

[3]Robert A. Baker, *The Southern Baptist Convention and Its People, 1607-1972* (Nashville: Broadman Press, 1974), p. 158.

[4]Robert A. Baker, *A Baptist Source Book* (Nashville: Broadman Press, 1966), pp. 92-93.

April 29—Rediscovering the Ancient Command of Christ

Scripture: John 20:21

Persecution had finally subsided when Baptists began to look on the fields of the world that were "white unto harvest." Baptists in

England had formed "The Particular Baptist Society for Propagation of the Gospel among the Heathen" in 1792. The Philadelphia Association in their annual meetings of October 1800 considered the formation of a missionary society that they might send out missionaries into the expanding nation.[1] Before the conclusion of the eighteenth century, many of the state associations were commissioning and supporting missionaries and pastors on the frontiers. But

> the earliest society formed by Baptists in America with a distinctive missionary purpose was the Massachusetts Baptist Missionary Society, formed in Boston in 1802. The purpose was the evangelization of frontier communities. Vail in *The Morning Hour of American Baptist Missions* names two other projected societies, Philadelphia and Rensselaerville, N.Y., which were initiated in 1800, but failed to materialize before the Boston group completed its organization. . . . The founders of the Massachusetts society specifically intended to send preachers to the isolated settlements where preaching was a rarity.[2]

Pastors Samuel Stillman of Boston's First Baptist Church and Thomas Baldwin of Boston's Second Baptist Church were the prime movers behind the establishing of the mission, and the two churches issued a call to the other state churches to unite for the purpose of the ongoing of the gospel. The appeal was dated April 29, 1802, and the meeting was held in the First Baptist Church. "The object of this Society shall be to furnish occasional preaching, and to promote the knowledge of evangelistic truth in the new settlements within these United States; or further if circumstance should render it proper." "At once they sent out their first missionaries: John Tripp, Isaac Case and Joseph Cornell. . . . The three were to find their own horses, but they were to have a weekly salary of five dollars plus expenses. They were to keep clear of politics, to keep an exact journal, and primarily to evangelize and encourage those people so sadly deprived, by distance and isolation, of church ministries."[3]

In 1803 the society established *The Massachusetts Missionary Magazine,* and challenging articles from outstanding pastors and actual reports from the missionaries' journals were used of God to stir the hearts of believers to extend their giving. By May of 1810, the society could report that a dozen missionaries had served during the preceding year. It is noteworthy that it was through the reading of the September 1809 issue of this magazine that Adoniram Judson was stirred so as to offer himself for missionary service to India. Three years later the Judsons and Luther Rice went to the field as Congregational missionaries and were converted to Baptist views. Rice returned to America to raise support for the Judsons, and in 1814, "The General Missionary

Convention of the Baptist Denomination in the United States of America for Foreign Missions'' was born. May we be obedient today to the Great Commision of our Lord Jesus Christ!

DLC

---

[1]A. D. Gillette, ed., *Minutes of the Philadelphia Baptist Association from A.D. 1707 to A.D. 1807* (Philadelphia: American Baptist Publication Society, 1851), p. 350.

[2]David Collier Woolley, ed., *Baptist Advance* (Philadelphia: Broadman Press, 1964), p. 25.

[3]John Woolman Brush, *Baptists in Massachusetts* (Valley Forge, Pa.: Judson Press, 1979), p. 14.

April 30—Sunday School: Source of Spiritual Blessing

Scripture: II Timothy 2:15

The first Sunday school in America was founded in September of 1799 in Pawtucket, Rhode Island, and for twenty-five years it was conducted as a day school on Sundays with pupils using spelling books as part of their equipment. In time, pastors began to envision the possibilities of spiritually-oriented Sunday schools, and the course of study was turned to the Word of God. The Sunday school has become a great tool of evangelism. One cannot help but wonder where Christianity would be today in America without local Sunday schools! The first Sunday school in Philadelphia was organized in 1815 and the first in Boston in 1816. By 1824 the ''Latter Day Luminary,'' a Baptist magazine for promoting missions, reported, ''The Sunday School properly conducted is the greatest and most successful opponent of the Prince of darkness. . . . Let these schools be cherished, let them be increased; soon the solitary place shall be glad for them, and the wilderness shall blossom as the rose.''

As with so much Baptist growth, there was no ''master plan'' and the Sunday schools proliferated spontaneously. Literature was needed both to train teachers and provide spiritual material for the students. In time, Sunday school associations appeared, but these did not meet the need of Baptist churches, for literature had to be supplied that taught the Baptist distinctives. One of the first to see this need was Ira M. Allen, agent of the Baptist General Tract Society. In 1832 Allen wrote, ''As it is, a part of the truth of God is excluded from all the Sunday

School books published by the American Union, which furnish the principal reading for hundreds of thousands of youth throughout the land. And we, as a denomination, have not a single book for Sunday Schools, containing our distinguishing sentiments.''[1]

As pressure mounted upon the members of the Triennial Convention to provide something for Baptist Sunday schools, at the triennial session in Richmond, Virginia, in 1835 that body requested the Baptist General Tract Society to change its constitution so that, in addition to its tract work, it might ''publish and distribute books for family use and Sunday Schools.'' The Hudson River Association (New York) in 1839 pressed the ''urgent need of a Baptist Sunday-school union to furnish a juvenile literature corresponding to Baptist convictions.''[2]

''This was finally accomplished on April 30, 1840, in New York City, when representations from fifteen states, from New Hampshire to Louisiana, voted to change the complexion and name of the tract society to 'The American Baptist Publication and Sunday School Society.' ''[3] For the first time, it was possible for Baptist Sunday schools to secure biographical, doctrinal, and historical material written from a Baptist perspective. Of course, just a few years later, the division came between Baptists of the North and South, and in this century, doctrinal disunions have caused the establishment of many Baptist publishing houses that provide literature for Baptist Sunday schools in associations with diverse doctrinal, ethnic, and cultural differences. However, we rejoice in the vision of the dissemination of our doctrines through the printed page for worldwide use!

DLC

---

[1]Lemuel Call Barnes, Mary Clark Barnes, and Edward M. Stephenson, *Pioneers of Light* (Philadelphia: American Baptist Publication Society, 1924), p. 115.

[2]Daniel Gurden Stevens, *The First Hundred Years of the American Baptist Publication Society* (Philadelphia: American Baptist Publication Society, n.d.), p. 21.

[3]Jesse L. Boyd, *A History of Baptists in America Prior to 1845* (New York: American Press, 1957), p. 113.

May

May 1—The Baptist Vision: Freedom for All

Scripture: Psalm 28

The compelling love of freedom predictably positioned Baptists with the Patriots during the Revolutionary War. Ministers of the Church of England, relishing their position as the "Established Church" in several colonies, favored the Tories rather than the Patriots. Baptists, on the other hand, served General Washington's army well, for "Baptist ministers were eager to go to the army as chaplains. Leading pastors from the East, from the Middle States, and from the South were with their armed brethren in all the toils, privations and perils of the Revolutionary War."[1] Among these chaplains were the Reverend David Jones, the Reverend John Gano, and the Reverend David Avery.

When Baptists from Virginia expressed grave concern about the security of religious freedom under the newly proposed Constitution of the United States, George Washington wrote them: "I recollect with satisfaction that the religious society of which you are members has been throughout America, uniformly and almost unanimously, the firm friends of civil liberty, and the persevering promoters of our glorious Revolution."[2] Morgan Edwards, Baptist preacher and historian from Wales, is apparently the only prominent Baptist who favored the Tories. The Philadelphia Committee of Safety placed Edwards under "house arrest" as a Loyalist in 1776, and though he had been a "Traveling Evangelist" for the Philadelphia Association since 1771, his travel was limited to the vicinity of his Newark, Delaware, home for five years. He seems to have been the only exception to American patriotism among the Baptists of that time.

Indeed, even the Baptists in England favored an American victory during the Revolutionary War, for apparently they feared losing their religious freedom. In a letter addressed to Dr. James Manning, president of Brown University, dated May 1, 1784, Dr. John Rippon of England said:

> I believe all of our Baptist ministers in town, except two, and most of our brethren in the country were on the side of the Americans in the late dispute. . . . We wept when the thirsty plains drank the blood of our departed heroes, and the shout of a king was among us when your well fought battles were crowned with victory; and to this hour we believe that the independence of America will, for a while, secure the liberty of this country, but if that continent had been reduced, Britain would not have long been free.[3]

Baptists were among the first of the religious bodies to recognize the authority of the Continental Congress. With the completion of the Constitution, Baptists were not unanimously in favor of ratification, but only because the Constitution did not have affixed to it a "Bill of Rights." Virginia had enacted its famous "Act of Religious Freedom" in 1786, and until the Baptists were assured by James Madison that the National Constitution would also have a "Bill of Rights," the Baptists were hesitant to ratify. This situation will be discussed in more detail later in this volume. Baptists have always championed freedom. One of our basic tenets is the liberty of conscience for all. Thank God for such a heritage, for this has made America the land of the free!

DLC

---

[1]William Cathcart, *Baptist Patriots in the American Revolution* (Grand Rapids: Guardian Press, 1976), p. 34.

[2]Robert A. Baker, *A Baptist Source Book* (Nashville: Broadman Press, 1966), p. 45.

[3]John T. Christian, *A History of the Baptists* (1922; reprint ed., Nashville: Broadman Press, 1926), 2:228.

May 2—Joan Boucher Loved, Lived, and Died in Truth

Scripture: III John

Joan Boucher, known also as Joan of Kent in England, was a lady of note, possessing much wealth. She was also well known at the palace in the days of King Henry VIII and King Edward VI. Joan belonged to the Anabaptist Assembly in Kent and with her friend Anne Askew was devoted to the study and circulation of Tyndale's translation which had been printed at Cologne in 1534. It is reported that she carried copies of this prohibited book under her clothing on her visits to the court and very likely to the prisons also, which she visited often and where she used her wealth to relieve those who suffered for Jesus' sake.[1]

Joan was arrested in May of 1549 and was exposed to cruel interrogations. She was examined and cross-examined, entreated and threatened, but she would not move from her faith. The whole futile operation was a travesty of properly exercised authority. If she were an empty-headed woman, as they pretended, they brought no honor to themselves in spending eighteen months of their time, before and during her imprisonment, trying to prove her a heretic. Lord Richie kept her at his house for two weeks as Bishops Cranmer and Ridley of the Church of England attempted to dissuade her from her Baptist convictions. Her judges called her demeaning titles but not "lady," which her parentage, position, and character demanded.

Foxe, also of the Church of England but of a tender heart, tried to save her and to induce the Vicar, John Rogers of St. Sepulcher, to help him. Rogers refused, however, believing that Joan ought to be executed, and reportedly, he spoke lightly of death by burning. Only five years later, Rogers's poor wife and eight children saw him consumed by flames at Smithfield, London, as he became the first martyr under Bloody Mary's reign.

Joan Boucher suffered amongst the flames May 2, 1550, to the eternal disgrace of all concerned. Common decency might have spared her the mockery of having Bishop Scorey preach to her while at the stake and vilify her there under pretense of pious exhortation. Yet possibly her last act did him a service which he needed very much and which had never been done for him previously. Her sermon to him is immortal, while his to her has long since been forgotten. Listening to him just before her soul ascended to heaven in the flame, she said in reply, "You lie like a rogue. Go read the Scriptures!"[2]

She believed in Christ's miraculous incarnation but rejected the doctrine of the immaculate conception of Mary and her subsequent sinlessness, insisting that Mary, like other women, needed to rejoice in God her Savior. Joan was a woman dedicated to God and His Word. While men of rank and station in this life capitulated, she stood firm as a lady of strong conviction and Christian character. We thank God for courageous women who, through sufferings, remained faithful to God's truth. Many women are included in God's roll of the faithful.

EWT

---

[1]Thomas Armitage, *The History of the Baptists* (1890; reprint ed., Watertown, Wis.: Maranatha Baptist Press, 1976), 1:449.

[2]Ibid., p. 450.

May 3—A Snowstorm That Changed a Life

Scripture: II Timothy 3:10-17

Charles Haddon Spurgeon was born in 1834, the second of ten children born to Pastor John Spurgeon and his wife. For a number of years in his childhood, young Charles lived with his grandparents in Stambourne, England, where his grandfather, the Reverend James Spurgeon, was the minister of the Congregational (Independent) Church. Up to the age of sixteen, the young man had no real assurance of salvation, though he had thought deeply of Christian doctrine. Then, on the first Sunday in January, 1850, a snowstorm kept him from visiting a certain church toward which he had started, and he entered a little Primitive Methodist building with about twelve other worshipers. The scheduled speaker could not keep his appointment, and one of the men attempted to preach. The text was Isaiah 45:22, "Look unto me, and be ye saved, all the ends of the earth: for I am God, and there is none else." Soon the preacher exhausted his thoughts but looking straight at young Spurgeon, he cried: "Young man, you look very miserable! You always will be miserable—miserable in life and miserable in death, if you don't obey my text: but if you obey now, this moment you will be saved. Young man, look to Jesus! Look! Look! Look! You have nothing to do but to look and live."[1]

Young Spurgeon heard, not the voice of the inept preacher, but the voice of the Spirit of God and was gloriously saved. He wrote out a covenant with the Lord and signed it. In it he declared his intention of serving the Lord the rest of his life. His service began immediately. The young man remembered the time when as an unsaved youth he had determined "that if ever Divine grace should work a change in [him], [he] would be baptized."[2] But the closest Baptist pastor was eight miles away! He began to correspond with the Reverend W. W. Cantlow, and in time, a date was set for a baptismal service. In writing a sweet letter to his parents for permission to be immersed, young Spurgeon said, "As Mr. Cantlow's baptizing season will come round this month, I have humbly to beg your consent, as I will not act against your will, and should very much like to commune next month. I have no doubt of your permission. We are all one in Christ Jesus; forms and ceremonies, I trust, will not make us divided.''[3] ''He walked from New Market to Isleham, seven miles, on May 3rd, 1850, where Rev. Mr. Cantlow buried him with Christ in baptism.''[4]

Some time later his mother said to him, ''Ah, Charles! I often prayed the Lord to make you a Christian, but I never asked that you might become a Baptist.'' With his typical humor, Spurgeon replied, ''Ah mother! The Lord has answered your prayer with His usual bounty, and given you exceeding abundantly above what you asked or thought.''[5]

Spurgeon testified continually of the spiritual impact that his baptism had in his life, and soon afterwards he was preaching. Volumes have been written concerning his accomplishments, but perhaps the most important contribution he made to Baptists was the restoration of evangelism to its true place, as he made it the very center of his whole life's ministry!

DLC

---

[1]Arnold A. Dallimore, *Spurgeon* (Chicago: Moody Press, 1984), p. 19.

[2]Ibid., p. 25.

[3]Charles H. Spurgeon, *Autobiography of Charles H. Spurgeon* (Philadelphia: American Baptist Publication Company, n.d.), 1:122.

[4]Thomas Armitage, *The History of the Baptists* (1890; reprint ed., Watertown, Wis: Maranatha Baptist Press, 1976), p. 596.

[5]Spurgeon, p. 69.

May 4—Slavery! An American Tragedy

Scripture: I Peter 2:13-25

The issue of slavery in America was doubtless the most divisive issue ever to confront our nation. The matter was many faceted, for it was surely a social and moral problem, but simultaneously it projected itself in the political, economic, and religious arenas as well. Baptists in the South had initially grown among that portion of the population that was in the lower economic class, and these were surely nonslaveholders. This accounts for the fact that the Baptists in the Southern states provided much of the opposition to slavery that existed. The more affluent plantation owners were profiting most from the dread practice, but these were not primarily Baptists. Because of their strong numerical representation in the South in modern days, many have assumed that the tragedy of slavery was a "Baptist problem," but such was not the case.

The political options were being considered by national leaders. Abraham Lincoln, when addressing the border states in behalf of compensated emancipation, on July 12, 1862, said, "I do not speak of emancipation at once, but of a decision at once to emancipate gradually. Room in South America for colonization can be obtained cheaply and in abundance, and when numbers shall be large enough to be company and encouragement for one another, the freed people will not be reluctant to go."[1]

The whole nation was astir, and controversy raged. "Baptists in the Southern states contributed their part of the opposition of slavery. . . . In Virginia, Kentucky and other states, associations passed resolutions against slavery. . . . Elihu Embree published in Jonesborough, Tennessee, in 1820, *The Emancipator,* the first antislavery paper in the United States."[2]

Agitation among Baptists was stimulated by the British brethren after the English Parliament passed legislation to eliminate slavery in the British West Indies. In 1835 British Baptists sent two English abolitionists as "fraternal delegates" to the Triennial Convention which was held in Richmond, Virginia.

> These brethren . . . were introduced also for the first time to first-hand information concerning the American number-one problem—slavery. Dr. Cox, one of the British delegates, preached in the First Church on the Sunday morning preceding the opening of the Triennial Convention. On that afternoon he went again to the First Church, where he witnessed with amazement and emotion, the great numbers of colored worshipers present. As this group clasped hands and sang, their bodies swaying in the rhythm of the music, the Englishman's enthusiasm broke the bounds of traditional British reserve. He asked permission to speak to them; he clasped their hands; he saw with his own eyes the overruling Providence of God in using the channel of slavery to bring to these sons and daughters of Africa the light of the gospel.[3]

Step by step the pressures mounted to abolish slavery, and on May 4, 1843, Baptist abolitionists met in Tremont Chapel (Boston) to organize a mission society which would support both foreign and home missionaries and would be "separated from all connection with the known evils of slavery." The die was cast, and Baptists, like all other Americans, would be divided and experience the terrible results of the Civil War.

DLC

---

[1]*Speeches and Letters of Abraham Lincoln, 1832-1865* (New York: E. P. Dutton and Co., 1907), p. 190.

[2]Robert A. Baker, *The Southern Baptist Convention and Its People, 1607–1972* (Nashville: Broadman Press, 1974), p. 155.

[3]Blanche Sydnor White, *First Baptist Church—Richmond, 1780–1955* (Richmond: Whittet and Shepperson, 1955), pp. 51-52.

May 5—"From My Palace in Culpeper"

Scripture: Psalm 48

In the early years of my ministry, on my way to preach in some of the old, historic Baptist churches of Virginia, I would pass the Berryville Baptist Church, where a monument is erected in the churchyard to

> the memory of James Ireland Minister of the Gospel. Born in Edinburg, Scotland, converted in Frederick County, Virginia . . . imprisoned at Culpeper, Virginia for preaching the Gospel, organizer of Baptist churches, pastor of Buck Marsh Church 1788 to 1806. His body lies in Buck Marsh Cemetery near here.
>
> In gratitude for the blessings of spiritual religion and freedom of conscience won in part through his suffering, this memorial is erected by the Baptists of Virginia.

There was another monument forged in his memory in the form of a church bell with the inscription "To the memory of James Ireland, Born 1748 died 1806." The intention of the Culpeper Baptist Church in Culpeper, Virginia, where James Ireland had been imprisoned, was "so that imagination, when our bell is rung, may hear James Ireland calling us forth."[1]

Why is all this attention called to one who was known as "Little Jamie Ireland"? After a turbulent youth in Scotland, where he was reared in a Presbyterian home, he came to Virginia and ultimately took up residence near New Market, Shenandoah County, Virginia, where he worked as a schoolteacher. After a long period of conviction of sin and efforts through religious exercises to receive relief of soul, he came to the knowledge of salvation by grace through faith alone in our Lord Jesus Christ.

He became a fearless and courageous proclaimer of this message and was followed with great persecution. On one occasion in Culpeper County, while he was praying after a preaching service, he was seized by the collar by two men and given the ultimatum of promising not to preach there any longer or going to jail. He chose the latter alternative, and after a few days he was incarcerated in Culpeper. Through the jail bars he preached in spite of all the efforts to disturb him and his listeners. His detractors ran riding horses at a gallop through his hearers, urinated in his face as he preached, attempted to blow him up with gunpowder, and endeavored to suffocate him by burning brimstone and Indian pepper under the floor of his cell. A doctor and the jailer conspired to poison him. Ireland also was dunked in water and threatened with public whippings. When drunken rowdies were placed in his cell to harass him, he led several to personal faith in Jesus Christ. During this time, he wrote letters to individuals and churches which he headed "from my Palace in Culpeper." This resulted in the salvation of many souls who heard his letters read as well as those who heard him preach. He said, "My prison then was a place in which I enjoyed much of the divine presence; a day seldom passed without some signal token and manifestation of the divine goodness toward me."[2]

Even while he preached out of prison, he continued to be threatened with beatings and dunkings. On one occasion two women conspired to poison his family, which nearly resulted in Ireland's own death and did cause the death of one of his eight children. He bore the burden of ill health as a result of this maltreatment until his death May 5, 1806.[3]

God help us to raise more monuments to these forgotten heroes of the faith who established our Baptist heritage and religious liberty throughout the land.

EWT

---

[1]Lewis Peyton Little, *Imprisoned Preachers and Religious Liberty in Virginia* (Lynchburg, Va.: J. P. Bell Co., 1938), pp. 184-91.

[2]James Ireland, *The Life of the Rev. James Ireland,* ed. Arthur C. Johnson (1819; reprint ed., Ashland, Ky.: Economy Printers, n.d.), p. 106.

[3]Ibid., pp. 125-32.

May 6—A Preacher, a Missionary and a Soldier

Scripture: Judges 6

One cannot peruse the minutes of the Philadelphia Baptist Association from 1707 to 1807 without often seeing the name David Jones. He was born May 12, 1736, and he experienced salvation and was baptized May 6, 1758, when he was just turning twenty-two years of age.[1] We have read previously that his calling had led him into a life of adventure and great usefulness to his God and to his country. The minutes of this historic Baptist association contain this record of its October meeting in 1772: "A certificate was given to Brother David Jones, who intends to visit the western tribes of Indians the next winter, to ascertain his good standing with us. Also, at his request, a motion was made to recommend his case to the respective churches, as he must be at the expense of paying his interpreter five pounds per month; and the contribution made be sent by their messengers to the next Association. If not wanted, the money will be returned to the donors."[2]

We gather from this record that the early Baptist missionaries were thrust out by the Holy Spirit and provided for by the local churches according to the New Testament pattern at Antioch.

He wrote several circular letters to the churches making up the Philadelphia Association. He gave the purpose of their annual meetings when he wrote the encyclical in 1788. "The great design of our annual meetings is to promote the welfare of the church of Christ, by giving our advice in difficult cases, and by the use of every other means, to preserve the unity of the spirit in the bond of peace."[3] The minutes of this association demonstrate its respect for the local church by expressing the collective opinion of the association and by never issuing a mandate to any church. The association existed for the churches, never the churches for the association. The local church was always considered the highest ecclesiastical tribunal on earth.

These circular letters also revealed the prevailing spiritual condition and welfare of the churches and country. Days of fasting and prayer were often requested. Jones in writing the letter in 1798 mentioned,

> We have been once more prevented assembling in the City of Philadelphia by a dreadful visitation from God. Whatever may be the natural cause of this complaint, no doubt *SIN* is the procuring cause; nor can we reasonably expect a removal of the calamity without a suitable reformation among the inhabitants, for which we ought fervently to pray to God; and who knoweth but He may in His great mercy, graciously answer our supplications.[4]

The minutes of 1800 record that the association met in Philadelphia. The eleventh entry states, "Conscious that the interposing Providence of God hath preserved the City of Philadelphia, during the present season, from the malignant fever, and caused the earth to bring forth her fruits more abundantly than for some years past, the Association set apart, and recommend, Thursday the 13th of November next, to be observed as a day of thanksgiving by all the churches in our connection."[5] Apparently, the Philadelphia area suffered a plague of some magnitude and drought conditions that extended for some years.

May the life of David Jones demonstrate to us the wonderful providential care of God through wilderness and war, and may we in our day, when so many malignant diseases are prevalent, have the spirit of contrition for sins as did our Baptist forebears.

EWT

---

[1]Thomas Armitage, *The History of the Baptists* (1890; reprint ed., Watertown, Wis.: Maranatha Baptist Press, 1976), 2:794.

[2]A. D. Gilette, ed., *Minutes of the Philadelphia Baptist Association from A.D. 1707 to A.D. 1807* (Philadelphia: American Baptist Publication Society, 1851), p. 124.

[3]Ibid., p. 239.

[4]Ibid., p. 335.

[5]Ibid., p. 349.

May 7—A Small-Town Preacher with a Worldwide Vision

Scripture: Romans 10:9-17

Gloomy and fatalistic high Calvinism held sway in the pulpits of England in 1754 when Andrew Fuller was born in Cambridgeshire. This doctrinal interpretation held that only the "elect" could be saved, and no human agency could avert the execution of the tragic fiat of damnation. The result could be seen in the churches as that theology produced a numbing of evangelism. However, young Fuller was gloriously saved as a teen-ager, preached his first sermon when he was but seventeen, and was called and ordained as pastor of the little Baptist church in the village of Soham. Soon thereafter, the Reverend Mr. Fuller was married and served the small congregation for seven years. His salary was minimal, and he supplemented it as best he could and gave himself to prayer, study and the preaching of the cross. In 1781, he was called to a vigorous church in Kettering, in Northamptonshire, and there he ministered for thirty-two years until his death.

> [Andrew Fuller] had remarkable intellectual gifts. He saw clearly, wrote in a simple yet compact style, and spoke with natural fervor and strength. He dedicated all his energies and talents to God. His love for human souls caused him to swing away from the Calvinistic doctrines of iron-clad election and reprobation. Believing thus in a freer and more human Gospel he wrought with passionate intensity to awaken men to interest in world-evangelization. The combination of

> these attributes made him one of the most effective religious leaders of his age.[1]

His literary fame spread throughout England and America, and soon his doctrinal position, known as "a modified Calvinism," became the majority stance among Baptists.[2]

His organizational genius was felt in his association, for in 1784 he established the ministers' meetings and prayer bands. His own understanding of missionary obligation was growing, and later in 1784, he preached his famous sermon on the "The Gospel Worthy of All Acceptance." In 1786 he met William Carey, and their lifelong friendship developed. In 1791, Fuller preached a sermon on "The Pernicious Influences of Delay," and the following year Carey preached his soul-stirring message of missionary challenge. Surely the Holy Spirit was moving, and four months later the missionary society was formed that changed the whole outlook of the evangelical churches toward a lost world. Andrew Fuller was chosen the secretary for the society, and without trains, planes, and buses, he set out on horseback on rough country paths and miry roads through rain and sleet to stir churches for missions. Many miles were traveled in England, five tours were made in Scotland, and one trip to Ireland. He continued his pastorate throughout the twenty-three years as secretary until his death. He faced constant opposition from the high Calvinists, the English Government, and the East India Company, but even before his death he witnessed English and American Baptists transformed with a missionary spirit.

> In 1798 Princeton College conferred on him the honorary degree of D. D., which he declined. Yale College . . . followed the example of Princeton in 1805, with a similar declination. . . . His death, on May 7, 1815, excited a profound sensation, and occasioned general grief. . . . His church erected a beautiful monument, which commemorates in glowing words their exalted appreciation of his great worth.[3]

Surely he was one of the fathers of our modern-day missionary movement!

DLC

---

[1]Austen Kennedy de Blois, *Fighters for Freedom* (Philadelphia: Judson Press, 1929), p. 233.

[2]Ibid., p. 236.

[3]William Cathcart, *The Baptist Encyclopedia,* ed. Louis H. Everts (Philadelphia: Louis H. Everts, 1881), 1:421-22.

May 8—Seeking to Glorify God in Organization

Scripture: Psalm 16

For many years Baptists throughout America, without sectional distinctions, had cooperated in the work of missions. Gradual differences began to surface which were caused by cultural and geographical locations, but the matter came to a head with the issue of slavery. The period from 1832 to 1845 was a most difficult time of irritation, and finally in 1845, division came as the churches of the South concluded that they could best perform the work of missions by operating separately from the churches of the North.

In response to a call from the Board of the Virginia Foreign Baptist Missionary Society, a convention met in Augusta, Georgia, May 8, 1845. The division was inevitable, but what structure would the new Southern group take? "The General Missionary Convention of the Baptist Denomination in the United States of America, for Foreign Missions," which had been formed in 1814, came to be called the "Triennial Convention." For all intents and purposes, this was merely a foreign mission society for Baptist churches. In 1824 the American Baptist Publication Society grew out of the Baptist General Tract Society. To meet the needs in America, the American Baptist Home Mission Society had been formed in 1832. These organizations had been accustomed to holding annual meetings at the same place and at the same general time, but this was an inefficient arrangement and produced repetition of effort and competition for loyalty and support. Francis Wayland had championed the cause of independent societies to ensure autonomy of the local churches.

Dr. William B. Johnson had been a prime mover in the establishment of the Triennial Convention and now championed the Southern Baptist Convention. Johnson had witnessed both the successes and failures of the Triennial Convention. Having studied law prior to his conversion and call to preach, he possessed one of the most competent minds among Baptists of the South. At that time Johnson was president of the South Carolina Baptist Convention. He called a meeting of the State Convention a week prior to the proposed meeting of May 8 to discuss a new Baptist organization for the South. In that meeting, Johnson proposed a centralized body that would represent churches, thus protecting local church autonomy, and yet take control over all societies that might grow out of that convention. In the May 8th meeting in Augusta, Johnson's plan was adopted fully, and he was elected the first president of the Southern Baptist Convention. He served two terms in that capacity, from 1845 to 1851.

It is interesting to observe that today in the Baptist movement in America, churches are formed into associations, conventions, conferences, and fellowships. Leaders from all forms of Baptist church government seek to ensure that each system protects the autonomy of each local church, for this is one of the fundamental tenets of Baptists. Hiscox wrote, "All such Associations, Conventions, Minister's Meetings and the like, are entirely voluntary. No church or individual is obliged to unite with them; and if so united, can leave them when they wish."[1]

Thus was born the Southern Baptist Convention, which has grown to be the largest Baptist organization in the United States.

DLC

---

[1]Edward T. Hiscox, *The Baptist Directory* (New York: Sheldon and Co., 1866), pp. 131-32.

May 9—"So He Slew Me with the Word of His Mouth"

Scripture: Romans 7:1-14

Morgan Edwards was born May 9, 1722, and grew to manhood during the reign of George I (1714-27) and George II (1727-60). Both of these kings "were personally in favor not only of keeping religious liberty stretched to the furtherest limits it had at present reached, but of making its field yet wider."[1] Trevethin Parish, Monmouthshire, Wales, where Morgan Edwards was born, had a relationship to England and Wales, and many of the people spoke both English and Welsh. The parish also had become one of the centers of religious nonconformity a century before Edward's birth.

At age sixteen he broke with his Anglican heritage and embraced the principles of the Baptists. This cleavage could have been caused by the infectious enthusiasm of the young Baptist missionaries who were sent out in such large numbers that hardly a village in the eastern and western valleys of Monmouthshire was not visited. When he was pastor of the Baptist Church of Philadelphia many years later, he reminisced in a sermon as follows:

> I remember the time (and the place too) when I first gave myself up as a lost man; for til then I was halting between two opinions about it. Fearing it was so, made me uneasy, and hope it might not be so, kept me from yielding to it. But this sentence stuck on my mind in a light that it was not wont to do, 'I will by no means clear the guilty!' then said I, I am gone, for I am guilty: if I am not damned God must be a liar. So He slew me with the word of His mouth. Then this commandment came, and I died. Then I knew what sort of thing despair was. And you cannot imagine what jolt I felt, when I learnt so much of the Gospel as to know it was possible for me to be saved, and that God might stand to His word, and not send me to hell.[2]

Morgan Edwards probably received his early preaching experience as a participant in evangelistic crusades during the spiritual awakening that followed the preaching of George Whitefield. Edwards attended Bristol Academy, where he received instruction in Hebrew, Greek, church history, homiletics, and systematic theology. He admonished Baptist ministers who either could not or would not learn to speak or write proper English, believing that "words are to a preacher what tools are to a mechanic; and if a mechanic has not his tools in good order will he not be a botch after he has done his best?"[3]

He came to America in 1761 where, on the recommendation of Dr. John Gill, he became pastor of the Baptist church in Philadelphia, which experienced remarkable growth under his ministry. He had outstanding ability as a preacher and was scholarly in his sermon preparation. A decade later he resigned as pastor and was appointed traveling evangelist for the Philadelphia Association.

Edwards was very concerned with the need for education among the Baptist ministry and was influential in obtaining a charter for Rhode Island College, now known as Brown University. He made trips to the southern United States, Ireland, and England to raise funds for the college and to procure a library. As he traveled through the South, he compiled information about the Baptists, which helped him contribute to the historical records of Baptists in America. Those interested in Baptist history are indebted to him for much material that would have been unavailable without his efforts.

EWT

---

[1]Thomas R. McKibbens, Jr., and Kenneth L. Smith, *The Life and Works of Morgan Edwards* (New York: Arno Press, 1980), p. 2.

[2]Ibid., pp. 3-4.

[3]Ibid., p. 10.

May 10—Richard Furman, "The Apostle of Education" in the South

Scripture: Proverbs 1:1-6

As is true of many early Baptist preachers, Richard Furman began his life in the North at Aesopus, New York, in 1755, but while yet an infant, his parents moved to South Carolina and settled on the High Hills of Santee. It was here that he became a Christian, and at the age of eighteen, he began to preach with a remarkable degree of clearness, devotion, and power for a youth. He planted many churches which united with the Charleston Association. He was ordained May 10, 1774, and although he was converted to the principles of the Separate Baptists, he ultimately was called to pastor the Regular Baptist Church in Charleston, South Carolina, where he brought a spirit of fervent evangelism for thirty-eight years.[1]

He was twenty-two when the Revolution began, and he avowed himself a firm Whig and threw all his powers into the American cause. When the British invaded South Carolina, he was forced to retire to North Carolina and Virginia, and afterwards Cornwallis put a price on his head. While in Virginia, he became a personal friend of Patrick Henry, who presented him with certain books which have been cherished by his posterity.[2]

During the time that education was suspect for ministers in the South, particularly among the Separate Baptists who feared that schools would dilute Baptist spirituality, divert mission money, and lead to a hireling ministry, Richard Furman became known as the "Apostle of Education." He led the association to form a General Committee in 1790 to administer educational funds. This committee provided funds for scholarships to attend the Baptist college in Providence, Rhode Island, and for young men to study under pastors who would also lead them in the reading of theology. As the first president of the Triennial Convention in 1814, he sought to include Baptist education as part of the convention's work. In his presidential address he said, "It is deeply to be regretted that no more attention is paid to the improvement of the minds of pious youths who are called to the Gospel ministry."[3] Because of his leadership in this field, the first Baptist college in the South, located in Greenville, South Carolina, bears his name.

Furman became a wealthy land owner from investments he had made. He also owned slaves and articulated the most widely quoted defense of that system among the Baptists in the South. Using history and logic he wrote a detailed defense of slavery in 1822, but the heart of his argument was that "the right of holding slaves is clearly established in the Holy Scriptures both by precept and example."[4] Not all Baptists in the South were proslavery. Many argued for the freedom of the slaves, some even released their slaves, and others emigrated to the North. This issue caused a further expansion in the division between the Baptists in the North and the Baptists in the South. The final rupture came with the outbreak of the Civil War.

Although he defended slavery, Furman heartily supported education for Baptist preachers. Thank God for the abolishment of such an abominable and horrible institution from this nation which takes pride in its reputation of being the "land of the free and the home of the brave," and may we praise the Lord for the fervent advocates of Christian education.

EWT

---

[1]H. Leon McBeth, *The Baptist Heritage* (Nashville: Broadman Press, 1987), p. 220.

[2]Thomas Armitage, *The History of the Baptists* (1890; reprint ed., Watertown, Wis.: Maranatha Baptist Press, 1976), 2:812-13.

[3]McBeth, pp. 352-55.

[4]Ibid., p. 384.

May 11—John Hart: A True Christian Patriot

Scripture: Esther 4

John Hart was not a preacher or orator, but he made his mark as a patriot during the period preceding the birth of our great Republic. Hart entered the Continental Congress in 1774 when he was about sixty years old, and in 1776 he took his place among the signers of the Declaration of Independence.

> Two days before it [the Declaration of Independence] was given to the world the British landed a powerful army on Staten Island. . . . His residence was on the highway of the enemy and his signature was sure to bring down their vengeance in a week or two; he knew that everything which he owned except the soil would be destroyed, his dear ones scattered, and his life taken if by the providence of the Evil

> One he was captured, and yet he did not hesitate to sign . . . though it might prove his own death-warrant.[1]

In the days that followed, he returned home to find that his family had fled, his crops had been burned, and his livestock had been driven away. He was now a fugitive and slept in caves, thickets, and even one night in a doghouse, where he shared the protection with the canine occupant. He was continually on the move and was unable to sleep in the same place on consecutive nights. During this time his wife became gravely ill, and he could not visit her, but his spirit could not be broken. After the Battle of Princeton, he returned and convened the legislature at Trenton.

In 1776 he was elected Speaker of the House of Assembly and had that same honor conferred upon him for the next two years as well. His neighbors called him ''Honest John Hart.'' Hart built the Baptist church building of Hopewell, New Jersey, and provided land as well for a church cemetery. John Hart passed away on May 11, 1779, exhausted from his labors and suffering from his many privations.

In 1865 a fine monumental shaft of Quincy granite was erected by the state of New Jersey near the Hopewell Baptist Church to honor the Baptist patriot. At the dedication of the monument on July 4, 1865, Governor Joel Parker gave a stirring oration. In part he said:

> As his public career was without blemish so was his private life pure and exemplary. He was a consistent member of old Hopewell Baptist Church. . . . He was a true patriot. I am of opinion, after a careful examination of the history of New Jersey during and immediately preceding the Revolutionary War, that John Hart had greater experience in the colonial and State Legislation of that day than any of his contemporaries, and that no man exercised greater influence in giving direction to the public opinion which culminated in independence.[2]

John Hart was not a professional politician. Rather he led the way with brave, sacrificial deeds. Such leadership is exactly what is needed in America today! The blessed tenet of ''Separation of Church and State'' was never meant to divorce the Christian virtues of morality as set forth in the Word of God from the realm of government. May we dedicate ourselves to stand for truth and thus influence our nation by the very power of our convictions of righteousness!

DLC

---

[1]William Cathcart, *The Baptists and the American Revolution* (Grand Rapids: Guardian Press, 1976), pp. 51-52.

[2]William Cathcart, *The Baptist Encyclopedia,* ed. Louis H. Everts (Philadelphia: Louis H. Everts, 1881), 1:505.

May 12—Love the Word of God Above the Word of Man

Scripture: Psalm 138

The Bible, being the pure unadulterated Word of God, is the basis of Baptist faith and practice. Therefore, Baptists have always been sincerely interested in disseminating the Scriptures far and wide. There was no question that Baptists would support the American Bible Society, which was composed of members of many evangelical denominations. In time, Baptists served on the Board of Managers of the Society, but the Reverend Spencer Houghton Cone, pastor of the Oliver Street Baptist Church in New York, was the only Baptist committee member.

William Carey had excelled as a linguist in his missionary work in India, and during the last years of his life, Dr. William Yates was his associate and then successor. In the course of time, Dr. Yates and the Reverend William Pierce revised the work on the Bengali translation, which was acknowledged to be one of the best ever made into a foreign language. They translated the word *baptizō* into the Bengali equivalent "immerse," and the British and Foreign Bible Society refused to print it. Then application was made to the American Bible Society, and though the contributions of the Baptist churches were sizable, the American Bible Society also refused. Baptists in America had given almost one hundred thousand dollars to the Society, but the Society had appropriated less than twenty-nine thousand dollars to aid in the translations made by Baptist missionaries. The Society patronized a version which translated *baptizō* with the word "sprinkle," but they considered the Baptists sectarian for insisting on translating the Greek word as "immerse." Dr. Cone argued that it was radically wrong for the Society to attempt to control the consciences of well-qualified missionaries or to decide what words they should *transfer* into translations and what words they should *translate*.

In the session in which the American Bible Society exiled the Baptists from their ranks, a gentleman defending pedobaptism rose to speak. He argued that warfare is perpetual for Christians, and we are all in one large army. The enemy is poised to strike, and a regiment that does not continue to show the solid front is guilty of desertion. No sooner had the speech ended when Cone stood and said,

"Mr. Chairman:

'There is a tide in the affairs of men
Which taken at the flood leads on to fortune;
Neglected, all our lives afterward
Are bound in shallows and miseries.'

On that tide my denomination is launched. It has risen to their feet. It commands them to embark. They dare not disobey the God they serve. They dare not cover up His truth, forsake high fortune, and incur the just retribution of being bound in shallows and in miseries all their life after. Sir, I love the army, but I love my regiment better, and whether they fall amid the mountains of America, or on the plains of Burmah, I fall with them!"[1]

Only one course of action was left to the Baptists. "On May 12, 1836, a large convention met in the Oliver Street church, New York, and after discussion, proceeded to organize the American and Foreign Bible Society. Rev. Spencer H. Cone . . . was its first president."[2]

May God's inspired, infallible, inerrant Word be our standard in our day!

DLC

---

[1]Edward W. Cone and Spencer W. Cone, *Some Account of the Life of Spencer Houghton Cone* (New York: Livermore and Rudd, 1856), p. 323.

[2]Edward T. Hiscox, *The Baptist Directory* (New York: Sheldon and Co., 1866), p. 276.

May 13—The Conversion of a Church

Scripture: Acts 8:26-40

The Congregational church in Sedgwick, Maine, had enjoyed the ministry of the Reverend Daniel Merrill for twelve years. During that time, the church had grown to be one of the largest of the denomination's churches in the state. However, when several of his ministerial students became Baptists, the Reverend Mr. Merrill determined to restudy the matter of baptism and write a book on the subject which would protect against such losses. The pastor already had what he called an "unconquered antipathy" toward the Baptists, and such a volume would be invaluable to many in refuting what he considered heresy.[1] For more than two years he searched the Scriptures but he was driven to the realization that the Bible did not support his long-held position.

The matter came to a head when a group of children were presented to be sprinkled and the pastor could no longer with a fully clear conscience perform the rite. Thus Merrill called the church membership to observe a day of fasting and prayer that the Lord might give him light and remove all doubts. For several months Merrill continued in agony of heart for, as he confessed, he "could not bear the idea of being called one [a Baptist]."[2] But as he became submissive to the will of God, he discovered peace in the matter. In October of 1804 he began a series of seven sermons to his congregation on the mode and candidates of baptism. Immediate opposition arose, and seven men petitioned the selectmen of Sedgwick to call a town meeting to act on the authority and propriety of their pastor's action. The meeting was held on January 18, 1805, and amazingly the selectmen concurred with Merrill's actions.

On February 28, 1805, the congregation voted unanimously to call for a council of Baptist ministers to administer New Testament immersion, to constitute them as a Baptist church, and to ordain Daniel Merrill as their pastor. The Reverends Thomas Baldwin of Boston, John Pitman of Rhode Island, and Elisha Williams of Massachusetts responded and arrived in Sedgwick on May 11, 1805. Immediately the Council members preached to the congregation, and on Monday, after a sermon by Williams, the Council examined candidates for baptism, and the interviews continued on Tuesday morning. At 10:30 that morning, the immersing of candidates began. After prayer, Baldwin and Merrill entered the water, repeating the words, "And they went down both into the water, both Philip and the eunuch, and he baptized him." After Rev. Merrill's baptism, Mr. Williams led Mrs. Merrill into the water, repeating the words: "And they were both righteous before God, walking in all the commandments and ordinances of the Lord blameless." In all, sixty-six candidates were baptized on May 13, 1805, and nineteen more were baptized on the following day.

On Wednesday afternoon the newly baptized group met with the Council members to form their church organization. The Council ordained Merrill as a Baptist pastor, and the Reverend Isaac Case gave the congregation the hand of fellowship as "a sister Church of Christ." Thus concluded the remarkable story of the conversion of a pastor and his people to the principles of the Baptists and the willingness to bear what at one time seemed to them an odious name!

DLC

---

[1]Henry S. Burrage, *History of the Baptists in Maine* (Portland, Maine: Marks Printing House, 1904), p. 143.

[2]Ibid.

May 14—Remove Not the Ancient Landmark

Scripture: Proverbs 22

On a hot, sultry August day in 1945, I hitchhiked across the northern Virginia landscape toward New Market, Virginia, where the historic Ketocton Association of Regular Baptists was convening. The Blue Ridge and Massanutten mountains shimmered in the late summer humidity, and I wondered whether I would arrive in time for the last session. The association had been assembling on the Friday, Saturday, and Sunday before the third Sunday in August since 1766. The year 1945 marked the one hundred and seventy-ninth anniversary session because the Revolutionary and Civil Wars had interrupted the annual meetings for a few years. Meeting with this church at that time was somewhat a joyous and historic occasion, for just a few days before, World War II had come to a close after over fifty million lives had been lost. Upon arrival, I looked across the street from the present building and saw the log edifice where Smith's Creek Regular Baptist Church met when it was constituted in 1756. I was nearly nineteen years old in 1945 and did not really appreciate the significance of the occasion or the place where we met. Being asked to preach that afternoon, I began a long relationship with the congregation and continued an even longer relationship with this ancient association, having preached among them since I was sixteen years old.

Two years after the Smith's Creek church was constituted, Anderson Moffett became its pastor. Moffett also began preaching at the early age of seventeen. I was standing in the church parsonage, some two miles west of New Market, when I looked across a field and exclaimed to the pastor, Nelson Pettit, "Elder Anderson Moffett and his wife Barbara are buried in that little grave plot that is overgrown with sassafras, locust, sage, and briars." My reading had described the place of their burial, and upon investigation the next morning, we found the proof of my speculation as we read the following upon a large stone placed over the grave: "In the memory of the many virtues of Anderson Moffett who was for upwards of 70 years a pious minister of the Regular Baptist Denomination, and for more than 50 years pastor of Smith's Creek Church. Born in

Fauquier August 28th, 1746, and died in Rockingham County, Virginia, May 14th, 1835.''

The sad part of this report is that Anderson Moffett was among those faithful ministers who resided in the Culpeper jail with others of our forefathers when the enemies of the gospel of God's grace were raging against those who proclaimed it. Records of Moffett's life and imprisonment were destroyed by fire after he had become so feeble with age that he could not recall them for posterity.[1] This faithful servant's grave, along with many others commemorating Baptists who planted churches across the land and paid the price through their sufferings for our freedom and were largely responsible for our Bill of Rights, is desecrated with weeds and brush. Even more alarming, we are losing these memorials of our sacred Baptist heritage for future generations. These faithful servants of God established and preserved the great heritage of liberty and truth we enjoy today. They are worthy to be memorialized, and our posterity deserves the memory and the principles for which they stood and suffered. May our Lord raise up a host of faithful people to help preserve these important landmarks. ''Remove not the ancient landmark, which thy fathers have set'' (Prov. 22:28).

EWT

---

[1]Lewis Peyton Little, *Imprisoned Preachers and Religious Liberty in Virginia* (Lynchburg, Va.: J. P. Bell Co., 1938), pp. 428-34.

May 15—A Prison, a Pistol, and a Preacher

Scripture: Psalm 64

Elder John Tanner appears to have begun his ministerial career in Halifax County, North Carolina, as early as 1773, having planted a small assembly of believers in Rocky Swamp. He also carried out an itinerant ministry which took him to Chesterfield County, Virginia, where he ran into conflict with the ecclesiastical and civil authorities. There was a Colonel Achibald Cary who seemed to take pleasure in apprehending and imprisoning Baptist preachers. John Tanner on May 15, 1773, ''did on his examination confess that he has divers times convened numbers of people in this County and more particular on this day did convene numbers and preach to them in this County, not being qualified by law so to do, which is contrary to law and tends to disturb the peace and good government of this colony."[1]

One can clearly see by this example that there were no definite laws forbidding preaching the gospel in the colony and that the enemies of the gospel of God's grace, such as Colonel Cary, had to use terms such as *disturbing the peace* and *vagrancy* to apprehend and imprison God's servants.

Tanner encountered other perils during the course of his ministry. A certain woman in the town of Windsor, North Carolina, was converted to Christ under the ministry of Elder Dargan, applied for baptism and church membership, and was received. Her husband, a great persecutor of the Baptists, was violently opposed to her baptism and threatened that if any man baptized his wife he would shoot him. Accordingly, baptism was deferred for some considerable time. Elder Dargan, being an infirm man, often asked visiting ministers to baptize for him. John Tanner, being present at a meeting, was asked by Elder Dargan to baptize Sister Dawson which Tanner proceeded to do. "Whether Elder Tanner was apprised of Dawson's threatenings or not; or whether he thought it was his duty to obey God rather than man, we are unable to say; but so it was he baptized Sister Dawson."[2]

At a later date, Mr. Dawson heard that Tanner was scheduled to preach at Sandy Run Meeting House and lay in wait for him. He shot Tanner with a horseman's large pistol at close range, sending seventeen shots into his thigh. Tanner lay in a nearby house for several weeks near death, but God in His grace spared the preacher's life. Dawson, fearing Tanner would die, sent a doctor up to attend him. Tanner never sought for any legal redress against Dawson but considered his wounds persecution for Christ's sake.

Tanner later moved to Kentucky where he planted Tates Creek Church in Madison County. Later he relocated in Fayette County and then on to Shelby County. He concluded his ministry in Missouri. Like the apostles of the New Testament, who were "scattered abroad," Tanner went everywhere preaching Christ and establishing churches. May we ever be grateful for these early missionaries who endured the rigors and perils of pioneering and the fires of persecution to spread the gospel of Jesus Christ throughout the land.

EWT

---

[1]Lewis Peyton Little, *Imprisoned Preachers and Religious Liberty in Virginia* (Lynchburg, Va.: J. P. Bell Co., 1938), p. 334.

[2]Ibid., p. 337.

May 16—The Young Orator Who Made Good

Scripture: Colossians 3:22-24

When the Southern Baptist Convention met in Washington, D.C., in 1920, no auditorium could be found that was large enough to accommodate all who wanted to hear George W. Truett. Thus it was that on May 16, 1920,

> he spoke from the steps of the nation's Capitol to more than fifteen thousand, including members of both houses of the Congress, army and navy officials, Supreme Court justices, editors, and citizens in every field of endeavor. . . . He chose for his subject "Religious Freedom." Immediately the vast throng perceived that this supreme orator was not trying to beguile them by some wizardry of language in behalf of his sect, but speaking as they would have him speak for all Americans—for what the founders struggled for and bequeathed to mankind . . . a free church in a free state.[1]

George W. Truett was surely one of the greatest orators that America ever produced. We have already examined the experience that God allowed in his life to fashion him into such a great preacher of the gospel (cf. February 9), but from his youth, he was obviously a gifted young man.

In 1888, young Truett attended the Georgia Baptist Convention. He was awed at the large gathering of "messengers" in the big county courtroom. He was hidden from view in the rear of the auditorium as one of the messengers presented the merits of Mercer University to the Convention. In the midst of his presentation, Fred McConnell

> paused and said, "Brethren, if you don't believe me [concerning the impact of Mercer upon young students for the ministry], I'll show you. George Truett, come to the platform and tell them!" Looking intently through the audience, he called, "George, where are you?" Disappointed, he said, "I do believe in my soul, the boy has got scared and run off!"
>
> Someone near the door reassured, "Here he is!" and conducting the pale stripling through the jammed aisles, he led him to the front.
>
> Young Truett stood speechless for a moment, then commenced tremblingly: "Ladies and gentlemen, I have never seen such a fine body of people as this before. In truth, I am really scared. My knees are making war on each other, and I hardly know which one of my father's sons I am."

> No longer hesitant, he proceeded "in a voice which has since thrilled millions," reported a biographer. He paid tribute to Mercer in beautiful words, in cadences that balanced commanding thoughts, captivating the audience. Presently men whispered, "Who in the world is this boy? Where did he learn to speak like that?" Onward he sped, upward like an eagle in flight, to tell them of what Christian education was doing.[2]

George Truett knew well the Baptist heritage of the separation of church and state and the tenet of soul liberty. While speaking to hundreds of our military in France in 1918, he said, "As a Baptist, believing in the competency of the individual in all matters of the soul, I would rejoice to see men everywhere voluntarily accept the tenets of my faith, but if by the pressure of the weight of my little finger I could physically coerce every person in the world to become a Baptist, I would withhold the pressure."[3]

May we in our day determine to use what talents God has given us to proclaim the gospel and reiterate our historical Baptist/biblical principles in a day of philosophical fog.

DLC

---

[1]Joseph Martin Dawson, *Baptists and the American Republic* (Nashville: Broadman Press, 1956), pp. 220-21.

[2]Ibid., pp. 213-14.

[3]Ibid., p. 220.

May 17—"Must I Go, and Empty-Handed?"

Scripture: Psalm 126

Charles C. Luther was raised in a godly home and grew up with the influence of a Baptist church in Worcester, Massachusetts, but he was not converted until his senior year of college. Born on May 17, 1847, Luther grew up with a love of journalism. After finishing his college preparatory course, he was employed for two years in that field before entering Brown University, where he graduated in 1871.[1] His intention upon completion of his academic course was to make journalism his vocation for life, and thus for the next five years, he was connected with the newspapers in Springfield, Massachusetts.

Gradually the Lord moved upon Luther's heart, and gifted with a fine voice, he left that field of endeavor. For a year he traveled with

Evangelist S. H. Pratt as a gospel musician. Still, there was a longing in Luther's heart to do more. Soon he found himself preaching, and in a short time he was serving regularly in the field of evangelism, primarily in Massachusetts and Rhode Island, though his ministry also took him to New Hampshire, Connecticut, New York, New Jersey, and Pennsylvania. Luther was in demand, and his meetings resulted in blessed additions of converts in the churches that he serviced.

In 1891 Luther was invited to assume the pastorate of the Baptist church in Bridgeport, Connecticut, where he served faithfully for two years. During his pastorate, he arranged meetings with Evangelist A. G. Upham, and the evangelist chose as his subject, "Stars for Your Crown," or "The Importance of Witnessing."[2] In the sermon Upham referred to a young man who, a month after his salvation, was injured fatally in an accident. As his condition became apparent, the young man was visited in the hospital by a friend who sought to confirm his genuine trust in Christ. The dying young man said, "No, I am not afraid. Jesus saves me now. But, I have not been able to lead even one such as I was, to Christ in the time I have known Him. No, I am not afraid to die; but oh! If I go—must I go and empty-handed?"

The illustration gripped Pastor Luther's heart, and as the evangelist continued his message, the pastor took out a piece of paper and began to write the words, "Must I go, and empty-handed? / Thus my dear Redeemer meet? / Not one day of service give Him, / Lay no trophy at His feet?"

Luther wrote approximately twenty-five sacred songs, and in 1887 he gathered his hymns, along with others, into a printed work entitled "Beautiful Beckoning Hands." But none of his hymns have experienced the wide use of the one alluded to above. In all, he wrote five stanzas to the hymn, and the demanding words of the last stanza call upon every child of God to redeem the time in Christ's service. The words are a fitting challenge today, for he wrote: "O, ye saints, arouse, be earnest, / Up and work while yet 'tis day; / Ere the night of death o'ertake thee, / Strive for souls while still you may." Luther committed the words of this hymn to George C. Stebbins, Baptist hymnologist, who wrote the music. May we allow the Lord to make us fruitful witnesses that we might not be empty-handed!

DLC

---

[1]Henry S. Burrage, *Baptist Hymn Writers and Their Hymns* (Portland, Maine: Thurston and Co., 1883), p. 512.

[2]Alfred B. Smith, *Al Smith's Treasury of Hymn Histories* (Greenville, S.C.: Better Music Publications, 1985), p. 43.

May 18—Missions Is Still the Need of the World!

Scripture: John 4:34-38

The commission of our Lord for His followers to go into all the world and preach the gospel to every creature had not changed, but persecution had made this a virtual impossibility until religious freedom was gained. In America, even after Baptists had experienced such liberty, they were slow to respond to a worldwide vision. Being primarily a rural people, they were content to reach only their immediate vicinity, and thus the true missionary spirit was dormant. Doubtless they knew little about the heathen nations around the world. In the main cities there was a stirring inspired by the accounts of William Carey, and offerings were sent to assist the efforts in India. Gradually a few local foreign mission societies were formed in America, but no concerted national effort was envisioned among the Baptists.

All of this changed dramatically with the conversion of the Judsons and Luther Rice to Baptist views as the Congregational missionaries sailed for India. Rice returned to America to encourage Baptist support of the Judsons, who had written to outstanding Baptist leaders concerning the need. To Thomas Baldwin of Boston, Judson wrote: "Should there be formed a Baptist Society for the support of missions in these parts, I shall be ready to consider myself their missionary."[1] Dr. Baldwin invited pastors of Massachusetts to his home to discuss the matter. The ministers were thrilled and immediately formed "The Baptist Society for Propagating the Gospel in India and other Foreign Parts," but as yet the Baptists had no national body for cooperative action.

Luther Rice met with the Baptist pastors in Boston, and they urged him to visit Baptist pastors throughout the North. He met with the Philadelphia Association, and everywhere he went he met with enthusiasm. Rice traveled into the South, and the response was gratifying. Offerings were being received to assist the Judsons, but still a national society was needed. Rice met William B. Johnson of Savannah and shared with him the vision of a general missionary society which would represent all of the local missionary societies. Dr. Johnson agreed to the proposed plan, and in response to a call for delegates to meet in a central location for discussions of the proposal, twenty-six ministers and seven laymen met on Wednesday, May 18, 1814, in Philadelphia.

The outcome was the formation of "The General Missionary Convention of the Baptist Denomination in the United States of America for Foreign Missions." The Society was to meet triennially and thus came to be called the "Triennial Convention."

The first missionaries of the newly formed society, of course, were Adoniram and Ann Judson, and its first field was Burma. The Judsons had gone to Burma when the East India Company refused to allow work in India. It is interesting to note that it was seven years after Judson left America that he had his first convert, and the Judsons suffered a great deal in establishing the work, but God vindicated the work with many converts in later years. New fields were soon opened, and until the sectional division among Baptists in America, the Lord was pleased to use the "Triennial Convention" as a united Baptist effort to come to terms with the Great Commission. May we in our days lift up our eyes on the fields of the world that are white unto harvest!

DLC

---

[1]Jesse L. Boyd, *A History of Baptists in America Prior to 1845* (New York: American Press, 1957), p. 86.

May 19—Uniformity, Conformity, and Dissent

Scripture: Isaiah 14:1-15

The issue of church/state relationship has its roots in the age-old struggle of Satan and the Caesars of this world system to "ascend above the heights of the clouds" and "be like the most High" (Isa. 14:14). God's will concerning this relationship is clearly set forth by His forbidding a Levite to be a king or anyone of the tribe of Judah to be a priest. Saul was rejected by God when he unlawfully usurped the priest's office and sacrificed to the Lord. Only Jesus Christ, who was after the order of Melchisedec, could rightly serve as priest and king.

After the elections of 1661 in England, the Anglican church dominated Parliament and influenced it to approve a revision of the Anglican Book of Common Prayer. The Act of Uniformity soon followed. It received the royal assent on May 19, 1662, requiring that all ministers should have received episcopal ordination and that, on pain of deprivation of every ecclesiastical office held, each minister must, upon some Lord's Day before the Feast of St. Bartholomew (August 24), publicly assert his "unfeigned assent and consent to all and everything contained and prescribed in and by . . . the Book of Common Prayer." Some seven hundred ministers, whose appointments had been made during the Interregnum, had already been compelled to vacate their livings by various kinds of pressures before this and were joined by one thousand more who felt they were unable to make such declarations.

The Baptists rejected the whole concept of an established church and its methods of appointment and payment even if they were qualified to receive them. Many of the rejected ministers became Baptists. It was estimated that a total of 1,760 ministers were ultimately ejected, many of these because they had given judgment against infant baptism.[1]

The indirect consequence for Baptists was considerable. First, when so many men and their congregations left the established church, it meant that Dissent, as a body, was now more likely to survive than if it had been reduced to a few Independents, Baptists, and Quakers. Secondly, a number of the ejected ministers and their people, in considering the whole question of their convictions, themselves became Baptists. This led to the founding of a number of new Baptist churches during the time of persecution.

The Act of Uniformity emphasized that the government envisaged one church with no alternative forms of worship, even if they were self-supporting and receiving no financial help from the government. During this period people were arrested "for either non-attendance at their parish church" or "for maliciously and seditiously assembling in unlawful conventicles under pretence of religion."[2]

Persecution was patchy depending on local personalities and relationships. In some places it is amazing that congregations survived at all, but it is clear that neither in the central government nor in local circumstances was there a consistent will to root out all dissent. The sentences ranged from fines, to imprisonment, to exile, and to threats of execution.

Our religious liberty did not come overnight but is the fruit we enjoy after centuries of struggle and suffering. May we cherish it and be militant to stand against all legislation that would limit our freedom of conscience and promote a church-state or a state-church.

EWT

---

[1]B. R. White, *A History of the English Baptists* (n.p.: American Baptist Historical Society, n.d.), 1:102-3.

[2]Ibid. p. 104.

May 20—George Leile: From Man's Slave to God's Slave

Scripture: Psalm 116:16-19

A previous entry mentions George Leile, America's first missionary (January 20). Leile was born in Virginia, probably about 1750, and was a slave of Deacon Henry Sharp. Leile was saved during his youth and early showed both an interest in and an aptitude for preaching.[1] When Deacon Sharp moved to Burke County, Georgia, a few years before the Revolutionary War, Leile, of course, accompanied him there. Married in early adulthood, Leile and his wife had three sons and a daughter. Sharp was a considerate master and soon emancipated Leile that he might give full time to preaching the gospel.[2] Apparently, Henry Sharp's family did not concur with his action in freeing Leile, for after Sharp's death, his heirs sought to re-enslave Leile, who then fled to the British for protection.[3] This was a natural thing for him to do, for his concern for freedom from slavery fired his support of the British during the Revolutionary War.[4]

Ordained on May 20, 1775, Leile labored around the Savannah area with much success during the Revolutionary War,[5] but at the conclusion of the conflict, he borrowed seven hundred dollars to move his family out of the reach of the Sharp heirs. Going to Jamaica as the indentured servant of Colonel Kirkland, an English officer, he was employed by the governor of the island, General Campbell. He worked and in a year paid his indebtedness and was given his certificate of manumission and launched into his ministry in Jamaica. Leile was a fiery preacher, and with four men who had emigrated from America, he began the first black Baptist church on the island. Soon strong opposition was experienced from the established Church of England. His meetings were often interrupted, and he was cruelly persecuted. Once he was imprisoned and charged with preaching "sedition," which was a capital offense under the law. He and several of his companions were tried for their lives. He barely escaped the death penalty, but another companion-preacher was hanged.[6]

This surely would have been enough to have discouraged others, but not George Leile! In a few years the church had grown to five hundred members, and Leile trained his men to carry the work out into the rural areas. With the help of influential friends, funds were secured from England, and a permanent building was erected to serve the congregation. Leile had arrived in Jamaica in 1783, and in 1842 more than fifty missionaries were sent from the island to minister in Africa. Thus, George Leile was not only the first missionary to leave the shores of America, but he was the first of his race to send missionaries back to his native land.

George Leile died in 1828, but his lasting contribution to the gospel was acknowledged in 1916, as contributions from Africa and almost every state in the United States provided funds for the erection of a monument in the yard of the First Bryan Baptist Church in Savannah, Georgia. George Leile was indeed an unusual man who was possessed with an overwhelming desire to serve his Savior.

DLC

---

[1]H. Leon McBeth, *The Baptist Heritage* (Nashville: Broadman Press, 1987), p. 779.

[2]Davis Collier Woolley, *Baptist Advance* (Nashville: Broadman Press, 1964), p. 193.

[3]McBeth, p. 779.

[4]Robert G. Gardner, *A History of the Georgia Baptist Association, 1784–1984* (Georgia Baptist Historical Society, 1988), p. 16.

[5]Ibid., p. 194.

[6]Jesse L. Boyd, *A History of Baptists in America Prior to 1845* (New York: American Press, 1957), p. 148.

May 21—A Good Man with a Good Testimony

Scripture: I Timothy 3:1-7

In the annals of history there are great men of God of whom there is very little said or written, and so it was with Elisha Callender. He was as Enoch in testimony, who ‘‘was translated that he should not see death; and was not found, because God had translated him: for before his translation he had this testimony, that he pleased God’’ (Heb. 11:5). Callender was not translated, but he ‘‘pleased God’’ and was as those unnamed witnesses ‘‘(of whom the world was not worthy:) they wandered in deserts, and in mountains, and in dens and caves of the earth’’ (Heb. 11:38).

The little that is said of Callender indicates that he was of a family of the faith that generated something in the world in which they lived. He was the son of Ellis Callender, the pastor of the Baptist church in

Boston, and uncle of John Callender and John Comer, outstanding preachers of Rhode Island. It is a well-known principle that a godly line is generated and established as a testimony to an ungodly world. And "he being dead yet speaketh" (Heb. 11:4).

Elisha Callender was of the Harvard graduating class of 1710 and was the first native Baptist preacher in this country who had received a college education.[1] This was the college from which Henry Dunster was forced to resign when he embraced Baptist principles in the rejection of infant baptism and of the right of the secular powers to interfere in religious affairs.

Elisha Callender was ordained May 21, 1718.[2] By this time the spirituality and testimony of the Baptists had so commended them to the respect of the better portion of the community that the three principal clergymen in Boston—Increase Mather, Cotton Mather, and John Webb—not only consented to be present at his ordination but Mr. Mather most cheerfully preached the ordination sermon. He selected as his subject "Good Men United," and before the whole colony, he condemned the "wholesale severities," which he called "cruel wrath," and said, "New England also has, in some former times, done something of this aspect, which would not now be so well approved of, in which if the brethren in whose house we are now convened met with anything too unbrotherly, they now with satisfaction hear us expressing our dislike of everything that has looked like persecution in the days that have passed over us."[3]

Spiritual prosperity attended Callender's ministry as pastor of the church in Boston. Scarcely did a month pass without some professions of faith. In his twentieth year of ministry, he was cut down by death. It was through the testimony of men like Elisha Callender that by 1729 the bitterness of the General Court of Massachusetts against the Baptists relaxed to the point that they were exempt from paying parish ministerial taxes if they alleged a scruple of conscience in the matter.

May God give us pastoral leadership that will "have a good report of them which are without" (I Tim. 3:7).

EWT

---

[1]William Cathcart, *The Baptist Encyclopedia,* ed. Louis H. Everts (Philadelphia: Louis H. Everts, 1881), 2:177.

[2]Thomas Armitage, *The History of the Baptists* (1890; reprint ed., Watertown, Wis.: Maranatha Baptist Press, 1976), 2:718.

[3]Ibid.

May 22—A Historian Who Made History

Scripture: II Peter 1:10-14

On a tombstone in the burial ground of Nonconformists in London called "Bunhill Fields," one can find these words:

> Here lies interred the mortal remains of the Rev. Joseph Ivimey, in his lifetime the respected pastor of the Baptist Church, which met in Eagle Street, Red Lion Square, for upwards of 29 years. He departed this life on the 8th day of February, 1834, aged 60 years.
>
> "GRACE REIGNS."

Joseph Ivimey was born at Ringwood, England, on May 22, 1773, into a family of eight children. Being the oldest, he was early taught the trade of a tailor, and his education was limited. The family's religious instruction was minimal, and that which he received was of an Arian nature. While still in his youth, he was assigned to an uncle, and for the first time in his young life he heard the gospel clearly preached. Though still in a state of spiritual confusion, he had a desire to hear the gospel faithfully preached, and he often walked nine miles with two friends to Wimbourne, England, for that privilege.

In 1794 young Ivimey moved to Portsea, and "he became a member of the Baptist church in that town, which was under the pastoral care of Mr. Daniel Miall."[1] Soon he was persuaded to try village preaching, and though his own evaluation of his efforts was not too pleasing, apparently others thought differently. In a short time he was called to assist Mr. Lovegrove, pastor in Wallingford. "But receiving an invitation from the Baptist church at Eagle Street, London, to preach for three Lord's days, he acceded to the request."[2] He was called by that congregation and was ordained on January 16, 1805. As his tombstone reminds us, for the next twenty-nine years he led "the forces of the Baptist denomination. Joseph Ivimey's services can hardly be overestimated. For many years he was the moving spirit in the London Churches."[3] He authored the four-volume *History of the English Baptist,* which is considered the finest of its kind. His literary work was done while he was suffering from extreme bodily weakness caused by asthma and other difficulties.

Pastor Ivimey encouraged many young men to consider Christian service. In the arena of religious freedom, Ivimey was at the fore. He never feared controversy and was known for his appearance in the House of Lords.

As his physical condition worsened, Ivimey thought and talked a great deal about heaven. He preached his last sermon on December 8, 1833, and his text was: "I know Whom I have believed, and am persuaded that He is able to keep that which I have committed unto Him against that day." As death approached, his mind was calm, and when the words, "And the blood of Jesus Christ cleanseth us from all sin," were read, he cried, "Ah! that is it! There's the foundation, there's my hope." His last request was to be raised up. Then, looking at his wife, his dying words were, "It's all over."

"In his will he had stated his wishes with respect to his funeral, in the following words, 'I desire to be buried in my family grave in Bunhill Fields, and that on the head-stone, after my name and date, there be added, and that only, GRACE REIGNS.' "[4]

The pastor/historian thus passed into the presence of His Lord with great peace and assurance of faith!

DLC

---

[1]John C. Carlile, *The Story of the English Baptists* (London: James Clarke and Co., 1905), p. 215.

[2]Alfred W. Light, *Bunhill Fields* (London: C. J. Farncombe and Sons, 1915), p. 113.

[3]Carlile, p. 216.

[4]Light, p. 117.

May 23—To Lay on Hands, or Not to Lay on Hands

Scripture: Hebrews 6

Some of God's choice servants live long and useful lives, and we find much material that describes in detail their accomplishments and adventures as they sojourned through this life. There were others who were just as godly and effective whose lives are not recorded in the annals of men because in the providential will of God their journey came to a quick and abrupt end early in life. We can be assured their deeds and faithfulness are recorded in heaven.

An exception to this rule is John Comer, who lived a few months shy of thirty years. Usually we have a record of such men because they kept a journal of their activities that was preserved by their families. Thus it was with John Comer.

After his conversion experience, which will be addressed at a later date in this volume, Comer adopted the sentiments of the Baptists and was baptized by the renowned Elisha Callender, who was pastor of the Baptist church in Boston. Soon after uniting with this church, he began preaching in 1725.

It appears to have been the practice of these early Baptists in America to place a young preacher with a reputable, older, experienced man. This was the case of Comer, and he was ordained co-pastor with Elder William Peckham of the Newport Church.

Here his ministry was short and effective, but we receive some insight into the practices and controversies that prevailed among the churches of his time. As we have seen in England, many of the Baptist churches had no congregational singing. This was also true at the Newport Church until Comer introduced singing as a part of their services. For a while the cause of their not singing had probably been the persecution that forced the believers into hiding, because singing would have revealed their secret meeting places. Soon no singing became a practice, persecution or no persecution, and singing was considered unspiritual by some.

The practice of the laying on of hands after baptism was adhered to by some congregations, and others were divided relative to this practice. The so-called Six Principle Baptists held tenaciously to the laying on of hands. The Newport Church no longer used this mode of initiation of newly baptized members into full fellowship of the church. Comer's attempt to have it uniformly observed was the cause of his dismissal from this pastoral charge in 1729.

Comer then preached as a supply for two years in the Second Baptist Church in Newport, after which he became the pastor of a church of his own order in the southern part of Old Rehoboth, near to Swansea, about ten miles from Providence, Rhode Island. Here he died of the dreaded disease of consumption (tuberculosis) on May 23, 1734.[1] He was a gentleman of education, of piety, and of great success in his calling. During his brief life, Comer collected a large body of facts, intending at some future time to write the history of the early American Baptist churches. His records became a source of blessing to others in their research to preserve such histories.

EWT

---

[1]William P. Sprague, *Annals of the American Pulpit* (New York: Robert Carter and Bros., 1865), p. 42.

May 24—A Preacher Who Was Worth $170

Scripture: Acts 20:17-24

We have already mentioned the baptism of James Lemen, his wife, and two others by Elder Dodge of Kentucky in 1794. "James Lemen, Sr., his wife and several of his neighbors, having been converted to the Baptist faith by an itinerant preacher from Kentucky, organized themselves into a Baptist church at a meeting held in the south room (of Lemen's home) on May 24, 1796."[1]

Lemen, who had served as an American soldier in the Revolutionary War, arrived in Illinois in 1786, having come from Virginia. Soon he and his family were introduced to the sterner side of frontier life. "The very summer of their arrival Mrs. Lemen's sister and her husband, James Andrews, were killed by the Indians, and their two little daughters carried captive to Prairie du Chien, Wisconsin. There one died. The other, a reward being offered, was recovered through French traders. Tragedies like this were frequent for several years. In two years, 1789-90, one-tenth of the total American population perished by Indian wars and murders."[2]

It was into that environment that James Smith, a Separate Baptist preacher from Kentucky, went with the gospel in 1787. Smith was "the first evangelical minister to visit Illinois."[3] In 1790 Elder Smith entered Illinois again to preach the gospel, and a number of people were converted under his ministry.

> In the midst of the work Elder Smith was captured by the Indians. In the party was a Mrs. Huff . . . with her little child. She had been under spiritual concern for some time, and while the savages were putting her to death Elder Smith fell on his knees praying for her, and in that attitude he was taken. On this account, and because of his praying and singing while they traveled, the Indians were afraid of him. He was taken to Vincennes, from whence word came through the traders . . . that he would be returned for a suitable ransom.[4]

"So much was he esteemed by the few poor settlers, among whom he had preached, that they raised $170, with which they ransomed him and returned him to his friends in Kentucky."[5]

One historian tells us that Elder James Smith returned to preach again in Illinois. These frontier Baptist preachers fearlessly answered the call of God, and they were amazing men. One of Elder Smith's sons was later elected the governor of Texas. Apparently, Smith did not preach merely to the emotions, for the converts continued on in the ways of the Lord. Family altars were established in the homes of the converts, and this resulted in a large number of preachers going out from that area to preach the gospel. In the absence of the ministry of regular preachers, the male converts directed their own services, led in prayer, and exhorted, explaining the portion of the Bible as they read.

We must also observe that in the house that cradled the first Baptist church in Illinois, the battle of slavery in the northwest territory was also fought. James Lemen, Sr., prepared a petition that was circulated among the pioneers and was successful in opposing the efforts of William Henry Harrison, then the governor of the Northwest Territory, who desired to introduce slavery into the section. We honor the memory of James Smith and the pioneer Baptist preachers who were willing to spend and be spent for the gospel!

DLC

---

[1]J. F. Breen, "The House of Genesis," *The Baptist,* 4 Feb. 1920, p. 442.

[2]Edward P. Brand, *Illinois Baptists: A History* (Bloomington, Ill.: Pantagraph Printing, 1930), pp. 20-21.

[3]William Cathcart, *The Baptist Encyclopedia,* ed. Louis H. Everts (Philadelphia: Louis H. Everts, 1881), 2:683.

[4]Brand, p. 22.

[5]J. H. Spencer, *A History of Kentucky Baptists from 1769 to 1885* (Cincinnati: J. R. Baumes, 1886), 2:86-87.

May 25—The Reuniting of God's Martyrs

Scripture: Psalm 66

Michael Sattler was born in Germany around 1490. At an early age he entered the Benedictine Monastery and attended lectures at a local university. It was at this time that he obtained a knowledge of the Greek and Hebrew languages. During his stay in the monastery, he began a study of the Pauline Epistles and embraced the evangelical faith. His dissatisfaction with the vice and hypocrisy of his fellow monks precipitated a severance of all ties to the Church of Rome.

Ferdinand of Austria announced a policy of heresy extermination which forced Sattler and his wife, whom he had married upon leaving the monastery, to flee to Switzerland. There he came under the influence of Wilhelm Reublin and became an Anabaptist. He soon became a prominent preacher and leader among the Anabaptists and held clandestine meetings in the forests. These meetings were soon discovered, and Sattler was expelled from Zurich.

After a brief stay among the Reformers in Strassburg, Austria, where Sattler attempted unsuccessfully to win some of their leaders to Baptist principles, he returned to Horb, Germany, at the invitation of Reublin. He preached at a conference of Anabaptists at Schleitheim, where a confession of faith, which he probably wrote, was approved. This Schleitheim Confession was not a doctrinal formulation but articles in the nature of a church manual. An implied theology was present in this work. There were articles concerning baptism, communion, discipline, the sword, and relationships to government.

While the Schleitheim meeting was in progress, the Anabaptists were discovered by the authorities in Rottenburg. Sattler, his wife, and others were arrested upon their return to Horb. Finding the Schleitheim Confession and other documents in Sattler's possession, the church-state authorities immediately saw the importance of this man. He was moved to the tower of Binsdorf. Anticipating his execution, he wrote a deeply moving letter of consolation to his beloved congregation.

When the trial began, fourteen defendants sat on the bench of the accused, and Sattler was their spokesman. "The judges laughed at his discourse, and after consultation, the town clerk of Ensesheim said: 'Oh you infamous, desperate villain and monk, you would have us engage with you in a discussion! The executioner will dispute with you, we think for a certainty.' Sattler exclaimed, 'Let the will of God be done.' "[1]

Execution took place on May 25, 1527.[2] It began at the marketplace, where a piece was cut from Sattler's tongue. Pieces of flesh were torn from his body with red-hot tongs. The tongs were applied five times more on the way to the execution. Still able to speak, Sattler prayed for his persecutors. After being bound by a rope to a ladder and pushed into the fire, he admonished the people, the judges, and the mayor to repent and be converted. Then he prayed, "Almighty God, Thou art the Way and the Truth: because I have not been shown to be in error, I will with thy help this day testify to the truth and seal it with my blood."[3]

As soon as the ropes burned and released his hands, he raised the two forefingers of his hands, giving the promised signal that a martyr's death was bearable, and exclaimed, "Father, I commend my spirit into Thy hands."

After every attempt to secure a recantation from his faithful wife failed, she was drowned eight days later and was reunited with her husband in the presence of their Lord.

EWT

---

[1]William R. Estep, *The Anabaptist Story* (Nashville: Broadman Press, 1963), p. 43.

[2]Joseph Meyer, *Baptist Establishers of Religious Liberty* (Chicago: Published by the author, 1923), p. 108.

[3]Estep, p. 44.

May 26—The Bold Preacher Who Fled Fast

Scripture: II Samuel 21:10-14

Toliver Craig and his wife, of Orange County, Virginia, were the parents of three sons who became Baptist preachers. They had very effective ministries in the area surrounding their home. David Thomas, the Regular Baptist, and Samuel Harriss and James Read, the Separate Baptists, had introduced the gospel of the grace of God into their community. It was not long until the Craig family became flaming evangels, preaching the Word of God everywhere and anytime they had opportunity.

As a result of this zeal, the sons Elijah and Lewis Craig found themselves in the county jail. Elijah was incarcerated four times, twice each in Culpeper and Orange County jails. Lewis was imprisoned only twice, once in Caroline County and once in Spotsylvania County, although he was arrested four times.[1] These imprisonments were for preaching the gospel of the Son of God without state-church ordination or state licensure, although they were charged with being vagrants, strollers, or disturbers of the peace.

These brothers probably appeared eccentric in their day, but their younger brother, Joseph, was a very unusual man. He was a man of small stature, stooping shoulders, and hardy complexion. He was very active in business and persevered as a traveling preacher. There is a court record in Orange County Court House dated May 26, 1768, charging him and several others with absenting themselves from the parish church.[2] This may have been due to his conversion experience prior to that date and his presence at Baptist meetings. In spite of several charges against him, to our knowledge he never saw the inside of a jail, doubtless due to the fact that he was a fast runner. John Taylor in his biographical sketches states,

> I will name a few instances of his singularity. I do not recollect, though a zealous preacher, that his persecutors ever got him into prison, he had a method to baffle them. He was once preaching at a place (Guinea Bridge Church), and the officers came after him; stepping out at a back door, he ran into a swamp supposing he was safe, but they took his track with a gang of dogs; to evade the dogs he betook himself to a tree, from which his pursuers shook him down, as if he were a wild beast, and demanded his going with them to Court. After reasoning with them a while, he refused to go; but they forced him on a horse, and perhaps tied his hands. On his way he reasoned thus: 'God's men ought not go to prison. I will have no hand in it—' and threw himself off the horse, and would neither ride nor walk; behaving perhaps (like a mad man) as David did, before Achish, King of Gath.—I Samuel 21:10. They let him go.[3]

Joseph assisted his brother Lewis in the pastorate at Upper Spotsylvania and Fredericksburg, Virginia, while also carrying out his ministry as an itinerant preacher with good success. The Word of God grew mightily among them. In 1781 he and his brother Lewis led between five and six hundred people across the mountains into Kentucky. Two hundred of these people were members of their own Baptist church. The preachers and people went in this mass migration as a "traveling church." After stopping at several places in Kentucky, they finally settled at South Elkton, where they established the first Baptist church in Kentucky. This action surely accounts for the temporary ceasing of the organized ministry of the Upper Branch and Fredericksburg Branch of the Upper Spotsylvania Baptist Church in Virginia.

EWT

---

[1]Lewis Peyton Little, *Imprisoned Preachers and Religious Liberty in Virginia* (Lynchburg, Va.: J. P. Bell Co., 1938), pp. 516-17.

[2]Oscar H. Darter, *The History of Fredericksburg Baptist Church* (Richmond: Garrett and Massie, 1960), pp. 44-45.

[3]Ibid., p. 45.

May 27—The Birth of a Baby Planted a Church

Scripture: Luke 1:1-17

There is abundant proof that, in many thoughtful minds, serious doubts had arisen among the Congregationalists of Massachusetts concerning the scriptural authority for infant baptism and the right of the secular power to interfere in religious affairs. Henry Dunster, who had been compelled to resign his presidency of Harvard College and was publicly admonished and put under bonds, had done much to bring about this thoughtfulness.

Dunster had great influence on the mind of Thomas Gould, a member of the Congregational Church of Charlestown. When a son was born into his home, Gould called his neighbors in to rejoice with him and to unite in thanks to God for this precious gift. He withheld the child from baptism and was summoned to appear before the church to answer why the child had not been sprinkled. He still refused to comply and was suspended from Communion. He was repeatedly brought before the Middlesex Court on charges relating to the "ordinance of Christ."

On March 3, 1668, Gould was brought before the Court of Assistants in Boston. The court, concluding that fines and imprisonments did nothing to win him and having a wholesome dread of repeating the Holmes whipping experiment, decided to belittle Gould and company by a free and public debate on the grounds of their practice. "Whether it be justifiable by the Word of God for these persons and their company to depart from the communion of these churches, and set up an assembly here in the way of Anabaptism, and whether such a practice is to be allowed by the government of this jurisdiction?"

Gould was to inform his Baptist brethren to appear, and the Baptist Church at Newport sent a delegation of three to assist their brethren in the debate. After two days of denunciation of the Baptists, who were not allowed to reply, the authorities claimed a victory. Gould was sentenced to exile from Massachusetts on May 27, 1668.[1]

These and other Baptists were forbidden again and again to hold meetings. The General Court took this action because of the pressure by elders of the state church. In an address from the state church convention April 30, 1668, the elders stated, "Touching the case of those that set up an assembly here in the way of Anabaptism . . . it belongs to the Civil Magistrates to restrain and suppress these open enormities in religion."[2]

After a long contest, the struggling young Baptist church, which had been first organized in Charlestown and then moved to Noddle's Island, ventured to relocate in Boston. There they quietly built a small meeting-house only to have the authorities nail it shut for a number of years.

The Baptist church in Boston was planted in the midst of great debate, turmoil, and persecution that began with the birth of a child. Some great ministries have had small beginnings and have struggled for decades in toil and suffering with the founders never realizing the full blessing of their labors.

EWT

---

[1]Gordon Carruth, ed., *Encyclopedia of American Facts and Dates* (New York: Thomas W. Crowell Co., 1956), p. 27.

[2]Thomas Armitage, *The History of the Baptists* (1890; reprint ed., Watertown, Wis.: Maranatha Baptist Press, 1976), 2:699-702.

May 28—A Ferocious Foe, a Fearless Woman, and a Fainting Wife

Scripture: Acts 9:20-25

Early Baptist pioneer preachers often paid a severe price in carrying the gospel into new areas. This was surely true when the gospel was introduced in "Natchez Country" in Mississippi. After a harrowing trip from South Carolina, a small group of emigrants made their way down the Tennessee River in three boats and were attacked by Cherokee Indians. The last boat was boarded by the Indians, and all but one passenger was slain.

Those in the first two boats succeeded in making it to the mouth of Cole's Creek, about twenty miles north of Natchez, and settled about ten miles from the Tennessee River. Among the group was Richard Curtis, Jr., who had been born in Virginia on May 28, 1756. A licensed Baptist preacher, he began ministering in the settlement, and in 1791 the Salem Baptist Church was established. The community grew, sinners came to know Christ and desired to be baptized and unite with the church, but Pastor Curtis was not ordained. It was felt advisable to correspond with the parent church in South Carolina for direction. The answer finally arrived, "That there was no law against necessity, and under the present stress of circumstances the members ought to assemble and formally appoint one of their number, by election, to baptize the converts."[1] This was done, and the work went forward without an ordained minister.

"Manuel de Lemos Gayoso, the Spanish Governor of the Natchez District (1789-1797) and Governor of Louisiana until his death" ruled the land, and religious freedom was unknown.[2] The Baptists worshipped secretly until one, Stephen De Alvo, was saved. He renounced Catholicism and united with the Baptists. This resulted in stringent persecution of the Baptists and an order from Gayoso that the Baptists "desist from their heretical psalm-singing, praying, and preaching in public or they would be subjected to sundry pains and penalties." In August of 1795, Gayoso sent his militia to arrest Curtis and to deport him to the mines in Mexico to work the rest of his life. Sentries had been posted by the Baptists, and warning was given in time for Curtis, Bill Hamberlin, and Steve De Alvo to escape and hide. The officer threatened the remainder that anyone aiding in the concealment or escape of the three men would themselves suffer banishment to the Mexican mines.

There was nothing for the three men to do but to leave the Natchez Country. The men of the church were reluctant to take supplies to the place of concealment, but a bold lady, Cloe Holt, volunteered for the dangerous mission and was completely successful. After the tedious trip, the men arrived at Great Pedee, South Carolina, and in time Richard Curtis was ordained. In the "Natchez Country" the Baptists continued their secret services. When the territory passed under the control of Georgia and was recognized as United States property, Curtis and his companions returned with joyful hearts. Curtis's wife, not knowing of his return, fainted when she saw him standing in the pulpit to preach. Richard Curtis "helped in the organization of the first association . . . in 1806 and attended the association for the last time Oct. 19, 1811, a few days before his death."[3] A marble monument stands in the cemetery of the Ebenezer Church near Beaver Creek as a reminder of this pioneer Baptist hero.

DLC

---

[1]John T. Christian, *A History of the Baptists* (1922; reprint ed., Nashville: Broadman Press, 1926), 1:334.

[2]Dan and Inez Morris, *Who Was Who in American Politics* (New York: Hawthorn Books, 1974), p. 257.

[3]Norman Wade Cox, ed., *Encyclopedia of Southern Baptists* (Nashville: Broadman Press, 1958), 1:344.

May 29—A Hostile Investigation Produced an Ordination

Scripture: III John

Early in life, John Gano professed conversion to Christ and was strongly inclined to unite with the Presbyterian church; but doubting the scriptural authority for infant baptism, he entered into an elaborate investigation of the subject. He read many books and had many conversations with Presbyterian ministers, only to become more and more convinced of the truth of Baptist principles. He had an extensive conversation with the renowned Gilbert Tennent, who at the close of the interview said, "Dear young man, if the Devil cannot destroy your soul he will endeavor to destroy your comfort and usefulness, and therefore, do not always be doubting in this matter. If you cannot think as I do, think for yourself."

Sometime after this, having obtained permission from his father, who was Presbyterian, he was baptized and united with the Baptist church at Hopewell, New Jersey.[1]

Soon after he was baptized, Gano became much exercised in mind about preaching Christ to dying sinners. One morning after he began plowing in his field, the words, "Warn the people, or their blood will I require at your hands," came to him with such force that he became insensible to his work. When he came to his senses, he was wet with rain, and the horses were greatly fatigued. Under this burden of God's calling, he applied himself to study in preparation to enter upon his duty. Before being licensed to preach, he accompanied David Thomas and Benjamin Miller on a missionary tour of Virginia. Their principal mission was to set in order a small church on Opecon Creek which was in a deplorable condition. The church had only three members able to give an account of their conversion. On this occasion Gano exhorted and taught some of the people. Upon returning home, his church called him to account for preaching without license but before proceeding to condemn him, they requested that he preach there to them. His preaching so favorably impressed the congregation that they called for his ordination which took place on May 29, 1754.[2]

Sometime later he was sent by the Philadelphia Association to the South as a missionary. His journey took him as far as Charleston, South Carolina, where he preached for Mr. Oliver Hart. In his journal Gano wrote of the service: "When I arose to speak, the sight of so brilliant an audience, among whom were twelve ministers and one of whom was Mr. George Whitefield, for a moment brought the fear of man upon me; but, blessed be the Lord! I was soon relieved of this embarrassment. The thought passed my mind, I had none to fear and obey but the Lord."[3]

Gano traveled on numerous occasions into the South, where he carried out a ministry of encouraging pastors, assisting in planting churches, and fervently evangelizing. Wherever he preached, he recorded the events of his ministry as well as the rise, progress, and spiritual welfare of the Baptists. Fortunately, John Gano's journal has given rich insights into the Baptist ministry during the Revolutionary War.

EWT

---

[1]J. H. Spencer, *A History of Kentucky Baptists from 1769 to 1885* (Cincinnati: J. R. Baumes, 1886), 1:117.

[2]Thomas Armitage, *The History of the Baptists* (1890; reprint ed., Watertown, Wis.: Maranatha Baptist Press, 1976), 2:753.

[3]Ibid., p. 754

May 30—A Chaplain Challenges the Command

Scripture: Daniel 1:8-21

Thomas B. Montanye was seventeen years of age when he was saved and then baptized by the Reverend John Gano in the First Baptist Church of New York City. Soon after the teen-ager was saved, his sister followed his pathway, and this greatly disturbed their father, for Benjamin Montanye was a very active member in the Dutch Reformed Church of that city. The result of the conversion of these youths to the Baptist persuasion forced Mr. Montanye to a new examination of baptism in the New Testament, and in time he too was immersed and became a Baptist. In fact, Benjamin Montanye was soon called to preach, and after helping in the organization of a Baptist church in the city, he accepted the call to a church in Deer Park, New York, and continued there in the pastorate until his death in his eighty-third year.

In the meantime, young Thomas Montanye also revealed the gift of preaching. In his nineteenth year he was ordained as pastor of the Baptist church in Warwick, New Jersey, where he served for more than twelve years. His preaching was powerful, and the work flourished. In one year alone, more than a hundred and fifty were added to the membership of the church. During this period, the Reverend Mr. Montanye served in various offices of the Warwick Baptist Association, as is revealed in the minutes of that organization for May 30, 1797. His abilities and successes attracted the attention of others, and in 1801 he was called to the church in Southampton in Bucks County, Pennsylvania, where he served until his death on September 27, 1829.

When the War of 1812 broke out with Great Britain, Montanye received a chaplain's commission. On one occasion, "a general drill and review of the army had been ordered for the morning of the Sabbath, at the same hour when preaching had hitherto been the 'order of the day.' " He went to "the quarters of the General in command and stated to him, in a dignified and courteous manner, that he held a commission from his country, and also from his God; that, by virtue of his latter commission, he was superior in command on the Sabbath to any of the military; that the general order for a review would interfere with orders from a higher source; and that, consequently, the review could not and must not take place.''[1] The Word of God was honored and the review postponed.

Montanye had possessed a strong physical constitution until 1829, when he suffered an attack of jaundice. In July he seemed to improve somewhat, but soon his condition worsened, and he preached his last sermon in September. Talking to a fellow pastor, Brother Montanye gave the following testimony: ''I go to the footstool of mercy as a poor, unworthy sinner, resting my whole salvation on the merits of the Lord Jesus Christ.''[2] On the day before his death, as a pastor friend left his company, he said, ''Farewell in Christ Jesus; you can fare well no where else.''[3] Montanye died on September 27, 1829, and as his remains were buried in the church cemetery at Northampton, an immense crowd of sympathizing friends showed their love for his fruitful life of faithful service to his Lord.

DLC

---

[1]William B. Sprague, *Annals of the American Pulpit* (New York: Robert Carter and Bros., 1865), 6:266.

[2]Ibid., p. 267.

[3]Ibid.

May 31—As You Therefore Go, Preach

Scripture: Romans 15:18-33

Elder John Bryce was born of Scotch parents in Goochland County, Virginia, May 31, 1784. His parents were strict churchmen, and he was confirmed in the Episcopal Church. Convicted under the preaching of Andrew Broadus, at the age of twenty-one, he united with a small Baptist church in his native county. About the same time, he was admitted to the bar, and for a considerable time he practiced law and preached the gospel in Richmond and Lynchburg. He was master in chancery for some years under Chief Justice John Marshall.

Bryce served as a chaplain one year in the United States Army during the War of 1812. He was pastor of churches in Fredericksburg and Alexandria, Virginia, and played a leading role among the Baptists of Virginia. He was influential in the organization of Columbian College in Washington, D.C., and was an active member of the American Colonization Society. At one time, he liberated about forty of his slaves and sent them to Liberia, Africa.

Bryce moved to Georgetown, Kentucky, where he established himself in the practice of law, took part in the political affairs of the state, and helped establish Georgetown College. He located in Crawfordsville, Indiana, where he remained ten years preaching, practicing law, and representing his county in the state legislature.

In 1844 Bryce was appointed surveyor of Shreveport, Louisiana. This appointment took place while the annexation of Texas to the United States was pending, and Bryce was supposed to have been President Tyler's confidential agent in that important event. After his term of office expired, he was elected mayor of Shreveport. Oscar Harter tells us in his *History of Fredericksburg Baptist Church,* "While in Shreveport [Bryce] performed the most important works of his life in the ministry. When he arrived in Shreveport, in 1844, he supposed there was not a Baptist Church or another Baptist preacher within 200 miles of him; when he left there in 1851 there were about 20 churches and two associations in the region. He was instrumental in accomplishing this great work despite the fact that the ground was being contested by Bishop Polk."[1]

Bryce returned to Kentucky in 1851 and pastored the church in Henderson. Here he invested the latter years of a long and eventful life. His profession as attorney took him to various places as the nation spread westward. His calling as a preacher constrained him to obey the commission of his Lord, "As you therefore go, make disciples." The imperative is to "make disciples" as the circumstances of life thrust us into many different locations in this world. Even the Christians in the prisons of Russia of our day felt that they were missionaries throughout the Gulag Archipelago. John Bryce was aware of the divine imperative upon his life and faithfully made disciples and planted churches. Because of men such as he, as the settlers moved westward so did the gospel, and Baptist churches were planted as a permanent testimony throughout the land. God grant that future generations will be motivated by the love of Christ to carry on with the great imperative.

EWT

---

[1]Oscar H. Darter, *The History of Fredericksburg Baptist Church* (Richmond: Garrett and Massie, 1959), p. 59.

June

June 1—"Majestic Sweetness Sits Enthroned"

Scripture: Psalm 119:33-40

For years the family name "Stennett" was synonymous with "Baptist preacher" in England, for our subject's "great-grandfather Edward, the grandfather Joseph, and the father . . . whose name was also Joseph, were noted ministers and citizens in that day."[1] Furthermore, "his brother, Joseph Stennett, and his son, Joseph Stennett, were (also) Baptist ministers."[2] Samuel Stennett was, however, "the most famous in this preaching family."[3]

Born in Exeter in 1727 and provided with an excellent education, Samuel Stennett became proficient in the Greek, Latin, and Oriental languages. Along with his academic ability, Samuel Stennett found early consecration to the things of God, for in his youth, he fell under conviction and as a young man was baptized by his father and admitted to church membership. Thus began an association with the Baptist church in Little Wild Street that would last for over fifty years. On June 30, 1747, the church called young Stennett to assist his father, but he did not accept the call for a year. Ten years later he was called to succeed his father as pastor. On entering the pastorate, Stennett said to the congregation, "I tremble at the thought." His ordination took place on June 1, 1758, and was led by the famed theologian, Dr. John Gill. For forty-seven years Stennett served the church and was an outstanding leader for religious liberty. Numerical growth was experienced during his ministry, and the church building had to be rebuilt. He attracted an educated following, including the famed philanthropist, John Howard. In 1763 Samuel Stennett was awarded the Doctor of Divinity degree by King's College in Aberdeen.

Stennett wrote several meaningful volumes, but more importantly, several of his hymns have survived the test of time and are still known among God's people. He wrote ''Majestic Sweetness Sits Enthroned'' and ''On Jordan's Stormy Banks I Stand.'' For over two hundred years, those hymns of praise have been used to encourage saints in adoration and anticipation.

The death of Mrs. Stennett was a great blow to the man of God. Though she had not been strong for some time, she was confined to bed for only about a week before she died. In a short time Dr. Stennett would be joining his wife in our Lord's presence, but he was more earnest than ever before. His sermons during his sorrow were long remembered for their vibrancy and content. He seemed to sense that his own time was limited and began praying that God might give him an easy passage. The Lord heard and answered his petition. During his last illness, Stennett spoke in glowing terms of Christ's finished work. He said, ''When I reflect upon the suffering of Christ, I am ready to say, 'What have I been thinking of all my life?' What He did and suffered are now my only support.'' And again he exclaimed to his son, ''Christ is to me the chief among ten thousand, and the altogether lovely.''[4]

On August 25, 1795, in his sixty-eighth year, Samuel Stennett passed into glory. His body was laid to rest in Bunhill Fields along with so many other Baptists and dissenters. Because of his ministry and music, we can say of Stennett, ''He being dead yet speaketh.''

DLC

---

[1]Alfred W. Light, *Bunhill Fields* (London: C. J. Farncombe and Sons, 1915), p. 179.

[2]William Cathcart, *The Baptist Encyclopedia,* ed. Louis H. Everts (Philadelphia: Louis H. Everts, 1881), 1:1102.

[3]Thomas Armitage, *The History of the Baptists* (1890; reprint ed., Watertown, Wis.: Maranatha Baptist Press, 1976), p. 563.

[4]Light, p. 183.

June 2—From the Plow to the Prison

Scripture: Luke 9:57-62

Elijah Craig was one of the well-known ''Craig Brothers.'' He came under the preaching of David Thomas, a Regular Baptist, in the year of 1764 and professed his faith in Jesus Christ. The next year he, along with others, was encouraged by Samuel Harriss, the Separate Baptist, to hold meetings in his neighborhood for the encouragement of the young converts and their mutual edification. Craig continued to preach the Word of God from house to house during the week, and on Sunday he used his tobacco barn for their place of assembly. He, like his brothers, had a limited education, but he applied himself to personal study and became a fruitful evangelist. He was considered by many to be the most effective preacher of the three brothers.[1]

In the year of 1766, sometime after he had begun his ministry, Craig traveled into North Carolina, where he persuaded James Read to come and baptize the young converts, himself being one of them. He now devoted himself to preaching with great zeal, was ordained June 2, 1770, and became the first pastor of Blue Run and Rapidan Churches, which were both constituted December 4, 1769. These churches exist today in the community where the writer lives, and Blue Run is known as the mother church of many other churches in a wide area. It was also at Blue Run that the First Separate Baptist Association in Virginia was held, with Elder Samuel Harriss as moderator and John Waller, Jr., as clerk.[2] Dr. Robert B. Semple relates,

> He was certainly a great blessing to Blue Run Church: for under his care they flourished. He was accounted a preacher of considerable talents for that day; which united to his zeal, honored him with the attention of his persecutor. They sent the sheriff and posse after him, when at his plough. He was taken before the magistrates of Culpeper. They without hearing arguments pro or con, ordered him to jail. At court, he, with others, was arraigned. One of the lawyers told the court, they had better discharge them; for that oppressing them, would rather advance than retard them. He said that they were like a bed of camomile; the more they were trod, the more they would spread. The court thought otherwise, and determined to imprison them. Some of the court were of the opinion that they ought to be confined in close dungeon; but the majority were for giving them the bounds. Mr. Craig says they were fed on rye bread and water, to the injury of their health. After staying there one month he gave bond for good behavior, and came out. He was also confined in Orange jail, at another time.[3]

Craig was imprisoned four times: twice in Culpeper, and twice in Orange County for preaching the gospel of the grace of God.

Craig was very useful in Virginia and served there until he migrated to Kentucky in 1786 to join his brothers. There he became an enterprising businessman. He bought one thousand acres of land and laid out a town on it which was first called Lebanon but afterwards Georgetown. No one can deny that Craig should be counted among the faithful servants of God who fearlessly faced the enemy and planted churches in spite of the persecution brought to bear upon him. The fruit of Elijah Craig's ministry remains in the liberty we enjoy and the little churches scattered over the hills of Virginia.[4]

EWT

---

[1]J. H. Spencer, *A History of Kentucky Baptists from 1769 to 1885* (Cincinnati: J. R. Baumes, 1886), 1:87.

[2]Lewis Peyton Little, *Imprisoned Preachers and Religious Liberty in Virginia* (Lynchburg, Va.: J. P. Bell Co., 1938), pp. 144-45.

[3]Robert B. Semple, *A History of the Rise and Progress of the Baptists in Virginia* (Richmond: Published by the author, 1810), pp. 415-16.

[4]Spencer, p. 87.

June 3—"Wilt Thou Go with This Man?"

Scripture: Genesis 24:15-60

What unusual youths! Both Edward Payson Scott and Miss Anna Kay broke off engagements for marriage when prospective mates were unwilling to go to the mission field! Before ever meeting her, Edward proposed marriage. In correspondence he asked if Anna "could favorably consider the idea of going with him as his wife to Assam, in case a personal visit from him should so incline (her)."[1] She consented to the visit and ultimately agreed to marry E. P. Scott, missionary appointee to Assam. Then they sought and obtained the blessing of her parents as well. At her parents' home, a former pastor was visiting, and he read for family devotions the decision of Rebekah when she was asked, "Wilt thou go with this man? And she said, I will go" (Gen. 24:58). [2] E. P. Scott returned home with the understanding that he would return for the wedding in the Baptist church in Payson, Illinois, on April 30, 1861.

April was an important month to the Scotts, for he was born April 7, 1832, and she on April 20, 1838. Both were baptized in April, and, of course, they were married that month. However, due to the beginning of the Civil War, Dr. and Mrs. E. P. Scott were asked to postpone their departure for Assam, and thus he served in two churches as pastor. Finally they left for the field on June 20, 1862, and arrived in Calcutta on October 20. After laboring for seven years, E. P. Scott determined in 1869 to carry the gospel to one of the most dangerous Naga tribes.

> A young Naga man who wished to marry must show thirty skulls of human beings before he was considered brave enough to defend a wife. These skulls were worn as a necklace. . . . Naga men all carried long spears and sometimes they were poisoned ones which carried death to their enemies. . . . With his violin in hand and a prayer for these savage men, he assayed to enter . . . their hills. . . . When he reached this place, he found twelve savage warrior chiefs ranged on either side of this narrow defile. They raised their spears as Scott approached as if to pierce him with them all. Just at this moment the violin poured forth its sweet strains, and the voice of the singer rang out in the words, "Am I a soldier of the Cross?"[3]

Thus it was that the door was opened, and the gospel did its mighty work as God used music as the key to open the door.

Asiatic cholera swept the area, and as the Reverend Dr. Scott ministered to the sick, he himself came down with the dread disease. On May 18, 1869, as he neared death, his wife asked him if he had peace. He answered, "Yes, perfect peace," and he entered the land of the well! Mrs. Scott remained for several years, but in 1873 she returned to America with her three children. Mrs. Anna Kay Scott entered medical school and graduated as a medical doctor. For twelve years she practiced medicine in Cleveland, Ohio. When her children were grown, Dr. Anna Kay Scott was ready to resume her missionary labors, for the call of God is without repentance. Because the need for a medical doctor was greater in Swatow, China, than in Assam, she was reappointed by the Women's Baptist Missionary Society of the West and arrived in China on November 15, 1889. As word of her abilities circulated, patients came from far and near. She would often see two hundred patients in a day with her schedule beginning at 4:00 A.M. and continuing until 10:00 P.M. Dr. Scott found it necessary in August of 1900 to leave China for Japan because of factional fighting in Swatow. She had been fully fifty years old when she had gone to China, and the pressures of learning the new language, ministering to the sick, supervising the building of medical facilities, and fulfilling other responsibilities were overwhelming. Health demanded that she leave for the States in 1904, but two years in the homeland found her well enough to return in November of 1907. Dr. Scott continued her responsibilities until her granddaughter, Dr. Mildred Scott, could succeed her. Dr. Scott arrived back in Chicago on June 3, 1914,[4] thus completing her missionary life. She passed into the Lord's presence on October 18, 1923, in Granville, Ohio.

DLC

---

[1]Anna Kay Scott, *An Autobiography of Anna Kay Scott, M.D.* (Chicago: Published by the author, 1917), p. 24.

[2]Ibid., p. 25.

[3]Ibid., pp. 38-39.

[4]Missionary Register of the American Baptist Missionary Union, American Baptists Missionary Society Archives, Valley Forge, Pa.

June 4—"Would the Nightingale Care If the Toad Despised Her Singing?"

Scripture: Psalm 77

It all began in a meetinghouse yard June 4, 1768, when the sheriff of Spotsylvania County, Virginia, seized John Waller, Lewis Craig, James Childs, James Reed, and William Mash. Three magistrates were standing in that yard and bound them under penalty of one thousand pounds apiece to appear in court two days later. The courthouse of Spotsylvania County and the county jail were then located in Fredericksburg but have subsequently been moved to Spotsylvania Court House, Virginia. According to Oscar H. Darter in his *History of Fredericksburg Baptist Church,* "the prison where these men were incarcerated was probably the old stone edifice still standing at the foot of William Street near the William Street Bridge; it fits all the details of evidence involved in and deduced from the case, as described by one contemporary (Mr. Edwards) and by an authority on Baptist History in Virginia (Dr. Semple)."[1]

Semple tells us that it was "the first instance of actual imprisonment, we believe, that ever took place in Virginia. . . . At court they were arraigned as disturbers of the peace; on their trial, they were vehemently accused, by a lawyer, who said to the court, 'May it please your worships these men are great disturbers of the peace, they cannot meet a man upon the road, but they must ram a text of Scripture down his throat.' "[2]

As they passed through the streets of Fredericksburg toward the old stone gaol, locked arm in arm, they sang the old hymn:

Broad is the road that leads to death,
And thousands walk together there;
But wisdom shows a narrow path,
With here and there a traveler.

Deny thyself and take thy cross,
Is the Redeemer's great command;
Nature must count her gold but dross
If she would gain this heavenly land.

> The fearful soul that tires and faints,
> And walks the ways of God no more,
> Is but esteemed almost a saint,
> And makes his own destruction sure.
>
> Lord, let not all my hopes be vain,
> Create my heart entirely new,
> Which hypocrites could ne'er attain
> Which false apostates never knew.
>
> These men could sing, like the Apostles in the jail at Philippi, under the most trying circumstances, because there was joy in their souls. If there were those who ridiculed them as they went through the streets singing that resounding song, what did they care? What would the nightingale care if the toad despised her singing? She would sing on and leave the cold toad to his grouchy thoughts and shadows. And what cared these preachers for the sneers and scoffs of men who grovel upon the earth? They sang on in the ear and the bosom of God.[3]

This scene did impress some and, as Semple records, had an awful appearance. It was so awesome that while other counties continued for some time imprisoning Baptist preachers, Spotsylvania never dared to repeat the experiment.

EWT

---

[1]Oscar H. Darter, *The History of Fredericksburg Baptist Church* (Richmond: Garrett and Massie, 1960), p. 18.

[2]Robert B. Semple, *A History of the Rise and Progress of the Baptists in Virginia* (Richmond: Published by the author, 1810), pp. 415-16.

[3]Lewis Peyton Little, *Imprisoned Preachers and Religious Liberty in Virginia* (Lynchburg, Va.: J. P. Bell Co., 1938), p. 97.

June 5—From Heresy to Harmony

Scripture: Psalm 32

The English Baptist triumvirate in India, composed of William Carey, William Ward, and Joshua Marshman, was interested in the souls of men regardless of their background. Thus when they encountered a young American in Calcutta, India, they presented the Savior, Jesus Christ, in all His sacred claims, beginning with His deity.

Nathaniel Williams was that young American, and the impression of the witness of those three missionaries registered deeply in his heart. But let me share some of the background of the young man who is our focus.

Nathaniel Williams had been born in Salem, Massachusetts, on August 24, 1784. He grew up with Unitarian influences, and the religious convictions of those formative days extended through his early life. While still in his youth, Williams found employment with his uncle and eventually was sent to India on one of his uncle's ships that was trading in Calcutta. At that time, young Williams met the English missionaries. Coming under great conviction, he submitted to the Savior's atonement and was saved. He made public profession of his faith, was baptized by the Reverend Lucius Bolles, and became a member of the First Baptist Church of Salem on June 5, 1808.[1]

The First Baptist Church of Salem had been formed three years previously with only twenty-four members. Bolles was the first pastor, and Nathaniel Williams could not have been placed in a finer institution for training. The church experienced continual growth, and Pastor Bolles was an excellent teacher-pastor. In time Williams became a deacon, and in July 1812 he was licensed to preach. Abandoning a lucrative business, Williams gave himself to study that he might enter the ministry. Finally, in August of 1816, he was ordained at Beverly, Massachusetts, and ministered there for nine years. The next eleven years found Williams pastoring in New Hampshire, Vermont, and again in Massachusetts, and then he returned to the church in Beverly as pastor.

In 1820 the Reverend Mr. Williams was appointed a member of the convention that was chosen to revise the constitution of the state of Massachusetts. Gifted as a polemicist with qualities of intelligence and dignity in debate, he and Dr. Thomas Baldwin, pastor of the Second Baptist Church of Boston, were largely responsible for bringing about the modification in the state constitution. This revision secured equal rights of conscience in religious matters to all the citizens of the Commonwealth. Because of Williams's reputation as a diligent student, Brown University conferred upon him the honorary degree of Master of Arts in 1824.

Following a full life of ministry, Pastor and Mrs. Williams retired to their son's home in Maine in 1846, but in 1852 they moved to Boston, and Williams was busy almost every Lord's Day preaching in the city. On May 27, 1853, the Lord called His servant home to glory, and thus came to a close an interesting and useful earthly journey that began in heresy and concluded in harmony with the gospel.

DLC

---

[1]William Cathcart, *The Baptist Encyclopedia,* ed. Louis H. Everts (Philadelphia: Louis H. Everts, 1881), 2:1249.

June 6—Their Preaching Was a Matter of Right

Scripture: Esther 4

A full day had passed since the apprehension of the four preachers and the exhorter in the meetinghouse yard. According to their bond they were now appearing in court June 6, 1768, and were being accused, as many other Baptists were subsequently accused, of being vagrants, strollers, and disturbers of the peace. The only real disturbers of the peace were the ruffians who would pelt them with apples and stones, drag them from the pulpits, beat them with fists, pound their heads on the ground, and on occasions duck them in water until they nearly drowned. Their only supposed crimes were quoting Scripture, preaching the gospel of the grace of God, and condemning the vices of the state-supported clergy.

John Waller, one of the accused, made his own and his brethren's defense so ingeniously that the court was somewhat puzzled to know how to dispose of them. Waller was capable of this feat, being a brilliant, talented scholar and having received his education from private tutors. Though bred a churchman, he was distinguished from other John Wallers by the title "Swearing Jack" because of his profane speech. He was converted and embraced the principles of the Baptists as a result of sitting on the grand jury before whom Lewis Craig gave testimony. The court offered to release Waller and the others if they would promise to preach no more in the county for a year and a day. They dared not obey this mandate because it was in conflict with the supreme command of their God, their sovereign, but they could cheerfully submit to the penalty which unjust human law inflicted, thus demonstrating its oppressive injustice and paving the way for its repeal.

There has been a speech widely publicized that Patrick Henry supposedly made in defense of these men. Some historians declare that he was not even present. Others believe that he was present but that the published speech was not his but was written later, and yet others defend the validity of the speech. It is well documented that Waller defended the group and that they spent many days in the jail. It is also well known that Patrick Henry was a friend of the Baptists, defended some of them in court, paid some of their fines, and assisted them in many ways.[1]

During their confinement, they preached through the grates, and Morgan Edwards records that they made "very serious impressions on the minds of eleven heads of families and some of their domesticks [domestics] with many others. The populace doing everything they could invent to keep the people off and to plague the prisoners, till at last they let the prisoners out in order to get rid of them."

An Anglican rector who had previously debated with John Corbley after one of Corbley's sermons and had verbally attacked Corbley from his pulpit visited these prisoners and entered into a friendly conversation upon the subject of religion. Before he left them, he offered to give security if they chose to give bond. Not all among the state clergy were in sympathy with such persecution.

Having a petition for their release refused on July 4, 1768, Lewis Craig entered into a recognizance to carry it to the General Court in Williamsburg. He and Benjamin Waller, upon presenting the petition, received a letter from the attorney general, John Randolph, Jr., to the deputy governor, John Blair, advising that "their petition was a matter of right" and suggesting he write the "king's attorney" of Spotsylvania County that he was not to "molest these conscientious people, so long as they behaved themselves in a manner becoming pious Christians, and in obedience to the laws."[2]

EWT

---

[1]Lewis Peyton Little, *Imprisoned Preachers and Religious Liberty in Virginia* (Lynchburg, Va.: J. P. Bell Co., 1938), p. 95.

[2]Ibid., p. 99.

June 7—Racked, Scourged, and Burned for Christ

Scripture: Daniel 3

On June 7, 1561, the Margrave of Antwerp went out with a great number of people, well armed with staves, and apprehended Joos Verbeek, a minister of God's word and of His church. On the 9th of June, Verbeek was allowed to offer his defense. He very freely confessed his faith and also his office, which the Margrave and gentlemen ridiculed. Verbeek was likewise very severely tortured, but through it all God preserved his lips from giving information about anyone else though he was so unmercifully handled that a cord bound around his body broke. Twice in four days he had to endure the rack. He was scourged until the blood flowed. He patiently endured it all, but greatly lamented that his persecutors had broken or so lamed his right hand by the torture that he was disabled from writing.

Having confessed his faith, baptism, and doctrine, and not being permitted to say any more, Verbeek heard the sentence pronounced. He spoke to the people: "Dear fellow citizens; I have lived here eleven years, and no one can bring any complaints against me, for I have done wrong to no one, and my life and doctrine agree with the Word of God." "That is true," exclaimed a brother, which the constables hearing, they rose up and inquired who it was, but they did not find him. Joos Verbeek said, "He who delivered Daniel from the lion's den, will likewise preserve me; for I suffer not for evil doing, but for the name of the Lord." "That is true," cried a brother. Others called out, "Be valiant, dear brother." Joos said boldly and cheerfully, "Dear fellow citizens, thus must all God's children suffer; the saints of God, the prophets, and many godly men have trodden this path before me."

When Verbeek approached the straw hut and stood before the door in which he was to present himself as a burnt offering, he lifted up his eyes to heaven, and said, "O holy Father, support thy servant in this time of need." The executioner's man wished to put a cord with a knot in his mouth to prevent his speaking; nevertheless, he was not silent, for he was heard to exclaim, "O Lord, Thou Son of David, have mercy upon me."

The executioner performed his work with fear and trembling. When the fire was kindled, Verbeek exclaimed, "O Heavenly Father, into Thy hands I commend my spirit. O Lord of Hosts, who separated me from my mother's womb, be with Thy servant in this last distress which I suffer for Thy name." He once more exclaimed, "O Heavenly Father, into Thy hands I commend my spirit," and presented a peaceful burnt sacrifice, an example to us all.[1]

During his imprisonment, Verbeek wrote a short letter to his wife and family with his left hand, his right being maimed. "I salute you most heartily, and all my five children. Bring them up in the admonition of the Lord. Be in behavior as becometh holy women. Teach the young women to be sober, to love their husbands, to be chaste, modest, obedient to their husbands, and steadfastly continue to keep the rule according to which you now walk. The Lord qualify you for all good works in what may become your calling. I commend you to the Lord and the word of His grace. May He grant us to see each other in eternity."

And may God grant us all to assemble with these martyred saints in the presence of our Lord.

EWT

---

[1]T. J. Van Braght, trans., and Edward Bean Underhill, ed., *A Martyrology of the Churches of Christ Commonly Called Baptists* (London: J. Haddon and Son, 1853), 2:303-5.

June 8—A Versatile Christian Champion

Scripture: Matthew 3:1-7

Robert Robinson was born on October 8, 1735, and gave promise of becoming an excellent student. However, with the death of his father when Robert was only fourteen, it was necessary for him to leave school and enter into an apprenticeship in London. By rising early to read, he was able to maintain his acquaintance with the classical languages and French in order to expand his education.

In 1752 Robinson went to hear George Whitefield preach, and the text from Matthew 3:7 burned its way into his conscience. "The convictions of sin thus aroused held possession of his mind, and he obtained no relief until December 10, 1755, when, to use his own words, 'he found full and free forgiveness through the precious blood of Jesus Christ.' "[1]

When Robinson was twenty-one, his indebtedness for his business training was cleared, and he remained at his employment for some time. He attended Whitefield's Tabernacle that was commonly called "The Soul Trap." Many of Robinson's friends thought that he exhibited the gifts suitable to the ministry, but it was not until 1758, while visiting relatives in Norfolk, that he ventured to minister God's Word. His preaching met with immediate success, and he was urged to enter the ministry of the Church of England, but he declined the offer.

Robinson had never questioned the matter of baptism until visiting the christening ceremony of a child. Because of a chance remark, he carefully studied the subject and became a Baptist by conviction! He received believer's baptism and soon left Norwich for Cambridge and was invited to preach in the Baptist church. For two years the congregation asked him to become their pastor. He continued his ministry without accepting the pastorate until May 28, 1761, when he assumed that position. The church grew rapidly, and members of the university became regular attendants. By 1764 the church needed a new building, and a new edifice which would seat six hundred was built. Robinson's influence grew, and he was in demand for preaching in the surrounding area. A gifted author as well, he also wrote the favorite hymn "Come, Thou Fount of Every Blessing," which is still enjoyed in our day.

While in Birmingham, England, on a preaching tour, Robinson died, and he was succeeded at Cambridge by the Reverend Robert Hall. The scholarly Robert Hall wrote the following epitaph which was mounted in the Cambridge church:

> Sacred to the memory of the Rev. Robert Robinson, of Cambridge, the intrepid champion of liberty, civil and religious. Endowed with a genius brilliant and penetrating, united to an indefatigable industry, his mind was richly furnished with an inexhaustible variety of knowledge. His eloquence was the delight of every assembly, and his conversation the charm of every private circle. In him the erudition of the scholar, the discrimination of the historian, the boldness of the reformer, were united in an eminent degree with the virtues which adorn the man and Christian. He died at Birmingham on the 8th of June, 1790, aged 54, and was buried near this spot.[2]

Robert Robinson has been called "one of the most eminent names in Baptist history," and we honor his blessed memory on this, the anniversary of his home going.

DLC

---

[1]William Cathcart, *The Baptist Encyclopedia,* ed. Louis H. Everts (Philadelphia: Louis H. Everts, 1881), 2:997.

[2]John C. Carlile, *The Story of the English Baptists* (London: James Clarke and Co., 1905), p. 160.

June 9—He Worketh All Things After the Council of His Own Will

Scripture: Matthew 11:1-19

John Corbley was born in Ireland in 1733, and when he was fourteen, he agreed to serve four years as an indentured servant in return for his passage to Pennsylvania. When he had fulfilled his time, he moved to Winchester, Virginia, and ultimately to Berkley County, where in a conversation with Elder John Gerrard he experienced salvation in Christ. Soon after his baptism he began to preach.

Few men suffered for the cause of Christ as did John Corbley. He spent considerable time in the Culpeper and Orange jails, preaching from the grates and receiving the same treatment as his contemporaries. After his liberation, he was often threatened with death, frequently taken from the jail, and cruelly beaten after being dragged about by the hair of his head.

Prior to 1771, Corbley and his family moved to Redstone, a frontier settlement in western Pennsylvania, where he planted the Goshen Baptist Church. He planted thirty other churches in Virginia (now West Virginia), Pennsylvania, and Kentucky, where he lived a short period of time before returning to Pennsylvania. The Goshen Church is now known as the John Corbley Memorial Baptist Church.

One of Corbley's most severe trials took place as he and his family were walking to church, a one-mile distance from their home. He related the experience in a letter to the Reverend William Rogers, pastor of the Baptist church in Philadelphia.

> Not suspecting any danger, I walked behind 200 yards, with my Bible in my hand, meditating. . . . As I was thus employed, all of a sudden, I was greatly alarmed with the frightful shrieks of my dear family before me. . . . I immediately ran with all the speed I could, vainly hunting a club as I ran, till I got within forty yards of them; my poor wife seeing me, cried to me to make my escape. . . . An Indian ran up to shoot me. I had to strip, and by doing so outran him. My wife had a sucking child in her arms; this little infant they killed and scalped. They then struck my wife several times, but not getting her down, the Indian who aimed to shoot me, ran to her, shot her through the body, and scalped her. My little boy, an only son, about six years old, they sunk the hatchet into his brains, and thus dispatched him. A daughter, besides the infant, they also killed and scalped.

Corbley goes on to describe the scalping of two other daughters who survived, and he relates the difficulty he was having with their physical and emotional problems following this vicious attack.

He concludes by saying, "Amidst it all, for what purpose, Jehovah only knows, [I was] redeemed from surrounding death. . . . Oh, may I spend [my life] to the praise and glory of his grace, who worketh all things after the council of his own will. The government of the world and of the church, is in his hands. . . . May it be taught the important lesson of acquiescing in all his dispensations."[1]

John Corbley died June 9, 1803, and it is recorded on his tombstone:

> Death, thou hast conquered me;
> I by thy dart am slain;
> But Jesus Christ shall conquer thee,
> And I shall rise again.[2]

EWT

---

[1]Archibald Loudon, *A Selection of Some of the Most Interesting Narratives of Outrages Committed by the Indians in Their Wars with the White People* (Carlisle, Pa.: n.p. 1808), 1:60-62.

[2]Lewis Peyton Little, *Imprisoned Preachers and Religious Liberty in Virginia* (Lynchburg, Va.: J. P. Bell Co., 1938), p. 139.

June 10—Targets of Persecution

Scripture: Matthew 10:16-21

"On the 10th of June, 1535, a furious edict was published at Brussels. Death by fire was the punishment on all Baptists who should be detected and should refuse to abjure. If they recanted they were still to die, but not by fire; the men were to be put to death by the sword, 'the women in a sunken pit.' Those who resisted the operation of the edict by failing to deliver up Baptists [Anabaptists] to the authorities, were to suffer the same punishment as accomplices."[1]

What a troublesome time in which to live! Religious freedom was unknown to Anabaptists, and they were forced to worship covertly, away from the prying eyes of the world. Spies were to be found everywhere because informers were promised one-third of the confiscated estates of the dread Anabaptists!

Perhaps the actual wording of a portion of the edict might prove enlightening as to the pressures that our forefathers experienced.

> In order to provide against and remedy the errors and seductions which many sectaries and authors of mischief, with their followers, have dared to sow and spread in our possessions, in opposition to our holy Christian faith, the sacraments and commands of the holy church our mother; we have at various times decreed . . . many mandates containing statutes, edicts, ordinances, together with punishments that transgressors should suffer; in order that by such means the common and simple people might guard themselves against the aforesaid errors and abuses, and that their chief promoters might be punished and corrected as an example to all.
>
> And it having come to our knowledge that . . . many and various sectaries, even some who are denominated Anabaptist or rebaptizers, have promoted . . . their said abuses and errors, in order to mislead the same . . . to the great scandal and contempt of the sacrament of holy baptism, and of our edicts, statutes, and ordinances:
>
> Therefore, being desirous to provide against and remedy the same, we summon and command, that, from this time . . . you make proclamation in all the parts of limits of your jurisdiction, that all who are,

> or shall be found to be, infected by the cursed sect of Anabaptists, or rebaptizers, of what state or condition they may be, abettors, followers, and accomplices, shall suffer the forfeiture of life and estate, and shall without delay, be brought to the severest punishment.[2]

There are several other paragraphs of the edict, but this example is typical of the many edicts issued by the Roman Catholic and even Protestant leaders who harmonized only at the point of persecuting the re-baptizers. Catholics and some reformers believed that "re-baptism" was a repudiation of the baptism by the state church, which they considered salvation. Anabaptists did not accept "sacramental grace" and "infant sprinkling." They denied that they were *re*-baptizers at all! Thank God for grace in Christ and the privilege of obeying His ordinance as a testimony! Praise the Lord for our glorious freedom of religion and liberty of conscience to serve Him without man's dictates!

DLC

---

[1]J. M. Cramp, *Baptist History* (London: Elliott Stock, 1870), pp. 168-69.

[2]Joseph Meyer, ed., *Baptist Establishers of Religious Liberty* (Chicago: Privately printed, 1923), p. 99.

June 11—Heap Coals of Fire on Their Heads

Scripture: Matthew 5:43-48; Proverbs 25:22

The associations of Baptist churches have long been a blessing in the ongoing of the gospel. In early America, growth was slow in the original associations, for local churches insisted on maintaining their autonomy. The work of the associations, however, was vital, for it was meant to assist churches in doing collectively what could not be accomplished by individual effort. "Baptist churches are independent, and consequently the business of Association is not authoritative; they may advise, and indeed urge advice, but cannot compel."[1] Furthermore, an association provides for fellowship, encouragement, and strength, which is provided by a combined voice.

When the Particular Baptists of England wished to establish a doctrinal statement in 1689, they called for a General Assembly and invited over one hundred churches, requesting that each send two messengers to the meeting. "Though the Assembly strongly maintained the independency of the local church, it gave advice on several questions that had been submitted. 'Our whole intendment is to be helpers together of one another by way of counsel and advice in the right understanding of that perfect rule which our Lord Jesus, the Bishop of our souls, hath thereby prescribed.' "[2]

The Separate Baptists in Virginia had divided into two associations for the convenience of the messengers, and on May 14, 1774, the Southern District met in the Banister Baptist Church of Halifax County. There they transacted one of the most important aspects of an associational ministry, a phase that is all but dead among us in these days. For three or four years there had been severe persecutions against the Baptists in many parts of Virginia. Letters were received at this association from preachers confined in prison, particularly from David Tinsley, then in the Chesterfield jail. The hearts of their brethren were affected at their sufferings, in consequence of which it was agreed to raise contributions for their aid. The following resolution was also entered into: "Agreed to set apart the second and third Saturdays in June as public fast days, in behalf of our poor blind persecutors, and for the releasement of our brethren."[3]

Those two days of prayer were Saturday, June 11, and Saturday, June 18, 1774, and the saints prayed for the enlightenment of the spiritually blind persecutors and the freedom of their ministers. We ought not to be surprised to observe that during that decade, the Separate Baptists "achieved their greatest growth . . . with 221 churches and unconstituted local bodies with 9,842 members."[4] Some of the persecutors were converted and became Baptist preachers, and freedom of religion was gained for the whole state of Virginia.

A revival of ancient practice would prove refreshing in Baptist associations in America today! Days of "fasting and prayer" rather than politicking, preaching instead of picketing before state capitols, and power with God rather than publicity before men are needed in our day, even as they were in early America. We should pray that our associations will again become the powerful force that our forefathers envisioned them to be.

DLC

---

[1]Robert Baylor Semple, *History of the Baptists in Virginia,* rev. ed. (Lafayette, Tenn.: Church History Research and Archives, 1976), p. 62.

[2]B. A. Ramsbottom, *Stranger Than Fiction* (Harpenden, England: Gospel Standard Trust Publications, 1989), p. 85.

[3]Semple, p. 78.

[4]Robert G. Gardner, *A History of the Georgia Baptist Association, 1784–1984* (Atlanta: Georgia Baptist Historical Society, 1988), p. 15.

June 12—Toleration or Free Exercise of Religion, the Question Settled

Scripture: Acts 23:1-11

When the General Association met at Dupuy's meetinghouse on the second Saturday in August 1775, the ferment in the colony of Virginia, as well as in the other colonies, in determining to resist the oppression of the political and religious establishment, produced a very favorable season for the Baptists. They were, to a man, in favor of any revolution by which they could obtain freedom of religion, having been ground under by Virginia's interpretation of toleration under British laws. They resolved at this session to circulate petitions to the Virginia Convention, or General Assembly, throughout the colony, asking that the state church establishment be abolished and that religious societies be protected in the peaceable enjoyment of their own religious principles and modes of worship. They appointed Jeremiah Walker, John Williams, and George Roberts to wait on the legislature with these petitions.

On June 12, 1776, the Virginia Declaration of Rights was adopted but not until its author, George Mason, and the committee of the whole consented, at the urging of young James Madison, to an amendment of the 16th article. The article originally stated:

> That religion, or the duty we owe to our Creator, and the manner of discharging it, can be directed only by reason and conviction, and not by force or violence; and, therefore, that all men should enjoy the fullest *toleration* in the exercise or religion, according to the dictates of conscience, unpunished and unrestrained by the magistrate, unless, under the color of religion, any man disturb the peace, the happiness, or the safety of society; and that it is the mutual duty of all to practice Christian forbearance, love, and charity for each other."

Mason and the committee accepted the amendment which read: "That religion, or the duty which we owe our Creator, and the manner of discharging it, can be directed by reason and conviction, not by force or violence; and, therefore, all men are equally entitled to the *free exercise* of religion according to the dictates of conscience, and that it is the mutual duty of all to practice Christian forbearance, love, and charity towards each other."[1]

The difference between the article and the amendment is between the free exercise of religion and toleration. Where did the young James

Madison learn this principle? From the Baptists and their persecution in Orange and Culpeper Counties, Virginia. Also this Declaration of Rights became the pattern of many other colonial declarations. Article 16 was the basis of the *establishment and free exercise* clauses of our federal Constitution.

May we never forget and may we pass on to our posterity that a vital part of our Baptist heritage involves religious liberty in America. Thanks be unto God for great statesmen, such as Madison, who were sensitive and knowledgeable of the needs of our oppressed forefathers and that they had the wisdom to devise or develop a constitution that has enabled us to evangelize our nation. May other peoples of the world be as blessed. God help us to be thankful and instill biblical principles of salvation and government into the hearts of future generations.

EWT

---

[1]Charles F. James, *A Documentary History of the Struggle for Religious Liberty in Virginia* (1900; reprint ed., Da Capo Press, New York: 1971), pp. 62-63.

June 13—They Spake with Boldness and Exhorted the People to Repentance

Scripture: Acts 17:15-34

Hans Mandemaker, a minister of the Word of God and of His church, was apprehended for the word and faith of Jesus Christ in Bavaria, together with Juriaen Raek, a deacon, and Eustachius Kuter. They were taken to Innsbruck and delivered into the hands of the magistrate. Mandemaker was confined in a deep tower in which were many worms and other creatures. The bats flew about him, the mice ran away with his food, and among them he incurred much danger which would have frightened anyone without a firm confidence in God. The other two brethren were incarcerated in the round tower in Innsbruck. They were dealt with separately and rigorously, but they replied faithfully to many articles which were committed to writing.

On the thirteenth day of June in 1560, they were condemned to death. At the passing of the sentence, a great number of people were present. They freely addressed the judges of the court and the jury, proving to them that the sentence, in the presence of God, passed upon innocent men, would rise up in judgment against them to their condemnation for having condemned innocent blood. When they replied that they were obliged to judge according to the emperor's command and proclamation, Hans Mandemaker said, "O ye blind judges! You are to judge according to your own heart and conscience, as you will have to answer for it in the presence of God. If then you judge and pass sentence, according to the emperor's proclamation, how will you answer before God?"[1]

They all spake with boldness and exhorted the people to repent, to forsake their sins, and to tread the path of truth; it was the truth for which this day they should suffer. A brother, Lenaert Dax, went and gave them his hand, and they took leave of each other. By this they were greatly cheered, praising God that they had seen a pious person who would relate their end to their brethren and the church.

Their sentence was read along with some articles which included that they did not believe that the holy body of Jesus Christ was in the sacrament but they observed the Lord's Supper in the same manner that Christ kept it with His disciples, and that they did not approve of infant baptism.

After this they were led to the place of execution called the Swine Acre near a sheepfold. Kuter was first beheaded, after which Juriaen Raek stepped cheerfully forward to the executioner and said, "Here I leave wife and child, house and goods, body and life, for the sake and truth of God." He knelt down, and the executioner beheaded him.

Thus they voluntarily and patiently bore testimony to their faith in Christ—by their words, their life, and death; yea, their bodies and their blood.

EWT

---

[1]T. J. Van Braght, trans., and Edward Bean Underhill, ed., *A Martyrology of the Churches of Christ Commonly Called Baptists* (London: J. Haddon and Son, 1853), 2:285-88.

June 14—A Brief Ministry in Violent Times

Scripture: Acts 19:23-41

Daniel Fristoe was one of a number of effective preachers who were called forth under the preaching of David Thomas. Fristoe, his brother William, and Jeremiah Moore were the product of the ministry of the Chappawamsick Church around which swirled controversy and violence from certain citizens in Stafford and Prince William Counties, Virginia. This did not deter the zealous efforts of Daniel Fristoe to preach the gospel of the grace of God and to plant churches in northern Virginia.

Several years after Fristoe's conversion in 1755, he was ordained to the regular work of the ministry on June 14, 1771. This was just one day after John Young was haled into court in Caroline County for preaching without a license. According to Fristoe's diary, the day following his ordination he met with the brethren in Fauquier County where they were examining some candidates for baptism. As the candidates were relating their conversion experiences, "one James Naylor came into the assembly and began to curse and swear and be very outrageous until at last he blasphemed God and threw himself on the ground, breaking the ground and tumbling like a fish taken out of the water, until at last one man for ten shillings tied him and took him away; after which the congregation (which was very numerous) had peace; and 16 persons were adjudged proper subjects for baptism."

The next day (being Sunday) about two thousand people came together. After the preaching, thirteen others were examined and deemed worthy of baptism. Fristoe baptized twenty-nine people before this great multitude. The trees overhanging the water became so overloaded with spectators that many of them fell, delivering their burden of people into the water. Fortunately no one was hurt. They then moved to a field and made a circle in the center where Fristoe laid hands on the persons baptized, which was the practice of many of the Regular Baptists at that time. The multitude stood around weeping. Fristoe records, "When we sang, 'Come We That Love the Lord', they were so affected that they lifted their hands and faces toward heaven and I discovered such cheerful countenances in the midst of the flowing tears as I had never seen before."[1] He declared that he had never seen such an appearance of God's working and the devil's raging at one time in one place as he did at that time when he was beginning his ministry as an ordained preacher.

Fristoe personally suffered from the mob's violence. He met with great opposition and once had a gun presented to his breast and a warrant sworn against him. His ministerial career was brief. Having been appointed messenger from Ketocton to the Philadelphia Association, he was, while in Philadelphia, seized with the smallpox, from which he never recovered. He died far from home in the thirty-fifth year of his life. His body was buried at the Baptist Church of Philadelphia, far from his faithful wife and seven children as well as the churches he had served so faithfully. Many a servant of God has died far from his earthly home and loved ones, only to be welcomed into the presence of his Savior and rejoicing saints.

EWT

---

[1]Lewis Peyton Little, *Imprisoned Preachers and Religious Liberty in Virginia* (Lynchburg, Va.: J. P. Bell Co., 1938), pp. 242-45.

June 15—He Pursued Law Then Preached Jesus Christ

Scripture: Romans 8:31-39

Many young men have entered college and had their faith shaken terribly by ungodly professors, along with the pressures of their peers. This led them to forsake the spiritual heritage of their fathers and the pure moral instruction of their mothers. On the other hand, some college students were so influenced by the claims of the gospel that their Christian witness prompted fellow students and professors to receive Jesus Christ as their Savior. Such was the case of Edward Miles Jerome, who was born June 15, 1826, and graduated from Yale in 1850.[1]

While he was a sophomore at Yale, he was converted to Christ. There have been times that the spiritual interest and testimonies of students and professors have initiated spiritual awakenings on college campuses. Some say that the "Haystack Prayer Meeting" marked the birth of the American foreign missions movement. This meeting took place at Williams College in Massachusetts, where a group known as the "Brethren" met regularly for prayer and discussion. Out of this awakening or revival came missionaries like Judson, Mills, and Rice.

At Yale, Edward Jerome was not a student in the Divinity School. Rather he pursued and graduated with a law degree. His early church relationships were with the Congregationalists. After being admitted to the bar, he pursued a vocation in business in New York by managing his father's business there.

After a few years, Jerome became persuaded that Baptist principles and doctrine were biblical. Though not a divinity student, his legal mind was enlightened by the Holy Spirit. He became a Baptist, was baptized, and united with the First Baptist Church of Hartford, Connecticut. It was there that he began his theological studies and was licensed by that church to teach and preach the Scriptures. He was ordained in 1859 as an evangelist in Holyoke, Massachusetts, and began his ministry preaching and supplying pulpits. He soon settled into a pastorate and served in this office for several years until he suffered an infection in his throat that disabled him. He attempted preaching afterwards, but failing health would not permit him to continue. Fortunately, he had developed excellent writing skills and was able to use these when he lost his ability to preach.

It is amazing how many who prepared for the legal profession ended up being very effective preachers. Charles G. Finney is an example of this as well as Edward Jerome. Even the Apostle Paul sounds like one schooled in law when he writes, "Who shall lay any thing to the charge of God's elect? It is God that justifieth. Who is he that condemneth? It is Christ that died, yea rather, that is risen again, who is even at the right hand of God, who also maketh intercession for us. Who shall separate us from the love of Christ? shall tribulation, or distress, or persecution, or famine, or nakedness, or peril, or sword?" (Rom. 8:33-35).

Some of the most persuasive and effective evangelists at one time had prepared for and entered the legal profession before answering the call to preach. It is wonderful to look back and see how God put all the preparation together to make us into that instrument He desired to use. Sometimes He then permits an infirmity to guide us into a ministry that utilizes a skill that we possibly never considered as the major ability that God would use in His service.

Edward Jerome's preaching and writing were doctrinally clear and were presented in an evangelical, earnest, and effective manner. He entered into the presence of his Lord on June 8, 1891.[2]

EWT

---

[1]William Cathcart, *The Baptist Encyclopedia,* ed. Louis H. Everts (Philadelphia: Louis H. Everts, 1881), 1:599.

[2]Philip S. Evans, *History of the Connecticut Baptist State Convention* (Hartford: Smith-Linsley Co., 1909), p. 256.

June 16—An Exile and a Compact of Freedom

Scripture: Isaiah 55

When the court-appointed Mr. Hooker failed to turn Roger Williams from what were considered religious errors in October of 1635, the court ordered Williams exiled within six weeks. The Boston court postponed the deadline of his departure until the spring of 1636, on condition that he would not further disseminate his views. When they heard that he held private meetings, continued to preach his radical views, and drew away as many as twenty followers with whom he planned to set up a rival colony, they moved at once to arrest him and to put him on a ship ready to sail for England. Governor Winthrop, for whatever reason, secretly notified him, and Williams fled into the cold wilderness in January 1636.

Williams would not have survived if he had not already befriended the Indians. He later said of his winter experience: "I was unmercifully driven from my chamber to a winter's flight, exposed to the miseries, poverties, necessities, wants, debts, hardships of sea and land in a banished condition. . . . I was sorely tossed for one fourteen weeks in bitter winter season, not knowing what bread and bed did mean . . . exposed to a winter's miseries in a howling wilderness of frost and snow."[1]

In June 1636, Williams and several friends from Salem established the nucleus of Providence Plantations just outside the Massachusetts Bay jurisdiction. He named the settlement to commemorate God's providence to him in his distress. Until they could apply for a proper charter from England, they drew up a compact on June 16, 1636, promising to abide by "such orders and agreements as shall be made by the greater number of the present householders . . . only in civil things." The charter of 1663 provided that "no person within said colony, at any time hereafter shall be in any wise molested, punished, disquieted, or called in question for any differences of opinion in matters of religion, and do not actually disturb the civil peace of said colony; but that all and any persons may from time to time, and at all times hereafter freely and fully have and enjoy his and their own judgments and consciences in matters of religious concernment."[2]

Williams lost confidence in the authority but not the mode of his baptism at the hands of one Ezekiel Holliman, a layman from Salem. He repudiated it because he took the view that for church ordinances to be valid, they must be traced back by unbroken succession to the apostles. Williams believed that when the ordinances were interrupted, there could be no new beginning until Christ sent a new apostle to reinstate them. From that time Williams became what was called a "Seeker" and did not unite with any communion of believers.

Whether we consider him a real Baptist or not, we acknowledge that he was one of the most important thinkers in America and that we owe him a great debt of gratitude for the religious liberty we enjoy today.

EWT

---

[1]H. Leon McBeth, *The Baptist Heritage* (Nashville: Broadman Press, 1987), p. 129.
[2]Ibid., p. 130.

June 17—Obedience Results in Blessing

Scripture: Proverbs 16:7

Adoniram and Ann Judson sailed from Salem on their way to India on February 19, 1812. War was everywhere. Napoleon and his French army had been considered a menace to the world, but he was just experiencing the disaster of his Russian invasion. South America was awakening to the force of Simón Bolívar's struggle for liberty, and the United States was on the verge of war with Great Britain. Another war, however, was about to break out in the hearts of the Judsons as they considered the subject of baptism for four months aboard ship. The four-month trip with the monotony of the rocking ship and the seasickness was one thing, but the battle of heart and mind was far worse! The heat in crossing the equator and the rough, rainy weather around the Cape of Good Hope were a trial but nothing like the conflict that must have gone on in the hearts of these two who changed the course of Baptists in America more than any other two people!

Ann was concerned as she saw her husband being drawn logically to a Baptist persuasion. Three major problems presented themselves to Ann's mind as she considered such a catastrophe: schooled in Congregationalism by parents, raised in a Congregational church, sent out by the Congregational Board and accompanied by dear Congregational friends . . . and leave it all? Aboard their ship were the Reverend Mr. and Mrs. Samuel Newell, companions in the gospel. Ann and Harriett Newell had been schoolmates, and now to break such a relationship? Ann wrote, "We anticipate the loss of reputation and of the affection and esteem of many of our American friends. But the most trying circumstance attending this change, and that which has caused most pain, is the separation which must take place between us and our dear missionary associates."[1]

The second source of trial was that they would doubtless be cut off from support by the Board of Commissioners. After all, the Baptists did not have a mission agency that could pick up their support, and in reality, they were untried missionaries. Who would venture to support them? Ann wrote to her parents, "These things were very trying to us, and caused our hearts to bleed for anguish. We felt we had no home in this world, and no friend but each other."

Last of all, Ann realized that the Baptists were looked down upon in America. Being faithful to a tender conscience, Baptists were considered rather "peculiar" by the more established churches. Whether their activities were concealed or revealed, Baptists were the objects of some contempt, and union with them surely would "wound and grieve her dear Christian friends in America."

The Judsons landed at Calcutta on June 17, 1812.[2] Ann had threatened that even though Adoniram might become a Baptist, she would not. For two more months the young missionaries studied the subject, and on September 6, they were immersed at the Baptist chapel in Calcutta.[3] At great price the Judsons had put conviction ahead of convenience, and God rewarded them with fruitfulness that only eternity can reveal. They were not guided by the crowd, nor by friends, but by God and His Word. What an important lesson this is for our generation!

DLC

---

[1]Walter N. Wyeth, *Ann H. Judson* (Cincinnati: n.p. 1888), p. 44.

[2]Walter Sinclair Stewart, *Early Baptist Missionaries and Pioneers* (Philadelphia: Judson Press, 1925), p. 88.

[3]G. Winfred Hervey, *The Story of Baptist Missions in Foreign Lands* (St. Louis: C. R. Barnes Publishing Co., 1892), p. 113.

June 18—The Peril of the Gospel's Advance

Scripture: II Corinthians 11:23-28

Severns Valley, Kentucky (now the site of Elizabethtown), was the location of the first Baptist church formed in the state and actually in the great Mississippi Valley. The area was a dense and unexplored forest inhabited only by a few pioneering families and wild Indians. Were we able to transport ourselves back in time to June 18, 1781, we would doubtless feel out of place, for the men were dressed partly in Indian costume with leather leggings, moccasins, and hats made of buffalo wool, rolled around white oak splints. The women were adorned with bed-gown and petticoats made entirely of buffalo wool. Perhaps even more startling would be the fact that the men were armed with rifle in hand and tomahawk in readiness, for Indians might attack at any moment. The guard at the door was ever watchful.

Under such a setting, eighteen members constituted the church, and John Gerrard was ordained as their pastor. Not much is known concerning the history of this first Baptist pastor to serve in Kentucky, and indeed, his tenure of office as pastor of the Severns Valley Baptist Church was short-lived. Gerrard was the first who discharged the functions of the pastoral office in the great valley between the Allegheny and Rocky mountains, and his experiences certainly were unique. Sometimes, Gerrard would deliver his sermons in a humble, round log cabin with earthen floor or, when peace again seemed assured, under the shade of some spreading tree. Let us always remember to thank God for the faithfulness of those early pioneers, for in time, the Severn's Valley congregation matured, and some eminent ministers of the gospel ministry were sent out from their midst. Their appearance was not of choice but of circumstance, but they were distinguished citizens in the community, and some of the original members had geographic areas named for them. LaRue County, Kentucky, was named for John LaRue, and Hodgenville was named for Robert Hodgen. Thomas Helm of that original number was the grandfather of Kentucky's governor, John LaRue Helm. These individuals were of hardy stock that could face the trials and, because of their faith in God's Word, could persevere and plant a colony. On October 29, 1785, the Severns Valley Baptist Church joined with three other churches to form the first association of churches in Kentucky, but the clerk's minutes note that the church was pastorless!

After serving as pastor for about eleven months, the Reverend John Gerrard took his rifle and went out to hunt for wild game to provide food for his family. The neighboring forest provided an abundance of prey for the table, but there was ever-lurking danger in the Indian-infested wilderness as well. Through the afternoon and evening hours, his wife and daughter awaited his return but in vain. Gerrard never was found. Surely he was killed by the wild Indians who roamed the forests.

"Our knowledge of him may be summed up in a single sentence. . . . 'Like John the Baptist, he came preaching in the wilderness, and, like Moses, no man knoweth of his sepulchre until this day.' "[1] May God rekindle the pioneering spirit among Baptists to carry the gospel around the world!

DLC

---

[1]J. H. Spencer, *A History of Kentucky Baptists from 1769 to 1885* (Cincinnati: J. R. Baumes, 1886), 1:22-23.

June 19—From a Proper Child to the Prince of Preachers

Scripture: I Samuel 2:1-10

No life story of Charles Haddon Spurgeon would be complete if it did not contain some account of his godly ancestors. When the Duke of Alva died in 1589, his wicked boast that he had sent to the executioners no less than eighteen thousand persons was not forgotten. That number represented the actual martyrs of the faith. Many other thousands were driven into exile. Among these were the progenitors of the English Spurgeons. These Dutch Christians brought to England their quiet energy and true godliness. Even in Spurgeon's physique, one can see a resemblance to these godly Dutchmen.

The great-grandfather of Charles Spurgeon, John Spurgeon, was a man of the true Puritan type, and his wife was akin to him in mind, principles, and life. James Spurgeon was a son of this godly couple and became pastor of the Independent Church in Stambourne, Essex, which he pastored for fifty-four years. His son, John, the father of Charles, was a businessman who also discharged his duties as pastor of the Independent Church at Tollesbury. In middle life, John began devoting all his time and energies to the ministry.

Charles Haddon Spurgeon was the first-born of seventeen children and was born on June 19, 1834. Almost as soon as he was old enough to leave home, he went to his grandfather's house. Under his grandfather's oversight and the devoted guidance of an aunt, Charles developed into a thoughtful boy, commonly fonder of his books than of his play.[1]

A pious minister, Richard Knill, who was visiting his grandfather, took an interest in this young lad as he was waiting some days for a preaching engagement. Spurgeon wrote some years later, "Calling the family together, [Mr. Knill] took me on his knee, and I distinctly remember his saying: 'I do not know how it is, but I feel a solemn presentiment that this child will preach the Gospel to thousands, and God will bless him to many souls.' "[2] There are many lives that touch a person, and among the most important are those choice servants of God who are invited to enjoy the hospitality of a home. They often make a deep, indelible impression on a young heart.

Of course, there is often no greater influence on a man's life than his mother. Mrs. Spurgeon trained her children with prayerful concern, and she was rewarded by seeing each one of them make a public profession of their faith in Christ. Two of her sons were preachers, and one of her daughters was the wife of a minister. Speaking one day to her son, Mrs. Spurgeon said, "Ah, Charley, I have often prayed that you might be saved, but never that you should become a Baptist." To this remark, Charles replied, "God has answered your prayer, mother, with His usual bounty, and given you more than you asked."[3]

We cannot overemphasize the importance of those influences in the early life of a child. Many saw the boy Spurgeon through the eyes of faith the same as Moses' parents saw Moses as a "proper child." This "proper child," Charles Haddon Spurgeon, became known as the "Prince of Preachers"! Lord, give us eyes of faith to see our children.

EWT

---

[1]R. Shindler, *From the Usher's Desk to the Tabernacle Pulpit* (London: Passmore and Alabaster, 1892), pp. 4-22.

[2]Ibid., p. 28.

[3]Henry D. Northrop, *Life and Works of Rev. Charles H. Spurgeon* (Philadelphia: Monarch Book Co., 1891), p. 23.

June 20—They Gave Themselves to the Lord as a People of God

Scripture: Philippians 1:1-11

It is interesting to note how our Lord took humble people across great stretches of ocean, planted them on a vast continent, brought them together, and established local churches. Generally, they were feeble numerically, but the seed sown was nurtured and, during times of spiritual awakening, multiplied amazingly. It is interesting to see how the churches of the Philadelphia Association of Regular Baptists began. The church at Montgomery is an example.

> In the year 1710, John Evans, and Sarah, his wife, from a church in Carmarthenshire, in South Wales, (James James, minister) came over and settled in Montgomery aforesaid. In 1711, came John James and Elizabeth, his wife, from Pembrokeshire, members of the church at Rhydwillym, (John Jenkins, minister) and settled in the same neighborhood. After some time Mr. Abel Morgan visited them, and preached to as many as came to hear, at the house of John Evans; and after his visiting for sometime, as often as he could, several persons were proposed for baptism, which was administered by Mr. Morgan. In the year 1719, it was moved to them either to join with some neighboring church, as that of Pennepek, being the nighest, or to be settled in gospel order as a distinct church by themselves. Upon which they consulted, and concluded, by reason of the distance of the place and diversity of language, they understanding very little English, to be rather a church by themselves. Their conclusion being approved by Mr. Morgan, a day was set apart for the solemnizing of this great work, being the 20th day of June, 1719; and Mr. Abel Morgan, and Mr. Samuel Jones, being spent in fasting and prayer, with a sermon being preached by Mr. Morgan, suitable to the occasion, they proceeded. Being asked whether they were desirous and willing to settle together as a church of Jesus Christ, they all answered in the affirmative; and being asked whether they were acquainted with one another's principles, and satisfied with one another's graces and conversation, it was also answered in the affirmative; and then for a demonstration of their giving of themselves up, severally and jointly, to the Lord, as a people of God and a church of Jesus Christ, they all lifted up their right hand. Then they were directed to take one another

by the hand, in token of their union, declaring, at the same time, that they had given themselves to God, so they did give themselves to one another by the will of God, 2 Cor. 7:5, to be a church according to the gospel; to worship God and maintain the doctrines of the gospel, according to their ability, and to edify one another. Then were they pronounced and declared to be a church of Jesus Christ; a right hand of fellowship was given to them as a sister church, with exhortations and instructions suitable to the station and relation they now stood in; and the whole was finished with solemn prayer to God for a blessing on the work of the day. Their number, nine or ten persons.[1]

It is true that "from small acorns mighty oaks are grown." Our spiritual fathers were more concerned with purity of doctrine and life than large numbers. God's heritage is a "little flock."

EWT

---

[1]A. G. Gillette, ed., *Minutes of the Philadelphia Baptist Association from* A.D. *1707 to* A.D. *1807* (1851; reprint ed., Minneapolis: James Publishing Co., n.d.), p. 19.

June 21—An Ambassador for Jesus Christ

Scripture: Romans 15:14-33

George Pleasant Bostick was the fifth son of fifteen children, three of whom became missionaries to China. These three gave a total of 110 years to reaching the Chinese with the gospel of Jesus Christ. For many years their mother prayed that God would call at least one of her sons to be a preacher of the gospel. When G. P., as he was affectionately known by his family and friends, answered God's call to China, she was apprehensive, but later when her youngest son, W. D., and youngest daughter, Addie, also went to China, she exclaimed with joy, "If I could feel as confident and happy about the other children as I do about these three, I would be willing for them to go to China. What a privilege and honor!"

G. P. Bostick was converted to Christ at an early age and was shortly afterward baptized into Floyd's Creek Baptist Church in North Carolina. Soon after, he had a clear definite call to preach. The church recognized his call and licensed him to exercise his gifts. He was later ordained at the New Hope Baptist Church near Raleigh, North Carolina. He was a joyful ambassador for Christ, yielding to God fifty-two of the sixty-eight years of his life.

While in seminary, Bostick pastored a small country church and, upon graduation, went to Concord, North Carolina, where he planted the first Baptist church in that city. He later answered the call to the First Baptist Church of Durham, North Carolina, where he soon found that it was not to be his life's work. God called him to China while in this pastorate, and he, his wife, and ten-month-old daughter left for Shantung Province, China. There he spent thirty-seven years of his life as a pioneer missionary. Many times as he pushed on into the interior of China, it seemed as if his life would be terminated. He was often surrounded with violence as he experienced the Boxer Rebellion, and twenty-five years later, their city of Pochow was captured by bandits and held for fifteen days in an orgy of pillage, murder, rape, and destruction of property.

Bostick was essentially a pioneer from the very beginning of his life. He was ever reaching onward and forward, moving on to the regions beyond where the gospel had never been preached. He also experienced deep sorrow in losing the wife of his youth and, later, the fine consecrated missionary whom he met in China and married. In both instances, he was a great distance from home when they died suddenly, and both were buried before he could return home. During that period many other faithful missionaries, such as Judson, were having similar experiences.

After this, while on furlough, Bostick met and married Lena Stover, my great-aunt. She assumed the responsibility for his family and was his devoted wife for the last fourteen years of his life. He contracted typhus fever and never fully recovered. On the occasion of his death, she testified, "He loved life in all its fullness, for God and family and humanity. He died as he had lived. I have never seen such a passing; a going out, as it seemed to me. He was in a coma. . . . On the borderline he called the names of loved ones who had gone on before."[1]

He joined those loved ones June 21, 1926. George Pleasant Bostick was one of those early pioneer missionaries who opened a great nation to the gospel of Jesus Christ. God grant us leadership in world evangelism with the same devoted, courageous, pioneer spirit.

EWT

---

[1]Lena Stover Bostick, *An Ambassador for Christ* (Luray, Va.: Lauch and Co., 1959), pp. 33-34.

June 22—She Kindled the Fires to Burn the Anabaptists

Scripture: Psalm 39

Hendrick Terwoort was not an English subject but a Fleming by birth and of a fine mind. Persecuted in his own land for his love for

Christ, he fled and asked protection of the Protestant Queen Elizabeth, the head of the English Church. Terwoort ultimately discovered that he had misplaced his confidence, for Elizabeth had him roasted alive at Smithfield, June 22, 1575.[1]

While in prison, Terwoort wrote a confession of faith that rejected infant baptism and held that a Christian should not make an oath or bear arms, that Anabaptists "believe and confess that magistrates are set and ordained of God, to punish the evil and protect the good," that they pray for them and are subject to them in every good work, and that they revere the "gracious queen" as a sovereign. He sent a copy to Elizabeth, but her heart was set against him. At the age of twenty-five, Terwoort was put to death because he would not make his conscience Elizabeth's footstool.

Terwoort was not a singular case. Bishop Jewel complained of a "large and unauspicious crop of Anabaptists" in Elizabeth's reign. She not only ordered them out of her kingdom, but in good earnest, kindled the fires to burn them. She pursued them more and more until they were driven in all directions. A large part fled to Holland, where at that time they enjoyed more toleration. Some remained in England, and they had several secret conventicles in London; some of their ministers had been educated at the universities.

Dr. Some wrote a treatise, attacking them and their faith. His charges against the Baptists were

> that they insisted on maintaining all ministers of the gospel by the voluntary contributions of the people; that the civil power has no right to make and impose ecclesiastical laws; that the people have the right to chose their own pastors; that the High Commission Court was an anti-Christian usurpation; that those qualified to preach ought not to be hindered by the civil power . . . that the baptism of Rome is invalid; that a gospel constitution and discipline are essential to a true church; and that the worship of God in the Church of England, is in many things defective. For these views they were accounted as heretics and suffered so severely from 1590 to 1630 we find but slight trace of Baptists in England during that period.[2]

Baptists were hated by the bishops, who falsely accused them of having no reverence for authority, seeking to overthrow government, being full of pride and contempt, being entirely interested in being schismatic, and desiring to be free from all laws. They were considered great hypocrites, feigning holiness of life.

Our American forefathers also stood for these principles. Thank God for saints who propagated liberty of conscience and endured persecution so that we might have religious freedom.

EWT

---

[1]Thomas Armitage, *The History of the Baptists* (1890; reprint ed., Watertown, Wis.: Maranatha Baptist Press, 1976), 1:451.

[2]Ibid., pp. 451-52.

June 23—When God Provided Harmony in Medley

Scripture: Psalm 94:9-23

When war broke out between England and France in 1755, the sixteen-year-old English novice in the cloth trade was glad, for it meant he could serve out his apprenticeship in the British navy, if he so chose. Thus it was that Samuel Medley, who had been born on June 23, 1738, found himself in the famed Battle of Cape Lagos.[1] He was wounded as the battle raged, and the greater part of the calf of one of his legs was shot away. The leg did not heal, and in time, the ship's surgeon told him that gangrene had set in and amputation was imperative. Young Medley was filled with horror, and the doctor granted one more day before surgery. Medley began to think of his godly father and grandfather and remembered a Bible in his trunk. Sending for it, he spent the night reading the Bible and praying. The next morning when the surgeon returned, he was amazed at the healing that had begun, and no operation was necessary. Rather than being led to repentance, Medley rejoiced in his good fortune and turned again from the Lord.

Having to convalesce before continuing to pursue his aspirations of advancement in the navy, Samuel Medley went to his grandfather's home in London. The old gentleman, William Tonge, was an educated and godly man, serving as a deacon in Dr. Andrew Gifford's pastorate at Eagle Street. The elderly gentleman witnessed to and warned his grandson, but young Medley was unconcerned. Then one Sunday evening the grandfather chose to read Medley a sermon by Dr. Isaac Watts, and the Holy Spirit brought conviction and worked a wonderful transformation in the young sailor's life. What a change resulted! Day by day Samuel Medley studied in his grandfather's library. He was twenty-two years old now, and there was no time to lose. He was baptized in December of 1760 by Dr. Gifford. He learned both Hebrew and Greek and prayerfully studied the Word of God.

In April of 1762, he married, and into their home were born seven daughters and one son. By 1766 Samuel Medley began to preach, and in 1767 he was called to pastor the Baptist church in Watford. His four-and-a-half-year ministry there was difficult, for the church was small and could not support him. Thus when a call came from Liverpool to the Particular Baptist Church, he accepted. The Medley family moved to Liverpool in the beginning of 1772, and Pastor Medley spent the rest of his life serving that congregation. Growth was immediate and continual, with expansion of the facility first and construction of a completely new chapel later.

Medley's usual day began in the study soon after his 4:00 A.M. rising. Private devotions and study were observed until ten o'clock, and then the various pastoral responsibilities among his people took place. He loved to witness to the sailors in his seaport city, and he had a keen interest in youth. The pastor loved music and wrote much poetry that found its way into useful hymns.

The man of God approached death in his sixty-first year, and on his deathbed he said, " 'I am now a poor shattered bark, just about to enter the blissful harbour: and O, how sweet will be the port after the storm.' . . . His last words were, 'Glory! Glory! Glory! Home! Home!' He died on July 17th, 1799,"[2] and thus ended a glorious journey in the grace of God.

DLC

---

[1]William D. Blake, *An Almanac of the Christian Church* (Minneapolis: Bethany House Publishers, 1987), p. 174.

[2]B. A. Ramsbottom, *Samuel Medley—Preacher, Pastor, Poet* (Rushden, Northamptonshire, England: Fauconberg Press, 1978), p. 11.

June 24—Second-Generation Preacher Makes Good

Scripture: Proverbs 1:1-9

We have already considered the Reverend David Jones, America's first Baptist chaplain to the military. Jones had served under General Horatio Gates in 1776 and apparently was so impressed with the General that he named his youngest son "Horatio Gates Jones" at the baby's birth on February 11, 1777, in Chester County, Pennsylvania. The young Horatio Jones grew to maturity in Chester and Bucks Counties and availed himself of the education that the local schools provided. At age nineteen, he was sent to an academy at Bordentown, New Jersey, and studied there under the celebrated Dr. William Staughton. On June 24, 1798, the young man professed his faith in Jesus Christ and was baptized and welcomed into the membership of the Valley Church.

Horatio returned to farming, but being a gifted speaker, he soon acquired a prominent position politically. Conviction that he had been called to preach, however, overcame all political aspirations. The Valley Church recognized his divine call and licensed him to preach in September of 1801. He ministered throughout the region until he was asked to accept the pastorate in Salem, New Jersey. He was ordained there on February 13, 1802. On that occasion, his aging father gave him the charge, saying "My son, in your preaching, don't put the rack too high. Some ministers put the rack so high that the little lambs can't get a bite. Put the rack low, and then the old sheep can get the fodder, and the lambs too."[1] His ministry was blessed of the Lord, and the church grew rapidly, but after three years, he was forced to resign when the climate there brought on a failure of his health.

Mr. and Mrs. Jones moved to their farm about five miles north of Philadelphia on the River Schuykill, and as his health allowed, he preached as opportunities were offered. During that time, he ministered at "Thompson's Meeting-house" in Lower Merion, Montgomery County, Pennsylvania. The building belonged to a Presbyterian, the Honorable Charles Thompson, first secretary of the Continental Congress. Thompson was a Greek scholar and had taught in the College of Philadelphia. Though he lived six miles from the "Meeting-house," Thompson attended the services directed by the Reverend Mr. Jones for three years. During that period, Jones's labors appeared to be fruitless, but in May 1808, he baptized his first convert in a local mill stream. More conversions and baptisms followed, and in September of 1808, the Lower Merion Baptist Church was organized with nineteen members. "In two years' time a meeting-house was built on a lot of ground, the gift of Thompson. . . . The Lower Merion Church . . . continued under his care for a period of forty-five years."[2]

Jones's ministry found him constantly visiting his people, and he served in civil affairs, filling many important posts but not with profit. He was a member of the Board of Managers in 1814 when the Baptist Board of Foreign Missions was organized in Philadelphia. He also exercised his influence in educational efforts to train young ministers. In 1812 Brown University conferred on him the degree of Master of Arts, and in 1852 the University of Lewisburg made him their first chancellor and bestowed on him their first Doctor of Divinity degree. The Reverend Horatio Jones passed into the presence of the Lord on December 12, 1853. We pause to honor his memory on the anniversary of his spiritual birth.

DLC

---

[1]William B. Sprague, *Annals of the American Pulpit* (New York: Robert Carter and Bros., 1865), 6:453.

[2]William Cathcart, *The Baptist Encyclopedia,* ed. Louis H. Everts (Philadelphia: Louis H. Everts, 1881), 1:614.

June 25—Martyrs: Triumphant in the Flames

Scripture: II Corinthians 12:1-10

Among the Anabaptist martyrs worthy of our remembrance is one Thomas Hawkes, who, with six others, was condemned to death on February 9, 1555. Hawkes was a young man of good stature who had been in the service of the Earl of Oxford. He was well versed in the Scriptures, and thus he had refused to have his child baptized in the Roman Church.[1] After being arrested, he was held prisoner in the gatehouse for many terrible months as he was being tried by the infamous Bishop Edmund Bonner of London. After Hawkes endured the agony of the long incarceration, Bishop Bonner finally decided upon the death penalty.

A short while before Hawkes's death, a group of his friends promised to pray for him in the dread hour of trial and asked for a sign if he realized that Christ was with him in the torture. He agreed with their request and decided that he would lift up his hands in token that he was at peace.

The day of his execution—June 25, 1555—arrived, and Hawkes was led away to the stake by Lord Rich where Hawkes would become a fiery sacrifice on the altar of religious prejudice. When he came to the post where he would be burned, a heavy chain was thrown around his waist, and he was secured. After bearing witness to those close at hand, he poured out his heart to God in prayer, and the fire was kindled. The sun shone brightly on those assembled to see him die, but a group of friends stood praying and straining eager eyes for the gesture of victory.

The victim did not move and slowly the flames enveloped his body.

> When he had continued long in it, and his speech was taken away by violence of the flame, his skin drawn together, and his fingers consumed with the fire, so that it was thought that he was gone, suddenly and contrary to all expectation, this good man being mindful of his promise, reached up his hands burning in flames over his head to the living God, and with great rejoicing as it seemed, struck or clapped them three times together. A great shout followed this wonderful circumstance, and then this blessed martyr of Christ, sinking down in the fire, gave up his spirit.[2]

The grace of God was sufficient, and this truth was proved time and again. Bishop Bonner had examined Rob Smith upon his refusal to allow infant baptism. Smith declared, "To judge children damned that be not baptized is wicked," and his fate was also sealed. At his execution on August 8 at Uxbridge, he was left a charred black mass supposed to be dead, but, to the consternation of the crowd, he rose, and lifting up the burned stumps of his arms, "endeavoured to sing praises to God before his spirit took its flight."[3]

Not only did the Anabaptists suffer, but on October 17, 1555, the outstanding bishops of the Church of England endured martyrdom. As they approached the stake, Ridley said to Latimer, "Be of good heart, brother, for God will either assuage the fury of the flame, or else strengthen us to abide it." As the fire was lit, Latimer cried to Ridley, "Be of good cheer, Ridley; and play the man. We shall this day, by God's grace, light up such a candle in England, as I trust, will never be put out."[4] It is evident that many suffered and that Anabaptists were marked out for great cruelty.

DLC

---

[1]John C. Carlile, *The Story of the English Baptists* (London: James Clarke and Co., 1905), p. 32.

[2]William Byron Forbush, ed., *Foxe's Book of Martyrs* (Philadelphia: John C. Winston Co., 1926), p. 227.

[3]Carlile, p. 33.

[4]Forbush, p. 237.

June 26—A Fearless Ambassador of Christ

Scripture: Luke 10:30-37

I. B. Kimbrough was born in Tennessee in 1826. Not until he was saved and called of God to preach did he begin to give himself to the matter of study. Being a farmer, he used every opportunity to read. He outfitted a shelf between the handles on his plow and placed a book upon the board so that he might read as he cultivated the fields. Being ordained in 1848, Kimbrough continued his practice of disciplined study and became a logical thinker and convincing preacher of his day. While ministering in Tennessee, Kimbrough at one time served as the financial agent of Carson and Newman College and traveled extensively in his state attempting to raise money with which to train young Baptist preachers.

In 1879 he moved to Texas and preached for twenty-three years in the Lone Star State until his death in 1902. Testimony concerning the Reverend Mr. Kimbrough assures us that he pursued his ministry with "a tenacity for the truth that would make no compromise with error and would yield not a hair's breadth in his conflict with heresy.''[1]

This description of his life is surely validated by an account which he shared in the Texas State Convention session on June 26, 1886, at Waco, Texas. Dr. Kimbrough recalled an incident from his days in Tennessee and his work with Carson and Newman College. As he was traveling from one appointment to another through a secluded forest, he was confronted by two highwaymen. Holding their guns on the man of God, they insisted that he dismount from his horse and hand over all his money.

> ''Very well, gentlemen, please give me a little time, and I will obey your orders,'' Kimbrough responded. After dismounting, he laid his money in two piles, then turning to the highwaymen he said: ''Gentlemen, this small pile of money is mine: you are at liberty to rob me of that; the larger pile is God's money, and I dare you to touch it. I collected it for the young preachers of the state who are struggling for an education at Carson and Newman College.''
>
> The earnestness and courage of the man attracted the attention of the robbers, and they began to inquire into the work in which he was engaged. He told them he was a Baptist preacher and explained to them his mission. After hearing what he had to say, the elder of the two men said: ''We will not take either your money or the money of the young preachers.''
>
> Turning to the young men, and looking them full in the face, Dr. Kimbrough added: ''Young men, you are in a mighty bad business. I believe you ought to give it up. In the meantime, I will be grateful if you will help me in the work in which I am engaged.''
>
> Following this appeal, the robbers gave him $5 each for the young preachers, whereupon the faithful minister mounted his horse, and all rode away, going in different directions.[2]

I. B. Kimbrough was a fearless ambassador of Jesus Christ! May we purpose to follow his courageous example in our day, when the gospel pathway is threatened in much more insidious manners.

DLC

---

[1]L. R. Elliott, ed., *Centennial Story of Texas Baptists* (Dallas: Baptist General Convention of Texas, 1936), p. 106.

[2]B. F. Riley, *History of the Baptists in Texas* (Dallas: Published by the author, 1907), pp. 302-3.

June 27—Living Sacrifices for God's Honor

Scripture: Hebrews 11:32-40

Roger Holland had come from the affluent family of Sir Robert Holland, but the family had fallen on hard times, and young Roger became a merchant-tailor apprentice to Master Kempton in London. The young man had been given thirty pounds to relay to his master, but Roger had rather entered into a period of revelry and soon gambled the money away. In shame and fear he determined to escape to France and rebuild his life, but he returned early one morning to his master's house and conversed with a servant girl, admitting his folly and asking a favor of her. He wanted to leave a note for his master acknowledging his debt and pledging to repay if ever he were able, but requesting that Master Kempton keep the transaction a secret for fear of the disgrace it would bring upon Roger's father.

Elizabeth, the maid, exhibited her Christian charity by presenting Roger with thirty pounds which she had just received as a legacy. However, she demanded that she would keep the note on the condition that he would reform his life, dispose of his books on Catholicism, begin attending the preaching of Dissenters, and read the Scriptures faithfully. Furthermore, she insisted that if she ever heard of his return to his old lifestyle, she would reveal the note to his master. Within half a year, Roger Holland became a zealous follower of the Lord Jesus and then led his father to the Lord. His father, whose situation had improved, rewarded him with forty pounds that Roger might begin a business in London. Roger returned to the house, repaid Elizabeth the thirty pounds, and proposed marriage. In the first year of the reign of Bloody Mary, Roger and Elizabeth were married.

Apparently, Roger Holland became a member of the Hill Cliffe Baptist Church about this time. "Two of the signatories to the letter of 1654 from Hill Cliffe are of the same name, Holland. This points to, at any rate, a probability of his having been a Hill Cliffe Baptist, perhaps minister there."[1]

On one occasion as forty people gathered for a service of prayer and the expounding of the Word,

> twenty-seven of them were carried before Sir Roger Cholmly. Some of the women made their escape, twenty-two were committed to Newgate, who continued in prison seven weeks. Previous to their examination, they were informed by the keeper, Alexander, that nothing

> more was requisite to procure their discharge, than to hear Mass. Easy as this condition may seem, these martyrs valued their purity of conscience more than loss of life or property; hence, thirteen were burnt, seven at Smithfield, and six at Brentford; two died in prison, and the other seven were providentially preserved. . . . They were sent to Newgate, June 16, 1558, and were executed on the twenty-seventh.[2]

As was so often the case, Roger Holland's death at Smithfield instead of destroying the faith of the Baptists only made it stronger. His relatives and friends were afterward more determined than ever to uphold the principles for which he died! May we with these heroes of the faith and with the hymn writer state and mean, "Thou (my Lord) art more than life to me," for then our lives shall be in a true sense "living sacrifices" for God's honor.

EWT

---

[1]James Kenworthy, *History of the Baptist Church at Hill Cliffe* (1882; reprint ed., Gallatin, Tenn.: Church History Research and Archives, 1987), p. 38.

[2]William Byron Forbush, ed., *Foxe's Book of Martyrs* (Philadelphia: John C. Winston Co., 1926), p. 269.

June 28—The Pastor Who Couldn't Ignore Immersion

Scripture: Romans 6:1-10

Milo P. Jewett was born in Johnsbury, Vermont, on April 27, 1808, into the family of Dr. and Mrs. Calvin Jewett. Being the son of a medical doctor, young Jewett was offered the opportunity of a fine education and graduated from Dartmouth College in 1828. Looking forward to a career in the legal profession, Jewett spent a year in a law office in New Hampshire, but in 1830 he abandoned law and entered Andover Seminary. His brilliant mind fully equipped him for the field of education, and "he decided that teaching and not preaching was the work for which God had fitted him. . . . In 1834 (he) accepted a professorship in Marietta College, Marietta, Ohio."[1]

Professor Jewett was persuaded to accept the pastorate of a Presbyterian church along with his educational duties, and for two years he served as pastor-professor. A disturbing situation developed which changed Jewett's life, and that we might hear it in his own words, we quote from a letter he wrote from Marietta College, dated June 28, 1838:

> Perhaps you know I have preached for about two years past to a Presbyterian church in the country. Some eighteen months ago, an elder of that church became a Baptist. On the occasion of his baptism, a sermon was preached by Rev. Hiram Gear, the Baptist minister in Marietta. This sermon disturbed several members of my church, and the session requested me to preach on baptism, in reply. I declined, saying, the best way to manage the excitement was, totally to disregard it. . . . Soon the session applied to me a second time, insisting that I must preach on the subject; several members of the church were in trouble, and a discourse must be delivered. Finding that the interest in the subject was not likely to die by neglect on my part, I told the church I would prepare a discourse as soon as practicable. . . .
>
> Thus compelled to write, I determined to go into an original investigation of the whole matter, proceeding just as if I had never heard or read anything on either side, and endeavoring, with a spirit of candid and prayerful inquiry, to seek after the mind of Christ. . . . I . . . entered upon an investigation of the original Scriptures relative to the language used respecting the ordinance. . . . Thus passed some months. . . . I was compelled to admit, as a philologist and interpreter of the Bible, that immersion, and that only, is the baptism which Christ enjoins.
>
> Afterwards I took up infant baptism; and here I found myself in clouds and darkness. . . . I would lay down the subject for weeks, then resume it, till, some three or four months ago, I was obliged, in the fear of God, to conclude that none but believers in Jesus have a right to the ordinance of Jesus.[2]

In January 1839 Jewett was baptized and united with the Baptist church in Marietta. Then resigning from the college, he went south to Marion, Alabama, where he established the Judson Female Institute. He was ordained into the Baptist ministry in 1839 and founded *Alabama Baptist,* which became the Baptist magazine of the state. In later life he returned to the North and became the first president of Vassar College. After losing his eyesight, the Reverend Mr. Jewett resigned from the college and moved to Milwaukee, Wisconsin. He continued to be active in the Lord's work, both as a college administrator and church member.

In 1840 he authored *Jewett on Baptism,* and the volume was blessed by the Lord in helping many to see the spiritual truth of the ordinance. Jewett passed into the Lord's presence in 1882 after a full life of spiritual obedience and service.

DLC

---

[1]William Cathcart, *The Baptist Encyclopedia,* ed. Louis H. Everts (Philadelphia: Louis H. Everts, 1881), 1:603.

[2]Milo P. Jewett, *The Mode and Subjects of Baptism* (Philadelphia: American Baptist Publication and Sunday School Society, 1845), p. 7-9.

June 29—A Man for an Hour of Great Travail

Scripture: Ephesians 1

During the years 1860 to 1865, our nation was convulsed in a horrible civil conflict that ultimately claimed hundreds of thousands of lives, both Northerners and Southerners. The pain and suffering defies imagination. Scarcely a family existed that was not touched by death. In some instances the future posterity of the family was entirely wiped out. One mother in North Carolina lost all six of her sons on the battlefields.

Out of such travail often comes a new sense of the frailty of humanity and the need for God. Thus it was with thousands in both armies who came into vital union with Jesus Christ, many just a short time before being violently swept into eternity. Others returned home horribly maimed and desperately ill from the malignant plagues that swept through the camps and prisons. The citizenry at home were shaken to their foundations as they saw the cream of their youth come streaming back into their communities wounded and sickly, having been aged far beyond their years by the horrors of war. The churches were brought to a place of spiritual sobriety and, in some instances, revival as a direct result of this terrible civil convulsion.

In the midst of this turmoil, Adoniram Judson Gordon was ordained into the gospel ministry June 29, 1863, and became pastor at Jamaica Plain, Massachusetts.[1] His name, Adoniram Judson, was prophetic, because his new birth kindled an evangelical spirit that permeated every area of his life and ministry. We have previously noted that he was actively involved with the great evangelist Dwight L. Moody and Moody's evangelistic campaigns as well as being an active soulwinner in his own ministry at Clarendon Street Baptist Church in Boston.

This evangelical spirit permeated Gordon's writing also. His pen produced many hymns and books which emphasized the need of the power of the Holy Spirit for the Christian to carry out his witness and ministry for the glory of Jesus Christ. In his introduction of his book *In Christ*, Gordon gives us some insight into his heart and ministry.

> Life is still of God, but it has this new dependency *"in Christ."* "Of Him are ye *in Christ Jesus*." The obligation to labor remains unchanged, but a new motive and a new sanctity are given to it by its relationship to Christ. "Forasmuch as ye know that your labor is not in vain *in the Lord*." The marriage relationship is stamped with this new

signet, "Only *in the Lord.*" Filial obedience is exalted into direct connection with the Son of God. "Children obey your parents *in the Lord.*" Daily life becomes "a good conversation *in Christ.*" Joy and sorrow, triumph and suffering, are all *in Christ*. Even truth, as though needing a fresh baptism is viewed henceforth "as it is *in Jesus.*" Death remains, but it is robbed of its sting and crowned with a beatitude, because *in Christ*. "Blessed are the dead who die *in the Lord.*"[2]

Reading Gordon's works not only reveals the depth of thought and spirituality that characterized his life, but also provokes a spiritual and intellectual exercise that benefits the reader. All that one may read by Gordon may not be in agreement with our interpretations, but his works provoke a deeper examination of our conclusions to see if they are true.

EWT

---

[1]Norman Wade Cox, ed., *Encyclopedia of Southern Baptists* (Nashville: Broadman Press, 1958), 1:570-71.

[2]A. J. Gordon, *In Christ* (New York: Fleming H. Revell Co., 1880), p. 12.

June 30—He Gave His Scalp and Received a Crown

Scripture: I Corinthians 15:20-34

According to the First Annual Report of the State Historical Society of North Dakota to the governor of North Dakota for the year ending June 30, 1906, Elijah Terry, a Baptist missionary, was killed by the Sioux Indians June 28, 1852.[1] He was a member of the First Baptist Church in St. Paul, Minnesota, when he came in contact with James Tanner, a half-breed whose father was stolen in childhood by a band of Shawnee Indians in Kentucky in 1789. Having been adopted into their tribe, he married an Indian and spent his life among them. His son James was educated in the best schools available for Indians. He served for several years as an interpreter and assistant in Methodist Missions at Sandy Lake and other stations among the Indians along the upper Mississippi River.

After careful Bible study, Tanner became a Baptist. During a severe winter, he walked to the nearest Baptist church and minister, possibly in St. Paul, in order to be scripturally baptized. He then went east, where he enlisted the interest of some Baptists in Philadelphia and elsewhere to support the teaching of the gospel to the Indians in the Dakota Territory.

On his return, Tanner solicited the assistance of Elijah Terry to carry out a plan to erect a log building in which they could teach the Indians and half-breeds and conduct gospel services. It was in the construction of this building that young Terry lost his life. While Tanner went to a nearby town to sharpen his broad-ax, Terry and a Frenchman went to the woods to score timber. Tanner relates:

> When I got near town a half-breed came running after me and called out that our comrades were killed. I instantly went back home, where I found the Frenchman badly wounded under the chin. After enquiring for my wife and children and finding them hid in the grass, I, with some armed half-breeds who had just arrived, went in search of Brother Terry. . . . They found him . . . with two arrows sunk deep in his back . . . a bullet hole in his left arm . . . a gash behind his left ear, a piece of scalp about seven inches long and four inches wide taken off, and two marks as if they were made with a blade of a hatchet on his back.[2]

Terry and the Frenchman had been walking along singing hymns when a party of Sioux Indians fell upon them. It was with difficulty that Tanner was able to secure a place from the Catholic priest to have Terry's body buried in the only cemetery in the vicinity, but there was rejoicing in heaven as the angels ushered his spirit into the presence of the Lord. Later, the Baptists of North Dakota removed his body to the Presbyterian cemetery in Wahalla and placed an appropriate monument over his grave. The martyred saints of the westward missionary movement should be memorialized so that we will remember the sacrifices they made to evangelize everyone, including the native Indian people.

EWT

---

[1]Linda W. Slaughter, *Leaves from Northwestern History* (Bismarck: Historical Society of North Dakota, 1906), 1:252.

[2]Ibid., p. 253.

July

July 1—Baptism: Threat to State Church Power

Scripture: Genesis 39

King Christian the Sixth was upon the throne of Norway and Denmark when Soren Bolle immersed Johannes Halvorsen, a shoemaker, on July 1, 1742, in the river that flows through Drammen. On July 8 Halvorsen immersed Bolle, Nills Buttedahl, two others, and then Bolle immersed his wife. He testified that all "this was not done in secret but openly before the eyes of everybody, in order that they might show the world that they were true disciples of Christ." There were no Baptists in Norway, and the state church was Lutheran, but Bolle, having prepared for the Lutheran ministry, was dissatisfied in his learning and could not subscribe to the doctrines of the state church.

From time to time throughout history, groups of people have come to the position of believer's immersion without any connections to Baptists elsewhere. The first person to administer the ordinance had never been immersed. He then either immersed himself (this is called "sebaptism") or immersed someone else who then immersed him. In almost every case when the first administrator had not been immersed by another, those whom he baptized lacked the assurance of the validity of their baptism due to a lack of succession.

Our purpose is not to claim that this was the beginning of the actual work of Baptists in Norway but rather to point out that when obedience to the ordinance of "believer's immersion" was practiced, the wrath of the state church and government soon followed. Soren Bolle was summoned before the magistrate, and in his defense he stated, "In regard to infant baptism my heart would rejoice if anybody could show me, out of the Bible, one word that speaks about it, because what we say or do must be founded on the Scriptures. I do not dare to do anything else but what I find in the Scriptures, because they shall judge me one day, and I can not follow old customs.''[1]

These converts to the Baptist principles soon discovered that it would not be easy to pursue the dictates of their conscience, for Bolle and Halvorsen were arrested and placed in separate cells. Bolle's home was searched and his writings taken, and for days the two men were examined by two priests. The men were then sent to Oslo to prison and again were placed in separate cells without the right to communicate with friends. Persecution in Drammen continued with the arrests of Jorgen Kleinow, Nills Buttedahl, and Jorgen Nicolaysen, and to assure that these might not seek converts, they too were sent to Oslo and placed in the penitentiary. Buttedahl's home was confiscated and sold to pay the expenses for the imprisonment of the group.

These forerunners of the Baptist cause may not be considered Baptists by some, but the treatment they received from the state church and government is reminiscent of the persecution Baptists have endured elsewhere. In 1743 Bolle, Halvorsen, Buttedahl, and Kleinow were sent into exile to the city of Altona, which had some religious liberty.

Whether or not these men are claimed as ''Baptists,'' they surely prepared the way for the later Baptists in Norway and exhibited a willing spirit of suffering for freedom of conscience.

DLC

---

[1]P. Stiansen, *History of the Baptists in Norway* (Chicago: Blessing Press, 1933), p. 32.

July 2—A Godly Family That Followed the Lord

Scripture: Psalm 27

As a lad, Andrew Gifford must have thrilled to the accounts given to him by his father concerning earlier trials of Baptist preachers. His father, the Reverend Emmanuel Gifford, was one of seven children and served as a sentinel as Andrew's grandfather preached the gospel in the Bristol, England, area. The grandfather's name was also ''Andrew Gifford,'' and he was imprisoned at least four times for the cause of Christ. King Charles II gave them a very brief time of relief in 1672 with his ''Declaration of Indulgence,'' but religious freedom was yet unknown. On September 5, 1672, Andrew's grandfather was granted a license which read in part, ''In pursuance of our declaration of the

15th of March, 1671-72, we do hereby permit and license Andrew Gifford, of our city of Bristol, of the persuasion commonly called Baptist, to be a teacher, and to teach in any place licensed, and allowed by us, according to the said declaration.''[1] But the persecution soon returned.

Surely Andrew's father, Emmanuel, told of his own experience when, as an eleven- or twelve-year-old sentry, he was discovered by intended persecutors and violently pursued. Becoming exhausted, he took refuge under a staircase, and as he hid, the ruffians ran by swearing that if they caught him they would do physical mayhem! But God gave deliverance to the Baptists in their worship and to young Emmanuel as well.[2]

With such a heritage, young Andrew Gifford was raised in Bristol and was baptized when he was fifteen years old. He was trained in a local academy, and when his father died, Andrew was twenty-four and preaching the gospel. He was not ashamed of the legacy left to him by his father and grandfather, but rather rejoiced in their faithfulness to the gospel and became one of the outstanding Baptists of his day. For almost sixty years he preached the Word of God with great success as ''his church was enlarged several times to provide room for the congregations that listened with profit and pleasure to his expositions.''[3]

We have introduced the actual ministry of Andrew Gifford previously (February 20) and have observed that he entered heaven on June 19, 1784. But let us go again to Bunhill Fields and consider the words of John Ryland as he stood on a tombstone in the early morning hours, addressing two hundred ministers and a vast multitude of others as well, on Friday, July 2, 1784. He closed his address by saying:

> Farewell, thou dear old man! We leave thee in the possession of Death until the Resurrection Day, but we will bear witness against thee, O King of terrors, at the mouth of this dungeon—thou shalt not always have possession of this dead body; it shall be demanded of thee by the great Conqueror, and at that moment thou shalt resign thy prisoner. O ye ministers of Christ, ye people of God, ye surrounding spectators, prepare, prepare to meet this old servant of Christ at that day, that hour when this whole place shall be nothing but life, and death shall be swallowed up in victory.[4]

Again, we have seen the torch of Baptist truth passed from generation to generation even in the midst of adversity. May each of us determine to provide such a spiritual inheritance that our children shall follow in our train!

DLC

---

[1]Thomas Crosby, *The History of the English Baptists* (1783-40; reprint ed., Lafayette, Tenn.: Church History Research and Archives, 1979), 3:154.

[2]Ibid., pp. 152-53.

[3]John C. Carlile, *The Story of the English Baptists* (London: James Clarke and Co., 1905), p. 161.

[4]Alfred W. Light, *Bunhill Fields* (London: C. J. Farncombe and Sons, 1915), p. 66.

July 3—The Great Answer of Faithful Prayer

Scripture: Acts 2

The Reverend John E. Clough was born July 16, 1836, in New York. Soon afterwards his family moved to Illinois and finally to Iowa. As a young man Clough served as a surveyor in Minnesota and then decided to enter college to become a lawyer. While training in Burlington, Iowa, in 1857, he was brought under spiritual conviction and was gloriously saved. Believing he was called to proclaim the gospel to those who had never heard, he trained at Upper Iowa University and graduated in 1862. Clough's appointment as a Baptist missionary to India took place in August of 1864, and he arrived in that country in March of 1865.

The missionary work with the Telugus had begun in 1836 under the direction of the Reverend S. S. Day and the Reverend Stephen Van Husen. The first twenty years were very discouraging, and many recommended abandoning the effort. The Reverend Lyman Jewett joined the mission in 1849, and in 1852 he and his wife visited Ongole. Before leaving the place, they climbed a slope which overlooked the village and prayed that God would send a missionary to Ongole and the region.

Upon arriving in India, John E. Clough worked more than a year among the Telugus in the city of Nellore, but in September of 1866, in answer to the Jewett's prayer, he relocated in Ongole, and a modern miracle of missions began! On January 1, 1867, he organized a church with eight members, and by the end of 1879, that church had grown to 13,106 members with forty-six national preachers and thirty assistants. The amazing story of such tremendous growth is well rehearsed, for it was nothing less than "a mighty outpouring of the Spirit of God (that) brought the multitude to Jesus."[1]

Clough's methods were biblical and saturated in prayer. Tent meetings of evangelism were held, the nationals were trained, and a circuit was established which contained more than eighty villages forty miles around Ongole. As the work grew, other missionaries were sent. Clough was joined by A. V. Timpany in 1868, John McLaurin in 1870, David Downie in 1873, and W. W. Campbell in 1874. These men and their wives were of great assistance to Clough.

The next three years were a time of trial, for the area was hit with a year of famine, a year of cholera, and still another year of famine. During these years, the government came to the aid of the perishing people by employing them in digging canals for the development of the country. Clough took contracts for this work and organized the people. He paid good wages to the starving nationals, and while they labored for their bread, his national preachers gave forth the gospel. "Many asked for baptism, but he refused to baptize any while the famine lasted lest they should profess Christianity from wrong motives. When the three years of pestilence and famine were over, he offered baptism to all true believers. July 3, 1878, two thousand, two hundred and twenty-two were immersed upon their profession of faith."[2] From June 16 to July 31, 1878, eight thousand six hundred and ninety-one had been immersed upon their profession of faith! What caused such results? Surely God answered the prayers of the Jewetts, and a mighty outpouring of the Spirit of God brought souls to Christ. Our missionaries around the world still need prayer partners in our day!

DLC

---

[1]William Cathcart, *The Baptist Encyclopedia,* ed. Louis H. Everts (Philadelphia: Louis H. Everts, 1881), 1:234.

[2]Thomas Armitage, *The History of the Baptists* (1890; reprint ed., Watertown, Wis.: Maranatha Baptist Press, 1976), 2:823-24.

July 4—Run, Speak to This Young Man

Scripture: Zechariah 2

John Waller was one of the more able preachers of his time. As we have seen, before his conversion, his capability in profanity earned him the sobriquet of "Swearin' Jack." His ability in the pulpit in preaching the gospel of Jesus Christ and pointing out the errors of the dominant religious system of his day attracted the attention of the religious and civil authorities. Besides spending a total of one hundred and thirteen days in four different county jails for preaching, Waller was subject to severe physical abuse. John Waller gave the following account of one such attack that took place in Caroline County, Virginia, during a worship service in a home.

> While he was singing the Parson of the Parish would keep running the end of his horse whip in his mouth, laying his whip across the hymn book, etc. When done singing he proceeded to prayer. In it he was violently jerked off the stage; they caught him by the back part of his neck, beat his head against the ground, sometimes up, sometimes down, they carried him through a gate that stood some considerable distance, where a gentleman gave him something not much less than twenty lashes with his horse whip. After they carried him through a long lane they stopped in order for him to dispute with the parson. The parson came up, gave him abominable ill language, and away he went with his clerk and one more. Then Brother Waller was released, went back singing praise to God, mounted the stage and preached with a great deal of liberty.[1]

Another time while he was preaching, a huge fellow pulled him down and dragged him about by his hair. A second, as stout as the first, ran to rescue Waller. One took hold of one hand and the other of the other hand so that between friend and foe poor Waller was about to lose both arms. The hurt remained with him for many weeks.[2]

On November 8, 1793, he moved to the state of South Carolina. John Waller's daughter had married Elder Abraham Marshall, a Baptist evangelist and son of the well-known preacher and church planter, Daniel Marshall. Some speculate that she was Waller's favorite daughter and he desired to be near them. Also good land could be purchased cheaply there, and he felt that his labors had come to an end in Virginia. Waller's work in his new home was blessed as he helped to establish two churches, but his ministry never had the impact of his ministry in Virginia.

He preached thirty-five years, baptized more than two thousand persons, assisted in ordaining twenty-seven ministers and in constituting eighteen churches. His last sermon, at the funeral of a young man, was taken from Zechariah 2:4, "Run, speak to this young man." He addressed the young in feeble, touching strains, saying that it was his last sermon. He spoke until his strength failed and then tottered to a bed from which he was carried to his house. He died July 4, 1802, in his sixty-second year.

John Waller represents, on this birthday of our great nation, the men and women who paid a dear price for religious liberty. He carried the scars of his scourging to his grave, which is located in the Waller-Hackett family burial ground in Abbeville County, near Greenwood, South Carolina.[3]

EWT

---

[1]Lewis Peyton Little, *Imprisoned Preachers and Religious Liberty in Virginia* (Lynchburg, Va.: J. P. Bell Co., 1938), pp. 230-31.

[2]Ibid., p. 233.

[3]Ibid., pp. 411-12.

July 5—Religious Systems Are Enemies of True Biblical Christianity

Scripture: Esther 3

The true nature of a church state and/or a state church is often revealed as one studies church history. Some of the most unrelenting and cruel punishments have been legislated by such unscriptural tribunals. In many cases, they have carried them out with ferocity as great as, if not greater than, the ferocity of pagan religio-political systems. Any challenge or threat to their self-appointed authority is met with verbal and physical attack of the most deceitful and contemptuous spirit. The blood of the Baptists and others who desired to worship God and to carry out His commission according to conscience and not human legislation is a testimony to this.

Such was the character and nature of the Massachusetts Bay Colony as revealed in its attack on Baptists, especially in its persecution of John Clarke and Obadiah Holmes. John Spur testified that John Cotton was the Puritan preacher and also the prosecuting attorney at the trial of Clarke and Holmes. Prior to the sentencing, Cotton "preached . . . that denying infants' baptism would overthrow all; and this was a capital offense; and therefore they were soul murderers."[1] After this, Cotton requested the death sentence.

Holmes's whipping, which is recorded elsewhere, nearly fulfilled that request for capital judgment. The brutality of the scourging was so severe that Holmes required the attention of a physician. Those who carried out the sentence were so incensed at those who gave any comfort to Holmes that the surgeon who dressed his wounds became the object of inquiry and interrogation.

John Spur and John Hazel also came and gave expression of concern and sympathy to Holmes. Holmes testified that they shook his hand but "did use no words of contempt or reproach unto any." He said that Hazel said nothing and that Spur said, "Blessed be the Lord."[2] Another testified that "John Spur came and met him presently, laughing in his face, saying, 'blessed be God for thee, brother'; and so did go with him laughing upon him up towards the prison." This was not a laugh of derision but of encouragement and rejoicing that God had sustained Holmes.

For this kindness, Spur and Hazel were taken by warrants "dated the 5th of the 7th month, 1651. By the court. Increase Newell."[3] Someone paid their fines just before they went to the whipping post, and Spur and Hazel were released. The principal complaints lodged by these Baptists were that they were refused the privileges of Englishmen to have counsel, to be tried by jury, and to know what law they had transgressed. To this last, Governor Endicott replied, "You have denied infant baptism, and deserve to die; I will have no such trash brought to our jurisdiction."

Religious systems are often great enemies to biblical Christianity!

EWT

---

[1]Albert Henry Newman, *A History of the Baptist Churches in the United States* (Philadelphia: American Baptist Publication Society, 1915), p. 138.

[2]Isaac Backus, *A History of the Baptists in New England,* ed. Charles G. Sommers (1846; reprint ed., New York: Lewis Colby and Co., n.d.), p. 113.

[3]Morgan Edwards, *Materials Toward a History of the Baptists* (Danielsville, Ga.: Heritage Papers, 1984), 1:213.

July 6—The Miracle of God's Appointments

Scripture: Acts 8:26-40

Dr. Barnas Sears was destined to become distinguished among Baptists in America as an educator and author, but he is best known for a single event in his life that he performed thousands of miles from his American home while he was in Germany. The event also took place in the covering of darkness.

Born in Sandisfield, Massachusetts, on November 19, 1802, young Barnas was trained in the best schools of the vicinity and entered Brown University, where he graduated with the highest honors of his class in 1825. He continued his theological course of study at Newton Theological Institution and upon graduation was called to pastor the First Baptist Church of Hartford, Connecticut. Following two years in the pastorate, Sears was invited to become a professor at Hamilton Literary and Theological Institution and remained there until 1833. His resignation was submitted that he might be enabled to travel to Germany to further his training.

Providentially, God had been moving on the heart of J. G. Oncken. We have observed elsewhere that Oncken had become convinced of the necessity of immersion to obey the Lord's command, but there was no one to perform the ordinance for the man of God and six others who had come to the same conviction. Oncken had written to Baptists in England and one had suggested "Se-Baptism" (i.e. self-baptism), but Oncken could not accept this as being the will of God. Others had invited him to England for the fulfillment of the ordinance, but he could not spare the time from the great work that God was accomplishing through his efforts. How wonderful then that according to God's schedule the Baptist leader from America should come upon the scene. "On April 22, 1834, at Altona, opposite Hamburg, he (Dr. Sears) baptized, in the Elbe, J. C. Oncken and six others, who, through the influence of Calvin Tibbs, a sea captain, had been led to adopt Baptist views."[1] Though Dr. Barnas Sears returned to the States and had a long and influential ministry among Baptists, I believe the greatest event of his ministerial service was the privilege of baptizing such a man as J. G. Oncken and thus sharing in the victories of Oncken in Germany and much of Europe (cf. entries on January 2 and January 26).

Upon his return to America, Dr. Sears became the president of Newton Theological Seminary. In 1848 he was elected secretary and executive agent of the Massachusetts Board of Education. In 1855 he became president of Brown University. In 1841 Harvard conferred the honorary Doctor of Divinity degree upon Sears, and in 1861 Yale honored him with an LL.D.

When George Peabody set up a large trust fund for the cause of education in the South following the Civil War, the board, to which the administration of the fund was committed, invited Dr. Sears to suggest a plan for the use of the fund, and then they requested that he administer the plan. To better accomplish his work, Dr. Sears moved to Staunton, Virginia, and worked among the Baptist people of that state. He pursued that labor from March 20, 1867, until his death on July 6, 1880.

Surely this was a rewarding life and one full of challenges and opportunities. But the most memorable blessing of all his service took place in the shadows of evening for fear of the reprisal of the state church in Germany when Dr. Sears assisted the Reverend Mr. Oncken in the obedience of baptism that helped produce such a rich, full ministry that so blessed Europe.

DLC

---

[1]George Braxton Taylor, *Virginia Baptist Ministers,* Third Series (Lynchburg, Va.: J. P. Bell Co., 1912), p. 332.

July 7—125 Years: A Ministerial Record

Scripture: Ephesians 1

We have previously considered the martyrdom of Edward Wightman (April 11) in England and mentioned the fact that his offspring were active in the Baptist ministry in early America. "Valentine Wightman was a descendant of Edward Wightman, who was burnt for heresy, at Litchfield, in England, in 1612. Of the Wightmans, there came to this country five brothers, all Baptists—two were preachers; two were deacons; one a private member of the church. Valentine was a son of one of these five."[1]

Valentine Wightman was born in Kingston, Rhode Island, in 1681. In 1705 he was licensed to preach, moved to Groton, Connecticut, and planted the first Baptist church in the colony of Connecticut. His fame spread after he successfully debated the Reverend John Bulkey in a seven-hour debate on June 7, 1727, on the subject of baptism. In 1712 he traveled to New York City to preach, and with continuing visits over a two-year period, Wightman baptized seven men and five women. In 1714 Wightman planted the first Baptist church in the state of New York with these twelve members. Valentine died on June 9, 1747, after completing a ministry of forty-two years in Groton.

The work in Groton continued under the direction of the Wightmans, for in 1754 Timothy Wightman, Valentine's son, was called to the pastorate. In the interval between 1747 and 1754, the church had declined, but Timothy steadied the work and experienced great revivals in 1764, 1775, 1784, and 1786-87. The church continually grew and was enabled to establish a second Baptist church in Groton in 1765. It should be noted that Timothy's ministry encompassed the period of the Revolutionary War, and the pastor ministered to his wounded countrymen. He and the church stood in defense of the principles of liberty for our newly forming nation. After a severe illness, Timothy Wightman died on November 14, 1796, having faithfully served for forty-two years the church that his father had founded.

On August 16, 1766, John Gano Wightman, Timothy's youngest son, was born. The youngster was named after the famed John Gano, pastor of the First Baptist Church of New York City. John Wightman was baptized upon his profession of faith in 1797, and it soon became evident that he was called of God to follow in the footsteps of his father and grandfather in the work of the ministry. He was ordained and accepted the call of the Groton church on August 13, 1800. His first wife died in 1816, and on July 7, 1817, he married Bridget Allyn who served faithfully at his side for several years. During his ministry, the church experienced at least ten seasons of refreshing revival. The Groton church established a sister church in Groton in 1831. John was honored by the Association of Churches, being often called upon to serve as the presiding officer, and he exhibited outstanding executive ability. John Wightman died on July 13, 1841, and thus concluded a ministry of one hundred and twenty-five years as grandfather, father, and son led the work in Groton. Interestingly, on June 12, 1864, the Reverend Palmer G. Wightman, grandson of the Reverend John Gano Wightman, was ordained pastor of the Groton church, and a great revival necessitated yet another building program.[2] May God grant us a multitude of such spiritually serving families in the cause of Jesus Christ in our day!

DLC

---

[1]William B. Sprague, *Annals of the American Pulpit* (New York: Robert Carter and Bros., 1865), 6:26.

[2]*Connecticut Church Records,* pp. 2-3.

July 8—A Principle of Conviction, Not a Preference of Convenience

Scripture: I Kings 21

Most sacredly has Rhode Island guarded the hallowed trust committed to her charge, for no man has ever been persecuted in that sovereignty for his religious opinions and practices from its first settlement in 1636. Roger Williams obtained the first charter in 1643 or 1644, and the first body of laws was drawn under it in 1647. At the close of these civil enactments under this charter these words were added: "And otherwise than this what is herein forbidden, all men may walk as their consciences persuade them, every one in the name of his God. And let the lambs of the Most High walk in this colony without molestation in the name of Jehovah their God forever.[1]

This charter united Providence and Newport into one body politic by the name of "The Incorporation of Providence Plantations in the Narragansett Bay of New England." But finding some defects in this charter, they sent Elder John Clarke to England to solicit a better one. He invested twelve years of his life and a great deal of his money in this solicitation. This second charter bears the date of July 8, 1663.[2]

A few years earlier, in 1656, the Rhode Island founders' conviction of religious freedom was severely tested by their neighbors in the colonies of Plymouth, Massachusetts, Connecticut, and New Haven. These neighbors pressed them hard to give up the principle of religious liberty and to join in their confederacy to crush the Quakers and prevent any more of them from coming to New England. This the founders refused to do and sent the following answer: ''We shall strictly adhere to the foundation principle on which this colony was first settled, to wit, that every man who submits to the civil authority may peaceably worship God according to the dictates of his own conscience without molestation.''[3]

This answer made these neighboring colonies hate them more and seek their ruin by violent actions and by slanderous words that reached England. The slander in England was so great that Roger Williams was forced to return to his native land to defend the actions of Rhode Island. Thus he recorded the event: ''I spent almost five years time with the State of England to keep off the rage of the English against us.''

The adjacent neighbors also encouraged the Pumham Indians to harass the Rhode Island people to the great loss of property, and the Indian leader Myantonomo was put to death for his attachment to Providence. When the people of Rhode Island were in imminent danger, they were not allowed to buy ammunition. Some of their houses were besieged, and some residents were taken to Boston where they were inhumanly treated.

We are thankful as Baptists to have an heritage of forerunners who persecuted no one and who stood for liberty of conscience for all. May we, as they, be willing to jeopardize our property and our very lives for this same principle as a conviction and not merely as a preference of convenience.

EWT

---

[1]Thomas Armitage, *The History of the Baptists* (1890; reprint ed., Watertown, Wis.: Maranatha Baptist Press, 1976), 1:649.

[2]Morgan Edwards, *Materials Toward a History of the Baptists* (Danielsville, Ga.: Heritage Papers, 1984), p. 160.

[3]Ibid., p. 161.

July 9—A Man Whose Heart Was Ever in Burma

Scripture: Acts 16:9-10

Joseph Getchell Binney, the third child in a rather affluent family, was born in Boston in December 1807. Born to parents of robust health, the baby seemed strong until the end of his first year, when Joseph contracted whooping cough. Recovery was very slow, and the effects endured throughout Joseph's lifetime. Joshua Binney, Joseph's father, was a successful businessman, but when Joseph was ten years old, his father signed a note as surety for a business acquaintance. Within a year the friend had defaulted, and Joseph's father was reduced to poverty. Unable to face his friends, Joshua Binney moved out, and Mrs. Binney did all in her power to keep the family together. When Joseph was about twelve, his mother passed away. Joseph's father returned home, and Joseph's grandmother moved in with the family to assist.

Joseph G. Binney was saved at twenty years of age, and he wrote, "About a month after my conversion, I became a member of Park Street Church (Congregational), and about the same time commenced a course of education with the design of becoming a Foreign Missionary."[1] Pursuing that wish, J. G. Binney entered Yale College, and during his course of study, he was invited to debate on the subject of "baptism." Like many other serious pedobaptists, young Binney became convinced with careful study that only believer's immersion was taught in the Bible. He was baptized in 1830, united with a Baptist church, and was soon licensed to preach. After becoming a Baptist, he enrolled in Newton Theological Seminary, but before he finished his course, his health failed. He feared that he would never be able to serve in the ministry. The Lord opened the door to a small pastorate where he could study and rest, and his health returned. The congregation built a new edifice, Joseph Binney was ordained, and in 1833 he married Miss Juliette Pattison.

The severities of the New England winters were physically difficult on Binney, and thus in 1837, he accepted the call to pastor in Savannah, Georgia, and remained there until 1843. The congregation increased significantly, and their interest in foreign missions was spurred.

A growing need "to establish and conduct a school for the training of a native ministry among the Karens" in Burma caused the Triennial Convention to call for assistance from Dr. Binney.[2] This was a dream come true, and the Binneys left in November 1843. In May 1845 a school was opened in Maulmain with thirteen adult students, all converted from heathenism. After five grueling years, Mrs. Binney's health broke, and the couple was forced to return to the States. For a brief period Dr. Binney pastored and was then invited to accept the presidency of the Columbian College. As he served in that capacity, his heart was still in Burma. Thus he resigned as president to again become a missionary, sailing for Burma in 1859. The school was now moved to Rangoon and opened with eighty students. Dr. Binney and his wife carried the full load as he preached, translated, and published. His strength was weakening, and in 1875 he was compelled to leave Burma again. On furlough, his health improved, and he began preaching and was soon offered a pastorate in Savannah, Georgia. He accepted, but his heart remained in Burma. On July 9, 1877, he resigned his church that he might return to his first love. The Binneys sailed in the fall of 1877, but he died on November 26 and was buried in the Indian Ocean. Dr. Binney was outstanding as a preacher and teacher, but his heart for the heathen marked him above his peers and causes us to rejoice today in the memory of this dear warrior of the Lord Jesus Christ.

DLC

---

[1]Mrs. J. G. Binney, *Twenty-Six Years in Burma* (Philadelphia: American Baptist Publication Society, 1880), p. 31.

[2]William Cathcart, *The Baptist Encyclopedia,* ed. Louis H. Everts (Philadelphia: Louis H. Everts, 1881), 1:100.

July 10—"The Queen of Female Missionaries"

Scripture: Jeremiah 33:3

Mrs. M. B. Ingalls has been called "The Queen of female missionaries" by Dr. S. F. Smith,[1] and we can begin to understand the title when we consider her life. Mrs. Ingalls sailed for her field of labor on July 10, 1851, as the second wife of the Reverend L. Ingalls. The couple was transferred from the Arracan Mission to the Burmese department of the Rangoon Mission and labored as a team until the death of Ingalls on March 14, 1856. Many in the States felt that Mrs. Ingalls should return home, but she was constrained by the Holy Spirit to continue in the work, and "the most remarkable success followed her labors—a success in some respects unprecedented in the history of the Burmese Missions."[2] Mrs. Ingalls "remained for forty-six years of further service in Rangoon and Thonze."[3]

She endured two fires on the field that destroyed virtually all of her personal property, but she resolutely continued with her labors. She returned twice to America on furlough and raised support as she awakened deep interest in the churches she visited for the cause of Christ in Burma. On one occasion Mrs. Ingalls returned to the States when her health failed. It took over two years for her to recover. While many thought she should again remain in her homeland, Mrs. Ingalls persisted in following the call of God and returned alone to the field.

While she was in charge of a lonely station, Mrs. Ingalls was holding an evening class in her bungalow when one of the nationals rushed in with great fear to report that the chief of a hostile tribe and his warriors were approaching her home. There was no time to escape, and in a few moments she heard the tramp of marching feet.

> The door was opened, and a swarm of wild men, with flashing eyes, poured into the room. She alone was calm and self-possessed, receiving them kindly as if they were friends. They seemed for a moment subdued by her manner; and, as if by inspiration, she seized the opportunity to divert their attention by stories about America, telling them among other things of Colt's revolver, laying her hand as she spoke, upon the pistol her lamented husband had presented her. The chief listened with scorn and incredulity pictured upon his face. Then, suddenly picking up a piece of paper, he stuck it upon the wall, and cried, 'Shoot.' For a second her heart trembled; she did not know that the pistol was loaded, nor how to use it, for she had never fired one in her life. But again, sending to heaven a swift petition for help, she took aim and fired. The ball pierced the centre of the target. Instantly, as if shot, or perhaps expecting that ball would follow ball, the wild natives rushed from the place, and the missionary widow and her frightened flock fell on their knees to render thanks to their Divine Protector.[4]

In April 1890, while speaking to a group of ladies in America, Mrs. Ingalls spoke of the "attempts of the Dacoits to terrorize her, and exhibited a placard (which had been) nailed to the door of her chapel, offering $10,000 for her head."[5] Believing that she was immortal in the hands of God, Mrs. Ingalls served the Lord faithfully amid great dangers, and we honor her memory as one of the great soldiers in our Lord's missionary army.

DLC

---

[1]G. Winfred Hervey, *The Story of Baptist Missions in Foreign Lands* (St. Louis: C. R. Barnes Publishing Co., 1892), p. 877.

[2]William Cathcart, *The Baptist Encyclopedia,* ed. Louis H. Everts (Philadelphia: Louis H. Everts, 1881), 1:581.

[3]Hervey, p. 940.

[4]Ibid., p. 868.

[5]Maung Shwe Wa, *Burma Baptist Chronicle* (Rangoon: Burma Baptist Convention, 1963), p. 158.

July 11—Biblical Truth: The Basis of Spiritual Union

Scripture: Jeremiah 6:16-30

We have seen that one of the points of contention delaying the union of the Regular Baptists and Separate Baptists in Virginia was that the Regulars had adopted a summary of the Philadelphia Confession of Faith which was the English Centenary Confession of Faith of 1689. The writer of an article concerning the importance of teaching our children in *The Old Paths* of 1897 said, "There can be no spiritual union not based on the knowledge, experience and doing of the truth."[1]

The Baptists in England had undergone not only physical persecution because of their biblical principles but also vicious verbal attacks misrepresenting their profession of faith. A note was addressed to "the judicious and impartial reader" of the 1689 Confession as follows:

> It is now many years since divers of us (with other sober Christians then living and walking in the way of the Lord, that we profess), did conceive ourselves to be under necessity of publishing a Confession of our Faith, for the information and satisfaction of those that did not thoroughly understand what our principles were, or had entertained prejudices against our profession, by reason of the strange representation of them, by some men of note who had taken very wrong measures, and accordingly led others into misapprehensions of us and them: and this was first put forth in 1643, in the name of seven congregations then gathered in London.[2]

By the year 1689 the seven churches represented had expanded to "upwards of one-hundred baptized congregations in England and Wales (denying Arminianism) being met together in London, from the third of the seventh month to the eleventh of the same, 1689, to consider some things that might be for the glory of God, and the good of these congregations."[3]

In reading the differing preambles to the various editions of the articles of faith, it is very clear that the reporting was just as biased, inaccurate, and often as dishonest as the misrepresentations of fundamentalist, Bible-believing Christians by the media of our day. The major concerns of those great men of God who affixed their names to those truths set forth was that the general public clearly understood those principles for which they stood, lived, and died, and that they would have a basis upon which they could order their homes and catechize their children, as well as a guide for exercising discipline and maintaining purity in their congregations.

May our Lord revive the same concerns in our churches and homes in this day of religious pragmatism which has led us to place great emphasis on methodology while spiritual purity and maturity, grounded in the principles of God's Word, are sadly neglected. Today it seems that success and spirituality are measured in numbers rather than in holiness.

EWT

---

[1]J. B. McInturff, *The Old Paths: They Being Dead Yet Speak* (Woodstock, Va.: W. N. Grabill, 1897), p. 1.

[2]Edward Bean Underhill, ed., *Confessions of Faith and Other Documents Illustrative of the History of the Baptist Churches of England in the 17th Century* (London: Haddon Bros., 1845), p. 173.

[3]Ibid., p. 171.

July 12—Baptists Receive the Wrath of All State Religions

Scripture: Acts 28:17-31

Sadly, we must be consistent with our reporting that the Protestant reformers were sometimes as guilty of atrocities as the Romanists and that more often than not, Anabaptists and Baptists were the objects of their violence. "Catholics and Protestants taught that tradition, reason and Scripture made it the pious duty of saints to torture and burn men as heretics out of pure love for their holiness and salvation. Protestants told them that it was a sacred duty to slaughter those as schismatics, sectaries, malignants, who corrupted the Church and would not live in peace with the Reformed."[1]

The sad instances of persecution practiced against the Baptists by the Protestants in King Edward VI's reign are in the Latin version of *Foxe's Book of Martyrs* but were left out of his English edition in order to protect the reputation of some of the martyrs of Queen Mary's day who had persecuted the Baptists during Edward's reign. John Rogers, one of Foxe's friends, called for the death of those who opposed the baptism of infants. It is reported that Rogers declared "That burning alive was no cruel death, but easy enough." It is believed it was Foxe who responded, "Well perhaps, it may so happen, that you yourselves shall have your hands full of this mild burning." And so it came to pass, and Rogers was the first man who was burned in Queen Mary's time.[2]

During the last year of King Edward's reign, Humphry Middleton was kept prisoner by the archbishop and was dreadfully tormented by him. On the occasion of being condemned in open court, Middleton said unto him, "Well, reverend Sir, pass what sentence you think fit upon us: but that you may not say you were not forewarned, I testify that your own turn will be next." And accordingly it came to pass; for a little while after, King Edward died, and the bishops were cast into prison. Humphry Middleton, however, was burned at Canterbury, July 12, 1555, during the reign of Mary.[3]

It seems at that period the contention was not so much over the mode of baptism but the time. Some reformers immersed but also taught that baptism put away original sin. The disputation relating to infant baptism and believer's baptism was so hot during the reign of Mary that the crowded prisons were filled with controversy between the different groups of prisoners over the nature of baptism.

We must keep in mind that the nature of the systems of theology of state churches oftentimes became the foundation of persecution. In contrast, there is no record of persecution carried out by Baptists.

EWT

---

[1]Thomas Armitage, *The History of the Baptists* (1890; reprint ed., Watertown, Wis.: Maranatha Baptist Press, 1976), 1:876.

[2]Thomas Crosby, *The History of the English Baptists* (1738-40; reprint ed., Lafayette, Tenn.: Church History Research and Archives, 1979), pp. 58-61.

[3]J. M. Cramp, *Baptist History* (London: Elliott Stock, 1870), p. 216.

July 13—Strong Drink Is a Mocker

Scripture: Proverbs 20:1

William Rufus Powell was blessed in being born into a godly home where daily family devotions were conducted by his father. Born on November 13, 1808, he knew the youthful joy of having a father with sterling integrity and a mother with convictions that she did not hesitate to announce and defend. The home was the center of much fellowship. The pastor often visited, and journeying preachers availed themselves of a "prophet's chamber." The sweet, uplifting influences abounded during William's youth, but when he was only eight years old, his mother died. Though his father and older sisters did their best to continue the fine traditions, the mother's touch surely must have been missed.

William's education was promising under the tutelage of the Reverend Herndon Frazer. Young William set his goal to pursue the study of law, and thus at age seventeen he moved from home and boarded at the home of Captain Therit Towles, a widower. Captain Towles's only daughter Mary was making her home with an aunt in Culpeper, Virginia, and she and her aunt often visited Captain Towles. William Powell had become a schoolmaster, and at twenty-one years of age he asked Mary to become his wife. In a short time, William became a deputy-sheriff with his father-in-law and settled down to a farmer's life on a plantation. The environment was far different from that of his youth. Sumptuous meals and sparkling wines led to much drunken revelry, but though Powell gave much time to playing cards, dancing, and fox hunting, he kept himself from the tippling of alcohol. In spite of all the activities of such a merry life, he managed to read widely, and his quest for knowledge kept him up late into the night, reading as many volumes as possible. He so established this habit that throughout his life four hours of sleep a night was all that he demanded!

In continual correspondence, a godly sister urged him to give heed to spiritual matters, but her warnings seemed to no avail. However, when his wife asked him to attend the Mine Run Baptist Church, William decided to go and hear the Reverend Philip Pendleton, a man of deep piety. William's heart was strangely moved, and the Bible became vital to him. He found a little grove where he cried out to God in prayer for pardon. The Lord responded with the deep peace of salvation, and the next Sunday morning William made an open profession of faith at Craig's Meeting House. Soon thereafter he and Mary were baptized into the fellowship of the Mine Run Church, and before long, William Powell was licensed to preach and became assistant to Pendleton. Upon the pastor's death, William Powell was ordained in 1836 and succeeded Pendleton as pastor of the Mine Run Church. He was a zealous advocate of missions, and during the early years of his ministry, he was perhaps the most popular of the preachers in the association.

William Rufus Powell is best known, however, for his position in relation to strong drink and the child of God. "He contended that the church should not allow the use of ardent spirits as a beverage by its members. He believed in total abstinence.''[1] Turmoil over this issue soon developed in the churches and association. Because the majority of the believers did not sustain their pastor's position, Powell left his church and formed another. Thank God for men of conviction, for in time Powell's view became the position of the Baptists!

The Reverend Mr. Powell passed away on July 13, 1859. His last sermon had for its text, ''Which hope we have as an anchor of the soul.'' During his last days, William called upon his family and friends to sing his favorite hymn, ''How Firm a Foundation,'' and in the reconciliation of the cross, he passed into the presence of the Lord with great victory. Thank God for the memory of William Rufus Powell—a Baptist leader of conviction!

DLC

---

[1]George Braxton Taylor, *Virginia Baptist Ministers,* Third Series (Lynchburg, Va.: J. P. Bell Co., 1912), pp. 15-16.

July 14—A New Testament in Siamese That They Fear Not

Scripture: I John 4:17-21

John Taylor Jones was born at New Ipswich, New Hampshire. When he was about fifteen years of age, he made a profession of faith and joined the Congregational Church in Ashby, Massachusetts. During his theological studies, Jones experienced a change in his thinking relating to the mode and subjects of baptism. In 1828 he was baptized by Pastor Malcom and joined the Federal Street Baptist Church in Boston. On July 14, 1830, he was married to Eliza Grew, and within seven months, they were on their way to Burma as missionaries.[1]

Upon arrival in Burma, Jones addressed himself with great zeal to his missionary work and soon became proficient in the Burman and Taling languages. He seemed to be especially drawn to the Talings, a tribal people, and believing there was great opportunity to preach to them in Siam (Thailand), he departed for that country to carry out that purpose. The Lord had another purpose for him, which was a special mission to translate the New Testament into the Siamese language. Jones engaged in this work with great interest and completed it in October of 1843. His translation of the New Testament ''compares favorably with the translation of the New Testament made in any of the Asiatic languages, including the lifework of such men as Carey, Marshman, Judson, and Morrison, and their worthy successors."[2]

During his last visit to New York, Jones is quoted as saying,

> There is one thing which distinguishes Christianity from every false religion. It is the only religion that can take away the fear of death. I never knew a dying heathen in Siam, or anywhere else, that was not afraid, terribly afraid, of death. And there was nothing that struck the Siamese people with greater astonishment than a remark that my dear departed wife made, in Siamese, to her native nurse, shortly before her death; "I am not afraid to die." For weeks after her death, the Siamese people would come to me, as though incredulous that such a thing could be, and ask, "Teacher, is it really true that a person had died and was not afraid to die? Can it be possible?" And when assured that it was even so, they would say, "Wonderful, wonderful, that a person should die and not be afraid."[3]

With Jones, Christianity was not so much a feeling as a principle; not so much an occasional impulse as an equitable and ever-acting power. He rejoiced in the sunshine of prosperity, but he toiled on with steady zeal under the deepest shade. Jones was said to be more eloquent in Siamese than in English. His death was very edifying. In his last hours three Siamese schoolgirls were brought to his bedside. He testified so sweetly to them: "You have often heard me tell you that the affairs of this world are of short duration." In this way the man of God prepared them for his death. This modest, unassuming man slipped out of this life to his eternal home, leaving the words of eternal life with the people of Siam.

EWT

---

[1]William B. Sprague, *Annals of the American Pulpit* (New York: Robert Carter and Bros., 1865), 6:772-73.

[2]William Cathcart, *The Baptist Encyclopedia,* ed. Louis H. Everts (Philadelphia: Louis H. Everts, 1881), 1:616.

[3]G. Winfred Hervey, *The Story of Baptist Missions in Foreign Lands* (St. Louis: C. R. Barnes Publishing Co., 1892), pp. 464-65.

July 15—God's Men from a Church Named Polecat

Scripture: II Thessalonians 3:1-5

If you were asked of which church you were a member, how would you like to answer "Polecat"? That is exactly what the early Baptists answered in the southwestern part of Caroline County, Virginia. John Burrus, a licensed minister among them, was apprehended and haled into court along with three laymen: Bartholomew Choning, James Goolrich, and Edward Herndon. During the same period, Elijah Craig spent time in the same jail at Bowling Green, Virginia. All of them were incarcerated because they, like the polecat, had become a stench in the religious nostrils of the established church for preaching the gospel without state church ordination or proper license. The church was later named Burrus Meeting House after the venerable preacher, and when the church was moved from near Polecat Creek to the White Oak Seats, the name of the church became Carmel.[1]

Carmel Church is still located on U.S. Highway 1, just north of Richmond, Virginia, one mile west off Interstate 95. In the churchyard is a memorial to these men and all who suffered incarceration for the sake of the gospel. Inside the church is a famous painting by Sidney King of Patrick Henry defending the five Baptist preachers in Fredericksburg, Virginia, at an earlier date. If you are traveling on I-95 in that area, it would be worthwhile to look for the sign "Carmel Church" and take that exit west and pause there a few moments to reflect on our great Baptist heritage.

Choning, Goolrich, and Herndon were not ministers, but they did exercise the gift of exhortation. They were fearless men and were accused of "jamming a Scripture verse down the throat of every man they met upon the road." They were evidently apprehended and imprisoned to await their trial July 15, 1771.[2] After the trial, the court record "ordered [that] they be remanded back to the gaol."

In the last two decades of the eighteenth century, the Burrus Church was one of considerable prominence. The association met there in 1788, 1793, and 1797. Following that, there was a decline to the point of considering dissolving the congregation and joining together with a sister church. In 1808 they experienced revival under the able leadership of Andrew Broadus. We are to this day thankful for God's providential care for this church and for its continuance as a living memorial to our spiritual heritage. The church still stands against the forces that would bring our ministers back under state licensure and thus state control.

May we all persevere, as this church has done, in preserving the landmarks and in teaching future generations the "fundamental principles" of our Baptist faith which are essential to the preservation of religious liberty for all throughout the land.

EWT

---

[1]Lewis Peyton Little, *Imprisoned Preachers and Religious Liberty in Virginia* (Lynchburg, Va.: J. P. Bell Co., 1938), pp. 245-47.

[2]Homer Massey, ed., *Forgotten Facts of Virginia's History* (Norfolk, Va.: Published by the author, n.d.), p. 6.

July 16—Baptists Desired Freedom, Not Toleration

Scripture: Luke 13:32-33

Baptists have always chafed under the system of coercion for religious support for an established church. The New Testament principle of voluntarism is cherished by the Baptists and is so ingrained in their hearts and minds that the members of the First Baptist Church of Middleborough, Massachusetts, must have been sorely grieved when they read the following notice, which was posted by the Reverend Isaac Backus on July 16, 1759.

> Whereas by a late Law of this Province it is enacted that a List of the Names of those who belong to each Baptist Society (Church) must be taken each year and given in to the Assessors before the 20th of July or else they will stand liable to be Rated to the ministers where they live: Therefore this is to Notifie all who belong to the Baptist Society who usually meet for public worship in this place that a meeting is appointed by the Committee to be at our meeting house on Monday the 16th Instant at two of the clock in the afternoon for each one that is seriously of our persuasion to appear in that a List may be taken agreeable to said Acts.[1]

Isaac Backus spent a great deal of time fighting to eradicate state support for the Standing Order churches. Not only did this practice impose "taxation without representation" upon Baptists, but it also robbed the local Baptist churches from building their own buildings, supporting their pastors, and establishing colleges to train preachers and expand their ministries. Some might have thought that the Baptists would have been satisfied in registering and thus being free of the "church tax," but this concession would provide only a measured toleration. Baptists could never be happy until they obtained a complete abolition of such a "church tax."

Baptists rejoiced a few years later when Virginia's famous Act for Religious Freedom was enacted in January 1786. The document read in part,

> Whereas, Almighty God hath created the mind free; . . . that to compel a man to furnish contributions of money for the propagation of opinions which he disbelieves, is sinful and tyrannical, and even the forcing him to support this or that teacher of his own religious persuasion, is depriving him of the comfortable liberty of giving his contributions to the particular pastor whose morals he would make his pattern. . . . Be it enacted by the General Assembly, That no man shall otherwise suffer on account of his religious opinions or belief; but that all men shall be free to profess, and by argument to maintain, their opinions in matters of religion, and that the same in no wise diminish, enlarge or affect their civil capacities.[2]

Liberty of conscience must be preserved at all cost! Baptists have always believed that "persecution for difference in religion is a monstrous and cruel beast, that destroyeth both prince and people, hindereth the Gospel of Christ, and scattereth his disciples that witness and profess His name."[3] May God make Baptists today real champions of liberty!

DLC

---

[1]Isaac Backus, *The Diary of Isaac Backus,* ed. William G. McLoughlin (Providence: Brown University Press, 1979), 1:513-14.

[2]Act of Religious Freedom from the *Code of Virginia.*

[3]Leonard Busher, *Religions Peace: A Plea for Liberty of Conscience* (London: John Sweeting, 1646), p. 41.

July 17—Another Look at the Terrible Practice of Slavery

Scripture: Colossians 3:22–4:1

Modern-day Americans are aghast when confronted with the calamity of slavery as it was practiced among Baptists in our land. It is no comfort of heart to realize that Baptists were not alone in this practice, but the relationship the slaves held with the white membership of the churches is a subject of widespread ignorance both in the North and the South.

Wonderfully the grace of God was operative. In the records of the Kiokee Church (Georgia), a thrilling account exists of the conversion of "Brother Billy, 'about one hundred years old,' formerly a slave but at that time, 'a free man of color.' "[1] This took place on July 17, 1841, and "Billy" united with the church.

Some evidence exists that causes us to believe that the slave members of Baptist churches were allowed to vote. As with the white males, black male members were ''assessed'' for church expenses and required to attend business meetings.[2] The females, black and white, did not vote in the business matters of the churches.

The slave membership of many Baptist churches greatly outnumbered the whites, and thus the churches often appointed spiritually faithful slaves to serve as a discipline committee among their own. The churches chastened their slave membership primarily for problems of morals and honesty, and they chastised their slaveholder members for these infractions as well as for cruelty and barbarity to their slaves. It is apparent that slaves were better off being owned by Christians than by unbelievers! This in no way condones slavery but merely emphasizes a historical fact.

Black slave preachers were licensed and ordained by the Baptist churches, and the impact of those slave preachers was unique! Much of the evangelism among the slaves resulted from the preaching on the plantations by these faithful men who were slaves twofold: first to the Lord Jesus Christ and then to an earthly master.

Segregation in the services was always maintained. In some of the old church buildings in the areas where slavery was practiced, one can still observe ''slave balconies.'' In other church buildings a portion of the facility was designated for the slave members.

Even following the Civil War, former slaves were being received into the membership of Baptist churches in the South. However, we have pointed out that the Baptists in the South often assisted the former slaves by helping them establish their own churches, granting them letters of dismission, and maintaining a fraternal relationship with the new assemblies. The persecution that black Baptist preachers experienced originated not from believers but rather from the unregenerate of the population.

These observations are not intended as an attempt to excuse slavery. The authors merely wish to show that racial relationships were far superior among those who were related in the brotherhood in Christ. The greatest liberating force known to man is the glorious gospel of the Lord Jesus Christ!

DLC

---

[1]James Donovan Mosteller, *A History of the Kiokee Baptist Church in Georgia* (Ann Arbor: Edwards Brothers, 1952), p. 180.

[2]Ibid., pp. 181-82.

July 18—For I Know Whom I Have Believed

Scripture: II Timothy 1:1-12

Many times the great wives behind the great men of God are ignored. The Baptist pastor Benjamin Keach, whose birth, conversion, and call to preach are mentioned elsewhere in this volume, was blessed with a wonderful wife. This godly lady, who had borne him five children in the space of ten years, died in 1670, and Keach wrote a poem in her memory entitled "A Pillar Set Up." In this poem

> he gave her a very great and noble character, commending her for her zeal for the truth, sincerity in religion, uncommon love to the saints, and her content in whatsoever condition of life God was pleased to bring her to. He particularly observes, how great an help, and comfort, she was to him in his suffering for the cause of Christ, visiting, and taking all possible care of him while in prison, instead of tempting him to use any base means for delivery out of his troubles, encouraging him to go on, and counting it an honor done them both, in that they were called to suffer for the sake of Christ. She was of an heavenly conversation, her discourse was savoury, and for the most part about divine things, seeking the spiritual good of those with whom she conversed. So successful was she herein, that some have acknowledged, that their conversion to God was thro' the conversation they had with her.[1]

Two years after his first wife's death, he married a widow of extraordinary piety with whom he lived thirty-two years. His second wife, Susanna Partridge, bore him five daughters, the youngest of whom married Thomas Crosby, a renowned Baptist historian. After the death of Benjamin Keach, Susanna lived with her daughter and son-in-law, and Crosby wrote of her, "She lived with me . . . the last twenty years of her life. I must say, that she walked before God in truth, and with a perfect heart, and did that which was good in His sight. She lived in peace, without spot and blameless."[2] Crosby paid further tribute to the godly heritage of his father-in-law's family: "I have been blessed with the happiness of a good wife, the youngest offspring of the reverend gentleman whose memory is hereby revived [i.e., Benjamin Keach]; so the many years I have enjoyed this blessing have given me an opportunity of being more particular, than in the many worthies in this history mentioned."[3]

Many godly wives saw their husbands pilloried, imprisoned, and treated roughly, and the encouragement that these women provided cannot be measured. Benjamin Keach's stand was constantly challenged by the religious establishment of his day, which kept him under the pressure of writing treatises and defenses upholding the principles of Baptists in answer to some of the most able defenders of pedobaptism of his day, including Richard Baxter. ''The hardships that he suffered for asserting believers baptism in opposition to that of infants, did not in the least influence his judgment, nor abate his zeal for that principle; for he was afterwards one of the most noted advocates in his day for it.''[4]

Keach continued in his ministry until his death July 18, 1704. On his deathbed he requested that Joseph Stennet preach his funeral sermon from these words: ''For I know whom I have believed, and am persuaded that He is able to keep that which I have committed unto Him against that day.''[5] We should be grateful for the memory of godly men, but we should also be thankful for their wives who stood with them in many sufferings and trials.

EWT

---

[1]Thomas Crosby, *The History of the English Baptists* (1738-40; reprint ed., Lafayette, Tenn.: Church History Research and Archives, 1979), 4:274.

[2]Ibid., p. 275.

[3]Ibid., p. 268.

[4]Ibid., p. 276.

[5]Ibid., p. 308.

July 19—The Brilliant Eye That Shone Like a Star

Scripture: Proverbs 11:30; Daniel 12:3

The impoverished Welsh family rejoiced on Christmas Day, 1766, as God blessed their home with a little son. The baby was named ''Christmas'' for the day, and so was born he who was to become the outstanding Welsh preacher and perhaps the greatest Baptist preacher that Great Britain ever produced!

Christmas Evans was raised in poverty, and his father died when the lad was only nine years old. He spent the next few years in the home of a disreputable uncle, and when he was fifteen, Christmas still could not read. There was never an opportunity to receive an education, but at eighteen, Christmas was converted and joined the Presbyterians. The young man was about six feet tall and had the build of an athlete. His very presence spoke of leadership, and he was urged to preach.

The amazing development of Christmas's untrained mind is a story all in itself. "He learned to read his Welsh Bible in the course of a month. . . . His intense thirst for knowledge led him to borrow and read every book that the scant libraries of the neighborhood afforded."[1] "He became skilled in Hebrew, Greek and English."[2]

Christmas cherished the desire to preach while still in fellowship with the pedobaptists. With a wish to expose the Anabaptists (as he called them), he studied his New Testament carefully. The result he has recorded for us: "Having read the New Testament through, I found not a single verse in favor of infant sprinkling, while about forty passages seemed to testify clearly for baptism on a profession of faith."[3] In 1788 Christmas was immersed in the River Duar by the Reverend Timothy Thomas.

Pastor Evans began his pastoral ministry in Lleyn in Caernarvon where he labored until he was called to the Isle of Anglesea in 1791. There were two chapels and eight preaching stations. Spiritual deadness was pervasive when he began his thirty-five year ministry there. However, in a short time the Isle was revived, and by 1826 the preaching stations had multiplied to scores, and twenty-eight preachers flooded the Isle with the message of grace.

During his pastorate on the Isle, Christmas traveled to Velin Voel to attend associational meetings in 1794. After two ministers had addressed the assembly in the heat of the open air, Christmas Evans was asked to speak. He preached for three hours, and from the outset the audience thrilled to his ministry. The message was on the demoniac of Gadara, and this famed sermon became the trademark of Evans. During his ministry he preached one hundred and sixty-three times before Baptist associations.

After short pastorates in Caperhilly, Cardiff, and again in Caernarvon, the man of God died on July 19, 1838, in his seventy-second year. In early life Christmas lost an eye, and the account of Robert Hall is thus to be understood: "Robert Hall said of him that he was 'the tallest, stoutest, greatest man he ever saw; that he had but one eye, if it could be called an eye; it was more a brilliant star; it shined like Venus! and would lead an army through a forest on a dark night.' "[4]

On his deathbed, the man of God referred to a verse in an old Welsh hymn, then waved his hand as if with Elijah in the chariot of fire, and cried: "Wheel about, coachman, drive on!"

DLC

---

[1]William Cathcart, *The Baptist Encyclopedia,* ed. Louis H. Everts (Philadelphia: Louis H. Everts, 1881), 2:832.

[2]Norman Wade Cox, ed., *Encyclopedia of Southern Baptists* (Nashville: Broadman Press, 1958), 1:427.

[3]Cathcart, p. 382.

[4]Thomas Armitage, *The History of the Baptists* (1890; reprint ed., Watertown, Wis.: Maranatha Baptist Press, 1976), 2:612.

July 20—A Short but Fruitful Life

Scripture: Numbers 14:24; 32:12; Joshua 14:8,9,14

The Reverend Samuel Pearce was ordained in 1789 as pastor of the Cannon Street Baptist Church in Birmingham, England, and he served that church until his death on October 10, 1799. Pearce was a dear friend of William Carey before the beginning of the missionary enterprise, and he was one of the warmest advocates of the cause of worldwide missions that the world has ever known. He was personally desirous of going with Carey to India, but the board of the Missionary Society, realizing his physical frailties, convinced him that he was invaluable to the cause of missions in England, and he willingly gave himself to that ministry. Pearce's eloquence in the pulpit stirred many throughout his homeland and in Ireland to volunteer for and support the work that was being carried on in India. His continual letters to Carey revealed a tenderness of heart for the work that constantly drove him. As a staunch prayer warrior, Pearce carried every matter to the Lord and expected and received answers to his prayers. In 1794 he wrote to the ministers in the United States urging the formation of an American Baptist foreign missionary society, and credit must be given to Pastor Pearce, for the seed fell on good soil and bore fruit a hundredfold.

What caused such an unsatiated desire in the heart of Samuel Pearce to get out the redemptive message? That question is best answered in knowing something of his background. Samuel Pearce was born in Birmingham, England, on July 20, 1766. As a lad he experienced seasons of distressing conviction as he considered his sin. When he was fifteen, he was in the house of a man who was dying, and the man in despair cried out, "I am damned forever." Hearing those words, young Pearce was filled with terror. The fate of the dying man and his own sinfulness filled him with anguish. For a year Pearce grappled with his own condition until hearing the Reverend Mr. Birt of Plymouth, England. He was pointed to the Lamb of God and, turning to the Lord, found full assurance and peace with God.

Soon after his wonderful salvation was realized, "he made a covenant with Jehovah, signing it with his own blood, pledging himself completely to the Lord."[1] Though that resolution was firmly made, Samuel Pearce was trusting strongly in the flesh, and he partly broke his vow. Again despair overcame him until the Redeemer made Himself known to the young man, and from that time, he became a "living sacrifice."

Samuel Pearce was trained for the ministry at the Bristol College, and during his collegiate life he was often engaged in preaching among the poor and neglected in the city. His subject matter always focused on the Savior's death upon Calvary.

Though Pearce's ministerial life lasted only ten years, William Cathcart has said, "Measured by usefulness instead of years this young pastor preached for at least a century."[2] In the late eighteenth century, to die by consumption was to be dreaded, but when he understood he was thus dying, Pearce said, "Oh my Lord, if by this death I can most glorify Thee, I prefer it to all others."[3] On his dying day he said to his wife, "O my dear! What shall I do? But why do I complain? He makes all my bed in my sickness." When Mrs. Pearce stated, "Jesus can make a dying bed feel soft as downy pillows are," he responded, "Yes, He can; He does; I feel it."[4] And so God's servant victoriously fell asleep in our Lord Jesus Christ!

DLC

---

[1]William Cathcart, *The Baptist Encyclopedia,* ed. Louis H. Everts (Philadelphia: Louis H. Everts, 1881), 2:890.

[2]Ibid., p. 891.

[3]Andrew Fuller, comp., and Levi L. Hill, ed., *Memoirs of the Late Rev. Samuel Pearce* (1846; reprint ed., New York: Lewis Colby and Co., n.d.), 3:341.

[4]Ibid., pp. 383-84.

July 21—A Remarkable Missionary to Africa

Scripture: Psalm 23

An emaciated old missionary spokesman stood before a united assembly of Baptists in Glasgow, Scotland, in 1879 and lifted his voice as he said, "Oh, that I had another life to go out to Africa. The field is white, and the multitudes are in darkness still."[1] This was the last public speech of Alfred Saker, veteran missionary to Africa. The Dark Continent's best-known missionary, David Livingstone, wrote about Saker and said, "Take it all in all, specially having regard to its many-sided character, the work of Alfred Saker at Cameroons and Victoria is, in my judgment, the most remarkable on the African Coast."[2]

Alfred Saker, who for more than thirty-seven years served as an English Baptist missionary in Western Africa, was born on July 21, 1814, in the parish of Wrothan, Kent, England. He was a thin, frail boy from a large family, and though he loved reading, he could not pursue his education because it was necessary to enter the work force. He labored with his father, who was a millwright and engineer, and received valuable information that could be transformed into useful labor years later in Africa.

Young Saker was saved when he was sixteen years old when he wandered into a Sunday evening gospel service in a little chapel in Sevenoaks where he had been sent by his father to assist in the millwright business. Returning home he became active in the local Baptist church and was baptized in 1834. Upon the death of his father, Saker moved to Devonport for employment and in 1839 married Miss Helen Jessup. Both united with the Morice Square Baptist Church in that city.

Since his conversion, Alfred Saker had been interested in missions, and his wife shared in this concern. The Sakers offered themselves to the Baptist Missionary Society for service in Africa. In a group of eight, the Sakers landed in Februrary 1844, and the outstanding ministry of Alfred Saker began. Though he was never physically robust, Saker's energy seemed inexhaustible. One by one the other laborers were forced to leave because the climate seemed lethal to most Europeans. To be sure, Saker suffered greatly from fever and debility, but he persisted in working with the tribes on the mainland at the mouth of the Cameroons River, and he personally built himself a home there, reduced their language to writing, and formed a school within the first two years of his labors. His home church sent a printing press, and he printed portions of the New Testament and school texts. In 1849 a church was formed. Saker introduced agriculture and taught industrial arts to the nationals, producing carpenters, smiths, and bricklayers. In 1853 the Spanish government insisted that the Baptists depart and suppressed all Protestant worship. Saker and his congregation moved en masse to Amboises Bay, where he purchased a tract of land from the Bambia chief. Again the missionary led with untiring personal efforts, and soon a new colony with homes and gardens was built. The indomitable missionary translated the Bible into Dualla in 1862 and then revised it completely by 1872. At least five times he returned to England to rebuild his health, but he never stayed longer than necessary, for the consuming passion of his life had been to work for the salvation of Africans. Broken in body, Saker returned for the last time to England in 1876, and as his health returned, he visited churches to challenge young men for Africa. He whose life text had been, "For Thou art with me," passed into the Lord's presence in March 1880 and doubtless said, "Now I am with Thee!"

DLC

---

[1]Walter Sinclair Stewart, *Early Baptist Missionaries and Pioneers* (Philadelphia: Judson Press, 1925), p. 149.

[2]Ibid., p. 192.

July 22—An Effective Preacher for Eventful Times

Scripture: Haggai 2

John Gano was a direct descendant of the Huguenots of France. His great-grandfather Francis was obliged to flee from the persecution that resulted from the bloody edict revoking the Edict of Nantes. Francis Gano settled in New Rochelle, New York. His son Stephen raised six sons, one of whom was John's father, Daniel. Daniel and his wife, Sarah Britton, were eminently pious people, he being a Presbyterian and she a Baptist. John, the fifth child and third son of this union, was born July 22, 1727, and embraced the Baptist convictions of his mother as a youth.

After carrying out an itinerant preaching ministry throughout the South, John Gano accepted a call to take charge of an infant church at the "Jersey Settlement" in North Carolina. The church grew to be large and his ministry abundantly useful throughout that region of the country. Upon an outbreak of a war with the Cherokee Indians, he moved to New Jersey.

On June 19, 1762, the First Baptist Church of New York City was constituted by Benjamin Miller and John Gano.[1] The latter immediately became its pastor. He also accepted the pastoral care of the Baptist church in Philadelphia, and for a number of years, he was the pastor of all Baptists in the two largest cities on the American continent. The church in New York prospered so much under his ministry that they had to enlarge the meetinghouse in 1763. He possessed excellent pulpit talents, and crowds flocked to hear him expound the Word of God.

During the Revolutionary War, the church was dispersed and its records suspended. No baptisms are recorded from April 24, 1776, to September 4, 1784.[2] The British forces occupied the city for more than seven years, and Gano served in the Revolutionary Army for that period of time as a chaplain. No city in America was occupied as long by the enemy and suffered so much as did the city of New York. Its inhabitants found shelter in other colonies, while the Tories made it their place of refuge. Pestilence and two great fires swept it, and the soldiers inflicted all the damage that they could. At the opening of the war, there were nineteen churches in the city, but when it closed, only nine of them could be used for worship. The Baptist meetinghouse, having been used for a horse stable, was almost in ruins. On his return to New York, Gano found emptiness, desolation, and ashes. He collected thirty-seven out of about two hundred of his former flock. Many had died, and others were scattered throughout every part of the new nation.

As soon as the building was decently cleaned, he rallied his people and preached to them from Haggai 2:3, "Who is left among you that saw this house in her first glory? And how do you see it now?" Under his ministry, the days of spiritual prosperity soon returned and lasted until he baptized his last convert on April 5, 1788, and left for Kentucky. During his pastorate of twenty-five years, he baptized 297 and received 23 by letter into the church. Armitage says, "He was one of the most remarkable men in America in all the resources which native strength, sound judgment, wit, ingenuity, retentive memory, zeal, and godliness furnish in times which try men's souls."[3]

EWT

---

[1]J. H. Spencer, *A History of Kentucky Baptists from 1769 to 1883* (Cincinnati: J. R. Baumes, 1886), 1:124.

[2]Thomas Armitage, *The History of the Baptists* (1890: reprint ed., Watertown, Wis.: Maranatha Baptist Press, 1976), 2:755.

[3]Ibid., pp. 754-56.

July 23—Baptist Growth in Sweden

Scripture: Acts 13:44-50

When he almost drowned, the thought of death and eternity became real in the life of the fourteen-year-old Andreas Wiberg. Young Wiberg had been born in 1816 in the northeastern part of Sweden. When he was nineteen and with a desire to show God his gratitude for being delivered from the premature death, he entered the University of Upsala with the ministry in mind. While a student, he realized his need of salvation and called upon the Lord. In 1843 he was ordained a minister in the state church (Lutheran), but he soon became dissatisfied with admitting the unconverted to the Lord's Supper, and he left his work as a minister. For two years he translated the works of Martin Luther and edited a religious paper. When Wiberg met other genuine believers in northern Sweden and expressed sympathy for their views, he became the subject of persecution.

In the spring of 1851, Wiberg visited Hamburg, Germany, and became acquainted with J. G. Oncken and the work of the Baptists. During his stay, he resisted the Baptist's doctrine, but upon leaving Germany, he was given a copy of "*Pengilly on Baptism* and on full examination, he adopted Baptist principles."[1] There was no one in Sweden to administer immersion, but in the providence of God, in 1852 his ship was detained in Copenhagen, and he met the Reverend F. O. Nilsson. Nilsson had previously introduced Baptist principles in Sweden but had been imprisoned and finally banished by the High Court of the Land. What a God-appointed meeting, for Nilsson baptized Wiberg "July 23, 1852, at eleven o'clock in the night, near the Island of Amager, a short distance from Copenhagen."[2] Even before his immersion, Wiberg had written a book on baptism in Sweden, and many had adopted Baptist views.

Though the Baptists in Sweden were subjected to bitter persecution, their number was close to five hundred when Wiberg arrived back from America in 1855. Wiberg returned to his native land after having been appointed the Director of the Labors of the American Baptist Publication Society for Sweden. On January 1, 1856, Wiberg began a Christian publication called *The Evangelist,* which had five hundred original subscribers. As the work of the Baptists grew in Sweden, a chapel was needed to solidify the gains. Thus, a twelve-hundred-seat auditorium was built in Stockholm. Baptists from England and America sent money to assist these Swedish brethren, but the persecution was far from over. While the presses could publish *The Evangelist* without trouble, Bible and tract distribution was more difficult. One of Wiberg's contemporaries, Mr. Hejdenberg, was summoned before the tribunals six times and was imprisoned in six different places from two to fourteen days each time. Another of the preachers was fined for preaching the gospel and thus desecrating the Sabbath. The persecutions seemed very severe, but as always, God gave grace and growth as a result of the suffering.

The Reverend Andreas Wiberg, who is considered the founder and builder of the Baptist witness in Sweden, passed away in 1887.

DLC

---

[1]Thomas Armitage, *The History of the Baptists* (1890; reprint ed., Watertown, Wis.: Maranatha Baptist Press, 1976), 2:833.

[2]William Cathcart, *The Baptist Encyclopedia,* ed. Louis H. Everts (Philadelphia: Louis H. Everts, 1881), 2:1240.

July 24—Bound and Drowned in the River Meuse for the Glory of God

Scripture: Matthew 25:31-46

Aeltgen Baten was an aged woman, and Maeyken Wouters was a young woman of about twenty-four years. Through the grace of God, they obtained the true knowledge of the gospel of Jesus Christ, believed the same, amended their lives according to its requirements, and were baptized upon their faith in Christ according to His commandment and the practice of the apostles.

This behavior could not be tolerated by the authorities of the state church; so they sent fourteen trappers (men who were charged to bring in those who offended the officials) to apprehend those two inoffensive women. On their way to prison, much sympathy was expressed for them. Maeyken said to them that she would rather go to prison for the testimony of Christ than go home.

They were imprisoned ten weeks in the officials' tower, where they were vexed with threatening and entreaties to turn from their faith. One bishop's chaplain came to Maeyken with bland words and a can of wine in the hope of getting her to recant. He appealed to her on bended knee, but she proved herself faithful and repelled the devil's deceit.

On another occasion an acquaintance appealed: "My dear friend Maeyken, oh that you would obey, and yield a point, to be released from these bonds. When you get out, you can live as before." She replied, "My dear friend, would you advise me this, that I should forsake God and become a child of the devil?" The man said, "Then you will have to die." Thereupon Maeyken said, "I should rather have this come to pass with us, than enjoy the light of day."

These two saints of God endured the worst tortures devised by depraved mankind, often fainting and being revived with dashes of cold water. They were so sustained by God that Aeltgen said, "Yes, if the door stood open, I should not wish to go away." In all their sufferings they were joyful in their God and thanked Him in their hearts and sang praises to Him in the prison.

Their sentences were that they be drowned by being cast alive, bound, from the Meuse River bridge. They were gagged, bound, and led to the bridge where their gags were removed. Aeltgen said, "O Lord, this is a beautiful city indeed; would that it repented with Nineveh," and as she commended herself to God, the executioner cast her from the bridge where she was instantly drowned. Maeyken said to the executioner, "Grant me, that in my greatest extremity I may pray to God and call upon Him." The executioner answered, "Pray to our lords the magistrates, and believe with us in the Romish Church, and you shall save your life." Maeyken said, "I have never done amiss to the magistrates; hence I also need not worship them." She was cast into the water, and with radiant countenance, she drifted upon the water for a long time until she was swallowed up into its depths. Thus these two faithful Christians began their lives in the presence of their Lord on July 24, 1595.[1]

EWT

---

[1]Thieleman J. van Braght, Jr., *The Bloody Theater; or, Martyrs Mirror of the Defenseless Christians* (Scottsdale, Pa.: Herald Press, 1950), pp. 1091-92.

July 25—"God's Ambassador to the Mississippi Valley"

Scripture: Luke 9:62

John Mason Peck was born on October 21, 1789, in Litchfield, Connecticut, while George Washington was serving his first term as president of our land. Washington would be called the "Father of America," but John Peck would become "God's Ambassador to the Mississippi Valley." In 1807 John Peck began teaching school but soon realized his weakness in grammar and determined to obtain more education. In 1809 John married Sally Paine, who proved to be an ideal wife for the pioneering life God planned for His servant.

When blessed with their first child, the Pecks hesitated to have the baby sprinkled. They began in earnest to study the Scriptures for spiritual light and decided that the Bible did not teach infant baptism. Upon moving to New York, they discovered that the nearest church was the Baptist church in New Durham, and there they adopted Baptist principles and were baptized in September of 1811. The church had services only once a month, and the people insisted that Peck preach to them when the pastor could not be present. He was licensed to preach and later assumed a pastorate. The Lord blessed his efforts, and for forty-six years his voice continued to proclaim the message of salvation.

The Pecks met the Reverend Luther Rice, and their hearts were turned toward the cause of missions. However, the Lord was not calling them to India but rather to the rugged western wilderness of America. Realizing his need for more training, Peck studied under Dr. William Staughton for a year in Philadelphia, and when the Triennial Convention met in that city in 1817, he volunteered and was accepted to service in the West, being commissioned on May 18, 1817.

John Peck was not yet twenty-eight years old when he wrote in his diary, "I have now put my hand to the plow. O Lord, may I never turn back—never regret this step. It is my duty to live, to labor, to die as a kind of pioneer in advancing the Gospel."[1] On July 25, 1817, with his wife and three little children in a small, one-horse wagon, the family began the journey of over a thousand miles that would consume over four months of laborious progress through regions that were undeveloped. On December 1 they entered St. Louis, and a whirlwind life of sacrifice and privations was underway! In April 1818 the first baptismal service took place in the Mississippi River in the midst of an iconoclastic environment where the Bible had been burned amid coarse songs and blasphemy. Peck began a Baptist church, making it the first base of operations in the West. He began his itinerant ministry, which would take him thousands of miles midst fierce opposition as he became inured to the cold and slept on the hard ground. He suffered hunger and fatigue and preached to Indians and hardy pioneers alike. In 1820 when his oldest son had died and his other children were sick, he too became seriously ill. At the same time, his support was cut off by the Baptist Convention. But he persevered, for he was intent on following the plow to the end of the furrow. He debated the antimissionary forces, established churches, and founded what later became Shurtleff College in Illinois. He established a Christian periodical and organized circuit-riding Baptist preachers.

Mrs. Peck died in 1856, and in an effort to temper his sorrow, John Peck set out to visit his children in Iowa. Peck's worn, tired body was racked with pain, and on March 14, 1858, heaven's gates opened to him. God's Ambassador to the West turned to a friend and said, "Only Christ is my Savior, my whole dependence," and with those words he finally took his hand from the plow that he might place it in the hand of his loving Savior and Lord.

DLC

---

[1]Charles L. White, *A Century of Faith* (Philadelphia: Judson Press, 1932), p. 31.

July 26—God's Purposes Manifest in the Planting of a Church

Scripture: Acts 14:1-18

In the planting of the first Baptist church in what was then the province of Maine, who would have thought that it was in the will and purpose of God to establish the Baptists hundreds of miles away in the South. This small group of believers immigrated to South Carolina and helped establish the first Baptist church in that area.

We also have insight as to the church-planting procedures of the early "Particular Baptists." The Baptist church in Boston granted a letter of approval and appointment on November 11, 1681, to William Screven "to exercise his gift in ye place where he lives or else where as the providence of God may cast him." Some months later they sent the following letter of approval for the establishing of a Baptist church in Maine:

> Upon serious and solemn consideration of the church about a motion or request made by severall members that lived att Kittery, y(et) they might become a Church & that they might p-ceed therein provided they were such as should be Approved for such A Foundacon work, the Church gave there grant and att ye time Appointed did send severall messengers to make y strict Inquiry and Examination as they ought in such A case who at there Returne brought y(et) Coppys here Inserted 26th of 7 mo 1682.
>
> The Church of Christ at Boston y(et) is baptized upon profession of faith haveing taken into serious consideration ye Request of our Brethren at Kittery Relating to there being A Church by themselves y(et) soe they might Injoy the precious ordinances of Christ which by reson of distance of habitason they butt seldome could enjoy have therefore thought meet to make Choice of us whose names are und'written as Messengers to Assist them in ye same and coming up to them we have found them A Competent Number and ye same faith with us for upon carefull examination of them in matters of Doctrine and practice & soe finding one with us by there (we hope) Conshiencous Acknowledgm(ent) of ye Confession of faith putt forth by ye

Eladers and Brethren of ye Churches in London and ye contry in England dated in ye year 1682.

And they haveing given themselves up to ye lord & too one Another in A Solemn Covenant to walk as said Covenant may Express & alsoe haveing Chosen theire officers whome they with us have Appointed and ordained, we doe therefore in ye name of ye lord Jesus & by the Appointm(ent) of his Church deliver them to be a Church of Christ in ye faith and order of ye Gospel.

signed by us in ye name of ye Church the 25 of 7 mo 1682.

Isaak Hull
Thomas Skinner
Phillipp Squire[1]

It is interesting to note the carefulness with which they carried out the examinations of the assembly and leadership, even though the process often required lengthy journeys by ship or over tortuous roads. This church, as in other instances, became a traveling church and established the gospel of God's grace in another remote area.

EWT

---

[1]Robert A. Baker, *A Baptist Source Book* (Nashville: Broadman Press, 1966), pp. 1-2.

July 27—Philadelphia, the First Baptist Association in America

Scripture: Acts 15:1-29

The churches making up the Philadelphia Association of Regular Baptists were provided members and ministers from the great Welsh migration in the late seventeenth and early eighteenth centuries. Welsh Baptists formed several of the early churches in Pennsylvania and provided leadership for others. Such leaders as Jenkins Jones, Abel Morgan, and Samuel Jones testify to the influence of the Welsh in their new country. The Philadelphia Association bore a distinctly Welsh flavor in its early days, bringing their tradition of great preaching, love of singing, and warm and fervent evangelism.[1]

The association originated in what they called general, and sometimes yearly, meetings. These meetings were instituted as early as 1688 and met alternately in May and September. The business of these meetings was chiefly confined to the ministry of the Word and the administration of the gospel ordinances. But at their meeting July 27,

1707, they seem to have taken more properly the form of an association, for then they had messengers from several churches and attended to their general concerns. We therefore date the beginning of this association from that time, though we might with but little impropriety extend it back some years.

They were a feeble, though faithful, band of believers at that time, consisting of but five churches: Lower Dublin, Piscataqua, Middletown, Cohansie, and Welsh Tract. There were only fourteen Baptist churches in all of the colonies at that time.

Some notes relating to this first associational meeting in America went as follows:

> It was concluded by several congregations, to make choice of some particular brethren, such as they thought most capable in every congregation, and those to meet at the yearly meeting to consult about such things as were wanting in the churches, and to set them in order. . . . It was then agreed, that a person that is a stranger, that has neither letter of recommendation, nor is known to be a person gifted, and of good conversation, shall not be admitted to preach, nor be entertained as a member in any of the baptized congregations in communion with each other.[2]

As the association grew and was loosely organized, it was deemed necessary to have articles of faith. At their meeting September 25, 1742, they voted to adopt and reprint "the confession of faith, set forth by the Elders of baptized congregations, met in London, A.D. 1689, with a short treatise of church discipline, to be annexed to the confession of faith."[3] They were careful to emphasize that it was not a creed but simply articles and a statement of faith. They desired no creed nor association to overlord the local church and thus wrote, "A Gospel church is the highest earthly ecclesiastical tribunal and is in nowise subject to any other church, or the decrees of associations or councils, but dependent for its acts on the Word and Spirit of God alone."[4]

This association, strongly believing in the sovereignty of God and autonomy of the local church, kept a spirit of evangelism and was responsible for establishing churches and associations throughout the land. God grant us the same scriptural balance.

EWT

---

[1]H. Leon McBeth, *The Baptist Heritage* (Nashville: Broadman Press, 1987), pp. 211-12.

[2]A. D. Gillette, ed., *Minutes of the Philadelphia Baptist Association from A.D. 1707 to A.D. 1807* (1851; reprint ed., Minneapolis: James Publishing Co., n.d.), p. 4.

[3]Ibid., p. 46.

[4]*Minutes of the Ketocton Association of Regular Baptists* (Luray, Va.: n.p., 1989), p. 43.

July 28—The Prison Couldn't Stop Their Witness

Scripture: Luke 21:12-13

We have previously considered the power of the state church in Norway and the antecedents of the Baptists in that country (July 1). Many soldiers had embraced Baptist principles, and on July 28, 1743, when ordered by their colonel to participate in a church parade, the soldiers refused. They assembled in front of the church, but the believers refused to enter and were arrested, and in January of 1744 they were brought before a court-martial. The verdict was given that Hans Pedersen should "work in iron" in one of the forts for three years, that Christopher Pedersen should "work in iron" for six months, and that the rest should be sent to prison in Oslo so that they might "work constantly and receive instruction, so they might change their mind."[1] King Christian VI changed the sentence, ordering all to be sent to the penitentiary in Oslo.

The officials had underestimated these Baptist prototypes, for they were a greater problem behind the prison walls than they were outside. Jorgen Nicolaysen was ordered to attend services in the prison chapel, and when he refused, he was dragged by force into the building. The king was reminded of his leniency toward Nicolaysen, and he responded by expressing his desire that the prisoner should be whipped and then be given religious instruction. The king's judgment was executed, but that did not stop the men. They continued to witness, and soon their influence was so great that other prisoners surrendered their lives to the Lord.

The bishop wrote the king on July 11, 1744, stating,

> The six military persons in the penitentiary have misused both your majesty's and God's grace and longsuffering. Six different priests have visited them, and have tried to bring them to repentance, but their work has been in vain. These Separatists are not only stubborn in regard to their own heresy, but they are trying to lead the other prisoners into the same heresy. I report this to your majesty in order that these prisoners may be removed from the penitentiary, as they are a burden to us, and a danger to the other prisoners."[2]

The king took the matter under consideration and decided ultimately that these "heretics" and Nicolaysen must be sent to some forts but not more than one to each fort, for more than one of these persons in one fort would do what had been done in the prison, and they would spiritually contaminate others and lead them as well to the spiritual principles that we today call the Baptist persuasion.

These progenitors of the Baptist cause believed that salvation is only through the new birth and is by faith alone. They maintained that the state should not control the church and that no one should use coercion in religious matters. The Bible, they believed, was to be the basis of faith and practice, and each believer was under the direct guidance of the Holy Spirit. They insisted that a call to preach the gospel came from God and not the king and that only those who were known as believers should be immersed. These tenets sound strangely current among Baptists of our day. We thank God for these early Norwegian believers and sense a blessed relationship of heart with their declaration of truth from above.

DLC

---

[1]P. Stiansen, *History of the Baptists in Norway* (Chicago: Blessing Press, 1933), p. 37.

[2]Ibid., p. 38.

July 29—Contrary Winds Deliver the Preacher

Scripture: Acts 27

Elijah Baker, one of the early Baptist ministers, was greatly used of God to establish churches in Virginia. It has been recorded that "through his instrumentality, all the churches between Hampton and Richmond City, were originated, and several on the eastern shore."[1] These successful efforts brought the wrath of Satan upon him, and he became the object of much abuse. He was often pelted with apples and stones while he was engaged in preaching.

On one occasion he was apprehended by some ruffians and placed on a privateer (privately-owned warship) with orders to land him on any coast out of America. He was compelled to work, and for refusing to comply but rather praying, preaching, and singing, he was ill used. The winds became contrary, keeping the ship in harbor, and Baker was placed on another ship, and that ship was also blown back into harbor. They thought it might be because they had Baker on board that the storm raged; so they placed him on a third ship. He asked the captain if he could sing and pray among the crew on Sunday. The captain attended and was convinced that he was a good man and set him at liberty on shore.

The imprisonment of Elijah Baker in the debtor's prison in Accomack, Virginia (which is the only prison of its kind still standing in Virginia), occurred two years after the General Assembly of the Commonwealth had passed a law which was to sweep away all existing laws restricting liberty to religious opinion and worship. It was the last occasion of imprisoning Baptist preachers. Probably because of this law, the wardens of the established church, instead of the state, were plaintiffs, and the charge was vagrancy instead of preaching without a license.

Baker was imprisoned the first day of July 1778. The case was continued on the 29th day of July, and it lasted until August 25, 1778, when the plaintiffs failed to appear, and the case was dismissed after Baker had spent fifty-six days in prison. As the other Baptists had done, he invested his time in preaching and prayer while confined.

In spite of the opposition and persecution, Baker succeeded in planting the first Baptist churches on the Eastern Shore of Virginia and Maryland. If you are ever on the Eastern Shore, it would be good to visit the memorial and the debtor's prison in Accomack. The memorial reads, ''Elijah Baker, Pioneer Baptist of the Eastern Shore of Virginia; Who landed at Hunt's Point, Old Plantation Creek, on Easter Sunday 1776 and the same day preached the first Baptist sermon 'At the end of a Horsing Tree.' Opposition of the Established Church caused him to be deported; but kind Providence brought him back. He was later imprisoned 56 days in the Old Debtor's Jail at Accomac for the crime of preaching the Gospel. Acts IV:19, 20.''

John Leland wrote that Baker was ''a man of low parentage, small learning and confined abilities. But with one talent, he did more than many do with five.''[2] God grant us more men of low estate who will yield their gifts and abilities to be invested in the lives of others for the glory of Jesus Christ. ''For ye see your calling, brethren, how that not many wise men after the flesh, not many mighty, not many noble, are called'' (I Cor.1:26).

EWT

---

[1]Lewis Peyton Little, *Imprisoned Preachers and Religious Liberty in Virginia* (Lynchburg, Va.: J. P. Bell Co., 1938), pp. 470-80.

[2]Ibid., p. 475.

July 30—Persecuted in England and in the Colonies

Scripture: Psalm 3

It is difficult to envision how such an event could happen, but the Reverend Thomas Patient, after coming from England to the "Land of the Free," was forced to return to Great Britain because of religious persecution.[1] But let us consider the phenomenon.

Thomas Patient was born in England, and it is thought that he was educated either at Oxford or Cambridge.[2] After becoming a Congregational minister, he emigrated to America. Meeting those who professed Baptist convictions, Patient re-examined the Scriptures pertinent to baptism. He concluded that "infant's baptism had no foundation in Scripture."[3] The Pilgrims had come to America to gain the right to worship according to the dictates of their own conscience, but the persecution that the Reverend Thomas Patient experienced caused him to return to his native land. We are thus reminded again that religious freedom was little known in the early days of the American colonies.

Returning to England, Patient served as co-pastor with the Reverend William Kiffin in London in 1640. Patient was one of the Baptist leaders who signed the Particular Baptist's Confession of Faith, which was put forth by seven Baptist churches in London in 1644. He has been spoken of as one "of the most prominent Baptists of those times."[4]

The English Parliament voted to appoint six ministers to preach in Dublin, Ireland, and the Reverend Mr. Patient accepted one of these appointments. His gift as an eloquent speaker made him a favorite, and he spoke to large audiences. He acted as chaplain for Colonel John Jones in Dublin. The colonel, who was actually the governor of Dublin, requested Patient to preach each Lord's Day in the Council of Dublin, and thus the aristocracy of the Anglo-Irish society heard a living gospel. From correspondence it is clear that Patient was personally acquainted with Oliver Cromwell during the British Commonwealth.

Patient baptized a large group in Dublin, and it is believed he founded the first Baptist church following the Reformation in Ireland. He apparently assisted in the establishment of the Baptist church at Cloughkeating. All the members of the congregation were tried for their lives, and the foreman of the jury vowed that all would be found guilty. But in the providence of God, the foreman died, and all the congregation was acquitted. Because he was willing to accept government remuneration for preaching, it is evident that the Baptists of London distanced themselves from Patient, but to him is ascribed the honor of building the first Baptist meetinghouse in Ireland.

After such a noteworthy and varied life, the man of God fell asleep in Jesus on July 30, 1666, having administered faithful service to His Savior in the New World as well as in England and Ireland. His Baptist conviction of immersion had cost him dearly, but the Lord honored His faithful servant.

DLC

---

[1]Thomas Crosby, *The History of English Baptists* (1738-40; reprint ed., Lafayette, Tenn.: Church History Research and Archives, 1979), 3:42.

[2]William Cathcart, *The Baptist Encyclopedia,* ed. Louis H. Everts (Philadelphia: Louis H. Everts, 1881), 2:886.

[3]Crosby, p. 42.

[4]John T. Christian, *A History of the Baptists* (1922; reprint ed., Nashville: Broadman Press, 1926), 2:256.

July 31—Is Anti-Pedobaptism a Capital Crime?

Scripture: Colossians 2:1-17

It had been a long walk of eighty miles for John Clarke, Obadiah Holmes, and an active Baptist layman, John Crandall. On their way to their blind friend's home in Lynn, Massachusetts, little did they know that they were being closely watched by the Massachusetts authorities. In the midst of their worship in Witter's house, a watching marshal and his deputies burst in and arrested them, took them to dinner, and then took them to a Puritan meeting that was obviously designed to show them the error of their ways. The three men entered, bowed to the assembly, sat down, and refused to remove their hats as a demonstration against the treatment they were receiving. They attempted to defend themselves but were silenced, and after the service were confined to a Boston jail, charged with being "certain erroneous persons, being strangers," though actually their offense was understood to be holding a religious meeting without license from the authorities.[1] Ultimately they were indicted for holding a private meeting, serving communion to an excommunicated person, rebaptizing converts, and other assorted offenses.

After spending ten days in jail, they were tried on July 31, 1651, before the court of assistants.[2] John Cotton, the Puritan preacher, had been invited to act as the prosecutor and state the case against the three heretics. Sitting in the prisoner's box, Clarke, Holmes, and Crandall heard him shout that the culprits denied the saving power of infant baptism, and thus they were soul murderers. This offense, declared Cotton with great fervor, deserved capital punishment just as did any other type of murder.

For their defense Clarke, Holmes, and Crandall admitted having a private service in a home, not a public service, and claimed that a home should not be invaded by civil authorities under the ancient English maxim that a man's house, however humble, is his castle.

Judge Endicott agreed with John Cotton that these three men should be put to death and made this accusation against them, "You go up and down, and secretly insinuate things into those that are weak, but you cannot maintain it before our ministers; you may try and dispute with them."[3] They were returned to jail where John Clarke wrote from prison to the court and proposed a fair debate upon his principles with any of their ministers. After setting out his principles in writing, there was talk that John Cotton would debate with him, but after consultation with others, Cotton declined.

These events finally resulted in Crandall's being released and Holmes and Clarke fined. Knowing that paying the fine would be an admission of guilt, they both refused, even though the alternative was the dreaded whipping post. The description of that terrible event will appear later in this volume.

Praise God for men of courage and conviction who laid the foundation for freedom of conscience in our nation. God give us men like them who will stand strong to preserve this cherished heritage for our generation and posterity.

EWT

---

[1]O. K. and Marjorie Armstrong, *Baptists Who Shaped a Nation* (Nashville: Broadman Press, 1975), pp. 57-58.

[2]Isaac Backus, *Your Baptist Heritage, 1620–1804* (1844; reprint ed., Little Rock: Challenge Press, 1976), p. 57.

[3]Ibid.

August

August 1—I Know I Shall Not Die Now

Scripture: Luke 9:18-26

John Comer was born in Boston, Massachusetts, on August 1, 1704, during a very unusual period in New England. Often Congregationalists and Baptists were members of the same Congregationalist churches. Comer's early spiritual exercises came under the ministry of the renowned Dr. Increase Mather. He occasionally had serious concerns about his soul. Then he caught the "distemper," of which he says,

> Nothing but the ghostly countenance of death, unprepared for, was before me, and no sight of a reconciled God, nor any sense of the application of the soul-cleansing blood of Christ to my distressed soul. I remained in extreme terror, until November 22, 1721. All the interval time I spent in looking over the affairs of my soul; and on that day I was taken sick. As soon as [my aunt] told me that the distemper appeared, all my fears entirely vanished, and a beam of comfort darted into my soul, and with it satisfaction from these words, "Thou shalt not die, but live and declare the works of the Lord." Yea, so great was my satisfaction, that immediately I replied, . . . Then I know I shall not die now; but gave me reason why I said so."[1]

After his recovery, Comer pursued his education at Cambridge and joined the Congregational Church. He believed it was very wrong when his intimate friend Ephraim Crafts joined the Baptist church in Boston. After debating with his friend and reading further concerning baptism, Comer had a change of mind but kept silent about it. Another experience of illness, the death of a very close friend, and a violent storm at sea,

> brought eternity so directly before him, as to spoil his plausible excuses for the neglect of baptism. He informs us, that those words of Christ, "Whosoever shall be ashamed of me, and of my words, in this

> adulterous and sinful generation, of him also shall the Son of Man be ashamed, when He cometh in the glory of his Father, with the holy angels.'' had such influence upon him, that after proper labors with those he was previously connected with, he was baptized, and joined the Baptist studies in a private way.[2]

He went on to pastor and co-pastor several churches in New England during a period when the people were somewhat remiss in church order and controversy prevailed concerning ordinances and practices. He not only succeeded in bringing order to some, introducing public singing to another, and carrying out heart-searching preaching that increased membership appreciably in the weaker churches, but he also raised opposition from those who resisted being stirred out of lethargy.

During a confused period in New England, Comer carried out his ministry with faithfulness, integrity, and soundness of mind. Though he was no exploding meteor, he was one of those who prepared the way for spiritual awakening by serving humbly in the circumstances of his life. May John Comer be an example to us, showing us that we may be ''way preparers'' even though we never see the full results of our ministries while yet upon this earth.

EWT

---

[1]Isaac Backus, *Your Baptist Heritage, 1620–1804* (1844; reprint ed., Little Rock: Challenge Press, 1976), p. 106.

[2]Ibid., pp. 106-7.

August 2—A Grandmother's Prayers Were Answered

Scripture: James 1:12

Stephen Gano was born on December 25, 1762, in New York City, where his father pastored the Gold Street Baptist Church. His parents planned for Stephen to enter Brown University, where his uncle, Dr. James Manning, was the president; but the Revolutionary War changed those plans. Stephen's father, the Reverend John Gano, entered the army as a chaplain, and thirteen-year-old Stephen was sent to another uncle, Dr. Stites, to be educated in the medical profession. While on the way to his uncle's home, he and his father stopped at his grandmother's house. She placed her hand on Stephen's head, prayed for his salvation, and said, ''Stephen, the Lord designs thee for a minister of the everlasting Gospel: be thou faithful unto death, and He will give thee a crown of life.''[2]

Thus, Stephen completed the medical course and became a doctor before he was saved. The young man entered the army as a surgeon, and in time he was called upon to serve on board a ship. The two-masted vessel ran upon a reef of rocks, and Gano was taken prisoner along with thirty-four others. They were all left on Turk's Island in the Caribbean to perish without food. Escaping from the island, the men made their way to St. Francis and there arranged to board a vessel for Philadelphia. Four days later, the British captured that ship, and Gano was placed in chains on a prison ship. In time he was repatriated in a prisoner exchange and soon set up his medical practice in Tappan, New York. After several years of medical practice, ''he was converted and in 1786 was set apart to the Gospel ministry.''

On August 2, 1786, Dr. Stephen Gano was ordained into the ministry by his father, uncle, and several other pastors in the Gold Street Baptist Church. After two brief but successful pastorates, in 1792 he received a unanimous invitation to the pastorate of the First Baptist Church in Providence, Rhode Island, where he served until his death. When he became pastor, the church numbered 165 members; however, during the thirty-six years of his ministry there, five new churches were born, and the membership of the First Baptist Church grew to 647.

First Baptist Church of Providence was one of the largest Baptist congregations in America. The members experienced frequent revival. In 1820 alone the records reveal that one hundred and forty-seven were baptized. Dr. Gano was a pre-eminent public speaker among the Baptists, and his executive ability was stellar. For nineteen years he served as moderator of the Warren Association. Few of the early Baptist leaders left a more hallowed influence on their hearers.

Dr. Gano outlived three wives, and at his death he left six daughters, four of whom were married to Baptist pastors. Though an invalid during his last years, he continued to preach until within three months of his death, which took place August 18, 1828. Dr. Stephen Gano was the son of a famous preacher, and his life honored his father's memory and faith.

DLC

---

[1]Thomas Armitage, *The History of the Baptists* (1890; reprint ed., Watertown, Wis.: Maranatha Baptist Press, 1976), 2:854.

[2]William B. Sprague, *Annals of the American Pulpit* (New York: Robert Carter and Bros., 1865), 6:232.

August 3—Another Baptist Preacher Who Gave His Life

Scripture: Mark 6:17-29

Baptist pastors were "marked" men in England when George Fownes became the pastor of the Baptist church in Broadmead, Bristol, in 1679. Thomas Ewins, a former pastor at Broadmead, had died as the result of his imprisonments while pastoring there (cf. April 26). Thomas Hardcastle, the next pastor, served from 1671 to 1678, and he was "imprisoned oft" and wrote blessed epistles to the saints from his Bristol cell to encourage and edify them.

George Fownes "was . . . born in Shropshire, bred up in school-learning in Shrewsbury; and his father dying, his mother sent him to Cambridge, where he was reckoned a considerable scholar, and one of a sharp wit."[1] Soon after his arrival in Bristol, new persecution broke out, and the authorities attempted to arrest Pastor Fownes. On August 3, 1680, Fownes proposed that the congregation seriously consider the steps that should be taken if the services were interrupted by law officers.[2] In essence they determined to continue their worship services unless the magistrate himself used violence. This tactic worked well until December 18, 1681, when the civil, ecclesiastical, and military powers invaded the house of God on the Lord's Day and Pastor Fownes was sent to prison at Newgate. After six weeks in jail, he appeared before the judge and was acquitted due to a flaw in the warrant.

Returning to his flock, he made arrangements, for safety's sake, to hold services in the fields rather than in their church building. Regardless of the weather, the saints gathered to worship and to hear the Word of God. In March of 1682 Pastor Fownes was arrested again on the highway in Kingswood for suspicion of coming from a meeting, though the accusers could not prove it. He was committed to Gloucester Jail, and his warrant was for six months. The persecutors declared publicly that he would not leave the jail alive. An effort was made to suborn witnesses, but this attempt proved futile. A jury was impaneled, and the man of God served as his own attorney. When the jury returned and pronounced the verdict of "not guilty," the bishop's chancellor, being one of the justices on the bench, said, "What! Not guilty?" The foreman reported the jury's findings, but the pastor was returned to prison in spite of the verdict. When his six months had ended, Pastor

Fownes demanded his freedom; however, a bond was demanded of him and the promise to cease preaching. He refused and requested a judicial inquest. Two justices appeared before the judge stating that if Fownes were released "he would draw all the country after him."[3] Thus it was that for the next two and a half years the dear man of God was held in the Gloucester prison until the Lord in mercy released him in death in December of 1685.

After the Act of Toleration, the Broadmead Church finally knew peace, and Pastor Fownes's son, George Fownes, became the pastor in 1693. In 1695 "the church built a new meeting-house 50 feet long by 40 feet, in the clear, and a vestry room 20 feet square."[4] How we ought to thank the Lord for staunch forebears who were willing to be faithful regardless of the cost.

DLC

---

[1]Thomas Crosby, *The History of the English Baptists* (1738-40; reprint ed., Lafayette, Tenn.: Church History Research and Archives, 1979), 3:28.

[2]Edward Terrill, *The Records of a Church of Christ Meeting in Broadmead, Bristol,* ed. Nathaniel Haycroft (London: J. Heaton and Son, 1865), p. 209.

[3]Crosby, p. 31.

[4]Terrill, p. 297.

August 4—I Am the Son of Charles Clay and Fear No Man

Scripture: II Samuel 23

Elder Eleazer Clay was one of those unusual men prepared for hard times. He was born a rugged Virginian August 4, 1744, and when just a boy of fourteen, he enlisted in the army of King George II and fought in the French and Indian War. In the providence of God, he moved to Chesterfield County, Virginia, and married Miss Jane Apperson. It was here that he came under considerable conviction of sin as a result of the preaching of William Webber, Joseph Anthony, and John Weatherford, who preached through the prison grates. Clay made his profession of faith in Jesus Christ in August of 1771, immediately became a member of the Baptist church, and was soon preaching the gospel of Jesus Christ.[1]

Colonel Cary, magistrate of the county and nemesis of the Baptist preachers in that area, was asked why he left Elder Clay unmolested and arrested others for preaching. The Colonel replied, "Mr. Clay has a livelihood, but these others were taken under a vagrant law." The "livelihood" was such that Elder Clay probably was the richest preacher in Virginia. He used his wealth to help the Baptist preachers in prison, and through his exertions and donations, a meetinghouse was built for the church he planted as the first Baptist church in Chesterfield County.

Clay was not without enemies. Preaching in a private house on one occasion, a man rode into the yard and asked for Clay. After being told that Clay was preaching in the house, he remarked: "I have come to cowhide him." This was reported to the preacher who replied: "I am the son of Charles Clay, and I fear no man. If I have to go out after him, I will give him one of the worst whippings he ever had in his life." The gentleman did not accomplish his objective.

Clay continued as a useful servant of Jesus Christ with unusual distinction and pastored the church he had planted for over sixty years. He loved the Word of God and read the New Testament once each month in addition to his Old Testament reading. He had a long life and went to his eternal reward in his 92nd year.

Although Eleazer Clay was never imprisoned, his brother, John Clay, served time in the jail for preaching. John established Black Creek Church in Hanover County and died when he was a comparatively young man. John Clay gave two outstanding sons to our young nation: Elder Porter Clay, a prominent preacher in Kentucky, and the Honorable Henry Clay, an illustrious statesman known as the "Millboy of the Slashes," who three times ran for the presidency of the United States. Henry Clay was a prominent and influential leader in his party for forty years.[2] God grant us courageous and tough leadership for this perilous time.

EWT

---

[1]Lewis Peyton Little, *Imprisoned Preachers and Religious Liberty in Virginia* (Lynchburg, Va.: J. P. Bell Co., 1938), pp. 214, 217.

[2]Ibid., pp. 218-19.

August 5—The Attitude of the Wicked Toward the Reverend Mr. Wickenden

Scripture: Psalm 10:1-8

In New England, Congregationalism claimed pre-emptive privileges; it was the religion of the State. The churches of that order were supported by a tax upon all of the inhabitants, irrespective of creed. Baptists not only had no legal recognition, but were treated as outlaws. In New York it was a little better. In that colony, under the Dutch, the Dutch Reformed Church was the established order. Peter Stuyvesant, their last governor, was bigoted and intolerant.[1]

Into that setting marched William Wickenden of Providence, Rhode Island. He was an elder of the second Providence church which was "vigorous . . . in propagating its notions."[2] We know little of the Reverend William Wickenden other than the fact that he was one of the earliest settlers in Providence, having moved there in 1636. He signed the first compact for Rhode Island in 1637 and served as a member of the legislature in 1648 and from 1651 to 1655 and again in 1664.

In 1655 the Reverend William Wickenden visited New York to preach the gospel. This information comes to us from an official paper on "The State of Religion" and was signed by two clergymen of the Dutch Reformed Church, Megapolensis and Drissius. The paper was dated at "Amsterdam, in N. Netherland," on August 5, 1657, and it was addressed to the "Classis of Amsterdam." The report pictures religion on Long Island, New York, in a sad condition and declares,

> Last year a fomenter of evil came there. He was a cobbler from Rhode Island, in New England, and stated that he was commissioned by Christ. He began to preach at Flushing and then went with the people into the river and dipped them. This becoming known here, the fiscaal [i.e., a government official] proceeded thither and brought him along. He was banished from the province.[3]

Very little additional information would be available to us were it not for quotations given by Armitage as follows:

> Both Broadhead and O'Callagan give a full account of his treatment in consequence. Under date of November 8th, 1656, O'Callagan says: "The Baptists at Flushing were the next to feel the wrath of the law. William Hallett, sheriff of that place, had dared to collect conventicles in his house, and to permit one William Wickendam (properly Wickenden) to explain and comment on God's Holy Word, and to administer sacraments, though not called thereto by any civil or clerical authority. He had, moreover, assisted at such meeting and afterward accepted from the said Wickendam's hands the breach in the form and manner the Lord's Supper is usually celebrated."[4]

For this violation of the statute, Hallett was removed from office and fined £50, which he was unable to pay and thus was banished. On the 8th of November, 1656, the General Assembly of New Netherland "ordained" that Wickenden should be fined one hundred pounds Flemish and be banished out of the province of New Netherland. However, before banishment, Wickenden was to remain a prisoner until the fine and cost of the process were paid. "The Council being informed, however, . . . that he was a very poor man, 'with a wife and many children' . . . the fine and costs were remitted, and he was condemned on the 11th of November 'to immediate banishment, under condition that if ever he be seen again in the province of New Netherland he shall be arrested and kept in confinement till the fine and costs are paid in full.' "[5]

Wickenden died in 1669. Thank God for our forebears and the religious freedom they gained!

DLC

---

[1]Charles Wesley Brooks, *A Century of Missions in the Empire State* (Philadelphia: America Baptist Publication Society, 1909), p. 28.

[2]Henry C. Vedder, *A Century of Baptist Achievement,* ed. A. H. Newman (Philadelphia: American Baptist Publication Society, 1901), p. 72.

[3]Thomas Armitage, *The History of the Baptists* (1890; reprint ed., Watertown, Wis.: Maranatha Baptist Press, 1976), 2:748.

[4]Ibid.

[5]Ibid., pp. 748-49.

August 6—A Pioneer Church for a Pioneer People

Scripture: Isaiah 8

On the third Sunday in August in 1945, I arose before daylight from my bunk at the Quantico Marine Corps Base and began a hitchhiking journey over the verdant hills of the Piedmont and across the Blue Ridge and Massanutten Mountains to the quaint village of New Market, Virginia, where the Ketocton Association of Regular Baptists was convened in its 179th anniversary session. The association was meeting with the historic Smith's Creek Church, which was constituted August 6, 1756.[1] Upon my arrival, I saw across the street an antique shop in a small log building. Little did I know at that time that it was the original meetinghouse in which the church assembled near Smith's Creek, after which it was named. Some years later, the building was moved to the campus of Ferrum College, a Methodist school in Southern Virginia. This was my first of many occasions to preach at this church over the past forty-eight years.

Baptists had lived in the area for at least eleven years prior to the constitution of the church. Some of them were from the Philadelphia Association, and at least one from New England, John Harrison, "wishing to be baptized, went as far as Oyster Bay, in Massachusetts, to obtain that ordinance.''[2] During this eleven year period, four notable preachers—Samuel Eaton, Benjamin Griffith, John Gano, and John Alderson—visited the neighborhood and preached among the people. Elder Alderson settled there and assumed the pastorate of the church from its organization for the next two years until he moved to Rockbridge County.

James Ireland had moved to the area and settled as a schoolteacher. He soon was converted and called to preach. He preached often at Smith's Creek Church as well as Mill Creek Church, which was also known as White House, where the believers assembled in the early days. Anderson Moffett, a fellowprisoner of Ireland in the Culpeper jail, assumed the pastorate and served the church for over fifty years. Moffett, a faithful preacher for seventy years, had suffered much for preaching the gospel of Jesus Christ.

Smith's Creek became a corresponding church of the Philadelphia Association but met yearly with Mill Creek (Frederick County), Broad Run, and Ketocton churches because of their remoteness from Philadelphia. They petitioned the Philadelphia Association for dismissal for the purpose of organizing in Virginia. This was granted in 1765, and on August 19, 1766, they met with the Ketocton Church and organized the Ketocton Association of Regular Baptists.

The Baptists in the valley of Northern Virginia have waxed and waned considerably down through the years. On that humid August day in 1945, as we celebrated the close of World War II, Smith's Creek Church was a numerically weak circuit church, meeting only once a month. We are grateful that it has seen times of refreshment in more recent years and is now a full-time active congregation in the valley that has planted many independent Baptist churches in more recent years. If you are in the beautiful Shenandoah Valley, stop at New Market and visit this Baptist landmark.

EWT

---

[1]Robert B. Semple, *History of the Baptists in Virginia,* rev. ed. (Lafayette, Tenn.: Church History Research and Archives, 1976), p. 377.

[2]Ibid.

August 7—Discipline in the Local Church

Scripture: I Corinthians 5:9-13

The desire of Baptist churches through the years to preserve an honored testimony is evident. Church discipline was practiced and meted out by the complete membership, and the purpose and intent were not to be punitive but rather purifying and restorative. The records of the Broadmead Church in Bristol, England, provide a good example, and the case of Jeremy Courtnay offers an excellent focus in point.

On September 8, 1677, six brethren visited Brother Courtnay to reprove and admonish him of "his sinne of drunkenness that hee was fallen into."[1] He declared his repentance and asked prayer. The men assured him that they expected a change of life in the matter. On December 12, 1677, "Br. Jeremy Courtnay was dealt with for drunkennesse, alsoe being now present. Hee hoped ye Lord would keepe him, hee should fall into that sinn noe more. Yett because hee had soe often given good words and failed, ye Church would trust him noe more, but waite to see some fruite; and Therefore pronounced, by one of ye Ruleing Elders, ye sentence of withdrawing from him alsoe."[2]

On March 7, 1678, the pastor admonished Jeremy Courtnay for the second time in the presence of the church. Brother Courtnay had fallen again, and on March 19, 1678, his wife asked that the brethren keep a day of solemn fasting and prayer for him in particular and accordingly they "kept a day of fasting and prayer att Br. Courtnay's house, ye 21st day of 3d month, 1678."[3] The pastor instructed the erring member and urged him to renounce and depart from his sin. Courtnay professed a willingness to do so, and the gathered men spent the remainder of the day in prayer for the offender.

Courtnay asked to be reinstated to his place in the church, and on July 3, 1678, the membership asked that he make public confession as to the dealing of the Lord in his life concerning the matter of drunkenness. The church agreed to watch over him until the next monthly "Day of Prayer."

Would to God that we could report a complete transformation of character, but on August 5, 1679, Brothers Bodenham and Snead were appointed to contact Brother Courtnay and inform him that he was expected to attend the meeting on the next "Day of Prayer" on August 7, 1679. Jeremy Courtnay did not attend, and the congregation, not finding the evidence of true repentance,

> did agree togeather to cast him out of ye Church: haveing sent two Brethren ye Lord's day before to him, to summon him to attend ye Congregation this day of prayer; but he came not. . . . Yet, Notwithstanding, ye Congregation proceeded to theire duty. And therefore, one of ye Ruleing Elders, Namely, Br. Terrill, by consent of ye Whole Congregation then assembled, did pronounce ye sentence. . . . This evening ended, with lamentation and sore trouble that wee were forced, for ye preservation of ye Glory of God and ye Churches purity, thus to proceed to our duty, as ye last means to endeavour his recovery.

> . . . For what Christ will Judge hereafter, his people should Judge here, and have noe fellowship with such workes of darkness.[4]

Do our modern-day churches preserve the "glory of God" and our churches' purity? The saints were long-suffering, but they were desirous of a virtuous testimony as well!

DLC

---

[1]Terrill, Edward, *The Records of A Church of Christ Meeting in Broadmead, Bristol*, ed. Nathaniel Haycroft (London: J. Heaton and Son, 1865), p. 164.

[2]Ibid., p. 170.

[3]Ibid., p. 178.

[4]Ibid., pp. 200-201.

August 8—Historically, Baptism Has Always Been Immersion

Scripture: Mark 1:9-11

The well-known Westminster Confession of Faith, "a creedal standard for all Presbyterian churches, (was) drawn up at Westminster (1643-46)."[1] "On June 1, 1643, the Commons voted 'for the calling an assembly of learned and godly divines' to meet 'at Westminster . . . on the first day of July.' "[2] The avowed purpose of the assembly was to enforce absolute doctrinal uniformity throughout England, Scotland, and Ireland. The assembly was composed of a few moderate Episcopalians, leading theologians representing the Puritans, Independents, and Scottish students of the Scripture. No Baptist theologians were invited or attended the proceedings. The Westminster Confession was for years the authority in the Presbyterian churches in the United States. When liberal leaders attempted a revision of the Westminster Confession of faith in America, a furor broke out among the Presbyterians, and in 1893 the attempt was defeated.

Modern-day Baptists are often surprised to discover that the theologians gathered at Westminster came very close to adopting immersion as their mode of baptism. One of the leading members of the Assembly was Dr. John Lightfoot, who kept a journal of the deliberations of the company. His

> entry [for] August 7, 1644 tells of a "great heat" in the debate of that day, when the Assembly was framing the "Directory" for baptism,

> as to whether dipping should be reserved or excluded, or whether "it was lawful and sufficient to besprinkle!" Coleman, called "Rabbi Coleman" because of his great Hebrew learning, contended with Lightfoot that *tauveleh*, the Hebrew word of dipping, demanded immersion "over head"; and Marshall, a famous pulpit orator, stood firmly by him in the debate, both contending that dipping was essential "in the first institution." Lightfoot says that when they came to the vote, "so many were unwilling to have dipping excluded that the vote came to an equality within one, for the one side was twenty-four, and the other twenty-five; the twenty-four for the reserving of dipping, and the twenty-five against it." "The business was recommitted," and the next day, (August 8, 1644) after another warm dispute, it was voted that " 'pouring or sprinkling water on the face' was sufficient and most expedient."[3]

How did this Presbyterian body, without a Baptist in it, come to such a "great heat" on the subject of immersion if it were a novelty and innovation among believers at that time in England? The answer is most clear! Immersion was practiced from the days of the New Testament. Dr. Philip Schaff, a member of the German Reformed church, wrote: "In England immersion was the *normal* [italics are his] mode down to the middle of the seventeenth century."[4] The *New Catholic Edition of the Holy Bible* with the imprimatur of Francis Cardinal Spellman states: "St. Paul alludes to the manner in which Baptism was ordinarily conferred in the primitive church, by immersion. The descent into the water is suggestive of the descent of the body into the grave, and the ascent is suggestive of the resurrection to a new life."[5]

The ordinance of believer's baptism is the age-old command given by our Lord to His churches and has historical perpetuity from the days of the apostles until now.

DLC

---

[1]Dirk Jellema, *The New International Dictionary of the Christian Church,* ed. J. D. Douglas (Grand Rapids: Zondervan Publishing House, 1974), p. 1039.

[2]Albert Henry Newman, *A Manual of Church History* (Philadelphia: American Baptist Publication Society, 1948), p. 286.

[3]Thomas Armitage, *The History of the Baptists* (1890; reprint ed., Watertown, Wis.: Maranatha Baptist Press, 1976), 1:438.

[4]Philip Schaff, *History of the Christian Church* (Grand Rapids: Eerdmans Publishing Co., 1958), 8:78.

[5]*New Catholic Edition of the Holy Bible* (New York: Catholic Book Publishing Co., 1954), p. 199.

August 9—A City Pastor, a Revolutionary Chaplain, a Wilderness Preacher

Scripture: Matthew 6:25-34

John Gano had a long and varied ministry as an itinerant preacher, as a pastor of churches in Philadelphia and New York, as one of the first Regents of New York University, as a Revolutionary War chaplain, and as a Kentucky wilderness preacher. During the Revolutionary War, his pastoral ministry was interrupted for more than eight years by occupying British troops. He served as chaplain in General George Washington's army, where he maintained the same purity of character and the same zeal and energy in the cause of Christ that he exhibited on the mission field and in the pastoral office.

Being an ardent patriot, at the outbreak of the war, Gano threw in his lot with the colonists and served as chaplain to General Clinton's New York Brigade. He was under fire at White Plains and displayed a cool and quiet courage which commanded the admiration of both men and officers. He described his conduct at Chatterlou's Hill:

> My station, in time of action, I knew to be among the surgeons, but in this battle, I somehow, got in the front of the regiment; yet I durst not quit my place, for fear of dampening the spirits of the soldiers, or of bringing on me an imputation of cowardice. Rather than do either I chose to risk my fate. This circumstance gave opportunity to the young officers of talking; and I believe it had a good effect upon some of them.[1]

He served with distinction at Fort Clinton and in the Western Campaign of 1779 against the Indians.

Although there is no documented evidence, three of John Gano's children testified that at the close of the war their father had baptized George Washington in the Hudson River. Washington is quoted as saying, "I have been investigating the Scripture, and I believe immersion to be the baptism taught in the Word of God, and I demand it at your hands. I do not wish any parade made or the army called out, but simply a quiet demonstration of the ordinance."[2]

Daniel Gano, one of Gano's sons and a captain of the artillery, was present and said that he, with about forty officers and men, accompanied the chaplain down to the Hudson River where the Reverend John Gano baptized George Washington.[3]

In 1908 E. T. Sanford of Manhattan's North Church commissioned a painting of Gano baptizing Washington. The painting was taken to the Baptist church at Asbury, New Jersey, where it hung until Mrs. Elizabeth Johnston, John Gano's great-granddaughter, presented it to William Jewell College, Liberty, Missouri, in 1926.

Gano completed his pastorate in New York, sold his possessions, and then migrated to Kentucky, where he joined the Craigs, Taylor, Dudley, and Hickman, evangelizing and planting churches. Among these brethren, who recognized him as a father in the gospel, he labored with faithfulness and efficiency for about ten years.

After sustaining injuries from a fall from his horse and after suffering a paralytic stroke, Gano recovered enough to participate in the "Great Revival" and preached a masterly discourse on the deity of Christ in defense of the truth of God against the inroads of Arianism. The next year, August 9, 1804, this venerable servant of Jesus Christ departed this life at his home near Frankfort, Kentucky.[4]

EWT

---

[1]"The Baptism of George Washington," Archives of First Baptist Church, New York, New York.

[2]Ibid.

[3]I. M. Haldeman, *The Truth About Baptism* (Bristol, Tenn.: Evangelistic Press, n.d.), pp. 50-51.

[4]J. H. Spencer, *A History of Kentucky Baptists from 1769 to 1885* (Cincinnati: J. R. Baumes, 1886), 1:126.

August 10—A Union in Revival

Scripture: Psalm 133

The Baptist General Committee of Virginia fulfilled a great need from its first session October 9, 1784, until its dissolution in 1799. The Commonwealth of Virginia, the nation, and the Baptists in America were in their formative years at this time. The Baptists sent memorials and remonstrances relating to the vital issues of religious liberty to the Virginia General Assembly by John Leland, Reuben Ford, and others.

On Friday, August 10, 1787, the General Committee also took up the subject of the union between the Regular and Separate Baptists. For many years the subject of union had been debated and concerns aired.

> The Regulars complained that the Separates were not sufficiently explicit in their principles, having never published or sanctioned any confession of faith; and that they kept within their communion many who were professed Armenians [*sic*], etc. To these things it was answered by the Separates that a large majority of them believed as much in their confession of faith as they did themselves, although they did not entirely approve of the practice of religious societies binding themselves too strictly by confessions of faith, seeing there was danger of their usurping too high a place.[1]

After considerable debate as to the propriety of having any confession of faith at all, the report of the committee was received with the following explanation in part:

> To prevent the confession of faith from usurping a tyrannical power over the conscience of any, we do not mean that every person is bound by the strict observance of everything therein contained; yet that it holds forth the essential truths of the Gospel, and that the doctrine of salvation by Christ and free, unmerited grace alone ought to be believed by every Christian and maintained by every minister of the Gospel. Upon these terms we are united; and desire hereafter that the names of Regular and Separate be buried in oblivion, and that, from henceforth we shall be known by the name of the United Baptist Churches of Christ in Virginia.[2]

This union took place during the time when a great spiritual awakening was taking place and bursting forth across the Commonwealth. To this day one can find churches that retain the title of "United Baptist Church." We should also take note that they used the term United Baptist churches (plural), not United Baptist church (singular). There is no such thing as the United Baptist church denomination.

The names Regular, Old School, New School, and others later surfaced in the debates relating to mission boards and church conventionism in the 1830s and 1840s. Great division took place in the 1880s and 1890s because of strict Calvinism which discredited human participation in the winning of the lost. The Primitives were antimissionary whereas the Regulars believed in doing everything possible to get the gospel out. Later in that century the controversy centered upon liberal theology. This division resulted in hyphenated Baptist names as various groups attempted to profess historical loyalty to their doctrinal position.

God's truth alone as in God's Word the Bible is the criterion of fellowship. The truth shall make you free to commune with God and fellowship with the redeemed (I John 1:7).

EWT

---

[1]Robert B. Semple, *History of the Baptists in Virginia,* rev. ed. (Lafayette, Tenn.: Church History Research and Archives, 1976), pp. 99-100.

[2]Ibid., p. 101.

August 11—Missionary Sacrifices Unknown to Others

Scripture: Psalm 127

Early American missionaries who labored in primitive surroundings in the uncivilized world were faced with tremendous hardships in taking their children into dangerous territory without either medical or educational opportunities. Fortunately, this situation has been remedied in recent years, but the first missionaries who decided to leave their children in America were greatly misunderstood. In 1838 Dr. and Mrs. Francis Mason made that decision, and Mrs. Mason wrote: "We have heard of the tortures of the Inquisition; but I do not know that they could exceed this self-sacrifice."[1]

Helen Maria Griggs was born in Massachusetts in 1806. On August 11, 1822, she was baptized and joined a Baptist church in Brookline upon her profession of faith. When still a small girl, Helen was very sick. Her mother prayed that the Lord would spare her, and at the same time, she unreservedly gave little Helen to God's will. Thus when several years passed and Helen told her mother of her call of God to Burma, the mother was fully willing for the Lord's direction.

Miss Griggs offered herself to go to Asia unmarried and alone, and the board grappled with this issue, for they had never previously sent out a single lady alone. However, upon examination she was appointed in December of 1829. The Lord of the harvest was working behind the scenes, and Francis Mason, then a student at Newton Theological Institution, met Miss Griggs. He too planned to go to Burma, and after a courtship of about five months, the two were married on May 23, 1830. As with other young missionaries, their honeymoon was spent aboard ship as they sailed the next day for Burma. Their trip took one hundred and twenty-two days, and they arrived at Calcutta.

Mrs. Mason's health provided problems for the missionary couple, but whenever she was able, she labored alongside her husband. Mrs. Mason became proficient in the Burmese and Sgau Karen languages and was able to teach and write in both. However, the matter of leaving her children came to pass after a furlough in the States. Many in the homeland criticized Mrs. Mason, and she was charged with having ''no more affection than a Sandwich Island mother.''[2] Editors of Christian periodicals had to go to her defense, and in a short time a drastic change for the better took place in public opinion. Four years later when Mrs. Grover Comstock left for Burma and parted from her children, announcement was made in the newspapers under the caption, ''The Noble Mother.''

The ordeal of leaving their children behind surely placed untold pressures on the missionaries. Tragically, Mrs. Mason suffered strange delusions and became somewhat demented. Her condition was such that Dr. Mason could care for her, and he reported that he had never seen her exhibit any anger. The Lord took Mrs. Mason to Himself on October 8, 1846, in her fortieth year. May we be reminded to pray for our missionaries as they face sacrifices that are totally unknown to those of us who operate the supply lines at home.

DLC

---

[1]G. Winfred Hervey, *The Story of Baptist Missions in Foreign Lands* (St. Louis: C. R. Barnes Publishing Co., 1892), p. 413.

[2]Ibid.

August 12—The Magistrate, the Parson, and the Baptist Preachers

Scripture: Acts 9:1-19

The following letter was written from Urbanna Prison, Middlesex County, Virginia, August 12, 1771, at the height of the persecution of Baptists in America. From this epistle we find that in two counties there were twelve Baptists in prison at one time, and it also gives us insight into the treatment they received as well as the success of their ministries while incarcerated.

> Dear Brother in the Lord:
>
> At a meeting which was held at Brother McCain's, in this county, last Saturday, while William Webber was addressing the congregation from James 2:18, there came running toward him, in a most furious rage, Captain James Montague, a magistrate of the county, followed by the parson of the parish and several others who seemed greatly exasperated. The magistrate and another took hold of Brother Webber, and dragging him from the stage, delivered him with Brethren Wafford, Robert Ware, Richard Falkner, James Greenwood, and myself,

into custody, and commanded that we should be brought before him for trial. Brother Wafford was severely scourged, and Brother Henry Street received one lash from one of the persecutors, who was prevented from proceeding to further violence by his companions; to be short, I may inform you that we were carried before the above-mentioned magistrate, who with the parson and some others, carried us one by one into a room and examined our pockets and wallets for firearms, etc., charging us with carrying on a mutiny against the authority of the land. Finding none, we were asked if we had license to preach in this county; and learning we had not, it was required of us to give bond and security not to preach anymore in the county, which we modestly refused to do, whereupon after dismissing Brother Wafford, with a charge to make his escape out of the county by twelve o'clock the next day on pain of imprisonment, and dismissing Brother Falkner, the rest of us were delivered to the sheriff and sent to close jail, with a charge not to allow us to walk in the air until court day. Blessed be God, the sheriff and jailer have treated us with as much kindness as could be expected from strangers. May the Lord reward them for it! Yesterday we had a large number of people hear us preach; and, among others, many of the great ones of the land, who behaved well while one of us discoursed on the new birth. We find the Lord gracious and kind to us beyond expression in our afflictions. We cannot tell how long we shall be kept in bonds; we therefore beseech, dear brother, that you and the church supplicate night and day for us, our benefactors, and our persecutors.

I have also to inform you that six of our brethren are confined in Caroline jail, viz. Brethren Lewis Craig, John Burrus, John Young, Edward Herndon, James Goodrick, and Bartholomew Cheming. The most dreadful threatenings are raised in the neighboring counties against the Lord's faithful and humble followers. Excuse haste. Adieu.

John Waller[1]

EWT

---

[1]Lewis Peyton Little, *Imprisoned Preachers and Religious Liberty in Virginia* (Lynchburg, Va.: J. P. Bell Co., 1938), pp. 275-76.

August 13—A Faithful Mother's Prayers Were Answered

Scripture: I Samuel 1

The honor of establishing the first Swedish Baptist church in America goes to the Reverend Gustaf Palmquist, but well might we honor the memory of his dear mother as well. Gustaf Palmquist was born on May 26, 1812, into a family of seven children during a time of great spiritual dearth in his homeland. Gustaf's mother came under deep conviction and turned to the parish priest for spiritual advice. She was merely assured that her deep piety was sufficient. Having no peace, Mrs. Palmquist sought out an old widow who was considered spiritually odd by the neighbors, and the widow pointed Gustaf's mother to the Lord. "Now began that work of grace which ultimately culminated in the founding of the Swedish Baptists of America."[1] Mrs. Palmquist began earnestly to pray for the salvation of her children, and our faithful God granted her petition, though Gustaf and his brother Per did not come into full assurance until eight years after their mother's death.

Gustaf had become a professor in a teachers' college in Stockholm. When he was thirty-two years of age, the peace of God finally became a reality in his life. Immediately he began to testify of his Savior. His vocal witness soon brought him into contact with Pastor F. G. Hedberg of Finland and the Reverend F. O. Nilsson, the exiled Baptist preacher. In Helsingland in northern Sweden, there was a group of believers who, in an attempt to escape persecution, determined to emigrate to America. They asked Gustaf Palmquist to accompany them and become their pastor. Believing the request was providential, Palmquist came to America and landed in New York in August of 1851. He was soon disheartened to learn that his flock was scattered over three states and there was no way that he could serve them as pastor.

Possessing the spirit of a pioneer, Palmquist traveled westward and made Rock Island, Illinois, his headquarters. He immediately began seeking out his countrymen and ministered to them wherever he found them, pointing them to Jesus as Savior. In 1851, having just returned from a tour of scattered Swedish communities in Iowa, Wisconsin, and Minnesota, Palmquist heard of a wonderful moving of the Spirit of God in the Baptist church at Galesburg, Illinois, and went to examine it. Palmquist was still a Lutheran, but now the seed of Baptist belief that had been planted in his heart in Sweden germinated. On June 27, 1852, he was baptized by immersion, and a month later he was ordained by the Galesburg church.

The Galesburg church commissioned Palmquist, without salary, to preach the gospel to the Swedish. He returned to Rock Island, and though now he experienced opposition due to his doctrinal change, the Lord granted him fruit. "Exactly forty-seven days after his own baptism he organized the first Swedish Baptist church in America. Only three members, two men and one woman! Undoubtedly it was the smallest church ever launched in our denomination."[2] Palmquist became the first pastor at the founding of the church on August 13, 1852.

The Lord accompanied His Word with blessing and power. The church grew, built an edifice, and reached out to begin other such churches. Ultimately the Swedish Baptist Conference was formed with the Reverend Mr. Palmquist as the first moderator.

May God give us mothers who are determined to claim their children for Christ in prayer.

DLC

---

[1]Adolf Olson, *A Centenary History* (Chicago: Baptist General Conference, n.d.), p. 33.

[2]Ibid., p. 35.

August 14—A Petition to Minister, a Declaration for Liberty

Scripture: Ezra 5

There were no other people more zealous in the support of the Revolution than the Baptists of Virginia, who had felt the scourge of an intolerant state church. Because Baptists were rallying to the cause of liberty in great numbers, the Baptist Association petitioned the Virginia Convention as follows in part:

> Alarmed at the shocking Oppression which in a British Cloud hangs over our American Continent, we, as a Society and part of the distressed State, have in our Association consider'd what part might be most prudent for the Baptists to act in the present unhappy Contest. After we had determined "that in some Cases it was lawful to go to War, and also for us to make a Military resistance against Great Britain, in regard of their unjust Invasion, and tyrannical Oppression of, and repeated Hostilities against America," our people were all left to act at Discretion with respect to inlisting, without falling under the Censure of our Community. And as some have inlisted, and many more likely so to do, who will have earnest Desires for their Ministers to preach to them during the Campaign, we therefore deligate and appoint our well-beloved Brethren in the Ministry, Elijah Craig, Lewis Craig, Jeremiah Walker and John Williams to present this address and to petition you that they may have free Liberty to preach to the Troops at convenient Times without molestation or abuse; and as we are conscious of their strong attachment to American Liberty, as well as their soundness in the principles of the Christian Religion, and great

> usefulness in the Work of the Ministry, we are willing they may come under your Examination in any Matters you may think requisite.
>
> We conclude with our earnest prayers to Almighty God for His Divine Blessing on your patriotic and laudable Resolves, for the good of Mankind and American Freedom, and for the success of our Armies in Defense of our Lives, Liberties and Properties. Amen.
>
> Sign'd by order and in behalf of the Association the 14th August, 1775.
>
> Sam'l Harriss, Moderator
> John Waller, Clerk

The Convention, under the date of Wednesday, August 16, 1775, issued the following resolution:

> Resolved, That it be an instruction to the commanding officers of the regiments or troops to be raised that they permit dissenting clergymen to celebrate divine worship, and to preach to the soldiers, or exhort, from time to time, as the various operations of the military service may permit, for the ease of such scrupulous consciences as may not choose to attend divine service as celebrated by the chaplain.[1]

Ultimately the Baptists supplied a greater percentage of chaplains to the Continental Army than any other religious society.

EWT

---

[1]Robert B. Semple, *History of the Baptists in Virginia,* rev. ed. (Lafayette, Tenn.: Church History Research and Archives, 1976), pp. 493-94.

August 15—A Moderator of a Wise and Moderate Spirit

Scripture: Acts 4:23-31

William Webber was considered one of the spiritual fathers and pioneers of the gospel in Virginia. He was born August 15, 1747, to parents of moderate means and received only three years of formal education. He became a carpenter and worked at that trade until hearing the preaching of John Waller, at which time he was converted to Jesus Christ and quickly became an exhorter.

Few men in Virginia suffered more persecutions than William Webber. He was among those who preached through the grates of the Chesterfield County jail, having spent three months of confinement there. Shortly after in the same year of 1771, he was taken from the platform in the midst of his message and was placed in the Middlesex County jail for forty-five days, where he, along with several others, preached twice a week through the bars to such as would hear.[1] Besides these imprisonments, he was roughly treated on many occasions. In spite of these things, the gospel prospered, and Baptist principles were embraced by many. These endeavors further resulted in the planting of numerous strong and fruitful churches such as Powhatan, out of which no less than fourteen preachers were called early in its history.[2]

Early in his ministry, Webber became pastor of the Dover Church in Goochland County, Virginia, and in spite of being in poor circumstances, he gave a great deal of time in his youth to preaching. As he grew older and his family larger, he found it necessary to limit his labors to his own and adjacent neighborhoods.

Semple says, "He was very successful in turning many to righteousness; and in the confirming the souls of his disciples. Mr. Webber was a man of talents. . . . He was a man of sound and correct judgment; well acquainted with mankind; well versed in the Scriptures; sound in the principles of the gospel, and ingenious in defending them against error."[3]

During the time that Baptists were uniting to petition the governing authorities concerning their grievances and liberty of conscience, they met in General Association or General Committee. William Webber was elected moderator in spite of the fact that older men of greater accomplishments and more refined powers were present. His election was prompted because of his soft, yet manly, affectionate attitude and methods. He was never influenced nor affected by the presence of others. William Webber was a man without guile.

God grant us such leadership in our day. We and our posterity will have to stand together for the preservation of those liberties our forefathers established. This we must do so that future generations may enjoy the freedoms, understand the principles, and observe the example of the proper spirit by which we conduct the business of the King of kings.

DLC

---

[1]Robert B. Semple, *A History of the Rise and Progress of the Baptists in Virginia* (Richmond: Published by the author, 1810), pp. 422-23.

[2]Robert B. Semple, *History of the Baptists in Virginia,* rev. ed. (Lafayette, Tenn.: Church History Research and Archives, 1976), pp. 264-65.

[3]Robert B. Semple, *A History of the Rise and Progress of the Baptists in Virginia,* pp. 424-25.

August 16—The Preacher: Not Physically Impressive, but Spiritually Powerful and Effective

Scripture: II Corinthians 11

Elder David Thomas was born August 16, 1732, and is described by William Fristoe, one of his sons in the ministry, as a distinguished, useful preacher, "whose fruitful mind, improved by close study, and aided by a supernatural influence enabled him in his public ministry to preach powerful, edifying and comfortably, so the saints were fed with marrow and fatness—and in his turn, a son of thunder, who could well discharge the artillery of Sinai, and exhibit the divine law to the arousing and alarming of many a poor sinner. He was a great patriot, and took an active part in our national revolution."[1]

David Thomas was a minister of the Philadelphia Association in Pennsylvania, and came to Berkley, Virginia, on a ministerial visit. Two men from Fauquier County became deeply concerned about their spiritual need. One of them, Peter Cornwell, had made a reformation of life, but by reading a sermon by George Whitefield, Cornwell realized he was lost and a stranger to the grace of God. These men traveled sixty miles over rough territory to hear the gospel. Upon hearing David Thomas, they were saved. They persuaded Thomas to come to the Broad Run area. This was around 1760, and his labors were so blessed that he resolved to become resident among them. A church was quickly constituted, and David Thomas was chosen pastor. He did not confine his ministry to one locality but proclaimed the gospel throughout northern Virginia with great response from his hearers. Churches were planted and men called to preach who later became outstanding lights in a dark period, influencing our statesmen in the behalf of the cause of religious liberty and freedom of conscience.

Some of the response was not at all favorable to Thomas. On one occasion a Captain Ball pulled him from the platform while he was preaching in a tobacco house and dragged him out of the place through a belligerent mob where individuals would clench their fists and gnash their teeth at him. His friends feared he would be pounded to pieces. At another time a man rushed toward him with a gun to shoot him. As he leveled the gun on the preacher, someone wrenched it from him, and a battle erupted in which many were injured. The revilings and slanders he met were innumerable.

William Wirt described Thomas in a letter: "He was so very near-sighted as to be almost blind; a very ungainly, little old man with a cracked voice, and odd and awkward in his delivery. Yet that man was very near running me mad. I was only sixteen or seventeen years old, extremely susceptible and tenderhearted, and he made such dead-sets at me, that I was within an ace of insanity. If my physician had not advised me to seek a southern climate . . . I should either have died in a lunatic asylum or become a Baptist preacher."[2]

In later life David Thomas carried his effective preaching into Kentucky, where he joined other Baptists who had migrated there in great numbers and were spreading the gospel of Jesus Christ. From there he departed for his eternal home.

EWT

---

[1]William Fristoe, *The History of the Ketocton Baptist Association, 1766-1808* (Staunton, Va.: William Gilman Lyford, 1808), p. 2.

[2]Lewis Peyton Little, *Imprisoned Preachers and Religious Liberty in Virginia* (Lynchburg, Va.: J. P. Bell Co., 1938), p. 40.

August 17—A Heroine Who Did What She Could

Scripture: Mark 14:1-9

The wives of pioneer missionaries in the early days of the expansion of the gospel into the far reaches of the world suffered many difficulties indeed. The story of Mrs. Ann Judson stirs one's heart when one considers the privations she endured while her beloved husband was imprisoned. However, little has been written concerning the wife of William Carey. Doubtless, some have been almost embarrassed to mention the fact that she died insane in her adopted land of India.

William Carey was born on August 17, 1761, and married Dorothy Plackett on June 10, 1781. The bride was five years his senior, and the couple shared a very meager lifestyle, but Carey considered his wife the "gift of God." Mrs. Carey's home village did not have a school, and thus she could not read or write when the young couple took love's oath in the church in Piddington, England. However, in the years that followed, Dorothy disciplined herself and learned to read and write, as one would expect, and her husband studied, preached to extend the kingdom, and made and mended shoes to help pay expenses.

One can only imagine the trauma that Mrs. Carey experienced when her husband announced that he had volunteered for missionary service in India. Mrs. Carey, along with Carey's church members, resisted her travel to India because she was expecting a baby. So, he planned to leave her with the children in England and to return in three years to pick them up when he was established in India. She also questioned whether her husband should go at all. After all, Carey was not robust, and she believed he could not endure the heat and hardships of India. The mental anguish must have been almost unbearable as Carey persevered. In time the family was taken to Piddington to remain with Dorothy's sister during his absence.

The pressure must have heightened as Carey "deputized" and made arrangements for his trip. However, as the time approached, officials would not allow Carey and his companion, Dr. Thomas, passage on the English ship to India. By the time that other arrangements could be made to travel aboard a Danish ship, Mrs. Carey had agreed to accompany her husband, and with her one-month-old son and three little ones, she boarded the ship for the five-month journey to Bengal. The long trip must have been tedious and trying.

The real trials began during their first year on the field when their money was exhausted and Mrs. Carey came down with a severe case of dysentery. "The mental disorder and distress, which harrowed Mrs. Carey . . . for the next thirteen years, dates from this misery. Ill with dysentery, her first-born son still worse; unable to afford even bread; appalled at their destitution in the strange and friendless city—her brain began to give way."[1]

Again in 1795 Mrs. Carey fell ill to dysentery, and "her spirit passed into a permanent gloom."[2] "Her mental distress had much worsened throughout her last five years. . . . [Carey] insisted on keeping her under his own compassionate care, till in the first week of December 1807 she emerged from the long fearsome tunnel into heaven's light and peace, into 'the rest that remaineth for the people of God.' "[3]

On William Carey's birth date we honor the memory of his "gift of God," who gave her all in the cause of missions. Dorothy Carey was a heroine of the faith!

DLC

---

[1]S. Pearce Carey, *William Carey* (London: Hodder and Stoughton, 1924), p. 145.

[2]Ibid., p. 162.

[3]Ibid., p. 271.

August 18—How Can You Win a One-sided Debate?

Scripture: Acts 22:1-22

The name of Thomas Gould was revered by early Baptists in Massachusetts because of nis adamant but gracious refusal in 1655 to have his infant sprinkled in the church of the standing order.[1] During the period of 1665 to 1670, Thomas Gould was "put in seven or eight courts."[2] The following is an account of this important event in his life.

Thomas Gould was a member of the Congregational church in Charlestown. When he and his wife were blessed with a baby, Gould ignored presenting the little son for "baptism." The pastor and the elders of the church admonished him in an interview, and Gould reported his response as follows: "My answer was, I did not see any rule of Christ for it, for that ordinance belongs to such as can make profession of their faith, as the Scripture doth plainly hold forth."[3] On December 30, 1656, Gould was suspended from Communion. His trials were just beginning however, for on April 7, 1657, he was called before the Middlesex Court. On February 28, 1664, he was haled before the Charlestown church for having a meeting of "Anabaptists" in his house. On October 11, 1665, he appeared before the Court of Assistants, charged with setting up a public meeting in opposition to the ordinance of Christ. At the same trial, Gould, along with Osborne, Drinker, Turner, and George, was "disfranchised" and threatened with imprisonment, for they declared their determination to continue their worship outside of the Congregational church. On April 17, 1666, Gould, Osborne, and George were presented to the grand jury at Cambridge for absence from the Congregational church "for one whole year." At that time they pled that they were members of a gospel church and attended worship regularly. For this "they were convicted of 'high presumption against the Lord and his holy appointments,' and were fined £4 each, and put under bonds of £20 each; but as they would not pay their fines, they were thrown into prison."[4]

On August 18, 1666, according to the General Court papers of Massachusetts, the Assistants' Court decided that Gould and Osborne could be freed if they would pay the fine and costs, but if they refused, they were to be banished. On March 3, 1668, Gould was brought before the Court of Assistants in Boston, and he was recommitted to prison. Being unable to dissuade Thomas Gould by force, the court decided to overwhelm his logic by allowing Gould, John Farnham, and Thomas Osborne the privilege of debating the subject of baptism on April 14 in the Congregational building in Boston. For two days the pedobaptists presented their case, but the Baptists were not allowed to reply. The authorities resorted again to fines and imprisonment, but seeing that Gould and his company could not be convinced, they were censured and, as much as possible, ignored.

Thomas Gould later wrote, "If eight or nine poor Anabaptists, as they call them, should be the destruction of their churches, their foundation must be sandy indeed."[5] From the trials of Gould, the First Baptist Church of Boston came into existence. Those who dared unite with that church suffered fines. Some were banished, but being unwilling to leave, they were imprisoned. Gould died in October of 1675, but his suffering was not without victory. Years later, Massachusetts, along with the whole nation, granted freedom of conscience for men to worship without fear or favor. Thank God for the faithful Thomas Gould!

DLC

---

[1]David Benedict, *A General History of the Baptist Denomination in America* (New York: Lewis Colby and Co., 1848), p. 380.

[2]David Weston, *The Baptists and the National Centenary,* ed. Lemuel Moss (Philadelphia: American Baptist Publication Society, 1876), p. 24.

[3]William Cathcart, *The Baptist Encyclopedia,* ed. Louis H. Everts (Philadelphia: Louis H. Everts, 1881), 1:461.

[4]Thomas Armitage, *The History of the Baptists* (1890; reprint ed., Watertown, Wis.: Maranatha Baptist Press, 1976), 2:700.

[5]Cathcart, p. 462.

August 19—Will the Baptist Preacher Dance?

Scripture: I John 2:15-17

We have previously considered the Reverend Hezekiah Smith (January 22), who pastored for forty years in Haverhill, Massachusetts, in a church that he had established. His ministry included not only his pastoral history and service as a chaplain in Washington's army but also his extensive travels in evangelistic tours throughout New Hampshire and Maine where he founded Baptist churches.

On August 19, 1770, Smith climaxed several months of itinerant preaching in New Hampshire with the formation of a Baptist church in Stratham, New Hampshire.[1] He had a continually exciting and fruitful ministry.

On one of his evangelistic-missionary trips into Maine, certain noteworthy events took place. Late one night he arrived at a hotel where he sought lodging for the night.

> A gathering crowd soon made him acquainted with the fact that a ball was to take place . . . that evening. Intending soon to seek the retirement of his room, he paid no attention to the . . . party near him, but was warming himself by the parlour fireside, in preparation for repose, when, to his surprise, he was waited upon by a deputation, with the request that he should join in the mirth of the evening. He politely declined; but they urged his acceptance. Again he begged to be excused, and again they insisted on having his company. At length, overcome by their entreaties, he accompanied them to the ball, where the assembly was waiting to commence the dance. His appearance being that of a gentleman, the company was desirous of showing him some marked respect; and united in inviting him to take the most prominent part in the performance. Finding himself, involuntarily, in this predicament, he resolved to make the best of it, and turn the whole affair, if possible, to some moral benefit. So, after having acknowledged, in his own easy and pleasant manner, the attention which had been shown him, he remarked that he had always made it a principle, through life, never to engage in any employment, without having first asked the blessing of God; and he presumed that the courtesy of the company would be farther extended to him, while he engaged in this imperative act of duty. Upon this, he immediately commenced a prayer. The singular turn which was thus given to the anticipated amusement of the evening, produced a remarkable effect. The commanding tones of his voice; his impressive style of supplicatory address; the fervour of his prayer, and the solemn allusions made in it, rivetted first upon himself every eye, and then upon his sentiments every heart, so that, before he closed, many were dissolved in tears.
>
> Finding, as he ended, the way quite prepared, he began . . . (an) address to the consciences of his audience, and continued it some length of time. The result was most happy. Suffice it to say, there was no . . . dance there, that evening. The company broke up with pensive thoughts. Many, who, to that hour, had been immersed in the . . . dissipating pleasures of this life, now resolved to break off their sins by righteousness, and seek a more solid and substantial good. A work of grace, of uncommon interest, commenced in the neighborhood, and, on the return of Mr. Smith in the following year to that region, he had the pleasure of receiving many of this same party, who had been raised . . . to a new life . . . of . . . Christian character.[2]

DLC

---

[1]Albert Henry Newman, *A History of the Baptist Churches in the United States* (Philadelphia: American Baptist Publication Society, 1915), p. 267.

[2]William B. Sprague, *Annals of the American Pulpit* (New York: Robert Carter and Bros., 1865), 6:99-100.

August 20—A Pacesetter in China

Scripture: Joshua 1:9

Jehu L. Shuck was born in Alexandria, Virginia, on September 4, 1812. We know little of the days of his youth, but he was educated in the Virginia Baptist Seminary, now the University of Richmond. Young Shuck proposed to Henrietta, the daughter of Dr. and Mrs. J. B. Jeter, and two days after their wedding in 1835, they were set apart as missionaries by the Triennial Baptist Convention and sailed for China on September 22, 1835. To Mrs. Shuck goes the honor of being the "first American evangelical woman missionary to go to China."[1]

Upon journeying to the "Portuguese territory of Macao on the China mainland in 1837, Shuck found a young man who, through his reading of Christian literature, had become prepared to accept Christ. Shuck thus was privileged to baptize the first Chinese convert to Christianity several years before a mission could be opened on the mainland of China!"[2]

In 1840 the agent from whom the Shucks received their financial support failed, and they relocated for safety in Hong Kong which was under British protection. There J. L. Shuck supported his family as he edited a paper and continued in his missionary work. In 1843 he established a church in Hong Kong with twenty-six members. However, in 1844 Mrs. Shuck passed away, and it was necessary for Mr. Shuck to return to the United States to make provision for his children. Yong-Seen-Sang (Seen-Sang corresponds to our "Mr.") was saved and had become a preacher, and thus he accompanied the missionary to the States in 1845 and 1846. "He was present at the first anniversary of the Southern Baptist Convention, which met in 1846 at Richmond, Virginia, and made an impressive address in reply to the welcome of the president of the Convention.[3] Yong traveled with Shuck, and together they were used of God in stirring up new interest for the evangelization of China.

In 1847 Shuck returned to China to labor in Shanghai. The need for a Christian physician was greatly felt. In response, Dr. and Mrs. J. Sexton James of Philadelphia were available and were sent to minister in medicine. Shuck and James had corresponded, and Shuck was anxiously awaiting the arrival of Dr. and Mrs. James. They made the trip to Hong Kong safely, but the schooner to Shanghai capsized in a sudden squall, and the medical missionaries went down with the ship. Shuck was crushed by this tragedy but ventured inland in 1850. Only the Chinese ports had been open to Christian preaching, but he was successful in establishing the first permanent foothold in the interior of China for the cause of Christ. However, as trials persisted and his second wife passed away, Shuck returned again to America.

Wishing to be nearer to his children, Shuck resigned from the foreign board and accepted an appointment from the domestic board of the Southern Baptist Convention to work among the Chinese in California. His first convert, "Wong Mui, returned to Canton and did faithful service as a native preacher."[4]

Having labored twenty-five years among the Chinese, J. L. Shuck moved to South Carolina in 1861, and he entered heaven two years later on August 20, 1863. His fifty-one years were fruitful, and he witnessed many "firsts" in the ongoing of the gospel among the Chinese.

DLC

---

[1]Norman Wade Cox, ed, *Encyclopedia of Southern Baptists* (Nashville: Broadman Press, 1958), 2:1201.

[2]David Collier Woolley, ed., *Baptist Advance* (Nashville: Broadman Press, 1964), p. 81.

[3]G. Winfred Hervey, *The Story of Baptist Missions in Foreign Lands* (St. Louis: C. R. Barnes Publishing Co., 1892), p. 473.

[4]Ibid., p. 522.

August 21—Wars Waged from Prison to Revolutionary Battlefields

Scripture: Exodus 17:8-16

The zeal with which the young preachers of Orange and Culpeper Counties carried out the commission of their Lord in Virginia was strong, and their convictions ran deep. At first they had no meetinghouses. This seeming hardship proved to be an asset rather than a liability because as they preached to large congregations in groves, from house to house, and even in tobacco warehouses, some donated land, and others provided materials and labor to construct a building. Thus did Nathaniel Saunders join others in building a 40 x 24 foot building to house the Mountain Run Church in Orange County, where he became pastor in 1767.

This did not limit the preaching of Saunders to a local site, for he continued his strong preaching against the inconsistencies of the established church's clergy and urged the people that they were in need of the new birth. This resulted in controversy in both verbal and written debates. Saunders received some kind letters but also some threatening and vindictive letters. Though he was summoned to court several times, he was convicted on only one occasion and served an unknown period of time in the Culpeper jail. Saunders, with some other Baptists of the period, initially accepted a license to preach in limited areas, such as one particular meetinghouse, but soon discovered that toleration was a means of taking away liberty, not granting it. In our day this injustice is practiced in Communist countries, and thus in Virginia, Baptists have fiercely resisted any type of licensure involving any local church ministry on the principle that licensure brings the church and state into a dangerous, intolerable, unscriptural, unconstitutional relationship.

A warrant for Nathaniel Saunder's arrest, dated August 21, 1773, also included William McClannahan, who became his fellow prisoner.[1] McClannahan was one of the boldest and most enterprising of the early Baptist preachers of Virginia. He was the first Baptist to preach the gospel of God's grace in the lower counties of the Northern Neck. One of the early converts of Westmoreland County wrote:

McClannahan I plainly see
Was instrumental in calling me;
And Fristoe, that dear man of love,
Preached I was born of God.

Captain McClannahan raised one of the companies of the Culpeper minutemen for the Revolutionary Army. He led them not only into battle but also in prayer, preaching to them regularly. His troops were principally Baptists, who were among the most strenuous supporters of liberty. The price of liberty was paid for in the jails as well as on the battlefields by men like Saunders and McClannahan.[2]

EWT

---

[1]Lewis Peyton Little, *Imprisoned Preachers and Religious Liberty in Virginia* (Lynchburg, Va.: J. P. Bell Co., 1938), p. 368.

[2]Ibid., pp. 273-74.

August 22—Isaac Backus, Religious Liberty's Apologist

Scripture: Nehemiah 13

As early as 1740 George Whitefield was preaching his revival sermons in New England. The Great Awakening had begun earlier in Jonathan Edward's church in Northampton, Massachusetts. The Norwich pastor, Benjamin Lord, was sympathetic toward the movement at the beginning and invited several outstanding revivalists to his church. Genuine assurance of salvation came to Widow Backus. Her son, working in the fields alone and contemplating the Scriptures and the ministry of the revivalists, was converted.

He became a full-fledged member of the Congregational church during a time of great controversy over the spiritual awakening. Those in favor of the awakening were known as "New Lights" and later "Separates," and those opposed were called "Old Lights." As the "New Lights" became convinced of error, they repudiated the Half-Way Covenant, embraced the need for a regenerate membership, and separated to form their own churches.

The result of all of this, as far as Backus was concerned, was that he preached a sermon in 1748 opposing infant baptism, but he was not immersed until August 22, 1751,[1] when he proved his conviction relative to believer's baptism. His complete, open espousal of Baptist beliefs in 1756 was no surprise because for years he had been preaching and defending the ideals for which Baptists were noted: believer's baptism for membership in the local church, spiritual liberty, the autonomy of each church congregation, and complete freedom from government control.[2] Backus, like many others of that period, deliberated on these principles and carefully considered them for a long period of time before publicly identifying with the despised Baptists.

At this time Backus became pastor of the First Baptist Church of Middleborough, Massachusetts, where he served until his death in 1806. During his Middleborough ministry, Backus continued his campaigns against taxation of religious bodies and the use of certificates of exemption, which were being forced on some Baptist congregations by the religious authorities. Backus denounced the scheme and contended that to sign the certificates before they could secure tax exemption was as much an invasion of personal rights as the tax itself. He finally condemned the practice when he said, "In all civil governments some are appointed for others, and have power to compel others to submit to their judgment; but our Lord has most plainly forbidden us, either to assume or submit to any such thing in religion."[3]

He later wrote an *Appeal to the Publick for Religious Liberty* in which he asserted, "It appears to us that the true difference and exact limits between ecclesiastical and civil governments is this, That the church is armed with light and truth, to pull down the strongholds of iniquity, and to gain souls to Christ and into His Church. . . . While the state is armed with the sword to guard the peace, and the civil rights of all persons and societies, and to punish those who violate the same."[4]

God grant us leadership that has the depth of conviction and the clear understanding of the biblical principles of church/state relationships to preserve religious liberty and freedom of conscience for our posterity. We must have "frequent recurrence to fundamental principles" for such to be maintained.[5]

EWT

---

[1]Robert C. Newman, *Baptists and the American Tradition* (Des Plaines, Ill.: Regular Baptist Press, 1976), p. 31.

[2]O. K. and Marjorie Armstrong, *Baptists Who Shaped a Nation* (Nashville: Broadman Press, 1975), pp. 88-89.

[3]Ibid., p. 90.

[4]Ibid., p. 92.

[5]George Mason, *Virginia Declaration of Rights,* June 12, 1776.

August 23—Revival Is the Need of the Hour Again

Scripture: Habakkuk 3:2

The debauchery of early America is well known. As settlers moved westward, there was little religious influence, and sin reigned.

> If a traveller had passed through the whole breadth of the settled portions of North America, in 1799, he would have heard the songs of the drunkard, the loud swearing and the obscenity of crowds around taverns, and the bold, blasphemous vaunting of infidels, in every village and hamlet. If he had returned in 1801, he would have heard, instead, the proclamation of the Gospel to awed multitudes, earnest prayers in the groves and forests, and songs of praise to God, along all the public thoroughfares.[1]

Virginia had experienced seasons of revival during the middle of the eighteenth century, but spiritual dearth existed in the areas west of the Allegheny Mountains, and wickedness increased. How refreshing to read of the great spiritual awakening! As with all such movings of the Holy Spirit, there were excesses that were of the flesh, but thankfully, the fleshly displays were rare among the Baptists. The revival spirit began among the Presbyterians and soon spread to the Methodists. The protracted "camp meetings," which became popular between 1827 and 1830, grew out of that period, and the Presbyterians and Methodists would join in united Communion services. After some initial participation in camp meetings, many Baptists, holding to a restrictive principle of Communion, would not participate and were not as involved in the fleshly excesses which persisted in some of the meetings. Although the modern-day Pentecostal movement did not begin for another century, strange phenomena began as the meetings continued into the early hours of the mornings. Many were genuinely converted, but the emotional spirit led to screaming, jerking, rolling, running, and even barking. The clamor and confusion in those meetings of intense excitement were out of character to the Regular Baptists and their "order." The Separate Baptists were known for their "ardor," but their meetings could not be considered in the same class.

Revival among the Baptists swept through the South, and the following letter, dated August 23, 1802, from David Lilly gives some of the thrilling details in South Carolina.

> A great work of God is going on in the upper parts of this State. Multitudes are made to cry out, "What shall we do to be saved?" A few days ago, I returned from our Association. We have had a truly refreshing season. A vast concourse of people assembled on Saturday, and considerable appearances of solemnity soon took place; but no uncommon effect till Sunday later in the evening. Then the Lord was pleased to manifest his power to many hearts.
>
> On Monday the work increased. The hearts of many were made to melt; and several men, noted for their impiety, were stricken and lay among the prostrate. I must acknowledge it was a memorable time with my soul. . . . The Association rose about 3 o'clock in the afternoon; and such a degree of brotherly affection as appeared among the ministers and messengers of the churches, I scarcely ever saw. It was enough to melt the heart of the greatest infidel living. . . . Be assured, my brother, the Lord is doing great things for his people in this country.[2]

The need of America again is revival. Baptist people ought to cry out to God for such a spiritual awakening in our day!

DLC

---

[1] J. H. Spencer, *A History of Kentucky Baptists from 1769 to 1885* (Cincinnati: J. R. Baumes, 1886), 1:505.

[2] Robert A. Baker, *A Baptist Source Book* (Nashville: Broadman Press, 1966), p. 49.

August 24—A Scholarly Presbyterian Becomes a Baptist

Scripture: John 7:40-53

During the decade of the 1650s, at least eleven Baptist churches were formed in Ireland. When Cromwell's army overran Ireland in 1649, its leadership consisted of many Baptists and Independents. Baptists abounded in his forces. Among them were twelve governors of towns and cities, ten colonels, four lieutenant colonels, ten majors, twenty captains, and twenty-three officers on the civil list who were Baptists. Most of these Baptist churches were founded and sustained by the officers and soldiers in Cromwell's army.[1]

London Baptists, responding to the appeal of the Irish Baptists, sent a number of preachers to Ireland. Among them was Thomas Patient, who formed a Baptist church at Waterford and by 1652 was preaching in Dublin. In 1653 a Baptist meetinghouse was erected under his leadership. Most of the early leaders, judging from their names, were English or Welsh.

> Along with their letter to London, the Irish Baptists listed twelve matters "requiring prayer by the churches." This list of spiritual priorities reveals much of the internal life of the churches at that time, with emphasis upon prayer for spiritual growth, more intense Bible study, closer personal communion with God, and more personal discipline in the Christian life. To keep these needs before them, they had set aside the first Wednesday of each month as a day of fasting and prayer.[2]

One of the most illustrious of the Irish Baptists, Alexander Carson was born in the north of Ireland in 1776. He settled as a Presbyterian pastor in 1798 at Tubbermore, where he received £100 per year from the government. He was a Greek scholar of the first order, and had he been willing to sign the "Standards" of the Church of Scotland, he could have become Professor of Greek in the University of Glasgow. He gradually adopted Baptist principles, gave up his Presbyterian pastorate and salary, and gathered a little band of Baptists about him in a church without a meetinghouse, while he himself endured deep poverty. In his day he was probably the leading scholar among the British Baptists and was a voluminous writer and profound reasoner. Carson's work on baptism has no superior and few equals. Some have called him the "Jonathan Edwards of Ireland."[3]

Carson was among those who operated a Baptist seminary at Bellina from 1830 to 1840. He also taught several ministerial candidates at his church in Tubbermore. Carson was one of those servants of God who came upon the scene when disorder and confusion prevailed. His life and ministry had a stabilizing effect that laid the groundwork for the "Prayer Meeting Revival" that spread from America to Ireland in the late 1850s, several years after Carson's death on August 24, 1844. Often the fruit of our labors does not come forth until we have entered into our rest after enduring the heat of the day of sowing and cultivating. See July 30th for additional details of Patient's life.

EWT

---

[1]Thomas Armitage, *The History of the Baptists* (1890; reprint ed., Watertown, Wis.: Maranatha Baptist Press, 1976), 2:570-71.

[2]H. Leon McBeth, *The Baptist Heritage* (Nashville: Broadman Press, 1987), p. 313.

[3]Armitage, p. 571.

August 25—A Little-known Martyr of the Communists

Scripture: Matthew 9:36

George and Ethel Birch, godly Presbyterian missionaries, were serving near Landaur, India, on September 12, 1918, when the Lord blessed them with a son named John. Two years later, because of recurring malaria experienced by George, Mr. and Mrs. Birch were forced to return to America. The family lived for some time in New Jersey. During that period, they discovered liberalism in their denomination and began to attend a Baptist church. Shortly thereafter, they were immersed.

At seven years of age, John Birch was converted and baptized, and it was apparent that the lad was mentally gifted. At the age of seven, he could read as well as the average adult, and his power of memory was awesome. Because of his ability, he was allowed to skip the sixth grade. Although this resulted in his early graduation, he was still at the head of his class. When John was eleven years of age, his heart was moved toward missionary service. In a missionary rally, he heard the challenge of worldwide missions, and he sat enthralled. Several days later his parents found a note John had left on the living room table which read, "The Lord is calling me to the mission field. I have the answer to the death wail of the lost."[1] From that day forward there was no question as to what John Birch would do with his life.

The family had continued to expand, and life was hard for the Birch clan. Thus when the Great Depression set in, the family moved down to Georgia. George's mother had passed away, and some of her estate near Macon, Georgia, had been given to them. In this new location, though there were now seven children to feed, John could attend nearby Mercer University. At Mercer, John excelled on the debate team, and his writing caused an English professor to urge him to become a professional writer. While in college he became embroiled in a theological controversy concerning the inroads of modernism at Mercer, but he graduated in 1939, magna cum laude. After finishing college, John completed a two-year course in one year in a small theological institute in Fort Worth, Texas, and then sailed for China in July of 1940, never to return to his homeland.

In one year John Birch could speak Chinese! After Pearl Harbor on December 7, 1941, the Japanese attempted to arrest John, but he escaped. He gave himself to the preaching of the gospel and to the encouraging of the saints as he traveled in war-torn China. Surely John Birch's fame would have grown had the English-speaking world known of his exploits and sacrifices for Christ. While traveling to minister to suffering believers, John was put in touch with Colonel Jimmy Doolittle and the four airmen from his plane. The plane had been ditched in China after their bombing raid on Tokyo. It was John Birch who led them to safety! Seeing the situation, Birch enlisted in the United States Army and served for some time as the Intelligence Officer for General C. L. Chennault. He was able, because of his knowledge of the language and culture of the people, to be of great help in setting up radio contacts. John knew the dangers of communism and witnessed its inroads. Unfortunately, official Washington was oblivious to the situation, and the Communists considered John Birch a dangerous enemy. Near the end of the Second World War, on August 25, 1945, John Birch was murdered by Chinese Communists in Hsuchow, China. His influence for Christ had spread over hundreds of miles where he was known to the nationals as "Bey Shang We," a title of respect. May God raise up another generation of people who have the answer to the death wail of the world and send them forth with His glorious gospel.

DLC

---

[1]James and Marti Hefley, *The Secret File of John Birch* (Wheaton, Ill.: Living Books, 1981), p. 36.

August 26—From Infant Baptism to Believers Baptism by Scriptural Study

Scripture: II Timothy 2:14-26

Benjamin Foster was born into a typical home of pious Congregationalist parents in Danvers, Massachusetts. After Foster received his early education in the town school, his parents saw to it that he further prepared for the university by continuing to study at the town school. At the age of eighteen, he was placed in Yale College in Connecticut. He distinguished himself by his outstanding moral life as well as his success in classical literature.

At this time there was much debate relative to the scriptural mode and candidates for baptism. Several tracts had appeared throughout the northern colonies, and there was no small disputation on the subject. Of course, baptism was debated often at Yale and was considered a proper subject for discussion. Because of his academic excellence and preparation, Foster was appointed to defend infant sprinkling. To prepare himself for the task, he endeavored to view the question in every light and from every angle. He carefully searched the Scriptures and studied the history of the church from the times of the apostles. The result, to his own astonishment and the surprise and chagrin of others, was very different from what was expected. When the day appointed for discussion arrived, to the amazement of the officers of the college, he avowed himself a decided convert to the doctrine of believers baptism, that only those who profess faith in Jesus Christ are to be the subjects of baptism and that immersion only is the mode of Christian baptism. He continued the rest of his life as a zealous and powerful advocate of these principles.

Foster graduated from Yale around the year of 1772, and soon thereafter he was baptized and joined the Baptist church in Boston. Under the pastoral care of Samuel Stillman, Foster continued his study of theology. He soon became pastor of the Baptist church in Leicester, Massachusetts, where he was ordained. He continued to preach and write tracts and ultimately answered the call of a Baptist church in Newport, Rhode Island, where his sphere of usefulness expanded and his opportunities for study increased.

In 1788 Foster received a unanimous call to the First Baptist Church in New York, where he continued in the pastorate until his death on August 26, 1798.[1] His death was brought about by yellow fever, which had reached epidemic proportions in New York in that year. When the dreadful disease began to prevail, Pastor Foster was frequent in his visits to pray and give comfort from God's Word. He was always willing to visit those terrible scenes of affliction from which many of the best of men shrunk back with terror.

As a scholar, particularly in the Greek, Hebrew, and Chaldean languages, Pastor Foster had few superiors. On his tomb in a New York cemetery is the following inscription: "As a scholar and divine, he excelled; as a preacher he was eminent; as a Christian he shone conspicuously; in his piety he was fervent; the church was comforted by his life, and it now laments his death."[2]

EWT

---

[1]Charles G. Sommers, ed., *A History of the Baptists in New England,* The Baptist Library, vol. 1 (New York: Lewis Colby and Co., n.d.), p. 297.

[2]Ibid.

August 27—An Early, Well-known Baptist Evangelist

Scripture: II Timothy 4:5

Jacob Knapp was born in an Episcopalian home on December 7, 1799, in Otsego County, New York. He was brought up in a religious environment and was taught the Creed and Catechism. When he was seventeen years old, his mother died, and he experienced deep anxiety about his own spiritual condition. Knapp was driven to seek spiritual life, and one Sunday morning, alone in a grove of trees, as he sought the Lord, he was saved and discovered the burden of sin removed. Soon after that experience, he visited a Baptist church in Masonville, New York, and witnessed the immersion of believers. In his own words he said, "This, thought I, is the way in which John the Baptist, Philip, and all the Apostles baptized."[1] Being only seventeen, he sought permission from his father to be immersed but was refused the privilege.

When his sons became twenty years of age, Mr. Knapp regarded them mature, and thus in 1819, Jacob was immersed upon his profession of faith. He had already been burdened to preach and sought an opportunity to further his education. The Hamilton Theological Seminary offered education to young men who had been licensed to preach, and in the spring of 1821, the Baptist church in Masonville licensed young Jacob. He entered the seminary on May 16, 1821, and graduated on June 1, 1824. Because he used his summer vacations as an opportunity to preach the gospel, it is not surprising that immediately following graduation, Knapp accepted a call to pastor in Springfield, New York. On August 27, 1824, he was ordained, and on September 1, he was married. During his six-year ministry in Springfield, he saw sixty people converted and added to the church. In September of 1830, he began a three-year pastorate in Watertown, New York. The blessings of God were evident as revival fires fell, and Pastor Knapp baptized about two hundred converts into the membership.

An amazing phenomenon took place in America about this time as successful "protracted meetings" were held. Charles G. Finney, who labored mainly among Presbyterians, was used greatly of God. Christians became concerned for a greater thrust in evangelism, and wherever Jacob Knapp was invited to preach, great results followed. Thus, he resigned his three-year pastorate at Watertown and began his labor as a "full-time" evangelist, remaining in that capacity for the next forty-two years of his life. He preached throughout New York and all of New England, with "his largest audiences . . . in Rochester (1839), New York (1840), Boston (1841) and Washington D.C. (1843)."[2]

In 1840 Evangelist Knapp moved his headquarters to Rockford, Illinois, and labored in the Midwest. However, in 1867 he went to California and preached among the churches there. "It is quite certain that no man in America ever equaled him in the number of his meetings, and in the extent of the territory they covered."[3] "It has been estimated that Elder Knapp preached 16,000 sermons; that one hundred thousand persons were converted under his labors . . . and . . . among the converts of his meetings two hundred fifty persons entered the ministry."[4]

The evangelist died on March 2, 1874. Knapp's funeral began at 1:00 P.M. the following Lord's Day and lasted until sunset. The crowd was so immense that it took almost an hour for the people to pass by the coffin and pay their final respects.

To Jacob Knapp goes the honor of being one of the first "Baptist evangelists" in the modern sense of the word, and we honor his memory on this, the anniversary of his ordination.

DLC

---

[1]J.D.C., ed., *Minutes of the Twenty-Ninth Annual Meeting of the Illinois Baptist Pastoral Union* (Aurora, Ill.: Knickerbocker and Hodder, 1874), p. 18.

[2]William Henry Brackney, *The Baptists* (New York: Greenwood Press, 1988), p. 213.

[3]J.D.C., p. 20.

[4]Ibid., p. 21.

August 28—The Wisdom of Age and the Zeal of Youth

Scripture: Philemon

A unique characteristic of the early Baptist preachers in Virginia was that a great majority of them were young and full of zeal for the Lord. Many of the Regular Baptists of Northern Virginia caught their fire from an older man, David Thomas. They often referred to him as "Old Father Thomas." Thomas was originally from the old Philadelphia Baptist Association and had moved to Virginia. Finding this group of young Virginia preachers, he fired their souls and also established them in sound doctrine without quenching their evangelistic zeal. Anderson Moffett was one of these young men. Moffett was born August 28, 1746, in Fauquier County. Thomas had preached and had planted the Broad Run Church in Fauquier County when Moffett was a youth.[1] Anderson Moffett was converted at an early age and began to preach when he was seventeen. We do not know at what age he was imprisoned in Culpeper. The following is a statement by Judge W. W. Moffett of Roanoke under the date of December 21, 1923. Judge Moffett alluded to information he had received from his father, John Moffett, concerning his uncle, Anderson Moffett, and the uncle's experience in Culpeper jail. This statement is important because it locates the old jail site, a landmark in Virginia Baptist history. This volume has mentioned that all of Anderson Moffett's records were destroyed by fire when he was an aged man and too weak to rewrite them. Our only evidence that he was a prisoner in Culpeper is gleaned from such verbal testimony. The Culpeper Baptist Church moved to a new location and still stands at the time of this writing.

> My father's plantation was in Culpeper, from ten to twelve miles of the courthouse. It must have been in the latter half of 1885, or the first part of 1886, that my father took me to Culpeper Court House. We were standing on the south side of the street looking at the Baptist Church on the north side of the same street. My father said to me pointing to the church, "There once stood the jail, and in that jail my uncle, Anderson Moffett, was imprisoned for preaching the Gospel." Then turning to his right and designating the house on the corner

diagonal from the Baptist Church, he said there was the home of two old people, Mr. and Mrs. Asher, who were ardent Baptists, and when that Baptist church was being built they sat under that tree (in the corner of their yard), watched its construction, rejoiced and thanked God for what He had done for the Baptists.[2]

Moffett was imprisoned along with many other young preachers in that jail. He was there when someone attempted to suffocate them by burning an Indian pepper plant under the jail floor. This incident evidently did not affect his health. God gave Moffett over seventy years of ministry, beginning when he was seventeen and ending in his eighty-ninth year after he had served Smith's Creek Regular Baptist Church for over fifty years.

God grant us zealous, faithful men in our day who will be granted longevity of life to establish a testimony for Jesus Christ and His church in many communities throughout our land.

EWT

---

[1]Inscription on Anderson Moffett's gravestone.

[2]Lewis Peyton Little, *Imprisoned Preachers and Religious Liberty in Virginia* (Lynchburg, Va.: J. P. Bell Co., 1938), p. 431.

August 29—A Well-Rounded, Faithful Man of God

Scripture: II Timothy 4:6

Thomas Baldwin was born on December 23, 1753, in Bozrah, Connecticut. Early in life he cultivated a taste for books and decided to prepare himself for the legal profession. When he was seventeen years of age, young Baldwin fell under conviction and called upon the Lord Jesus Christ as his personal Lord and Savior. Soon he felt he must declare himself in favor of Baptist doctrine. He severed his ties with the denomination in which he had been raised, and subsequently many of his friends parted company with him.

Upon moving to Canaan, New Hampshire, Baldwin, though a young man, was chosen to represent his village as legislator in the General Court of the State. However, the Master had other plans for him. In due time, Baldwin decided to spend his life in the work of the ministry. On June 11, 1783, Thomas Baldwin was ordained and for seven years performed the duties of pastor in the Baptist church in Canaan.

When the thirty-six-year-old pastor of the Second Baptist Church of Boston, Massachusetts, passed away, "the committee of the church . . . had their attention providentially directed to Rev. Thomas Baldwin, as a 'good minister of Jesus Christ.' "[1] He was invited to fill the pulpit for three months. "Soon a unanimous call was given him, and on the 11th of November, 1790, he was installed over the people, with whom he continued the rest of his useful life."[2] Baldwin pastored there for thirty-five years and became a dominant force among early Baptists in America.

Baldwin was an excellent pastor, and the church experienced continual growth. "In the year of 1791 not far from seventy were added to the church, and in 1803 commenced another revival, the fruit of which was an addition to the church of 212 persons."[3] "He also served as a member of the Constitutional Convention of Massachusetts, in 1821, and took an active part in its discussions."[4] The Baptist leader also served as a trustee of Brown University, Waterville College, and the Columbian College.

However, our chief interest in Dr. Thomas Baldwin centers in his missionary concern. On April 29, 1802, he co-authored the call for the establishment of the Massachusetts Baptist Missionary Society. In 1803 he became editor of the "Massachusetts Baptist Missionary Magazine" and served until his death. Dr. Baldwin received a letter from Adoniram Judson in February, 1813. Judson wrote, "Should there be formed a Baptist Society for the support of missions in these parts, I shall be ready to consider myself their missionary!"[5] Baldwin immediately invited several leading pastors from Massachusetts to meet and confer on the matter. The result was the organization of a temporary society to assist the Judsons until such time as the Baptists nationally could rally forces for the undertaking. Ultimately, with the formation of "The General Missionary Convention of the Baptist Denomination in the United States for Foreign Missions," Dr. Baldwin served as the secretary.

"The ministry of Dr. Baldwin continued till August 29, 1825, when after a long life, creditable to himself and eminently useful to the church of God, he was suddenly called to receive the 'crown of righteousness that fadeth not away.' "[6] We honor the memory of a pastor with a "missionary heart" and pray that the Lord will give us a host of such men in our day.

DLC

---

[1]David Benedict, *A General History of the Baptist Denomination in America* (New York: Lewis Colby and Co., 1848), p. 395.

[2]Ibid., p. 396.

[3]William Cathcart, *The Baptist Encyclopedia,* ed. Louis H. Everts (Philadelphia: Louis H. Everts, 1881), 1:63.

[4]Thomas Armitage, *The History of the Baptists* (1890; reprint ed., Watertown, Wis.: Maranatha Baptist Press, 1976), 2:853.

[5]Jesse L. Boyd, *A History of Baptists in America Prior to 1845* (New York: American Press, 1957), p. 86.

[6]Benedict, p. 396.

August 30—A Sunday School Revival Would Be Welcomed

Scripture: Proverbs 22:6

Historians commonly agree that the Sunday school movement must be credited to an Anglican layman, Robert Raikes of Gloucester, England. In 1780 Raikes pioneered with Sunday instruction for the underprivileged boys, and he hired teachers to instruct the lads in reading and writing. Child labor laws were unknown in England, and disadvantaged children were placed in the work force and were not privileged to obtain an education. We surely rejoice in the advancement engineered by the benevolent Raikes!

A Baptist layman, William Fox, "who was a godly member of the Baptist Church in Prescott street, Goodmans Fields, where he enjoyed the able and spiritual ministry of the eminent and learned Abraham Booth,"[1] must be considered the architect of the Bible-centered Sunday school known in modern times. Fox called a meeting, which was held on August 30, 1785, for the purpose of organizing a "Sunday School Society." It was resolved unanimously "that it is the opinion of this meeting that great benefit would accrue to the community at large from the adoption of such a measure, and that a Society be formed for carrying the same into immediate effect."[2] Doubtless the concept of having Sunday school just for children has added to the lack of emphasis on adult training in the Sunday school hour both in Great Britain and Canada.

When we consider the impact of the Sunday school historically in America, we cannot help but pause to thank God for the vision of William Fox. It has been reported that after visiting America, Alexis de Tocqueville said, "I sought in vain for the secret of America's greatness until I went into her Sunday schools and churches. Then I understood why France is a slave and America is free."

No one will ever be able to assess fully the value that the Sunday school movement has provided for America. Missionaries serve around the world today because of the vision that was imparted in a Sunday school class. Pastors stand behind the sacred desk today because in their youth a Sunday school worker took time to encourage them in the Word of God. It would be impossible to know how many well-adjusted homes exist because of the influence of the Sunday school during the formative years of life. J. Edgar Hoover, former Director of the Federal Bureau of Investigation, said, "Crime among youth would become practically negligible if the young people of America attended Sunday school regularly during their formative years."[3]

In our day we do well to understand that the Sunday school enables the church to renew that vision in every generation. Sunday school has had an inestimable influence on American society in the past, and by the grace of God, it can be a tool of God to revive our nation.

DLC

---

[1]W.H.H. March, *The Modern Sunday School* (Philadelphia: American Baptist Publication Society, 1874), p. 42.

[2]Joseph Ivimey, *Memoir of William Fox, Esq., Founder of the Sunday School Society,* ed. George Whightman (London: n.p., 1831), p. 34.

[3]J. Edgar Hoover, "Why I Believe in the Sunday School," *United Evangelical Action* 10 (September 1951): 5.

August 31—The Pilgrim Entered the Celestial City

Scripture: Revelation 21:9-27

While John Bunyan was a prisoner for preaching the glad tidings of salvation, he received the king's license to preach. It was one of the first to be granted. Probably because Bunyan refused to sign the license, His Majesty continued to keep him a prisoner more than six months after he licensed him. Bunyan had attended the Baptist meetings and regularly preached some four years before his release. In the eleventh year of his imprisonment, the congregation chose him for their pastor. He accepted the call and gave himself to serve Christ and His Church in that capacity. Only a man such as Bunyan could exercise his pastoral office in preaching among them as he continued a prisoner in the jail.[1]

So loving was Bunyan's disposition that the jailer was tender toward him all the time. He not only allowed Bunyan to visit his church frequently, without a guard, and to preach the gospel elsewhere, but he permitted Bunyan's blind daughter, Mary, to visit him regularly, with such little gifts as she could gather for his solace. She had great concern for him. She would put her delicate fingers to his eyes and cheeks to feel if the tears flowed that she might kiss them away.[2]

As a result of the intervention of a sailor who had spirited Charles II away to France during the Republican rebellion, with royal permission, four hundred and seventy-one Quakers and twenty Baptists and Independents, along with John Bunyan, were released. Bunyan immediately began his ministry of visiting the sick, preaching from house to house, planting churches in villages, and extending the influence of the gospel. When they opened a newly built meetinghouse, it was so thronged that many were constrained to stay outside. A great number were added to the church, and Bunyan's spirit was greatly refreshed. When he preached in London, the congregation was much more numerous than the meetinghouse would hold. About 1,200 attended a morning lecture on a weekday, in the winter at seven o'clock, and on the Lord's Day about 3,000, "so that he was pulled almost over people to get into the pulpit."[3]

While he was yet in prison, his little Mary entered the "Celestial Gate" before the hero of the "Den" as a true "shining one" to watch and wait for his coming. In 1688 he traveled to London to reconcile an alienated father and son and succeeded. On the journey a violent storm overtook him, and he contracted a fatal illness which took him to Jesus, the King in His beauty, and to Mary, his daughter, no longer blind. She raised not her hand to his cheek there, as her desire had been in the Bedford prison, for God had wiped away all tears from his eyes; and since then, the young and old pilgrims have dwelt together in the golden city.

His birth, recorded elsewhere in this volume, took place the same year as the passage of the "English Bill of Rights." His death, on August 31, 1688, was the year of the deliverance of England from popish tyranny. John Bunyan represents a great host of Baptists who loved liberty of conscience and were dedicated to their Lord and the principles of His Word.

EWT

---

[1]John Bunyan, "The Life of John Bunyan," *The Pilgrim's Progress from This World to That Which Is to Come* (New York: J. B. Hurst and Co., n.d.), p. 43.

[2]Thomas Armitage, *The History of the Baptists* (1890; reprint ed., Watertown, Wis.: Maranatha Baptist Press, 1976), 1:480.

[3]George Offar, "Memoir of John Bunyan," biographical sketch introducing *The Pilgrim's Progress* (London: Routledge, Warne, and Routledge, 1861), pp. xix-xxii.

September

September 1—Faith Stretched Her View to the Bright World of Eternal Life

Scripture: Philippians 1:20-30

Sarah Boardman and her husband George left the United States in July of 1825. The scene of their labors for Christ was to be among the Karen tribes of Burma. These tribes had been oppressed by their Burmese neighbors and lived hidden in the hills and forests. Shortly after the first fruits of George Boardman's ministry were baptized, "his joyful spirit ascended to its rest."[1] Although the Burmese received the gospel slowly, the Karen Christians soon numbered in the tens of thousands and were gathered into local churches. A college and seminary were established to train and send forth preachers and teachers among their people.

After George's death, Sarah Boardman became the second wife of widower Adoniram Judson, who said in a notice he prepared concerning her death, "He constantly thanks God that he has been blest with two of the best wives; he deeply feels that he has not improved those rich blessings as he ought; and it is most painful to reflect, that from the peculiar pressure of the missionary life, he has sometimes failed to treat those dear beings with that consideration, attention, and kindness, which their situation in a foreign heathen land ever demanded."[2]

Sarah had been prostrated by illness on the Isle of France where there was little expectation of her recovery, but they continued their passage toward America after an absence of twenty years. Though she had a longing desire to see once more her son George, her parents, and friends of her youth, she was constrained to say, " 'I am in a strait betwixt the two—let the will of God be done.' "

During her last days, Sarah spent much time praying for the early conversion of her children. Her husband expected to have the painful necessity of burying her at sea, but the ship came to anchor in the port of St. Helena, where at two o'clock in the morning of September 1, 1845, Judson, in his own words, "wishing to obtain one more token of recognition . . . roused her attention and said: 'Do you still love the Savior?' 'O yes' she replied; 'I ever love the Lord Jesus Christ.' I said again, 'Do you still love me?' She replied in the affirmative, by a peculiar expression of her own. 'Then give me one more kiss;' and we exchanged that token of love one more time.' "

After Sarah's burial, which was attended by a multitude of government officials, the personnel of the ships in harbor, and natives of the island, Judson relates, "I was obliged to hasten on board ship and immediately went to sea. On the following morning, no vestige of the island was visible in the distant horizon. For a few days in the solitude of my cabin, with my poor children crying around me, I could not help abandoning myself to heartbreaking sorrow. But the promises of the gospel came to my aid, and faith stretched her view to the bright world of eternal life, and anticipated a happy meeting with those beloved beings, whose bodies are moldering at Amherst and St. Helena."[3]

EWT

---

[1]Thomas Armitage, *The History of the Baptists* (1890; reprint ed., Watertown, Wis.: Maranatha Baptist Press, 1976), 2:816.

[2]John Dowling, *The Judson Offering* (New York: Lewis Colby and Co., 1846), p. 215.

[3]Ibid., p. 222.

September 2—When the Internal Revenue Service Collected Taxes for Churches

Scripture: Ezra 7:16

The ecclesiastical tax, which was approved by some colonies in early America and which forced Baptists to pay assessments for the upkeep of churches of various denominations, was most obnoxious to early Baptists. For many years Baptists, both men and women, suffered because of these regulations. On September 2, 1774, Mrs. Martha Kimball sent the following letter to the Reverend Isaac Backus relating her earlier experience:

> Mr. Backus, I understand that you are collecting materials for a Baptist History, in which you propose to let the public know how the Baptists have been oppressed in Massachusetts Bay. This is to let you know that in the year 1768, in a very cold night in winter, about nine or ten o'clock in the evening, I was taken prisoner, and carried by the collector in the town where I live, from my family, consisting of three small children, in order to be put in jail. It being a severe cold night, I concluded, by advice, while I was detained at a tavern in the way to jail some hours, to pay the sum of 4-8 L. M. (i.e., Legal Money), for which I was made a prisoner, it being for the ministerial rate. The reason why I refused paying it before, was because I was a Baptist, and belonged to the Baptist Society, in Haverhill, and had carried in a certificate to the assessors, and I suppose, according to law. Thus they dealt with a poor widow woman in Bradford, the relict of Solomon Kimball, late of the said town;—at whose house the Rev. Hezekiah Smith was shamefully treated by many of the people in Bradford, who came headed by the sheriff, Amos Mulliken, at a time when Mr. Smith was to preach a sermon in our house, at the request of my husband, and warmly contended with him, and threatened him if he did preach. Mr. Smith went to begin service by singing notwithstanding the noise, clamour, and threats of the people. But one of their number snatched the chair, behind which Mr. Smith stood, from before him. Upon which my husband desired Mr. Smith to tarry a little, till he quelled the tumult; but all his endeavours to silence them were in vain. Upon which my husband desired Mr. Smith to begin public service; which accordingly he did, and went through then without further molestation.
>
> Martha Kimball
>
> Bradford, Sept. 2nd, 1774.
>
> N.B. The above I can attest to. It may be observed that the tavern wither they took me is about two miles from my house. After I had paid what they demanded, then I had to return to my poor fatherless children, through the snow on foot, in the dead of the night, exposed to the severity of the cold.

The doctrine of the separation of church and state was unknown in colonial America, and Baptists were assessed for the support of ministers of the ''standing order'' churches. Even though Baptists had their own churches, which they were attempting to support financially, the authorities, who had escaped from one ecclesiastical establishment in Europe, founded another that functioned in the same way. Thank God for the sacrifice of our early Baptist forebears—men and women—who finally provided for this nation the freedom of conscience and full separation of church and state!

DLC

September 3—A Life of Continued Growth in Grace

Scripture: II Peter 3:18

Henry Jessey, the son of an Episcopalian clergyman, was born on September 3, 1601, at West Rounton, in Yorkshire, England. At age seventeen he was sent to St. John's College at Cambridge, and in six years he earned his Bachelor and Master of Arts degrees. It was at Cambridge, when Jessey was twenty-one years old, that he was converted. From that time, the young man determined to devote himself to the sacred office of the ministry.

Upon graduating from college, Jessey served as chaplain to the family of Bramton Gurdon in Suffolk and remained in that capacity for nine years. During that period, he continued in his quest for knowledge. In 1627 Jessey was removed for failing to use all the ceremonies of the Episcopal denomination and for removing a crucifix that had been set up in the church.

Sir Matthew Bointon now became Jessey's patron, and Jessey preached in two local parishes before moving to London in 1635. Jessey was often invited to preach for a congregation of Dissenters (Congregationalists) and in the course of time, he accepted the invitation to pastor the church. A year after he began that ministry, several members of the congregation embraced Baptist doctrine and left his charge. Again, in 1641 a larger group departed and when, in 1643 an even larger group separated from the Congregational church, Jessey began a diligent examination of the Scriptures concerning baptism. He held conferences with learned men of the pedobaptist persuasion and spent much time in study and prayer before changing his conviction relative to the *mode* of baptism. In 1642 he announced to his congregation that immersion appeared to him to be the right manner of baptism, and therefore he proposed that those who were baptized in the future would be immersed. For two or three years he immersed the children who were presented for baptism.

About 1644 the controversy as to the *subjects* of baptism was again addressed. Several in Jessey's congregation had come to believe that infant baptism was unscriptural, and in his study Pastor Jessey also came to that conclusion, but wanting to be sure of his position, he consulted with the outstanding Congregational pastors of the area. They could not dispel his newfound conviction, and in June of 1645, Pastor Jessey was immersed by the Reverend Hanserd Knollys. Prior to that time, Jessey on several occasions had been imprisoned for his preaching. On one occasion in April 1640, Jessey had been taken to the Tower and imprisoned by the order of Archbishop William Laud, and then a year later he was sentenced by the Lord Mayor. This oppression had caused his fame to spread, and thus it was an advantage to the Baptists to have a man of such notoriety and piety as part of their movement. However, Jessey continued with a loving attitude, even to those who abused him, and his spirit procured for him the esteem of leaders in all parties. Henry Jessey's influence for Baptist principles made him an outstanding example of Baptist devotion in England, and thus we rejoice in the story of his life.

DLC

September 4—From His Growth in Grace to Glory

Scripture: Proverbs 16:7

In our consideration of the Reverend Henry Jessey, we must not ignore the fact that he served for some time under Cromwell as a "Trier"; that is, he was a member of a committee formed by the government for the examination of candidates to remove "scandalous" clergymen. Some have looked askance at Baptist participation on such a committee and particularly at the fact that Jessey received payment from the government for ministering at St. George's church in Southwark on Sunday mornings. He continued his ministry in the afternoons among his own people simultaneously. However, we must consider the time in which the man of God lived and the need of the hour.

"The impartial reader will give due weight to the considerations which have been alleged in their defence, viz.:—that the scarcity of qualified ministers warranted them in taking this step, as they were thereby put in a position to preach the Gospel to thousands who would have been otherwise destitute of the means of grace; that they were bound to no forms and ceremonies, and allowed to conduct worship in whatever manner they pleased."[1]

Henry Jessey was a great scholar and had extensive knowledge of the Greek, Hebrew, Syriac, and Chaldee languages. He labored to produce a new translation of the Scriptures, but the restoration of the rule of the kings made impossible the completion of that project.

That he might be entirely devoted to the work of the ministry and to enable him to help families in financial need, Jessey chose never to marry. "There were above thirty families, who had all their subsistence from him, and were after his death exposed to great difficulties."[2]

Upon the restoration of the rule of the kings in England and the re-establishment of the Episcopal church as the official vehicle of worship, Jessey was again committed to prison. His cell became the doorway to heaven on September 4, 1663. As he lay dying, "one by his bedside said to him, 'They among whom you have laboured can witness that you have been a faithful servant of Christ, making His glory your utmost end for the good of souls.' 'Say no more than that,' he whispered, 'but exalt God.' "[3]

Henry Jessey was buried on September 7. It is reported that several thousand people of all denominations attended the service, bearing testimony to the worth of his ministry and to his character.

Obediah Wills had written against Jessey's acquired Baptist doctrines during the godly man's lifetime, but following Jessey's death, Wills wrote, "And such a frame of Spirit was there in that man of God, Mr. Jessey,—He, to my knowledge, was an Anti-pedobaptist of long-standing, as holy I conceive, as any of that judgment; of good learning and of a very tender conscience, and of so healing and uniting a spirit, that he esteemed it his duty, and pressed others to it, to keep up Christian communion with those that feared God tho' they differ'd about baptism. . . . I wish there were more such Anti-pedobaptists as he."[4]

May we so live that even our enemies might praise a blessed memory that we leave for Christ!

DLC

[1]J. M. Cramp, *Baptist History* (London: Elliott Stock, 1870), pp. 280-81.

[2]Thomas Crosby, *The History of the English Baptists* (1738-40; reprint ed., Lafayette, Tenn.: Church History Research and Archives, 1979), 1:316.

[3]John C. Carlile, *The Story of the English Baptists* (London: James Clarke and Co., 1905), p. 85.

[4]Crosby, pp. 321-22.

September 5—Though My Flesh Should Fail, God Will Not Fail

Scripture: Matthew 10:16-24

The trial judge agreed with the prosecutor, John Cotton, that John Clarke, Obadiah Holmes, and John Crandall deserved to be put to death, but he would let them off with a fine. If they did not pay the fine and immediately leave the territory of the colony, they should be well whipped. While Clarke, Holmes, and Crandall were confined once again to jail, friends in Newport raised the money for the fines of all three men. Crandall was released from the fine. John Clarke and Obadiah Holmes refused permission for their fines to be paid, believing it would be an admission of guilt. As Clarke was led to the whipping post, a friend pressed money into the hands of the Puritan official accompanying the party, and Clarke was released. "Agreeing to the payment of my fine would constitute admission of wrong-doing," Holmes continued to maintain.

As he was being stripped to the waist, Holmes preached a brief sermon to the dense crowd of men, women, and children that formed a circle about the whipping post, exhorting them to remain faithful to their beliefs. According to Holmes's own testimony, the flogger used a whip with three hard leather lashes, stopped three times to spit on his hands, and applied the whip with all his might. Each of the thirty strokes cut three gashes through the skin. Several voices were heard encouraging and praising him in spite of the hostility of the civil officers against such. In Holmes's own account, he said,

> As the man began to lay the strokes upon my back, I said to the people, though my flesh should fail, yet God will not fail: so it pleased the Lord to come in, and fill my heart and tongue as a vessel full, and with audible voice I break forth, praying the Lord not to lay this sin to their charge, and telling the people I found He did not fail me, and therefore now I should trust Him forever Who failed me not: for in truth, as the strokes fell upon me, I had such a spiritual manifestation of God's presence as I never had before, and the outward pain was so removed from me, that I could well bear it, yea, and in a manner felt it not, although it was grievous.[1]

After this scourging on September 5, 1651, Holmes was welcomed back to the peace and freedom of Newport. For twenty days and nights he could sleep only by lying on his stomach, or propped upon his knees and elbows.

Not only was our religious liberty purchased through the sufferings of men like Obadiah Holmes, but such incidents prompted the discussion of the right of civil authorities to enter a home without a warrant, just on suspicion that a crime was committed. The framers of our Constitution took note and provided Americans protection from such invasions of our homes. God help us to maintain such liberty by righteous living.

EWT

---

[1]O. K. and Marjorie Armstrong, *Baptists Who Shaped a Nation* (Nashville: Broadman Press, 1975), pp. 60-61.

September 6—"His Saviour Has the Charge of the Whole Affair"

Scripture: Philippians 1:1-11

As Thomas Cramp was sitting before the ordination council to be interrogated before being recommended to the pastoral care of the Baptist church of St. Peter's, Isle of Thanet, England, his vigorous four-year-old son John was at home, pulling up the broad beans out of the garden. Little did either know that this mischievous boy in a few short years would appear before the church and be accepted into its membership. However, on September 6, 1812, at the age of sixteen, John Cramp was baptized by his father.[1]

John immediately commenced the study of the Greek language and made great progress in studying the New Testament. He became very proficient in the Latin, Greek, and French languages and maintained a humble spirit, which was manifested when he said, "I first learned how to learn Latin." His zeal for God's Word was matched by his desire for the salvation of others. He began addressing the people at the weekly prayer meeting and continued until he left for his theological studies at Stepney Theological Institute which later became Stepney College. This was the beginning of a very fruitful ministry in England which was later continued in Canada. It is estimated that he preached 5,176 sermons during the course of his ministry.

After assisting his father in the pastorate for fourteen years and pastoring the church at Hastings, John Cramp was sent by a committee of the Canada Baptist Missionary Society to take charge of the Montreal Baptist College. This school was a citadel of Romanism, and he very well may have been motivated to write his well-known *Text Book of Popery* out of that experience. This book was just one of many publications relating to doctrinal truth and the practical application of that truth. In the estimation of many, his outstanding work was his *Baptist History, from the Foundation of the Christian Church to the Close of the Eighteenth Century*. In 1868, after great labor and research, this history was published. Every Baptist preacher and layman should have this volume in his library.

Dr. Cramp left Montreal to take the oversight of Acadia College. He served as president of this college until the infirmities of age compelled him to retire in 1869. He exerted great influence in the Maritime provinces through his labors in preparing men for the ministry, as a preacher of the gospel throughout that area, and by his extensive writing. He also was held in high esteem in the United States where his works have been widely circulated.

The Baptist church of Wolfville, where Acadia College was located, sent a resolution to Cramp's family upon the occasion of his death. It stated in part: "Dr. Cramp ever manifested a strong interest in the welfare of this church in her various enterprises. . . . He was jealously desirous for the welfare of the pastor of the church, and anxious that he should be upheld and supported by its members, both by their prayers and their contributions, to which his share was added with cheerful promptness."[2]

Among the manuscripts written by Dr. Cramp during the quiet years that followed his more active labors was one entitled *The Last Things*. In this he wrote, "There is one thing that is satisfying to the Christian. His Saviour has the charge of the whole affair. He employs His servants as He pleases. He calls them home when their work is done. He has the keys of the invisible world, and of death. When He turns the key, the door opens, and the believer enters the invisible abode. Till then he is a stranger and a pilgrim on earth."[3]

What joy, what comfort is found in a truly fulfilled life that is invested for the glory of Jesus Christ.

EWT

---

[1]T. A. Higgins, *The Life of John Mockett Cramp, D.D.* (Montreal: W. Drysdale and Co., 1887), p. 16.

[2]Ibid., p. 335.

[3]Ibid., pp. 366-67.

September 7—Luther Rice, a Beloved Man of Controversy

Scripture: Acts 26:19-32

No other subject is the object of discussion and the center of controversy like world evangelism. When we study the Baptist missionary movement in America, we find a great illustration of this controversy in the resulting division over missionary methods and the support of missionaries. In Virginia, the Regulars and Separates after long controversy had decided that those names be relegated into oblivion, and they would henceforth be known as the United Baptists of Virginia. This decision was soon reversed when on September 7, 1813, Luther Rice returned to kindle the fires of missionary zeal among the Baptists whose principles he had embraced while on his way to India. These fires were ignited among the churches, and not only were the people stirred, but Satan was also aroused to inflame some fires of controversy in an effort to sabotage the revival to evangelize the world.

It had been decided that Rice, because he was single, should return to America from India to enlist Baptist support for the missionary venture overseas. Neither Rice nor Judson, his colaborer, expected this trip would take more than a year or two. However, Rice never returned, ending his days in promoting missions and Christian education in America. This course of events caused some friction between these two great men. Judson never approved of Rice's failure to return, and for years the disagreement interrupted the warm fellowship they had enjoyed previously.

The fact that Rice did work well and that God prospered his work contributed to the way events unfolded. He traveled among the churches and associations, spellbinding audiences with his exciting messages on missions. At that time he was the rare person who had gone into the darkness of paganism and had returned to report what existed there. Although some independent mission societies existed, they provided primarily for preaching in the United States. "Before the end of 1813, at least seventeen local and regional societies had agreed to share in the foreign mission work."[1]

To catch the extent of Rice's vision and zeal, as well as to understand the influence of his Congregationalist background, it would be good to consider his statement: "While passing from Richmond to Petersburg in the stage, an enlarged view of the business opened upon my contemplation. The plan which suggested itself to my mind, that of forming one principal society in each state, bearing the name of the state, and others in the same state, auxiliary to that; and by these large, or state societies, delegates be appointed to form one general society."[2]

This plan came to fruition in the Triennial Convention of 1814. Luther Rice died in 1836, exhausted in body and soul. He labored to the last for his beloved Columbian College of Washington, D.C., and on his deathbed he instructed his friends to sell his horse, Columbus, and his sulky and to give the proceeds to the college. He died as he lived—alone. While his old colleagues overseas, the Judsons, were elevated in the hearts of the people, Rice, who labored at home, was vilified by many. Like all of us, Rice had faults, but now we have a renewed appreciation for the man, who gave all his energies and devotion to world evangelism and education among the Baptists.[3]

EWT

---

[1]H. Leon McBeth, *The Baptist Heritage* (Nashville: Broadman Press, 1987), p. 346.

[2]Ibid.

[3]Ibid.

September 8—"Congress Shall Make No Law Respecting an Establishment of Religion"

Scripture: Psalm 144

On a number of occasions the Congregationalists desired the Baptists to join them in combating heretical sects. Early on they petitioned the Baptists of Rhode Island to reject the Quakers who were settling within the bounds of their colony. Later, there was a letter received from the Convention of Congregational Ministers in Boston and presented to the Warren Baptist Association when it convened at Harvard September 8, 1790. They desired the Baptists to send a petition to Congress requesting their "attention to several impressions of the Bible now making, representing the importance of accuracy in these impressions; and earnestly praying that they would take such measures as the Constitution would permit, that no edition of the Bible, or its translation be published in America, without its being carefully inspected, and certified to be free from error." They desired the Baptist concurrence because of the Bible's "importance to all denominations of Christians, as they appeal to the Holy Bible as the standard of truth."[1]

The Baptists on this occasion felt under obligation to give early attention to the preservation of the purity of the Holy Scriptures and appointed a committee to prepare and transmit a petition to Congress on that important subject. Congress, they believed, had the right and duty to protect and promote evangelical Christianity for the good of society, and they assumed that the Holy Bible was accepted as the source of revealed authority by all denominations. Even later, the Baptists of New England suggested it would be proper for Congress to allocate some of the taxpayers' money for the support of foreign missions.

How easy it is to lose sight of the fundamental principles of liberty of conscience in a good cause. The end never justifies the means. We are thankful that the Virginia Baptists stood firm on principle even when they would have benefited materially from the General Assessment Bill. Their action in opposing a bill granting government subsidies for the support of religion paved the way for the passage of Virginia's "Act for Establishing Religious Freedom." We can be thankful that the National Congress did not respond favorably to these petitions to support religion but rather adopted the First Amendment to the Constitution. That blessed amendment begins with these words: "Congress shall make no law respecting an establishment of religion or prohibiting the free exercise thereof."[2]

There was grave danger in placing into the hands of government the power to determine who was the proper translator and what was the proper translation. We would be rendering unto Caesar God's truth. Certainly the proliferation of so many spurious translations and expansions of the Scriptures in our day would have appalled our Baptist forefathers, but we can thank God that our present liberal, humanistic Congress has no power to regulate the Scriptures in any way.

May we also remember George Mason's declaration when he wrote the Virginia Declaration of Rights: "That no free government or the blessing of liberty, can be preserved to any people but by a firm adherence to justice, moderation, temperance, frugality, and virtue, *and by frequent recurrence to fundamental principles.*"[3]

EWT

---

[1]William G. McLoughlin, ed., *The Diary of Isaac Backus* (Providence: Brown University Press, 1979), 3:1295.

[2]The Constitution of the United States, the First Amendment.

[3]Virginia Declaration of Rights, Article 15.

September 9—A Baptist "Samson" Stood to Preach

Scripture: Judges 14:6

We have alluded to the treatment given our Baptist forebears in America by the ruffians who threatened, beat, and dunked the faithful followers of our Lord. Reference has been made particularly to the abuse heaped upon two young Baptist ministers in Massachusetts (cf.

March 27). The Warren Association received a letter concerning the Pepperell riots of March 27 and June 16 and doubtless discussed the matter in their September 9, 1778, meeting as Isaac Backus reported.

Baptists did not on every occasion surrender to the maltreatment without resistance. David Thomas, perhaps the most learned and scholarly of the early Baptist preachers in Virginia, was frequently assaulted and disturbed. Thomas had been dragged from the church house during a service, and on another occasion an irate listener attempted to shoot him. At another time, when the ruffians of the nearby area had sworn to beat him, Thomas traveled thirty miles and invited Amos Thompson to preach for him. Amos Thompson was of immense size and fond of adventure, and he agreed to the request.

Dr. Archibald Alexander, a prominent Presbyterian minister, happened to be visiting the area, and he gives this account of the activities:

> The Rev. Amos Thompson, was a man of gigantic frame, but not in the least inclined to corpulency. His bodily strength was prodigious, several proofs of which I had from himself. . . . When they [Thomas and Thompson] arrived, a . . . multitude had assembled, some to hear the preacher, and some to see the sport [the beating of the Reverend David Thomas]. . . .
>
> While Mr. Thompson was at prayer, a company armed with bludgeons entered the house, and took their position just before the pulpit; but when they saw the brawny arm and undaunted appearance of the preacher, they became alarmed and permitted the service to go on to its conclusion. I ought to have stated, that at the close of his discourse, Mr. Thompson addressed himself directly to these men. . . . He, concluded by saying, that although he was a preacher, and a man of peace, he held it to be right, when attacked to defend himself, which he was ready and able to do. When the meeting was ended, he went out of the house and inquired for the captain of the band. Being led to the spot where they were collected, he approached this man, and asked him to go aside with him. A stout, bold-looking man walked off with him toward the woods, on entering which he appeared to be panic-struck, stopped, and raised his club. Thompson said, " 'Fie, man, what can you do with that?' " and in a moment wrested it out of his hand, adding that he intended no violence, but that if so disposed, he could hurl him to earth in a moment. The ruffian was completely overawed, and was glad to escape from so powerful an antagonist. . . . Thomas received no further molestation.[1]

The early Baptist preachers in pioneer America were often attacked by gangs of rowdies, but many times the hardy ministers were blessed with God-given strength that assisted them in their task of preaching the gospel. We rejoice today in America, not only for our hard-won freedom to worship, but in the protection afforded to one and all in their effort to follow the dictates of their conscience.

DLC

---

[1]Lewis Peyton Little, *Imprisoned Preachers and Religious Liberty in Virginia* (Lynchburg, Va.: J. P. Bell Co., 1938), pp. 43-44.

September 10—This New Doctrine, Shall He or Shall He Not Preach It?

Scripture: Acts 17:16-34

Lewis Lunsford, a gifted young preacher, began preaching in the counties of the Northern Neck of Virginia around 1773. His preaching was attended with great blessing, and believers were added to the Lord in most of the neighborhoods. This attracted the attention of the established clergy, who began to attack the Baptists from the pulpit.

On one occasion the parson in Richmond County announced that he was going to preach against the Baptists on a given Sunday. This attracted about seven hundred people from all quarters, which resulted in the balcony's cracking before the service started. The result caused panic to all and injury to those who had fallen and were trampled. Some never stopped running until they arrived home, supposing that God was sending judgment upon them. Others thought that the slaves were raising an insurrection. In spite of the confusion, the majority of the people remained. After the wild disturbance settled, they went in again and heard the parson say an abundance about the tenets and practice of the Anabaptists and assert as a fact that the present Baptists sprang from them and were to be equally avoided. He did not persuade all of his hearers that his claims were true.

These tactics were not successful in stopping the gospel of grace from being preached by these young Baptist evangels. Thus the enemy resorted to more serious and violent procedures. On a Lord's Day, September 10, 1775, Lewis Lunsford preached in Richmond County, Virginia, from the text: "And they took him, and brought him to Areopagus, saying, May we know what this new doctrine whereof thou speakest is?" (Acts 17:19). A constable came with a warrant to take him before a magistrate as an itinerant preacher. The constable politely chose not to execute the warrant until Lunsford had preached. There was contention among those of his opposition. Some wanted to see the warrant served and hurled stones at and in the house where he preached. Others declared that he should not be taken into custody. The constable, with hands trembling, said that he would not serve a warrant on so good a man. As contention ran high, another man took the warrant and with trembling hands touched Lunsford with the paper. It was reported that the man who delivered the warrant went insane afterwards. Lunsford attended the summons and appeared before the magistrate.[1]

The court determined that Lunsford had been guilty of breach of good behavior and that he must give security that he would not preach in Richmond county for a period of twelve months. He was advised by a voluntary attorney and some friends to post this security since he was soon to receive a license to preach. This never took place, and Lunsford always regretted his conduct on this occasion. He said his choice of not going to jail gave him more uneasiness than any other thing he had ever done.

Sometimes our most well-meaning friends give us advice during a crisis, and under the pressure of the circumstance, we make a decision against our conscience that we regret for the rest of our lives. Well-established principles ahead of time stand with us under duress.

EWT

---

[1]Lewis Peyton Little, *Imprisoned Preachers and Religious Liberty in Virginia* (Lynchburg, Va.: J. P. Bell Co., 1938), pp. 450-52.

September 11—Ninety-Three-Year-Old Preacher "Dies in the Saddle"

Scripture: Philippians 1:20-21

The name of Samuel Cartledge is not new in our consideration, for we viewed him when he was a young constable in Georgia and arrested the Reverend Daniel Marshall. We recounted that Samuel Cartledge was saved and after serving as a deacon in Kiokee, Georgia, was ordained and pastored faithfully for a number of years.

Cartledge was born July 15, 1750, near Rockingham, North Carolina. Samuel's father had been reared as a Quaker, but he married an Anglican woman, and the family assumed the Anglican faith. In that background young Samuel grew. He was confronted with the gospel by Mrs. Marshall at the arrest of her husband, Daniel, and in 1777 Samuel Cartledge was baptized by her husband. Before long, Cartledge was ordained as a deacon in the Kiokee Baptist Church. After being under the spiritual teaching of Daniel Marshall as a "licentiate" for several years, he was ordained into the gospel ministry by Abraham Marshall, Daniel's son, in 1789. Soon a fruitful ministry began which lasted more than fifty years.

After serving for a short time in Georgia, Cartledge "was recorded as a new minister in the Georgia Association in 1792."[1] He moved to South Carolina and became pastor of the Callahan's Mill Church "where he served . . . for over fifty years, until his death in 1843."[2] In those days, few rural churches held services every week, and often pastors served multiple churches and trained their deacons to care for the spiritual needs of the flock in their absence. Thus it was that in 1792 Cartledge accepted the oversight also of the Plum Branch Baptist Church and ministered there concurrently, serving there also for over fifty years. During his long ministry, he "served at least three other churches, but it is not clear how many years he remained at these."[3]

Of course, travel was limited to horseback, and the "work" of the ministry consisted of many grimy miles of laborious travel to preach the Word. The man of God is commissioned to "preach the word . . . in season, out of season," and the Reverend Mr. Cartledge did just that! For years, there was little moving of the Holy Spirit's power, but in 1830 revival swept the area. The man of God was now eighty years old, but "a series of meetings, in the day and at night, was held at the Callahan's Church, which continued two weeks. . . . A large number, especially of the young persons, became convicted and converted; and were baptized."[4] From 1827 through the revival of 1830, the membership of the Callahan Church had grown by almost two hundred per cent, and that with an eighty-year-old pastor! The lengthy obituary that announced his death claimed that thousands had been won to Christ through the ministry of Samuel Cartledge, and it spoke of his unquestionable zeal and piety.

Cartledge had four sons and a daughter and outlived two wives. When he was ninety-three years old, the pastor decided to travel back to Georgia to visit friends and to preach, but he was thrown from his horse and died on July 13, 1843. In family devotions that morning Cartledge had read, "For me to live is Christ, and to die is gain."

This date has been hallowed to our memory, for on September 11, 1843, the Edgefield Association passed resolutions to honor "our beloved and venerable Father in the Gospel, Elder S. Cartledge." Then they marched to the burial site to thank God for the memory of this faithful man of God.

DLC

---

[1]James Donovan Mosteller, *A History of the Kiokee Baptist Church in Georgia* (Ann Arbor: Edwards Brothers, 1952), p. 231.

[2]Tony W. Cartledge, ''Samuel Cartledge: Colonial 'Saul of Tarsus,' '' *Viewpoints—Georgia Baptist History* 8 (1982): 21.

[3]Ibid.

[4]Ibid., p. 22.

September 12—They Preached Christ on the Sabbath Contrary to Law

Scripture: Matthew 12:1-13

> To Samuel Perkins, of Windham, in Windham County, a Collector of Society Taxes in the first Society in Windham:
>
> Greeting: By authority of the State of Connecticut, you are hereby commanded forthwith to levy and collect of the persons named in the foregoing list herewith committed to you, each one his several proportion as therein set down, of the sum total of such list, being a rate agreed upon by the inhabitants of said Society, and to deliver and pay over the sums which you shall collect to the Treasurer of said Society within sixty days next coming; and if any person shall neglect or refuse to pay the sum at which he is assessed, you are hereby commanded to distrain the goods, chattels, or lands of such person so refusing; and the same being disposed of as the law directs, return the overplus, if any, to the respective owners; and for want of such goods, chattels, or lands whereon to make distress, you are to take the body or bodies of such persons so refusing, and them commit to the keeper of the gaol in said county of Windham within the prison, who is hereby commanded to receive and safe keep them until they pay and satisfy the aforesaid sums at which they are respectively assessed, together with your fees, unless said assessment, or any part thereof, be legally abated. Dated at Windham, this 12th day of September, 1794.
>
> JABEZ CLARKE, Just. Peace.'[1]

The above form is an example of the authority exercised by law in Connecticut, where fiery zealots continued to persecute Baptists who refused to pay the clerical tax. At one time a number of Baptists and their minister were taken in the very act of worshiping God. They were promptly incarcerated in the New London jail for attending a religious meeting ''contrary to law of the Sabbath Day.'' One prisoner was a babe at its mother's breast; the prison was fireless and the weather bitterly cold, yet the child lived and grew up to be a successful Baptist preacher.

Ebenezer Frothingham of Middletown wrote a book in 1767 in which he says that as a Separate Baptist, he was confined in Hartford prison for nearly five months for nothing but exhorting and warning the people after the public worship was finished and the assembly dismissed. While confined there, five others were imprisoned for the same crime.

In other cases in Connecticut, venerable ministers of the gospel were whipped at the town post or at the tail of an ox cart as they were driven through the town. Sometimes they were placarded and placed on horseback and otherwise ignominiously treated for preaching Christ.[2] When the minister's tax was to be collected, the dissenting layman's cow or the contents of his corn crib were seized and taken to the town post to be sold. The layman considered himself fortunate if he escaped the stocks.

In spite of this persecution, one Baptist church after another was planted and grew in various parts of Connecticut. The early Baptists obeyed the mandate, "As you therefore go, make disciples," and like the early disciples, they went everywhere preaching the gospel of Jesus Christ. We would do well to follow their example.

EWT

---

[1]Thomas Armitage, *The History of the Baptists* (1890; reprint ed., Watertown, Wis.: Maranatha Baptist Press, 1976), 2:741.

[2]Ibid., pp. 740-41.

September 13—The Prisoner Who Refused to Be Coerced

Scripture: Acts 16:30-40

Doubtless the public whipping of Obadiah Holmes in Boston's marketplace during the summer of 1651 was one of the most flagrant expressions of bigotry in the American colonies. Our interest now is centered on John Hazel, who, along with John Spur, approached Holmes after his scourging to console and encourage him. For their crime of showing compassion to the suffering Holmes, both men were summarily arrested and jailed. Spur, who had just two months previously been excommunicated from the Salem church for declaring his opposition to infant baptism, was fined forty shillings or the threat of a public beating. Though Spur declined the offer of a friend to pay the fine, the court accepted the payment and dismissed him immediately.

John Hazel's case was most interesting, for he was a man of at least sixty years of age, and his health was frail. Hazel's trial was set for September 6, and he was asked if he was in agreement with the actions of Obadiah Holmes in coming to Lynn to baptize and administer Communion. Hazel defended himself by answering that he was present to be questioned not for the actions of another but for his own deeds. He demanded to know what law he, John Hazel, had broken. The court realized that the old Baptist was quite crafty, and thus they returned him to jail for the night. When he entered the court the next day, the governor read his sentence, which was that he must pay forty shillings or be well whipped. Hazel requested a jury as an English subject and asked that the accusation be set before him as to what law he had broken. The magistrates answered that he was in contempt of authority for comforting a criminal. The canny old Baptist, however, saw the falsity of their argument and pointed out that if Holmes had been guilty of an infraction, the public whipping had satisfied the law and his guilt was removed! The magistrates then pursued the matter and suggested that if Hazel felt it necessary to have shown mercy to Holmes, he might have done it privately. Hazel answered that he was at liberty for that place was as free as any other. Hazel was then returned to jail until either the fine was paid (and he refused to comply) or the whipping was administered. However, the court reduced the number of stripes to ten, apparently because of the weakness of the older man.

Attempts were made to coerce Hazel with the threat of the whipping "tomorrow," but the prisoner was willing to accept the consequences and would not pay. Day after day, for five days such postponements were made. When it was clear that Hazel was equal to the threat, and surely public opinion would have turned upon the legal system with the abuse of an aging man, the jailer acknowledged to Hazel that he would not be whipped and that he was free to leave. Hazel demanded a discharge! Surely the court was totally embarrassed by this bitter defeat at the hands of an unlearned, but deeply principled, Baptist layman. Having previously suffered with Holmes in Rehoboth, Massachusetts, Hazel was no stranger to court proceedings and imprisonments.[1] He had come to believe that relief could come only in assuming a firm position and a determined stand against the tyranny.

"Hazel wrote his account of the episode on September 13, 1651, (and) a few days later he died from illness and age."[2] John Hazel was surely another unsung Baptist hero of the faith.

DLC

---

[1]Thomas Armitage, *The History of the Baptists* (1890; reprint ed., Watertown, Wis.: Maranatha Baptist Press, 1976), 2:679.

[2]Edwin S. Gaustad, *Baptist Piety* (Grand Rapids: Christian University Press, 1978), p. 32.

September 14—Bold Eccentrics for God's Truth

Scripture: Titus 2:11-15

The Second Baptist Church of Sutton, Massachusetts, was received into the Warren Association on September 14, 1768. This church was pastored by Jeremiah Barstow, who was converted to the New Light views around 1748 and felt called to preach. The strong impression to preach soon got him into trouble with the law when, in the same year, he was imprisoned for creating a disturbance because he interrupted a clergyman in the pulpit, asking for a chance to preach, and continuing to exhort the people after being turned out of the meetinghouse. This ultimately led to a movement to plant a Baptist church in Thompson, Connecticut. Sometimes the Lord uses the wrath of men to praise Him.

Perhaps he received some of his boldness from Ebenezer Moulton, who baptized him. This was the man of whom Isaac Backus wrote, "That Ebenezer Moulton of Brimfield, a Baptist Preacher, had been here among my people a preaching, and plunged some of them."[1] He went on to say that it had caused great contention among the people and brought trials to his own soul. This probably was a factor in persuading Backus of believers baptism and Baptist principles.

Moulton was an evangelist and a zealous promoter of the Separate Baptist movement in New England. He had been ordained by the First Baptist Church in Boston in 1741. He became very active in attempts to abolish religious taxes and was used in planting churches in Connecticut, Massachusetts, and Nova Scotia.

Barstow also resisted religious taxes and in 1750 was imprisoned for failure to pay his ministerial tax. He seemed to be a man who was always in "hot water" because he kept the water hot. In the same year he was mobbed and beaten in Brookfield, Massachusetts, in the presence of numerous clergymen and peace officers, because he announced to a crowd at the ordination of a standing clergyman that a Baptist preacher would be in town that evening to hold a meeting.

In that period of religious oppression in New England as men were carving out a new nation in a formidable wilderness, it took men with strength of character, depth of conviction, and boldness of purpose to propagate and promote the truth of God's grace. This was particularly true considering they were ministering among those who had the same qualities but were of different religious persuasions and were deeply entrenched into the social fiber of their communities.[2]

Barstow and Moulton would be considered eccentric, but after all, we are a "peculiar people, zealous of good works." God grant to us the same courage to propagate God's truth and to maintain it without apology for our separatist convictions.

EWT

---

[1]William G. McLoughlin, ed., *The Diary of Isaac Backus* (Providence: Brown University Press, 1979), 1:71.

[2]Ibid., 2:611.

September 15—Sunday School: Provider of Christian Leaders

Scripture: Deuteronomy 11:18-21

The first Sunday school in America was founded by Samuel Slater, who is regarded as the founder of the American cotton industry.[1] Slater came to America from England and from memory reproduced the cotton machinery with which he had worked there. In 1793 he established a factory in Pawtucket, Rhode Island, under the name of Almy, Brown & Slater.

Slater became aware of the ribald activities on Sundays of the young boys who were employed in the mill. One must remember that there were no child labor laws then, and the youthful employees desecrated the Lord's Day. He invited a group of boys to his home on Sundays with the purpose of establishing a Sunday school for them after the order of the Sunday school begun in England by Robert Raikes. Thus,

> on September 15th, 1799 . . . a Sunday School was established . . . by Samuel Slater for the benefit of the children employed in the cotton factory. . . . It was composed of seven boys . . . and . . . furnished secular instruction. . . . Its library consisted of two testaments and three Webster's spelling-books. . . . At a later date, as regular religious meetings had . . . been established in the village, the mighty possibilities of the Sunday School as an agent for religious culture were discerned and secular instruction was superseded by religious.[2]

In 1804 a young seminarian, the Reverend David Benedict, began preaching in Pawtucket and became pastor of the First Baptist Church. The young pastor started a Sunday school under the auspices of the church, and shortly thereafter, Mr. Slater's school was placed under Benedict's care as well. The secular instruction gave way to the sacred, and the Sunday school, as we know it, came into being in America. Near the close of his life, Benedict wrote, "Sunday Schools . . . which are now in such successful operation with us, and other communities in the land, were wholly unknown in my early day."[3]

Only eternity will reveal the results that Sunday schools have produced in America. While the Sunday school movement in Great Britain emphasized education, the American Sunday school featured evangelism. Robert Raikes and Samuel Slater were seeking a method of transforming young boys from waywardness to righteousness. Has the Sunday school succeeded? The record speaks for itself! It is maintained that "98 percent of all Sunday School trained boys and girls never get into serious trouble or crime."[4] What has the Sunday school done for local churches? Studies reveal that the Sunday school provides the church with sixty per cent of its evangelistic opportunities and eighty to eighty-five per cent of its members.[5] But perhaps even more important is the fact that from ninety to ninety-five per cent of all ministers, missionaries, evangelists, and full-time Christian workers come to Christ through the Sunday school effort.[6]

With these facts before us, we cannot but thank the Lord for the Baptist Sunday schools in America and the concern of Samuel Slater and vision of the Reverend David Benedict in instituting and developing the Baptist Sunday school. We need to pray that our vision of this institution shall not grow dim in time.

DLC

---

[1]*Webster's Biographical Dictionary* (Springfield, Mass.: G. and C. Merriam Co., Publishers, 1972), p. 1370.

[2]*Pawtucket* [R.I.] *Gazette & Chronicle*, 15 September 1876.

[3]David Benedict, *Fifty Years Among the Baptists* (New York: Sheldon and Co., 1860), p. 25.

[4]*Would You Cheat Your Child?* (Chicago: National Sunday School Association, n.d.), p. 2.

[5]*Our Most Indispensable Institution* (Chicago: National Sunday School Association, n.d.), p. 1.

[6]Ibid.

September 16—Outstanding Missionary to the Indians

Scripture: Psalm 96

Joseph Samuel Murrow served our Lord as a missionary among the American Indians for seventy-two years! Born in Georgia on June 7, 1835, into the home of a Methodist minister, Joseph Murrow doubtless heard the gospel early in life. He was nineteen years of age when he was converted and united with the local Baptist church. The next year he was licensed to preach. Young Murrow entered Mercer University in 1856 and was ordained by the First Baptist Church of Macon, Georgia, on September 16, 1857. The Domestic and Indian Mission Board of the Southern Baptist Convention appointed him a missionary to the Creek Indians. He entered into that ministry after marrying in Mississippi in November of 1857. To him goes the honor of organizing the first permanent Baptist church among the Seminoles in 1860. During the time he labored among the Seminoles, Murrow baptized two hundred people and is considered "the father of the mission work among the Seminoles."[1]

At the time of the Civil War, the Seminoles selected Murrow to serve as subsistence agent in the transactions with the government in securing food and supplies. Though cut off from the financial support of the Association, he did not cease his missionary activities. At the termination of the War Between the States, Murrow settled among the Choctaw Indians in Oklahoma and organized the Atoka Baptist Church in 1869. His labors included work in organizing the Sunday schools and establishing a strong association among the Indian churches.

By 1881 he was reported to have "preached thousands of sermons, traveled hundreds of thousands of miles, and baptized over a thousand Indians."[2] Throughout his lifetime of service, "he organized over 75 churches, baptized more than 2,000 converts, and assisted in ordaining 60 Indian preachers."[3] He became affectionately known among all the tribes as "Father Murrow." As an educator, in 1883 Father Murrow led in organizing the Baptist Missionary and Educational Convention of Indian Territory and was one of the founders of the Bacone College and Atoka Baptist Academy.

"Perhaps the crowning work of his life was the founding of the orphanage now called the Murrow Indian Orphans' Home—the only

Christian orphanage in existence primarily for Indians.''[4] At sixty-seven years of age, Father Murrow believed that his lifework among the Indians was drawing to a close. Thus, in 1902 he initiated the organization that he envisioned as the most important work of his life. In the first year of its operation, forty children were received into the orphanage. Murrow served as superintendent until 1907, when failing health forced him to step aside from that role of leadership. A conflict developed with the Home Mission Board of the Southern Baptist Convention when Murrow approached them about assuming the operation of the orphanage, and thus he returned to the Home Mission Society, and they took on the orphanage's management in 1909.

Throughout the rest of his life, Father Murrow remained as active in the Indian work as health would permit. Joseph Samuel Murrow died on June 7, 1929, in Atoka, Oklahoma, where he was buried.

DLC

---

[1]William Cathcart, *The Baptist Encyclopedia,* ed. Louis H. Everts (Philadelphia: Louis H. Everts, 1881), 2:825.

[2]Ibid., p. 826.

[3]Henry C. Vedder, *A Short History of Baptist Missions* (1907; reprint ed., Philadelphia: Judson Press, 1927), p. 463.

[4]Norman Wade Cox, ed., *Encyclopedia of Southern Baptists* (Nashville: Broadman Press, 1958), 2:931.

September 17—The Lion Who Became a Lamb

Scripture: Acts 8:36-37

In 1825 John Kerr assumed the pastorate of the First Baptist Church of Richmond, Virginia. Kerr had a stirring ministry and brought to the pulpit the ardor of an evangelist and the suave mannerisms of a politician, for he had served in both capacities. Since his licensing to preach, he had ministered in evangelism, and then for two terms he had served his countrymen in Congress.

Under his ministry in Richmond, he experienced great revivals, and in 1831 the church recorded 555 baptisms. Mrs. Archibald Thomas planned to be baptized and received into the membership of the First Baptist Church on September 17, 1826. Upon relating her plans to her husband, he was shocked. The church had no indoor baptistery, and therefore, immersions were held in a public place. In the thoughts of

Mr. Thomas, such a baptism was unconscionable, for it meant exposing oneself before a curious and perhaps vulgar audience. On the afternoon of the date, Catherine Thomas descended the staircase dressed to go to the baptism, and she met her husband in the hallway.

> "Where are you going?" he asked. "To follow my Lord in baptism," she replied. For a long moment husband and wife faced each other in silence. He was the first to lower his eyes. "Wait for me, please," he said. When he returned to the hall with hat and cane, his wife was amazed and troubled, for well she knew his quick temper. "Where are you going?" she asked. "I'm going with you," he replied. "If my wife is to be the object of scorn for rude people of the city, her husband's place is by her side to lend his protection."[1]

But what would he do? As we have said, she knew his quick temper, and once when John Leland was scheduled to baptize a woman and word came to her husband of the planned service, the unconverted, irate husband had stated his intention to murder the Baptist preacher and left for the service with gun in hand! To be sure, the resourceful Leland had circumvented the would-be murderer's plan,[2] but how would Mr. Thomas react?

> Together they entered the carriage and were driven to the place of baptism. There was the anticipated crowd . . . some reverent, some scornful, some curious. The minister explained the symbolism of believers' baptism and Archibald Thomas understood for the first time what conversion and baptism meant. Suddenly he stepped forward and asked courteously: "Is there anything in the regulations of your church which forbids the acceptance of a candidate for baptism at such a time?" "Nothing," Mr. Kerr replied, "provided the church is assured that the person who makes the request has repented of his sins and accepted Jesus Christ as his Saviour." "Then," Mr. Thomas said, "I wish to present myself as a candidate for baptism and membership in your church."[3]

The men were hastily called into a business session, and hearing a creditable expression of his faith, they accepted Archibald for baptism. He and Catherine were baptized with others on that occasion. "In the next business meeting of the church, Archibald Thomas took his place with his brethren and, until his death in 1861, he was one of the most effective members the church has had in her long history."[4]

DLC

---

[1]Blanche Sydnor White, *First Baptist Church—Richmond, 1780-1955* (Richmond: Whittet and Shepperson, 1955), p. 45.

[2]Norman Wade Cox, ed., *Encyclopedia of Southern Baptists* (Nashville: Broadman Press, 1958), 2:749.

[3]White, p. 45.

[4]Ibid., p. 46.

September 18—A Businessman Who Put God First

Scripture: Matthew 7:7-12

William Quarrier was born on September 29, 1829, in Scotland. When the lad was less than five years of age, his father died of cholera at sea, and his mother moved the family of three children to Glasgow. There were no child labor laws, and the little fellow was sent off to work in a shoe manufacturing shop for a shilling a week. At seven years of age, William was apprenticed to a shoemaker so that he might learn the trade during his youth.

As a youngster, little William envisioned growing to maturity and assisting others. William Quarrier later wrote, "When I was a little boy, I stood in the High Street of Glasgow, barefooted, bareheaded, cold and hungry, having tasted no food for a day and a half, and, as I gazed at each passer-by, wondering why they did not help such as I, a thought passed through my mind that I would not do as they when I would get the means to help others."[1]

Actually Quarrier was raised with very little religious instruction, but he visited the Blackfriars Street Baptist Church when he was a youth. When he was seventeen years old, he was converted under the ministry of the Reverend James Taylor, and he began to witness to others. As he became able, he supported his mother, and she began to attend the Blackfriars Street Church with him. Six years later she too was saved. In his faithfulness to witness of God's grace, the young man filled pew after pew of the church with his efforts. He put the Lord first in his business life, and once, when he was seeking financial help to open a shoe store, the potential creditor advised that young Quarrier might have to give up attendance at the weekly prayer meeting to be a successful entrepreneur. " 'My answer was,' he said, 'that if business required me to give up my obligations to Christ, I would relinquish it and remain as I was before—a resolution which I have no reason to regret since.' "[2]

Quarrier became a very successful businessman. He served as a deacon in the local church, and his enterprise expanded under the blessing of God. The successful businessman never forgot his youthful needs, and thus he spearheaded a movement to begin an orphanage.

That vision and effort resulted in "The Orphanage Homes of Scotland." During his lifetime, Quarrier erected or acquired sixty-four buildings which were continually filled in caring for the needs of boys and girls in his homeland. The story of God's direction and blessing could not be told in such a limited space, but in time Quarrier purchased sufficient land on which to build a complex that would serve the needs and provide for further expansion. A meaningful dedication was held, and the *North British Daily Mail* on September 18, 1878, reported, "It must have been with the liveliest satisfaction that Mr. Quarrier opened his Orphan Cottage Homes at Bridge of Weir yesterday." During the past fourteen years, "over a thousand . . . children . . . have been successfully laid hold of. . . . For a long time past he has had, on an average, a family of 200 helpless young people looking to him for daily bread."[3] As to the financial undergirding, Quarrier wrote that "in entire dependence upon God . . . no one would be called on for subscriptions, no names of donors would be published . . . but that everything should be committed to God in prayer."[4]

William Quarrier died on October 16, 1903, and over two thousand attended his funeral, which was conducted by his son-in-law, Pastor D. J. Findlay of Glasgow. Our hero of the day was a faithful Christian businessman who surely put the Lord Jesus Christ first in his life!

DLC

---

[1]Alexander Gammie, *A Romance of Faith* (London: Pickering and Inglis, n.d.), pp. 17-18.

[2]Ibid., pp. 34-35.

[3]Ibid., pp. 109, 111, 113.

[4]Ibid., p. 115.

September 19—"I Will Preach Publickly and from House to House"

Scripture: Acts 20:17-24

Mr. Hanserd Knollys was born in 1598 at Chalkwell in Lincolnshire, England. He descended from religious parents who took care to have him tutored in good literature and religious principles. He then was sent to Cambridge University, from which he graduated. While at the university, he lived a very pious life, daily spent time in the study of God's

Word, fasted, prayed, and maintained a strict examination of himself for sins with the purpose of repenting of them.

Knollys was ordained by the bishop of Peterborough as a deacon and then as a presbyter of the Church of England. He was a minister of the Church of England for nine years. Because he expressed his antipedobaptist convictions and his opposition to a national church as well as established uniformity, he was stoned out of the pulpit, locked out of the building, persecuted at petty sessions in the country, and sent as a prisoner to London. Upon being heard by the committee of examination, he was exonerated and set at liberty to preach.

At last Knollys renounced his established church ordination and set up a separate meetinghouse. Here the people flocked to him, and he regularly had a thousand hearers. Opponents warned his landlord to remove him from that place, and Knollys was summoned to appear before a committee of divines. Upon examination, he confessed that he had renounced the "holy orders" of the established church and said, "he was not ordain'd, in a church of God, according to the order of the Gospel, and then declared to them the manner of ordination used among the Baptists. At last the Chairman in the name of the committee commanded him to preach no more; but he told them he would preach the Gospel, both publickly and from house to house, saying it was more equal to obey Christ who commanded him, than those who forbad him, and so went his way."[1]

Frequently Knollys was hurried about from place to place by the evil of the times and the envy of his persecutors. First he and his family were forced from Lincolnshire to London, then from London to New England, and thence back again. Another time they were obliged to move from England into Wales and after this, twice from London to Lincolnshire. Another circuit was from London to Holland to Germany, back to Rotterdam, and then to London. While in New England, he was not tolerated in Boston, being called an antinomian; therefore, he went to Dover, where he preached for four years.

Knollys was well acquainted with the learned languages and had an extraordinary way of instructing youth. Many eminent persons, both for piety and learning, were trained by him. He baptized the eminent minister Henry Jessey (cf. the entries for September 3 and 4) of London and was one who signed the Baptist Confession of Faith in 1643. He continued his ministry in London through great changes and sufferings until he died in peace, September 19, 1691. Knollys was ninety-three years old at his death.[2]

EWT

---

[1]Thomas Crosby, *The History of the English Baptists* (1738-40; reprint ed., Lafayette, Tenn.: Church History Research and Archives, 1979), 1:226-30, 334-36.

[2]Isaac Backus, *Your Baptist Heritage, 1620–1804* (1844; reprint ed., Little Rock: Challenge Press, 1976), pp. 41-42.

September 20—Were They Baptist Dissenters or Sowers of Sedition?

Scripture: I Kings 22:1-40

The citizens of the plantations and settlements of Virginia were not always the most genteel kind of people. Most of them attended the established Church of England because it was mandated by law. Among the tax-supported clergy, there were those who had lost the respect of the people because of their licentious conduct, and the citizenry itself had fallen into a spiritual malaise.

When men like Nathaniel Saunders began to preach the necessity of the new birth, resulting in a holy life, many of the people, especially among the clergy and those in authority, were not pleased. To add to this displeasure, the zealous new converts to the Baptist principles had some harsh things to say about the lack of spirituality and moral integrity of some of the leadership of the established church. The countryside was set afire, not only by the gospel but also by the reactions to those accusations. This overwhelming response to the proclamation of truth was why magistrates were running hither and yon with warrants, often charging Baptist preachers with disturbing the peace.

The following is a copy of an actual warrant similar to many others issued at that time. The abbreviations at the beginning stand for "Culpeper" and "Scilicet."

> Culpr Sct:
>
> Whereas we have received Information that Nathaniel Saunders & William McClannahan stiling themselves Protestant Dissenters, does Teach & Preach Contrary to the Laws & usages of the Kingdom of Great Britian, raising Sedition & Stirring up Strife amongst his Majestie's Liege People.
>
> Therefore In his Majestie's Name we require you, Samuel Ferguson and John Lillard, to take Nathaniel Saunders and William McClannahan and their abettors and bring before some Justice of the Peace for the sd County to be Examined Touching the Charge, & we do hereby Command all his Majestie's Subjects to be Aiding and Assisting in the due Execution thereof.

Given under our hands this 21st day of August 1773

John Slaughter
George Wetheral

To the Sheriff Or any Constable of this County, or to Samuel Ferguson and John Lillard

Executed: Pr Samuel Ferguson John Lillard

At a court held for Culpeper County, September 20, 1773, Nathaniel Saunders appeared, was charged according to the warrant, and spoke in his own defense. He was bound in the sum of £200 ($973.30), which was an exorbitant sum that Saunders could not pay, and was prohibited "to teach, preach or Exhort for the space of one year," to which he could not consent.[1] He accepted the alternative of going to the Culpeper jail, where he spent an undetermined period of time. Culpeper imprisoned more preachers than any other county in Virginia.

EWT

---

[1]Lewis Peyton Little, *Imprisoned Preachers and Religious Liberty in Virginia* (Lynchburg, Va.: J. P. Bell Co., 1938), pp. 368-71.

September 21—Should Baptists Support All Faiths?

Scripture: Psalm 37:16

The ecclesiastical tax that Baptists were forced to pay for the support of the state church was ever a thorn to men of the Baptist persuasion.

> The town of Ashfield, Mass. was settled by Baptists. In 1770, a few Congregationalists built a meeting house, called a minister, and taxed the Baptists for his support. The greater part of his salary . . . came from Baptists. Because they refused to pay this burdensome tax, 398 acres of their land were seized, together with their homes, cattle, crops, and graveyards—constituting everything of many families, and sold to pay the tax. . . . The property was sold far below its value, and the . . . minister was one of the purchasers. . . .
>
> In 1774 the law of 1573, was renewed, Massachusetts requiring that certificates should be recorded in each parish where Baptists lived, in order to exempt them from tax for the state church support, for a copy of which certificate, a charge of four pense was made.[1]

The Warren Association met on September 14, 1774, and agreed to send the Reverend Isaac Backus to the First Continental Congress to present their petition before the delegates. It was at that time that John Adams, a delegate from Massachusetts and later president of the United States, said, "They might as well expect a change in the Solar system, as to expect that we would give up our ecclesiastical establishment," by which he meant the support of the Congregational churches by taxation. At the same time, Mr. Paine, also a member of the Massachusetts delegation said, "There was nothing of conscience in the matter; it was only a contending about a little money." Isaac Backus replied, "It is absolutely a point of conscience with me, for I cannot give in the certificates they require, without implicitly acknowledging that power in man which I believe belongs only to God."[2]

Isaac Backus says in his diary that on Wednesday, August 9, 1780, he returned from preaching in Mansfield and "found Elder [Isaiah] Parker of Harvard at my house, who came to ask advice about three of their Society [Church] who are in Worcester jail for ministerial taxes."[3] Nathan Willard and John Hawkes had been imprisoned for almost four months, and Oliver Wetherbee had been incarcerated for a month and a half for refusing to pay taxes to support Timothy Harrington, the Congregational preacher in Harvard, Massachusetts. Mr. Hawkes had been taxed £6.16.0 and Mr. Willard had been taxed £24.18.6. Backus visited the men in jail on September 21, and shortly after, Willard and Wetherbee were released, apparently without paying their fines.

It is difficult for us to realize that religious inequality and intolerance upheld by the civil power was ever practiced in the "Land of the Free," but the historical record speaks for itself. America did not practice freedom of conscience in the colonial days. The wonderful triumph of religious liberty is a tribute to men and women of conviction who were determined to pay whatever price was necessary to bring about its realization. The gift of religious freedom has been given our generation, but it is essential that we instruct our children in this little-known history, lest our posterity take freedom for granted and forfeit these liberties.

DLC

---

[1]Richard B. Cook, *The Story of the Baptists in All Ages and Countries* (Baltimore: H. M. Wharton and Co., 1886), pp. 232, 234.

[2]William G. McLoughlin, ed., *The Diary of Isaac Backus* (Providence: Brown University Press, 1979), 2:917.

[3]Ibid., p. 1055.

September 22—The One-Legged Preacher Who Walked on Ice

Scripture: Philippians 4:12-13

Fredrick Ludwig Rymker, the man who became known as the pioneer of the Baptist work in Norway, was born in Stige, Denmark, on September 22, 1819. Having been born to poor parents, the young man's education was meager, and he learned the trade of a shoemaker. However, at age twenty he went to sea.

Rymker sailed to New York and resided in a sailor's lodging house. While there he was invited by a believer to visit the Mariner's Temple, and he soon came to know Jesus Christ as his Savior. During the next year, he lost a leg in an accident and was fitted with a wooden leg. Upon returning to the Mariner's Temple, he was immersed and became a member of that church. He became a zealous witness for Christ and was licensed to preach in 1848. In 1850 Rymker was sent by the Baptist Women's Society as a missionary to Denmark.

Arriving back in Denmark, Rymker began to preach in Stige. Two years later he married and constructed a home with a meeting hall which could be used for church services. He was ordained in Copenhagen and began to publish the paper *Missionary Magazine for Baptized Christian Churches*. In the course of time, Rymker was asked to serve as a missionary in Norway and was promised $200 a year support for such service.

Rymker left for Norway on September 19, 1857. Traveling throughout the country to investigate potential opportunities, he preached to congregations of the "Free Church," but eventually, the "Free Church" pastors withdrew their fellowship from him because they feared a schism in their congregations regarding believers immersion. Settling near Porsgrund, Rymker began his work in earnest. He visited the town of Larvik and looked upon it as a mission station. Having no means of transportation, the one-legged preacher would walk to and from his preaching opportunities there—some twenty miles away. In good weather, he could cover that distance in eight or nine hours, but during the winter, it took much longer. "Once he fell on the icy road and broke his wooden leg, and he was lying on the road until somebody found him and drove him to town."[1]

Norway's 1845 law concerning "dissenters" stated that no one under nineteen years of age could leave the state church and no one was to perform the "sacraments" without his denomination's authority. Thus, a church had to be formed, and this event took place on January 6, 1861, with nine members.

Mrs. Kari Kristensdatter requested immersion, but her husband threatened there would be a baptism of blood. When Rymker arrived at the river to baptize the lady, "her husband with some of his friends were there, and each one of them carried an ax on his shoulder. The little group of Christians fell on their knees and asked for divine protection, and the baptism was performed without any disturbance."[2] The growth among the Baptists was surely slow, but the foundation was laid. "The result of about ten years' labor there was the formation of five or six churches, the ordination of two preachers . . . the conversion and baptism of between one hundred and fifty and two hundred Norwegians, scattered over a territory of two hundred miles."[3]

Thus, on the anniversary of his birth, we honor the memory of the one-legged, sacrificial, faithful preacher who resolutely served His Lord.

DLC

---

[1]P. Stiansen, *History of the Baptists in Norway* (Chicago: Blessing Press, 1933), p. 69.

[2]Ibid., pp. 72-73.

[3]Thomas Armitage, *The History of the Baptists* (1890; reprint ed., Watertown, Wis.: Maranatha Baptist Press, 1976), 2:831.

September 23—James Hickey, the Apostle of Mexico

Scripture: Matthew 13:34-43

James Hickey, like so many of the outstanding early missionaries, did not become a Baptist because he was reared in a Baptist family or because he sat under the ministry of a faithful Baptist pastor. His birthplace was Sligo, Cork County, Ireland, and his birth date was September 23, 1800. He was born of devout Roman Catholic parents who were dedicated to the upbringing of their son as a priest committed to the church. This goal seemingly was being accomplished when Hickey left home to attend the priest's college. He had been taught only the doctrines of the Roman Church. While at this college, much to his intense chagrin and shame, he discovered that immorality and drunkenness were the common practices of the teachers and students alike and that the entire leadership of this church was corrupt and rotten.[1]

At this time Hickey, who had high ideals, began to question the doctrine of a religious system that produced leadership with such corrupt conduct. Under the influence of a fine Protestant aunt and a young Christian woman with whom he was in love, he left the Roman Church. After his marriage, he entered a school of the Anglican Church but soon discovered that in many respects it was like the Roman Church. He left their fellowship and joined the small group of Evangelicals of Ireland known as Independents.

The example of the lives of William Carey and Adoniram Judson laid hold upon Hickey's life. Coupled with this inspiration, the loss of his beloved wife brought the loneliness that forced him more and more to seek the companionship of the Lord. In the year 1830, he began his work in the United States, where the pioneers were ever pushing westward. At this time, through his exposure to the Scriptures and the lives of the Baptist missionaries, he was fully persuaded of and embraced Baptist principles.

Mexico and the Spanish-speaking people had always been upon his heart. At the outbreak of the Civil War, Hickey crossed the Rio Grande and began his active ministry in Matamoros. These were also turbulent times in Mexico with much civil strife and the intervention of European nations into Mexico's internal affairs. This did not keep Hickey from dedicating himself that all men might come to know his Lord and Savior.

The country was enslaved for three hundred years by the Roman religion and superstition. The people, through the fear of the ecclesiastical powers, often reacted violently to the evangelism of this servant of God and his companions in the gospel who had joined him. Hickey suffered the privations of heat, cold, hunger, and thirst, and at the age of sixty-five, often rode horseback forty and fifty miles under a burning sun.

The passion of his life was to preach Christ. On January 30, 1864, Hickey organized the First Baptist Church of Monterrey. This was the first evangelical church started in Mexico. One of his converts wrote, "Let his name be embalmed, and his memory be dear to all who rejoice that Mexico first heard the Gospel from Baptist lips." He who came out of the darkness of Catholicism rejoiced when he was able to lead others from such a depth to the light of the knowledge of God. James Hickey well deserves to be called "the Apostle of Mexico."[2]

EWT

---

[1]Walter Sinclair Stewart, *Later Baptist Missionaries and Pioneers* (Philadelphia: Judson Press, 1928), 2:40.

[2]Ibid., p. 61.

September 24—Baptist Education: Training for Spiritual Leadership

Scripture: I Samuel 2:1-15

The idea that the Baptists were not at all interested in or concerned with an educated ministry in America is an absolutely false concept. Though many outstanding men were deprived of an early formal, classical education because their frontier upbringing did not provide such, many of them overcame this obstacle through the diligence of a godly mother and/or father, who provided means for the hungry heart and thirsty soul to receive enough education to understand the Bible and to prepare them for future opportunities.

The Baptists in the state of New York became interested in establishing a denominational school of higher learning in their state. "On the 24 of September, 1817, thirteen brethren met at the house of Deacon Jonathan Olmstead, in Hamilton, Madison County, and formed themselves into a society, to be known as 'The Baptist Educational Society of the State of New York.' Their chief treasures were in their faith and prayers. Each member was required to pay one dollar as a condition of membership. The special object of this was 'to educate pious young men for the ministry.' "[1]

Many of the early Baptist preachers, such as John Clarke and Henry Dunster, had been educated in England and later embraced Baptist principles. Dunster was forced to resign his presidency of Harvard College after fourteen years of service because he repudiated pedobaptism and a church-controlled state.

James Manning was a graduate of the College of New Jersey, later Princeton University, and was entrusted by the Philadelphia Association of Regular Baptists "with the arduous task of establishing a denominational college on some suitable part of this continent."[2] He began this task with one student. At the first commencement in 1769, he graduated seven. Manning saw at once that success depended upon the interest of the local churches. He and Hezekiah Smith determined to form an association with the double purpose of resisting the oppression of the Standing Order in New England and of securing an educated

Baptist ministry. This goal was accomplished at Warren in 1767 and continued when the institution moved to Providence in 1770. The Philadelphia and Warren Associations were intimately identified with the college for many years. Men such as John Gano, Isaac Backus, and Morgan Edwards supported and were clearly associated in the formation of that institution, which was founded to educate ministers. The school is now known as Brown University, the first Baptist institution of higher learning in America.

Additional consideration could be given to Luther Rice, who, as a Congregationalist missionary, became a Baptist onboard ship on his way to India. At the urging of Adoniram Judson, he returned to the United States to encourage and exhort Baptists to support world evangelism. A part of his vision was the founding of Columbian College, now George Washington University in Washington, D.C. The original purpose was to train preachers and missionaries.

Schools began springing up in the South as well under the able leadership of men like Richard Furman, who was the first president of "The Baptist General Convention for Foreign Missions," later known as the Triennial Convention. Furman University of Greenville, South Carolina, was named after him.

Baptist educators and educational institutions have played an important role in evangelizing our nation and the world. May God help us to raise up more such institutions throughout the world and protect them from apostasy.

EWT

---

[1]Lemuel Moss, ed., *The Baptists and the National Centenary* (Philadelphia: American Baptist Publication Society, 1876), p. 86.

[2]Thomas Armitage, *The History of the Baptists* (1890; reprint ed., Watertown, Wis.: Maranatha Baptist Press, 1976), 2:720.

September 25—Baptists and the Federal Bill of Rights

Scripture: II Chronicles 17:1-19

The final drafts of the twelve amendments (out of the many that had been suggested by James Madison and others) were passed by Congress on September 25, 1789, after only seven or eight days of debate, and were presented to the states for approval.[1] This action fulfilled the promise of Madison to John Leland and the Baptists when, as a delegate to the Virginia Constitutional Convention and later as a candidate from Orange County for the House of Representatives in the Congress of the United States, Madison solicited their support.

All this began with the influence of the Baptists upon Madison, Thomas Jefferson, Patrick Henry, and other leading statesmen in Virginia. The Baptists had been consistent in their convictions relating to liberty of conscience for many years. Their convictions were demonstrated by their willingness to suffer physical abuse and imprisonment. These convictions caused them to petition the Virginia legislature on many occasions.

Some years before when a committee was appointed by the Virginia legislature to write a Declaration of Rights, George Mason presented the articles, of which the 16th had the phrase "that all men should enjoy the fullest *toleration* in the exercise of religion." Madison raised an objection to the term *toleration* and offered the substitute "all men are equally entitled to the *free exercise* of religion according to the dictates of conscience." Toleration, Madison maintained, belonged to a system where there was an established church and where liberty was a thing granted, not of right, but of grace. He feared the power in the hands of a dominant religion to construe what "may disturb the peace, the happiness, or the safety of society," and he ventured to propose the substitute which was finally adopted. It marks an era in legislative history and is believed to be the first provision ever embodied in any constitution or law for the security of absolute equality before the law to all religious opinions.

Where did Madison learn the distinction between religious freedom and religious toleration? Surely it was from observing his Baptist neighbors who persistently taught that the civil magistrates had nothing to do with matters of religion and as a result had experienced persecutions. Jeremiah Walker, John Williams, and George Roberts were appointed by the Baptists to represent their views on such important occasions before the legislature and were doubtless on hand.[2]

It was John Leland, James Madison's near neighbor with whom Madison counseled on more than one occasion, who wrote, "Government should protect every man in thinking and speaking freely, and see that one does not abuse another. The liberty I contend for, is more than toleration. The very idea of toleration is despicable; it supposes that some have a pre-eminence above the rest to grant indulgence."

After a long, bitter struggle, religious freedom had triumphed in Virginia. The words of Virginia's Declaration of Rights were incorporated into the Federal Bill of Rights and began with "Congress shall make no law respecting an establishment of religion, or prohibiting the free exercise thereof.''

Thank God for the humble Baptists of Virginia who, after the century-old tradition of their forefathers, were faithful to the Baptist principle of separation of church and state. May we protect this liberty for our posterity.

EWT

---

[1]''The Annals of America,'' *Encyclopedia Britannica* (Chicago: Encyclopedia Britannica, Inc., 1976), 3:364.

[2]Charles F. James, *A Documentary History of the Struggle for Religious Liberty in Virginia* (1900; reprint ed., New York: Da Capo Press, 1971), pp. 62-64.

September 26—"Your Imprisonment Is Not a Punishment, But a Glory"

Scripture: II Chronicles 16

In 1763 the Elder David Thomas became the first Baptist preacher ever to proclaim the gospel of God's grace in the counties of Orange and Culpeper, Virginia. His preaching was in the power and demonstration of the Spirit. Mr. Nathaniel Saunders was among the ''first seals'' to his ministry. Many others were also baptized about the same time. In 1766 Saunders began to preach, and in 1768 he was ordained to the care of Mountain-Run Church, which was constituted at the same time. He held this position until the church was dissolved in 1782.[1]

These early men of God zealously preached with plain and forceful words on the absolute necessity of the new birth, making its application to the clergy and the laity of the established state church. Even among the Presbyterians this subject had been neglected. This stirred up the ire of many against these preachers, but the subject of the new birth was the object of much discussion in the community. Nathaniel Saunders was not remiss in the proclamation of this message and found himself the recipient of much correspondence, some of an appealing nature and other of a threatening nature, to cease and desist preaching thus. He was summoned to court on several occasions and confined, along with William McClannahan, in the Culpeper jail for an unknown period of time.

During this time, Saunders received the following interesting letter written September 26, 1773:

> Dear Brother—I hear you are put in prison for preaching the Gospel of Jesus Christ. Perhaps you think it hard. But O, what honor the Lord put upon you! I think you may be willing to suffer death now, seeing you are counted worthy to enter a dungeon for your Master's sake. Hold out, my dear brother! Remember your Master—your royal, heavenly, divine Master—was nailed to a cursed tree for us. O, to suffer for him is glory in the bud! O, never let it be said that a Baptist minister of Virginia ever wronged his conscience to get liberty, not to please God but himself! O, your imprisonment (which I am satisfied is not from any rash proceedings of your own) is not a punishment, but a glory! 'If you suffer with Him you shall also reign with Him.'
>
> Dear Brother, the bearer is waiting or I should have enlarged. This is only to let you know that I can pray for you with great freedom. Give my kind love to your fellow prisoner, though I know him not. I hope he is a dear child of God. Pray for me, for I need it. I remain, dear brother,
>
> Yours in our dear Lord Jesus,
> David Thomas[2]

Although David Thomas was never imprisoned himself, he underwent such violent persecution that his life was in peril on many occasions. He was the elder among elders in Virginia and had a tender, compassionate concern for their welfare as one can see from this epistle. God grant us that same love for one another in our times of testing, and may we communicate in writing so that our posterity may have a witness of our compassion and concern.

EWT

---

[1]Robert B. Semple, *A History of the Rise and Progress of the Baptists in Virginia* (Richmond: Published by the author, 1810), p. 177.

[2]Lewis Peyton Little, *Imprisoned Preachers and Religious Liberty in Virginia* (Lynchburg, Va.: J. P. Bell Co., 1938), pp. 372-73.

September 27—God's Apostle to a Suffering People

Scripture: II Timothy 2:1-8

Humphrey Posey was an eminent Baptist preacher of large stature, great abilities, and a great and benevolent heart. Dr. J. H. Campbell, in his *Georgia Baptists,* records his conviction ''that Humphrey Posey was naturally one of the greatest men, and, for his limited opportunities, one of the greatest preachers he has ever known. His person, his countenance, his voice, the throes of his gigantic mind, the conceptions of his large Christian soul—all proclaimed him great.''[1]

These qualities prepared him for the great work among the Cherokee Indians. In writing relative to the mission work, Posey said, ''They look to the religious societies for teachers, preachers, and farmers, as they have unanimously found out that Christians are their only friends, whose example they wish their rising generation to follow, and whose instruction they hope will prove a lasting blessing to their nation.''[2]

After securing the unanimous consent of the General Council of the Cherokees, Posey journeyed to Washington and was most kindly received by President Monroe and John C. Calhoun, who was then Secretary of War. Posey secured endorsement of his plan to establish a mission on the land set apart for that purpose at Valley Towns in Cherokee County, North Carolina. The plan was adopted by the Baptist Mission Board in Philadelphia, and he returned to provide a farm with three horses, wagons, tools, forty head of cattle, and about a hundred hogs. Soon he had about eighty acres enclosed and in cultivation.

Writing on September 27, 1821, Posey said, ''Our school is doing very well; 40 Cherokees are still improving very fast. . . . I humbly hope day is broke in this wilderness. I have been able to undergo the fatigues of my situation entirely cheerful since I understood the dear brethren and sisters were coming on this fall. O for a heart of thankfulness to the Great Giver of all good, for His loving-kindness to the children of men!''[3] The group from Philadelphia consisted of a company of 26 including a preacher, teachers, a blacksmith, farmers, and one who had studied medicine.

The labors of these faithful missionaries were fruitful. We find that up to the time of the removal of the Cherokees by order of the United States government in 1838, hundreds of them had been converted and formed into churches. At least one missionary, a teacher, followed them to their new home and continued to work for their spiritual good. In 1842 all the churches had meetinghouses, their own printing office, and in 1846 the translation of the New Testament. In 1863 there was an estimated 1,500 church members among the Cherokees.

In the midst of sufferings, atrocities, and injustices, God continued to call out a people for His name by using dedicated, godly men.

EWT

---

[1]William Cathcart, *The Baptist Encyclopedia,* ed. Louis H. Everts (Philadelphia: Louis H. Everts, 1881), 2:928.

[2]George Washington Paschal, *History of North Carolina Baptists* (Raleigh: Edwards and Broughton Co., 1955), 2:543.

[3]Ibid.

September 28—Unsung Baptist Pioneering Heroes

Scripture: Hebrews 11:38-40

Roswell Kimball was born on May 12, 1792, in Plainfield, New Hampshire, into the home of a Baptist pastor. He was trained early in Baptist doctrine and enjoyed the use of his father's library. He was converted at the age of eighteen, soon after his father's death. Five years later, he heard a sermon on missions that challenged him for life. A spiritual battle followed, and being unwilling to accept the call to preach the gospel, young Kimball determined to give himself rather to the practice of medicine. He completed the designated courses of study and became a successful physician. Still the peace he desired eluded him, and he did not have the joy of the Lord.

During his practice of medicine, Kimball became backslidden as a result of his refusal to obey the call of God. In consultation with his pastor, he decided that "obedience was better than sacrifice" and was licensed to preach by the Baptist church in Hartland, New York, on October 24, 1830. During the next five Sundays, he preached for his pastor, and revival fires fell with thirty-five being added to the church. With this confirmation of the Lord, Kimball was ordained in Hartland on September 28, 1831, when he was almost forty years of age.

During the next four years as Kimball pastored, large numbers were added to the church as the Spirit of God used Kimball's earnest, simple, direct preaching. However, Kimball's heart still burned toward the cause of missions, and thus, in 1835 under a commission from the American Bible Society, he emigrated with his family to Illinois and labored in that service until 1837. In 1839 he was appointed "General Agent (of the Illinois Baptist Convention) at a salary of $500."[1] For the next two years "he traveled, principally on horseback, thirteen thousand five hundred and sixty miles, and delivered six hundred and thirty-one sermons and addresses."[2]

The Reverend Mr. Kimball died "in the seventy-fourth year of his age, in strong faith in Christ, and with a glorious hope of a blessed immortality."[3]

We cannot help honoring the memory of the Baptist pioneers who were willing to minister in the wilderness though many times they had no place to sleep. The Reverend Jay Pruden of Michigan found himself in a violent snowstorm. While looking for lodging, he was invited into a humble home in which he found an elderly couple. He accepted their hospitality and attempted to witness to them, but the old man swore and refused the testimony. The missionary retired to rest with a heavy heart.

In the morning the elderly gentleman was waiting for the pioneer-preacher and said,

> "Stranger, have you a Bible?" He said, "Yes; but why do you ask such a question after last night's declarations?" The old man replied: "We want you to read it to us and pray with us." The colporter said: "I would like to know why you changed?" The old man said: "Stranger, do you know you talk in your sleep? . . . Well, wife and I have been kept awake by hearing you say every little while in your sleep, 'Oh, that they might know Jesus;' and we want to know Him."[4]

Such were the results wherever Baptist pioneer missionaries went westward with the gospel in the early 1800s in America. May God cause us to revere their memories and to determine to go forward to new regions beyond in our generation as well!

DLC

---

[1]Edward P. Brand, *Illinois Baptists: A History* (Bloomington, Ill.: Pantagraph Printing Co., 1930), p. 134.

[2]*Minutes of the Illinois Baptist Pastoral Union* (Alton, Ill.: S. V. Crossman and Co., 1865), p. 10.

[3]Ibid.

[4]M.E.D. Trowbridge, *History of Baptists in Michigan* (n.p.: Michigan Baptist State Convention, 1909), p. 203.

September 29—The Leading Baptist of the Seventeenth Century

Scripture: Job 23:10-14

When the plague swept London in 1625, killing an estimated one third of the population, little William Kiffin was but nine years old. He experienced six plague sores yet miraculously recovered, though he was left an orphan as his mother and father succumbed. Surely the providential hand of Almighty God was upon the boy, for he was to grow up to be "the most beloved Baptist of his time."[1] William Kiffin was regenerated in his teen years through the ministry of Puritan preachers. Around age twenty-two, Kiffin joined an Independent church in London. Later he came to Baptist convictions and united with the Baptist church that John Spilsbury was pastoring. In 1640 Spilsbury's church supervised the establishment of a "sister church" in Devonshire Square, and William Kiffin became pastor, serving in that capacity for the remaining sixty-one years of his life.

In the course of his life, Kiffin became one of the most successful businessmen in England as he carried on trade with foreign countries. Thus, he superintended the work of the church at Devonshire Square and used an assistant pastor to assist in the various responsibilities. "Kiffin's influence was very great. Macaulay says, 'Great as was the authority of Bunyan with the Baptists, William Kiffin's was greater still.' He had talents of the highest order; his education was respectable; his sagacity was uncommon; his manners were polished; his piety was known everywhere; and for half a century he was the first man in the Baptist denomination."[2]

With all of his personal success, William Kiffin suffered as few other men did. Though an advisor to the king, he was arrested many times. While he was incarcerated in the White Lion jail, some of the prisoners conspired to murder him, but God overruled and he was released. Later, he was accused of hiring men to kill the king, but the charges were miraculously dismissed by the king himself, and Kiffin was freed.

Personal sorrows harassed William Kiffin as well. His first son, also named William, died when he was only twenty years of age and was buried in Bunhill Fields. His second son traveled in Europe for reasons of health. That son's testimony for Christ to a Roman Catholic priest in Venice, Italy, caused the priest to poison him. Kiffin's daughter died soon after, and it was not long until death claimed his wife also. Through it all, Kiffin's faith remained strong, and his witness was undimmed. Perhaps the greatest trial of his life came when two of his beloved grandsons, Benjamin and William Hewling, were martyred for their faith. Later Kiffin wrote, "It was a great comfort to me, and still is, to observe what testimony they left behind them of that blessed interest they had in the Lord Jesus and holy confidence of their eternal happiness."[3]

William Kiffin's life spanned one of the most tumultuous centuries of the history of England. Kiffin passed into the presence of his Lord on September 29, 1701. The pastor-merchant had been raised up by God's providence so that his talents, influence, and wealth might be used to assist the persecuted brethren in the distressing period of Baptist suffering in England. Surely for half a century, William Kiffin was the "Father of the English Baptists."

DLC

---

[1]B. A. Ramsbottom, *Stranger Than Fiction* (Harpendon, England: Gospel Standard Trust Publications, 1989), p. 93.

[2]William Cathcart, *The Baptist Encyclopedia,* ed. Louis H. Everts (Philadelphia: Louis H. Everts, 1881), p. 655.

[3]Ramsbottom, p. 61.

September 30—In Youth They Faced Death with Joy and Peace

Scripture: Daniel 6

Upon Charles II's death, his brother James II ascended the throne of England. He was an avowed Catholic and was ready to re-establish Catholicism in England, regardless of what it might cost him. It was during his short reign (1685-88) that Benjamin and William Hewling surrendered their lives at a young age (Benjamin 22 and William 19) "for the English liberties, and the Protestant religion."[1]

They had been preceded in death by their father and had been brought up by a gentle mother and grandfather, William Kiffin, who was one of the wealthiest and most eminent preachers among the Baptists of that day. These young men, seeing popery encouraged and religious liberty likely to be invaded, furnished themselves with arms and joined the Duke of Monmouth in an unsuccessful struggle for civil and religious freedom. After the dispersing of the duke's army, they fled by ship but were driven back and forced to surrender themselves.

They were imprisoned in Newgate, where they were separated and their family forbidden to see them. Their grandfather made an appeal for the release of his grandsons, which was rejected by the king and those representing him. The Hewling brothers were transported from place to place and ultimately tried and condemned to death. Their sister was finally able to follow them and minister to some of their needs. She gave this account:

> They with great cheerfulness professed that they were better and in a more happy condition than ever in their lives, from the sense they had of the pardoning love of God in Jesus Christ to their souls; wholly referring themselves to their wise and gracious God to choose for

> them life or death. . . . "We know he is able to deliver; but if not blessed be His name; death is not terrible now, but desirable. As for the world, there is nothing in it to make it worth while to live, except we may be serviceable to God therein. Oh! God is a strong refuge: I have found Him so indeed."[2]

At the time of his execution, William wrote these few lines to a friend, "I am going to launch into eternity, I hope and trust, into the arms of my blessed redeemer; to Whom I commit you, and all my dear relations."

Benjamin received news of his brother's execution with great assurance and comfort, and as the hour of his own execution was near, he said, "When I have considered others under these circumstances, I have thought it very dreadful; but now God hath called me to it. . . . I can cheerfully embrace it as an easy passage to glory; and though death separates from the enjoyments of each other here, it will be for a very short time, and then we shall meet in such enjoyments as now we cannot conceive of, and forever enjoy each other's happiness."[3]

On September 30, 1685, Benjamin Hewling came to the place of execution, which was surrounded with spectators. His testimony of cheerfulness and joy gave evidence of the presence of God. There were all sorts of people present, including the soldiery, who were exceedingly affected and amazed at the composure and strength of this young martyr. God's grace is sufficient, no matter how trying the circumstance.

EWT

---

[1]J. Newton Brown, *Memorials of Baptist Martyrs* (Philadelphia: American Baptist Publication Society, 1854), p. 247.

[2]Ibid., p. 249.

[3]Ibid., p. 216.

October

October 1—New Hampshire's First Baptist Church

Scripture: I Peter 3:14-17

Though there is some question as to the date of the founding of the first Baptist church in New Hampshire (1750 or 1755), there is no doubt that Newtown (now Newton) was its location. The first record on the church books is October 1, 1767. We know nothing concerning the first days of the history of that church other than the fact that it was under attack by the standing order (state church), for we are given real insight into the earliest record extant.

The record is as follows:

1. John Wadleigh was chosen moderator.
2. Joseph Welch was chosen clerk.
3. Voted, To carry on Mr. Stewart's and Mr. Carter's lawsuits which are now in the law on account of rates imposed on them by the standing order.[1]

The remainder of the minutes dealt with the salary to be given to the pastor, Mr. Hovey. Three men were appointed to the oversight of securing the pastor's wages, and it was further decided that any men who refused to participate in providing the annual compensation of £50 would not have the protection of the local assembly against the demands of the standing order.

It was hoped that the case of Mr. Stewart and Mr. Carter could have been settled early in their favor, but such apparently was not so. Almost three years later the church met again (June 25, 1770) and spent the entire business meeting in discussion of the lawsuit.

Another historian has written, "It is as refreshing as a breeze from their own mountains to find so much human 'granite' in this little band of New Hampshire Baptists. They refuse to support a State Church by force, and they resolve to support their own chosen pastor cheerfully. . . . Such a Church deserved to live, and it exists today.''[2]

The work of the Baptists in New Hampshire grew very slowly following the establishment of the church in Newton. In his centennial address, William Lamson concluded his remarks by saying:

> Unquestionably the constant persecutions and repeated litigations to which the Baptists were subjected in those years had much to do in retarding their growth (in New Hampshire). The standing order believed that it was the church of God, and that it was truly serving God in compelling the Baptists and other Separatists into conformity, as they were in the prayer closet or in the worship of the sanctuary. Scattered over the state there may have been many of our faith who were longing and praying for the time when they should be permitted to worship God and obey his ordinances, with none to molest or make them afraid. But the difficulty, under the circumstances, of sustaining churches, deterred them from becoming organized. They were as sheep not having a shepherd.[3]

Baptists have ever maintained that the government has only to do with the collection of taxes, the protection of its citizenry, and the punishment of criminals who break the law and that the separation of church and state alone guarantees the freedom of worship. These principles are true and must ever characterize Baptist life and thought.

DLC

---

[1]John T. Christian, *A History of the Baptists* (1922; reprint ed., Nashville: Broadman Press, 1926), p. 144.

[2]Thomas Armitage, *The History of the Baptists* (1890; reprint ed., Watertown, Wis.: Maranatha Baptist Press, 1976), 2:765.

[3]Christian, p. 147.

October 2—Rediscovering the Great Commission

Scripture: Isaiah 54:2-3

When we consider the modern missionary movement among Baptists, it is necessary for us to realize that our forefathers were forced for years to worship in clandestine assemblies for fear of persecution. As a result, believers had long forgotten the Great Commission of our Lord. To be sure, there was personal witnessing, but it was well nigh impossible to carry the gospel into other nations of the world.

As God's people studied the Scriptures, God awakened their hearts to the great need. One group upon which the Holy Spirit moved was the Northamptonshire Baptist Association in England. "At the meeting of the association in 1784, at Nottingham, it was resolved to set apart an hour on the first Monday evening of every month, 'for extraordinary prayer for the revival of religion, and for the extending of Christ's kingdom in the world.' This suggestion proceeded from the venerable (John) Sutcliff."[1]

Continually from 1787 to 1790, the Reverend William Carey presented the importance of missionary effort. Few were found who sympathized with his entreaties. For example, on one occasion when Mr. Ryland requested one of the younger ministers to propose a topic of discussion, Carey suggested, "The duty of Christians to attempt the spread of the Gospel among heathen nations." Mr. Ryland censured Carey and referred to him as a mere enthusiast for considering such a notion.

However, Carey persisted in his passion for missions and wrote an essay entitled, "An Inquiry into the Obligation of Christians to Use Means for the Conversion of the Heathen." Thomas Potts had the essay printed in tract form, and the pamphlet had a marked influence.

At the May meeting of the Northamptonshire Association in 1792, Carey preached a sermon from Isaiah 54:2-3 and divided his message into two thrusts:

1. Expect great things from God;
2. Attempt great things for God.

The pastors were greatly moved and passed a resolution

> that against the next minister's meeting at Kettering, a plan should be prepared for the purpose of forming a society for propagating the Gospel among the heathen.
>
> At the Kettering meeting, on the second of October, the society was formally incorporated; and the first subscription, made on the spot, amounted to E13. 2s. 6d. This sum, though really small, was comparatively large; for it was the contribution of a few poor but enlightened servants of Jesus Christ.[2]

We honor William Carey and the pastors of the Northamptonshire Association for their vision of a lost world. On this date so many years ago, our brethren accepted anew the call of our Lord to take the gospel into all the world. The entries for April 4, July 20, and August 17 also address this subject. May we dedicate ourselves afresh to the task of worldwide evangelism in presenting the message of redemption as long as there are open doors. Our living Lord is still calling His own to go into all the world and preach the gospel to every person.

DLC

---

[1]F. A. Cox, *History of the Baptist Missionary Society* (London: T. Ward and G. J. Dyer, 1842), 1:10.

[2]Ibid., pp. 17-18.

October 3—A Physician, a Lawyer, and a Baptist Preacher

Scripture: Hebrews 6

John Clarke was an important instrument in the establishment of religious liberty in Rhode Island and the American colonies. It is interesting and somewhat confusing to note that many of these early Baptists in America, step by step, gradually embraced Baptist principles. Often they left the English state church and joined the ranks of the Dissenters because they were moved by the horrible persecutions of the sects, and thus they ultimately became persuaded of believers baptism and freedom of conscience as biblical truth. The corruption among the state-church clergy, spiritual deadness among the congregation, and the persecution of the Dissenters were often catalysts that triggered the Separatist movement.

This appears to be the case in the life of John Clarke, who was born in Suffolk County, England, on October 3, 1609, and received pedobaptism five days later.[1] It is clear that he was well educated, and because the University of Leyden shows a "Johannes Clarke" among its students in 1635, some conclude that he attended that famous Dutch school and while there became acquainted with Dutch Baptists. Clarke was a reputable physician, occasionally a lawyer, an able statesman and diplomat, and a successful Baptist pastor.

Exactly at what point John Clarke became a Baptist is not clear, but it is apparent that he was persuaded that Baptist principles had their origin in the Word of God, and these principles became deeply rooted convictions that motivated him to separate from the Puritan movement of New England. We do know that he was among those that were relieved of weapons by the Boston authorities in 1637 on suspicion of being "tinged with anabaptism."[2]

There was a church in Portsmouth by 1638 that had two factions. One group held for the authority of the "inner light," and the other held for the authority of the written Scripture. The controversy led to a division, and the church scattered. Clarke led a group and set up a church at Newport where, under his leadership, it became distinctly

Baptist and remained for the rest of the century as one of the leading Baptist churches in America.

Satan endeavored to destroy this small witness in its early years by introducing serious doctrinal differences. While Clarke and most of the members were Particular Baptists, the membership included some General Baptists as well. They were often called "Six Principle Baptists" because they insisted upon the six points of Hebrews 6:1-2, which included the laying on of hands following the baptism of new converts which Particular Baptists did not always follow. Around 1655 or 1656, the Newport Church split with the withdrawal of twenty-one members who held to general redemption, opposed singing as a part of worship, and practiced the laying on of hands. Later, Stephen Mumford, who is called the first "Sabbatarian" Baptist in America, came and propagated "seventh-day" views among the members.

John Clarke courageously faced many of the same problems we are confronted with today. Thank God for Clarke's courage, faithfulness, and perseverance. God grant us these qualities and also enable us to leave to our posterity a witness well-grounded in truth.

EWT

---

[1]H. Leon McBeth, *The Baptist Heritage* (Nashville: Broadman Press, 1987), p. 137.

[2]Ibid.

October 4—From a Barren Wilderness to a Fruitful Pulpit

Scripture: I Kings 19:9-21

Not all servants of God who were used effectually in propagating the gospel of Jesus Christ had the advantages of much formal education. God often used other means of molding their lives and preparing them for the great work they would accomplish. Thus it was in the life of John Peck, who was born October 31, 1789, in Stanford, New York, as the fifth son and eighth child of John and Sarah Peck.

When the boy was fifteen his father moved into a part of the state that was almost an unbroken wilderness. These primitive conditions necessitated the constant hard labor of John's brothers and deprived John of an early education. However, from his father John inherited the natural abilities, great energies, and capability to learn from observation and experience; from his mother's pious example and instruction, blended with uncommon native force of mind, great prudence, cheerfulness, and affection, his character was formed early in life. His mother, a member of a Baptist church, taught him how to pray and inspired him with a love of the Bible and an eager desire for knowledge. This instruction laid a broad and deep foundation for that intelligence and piety for which he was afterwards distinguished.[1]

The school of the wilderness with its hard labor of axe and plow, as well as its deprivations, did not discourage Peck's intense desire for education. Upon attaining adulthood, he purchased a small farm and continued to invest a portion of his time in labor and superintendence, but he also gave himself to self-education from such appropriate books that were available to provide a systematic course of study.

After making a profession of faith, Peck was baptized August 25, 1798, and became a member of the newly constituted Baptist church at Norwich, New York, when he reached his eighteenth year. Shortly thereafter, he began to preach as a licentiate and was married to Sarah Ferris, a daughter of Deacon Israel Ferris and sister to Elder Jonathan Ferris of the Baptist church at Norwich. Sarah made him an excellent wife and shared his joys, sorrows, and labors for almost a half century. In 1804 Peck accepted the pastorate of the First Baptist Church in Cazenovia, New York, where his labors were rewarded with great revivals and in-gatherings of large numbers of converts. He became the agent of the Baptist Missionary Convention and later the Baptist Home Mission Society. From 1839 to 1847, he reported that he had traveled 26,840 miles, received support for the society, assisted pastors, and preached revivals.

Peck's life was touched with trials, culminating with the death of his beloved wife Sarah, followed by the death of his youngest son, Linus, a few days later on October 4, 1847. Linus had just completed his ministerial training and had entered the ministry. He had given himself to care for an ailing brother in the faith, but contracting the disease, he joined his mother in the presence of the Lord.

At difficult times may we remember John Peck, who was conformed to the image of his Savior through the influence of a godly home, the rigors of taming a wilderness, the challenges of the ministry, and the sufferings of the loss of loved ones. May we be submissive to the discipline of trials and allow God to conform us to His will.

EWT

---

[1]William B. Sprague, *Annals of the American Pulpit* (New York: Robert Carter and Bros., 1865), 6:432.

October 5—Three Centuries with the Same Message

Scripture: Jeremiah 1:4-9

The earliest Baptist preachers in America were a vigorous, energetic group of men who were assured of their call of God and who were willing to give themselves at all costs to the ministry. In the eighteenth century, men such as Elisha Rich made a spiritual impact on their communities as they labored to support their families and preach the gospel. Ordained on October 5, 1774, Rich took the pastoral responsibility of the Chelmsford, Massachusetts, Baptist church. He used his skills as a blacksmith, gunsmith, farmer, and bookkeeper to sustain his family. Persecution was to be expected, and he suffered " 'no little rough opposition,' his livestock was injured, the pulpit in the meetinghouse was set to fall when he ascended it, and he was otherwise harassed."[1] But those hearty souls persevered, and the work of God expanded.

By the nineteenth century, the overt opposition had all but ended, but the same determination was revealed in the lives of Baptist pastors. The population had increased, and now many of the men of God found themselves responsible for overseeing the ministries of three or four scattered congregations. They continued to support their families, but now their ministerial responsibilities were multiplied. Such a man was the Reverend Christopher Columbus Metcalf, the author's grandfather. He was born on March 10, 1855, and ministered the Word of God faithfully for fifty-two years. For some time C. C. Metcalf served as a circuit-riding pastor in the hills of Kentucky and had the care of four churches. Though possessing a good formal training and having a sufficient pastoral library, Grandpa Metcalf farmed through the week, and then on Saturday at noon he mounted his horse and rode to his first church. Upon his arrival there, he would release his horse, and the animal would make its way back to its stall at home. Most of the churches had services on Saturday night and Sunday as well, for they had meetings on only one Sunday a month! Grandpa would preach on Saturday evening and then remain in the home of one of his deacons. Into the late hours of Saturday night, Metcalf would give the deacon instructions for Sunday school classes and services for the next three Sundays. Following the Sunday morning service, Pastor Metcalf would ride in someone's wagon in the direction of his home and then walk or "hitch" a ride back to his house. Grandpa did this so that the family would have the horse on Sunday! This schedule was repeated each Saturday as he left home at noon in a different direction that he might minister to yet another congregation.

America owes a great debt to ministers who invested their lives in spreading the gospel, for it was that message that became the foundation of our civilization. Those early preachers were willing to "spend and be spent" for the Lord Jesus Christ. Pastor Metcalf experienced times of refreshment when communities were transformed by the gospel. I have followed his path as a Baptist preacher in the twentieth century. Surely times have changed, but I cannot help wondering if we have a "professionalism" that negates the magnetism of the message. Surely it is only the Word of God activated by the Holy Spirit that produces life, but I wonder if our suave, smooth mannerisms have not served to produce a superficial form rather than a supernatural force for righteousness. May God give us that old-time tenacity and dedication to "minister and give" rather than to "perform and receive!"

DLC

---

[1]William G. McLoughlin, ed., *The Diary of Isaac Backus* (Providence: Brown University Press, 1979), 2:610.

October 6—Lies, the Tool of Satan Against God's Servants

Scripture: I Kings 21:1-15

Thomas Grantham, a faithful and laborious minister of Christ, began to seek the Lord very early. Upon publicly making a profession of his faith by being baptized, he joined himself to the church of the immersed which gathered at Boston, Lincolnshire, England, when he was about the age of nineteen. In exercising his gifts of preaching, Grantham soon became the object of Satan's hate and was thrown into the Lincoln jail. As was true of Bunyan and many other faithful sufferers for Christ, he occupied his time by writing. His first tract bore the title *The Prisoner Against the Prelate* and set forth the reasons for separation from the Church of England.[1]

A small group of believers in Lincolnshire who resolved to keep the biblical principle of immersion only upon profession of faith in Jesus Christ called Grantham to be their pastor when he was only twenty-two years of age. Under his ministry they grew and sent forth several ministers to preach the gospel. Though they were respected by many, their prosperity attracted the attention of the established clergy, who by warrants brought Thomas Grantham before the magistrates. The clergy had nothing but forged stories and lies to support their accusations. The magistrates, seeing through these false accusations, set Grantham and the others free. Satan often uses of false accusations to discredit and slander God's faithful servants. Much later, the former rector of Tattershall in Lincolnshire confessed to Thomas Blofield of Norwich on October 6, 1691, that he had lied about Grantham.[2]

In spite of all this, they went on cheerfully and publicly preached the Word of God, though they were often set upon by mobs who would rudely interrupt their discourses and drag them out of doors and stone them. As a result of the imprisonment of some one hundred Baptists, the levying of some three hundred fines, as well as presentments and excommunications by the hundreds in the commissary courts, Grantham and another messenger were sent by the Baptists to wait upon King Charles II with a humble remonstrance. After praising God for the indulgence and setting forth their rights of liberty of conscience, they besought the king "to leave them to the light of Scripture, with respect to the exercise of those spiritual gifts of prayer and preaching in their assemblies, according to their abilities for the edification of the church."[3]

It can be said that Thomas Grantham was the person who greatly encouraged the Baptists in their sufferings at Lincolnshire and directed them in all their proceedings. For every period of great persecution, God raises up men of deep conviction and strong character to lead His people. May our local churches provide the spiritual atmosphere that will cultivate many strong leaders for a future that holds many opportunities and many adversaries.

EWT

---

[1]Thomas Crosby, *The History of English Baptists* (1738-40; reprint ed., Lafayette, Tenn.: Church History Research and Archives, 1979), 3:77-78.

[2]Ibid., p. 262.

[3]Ibid.

October 7—The Golden-Voiced Orator

Scripture: John 1:29,36

Charles Haddon Spurgeon must have possessed an extraordinary vocal ability during his amazing ministry in London. One historian says, "He had the finest voice of any public man of his time."[1] We know also that George Whitefield also addressed huge crowds in America. "Benjamin Franklin measured the area reached by his voice and declared, 'I computed that he might well be heard by more than thirty thousand.' "[2] In these days of public address systems and lapel microphones, few preachers have cultivated the art of projecting their voices.

Return with me to the days of young Spurgeon. He was called to the New Park Street Church on April 19, 1854. Within a year's time, it was absolutely necessary to secure a larger building. In less than three years, the congregation had grown by 425 per cent! Thus, in February of 1855, the Exeter Hall was secured, and when the crowds continued to increase, the congregation moved on October 19, 1856, to the Royal Surrey Gardens. This edifice with its three tiers of galleries would seat twelve thousand persons. Since the days of Whitefield and Wesley, no preacher had ministered to so large an audience. When the doors were opened, waiting crowds poured in, filled every seat, and crowded the aisles. Thousands of others outside refused to leave. One Sunday as Spurgeon, only twenty-two years of age, rose to pray, someone in a gallery shouted, "Fire," and another voice on the ground floor called, "The galleries are falling," and yet another person shouted and panic struck the hall. People rushed to leave while those outside rushed to get in. Under all the force, a stair railing gave way, and pandemonium set it. Spurgeon tried to quiet the crowd, but his efforts were in vain. He went to a side room and, overcome with grief, fell to the floor. His deacons realized how sensitive their young pastor was, and they whisked him away to the suburbs. Tragically, seven persons died and twenty-eight were hospitalized. This was almost the undoing of the young pastor, but the Lord comforted his heart, and his burden was lifted. Spurgeon returned to the pulpit having missed just one Sunday.

For a period of three years, from November 1856 to December of 1859, the morning services were held in Surrey Hall, and the crowds were greater than ever. The average attendance for those three years was in excess of ten thousand.

> The all-time attendance record, "the greatest crowd ever addressed by a Gospel preacher," (to that time) was set on October 7, 1857, in Spurgeon's twenty-third year. The occasion was a fast-day service held in the central transept of the cyclopean Crystal Palace, a building so large that it was "apparently unenclosed for vastness." By turnstile count, 23,654 persons were present. . . .
>
> Another interesting incident in connection with this . . . meeting was Spurgeon's private afternoon acoustical test in the empty building. He lifted his golden voice and cried, "Behold the Lamb of God which taketh away the sin of the world." A workman in a high gallery heard

the voice, was smitten with conviction, put down his tools, went home, and after a season of spiritual struggle, found peace and life by beholding the Lamb of God.[3]

The golden voice of Charles Haddon Spurgeon was silenced in death on January 31, 1892, but I am sure in resonant tones, he shouted, "Worthy is the Lamb" as he beheld his Lord and Savior!

DLC

---

[1]John C. Carlile, *The Story of the English Baptists* (London: James Clarke and Co., 1905), p. 237.

[2]Arnold A. Dallimore, *George Whitefield* (London: Banner of Truth Trust, 1970), p. 296.

[3]Richard Ellsworth Day, *The Shadow of the Broad Brim* (Philadelphia: Judson Press, 1934), p. 98.

October 8—The Preaching, the Printing, the Prison, and the Pillory

Scripture: Galatians 6

Benjamin Keach had no small share in the sufferings of the Baptists in England during the persecutions of the middle seventeenth century. He was often seized while preaching and committed to prison, sometimes bound. Sometimes he was released upon bail, and sometimes his life was threatened.

On one such occasion when troopers were sent to Buckinghamshire to suppress the Dissenters, they discovered Keach preaching. Their rage was so great that they swore they would kill the preacher by trampling him to death with their horses. This they prepared to do by binding him and laying him on the ground. Just as they were about to spur their horses, an officer rode up and interposed, thus preventing their violent intentions. Instead Keach was tied and placed across the horse of one of the troopers and carried to the jail, where, after some hardships and suffering, he was released.[1]

Keach wrote a little book in 1664 entitled *The Child's Instructor; or, A New and Easier Primer*. Some of his friends desired him to print it for the use of their children, and thus he sent it to London, where it was published without his name affixed to it. In this book he asserted that infants ought not to be baptized, that laymen having abilities may preach the gospel, and that Christ would reign personally upon the earth in the latter day.

Soon a justice of the peace and a constable appeared at his door, seized all of his books that could be found, and bound him over to the court. His trial began October 8, 1664, and the judge's opening remarks reflected on Keach's character and profession. The judge accused him of wresting the Scriptures in his preaching and writing a creed to his own and other's destruction. Keach was not permitted by the judge to defend his writings. The judge said, "You shall not preach here, nor give the reasons of your damnable doctrine to seduce and infect the king's subjects."

Keach was denied a copy of the indictment, which was lengthy, before he made a plea. Thus he pleaded not guilty to the charges. He was once again denied the privilege of defending his writings. Following long deliberations and instructions from the judge, the jury reluctantly declared him guilty as charged. Obviously, the trial was carried on in a very arbitrary manner, and a verdict was extorted against him.

The judge sentenced Keach to prison for two weeks and to stand in the pillory in the market place at Aylesbury with a paper upon his head which accused him of publishing a schismatical book. He was to pay a fine of twenty pounds to give surety that he would appear in the next court to recant his doctrines. At another time Keach stood in the pillory at Winslow where the hangman carried out another part of the sentence by publicly burning his book before his eyes.[2]

The mob, who usually got sport out of hooting and pelting the pilloried with eggs, listened eagerly to Keach as he preached from the Scriptures. The sheriff was enraged and threatened to gag Keach. The incensed sheriff also accused Keach's faithful wife, who was standing by, of providing Keach with a Bible.

Benjamin Keach exhibited great courage under very trying circumstances, and God granted him a long and fruitful ministry. Lord, provide for us in the hour of our trial!

EWT

---

[1]Thomas Crosby, *The History of English Baptists* (1738-40; reprint ed., Lafayette, Tenn.: Church History Research and Archives, 1979), 2:185-208.

[2]Thomas Armitage, *The History of the Baptists* (1890; reprint ed., Watertown, Wis.: Maranatha Baptist Press, 1976), 2:547-48.

October 9—The "Real" McCoys

Scripture: Proverbs 23:29-31

Christiana Polk was well acquainted with the stories of the Indians in early America, for she was the daughter of Captain E. Polk, a soldier and pioneer of the country. Prior to Christiana's birth, her mother and three siblings had been captured by the Ottawa Indians and held prisoners for several years before being found and freed by the valiant husband and father. It is surely amazing, therefore, that following her marriage on October 6, 1803, to Mr. Isaac McCoy, the Lord should lead this splendid couple to pioneer missionary work among Indians of that tribe.

Surely no family made a greater sacrificial contribution in the spiritual welfare of the American Indians than the McCoy family. Isaac and Christiana had thirteen children, and they were all raised primarily in the moving frontiers. The children knew the privations of early missionary living but apparently entered willingly into the necessary sacrifices. This is evidenced by the fact that the two oldest sons, after having graduated from the Columbian College in Washington, D.C., and the Kentucky Medical College of Lexington, Kentucky, both died in severe weather as they traveled on behalf of the missionary labors of their father. The dedication of the family was a tribute indeed to Mrs. McCoy since her husband was gone so much of the time.

We have given a general description of the work of the Reverend Isaac McCoy in the entry of February 11. However, it is instructive to mention that he was ordained on October 13, 1810, by his father (the Reverend William McCoy) and the Reverend George Waller. Isaac's older brother, James McCoy, was an ordained pastor as was his younger brother, Rice McCoy. The younger brother is "supposed to have been the first white child born in the North Western Territory."[1]

The Reverend Isaac McCoy's life is amazing when we consider the fact that he authored a six hundred-page book on the *History of Baptist Indian Missions* without a "study" or secretarial help in the midst of his incessant traveling.

He also championed the cause of moving the Indians to west of the Mississippi, for "the first obstacle that he encountered, (in his effort to evangelize) and that which proved to be the greatest handicap to his work, was the white man's liquor among these Indians. This proved a veritable fire-water to them. They acted as men possessed when they drank this liquor."[2] McCoy became, therefore, one of the leading proponents of moving the Indians to the Far West.

Of all the "firsts" that were attained by the Reverend Isaac McCoy, one of the most interesting occurred on "October 9, 1825, [when] McCoy preached the first sermon in English ever delivered in Chicago or near its site."[3] Little could Isaac McCoy have envisioned the thriving metropolis that now sprawls in that area, and he shall ever have the honor of being Chicago's premier preacher! "His life and labors were truly the connecting link between barbarism and civilization in this region of the country and over a large portion of the West. His perseverance and devotion were morally and heroically sublime. For nearly thirty years he was the apostle to the Indians of the West.''[4]

DLC

[1]William B. Sprague, *Annals of the American Pulpit* (New York: Robert Carter and Bros., 1865), 6:544.

[2]Walter Sinclair Stewart, *Early Baptist Missionaries and Pioneers* (Philadelphia: Judson Press, 1925), p. 205.

[3]William Cathcart, *The Baptist Encyclopedia,* ed. Louis H. Everts (Philadelphia: Louis H. Everts, 1881), p. 766.

[4]Ibid., p. 767.

October 10—A God-Blessed Historian

Scripture: Psalm 78:4-7

David Benedict, the famed Baptist historian, was born into a splendid New England family that traced its roots back to 1500 in Nottinghamshire, England. David was born to Thomas and Abigail Benedict on October 10, 1779, and at an early age he cultivated an affection for reading. His greatest interest was in searching out histories, and he availed himself of such literature during every spare moment.

When the lad was fourteen, Benedict was apprenticed to a shoemaker and for seven years labored in that trade. His ability secured for him a proposal to form a partnership for the manufacturing and retailing of shoes, but his conversion at age twenty changed the course of his life. In December 1799 he was baptized in the Housatonic River and united with the First Baptist Church of Stratford. In 1802 he gave up his career as a shoemaker and entered the academy of the Reverend Stephen S. Nelson at Mount Pleasant, New York. During the next two years, he partially paid his expenses by tutoring younger pupils. Francis Wayland, future president of Brown University, was one of his students during that time.[1]

Upon completion of his studies under the Reverend Mr. Nelson's direction, Benedict entered Brown University in 1804 and graduated in 1806. He presented an oration on Ecclesiastic History at the graduation ceremonies that year. Two years later, Benedict was united in marriage to a daughter of Dr. Stephen Gano. The Benedicts were happily married for sixty years and had a family of nine sons and three daughters.

During his years of college training, Benedict preached for the Baptists in Pawtucket and spent his summers ministering there as well. This resulted in the establishment of the First Baptist Church of Pawtucket, and following his graduation, Benedict was ordained and became pastor of that church, a ministry he continued for twenty-five years. America's first Baptist Sunday school was begun there as well (cf. September 15). In 1816 the pastor was chosen to serve as a trustee of his alma mater, and at the time of his death, he had been the senior member of the board of trustees for sixteen years.

> Dr. Benedict had for many years been engaged in collecting materials for the *History of the Baptists in the United States*, and to some extent, in other countries, and had already printed several volumes relating to the subject. These materials had been collected in various journeys and by an extensive correspondence. He now determined to devote himself to the further prosecution of this and of kindred plans of literary labor. For the purpose of facilitating the correspondence which these plans involved, he obtained an appointment as postmaster at Pawtucket and held that office for ten years, the work, however, being principally done by his sons. In labors of this and of kindred kinds, he passed the remaining years of his long life, after retiring from the active ministry.[2]

There was no public transportation at that time. Benedict traveled throughout the young nation and territory on horseback, covering nearly four thousand miles. He then sent out questionnaires and, through extensive correspondence, compiled and completed his history, which appeared in 1813.

Dr. Benedict lived to the age of ninety-five. Up until his death on December 5, 1874, his eyesight was unimpaired, and he was able to write clearly both day and night. Baptists are indebted to David Benedict for preserving so well our Baptist annals for coming generations.

DLC

---

[1]Elizabeth J. Johnson and James Lucas Wheaton IV, "The Annotated Index—Reminiscences and New Series of Rev. David Benedict," *History of Pawtucket, Rhode Island* (Pawtucket, R.I.: Spaulding House Publishing Co., 1986), p. xi.

[2]*Representative Men and Old Families of Rhode Island* (Chicago: J. H. Beers and Co., 1908), p. 1466.

October 11—And Have You Shown It to Jesus?

Scripture: I Timothy 2:1-8

Samuel Harriss, like many of his contemporaries, began exhorting and preaching immediately after his conversion. This instant involvement probably came about because he was baptized by Daniel Marshall and joined Dutton Lane's church. No one could be under the influence of these men and not be ignited with the fire of evangelism. Semple states, "During the first years of his ministry, he often travelled with Mr. Marshall; and must have caught much of his spirit. For there is obviously a considerable resemblance in their manner."[1]

For the first six or seven years, Harriss's labors were confined to the adjacent counties of Virginia and North Carolina. He was ordained a ruling elder in Lane's church in 1759. "His manners were of the most winning sort; having a singular talent at touching the feelings. He scarcely ever went into a house without exhorting and praying for those he met there."[2]

We have previously noted that upon the invitation of Allen Wyley of Culpeper County, Virginia, Samuel Harriss crossed the James River, exhorting and praying at every house he visited until he reached Wyley's house (cf. January 12 entry). After preaching the first day without disturbance, Harriss was met the next day with sticks, whips, and clubs in the hands of an angry mob. That night he went to Orange County and preached with much effect. He continued there many days with great crowds following wherever he went. On this journey he sowed many good seeds which later brought forth a great harvest.

It was not until October 11, 1769, that Harriss was ordained as an evangelist. His first candidate for baptism after ordination was James Ireland, who had traveled from Shenandoah County to the home of Harriss. Ireland was later confined in Culpeper jail for preaching without licensure. He describes Harriss as follows:

> I saw him ordained and a moving time it was. He was considered a great man in the things of time and sense; but he shone more conspicuously in the horizon of the church, during the time of our sweet intercourse together, so that he was like another Paul among the churches. No man like minded with him, who like a blazing comet, would rush through the colony or state displaying the banners of his adorable Master, spreading His light and diffusing His heat to the consolation of thousands.[3]

The remarkable anecdotes told of Harriss are so numerous that they would fill a volume. Just before his death, when he was somewhat over seventy years of age, a criminal who had just been pardoned at the gallows met him on the road and showed him his reprieve. "Well," said Harriss, "and have you shown it to Jesus?" "No, Mr. Harriss, I want you to do that for me." The old man immediately descended from his horse in the road, and after the former prisoner also alighted, they both kneeled down. Harriss put one hand on the man's head and held the other upon the pardon, in behalf of the criminal. Harriss then returned thanks for the reprieve and thus prayed for the criminal to obtain God's pardon as well.[4]

EWT

---

[1]Robert B. Semple, *A History of the Rise and Progress of the Baptists in Virginia* (Richmond: Published by the author, 1810), p. 378.

[2]Ibid., p. 379.

[3]Lewis Peyton Little, *Imprisoned Preachers and Religious Liberty in Virginia* (Lynchburg, Va.: J. P. Bell Co., 1938), p. 151.

[4]Ibid., p. 157.

October 12—A Humble Patriot, Preacher, and Businessman

Scripture: Acts 18:1-11

In the annals of Baptist history there are multitudes of unsung heroes of the faith. Because there has not been the unscriptural establishment of a human religious hierarchy, their names have often disappeared from the records of this world, but they are recorded on the eternal annals of heaven.

Thus it was with John Pitman, who was born into a family that moved about frequently because of the father's mercantile pursuits. His father's death left his mother with several small children. In his youth his parents had taught him to reverence the Bible and to be faithful in church attendance. Because of the circumstances of his family, he was apprenticed as a rope-maker. He became increasingly dissolute and profane and continued in sin for a period of about four years. Sometime in 1769 he resolved to change his course and launch out into a life of self-righteous effort. He prayed three times a day, strictly observed the Sabbath, and fasted from Saturday until Sunday night. However, these works gave him no peace of heart or mind.

While in this state of mind, Pitman inquired of Dr. Stillman, pastor of the First Baptist Church of Boston. Stillman counseled him with the gospel of God's grace, and eventually Pitman experienced salvation, was baptized, and was received into the church.

When the British soldiers fired on the citizens of Boston, March 5, 1770, Pitman was close to one of the victims who was shot. He later mounted guard on that memorable night. He became a volunteer in the first battalion of the Pennsylvania militia, under the command of Colonel Dickenson.

John Pitman was engaged in secular business but accepted the call from the Baptist church in Upper Freehold, New Jersey, October 12, 1777.[1] His life testified of a great Christian firmness and showed that his patriotism was tempered and directed by his piety. As did many Baptists, he supported the American Revolution and continued with his secular occupation throughout much of his ministry. These men were engaged in many different kinds of professions and devoted no small part of their time to the study of God's Word. Pitman traveled extensively from Philadelphia to Rhode Island, going everywhere preaching the gospel, and, on many occasions, serving local churches when they were in need.

It was said of Pitman, "He was a man of remarkable firmness, and of great courage, physical and moral. . . . In all his dealings with his fellowman, he evinced the strictest integrity."[2]

May this go down as a memorial to the thousands of Baptist preachers who sustained their families with hard labor, burned the midnight oil to prepare their hearts and minds with the Word of the God to feed the flocks, and also evangelized their part of the great harvest field. Thank God He equips some men with the strength and stamina to carry on such a ministry.

EWT

---

[1]William B. Sprague, *Annals of the American Pulpit* (New York: Robert Carter and Bros., 1865), 6:198.

[2]Ibid., p. 199.

October 13—Humiliation, Fasting, and Prayer

Scripture: Matthew 22:1-14

The Philadelphia Association of Regular Baptists convened at Hopewell, New Jersey, October 13, 1778, and was opened with a suitable discourse from Elder Abel Morgan from Matthew 22:4. "Again he sent forth other servants, saying, Tell them which are bidden, Behold, I have prepared my dinner: my oxen and my fatlings are killed, and all things are ready; come unto the marriage." His message reflected the spirit of urgency that the entire association felt. The young nation was engaged in war with a formidable enemy, and things did not look good at all for the Continental Army. Their minutes record their concern:

> The Association, deeply impressed with a sense of the calamities of the times, the prevalence of vice and profanity, and the declension of vital piety:
>
> Resolved, To recommend to the churches to observe four days, the ensuing year, of humiliation, fasting and prayer, and abstinence from labor and recreation; viz., the second Thursday in November, February, May and August; and they entreat the same day religiously observed in a solemn and devout manner.[1]

The United States of America through the years has sent its young men by the hundreds of thousands into battles around the world. It seems that every generation needs to be ''deeply impressed'' with the calamities that confront it. How tragic that profanity, vice, and declension of personal piety characterize modern generations. These faults did not generally characterize the American Patriots of 1778. Surely every generation needs to humble itself before God, making similar confessions as the prophet Daniel, who prayed, ''We have sinned, and have committed iniquity, and have done wickedly, and have rebelled, even by departing from thy precepts and from thy judgments. . . . I ate no pleasant bread, neither came flesh nor wine in my mouth, neither did I anoint myself at all, till three whole weeks were fulfilled'' (Dan. 9:5; 10:3).

Current Christianity equates the matter of fasting to monastic living or to an act of religiosity. To complicate the matter, affluence makes it difficult for a people who have material abundance to understand the spiritual need for biblical fasting. May our Lord bring us to the awareness of spiritual and moral perils so that we might respond in humility, fasting, and prayer. Our forefathers experienced revival, and the nation enjoyed any number of spiritual awakenings. May our souls hunger and thirst for such seasons of refreshing; then may our spiritual leadership call the people apart and sanctify definite days of humiliation (repentance), fasting, and prayer. Our changeless God has promised to answer such intensity of heart.

''Wilt thou not revive us again: that thy people may rejoice in thee?'' (Ps. 85:6).

EWT

---

[1]A. D. Gillette, ed., *Minutes of the Philadelphia Baptist Association from A.D. 1707 to A.D. 1807* (1851; reprint ed., Minneapolis: James Publishing Co., n.d.), p. 159.

October 14—By Whom Should a Church Be Supported?

Scripture: Matthew 17:24-25

When the First Continental Congress met in 1774 in Philadelphia with delegates from all of the thirteen colonies except Georgia, they were intent upon discussing the common concerns of the uncertain future. Serving as agent for the Warren Baptist Association, the Reverend Isaac Backus appeared to petition the Congress for an end to the use of public funds for any church or religious group. He had already written an article entitled "An Appeal to the Public for Religious Liberty," and in it he had said,

> It appears to us that the true difference and exact limits between ecclesiastical and civil government is this, That the church is armed with light and truth, to pull down the strongholds of iniquity, and to gain souls to Christ, and into His Church . . . while the state is armed with the sword to guard the peace, and the civil rights of all persons and societies, and to punish those who violate the same. . . . I before declared that the Scripture is abundantly clear for a free support of ministers, but not a forced one; and observed, that there is as much difference between them, as there is between the power of truth in the mind and the power of the sword in the body.[1]

The call for the Continental Congress had originated in Massachusetts. Thus the Massachusetts Baptists arranged for a conference with the representatives from their state. The meeting took place on October 14, 1774, in Carpenters Hall. Dr. James Manning read the petition from the Association, and Isaac Backus explained it.

John Adams, leader of the Massachusetts delegation, was obviously upset by the plea from the Baptists. Answering the grievances of the Baptists, John Adams gave a lengthy speech, and Samuel Adams spoke as well. Both of them claimed, "There is indeed an ecclesiastical establishment in our province but a very slender one, hardly to be called an establishment."[2] In their lengthy reply, they attempted to divide the Baptist brethren, but Backus replied, "It is absolutely a point of conscience with me; for I cannot give in the certificates they require [i.e., a complicated exemption certificate], without implicitly acknowledging that power in man which I believe belongs only to God."[3]

"John Adams closed the four-hour discussion with a promise that the Massachusetts delegates would do what they could for the relief of the Baptists, then, according to Backus, added these words: 'Gentlemen, if you mean to try to effect a change in Massachusetts laws respecting religion, you may as well attempt to change the course of the sun in the heavens!' "[4]

Unfortunately, that promise was not kept. "John Adams returned home and reported that Mr. Backus had been to Philadelphia to try to break up the union of the colonies. It is well for us as a nation, that all the country's leaders had not the same contracted view of liberty."[5]

We thank God for other leaders who saw the issue more clearly, but we praise the Lord as well for our Baptist forefathers who refused to be intimidated and paid the price to secure religious freedom, not merely for those who agreed denominationally with them but for all Americans! Religious freedom as we know it today in our great land is, in large measure, attributable to our Baptist forefathers.

DLC

---

[1]O. K. and Marjorie Armstrong, *The Baptists in America* (New York: Doubleday and Co., 1979), p. 97.

[2]William G. McLoughlin, ed., *The Diary of Isaac Backus* (Providence: Brown University Press, 1979), 2:916.

[3]Ibid., p. 917.

[4]Armstrong and Armstrong, p. 99.

[5]Richard B. Cook, *The Story of the Baptists* (Baltimore: H. M. Wharton and Co., 1886), p. 236.

October 15—A Strong Woman of Faith Jailed

Scripture: Psalm 37:12-15

Previous entries have mentioned the unconscionable taxation of Baptists to support the established churches in the various colonies in early America. Doubtless, the situation in Massachusetts was the most severe. Women as well as aged men were imprisoned for their refusal to conform. The following letter from Mrs. Elizabeth Backus, a fifty-four-year-old widow and mother of the Reverend Isaac Backus, gives much light on the trials of that day.

> Norwich, Nov. 4th, 1752. My Dear Son, I have heard something of the trials amongst you of late, and I was grieved, till I had strength to

> give up the case to God, and leave my burden there. And now I would tell you something of our trials. Your brother Samuel lay in prison twenty days. October 15th, the collectors came to our house, and took me away to prison, about nine o'clock, in a dark, rainy night. Brothers Hill and Sabins were brought there the next night. We lay in prison thirteen days, and were then set at liberty, by what means I know not. Whilst I was there, a great many people came to see me, and some said one thing and some said another. Oh, the innumerable snares and temptations that beset me! more than I ever thought of before. But oh, the condescension of Heaven! though I was bound when I was cast into this furnace, yet I was loosed and found Jesus in the midst of a furnace with me. Oh, then I could give up my name, estate, family, life and breath, freely to God. Now the prison looked like a palace to me. I could bless God for all the laughs and scoffs made at me. Oh, the love flowed out to all mankind! then I could forgive as I would desire to be forgiven, and love my neighbor as myself. Deacon Griswold was put in prison the 8th of October; and yesterday old brother Grover; and they are in pursuit of others, all which calls for humiliation. The Church has appointed the 13th of November to be spent in prayer and fasting on that account. I do remember my love to you and your wife, and the dear children of God with you, begging your prayers for us in such a day of trial. We are all in tolerable health, expecting to see you. These from your loving mother, Elizabeth Backus.[1]

In 1770 when the Baptists of Ashfield, Massachusetts, refused to pay the tax for the support of the Congregational minister, ''398 acres of their land were seized, together with their homes, cattle, crops, and graveyards—constituting everything of many families, and sold to pay the tax.''[2] ''In the year 1728, an Act was passed by the General Court of Massachusetts, exempting Baptists from the tax; but as it relieved the persons only, but left the property still liable, it was of little service. Other acts were afterwards passed, to be in force for short periods, professedly to give relief; but they were clogged with so many difficulties and obnoxious conditions, that the Baptists continued to suffer, and in many places, and for many years.''[3]

''The persecutions of Baptists in Ashfield and Montague and Haverhill and Chelmsford and Bradford are known to all who know anything of our denominational history in New England, and its record is almost worthy to be bound in the same volume with the history of ecclesiastical persecution under Bloody Mary.''[4]

How unbelievable that elderly men and women would suffer because of their convictions. Such is our Baptist heritage, and we should praise God for it!

DLC

---

[1]Isaac Backus, *Your Baptist Heritage, 1620–1804,* (1844; reprint ed., Little Rock: Challenge Press, 1976), p. 127.

[2]Richard B. Cook, *The Story of the Baptists* (Baltimore: H. M. Wharton and Co., 1886), p. 234.

[3]J. M. Cramp, *Baptist History* (London: Elliott Stock, 1870), p. 454.

[4]Lemuel Moss, ed., *The Baptists and the National Centenary* (Philadelphia: American Baptist Publication Society, 1876), p. 22.

October 16—He Lived a Hero and Died a Martyr

Scripture: II Kings 23:1-30

John Moffett was born the youngest of four children to John and Sarah Moffett, October 16, 1858, in Culpeper County, Virginia. He was the great-nephew of the renowned Anderson Moffett, who began preaching at the age of seventeen and who was imprisoned in the Culpeper jail in colonial Virginia because he believed that the authority of Jesus Christ, who called him, was higher than the authority of the state that would regulate his ministry. John seemed to inherit the strength and courage of that Scotch-Irish family, who were "careful in business, true to their obligations, firm and unyielding in their avowed principles."[1]

The Civil War made a deep impression upon the young lad, as his home place became a vast arena where he viewed the devastation of that conflict. His father, from whom he received his first schooling, died when John was just nine years old, leaving his mother with four children and overwhelming grief. Shortly after the death of her husband, Sarah Moffett gathered her children around her bedside to read them an impassioned sermon on the awesome subject of heaven and hell by Charles Haddon Spurgeon. This made an impression on John, and later, at the age of fourteen, he was converted at a Methodist camp meeting. Ultimately he was baptized, along with his sister, in the Hazel River and joined the Gourdvine Baptist Church. During his teen years John was convinced that his life's calling was to be a minister.

After fulfilling some classical and biblical education, Moffett pastored some country churches, where he demonstrated a deep concern for the poor, needy, and orphaned. Upon accepting a call to the North Danville Baptist Church, he began "illustrating an abiding passion for two causes, the need for an orphanage and the need to combat the evils of alcohol." The former passion culminated in the founding of an orphanage in Salem, Virginia, while the latter resulted in a war with the liquor crowd that was well entrenched in the politics of that area. Surely his compassion for the poor and orphaned motivated him to fight the evil that causes so much poverty and neglect of children.

Moffett was a formidable force to contend with as he spoke and wrote against the evils of whiskey. The media of his day, as in ours, was lined up in favor of the moneyed liquor interests, forcing Moffett and his friends to publish a prohibitionist paper. Moffett attacked a politician named J. T. Clark, whom he believed to be controlled by the liquor crowd. Clark was so incensed that he gunned down Moffett on the street in Danville, Virginia, while the latter was on his way to a temperance meeting. The battle had waxed so hot and tempers had flared so out of control that "on the night of the murder, one of Clark's helpers went to a saloon and mockingly remarked that Clark 'had shot a dog in the street.' "

As his great-uncle Anderson Moffett was imprisoned for his faith nearly a century before, John Moffett was martyred for his stand against the curses of liquor and the criminal element that profits from the suffering and pain of others. The inscription on his tombstone best describes him: "He lived a hero and died a martyr."[3]

What a privilege to live and die for Jesus Christ and the principles of His Word! May we live by those same principles and not be governed by our lust for fame or fortune.

EWT

---

[1]Fred Anderson, "John Roberts Moffett: Virginia Baptists' Martyr for Temperance," *Virginia Baptist Register* (published by the Virginia Baptist Historical Society) No. 26 (1987), p. 1301.

[2]Ibid.

[3]Ibid.

October 17—A Missionary Conceived in His Father's Heart

Scripture: Hebrews 11:8-16

Missionaries are sometimes "born" before they are born. These potential "missionaries" are conceived in the hearts of parents who love the Lord and are committed to God's mandate to reach the world with the gospel. Such Christian parents dedicate their unborn children to the Lord.

A missionary was born in Darlington, South Carolina, on October 17, 1835, after much travail and prayer at the throne of grace. The future missionary was named Jesse Boardman Hartwell after his father and grandfather who were Baptist ministers. His father, an ardent friend of missions, dedicated Jesse to the work of world evangelism. When Luther Rice returned from India, he visited the Hartwell home. As Hartwell opened the door to meet his friend, he said, ''Brother Rice, my missionary has come,'' and that very day the baby was dedicated formally as a missionary to the perishing millions.[1]

We cannot overemphasize the importance of dedicating our children to the work of missions, even before birth. How many great men and women of God were presented to the Lord at birth and before? Hannah gave her son Samuel, even in her barrenness.

Jesse Hartwell made his profession of faith in Jesus Christ and was baptized July 14, 1850. After receiving his education and biblical training, he sailed for China with his wife Eliza in November of 1858. They labored there for many years, first in Shanghai and then at Tung Chau Foo in Northern China, where they opened a mission, organized a local church, and where Hartwell's first convert ultimately became a minister. Eliza died in China.

After an extended period, Hartwell married Eliza's sister Julia. Julia eventually experienced a lengthy period of sickness that caused the couple to return to the States. Being unwilling to remain inactive, they served as missionaries to the thousands of Chinese immigrants on the West Coast. The Hartwells' faithful labors resulted in the planting of a mission among the Chinese in San Francisco. This work became very successful.

In his youth the author was always taught the importance of courtesy and kindness toward women. This was especially true if a woman was expecting a child. Society has since learned that much is communicated to a child in the womb. How vitally important it is that parents recognize this potential of transmitting love to the unborn child. Because society has been influenced with secular humanistic concepts, many think of unborn children simply as fetuses and do not recognize the potential they contain.

May God help us to be sensitive to the fact that much is determined in the life of a person while this life is yet within the womb. The unborn share our emotions, hear our singing, conversations, and prayers. May more Christian parents communicate their love, joy, faith, and motivation to their unborn children. May these same parents dedicate their unborn children to the Lord as did the parents and grandparents of Jesse Boardman Hartwell.

God grant us the spirit of the Hartwells in dedicating and challenging our children to the work of world evangelism.

EWT

---

[1]William Cathcart, *The Baptist Encyclopedia,* ed. Louis H. Everts (Philadelphia: Louis H. Everts, 1881), 1:560-61.

October 18—A Puritan Solicitation to Persecute Baptists

Scripture: Mark 3:1-12

The stigma of those denominated Anabaptists in Germany, who had interpreted liberty as giving license to the flesh, clung tenaciously to many good Baptists who did not have the least odor of licentiousness upon them. These true Baptists had taken the Apostle Paul literally when he wrote to the Galatians, "For, brethren, ye have been called unto liberty; only use not liberty for an occasion to the flesh, but by love serve one another" (Gal. 5:13).

The enemies of the Baptists in England and New England would often refer to these Anabaptist antinomian renegades when they would attack the Baptists' doctrine and character. It was like setting up the proverbial straw man and knocking him down. This caused some misinformed, sincere citizens much concern and gave the Puritan religio-political hierarchy some ammunition to further attack the Baptists. Petitions came in from various places in Massachusetts requesting that the laws against the Baptists might be strengthened.

Massachusetts was not satisfied with persecution on its own account but wrote the Plymouth Colony to join them in their oppression of the Baptists. The following letter was written by the Court of Massachusetts Bay, October 18, 1649, to the colony of Plymouth:

> Honored and beloved Brethren:
>
> We have heretofore heard diverse Anabaptists, arisen up in your jurisdiction, and connived at; but being few, wee well hoped that it might have pleased God, by the endeavors of yourselves and faithful elders with you, to have reduced such erring men againe into the right way. But now, to our great grief, wee are credibly informed that your patient bearing with such men has produced another effect, namely, the multiplying and increasing of the same errors, and wee fear of other errors also, if timely care be not taken to supresse the same.

> Particularly wee understand that within a few weeks there have been in Sea Cuncke thirteen or fourteen persons rebaptized (a swift progress in one towne; yett wee heare not of any effectuall restriction is intended thereabouts). Lett it not, wee pray you, seem presumption in us to remind you hereof, nor that wee earnestly intreate you to take care as well of the suppressing of error, as the maintenance of the truth, God equally requiring the performance of both at the hands of Christian magistrates, but rather that you will consider our interest is concerned therein. The infection of such diseases, being so near us, one likely to spread into our jurisdiction. . . . Wee are united by confederacy, by faith, by neighborhood, by fellowship in our sufferings as exiles, and by other Christian bonds, and wee hope that neither Satan nor any of his instruments shall, by these or any other errors, disunite us of our so neere conjunction with you, but that wee shall both equally and zealously uphold all the truths of God revealed, that wee may render a comfortable account to Him that hath sett us in our places, and betrusted us with the keeping of both tables, of which will hoping, wee cease you further trouble, and rest.
>
> Your very loving Friends and Brethren.[1]

In the colonies there were united voices which proclaimed that the unjustified harshness against the Baptists and others was bad for the colonies. For a time this criticism caused the authorities to enforce the laws with greater force. The sufferings of our forefathers paved the way for ultimate and full religious liberty. The excesses of the pseudo-Baptists in Germany hindered religious liberty for many years. May we live sanctified, temperate lives in order to preserve our freedom and to spread the gospel throughout the world.

EWT

---

[1]John T. Christian, *A History of the Baptists* (1922; reprint ed., Nashville: Broadman Press, 1926), 2:58-59.

October 19—Another Candidate for the Crown of Life

Scripture: Luke 23:46; Acts 1:8

We have mentioned the persecution of the Baptists in England under the rule of the royal families of Great Britain. The martyrdom of the Reverend John James is a graphic illustration of that hatred.

John James was a Sabbatarian Baptist (i.e., he kept the Saturday Sabbath), and his congregation met in Bulstrake Alley, Whitechapel, London.

> It was the afternoon of October 19th (1661). The service had commenced. Mr. James was preaching the Gospel, when a justice of the peace entered to disperse the assembly. He ordered Mr. James to cease preaching, which the little man promptly declined to do. He then had him taken from the pulpit and conveyed to Newgate. He was charged with having used seditious language in his sermon, but he denied the charge in the most explicit terms. . . . In November Mr. James appeared in the dock. He pleaded "not guilty," and was again remanded. Afterward a verdict was given against him upon the evidence of profligate persons.

The injustice of the sentence was so great that Mrs. James petitioned King Charles to intercede, but the king treated Mrs. James with contempt and decreed that the sentence must be fulfilled and that James would be hanged.

The Reverend Mr. James responded to the verdict saying,

> There are two or three Scriptures I would like to leave with you. One is "As for me, do as seemeth good unto you but know ye for certain if ye put me to death ye shall surely bring innocent blood upon yourselves"; another is, "Precious in the sight of the Lord is the death of His saints;" and the last is, "He that toucheth the Lord's people toucheth the apple of His eye." I have no more to say for myself, but one word for my Lord, and I have done. The Lord Jesus Christ, the Son of God, is the King of England.[1]

"On the 26th of November, Mr. James was dragged . . . from Newgate to Tyburn, the place of execution. . . . In his address to the multitude, referring to his denominational sentiments, he said, 'I do own the title of a baptized believer. I own the ordinances and appointments of Jesus Christ.' "[2] "When he had finished, the executioner said, 'The Lord receive your soul, sir,' to which he replied, 'I thank thee,' and added, 'Father, into Thy hand I commit my spirit.' Immediately after[,] his body, separated into parts, was affixed to the gates of the city, and his head set upon a pole by the meeting-place where with his people he had worshipped God in peace."[3]

"John James was an inoffensive and benevolent man, free from any blemish in his character, and guiltless of every charge in the indictment. He was savagely murdered by Charles II, his courtiers, and his tools, the judges, to terrify the Dissenters, and especially the Baptists, into loyalty."[4]

May God give us the grace to stand firmly in our day even though such persecution might return. The word "witness" in Acts 1:8 is the word from which we get our word "martyrs." May we be "witnesses" and even willing to seal our "witness" as "martyrs" for Jesus Christ if that becomes necessary.

DLC

---

[1]John C. Carlile, *The Story of the English Baptists* (London: James Clarke and Co., 1905), p. 137.

[2]J. M. Cramp, *Baptist History* (London: Elliott Stock, 1870), pp. 290-91.

[3]Carlile, p. 138.

[4]William Cathcart, *The Baptist Encyclopedia,* ed. Louis H. Everts (Philadelphia: Louis H. Everts, 1881), 1:593.

October 20—A Faithful Member of a Godly Team

Scripture: Ecclesiastes 4:12

Solomon said, "A threefold cord is not quickly broken," and this principle is confirmed in the lives of William Carey, Joshua Marshman, and William Ward and their missionary labors in India. The three have been designated the "Serampore triumvirate," and their exploits of faith have thrilled Christians through the years. Surely the principle of sending a team of missionaries (as we discover often in the book of Acts) is one that mission boards of our day ought to seriously reconsider.

Just before sailing for India, the Lord caused William Carey's path to cross that of young William Ward. It was the spring of 1793, and Ward was just twenty-three years old, having been born on October 20, 1769. Ward was "a printer of Derby, who was visiting city friends. . . . Carey unfolded to him the desire and purpose of his heart respecting Biblical translations. Laying his hand on Ward's shoulder as they parted, he said, 'I hope, by God's blessing, to have the Bible translated and ready for the press in four or five years. . . . You must come and print it for us.' Neither ever forgot this."[1]

It was not until August of 1796 that William Ward was converted and, upon his baptism, united with the Baptist church in Hull. However, soon after that, a Christian friend, recognizing his gifts, offered to pay his expenses to study for the ministry. Thus Ward left the field of journalism and studied under Dr. John Fawcett at Ewood Hall, Yorkshire. Hearing again of the need of the Missionary Society for a printer to publish the Bengalee translation of the Scriptures, Ward offered himself for service in India and was accepted.

"On the 29th of May, 1799, (at the age of twenty-nine) he sailed with Dr. Marshman, Mr. Brunsdom, and Mr. Grant, with their families, for Bengal."[2] After being accepted by the society for service, Ward wrote as follows to William Carey:

> I know not whether you will remember a young man, a printer, walking with you from Rippon's Chapel one Sunday, and conversing with you on your journey to India. His services were accepted by the Society on the 16th (October, 1798). It was a happy meeting. . . . It is in my heart to live and die with you, to spend and be spent with you. I trust I shall have your prayers for a safe journey to you, and be refreshed by your presence. May God make me faithful unto death, giving me patience, fortitude and zeal for the great undertaking.[3]

The Lord graciously answered that desire, and Ward became an essential member of the triumvirate. In 1811 Ward published the first edition of the Bible for the Hindus. In 1819 he furloughed in England and "was the first missionary who had ever returned (to Great Britain) from the East."[4]

William Ward, though a printer, was well received in the pulpits of England. He even came to America for three months to raise funds for the Serampore College. Doubtless, the work in India could not have been accomplished without his expertise and strenuous efforts. He had wished to "live and die" with Carey. Ward returned to India in 1821. Following a brief illness, he passed away on May 7, 1823, in his fifty-fourth year, the first of the triumvirate to die. The three were united around our Lord's throne when Carey passed away on June 9, 1834, and Marshman joined them on December 4, 1837. The threefold cord is again intact.

DLC

---

[1]S. Pearce Carey, *William Carey* (London: Hodder and Stoughton, 1924), p. 119.

[2]John Brown Myers, *The Centenary Volume of the Baptist Mission Society* (London: Baptist Missionary Society, 1892), p. 276.

[3]Carey, p. 177.

[4]William Cathcart, *The Baptist Encyclopedia,* ed. Louis H. Everts (Philadelphia: Louis H. Everts, 1881), 2:1210.

October 21—A Preacher of Righteousness in the Wilderness

Scripture: Psalm 16:8

The Massachusetts Baptist Missionary Society was greatly used of God to make a spiritual impact upon the pioneering areas during the westward move of the population in early America. David Irish was one of the early rugged Baptist pioneers sent out to evangelize and establish churches in the frontier regions of our nation.

In 1794 the Reverend David Irish settled in Scipio, New York, and began preaching the gospel in the new settlements of Cayuga County. He was the ''pioneer preacher in that region'' and was doubtless the first minister of the gospel in that county.[1] In 1795 he established the first Baptist church there, but he had to endure much to obey the call of God.

> Elder Irish was indefatigable in labor, patient in fatigue, and easily surmounted many obstacles which would deter one possessed of a mind less resolute. Those who are acquainted with the state of the new and thinly inhabited countries, cannot form an idea of the qualities necessary to enable a minister of Christ to plant the Gospel in such an extensive region as was traversed by this valuable man. One instance which may serve to show what he had the fortitude and perseverance to go through, it is thought proper to relate. In 1799, being called with some of his brethren of the church in Scipio to assist in organizing a church Phelpstown, Malvern Hill, the roads at that time being totally impassable for traveling on horseback by reason of the great depth of mud and snow, he encouraged his brethren to undertake to travel on foot, a distance of thirty miles, which all but one accomplished. He baptized during his ministry 1,280 persons.[2]

In 1797 Irish planted the Baptist church in Manchester (then Farmington, New York), and this required a journey from his home in Scipio, fifty miles through sparsely settled country and much of the way through unbroken forest. In addition to his rugged work in Cayuga County, he penetrated the field then considered the ''Far West'' and evangelized the ''Holland Purchase.'' In 1810 Irish organized the Baptist church in Willink (Aurora), Erie County.

David Irish passed away on September 10, 1815, after a fruitful, pioneering-missionary life. The following quote is from his diary: ''The opportunity appeared exceedingly solemn and important. After sermon, we repaired to the water, singing one of Zion's songs. Here ten precious souls followed the blessed Redeemer into his watery tomb. . . . Joy lighted up in the countenance of the saints; while sinners trembled, as if the judgement day were approaching.''[3]

Thank God for those pioneering heroes! It is no wonder that one historian said, ''Were the same spirit of self-denying, consecrated zeal manifested in the ministry of today, there would be less moral destitution in our land.''[4] May we also dedicate ourselves to God's perfect will for the ongoing of the gospel at home and abroad.

DLC

---

[1]Charles Wesley Brooks, *A Century of Missions in the Empire State* (Philadelphia: American Baptist Publication Society, 1909), p. 33.

[2]Ibid., p. 46.

[3]John Woolman Brush, *Baptists in Massachusetts* (Valley Forge, Pa.: Judson Press, 1970), p. 21.

[4]Brooks, p. 260.

October 22—Perhaps Today?

Scripture: Luke 12:37-40

Through the years, Baptists have had the greatest doctrinal variety of all denominations. Doubtless this has been occasioned by our distinctive of soul liberty that allows every child of God to stand before the Lord on an equal level as each seeks to know the will of God. With no "priest-craft," each believer is to "study to shew himself approved" of the Lord, and this has resulted in Particular and General Baptists as well as many other variations.

In 1833 William Miller began to preach distinctive doctrines concerning the second coming of Jesus Christ and the end of the world. Miller was a member of the Baptist church in Low Hampton, New York, and was licensed to preach in that very year. He had few educational advantages, but he was a diligent student of the Bible and was intrigued by prophecy. With the limited library at his disposal, he concluded that the prophecies of Daniel pointed to A.D. 1843 as the year of the Lord's return. Miller preached with fervency and during that period many professions of faith were made, for hearers became convinced through the earnestness of Miller's preaching, his sincerity, and apparent familiarity with the Scriptures. Unfortunately, Miller's zeal surpassed his knowledge. The response was great. Throughout the northern tier of states from Maine to Michigan, farmers sold their property, dressed in white, and ascended the highest hills in their areas to await the Lord's return.

When 1843 passed and the Lord had not returned, Miller assumed that he was in error. Through revised calculations, he projected the second coming to be on October 22, 1844. Many who had accepted the original teaching now believed the new teaching, only to be devastated for the second time.

Miller was no charlatan who set these dates for his own aggrandizement. He was a sincere believer and loved the Lord. "Today he is usually referred to more or less with contempt, but those who knew him esteemed him highly for his intelligence, integrity and spiritual earnest. A fellow-Baptist, the scholarly Thomas Armitage, having conversed with Miller repeatedly, wrote of him as a man of 'sincerest devotion,' who was possessed of 'many excellencies and spotless character.' "[1]

It is instructive to note that Miller repudiated a cult that grew from his interpretation of prophecy and that claims him as one of their founders!

On November 10, 1844, Miller wrote an associate and "expressed sore disappointment at the failure of his prophecy, but added, 'I have fixed my mind on another time, and here I mean to stand until God gives me more light, and that is to-day, and to-day, and to-day, until He comes.' "[2]

Baptists have varied considerably in their interpretation of the doctrine of future things, but may God give us that purpose of heart in our lives to live every day looking for the coming again of our blessed Lord. May we begin each day with that blessed hope, praying, "Perhaps today," and may we retire every night with consoling, precious peace, praying, "Perhaps tonight."

DLC

---

[1]Norman F. Douty, *Another Look at Seventh-Day Adventism* (Grand Rapids: Baker Book House, 1962), p. 104.

[2]Henry S. Burrage, *History of the Baptists in Maine* (Portland, Maine: Marks Printing House, 1904), p. 200.

October 23—Betrayed by a Recipient of Charity

Scripture: Acts 9:36-43

The Rye-house Plot, as it was called, stands associated in English history with acts of atrocious cruelty, perpetrated under the color of the administration of justice. The perpetrators were said to have contemplated the assassination of Charles II, but of this accusation there is no evidence. Those accused of perpetrating the "plot" committed no overt act, and those executed died as the result of the most flagrant violation of law and justice.

Elizabeth Gaunt, a godly Baptist woman who lived in London, spent a great part of her life doing acts of charity, visiting jails, and looking after the poor of whatever religious persuasion they might be. However, her compassion became her undoing. An accused rebel was looking for refuge from his pursuers. Elizabeth, thinking him one who was escaping religious persecution, took him in while she looked for opportunity to send him out of the kingdom. He heard that Charles II would sooner pardon the rebels than those who harbored them. Upon receiving this information, he delivered himself up and accused her who had harbored him in exchange for his life. Elizabeth was seized, tried, and condemned, though there was no other witness to prove that she knew that the person she harbored was guilty of high treason. She truly thought she was protecting a nonconformist. Though in the eye of the law she was innocent and though witnesses were ready to attest to her virtues, the judge refused to let them testify and instructed the jury to find her guilty.

Elizabeth was condemned and burned, as the law directed in the case of women guilty of treason. She died with a steadfastness and cheerfulness that amazed all who saw it. She said that charity was as much a part of her religion as faith. She hoped she had reward with Him for whose sake she did this service, however unworthy the person was who made so ill a return for it. Elizabeth rejoiced that God had honored her to suffer by fire and that her suffering was a martyrdom for that religion which was all love.

William Penn, the Quaker, saw Elizabeth lay the straw about her for a speedy burning and witnessed her behavior that was in such a way that all the spectators were moved to tears. Not knowing whether she would have strength at the stake to speak because of weakness from her hard and severe imprisonment, Elizabeth left a short epistle in which she wrote: "Neither do I find in my heart the least regret at anything I have done in the service of my Lord and Master, Jesus Christ, in securing and succoring His poor sufferers, that have showed favor to His righteous cause."[1]

Elizabeth Gaunt was executed at Tyburn, near London, October 23, 1685. She is entitled to an eternal monument in the hearts of all true Christians as one who gave refuge and sustenance to God's servants who were fleeing the wrath of the Papist rulers. She was truly a Dorcas who "was full of good works and almsdeeds," (Acts 9:36). The annals of Baptist history are full of the deeds of godly women. May our generation add to those records women of Christian character and faithfulness.

EWT

---

[1]J. Newton Brown, *Memorials of Baptist Martyrs* (Philadelphia: American Baptist Publication Society, 1854), p. 301.

October 24—A Memorial to a Great Missionary Mother, Ann H. Judson

Scripture: Psalm 34

One of the great faults of this age of technical advancement is that we have instant communication with almost any place on earth and very little recording of that communication. The day of letter writing and journals is over, and thus we do not have the records in writing as in the days when missionaries wrote profusely, even though the messages took many months to arrive at their destinations. Through these old letters and journals, we have access to records of events and insights into the spiritual lives of great men and women. The life and work of Ann Hasseltine Judson was preserved in letters written by her husband, Adoniram, by Ann herself, and others.

She wrote from Rangoon, September 26, 1815:

> You doubtless are expecting to hear by this time of the Burmese inquiring what shall they do to be saved, and rejoicing that we have come to tell them how they shall escape eternal misery. Alas, you know not the difficulty of communicating the least truth to the dark mind of a heathen, particularly those heathen who have a conceited notion of their own wisdom and knowledge, and the superior excellence of their religious system.''
>
> I know, my dear mother, you long very much to see my dear son. I wish you were here to see him. He is a sprightly boy, and already begins to be very playful. We hope his life may be preserved, and his heart sanctified, that he may become a missionary among the Burmans.[1]

Sadly, she wrote on May 7, 1816, ''Death, regardless of our lonely situation, has entered our dwelling, and made one of the happiest families wretched. Our little Roger Williams, our only little darling boy, was three days ago laid in the silent grave. Eight months we enjoyed the precious little gift, in which time he had so completely entwined himself around his parents hearts, that his existence seemed necessary to their own. But God has taught us by afflictions, what we would not learn by mercies.''[2]

Adoniram Judson left his dear wife Ann for an extended journey that would consume several months. Writing a letter to Ann's mother he related, ''Our parting was much less painful than many others had been. We had been preserved through so many trails and vicissitudes, that a separation of three or four months, attended no hazards, to either party, seemed a light thing. We parted therefore, with cheerful hearts, confident of a speedy reunion, and indulging fond anticipations of future years of domestic happiness.''[3]

Little did he know that before he returned, his beloved Ann would be struck down by a violent fever and in a few days yield to death on October 24, 1826.

He concluded a later letter with these words:

> Where glories shine and pleasures roll,
> That charm, delight, transport the soul;
> And every panting wish shall be
> Possessed of boundless bliss in thee.
>
> And there my dear mother, we also soon shall be, uniting and participating in the felicities of heaven with her, for whom we now mourn. ''Amen—even so, come Lord Jesus.''[4]

EWT

---

[1]James D. Knowles, *Memoir of Ann H. Judson* (Philadelphia: American Baptist Publication Society, 1835), pp. 143-44.

[2]Ibid., p. 150.

[3]Ibid., p. 332.

[4]Ibid., p. 336.

October 25—The Little Foxes Spoil the Vines

Scripture: Acts 20:7-12

From the very beginning of the planting of local churches there have been people who needed disciplinary action. The Pastoral Epistles were written by the Apostle Paul to give exhortation and instruction on how to deal with these problems. He exhorts Timothy ''that thou mayest know how thou oughtest to behave thyself in the house of God, which is the church of the living God, the pillar and ground of the truth'' (I Tim. 3:15). He later says in his second letter, ''Preach the word; be instant in season, out of season; reprove, rebuke, exhort with all longsuffering and doctrine'' (II Tim. 4:2). The local church is important in its function, an organism; so ''let all things be done decently and in order.'' (I Cor. 14:40).

The early Baptist churches in England faced the same trivial problems of assembly that Baptist churches face today. The Baptist church at Tunbridge Wells, Kent, England, recorded:

> At the Church Meeting held at Brother Hills, the 25th of ye 10th month, 1702, we do agree upon these necessary things following as being good orders: . . . Unseasonable sleeping in ye meeting, to the shame of ye profession and griefe of ye Brotherhood, is in any wise to be Reprooved by ye Elder in ye same spirite of Meekness and Love upon ye same knowledge of his own or information of others as aforesaid. But if any shall be found to Tollerate themselves in such practices, as by their actions appear (tho' doubtless in words they will deny it), that they may be publikly Rebuked, that they may bear their shame.[1]

Similar church action was taken against being late for meetings. They considered it being a "church disorder," and deserved a reproof "by ye Elder." They withdrew fellowship and excommunicated one Ann Barton who had neglected the local Baptist church and returned to the state church. Also, one Joan Hunt was disciplined because she indulged in dancing, refused to hear the admonition of the church, and broke her promise to attend the assembly. One John Mercer was disciplined for drunkenness and swearing.

These problems which were commonplace then are also prevalent now. It is to our shame that very little church discipline is exercised today. Our forebears considered the congregation a spiritual family with the need of leadership to carry out discipline for its order and testimony to the world. Too many consider the local church a corporation ambitious only for numerical goals, with very little attention given to loving discipline that is intended to produce purity within the assembly.

Sleeping in the assembly and being late may seem trivial, but they are symptomatic of more serious spiritual problems. A careless spirit toward the body of believers when it assembles for worship, prayer, preaching, teaching, and fellowship reflects the deeper problem of indifference toward God, His Word and His Church. May we remember that it is "the little foxes, that spoil the vines" (Song of Sol. 2:15).

May we return to taking close personal care of the local church and each individual member. All churches have problems. We demonstrate our spiritual maturity by the way we deal with them. Problems do not go away when ignored, no matter how much we would like for that to take place. We can complicate them by trying to solve them with a wrong attitude. We must deal with them in love and on the principles of God's Word. Remember, "it is not a sin to have bed bugs, but it is a sin to keep them!"[2]

EWT

---

[1]John C. Carlile, *The Story of the English Baptists* (London: James Clarke and Co., 1905), pp. 104-5.

[2]My grandmother Mary Jones.

October 26—The Decease of the Wonderful Boy-Preacher—1793

Scripture: Isaiah 55

Lewis Lunsford was born in Stafford County, Virginia, around the year 1753. Early in his life, while attending William Fristoe's meetings, Lunsford was deeply convicted and gloriously saved through the gospel of God's grace. After being baptized by Fristoe, Lunsford began to stand up as an advocate for the gospel of Jesus Christ. Lunsford's talents commanded the attention of many and procured for him the appellation of "The Wonderful Boy." Wherever he placed his foot as a preacher, there was blessing, but his message also attracted opposition.

Sometime after his glorious conversion, there assembled a congregation at a stage built on the property of a Mr. Stephen Hall near Mundy's Point. After Lunsford had read his text, some who were well armed with staves and pistols drew near to attack him. Some of the irreligious part of the gathering who had assembled to hear him flew to a nearby fence and, in spite of Lunsford's plea to the contrary, made battle with his enemies by taking out the stakes and using them as weapons. Several, with pistols drawn, mounted the stage. The added weight caused the stage to collapse, and the commotion prompted a tumult which caused Lunsford to retire to Mr. Hall's house nearby. He was pursued by his opposers, who were unable to break in, and he was hidden in an upper room.

One of the armed ruffians thought himself a sensible debater and thought that he might by argumentation refute the principles Lunsford had set forth. The man was granted the privilege of entering the upstairs room to converse with Lunsford. When the man returned, his countenance was changed, and his friends wished to know the result of the conversation. His response was, "You had better converse with him yourselves. Never a man spake like this." They answered him, "Are ye also deceived?" This transformed ruffian, though desirous of further communication with Lunsford, never had the privilege of seeing him again. Unfortunately, he was taken by an untimely death.[1]

Though Lunsford had become ill, he would not stay away from the Dover Association meeting which convened about eighteen miles from his home. While there, he appeared so much better, and therefore he made appointments to preach in the lower part of Virginia. He began to carry out these appointments but soon became ill again. Apparently, pneumonia had set in. Lunsford preached his last sermon from Romans 5:1. "Therefore, being justified by faith, we have peace with God through our Lord Jesus Christ." On October 26, 1793, at the approximate age of forty, Lewis Lunsford fell asleep in the arms of Jesus.

Semple described Lunsford: "On his best strains he was more like an angel than a man. His countenance, lightened by an inward flame, seemed to shed beams of light wherever he turned. His voice, always harmonious, often seemed tuned by descending seraphs. His style and his manner were so sublime and so energetic that he was indeed an ambassador of the skies, sent down to command all men everywhere to repent."[2]

Lunsford's life was terminated in the prime of his life, leaving a family and a fruitful ministry. "For my thoughts are not your thoughts, neither are your ways my ways, saith the Lord" (Isa. 55:8).

EWT

---

[1]Lewis Peyton Little, *Imprisoned Preachers and Religious Liberty in Virginia* (Lynchburg, Va.: J. P. Bell Co., 1938), p. 467.

[2]Robert B. Semple, *A History of the Rise and Progress of the Baptists in Virginia* (Richmond: Published by the author, 1810), p. 473.

October 27—A Prodigal Son Reclaimed

Scripture: Luke 15:11-24

Elias Keach was born in 1667 in England. He was the only son of the Reverend Benjamin Keach, and like so many other sons of noble Christian families, he was not saved in his youth. At age nineteen, he traveled to America to seek his fortune. When he arrived in Pennsylvania, he was a wild young man, but "he dressed in black and wore a band in order to pass for a minister."[1] The name "Keach" was well known among the Baptists in the colonies, and soon the young man was invited to preach. Having been raised under the ministry of such an outstanding man of God, he mentally knew the message of grace.

"A crowd of people came to hear him, and concluding to brave the thing out he began to preach, but suddenly stopped short in his sermon. There was a stronger fluttering than he had counted on in his heart. . . . He was alarmed at his own boldness, stopped short, and the little flock at Lower Dublin thought him seized with sudden illness. When asked for the cause of his fear he burst into tears, confessed his imposture and threw himself upon the mercy of God for the pardons of all his sins."[2]

Young Mr. Keach returned to Pennepek and began to preach with great power. He organized the church and threw himself into the ministry with zeal. He preached at Trenton, Philadelphia, Middletown, Cohansey, Salem, and many other places, baptizing his converts into the church at Pennepek. With the exception of the believers at Coldspring, all the Baptists of New Jersey and Pennsylvania were connected with that church. He well may be considered the chief preacher of the Baptists in those parts of America during that time.

Keach married Mary Moore, the daughter of Chief Justice Moore of Pennsylvania, and pastored the Pennepek Church until 1689. When a doctrinal dispute erupted in that church, Keach resigned and apparently traveled throughout the colonies in the field of evangelism for two years. After that time, he returned to England with his wife and organized a church on Ayles Street, Goodman's Fields, in London, and preached to great crowds. In nine months he had baptized 130 into the fellowship of that church. Elias Keach died when he was only thirty-four years of age on October 27, 1701.[3]

Thus we have the history of an unbelieving preacher whose own sermon was used of the Holy Spirit to bring conviction and conversion in his own life! We are reminded again that God uses His Word to bring conviction, and we rejoice that such a rebellious farce became a regenerating force in the hands of God. When he arrived back in England, Elias labored with his father to produce an update of the Baptist Confession of Faith, and we can only imagine the thrill of his parents in their son's salvation. May this encourage Christian parents to realize that God's Word will not return unto Him void though they may not see the immediate results in the lives of their children.

Our responsibility is to train our children in the way they should go and to trust the Lord to regenerate them through His mighty power.

DLC

---

[1]Morgan Edwards, *Materials Toward a History of the Baptists* (Danielsville, Ga.: Heritage Papers, 1984), 1:7.

[2]Thomas Armitage, *The History of the Baptists* (1890; reprint ed., Watertown, Wis.: Maranatha Baptist Press, 1976), 2:708.

[3]J. M. Cramp, *Baptist History* (London: Elliott Stock, 1870), p. 480.

October 28—We Love Christ Better Than Sect and Truth Better Than Party

Scripture: Jeremiah 5:1-13

Charles Haddon Spurgeon was not only an eloquent, Spirit-filled preacher of the gospel but also a great apologist for the faith once delivered to the saints. Because of his popularity among the common people, he became the target of the fiery darts of the state-church clergy. He always seemed capable to reply with sharp thrusts from his intellectual sword and lively ammunition from his doctrinal battery.

The most trying contest came later in life and involved not another denomination but the Baptist Union of which he was a part. The seeds of controversy had been sown early among the pastors of the Union. The Baptist Union had modified its constitution away from a doctrinal base to a more functional base in 1873. There had been complaints for years about doctrinal deterioration in the Union. The controversy broke out with a series of articles in Spurgeon's magazine, *The Sword and Trowel.* The first article in March of 1887 was entitled "The Down Grade," and this title gave the name to the conflict known as the "Down Grade Controversy."[1]

One gains insight into the condition of the Union by that which Spurgeon wrote during the height of the dispute before he withdrew on October 28, 1887:

> No lover of the Gospel can conceal from himself the fact that the days are evil. A new religion has been initiated, which is no more Christianity than chalk is cheese, and this religion, being destitute of moral honesty, palms itself off as the old faith with slight improvements, and on this plea usurps pulpits which were erected for Gospel preaching. The Atonement is scouted, the inspiration of the Scripture is derided, the Holy Spirit is degraded into an influence, the punishment of sin is turned into fiction, and the Resurrection into a myth, and yet these enemies of our faith expect us to call them brethren, and maintain a confederacy with them!
>
> At the back of doctrinal falsehood comes a natural decline of spiritual life, evidenced by a taste for questionable amusements, and a weariness of devotional meetings.[2]

Spurgeon's early complaints centered upon three problems: the decline of prayer meetings among the Baptist churches, the worldliness of ministers relating to entertainment, and doctrinal problems which stemmed from the inroads of the "higher criticism" of that day.

This controversy, which extended over several years, isolated Mr. Spurgeon from many who refused to stand with him for the defense of biblical truth. Many believed that the grief and conflict of this battle hastened his death, which took place after a period of illness at Mentone in Southern France. His death occurred on January 31, 1892, when Spurgeon was only fifty-seven years of age. He left, by his testimony, a rich legacy of God's truth and volumes of biblical literature which have been translated into many languages and spread throughout the world.

In our day when apostasy abounds, God grant us men of God with like character and integrity to withstand the onslaught of those who would give mankind "chalk" instead of "cheese."

EWT

---

[1]H. Leon McBeth, *The Baptist Heritage* (Nashville: Broadman Press, 1987), pp. 302-3.

[2]Russell H. Conwell, *Life of Charles Haddon Spurgeon* (Philadelphia: Edgewood Publishing Co., 1892), pp. 469-70.

October 29—The Voice of a Prophet in Pagan New York

Scripture: Isaiah 8:20

John Roach Straton was born on April 6, 1875, in Evansville, Indiana, where his father was serving as pastor of the First Baptist Church. His parents had come to America ten years earlier from Scotland. The family later moved from Indiana to the South, where Straton served small churches in Alabama and Georgia. When he was twenty years of age, young John Straton entered Mercer University. His father died during his college career, which made the financing of his college work difficult. John completed only three years of college training.

John Roach Straton was converted while attending evangelistic meetings in Atlanta, Georgia, and following baptism he was encouraged by the noted evangelist, James Boardman Hawthorne, to attend the Southern Baptist Seminary. Straton was ordained in 1900 and pastored a small church in Louisville, Kentucky. Following his marriage in 1903, he moved to Texas. Straton served simultaneously as a pastor in Hubbard City, Texas, and as a professor at Baylor University from 1903 to 1905.

The great battle of fundamentalism began soon after the turn of the century, and Straton was in the midst of the fray. During his college years, he won the Georgia and Southern Intercollegiate Oratorical Championships and became known as a gifted orator and debater. After accepting the call to the Calvary Baptist Church of New York City in 1918, he became appalled by the moral decadence of society and became known as a reformer. He adopted sensational methods that kept him before the people, and he attacked the insufferable wickedness that he witnessed. "At the heart of Straton's Fundamentalism there came to be an emphasis on the infallibility of the Christian Scriptures."[1] The result of his aggressive denunciation of liberal theologians led to his being "frequently a guest speaker and debater on college campuses, lecturer at Bible conferences and summer assemblies, evangelist at revival services, and a regular contributor to newspapers throughout the country."[2]

For Straton, whether attacking vice or debating modernists, the key issue was the same—the all-importance of Scripture. Frequently he made the accusation that attacks on the Bible would lead to lawlessness and ultimately to the total demise of civilization.[3] "Straton's was truly the voice of a prophet in 'pagan New York City.' "[4]

Straton conducted tent meetings and street meetings throughout the area. He had an automobile outfitted with a portable pulpit that he had designed, and accompanied by a cornet soloist to attract crowds, he preached on the streets wherever he could gain an audience. Through radio station WQAO, which was owned by Calvary Baptist Church, his voice was known far and wide throughout the area. Straton was daring, innovative, and seemingly weariless, but the heavy schedule wore on him. His controversial methods produced a perpetual stormy environment, and though some were attracted to his ministry by the excitement, others of his own flock were repulsed. Living under continual tension doubtless led to the paralytic stroke which ultimately resulted in his death on October 29, 1929, in Clifton Spring, New York. How amazing that the death of this sincere man of God should occur on the same day as the catastrophic crash of the Stock Market on Wall Street! John Roach Straton was a unique man whose love of the Word and his Lord could never be questioned.

DLC

---

[1]C. Allyn Russell, *Voices of American Fundamentalism* (Philadelphia: Westminster Press, 1976), p. 51.

[2]Ibid., p. 50.

[3]George M. Marsden, *Fundamentalism and American Culture* (New York: Oxford University Press, 1980), p. 163.

[4]David O. Beale, *In Pursuit of Purity* (Greenville, S.C.: Unusual Publications, 1986), p. 212.

Ocotber 30—I Believe You Mean to Drown Me

Scripture: Psalm 76

David Barrow was born October 30, 1753, into a plain farm family in Brunswick County, Virginia. After he professed conversion at the age of sixteen, he was baptized by Zachariah Thompson and immediately began to exhort others to seek the Savior. Though he had received very little education earlier, after he married he studied grammar under Elder Jeremiah Walker and became an excellent grammarian. Barrow was ordained in 1771 and traveled and preached extensively in Virginia and North Carolina.[1]

Barrow became the pastor of Isle of Wight Church in 1744. His ministry was interrupted when he shouldered a musket in 1776 and entered the army to defend his newly established country. Barrow's exceptional deportment rendered him popular with all classes of men except the baser sort of "church men" who opposed the gospel of God's grace. His successful ministry was met with violent opposition and persecution.

On one occasion in 1778, David Barrow and Edward Mintz received an invitation to preach at the house of a gentleman who lived on the Nansemond River near the mouth of the James River. They were informed upon arrival that they might receive rough usage, and so it happened. "A gang of well dressed men came up to the stage, which had been erected under some trees, as soon as the hymn was given out, and sung one of their obscene songs. They then undertook to plunge both of the preachers. Mr. Barrow they plunged twice, pressed him into the mud, held him long under water, and came near drowning him."[2] At length Barrow replied, "I believe you mean to drown me."[3]

The whole assembly was shocked; the women shrieked, but no one interfered because about twenty stout men were engaged in this activity. Before Barrow and Mintz could change their clothes, they were driven off by these outrageous churchmen, who also abused the man who had invited them and anyone who spoke in favor of the preachers. Within a few weeks, three or four of the persecutors died in a very distracted manner.

Barrow and the other men of God disregarded the threatening orders and continued to preach without further molestation. Many believed and were baptized and were organized into a branch of the Western Branch Baptist Church at Shoulders Hill in January 1785.

The birth of early Baptist churches often came only after long and painful travail. God grant to us the same perseverance and humility in preaching the gospel and bringing forth infant churches throughout our nation and the world for the testimony of Jesus Christ.

EWT

---

[1]J. H. Spencer, *A History of Kentucky Baptists from 1769 to 1885* (Cincinnati: J. R. Baumes, 1886), 1:193.

[2]David Benedict, *A General History of the Baptist Denomination in America* (Boston: Manning and Loring, 1813), 2:249.

[3]Robert B. Semple, *A History of the Rise and Progress of the Baptists in Virginia* (Richmond: Published by the author, 1810), p. 357.

October 31—Printed Ridicule of the Baptists

Scripture: Luke 6:26

Our Lord warned in Luke 6:26, "Woe unto you, when all men shall speak well of you!" Our Baptist forefathers knew the fury of the tongue and pen as well as of the knife and sword. Speaking of John Waller and the early Separate Baptist preachers of Virginia, Lewis Peyton Little has written that "preachers of that day endured the most inhuman treatment and bodily suffering in order that they might make disciples for their Lord." And yet the bodily suffering and imprisonment in the county jails were not the worst features of their persecution. The bitter scorn and ridicule heaped upon them were much harder to bear than bodily pain. Take for example the following notice which appeared in the *Virginia Gazette* of October 31, 1771:

A Recipe to Make an Anabaptist Preacher in Two Days Time

Take the Herbs of Hypocrisy and Ambition, of each an Handful, of the Spirit of Pride two Drams, of the Seed of Dissention and Discord one Ounce, of the Flower of Formality three Scruples, of the Roots of Stubbornness and Obstinacy four Pounds; and bruise them altogether in the Mortar of Vain-Glory, with the Pestle of Contradiction, putting amongst them one Pint of the Spirit of Self-conceitedness. When it is luke-warm let the Dissenting Brother take two or three Spoonfuls of it, Morning and Evening before Exercise; and whilst his Mouth is full of the Electuary he will make a wry Face, wink with his

> Eyes, and squeeze out some Tears of Dissimulation. Then let him speak as the Spirit of Giddiness gives him Utterance. This will make the Schismatic endeavor to maintain his Doctrine, wound the Church, delude the People, justify their Proceedings of Illusions, foment Rebellion, and call it by the Name of Liberty of Conscience.[1]

We must realize that success will always bring criticism. Surely Charles H. Spurgeon experienced that in England! ''Spurgeon was so much in the public eye that they [i.e., newspaper editors] could not avoid mentioning him, and since they regarded him as a charlatan, they set out upon a campaign of bitter denunciation. Some of their statements were too crude or blasphemous to be repeated.''[2]

How should we react to the attacks upon our message and our motives? We should respond as Mr. Spurgeon did. He refused to dignify the attacks with a reply, though

> he was wounded in seeing himself thus accused and held up to ridicule. Mrs. Spurgeon gathered all the defamatory statements and pasted them in a scrapbook, till it finally became a huge volume. She also framed a text and hung it on the wall. It read: ''Blessed are ye, when men shall revile you, and persecute you, and shall say all manner of evil against you falsely, for My sake. Rejoice, and be exceeding glad: for great is your reward in Heaven: for so persecuted they the prophets which were before you.''[3]

Persecution, both verbal and physical, often comes during great strides forward in the work of God. Rather than dreading harassment, perhaps we should make sure we are ''transformers'' rather than ''conformers,'' for our Lord said, ''In the world ye shall have tribulation.''

DLC

---

[1]Lewis Peyton Little, *Imprisoned Preachers and Religious Liberty in Virginia* (Lynchburg, Va.: J. P. Bell Co., 1938), pp. 233-34.

[2]Arnold Dallimore, *Spurgeon* (1984; reprint ed., Glasgow: Banner of Truth Trust, 1985), p. 64.

[3]Ibid., pp. 66-67.

November

November 1—A Greatly Used Old-Time Evangelist

Scripture: II Kings 2:8-14

Mordecai F. Ham, Jr., was one of the most prominent, powerful evangelists of the first half of the twentieth century. Almost a third of a million additions to the family of God were produced through his efforts! These results are all the more amazing when we realize that Evangelist M. F. Ham was born in a rural area of Kentucky and had limited academic training. Actually, the evangelist was named after his grandfather, the Reverend Mordecai F. Ham, who was a leading pastor in the Bays Fork Association (Kentucky) and pastor of the Bethlehem Baptist Church for more than forty years. "It would be safe to say that more than 2,000 persons have been brought into the churches he (i.e., the grandfather) served."[1]

The evangelist's father was the Reverend Tobias J. Ham, only son of the older Reverend Mr. Ham. Tobias J. Ham made a profession of faith in 1866 and was baptized by his father. Ten years later, on February 4, 1876, he was ordained and "pastored fourteen churches, five of which he helped establish; baptized 1,500; and married 800 couples."[2] Mordecai, Jr., was the fourth of Tobias's six children and the oldest son. Born April 2, 1877, on a farm in Allen County, Kentucky, he grew up in an environment that treasured the work ethic. He labored in the fields after school with his preacher/father and matured from childhood through his teen years under the ministries of both his father and grandfather. Young Mr. Ham could not date his spiritual new birth but had the assurance of his salvation. At sixteen years of age, he was Sunday School Superintendent of the Baptist church in Greenwood, Kentucky. He was greatly influenced by his mother's Christian character and his father's nightly devotions, and soon he was overcome with an urge to preach.

The young man was privileged to have some limited training at Ogden College in Bowling Green, and at the same time he studied law privately. However, being too young to enter into the legal profession, he became a traveling salesman for a grocery firm. From 1897 to 1900, Ham was manager for a photographic company in Chicago and tried to withstand the call to preach. However, at the time of his grandfather's death on February 28, 1899, Ham witnessed the serenity of the old man of God, and on that occasion his father, and many others, prayed that his "grandfather's 'Prophet's Mantle' would fall on (him)."[3]

Mordecai Ham married in July of 1900 and then devoted himself completely to the task of preparing to preach. He placed himself under a strict reading regimen and faithfully sought the Lord. In September 1901, while visiting an associational meeting with his father, he was invited to speak. That event transformed his life, as doors began to open miraculously for him in evangelism. The accounts of the opposition toward and results of the meetings of Evangelist Ham are indeed thrilling. In an early meeting he was threatened by a ringleader of some moonshiners, but by the following night, the death angel had visited four of the gang. Fear fell upon the community, and eighty professed Jesus Christ as Savior.

By 1903 invitations were coming from outside Kentucky. Success crowned M. F. Ham's fifty-year ministry, even though persecution followed him frequently. "Neither the ruffians, of San Benito, Texas, who tried to take the evangelist out and tar and feather him, nor the liquor crowd of Salisbury, North Carolina, that shouted all one night, 'Hang Ham! Hang Ham' were able to slow his campaigns in twenty-two states.[4] Mordecai F. Ham passed into the presence of the Lord on November 1, 1961, and we cry out to our God, "Lord, do it again!"

DLC

---

[1]J. H. Spencer, *A History of Kentucky Baptists from 1769 to 1885* (Cincinnati: J. R. Baumes, 1886), 2:527.

[2]Edward E. Ham, *Fifty Years on the Battle Front with Christ* (Louisville: Old Kentucky Home Revivalist, 1950), p. 4.

[3]Ibid., p. 18.

[4]Ibid., p. 10

November 2—An Average Man Who Accomplished a Monumental Task

Scripture: I Corinthians 1:26-29

One cannot read of the advancement of the Baptist cause in America without often meeting the name of Daniel Marshall. This is amazing when one realizes that Marshall was not immersed until he was forty-eight years old. He was ordained three years later and began his Georgian ministry when he was sixty-five. Marshall died on November 2, 1784, at the age of seventy-eight. His service as a Baptist preacher spanned only twenty-seven years. We have also been informed that he was not a great pulpiteer nor a leader with great charisma. Morgan Edwards wrote, "His success is surprising when we consider that he is a man of no bright parts nor eloquence nor learning. Piety, earnestness and honesty are all he can boast of."[1] William L. Lumpkin added, "Daniel Marshall did not possess . . . conspicuous gifts . . . (and) he was certainly not as effective a preacher."[2] Then, quoting Morgan Edwards again, Lumpkin alluded to Marshall as "a weak man, a stammerer, no scholar."[3] In writing the life of his father, Daniel's son Abraham stated, "He was now called, as a licensed preacher, to the unrestrained exercise of his gifts; and though they were by no means above mediocrity, he was instrumental in awaking attention, in many of his hearers, to the interest of their souls."[4]

Those who actually heard Daniel Marshall made it clear that he was not a great orator, nor was he possessed of an unusual physical appearance or a magnetic personality. Yet, in spite of all of this, we consider his role in the expansion of the Sandy Creek Church in North Carolina. In seventeen years this church became "the mother, grandmother, and great-grandmother to forty-two churches,"[5] and we ask how could it be? We trace his activities and realize that the first Separate Baptist church in Virginia was founded by Marshall. We examine his service in South Carolina and find that he founded six churches there before entering Georgia in 1771. We have told the story of Marshall's treatment in Georgia by the state church (January 1), but when Daniel Marshall died on November 2, 1784, six more Baptist churches had been formed in Georgia, and he had presided at the organization of the Georgia Association. Again we ask ourselves how a man of apparently limited abilities could possibly accomplish so much for the glory of our Lord.

Several reasons can be given to account, in part, for such a fruitful life. First, Marshall possessed a determination that caused him to persevere. When he was arrested in Georgia for preaching as a Baptist, he refused to quit. "During the American Revolution, Marshall was the only minister of any denomination who continued his ministry in Georgia. . . . As a result of Marshall's labor even during the troubled times of the Revolution, . . . (churches) were sufficiently numerous to organize the Georgia Baptist Association."[6] Second, wherever Marshall ministered, he organized the converts. Not only did he enjoy evangelistic success, but Marshall organized the young believers into churches, and when churches were sufficient in number, he organized them into an association. Third, Marshall sought out converts whom he could train, and thus he multiplied his ministry. This principle was true in his life and ministry throughout the years. It is well illustrated in the thirteen years he preached in Georgia, for no less than fifteen men were personally trained by Daniel Marshall to carry the gospel to the surrounding areas.[7]

In 1904, the citizens of Appling, Georgia, erected a monument to the memory of the Reverend Daniel Marshall. On this anniversary of his death, we honor his memory and thank God for his service.

DLC

---

[1]Morgan Edwards, *Materials Toward a History of the Baptists* (Danielsville, Ga.: Heritage Papers, 1984), 2:144.

[2]William L. Lumpkin, *Baptist Foundations in the South* (Nashville: Broadman Press, 1961), p. 39.

[3]Ibid., p. 39.

[4]Charles G. Sommers, ed., *A History of the Baptists in New England,* The Baptist Library, vol. 1 (New York: Lewis Colby and Co., n.d.), p. 308.

[5]Edwards, p. 92.

[6]Norman Wade Cox, ed., *Encyclopedia of Southern Baptists* (Nashville: Broadman Press, 1958), 2:824.

[7]James Donovan Mosteller, *A History of the Kiokee Baptist Church in Georgia* (Ann Arbor: Edwards Bros., 1952), p. 126.

November 3—Roger Williams, a Danger to Ecclesiastical Tyrants

Scripture: Ezekiel 3:1-11

No one can consider religious freedom and soul liberty without immediately thinking of Roger Williams, though down through the ages there have been many shining lights in the struggle for liberty of conscience. In the history of the United States of America, none shone brighter than Roger Williams.

In spite of being born of poor parents, he received a good classical education. This opportunity came at the hands of a wealthy benefactor who saw that Williams was a gifted man. Having a quick mind and industrious spirit, he began to study law, but his heart soon turned to theology. As we look back into his life and the place of confrontation and leadership he ultimately assumed, we see that the legal studies were of considerable help, as was his grounding in biblical truth.

After he received Episcopal orders, Williams was placed in charge of a parish. His understanding of Christian liberty, however, would not permit him to continue under the heavy yoke of the established church. He soon separated from the communion of the Church of England and landed at Boston as a dissenter in search of evangelical liberty.

It was not long until Williams found that the colonists had set up a theocratic government in which none were admitted to the exercise of civil rights unless they were members of one of their state churches. Thus, offenses against religion were punishable by the magistrate. These things Williams abhorred, and he testified of his dislike from the very commencement of his residence. The Puritans had resisted the magistrate in England by refusing to obey him in things ecclesiastical and, in consequence, had gone into exile. They believed that the leadership of the Church of England was not guiding the church in a scriptural manner, and they were determined to construct a church that followed their understanding of the biblical model. The Puritans, however, did not believe in freedom of worship for those who disagreed with their system. They prepared to banish Williams for his belief that all men should have freedom of conscience to worship as they pleased without the interference of the state. The following sentence, placed upon Roger Williams November 3, 1635, points this out:

> Whereas, Mr. Roger Williams, one of the elders of the church at Salem, both broached and divulged divers new and dangerous opinions against the authority of the magistrates; has also writ letters of defamation, both of the magistrates and churches here, and that before any conviction, and yet maintaineth the same without any retraction; it is therefore ordered; that the said Mr. Williams shall depart out of this jurisdiction within six weeks now next ensuing, which, if he neglect to perform, it shall be lawful for the Governor and two of the magistrates to send him to some place out of this jurisdiction, not to return any more without license from the Court.[1]

We have previously seen that they meant what they said. When they had given a further period of grace, they, believing Williams had violated their terms, attempted to seize him and put him aboard ship for England. As the result of a secret warning from Governor Winthrop, he escaped their seizure by facing a terrible blizzard in the winter wilderness and spending a hard winter with the native Indians. Roger Williams demonstrated by the trials he was willing to endure that he had convictions and not mere preferences. The Puritans had strong convictions, but they were not willing to allow others to express their convictions. May God help us to have strong convictions and supply the grace to extend the principles thereof to others.

EWT

[1]J. M. Cramp, *Baptist History* (London: Elliott Stock, 1870), pp. 414-15.

November 4—A True Successor of Martyr John Huss

Scripture: Romans 12:18; Matthew 10:16

We have already observed (February 12) a résumé of the life of Henry Novotny, "The Bohemian Judson," and it is interesting to realize that he served in the same land as the martyred John Huss. More than a century prior to the Reformation of Luther and Calvin, John Huss had "appealed to the Bible as the only authority in religion; believed in the sole headship of Christ over the Church; (and) taught the priesthood of all believers."[1] Thus, in spite of the martyrdom of Huss on July 6, 1415, and the ensuing storms of persecution that "reduced the population of Bohemia from three million to eight hundred thousand," the seed of truth had been planted and sprouted to life in the days of Henry Novotny.[2]

On November 4, 1870,[3] Novotny entered seminary in Switzerland, and in 1875 he married Anna Kastomlatska. In 1881 he went with his wife and two children to Edinburgh, Scotland, to study in the Free College there. For some time he served in evangelism, but he lost his position as an evangelist when he embraced the Baptist position and was immersed on February 12, 1885, in the largest Baptist church on the continent by Pastor Charles Ondra in Lodz, Russian-Poland.

Returning to Prague, Bohemia, Novotny realized the fulfillment of his dream as sixteen members organized a Baptist church near Prague. Very little religious liberty was known, and Novotny was called before the court numerous times. During one period, it was necessary for him to report to the local authorities every Monday to narrate his activities in the ministry. When the law officials refused to allow the church to meet in their building, the pastor moved the services to his own home. As the work grew and he could not house the congregation, he rented a hall for the meetings. With increased attendance, the officials now insisted that services could only be held "in a dwelling place," and thus the pastor had one of his sons sleep in the rented building and then insisted it was "as his home." The magistrates became accustomed to the pastor as he appeared before them often, and some recognized his sound ideals. "Once when he was before the authorities, one of the judges after having been very cross with him, because of his endless preaching, called him into his private study. There he said to him: 'Now, Mr. Novotny, I speak to you as a friend, not as a judge, don't bother about us, if you can transgress the law very skillfully, do it, but we must not know anything about it.' "[4]

Novotny conducted seven services each Lord's Day. He not only preached but also played the organ and conducted the Sunday school. His dear wife Anna was a hearty soul as well. She was immersed in the icy Vltava River on March 24, 1885, when the ice had to be broken for her immersion. That act of obedience, even in the face of adversity, seems to have characterized her life of service with her husband.

The work of the Baptists grew under such direction, and Novotny's pen proved as strong as his pulpit ministry. His "literary work was done under the pre-war [First World War] Austrian government, which strictly censored printed material . . . religious or otherwise. Hence Mr. Novotny's writings were often confiscated, and several times he had to pay heavy fines."[5]

By the time of his home going, his son Joseph followed him in the pastorate, and the work had so proliferated that there were Baptist churches to be found in more than thirty towns in Bohemia. A number of young men had responded to the call to preach. The impact of Pastor Novotny's life will be fully appreciated only when we stand together in the presence of our rewarding Lord.

DLC

---

[1]J. N. Prestridge, *Modern Baptist Heroes and Martyrs* (Louisville: World Press, 1911), p. 72.

[2]Ibid., p. 73.

[3]Vaclav Vojta, *Czechoslovak Baptists* (Minneapolis: Czechoslovak Baptist Convention, 1941), p. 72.

[4]Prestridge, p. 162.

[5]Vojta, p. 63.

November 5—From the Prisons of Virginia to the Frontier of Pennsylvania

Scripture: Ezekiel 2

John Corbley was a man of deep convictions and, being born in Ireland, was a prime example of the "Fighting Irish." One biographer gives the following description: "The Rev. John Corbley was the type of man, who makes his own history by his vigorous and active life. When he took sides, it was not of the passive type of opposition, and right or wrong, he became a fighting champion for his chosen cause. He was a militant crusader for any cause or controversy he saw worthy of his efforts."[1]

His fight for religious liberty brought him into conflict with the state church in Virginia. In addition to Corbley's preaching through the grates of the notorious jail of Culpeper County, Virginia, the Order Book of Orange County for the years 1763-1769, page 514, records the following:

> This day (July 28, 1768) Allen Wiley, John Corbley, Elijah Craig and Thomas Chambers in Discharge of their Recognizance Entered into before Rowland Thomas Gent on being charged as Vagrant and Itinerant Persons and for assembling themselves unlawfully at Sundry Times and Places under the Denomination of Anabaptists and for Teaching and Preaching Schismatick Doctrines Whereupon the Court having Examined the Witnesses and heard the Counsel on both Sides are of the Opinion that the sd. Allen Wiley, John Corbley, Elijah Craig and Thomas Chambers are guilty of a Breach of Good Behaviour and Ordered that they enter into Bond.[2]

Under the Toleration Act of England, the officials could not prosecute the itinerant Baptist preachers for simply preaching and teaching; so they devised a way to bring them before the "Bar of Unjustice" on charges of vagrancy and disturbing the peace because they traveled widely and their success stirred up the state church clergy to wrath and violence. Corbley's familiarity with the courts and jails and Patrick Henry's friendship to the cause of the Baptists, possibly motivated Henry later to appoint Corbley a judge or justice of the peace of Monongalia County, Virginia, now West Virginia. However, Corbley was not on the great frontier to pursue law but to evangelize and plant churches. He soon moved back to Pennsylvania in the Redstone Settlement, and it was here that he spent the last years of his life.

These years were no less eventful and vigorous than the early ones, being filled with adventure and conflict as well as suffering. It was reported that he was imprisoned on a charge of complicity in the "Whiskey Rebellion" which involved the principle of "taxation without representation." Any threat to liberty and freedom certainly would challenge Corbley. It is also recorded that during this period members of his family, including his wife, were massacred by the Indians. The minutes of the Great Bethel Baptist Church of Uniontown, Pennsylvania, record that Corbley, one of the ablest preachers of his time at the age of forty-two, constituted a Baptist church at Forks-of-Cheat, now Stewartstown, West Virginia, with twelve members on November 5, 1775, and served as its first pastor.[3]

Corbley was one of those heroes among the Baptists on the early frontier of our great nation. These Baptist heroes were a peculiar stock of people with extraordinary conviction, strength of character, and a vigorous nature. They also were endowed with a physical stamina that helped them endure the rigors of frontier life and the punishment of prison cells. May our Lord raise up men and women with such qualities and constitutions to face the challenges of our day.

EWT

---

[1]Note from various historians of Green County Pioneers.

[2]Lewis Peyton Little, *Imprisoned Preachers and Religious Liberty in Virginia* (Lynchburg, Va.: J. P. Bell Co., 1938), pp. 135-36.

[3]Minutes of the Church Historical Committee, Great Bethel Baptist Church, Uniontown, Pa., pp. 17-18.

November 6—Preaching, Planting, Persevering, and Pushing On

Scripture: Luke 10:1-12

Elijah Baker was born in Lunenburg County, Virginia, in 1748. He was converted to Christ and was baptized in 1769 by the renowned Separate Baptist Samuel Harriss. Immediately after his baptism, he became a zealous witness for Christ and began to recommend the grace of God to all he met. Unlike so many of the early Virginia Baptist preachers who migrated westward and southward into Kentucky, the Carolinas, and Georgia, Elijah Baker carried the gospel eastward and planted all of the early Baptist churches between Richmond and Hampton in Virginia.[1]

Baker was carrying the gospel of God's grace into the very citadel of the established state church and aroused religious enemies on every hand to great anger and violence. Baker's ministry was greatly blessed in spite of the strong opposition of the state and church officials, as well as the mobs that pelted him with apples and stones. He was an itinerant minister all his life, preaching, planting, and moving on to other fields. Truly following the pattern of the Apostle Paul, he also attracted other men into the gospel ministry, having many Timothys who took the oversight of these tender, newly-planted churches.

Upon crossing to the Eastern Shore, Baker began his ministry under a huge white oak tree that measured ten feet in diameter. He continued a fruitful ministry in both Virginia and Maryland, planting no less than ten churches.[2] Baker had many friends. One was Dr. Richard Lemmon, in whose home Baker died November 6, 1798, at age fifty-six.

Dr. Lemmon wrote:

> In Mr. Baker I found the Israelite indeed, the humble Christian; the preacher of the Gospel in the simplicity of it; and the triumphant saint, in his last moments. In his preaching he was very plain; and generally experimental; always very express on the doctrine of regeneration; never entering upon the doctrines by which he conceived he should give offense to one or another. In his last illness, I attended his bedside, day and night, for three weeks; and had many agreeable conversations with him, on the glorious things of the kingdom of Christ. He retained his senses to the last minute; and seemed rather translated, than to suffer pain in his dissolution. Death was to him as familiar in his conversation as if he talked of an absent friend from whom he expected a visit.[3]

Clearly, Elijah Baker was a humble servant of God who enjoyed the fullness of the Holy Spirit, coupled with the strong characteristics of piety and importunity. These qualities brought forth a most fruitful ministry in establishing churches that bear testimony to this day to the gospel he preached and to his faithfulness in delivering it. God grant us many men of this quality for our generation and generations to come.

EWT

---

[1]Lewis Peyton Little, *Imprisoned Preachers and Religious Liberty in Virginia* (Lynchburg, Va.: J. P. Bell Co., 1938), p. 475.

[2]Robert B. Semple, *History of the Baptists in Virginia,* rev. ed. (Lafayette, Tenn.: Church History Research and Archives, 1976), p. 478.

[3]Little, p. 476.

November 7—Great Convictions of a Giant-Hearted Man

Scripture: II Timothy 4:1-5

At times the six-foot, three-inch Texan, B. H. Carroll, looked to be forty feet high to Dr. L. R. Scarborough, but it was Carroll's convictions and not his stature that caused the illusion.

While still a youth of sixteen, Carroll entered Baylor College, but at the outbreak of the Civil War, he joined the Texas Ranger service to guard the Texas border. In 1862 he enlisted in the army of the Confederate States and served for four years. He was wounded in Mansfield, Louisiana, in 1864.

Following a bitter battle with skepticism, Carroll was converted in 1865 and united with the Baptist church in Caldwell, Texas. In 1866 he was ordained to the gospel ministry and the same year married Ellen Virginia Bell. God blessed that union with nine children.

The Reverend B. H. Carroll preached in small churches in Burleson County for three years. In 1870 he was called as pastor of the First Baptist Church of Waco, Texas, and the congregation grew under his ministry. This location provided him the opportunity to lecture at the nearby Baylor Baptist College. Before long he gained a reputation as a superlative teacher. His unusual gifts as a preacher/teacher allowed him to continue his dual role as pastor/professor, and he taught theology and Bible at Baylor from 1872 until 1899, when he resigned his pastorate. His intense interest in higher education had won out.

In 1908 a full-fledged seminary was founded, and Dr. B. H. Carroll became the first president of the Southwestern Baptist Theological Seminary, which was located in Fort Worth, Texas. Always a great pulpiteer, Dr. Carroll was able to stimulate interest and confidence in those who heard him, and thus he was able to raise financial support. In the seminary's early years, he "sent an appeal to many pastors: 'I am up a tree. Can't you and your fine men help me?' One pastor wrote, 'I am in a hole. I must call my fine men together to raise $14,000.00 to pay on a pressing debt on our building. How can a man in a hole help a man up a tree?' Carroll replied: 'When you come up the tree to help me down, you will be out of your hole.' "[1] Carroll's ability and sense of humor saved the day on many occasions.

From the beginning of the seminary, Dr. L. R. Scarborough served as professor of evangelism. Dr. Carroll served as president from the seminary's founding until his death on November 11, 1914. The last year and a half of Carroll's life, he was ill, and Dr. Scarborough served the seminary as acting president. Just days prior to his death, Dr. Carroll called Dr. Scarborough to his bedside to instruct him, and L. R. Scarborough reports it as follows:

> B. H. Carroll, the greatest man I ever knew, . . . a few days before he died, expecting me, as he wanted me, to succeed him as president of the seminary, . . . pulled himself up by my chair with his hands, and looked me in the face. There were times when he looked like he was forty feet high. And he looked into my face and said, "My boy, on this Hill orthodoxy, the old truth is making one of its last stands and

> I want to deliver to you a charge. . . . You will be elected president of the seminary. I want you, if there ever comes heresy in your faculty, to take it to your faculty. If they won't hear you, take it to the trustees. If they won't hear you take it to the conventions that appointed them. If they won't hear you, take it to the common Baptists. . . . I charge you in the name of Jesus Christ to keep it lashed to the old Gospel of Jesus Christ.''[2]

We can only thank God for such loyalty to the message of saving grace and faithfulness to our Savior!

DLC

---

[1]Norman Wade Cox, ed., *Encyclopedia of Southern Baptists* (Nashville: Broadman Press, 1958), 1:233.

[2]L. R. Scarborough, *The Tears of Jesus* (New York: George H. Doran and Co., 1922), pp. 93-94.

November 8—More on the Wicked and William Wickenden

Scripture: Proverbs 16:1-12

The Dutch Reformed Church of New York contemptuously referred to William Wickeden as ''the cobbler'' who dipped his converts. It appears that he was the first Baptist to preach the gospel of the grace of God in the colony of New York. He had come from the citadel of religious liberty, Rhode Island, and was under the conviction that he was commissioned by Jesus Christ to preach His Word. He began preaching at Flushing and going to the river to dip the converts.

A previous entry (August 5) mentions that ''on the 8th of November, 1656 the General Assembly of New Netherland 'ordained' that Wickenden should be condemned to pay a fine of one hundred pounds Flemish and be banished from the province of New Netherland, 'the aforesaid Wickendam (Wickenden) to remain a prisoner till the fine and cost of the process shall be paid.' ''[1]

As was the case in Connecticut and Massachusetts, the more the Dutch authorities persecuted the ''heretics,'' the more restrictive the authorities became. Instead of relaxing their religious laws and allowing freedom of speech and conscience, they became more indignant and enlarged their legislation against what they considered heresy. Hence, on September 21, 1662, the authorities said that because they

> find by experience that their hitherto issued publications and edicts against conventicles and prohibited assemblies are not observed and obeyed as they ought, therefore, by these presents, they are not only renewed but enlarged in a manner following. Like as they have done heretofore, so they prohibit and interdict as yet, that besides the Reformed worship and service no conventicles or meetings shall be kept in this province, whether it be in houses, barns, ships, barks, nor in the woods or fields, upon forfeiture of fifty guldens for the first time, for every person, whether man or woman or child that shall have been present at such prohibited meetings, or shall have lent his house, barn or any place to that purpose; for ye second time twice as much, for the third time four times as much, and arbitrary punishment besides.[2]

Religious persecution prevailed against our Baptist forefathers in varying degrees from Georgia to Maine, and this persecution continues today in other nations where our brethren languish in prisons merely for assembling in their houses and forests in the name of Christ. Out of this crucible of suffering and oppression the Bill of Rights was born with its guarantees of freedom of religion, freedom of speech, the right to assemble peaceably, and the ability to petition the government. We can clearly see why our founders were eager to protect us from unreasonable search and seizure and to secure the right of a quick and fair trial. They had seen homes plundered, meetings desecrated, and preachers seized and held in prison for months on end. They were determined that this would never happen in the new nation. What a privilege to have such a great heritage as Baptists! Knowledge of the afflictions of our Baptist forefathers should motivate us, who have benefited so much from their sufferings, to determine that these principles of freedom be preserved for our posterity. We can accomplish this goal by teaching our offspring the history of men and women in other generations who paid a great price in order that we might enjoy our blessed freedom. We also should be vigilant in petitioning and being outspoken when these principles are threatened. We do well to pray for our persecuted brethren in other lands and, as it is possible, to communicate with them. May we never cease to lift our voices to our God in praise and thanksgiving for all His goodness and mercy.

EWT

---

[1]Thomas Armitage, *The History of the Baptists* (1890; reprint ed., Watertown, Wis.: Maranatha Baptist Press, 1976), 2:749.

[2]Ibid.

November 9—Perseverance Under Persecution Purchased Liberty of Conscience

Scripture: Acts 25:1-12

The spiritual awakening under the preaching and leadership of George Whitefield and Jonathan Edwards was sometimes called the "New Light Stir," and there was no greater "stir" than in the colony of Connecticut. The controversy continued for many years and centered on the Half-Way Covenant, pedobaptism, and freedom to worship God as regenerate people. Many of the Separates joined the Baptists and embraced their principles. The established church influenced the legislative and judicial systems to tighten the laws and the enforcement of regulating religious activity. "The Legislature not only enacted these severe and unprecedented laws, but they proceeded to deprive of their offices such of the justices of the peace and other officers as were New Lights, as they were called, or who favored their cause."[1]

Students were expelled from Yale College, and churches passed rules of excommunication such as the one passed August 9, 1745, by the Congregational Church at Middletown, Connecticut, stating, "When members of this church shall renounce infant baptism and embrace the Baptist principles and practice baptism by immersion, they shall be considered by that act as withdrawing their fellowship from this church, and we consider our covenant obligations with them as church members dissolved."[2]

When we remember that their membership and attendance were not a thing of choice but mandatory by law, we clearly see the injustice of such an act and the inconsistency of the religious system.

The venerable Judge William H. Potter said, "The unfortunate Separates were pursued into every calling, hunted out of every place of trust, hauled before clergy and church, dragged before magistrates, and suffered without stint and without much complaint countless civil and ecclesiastical penalties as heretics or felons, but oppression only confirmed their faith and thrust them into closer union with their Baptist fellow-sufferers, who as in duty bound, joyfully espoused the cause and rights of the Separates."[3]

Thus many New Lights, embracing the doctrines that Baptists had propagated and suffered for through many decades, united as individuals and entire congregations with Baptist churches.

The efforts of the Baptists to throw off the burden of oppression had continued many years. They had adopted resolutions in churches and associations, carried petitions from year to year to the legislatures, and sent capable counsel at great expense to seek redress of grievances. Elder Asahel Morse, who was baptized November 9, 1798, and was licensed to preach in 1799, became a member of the State Convention to frame a new state constitution in 1818. He wrote the article on religious liberty that secured the rights of conscience in the state of Connecticut. He was a man of great power and influence among the Baptists, and in 1820 he went to Philadelphia as a delegate from the Connecticut Baptist Missionary Board to the Baptist General Convention.[4]

We should be thankful for faithful men who have been willing to become involved by being the right man in the right place so that our liberties would be secured in every state throughout the land.

EWT

---

[1]Thomas Armitage, *The History of the Baptists* (1890; reprint ed., Watertown, Wis.: Maranatha Baptist Press, 1976), 2:742.

[2]Ibid., p. 742.

[3]Ibid., p. 743.

[4]William Cathcart, *The Baptist Encyclopedia,* ed. Louis H. Everts (Philadelphia: Louis H. Everts, 1881), 2:817-18.

November 10—West Africa's "Carey"

Scripture: Romans 8:31-32

''The Father of Western Africa Missions'' was about six feet tall, broad shouldered, and of erect frame.[1] He planted the ''Providence Baptist Church (which) was the first Baptist church in Africa and one of the earliest denominational movements on the continent.''[2] The missionary served as a medical officer, soldier, governmental inspector, and pastor as he led his flock in the work of evangelism and education. ''For many years after his death, there remained no other memorial of the great African than a little village in Liberia called by the name, 'Carey.' But in 1850 the late Reverend Eli Ball, of Virginia, while visiting all the Liberian Baptist missionary stations as agent of the Southern Baptist Convention, searched for the spot where he was buried, and after considerable difficulty he found it. The next year a marble monument was sent out and placed over the grave.''[3]

Who was this great missionary? His name was Lott Carey. He had been born a slave in Virginia. No record was kept of the birth of slaves; however, it appears that he was born about 1780. His father was a member of a Baptist church, and his mother made no profession of faith. As the lad grew, he became more intemperate and profane. In 1804 he began his work as a slave in a tobacco warehouse in Richmond. In 1807 he heard a sermon on the conversion of Nicodemus by the Reverend John Courtney, pastor of the First Baptist Church in Richmond. At that time Lott Carey was gloriously saved and his life transformed. He learned to read with the assistance of another warehouse slave and soon manifested a zeal to preach to those of his race.

Deacon William Crane of the First Baptist Church had begun a school for black men in 1815. Classes were held three nights each week. Twenty black men were enrolled, including Lott Carey. The regular course of study was supplemented with articles from various publications that Mr. Crane thought would be of interest and help. The missionary cause, which was of great concern to the teachers of the school, was reflected in the hearts of the student body.

Lott Carey lived frugally, and in 1813 he purchased his freedom and that of his two children for $850.00. In time he purchased a good farm for fifteen hundred dollars and worked for a salary of $800.00 annually. He was such a good worker that when he felt the call to go to Africa with the gospel, his employers offered him a twenty-five per cent raise if he would remain in their service. He was committed to God's call, however, and Mr. Crane recommended Carey and Collin Teague, a worker desirous of going with him, to the American Board of Foreign Missions.

> His farewell sermon, preached in the meeting-house of First Baptist Church, made a powerful and lasting impression. Mr. Crane had never heard him preach. But Teague had repeatedly said to him, "I can tell you, Sir, I don't hear any of your white ministers that can preach like Lott Carey." This testimony made Mr. Crane curious to hear him. His text was from Romans 8:32. "I have," says Mr. Crane, "a most vivid recollection of the manner to which, toward the close, he dwelt upon the word, 'freely.' " . . . He rang a succession of perhaps a dozen changes upon the word, in a manner that would not have dishonored Whitefield.[4]

On January 23, 1821, Carey and his little missionary group sailed from Norfolk, Virginia, aboard the "Nautilus" for Africa. His missionary career ended less than a decade later when he suffered an accident on November 10, 1828.

But for the adverse circumstances in which he was placed, Carey might have won a worldwide reputation as preacher, explorer, physician, general, or chief magistrate. As it was, he met and mastered the demoniac hordes as did David Livingstone when placed in a similar situation.[5]

Thank God for the sacred memory of Lott Carey, the slave of man who became the slave of Christ to Africa!

DLC

---

[1]Jesse L. Boyd, *A History of Baptists in America Prior to 1845* (New York: American Press, 1957), p. 150.

[2]Leroy Fitts, *A History of Black Baptists* (Nashville: Broadman Press, 1985), p. 111.

[3]A. H. Burlington, *The Story of Baptist Missions in Foreign Lands* (St. Louis: C. R. Barnes Publishing Co., 1892), p. 206.

[4]Ibid., p. 201.

[5]Ibid., p. 207.

November 11—A Little That Is Invested Well Will Bring Forth Much

Scripture: Psalm 126

As in many similar instances, it seems that the mother of Thomas Baldwin left early impressions of a fine moral and intellectual character on her son. His father was attached to the military service and rose to some distinction in the then Colonial Army. When Thomas was sixteen years old, his father having died previously, his mother remarried and moved to Canaan, New Hampshire. It was here that Baldwin represented the town in the state legislature at an early age and commenced his studies to fit himself for the legal profession.

After the death of his first-born child, in 1777 Baldwin resolved to make religion his first concern. It was not until 1780, through the influence of two Baptist preachers who had come to labor temporarily in the neighborhood, that he came to a full understanding of the gospel of the grace of God. Having been educated among the pedobaptists, he struggled with the subject of baptism. He became persuaded that the views in which he had been trained were unscriptural and that if he were to be obedient to his Lord, he must follow Him into the waters of baptism. This he did, knowing that it would meet with the disapproval and alienation of many of his friends. He determined that no earthly consideration should prevent him from carrying out his convictions, and he was baptized in the latter part of 1781.

Baldwin soon decided to invest his life in winning souls to Christ and building up the cause of Him who had by His grace brought him to the saving knowledge of the truth. In due time, he was set apart to the work of the ministry by ordination as an evangelist. For seven years he performed the duties of pastor of the Baptist church in Canaan with no stipulated salary. All he received did not average to more than forty dollars a year. Though generally home on Sunday, he spent a considerable amount of time traveling and preaching in destitute places. Sometimes he journeyed more than one hundred miles through wilderness, in the cold of winter, depending only on the charity of people and the strength of the Lord.

Baldwin answered the call to the Second Baptist Church in Boston, Massachusetts, and was installed November 11, 1790.[1] His ministry was soon blessed with abundant fruit. In 1791 seventy were added to the church, and they later experienced several glorious revivals, one of which resulted in twenty-one professions of faith.

Baldwin became a prolific writer, editor, and apologist for the principles of the Word of God which had formed his Baptist convictions. At the beginning of his ministry in Boston, he had read little and seen little, but God had given him an ability to think. He used and invested his talent well. The celebrated Andrew Fuller said of Baldwin's written works on baptism and other Baptist principles, that they were the ablest discussions of the questions Fuller had ever read.

May we diligently invest our abilities well, no matter how small we may consider them or how few our opportunities.

EWT

[1]William Sprague, *Annals of the American Pulpit* (New York: Robert Carter and Bros., 1865), 6:210.

November 12—If I Were Out of Prison Today, I Would Preach the Gospel Tomorrow

Scripture: John 3:22-36

The restoration of Charles II introduced a reign of terror and of suffering upon the Dissenters in England. If they met for worship, they were liable to be stripped of their property, consigned to a jail, and even put to death. During this time John Bunyan was afflicted by the decease of his beloved wife and mother of his four children. God in His mercy gave him a second wife who proved to be a most devoted and heroic woman in the hour of his greatest need.

While preaching to a small congregation at Samsel, Bunyan was arrested November 12, 1660, and hurried to the Bedford jail, located in one of the central piers of the bridge over the river Ouse.[1] One can hardly realize the miseries experienced when pious men and women were taken to such "dens" and thrust in, as Bunyan was, with the most depraved kind of felons.

After about seven weeks of imprisonment, he was tried before Justice Keeling, who pronounced him guilty of not submitting to the state church. He heard the judge declare, "You must be had back to prison, and there lie for three months; and then if you do not submit to go to church to hear divine service, and leave your preaching, you must be banished from the realm; and after that, if you be found in this realm without special license from the king, you must stretch by the neck for it, I tell you plainly." Bunyan responded by saying, "If I were out of prison today, I would preach the Gospel again tomorrow, by the help of God."

Bunyan described the parting from his wife and children as "the pulling the flesh from the bones. I saw I was as a man who was pulling down his house upon the head of his wife and children." He had particular compassion upon his little blind Mary, of whom he said, "Oh, the thoughts of the hardships I thought my poor blind one might go under, would break my heart in pieces."[2]

At the end of the three months, Bunyan became anxious to know what the enemies of the cross intended to do with him. In prison he was treated with the utmost trust and respect. It was thought that the imprisonment, as it stretched out to over twelve years, saved his life during a time when many were put to death for their faith. His heroic wife presented his petition for release and addressed the judge, "My lord, I have four small children that cannot help themselves, of which one is blind, and have nothing to live upon but the charity of good people." However, they continued his incarceration because he would not deny the lordship and ultimate authority of Jesus Christ over his life by ceasing to preach and accepting licensure from the state.

The Bible and *Foxe's Book of Martyrs* were his library. God granted him the tools of quill and ink and thus fulfilled His purposes in the writing of useful treatises, including *The Holy City, Christian Behavior, The Resurrection of the Dead, Grace Abounding to the Chief of Sinners,* and the immortal *Pilgrim's Progress*. This last volume graces libraries all over the world and has been translated into several languages, including Chinese, Hottentot, Greek, and Malay.

Prison walls may constitute God's open door to the world.

EWT

---

[1]George Offar, "Memoir of John Bunyan," biographical sketch introducing, *The Pilgrim's Progress* (London: Routledge, Warne and Routledge, 1861), p. x.

[2]Ibid., p. xii.

November 13—Toleration or Freedom of Conscience

Scripture: Romans 14:10-12

It disgusts many Americans today to think that anyone would be coerced into compliance to any religion against his will. We have been conditioned to believe in freedom of conscience due to its long practice in our land. But the truth is that "in 1644, a poor man by the name of (Thomas) Painter was suddenly turned anabaptist, and for refusing to have his child baptized, he was complained of to the court, who, with judicial dignity, interposed their authority in the case . . . and because the poor man gave it as his opinion that infant baptism was an anti-christian ordinance, he was tied up and whipped."[1]

Persecution often backfired on the perpetrators as it did in Massachusetts. The influence of the Baptists grew, and thus on November 13, 1644, the General Court passed the following law:

> Forasmuch as experience hath plentifully and often proved that since the first arising of the Anabaptists . . . they have been the incendiaries of commonwealths, and the infectors of persons in maine matters of religion, and the troublers of churches in all places where they have been, and that they have held the baptizing of infants unlawful, have usually held other errors in heresies together therewith, though they have (as other heretics use to do) concealed the same, till they spied out a fair advantage and opportunity to vent them, by way of question or scruple, and whereas divers of this kind have, since our coming into New England, appeared amongst ourselves, some whereof have (as others before them) denied the ordinance of magistracy, and the lawfulness of making warr, and others the lawfulness of magistrates . . . which opinions, if they should be connived at by us, are like to be increased amongst us, and so must necessarily bring guilt upon us, infection and trouble to the churches, and hazard to the whole commonwealth.
>
> It is ordered and agreed, that if any person or persons within this jurisdiction shall either openly condemne or oppose the baptizing of infants, or go about secretly to seduce others from their approbation or use thereof, or shall purposely depart the congregation at the

> administration of the ordinance, or shall deny the ordinance of magistracy, or their lawful right or authority to make warr . . . and shall appear to the court wilfully and obstinately to continue therein after due time and meanes of conviction, every such person or persons shall be sentenced to banishment.[2]

Evidently, the Puritans were strongly opposed to the Baptists of their day. This law was directed against the Baptists, but pressures mounted on the General Court so that, though they would not repeal the law, they publicly confessed "that the Baptists were 'peaceable' citizens amongst them."[3] In essence, they said that if the Baptists went about their worship without influencing others, the law would not be enacted against them.

We must again point out the difference in the Baptist position of religious liberty based on freedom of conscience and the religious toleration allowed by some "state churches." Baptists believe that "a free church in a free state is a New Testament principle. . . . The right of every soul to direct access to God is an inalienable right, with which the state must not interfere."[4] State churches have arrived at the position of allowing other churches to exist, but favorable laws and/or fiscal levies are often to be granted the favored church. This is thought by some to be "toleration," but Baptists believe that the end of governmental administration is equal justice under law. Baptists, therefore, repudiate every form of compulsion in religion or restraint of religious freedom. Let us pray for our nation that this principle which made us great shall be preserved for coming generations.

DLC

---

[1]David Benedict, *A General History of the Baptist Denomination* (New York: Lewis Colby and Co., 1848), p. 370.

[2]John T. Christian, *A History of the Baptists* (1922; reprint ed., Nashville: Broadman Press, 1926), p. 54.

[3]Thomas Armitage, *The History of the Baptists* (1890; reprint ed., Watertown, Wis.: Maranatha Baptist Press, 1976), 2:682.

[4]E. Y. Mullins, *Baptist Beliefs* (Philadelphia: Judson Press, 1925), pp. 72-73.

November 14—He Preached Emancipation

Scripture: I Peter 5

David Barrow, while contending for the liberty of the American colonies, was persuaded of universal liberty. Through this principle he came to the conclusion that it was sinful to hold slaves. Accordingly, he freed all his slaves; he owned a considerable number. "Although the measure proved his disinterested zeal to do right," remarks Mr. Semple, "it is questionable whether it was not, in the end[,] productive of more harm than good. While it lessened his resources at home, for maintaining a large family, it rendered him suspicious among his acquaintances, and probably in both ways limited his usefulness."[1]

Semple's remark gives insight into the response of many toward those who zealously took up the cause of emancipation. Many people opposed slavery, including some of our great statesmen. George Mason, a leading thinker in Virginia, cited the lack of a provision to abolish slavery as one of his reasons for refusing to sign the Constitution.

After laboring zealously in Virginia and North Carolina for over twenty years, Barrow moved to Montgomery County, Kentucky. He soon distinguished himself as a man of piety, talent, and usefulness. When some among the Baptists began to embrace Unitarianism, he was sent to convince the heretics of their apostasy. In 1803 he published a pamphlet on "The Trinity" which helped to check this growing heresy.

"Perhaps no minister in Kentucky enjoyed the confidence and esteem of his brethren, and the people generally, in a higher degree than did Mr. Barrow. But he did not long enjoy this popularity."[2] The people became stirred up concerning the subject of slavery. Because he propagated his emancipation views, the North District Association expelled Barrow from his seat in that body and also sent a committee to go to the church to accuse him there. The committee presented two alternatives: exclude Pastor Barrow from the church or be excluded from the association. There was no charge of immorality or doctrinal heresy against Barrow or his church. The complaint was that he preached emancipation. This demonstrated how far good and wise men will stray from Baptistic and biblical principles when stirred by the passion of controversy.

Barrow wrote a sixty-four page pamphlet on the evils of slavery that gained some converts to his convictions. He was an ardent member of a Baptist emancipation society called the "Friends of Humanity" and supported it with zeal until his death November 14, 1819.

The moral issues of an evil commerce were already being debated and were dividing good men even in the wilderness during the early history of our nation. A few years later, it became the catalyst that caused the eruption of a horrible conflict that convulsed the country, divided homes and churches, and plagues us even to this day. The conduct of men, good and bad, will influence future generations. God help us to influence our posterity for good.

EWT

---

[1]J. H. Spencer, *A History of Kentucky Baptists from 1769 to 1885* (Cincinnati: J. R. Baumes, 1886), 1:195.

[2]Ibid., p. 196.

November 15—Perish at Sea Before Disgracing the Cause You Go to Serve

Scripture: Lamentations 1:12-22

Why did over eight thousand persons assemble on the island of Jamaica for the memorial service for William Knibb who had died of yellow fever November 15, 1845, after only four days of illness? It was because Knibb, known as "the lion-hearted" and having been exposed to the severest trials, had been the major instrument to bring spiritual and bodily liberty to the slaves. Opposition to Knibb had come from the Roman and English clergy, the planters, the civil authorities, and the soldiers. Knibb bravely met and finally conquered all his adversaries.

Upon Knibb's departure from Market Street, Bristol, England, his invalid mother sat at a window early one morning, watching her Baptist missionary son depart for the West Indies. Having bade farewell, she called him back and said, "Remember, William, I would rather hear that you perished at sea, than that you had disgraced the cause you go to serve."[1] With this admonition ringing in his heart, he arrived in Jamaica and was brought face to face with the horrors of slavery. His whole manhood revolted, and he vowed that he would not rest until freedom was obtained. He wrote home, "The cursed blast of slavery has, like a pestilence, withered almost every moral bloom. I knew not how any person can feel a union with such a monster, such a child of hell. For myself, I feel a burning hatred against it, and look upon it as one of the most odious monsters that ever disgraced the earth."[2]

Knibb also reported that the prayer meeting at daybreak every Wednesday morning was attended by nearly a thousand slaves. Knibb was thrown into prison and charged with inciting the slaves to rebellion. He declined to leave the island, though a way of escape was offered him. At last the attorney general declared that there was no case against him.

Knibb returned to England on a holy crusade only to find that the missionary committee regarded slavery as a political question and required their representatives to be silent upon the subject. Knibb was advised to be prudent and temperate. To this he responded, "Myself, my wife, and my family are entirely dependent upon the Baptist Mission. We have landed without a shilling, and may at once be reduced to penury. But, if it be necessary, I will take them by the hand and walk barefoot through the kingdom but I will make known to the Christians of England what their brethren are suffering."[3]

And this he did, even when his coattails were pulled to silence him. He raised his voice and said, "Whatever be the consequences, I will speak. At the risk of my connection with the society and all that I hold dear I will avow this. If the friends of missions will not hear me I will tell it to my God, nor will I desist till the greatest of curses is removed, and 'Glory to God in the highest' is inscribed on the British flag."[4]

The Baptist churches responded with great generosity, and the British government made a grant to restore the loss caused by the destruction of mission premises. Knibb returned to Jamaica, and at midnight on July 31, 1838, fourteen thousand adult slaves and five thousand of their children gave thunderous thanksgiving and praise at that moment when the entire slave population was liberated. A mahogany coffin, packed with the whips, branding irons, and other symbols of their slavery, was lowered into a grave as Knibb cried, "The monster is dying, the monster is dead; let us bury him! The negro is free."

This account explains, in part, why so large a congregation gathered when the body of the forty-two-year-old missionary, William Knibb, was lowered to its rest to await its liberation from the grave at the coming of His Lord.

EWT

---

[1]G. Winfred Hervey, *The Story of Baptist Missions in Foreign Lands* (St. Louis: C. R. Barnes, 1892), p. 699.

[2]John C. Carlile, *The Story of the English Baptists* (London: James Clarke and Co., 1905), pp. 205-6.

[3]Ibid., pp. 206-7.

[4]Ibid., p. 207.

November 16—Abraham Marshall Baptizes a Preacher-Cousin

Scripture: Acts 18:7-8

Abraham Marshall was the subject of an earlier entry (March 31) which told how the bachelor pastor traveled for 2,200 miles in 1792 in search of his life partner. However, in 1786 Abraham had made a similar round-trip journey by horseback to Connecticut to care for matters of his deceased father's estate. The trip began on May 10, 1786, and the man of God was away from his beloved home state of Georgia until November 16 of that year.

Abraham's greatest delight was in preaching. At every opportunity on his trip he declared the gospel and defended the faith. Wherever he could find an open pulpit, Abraham Marshall witnessed God's blessing in the salvation of souls. As he journeyed northward, he chanced to meet a Mr. Winchester who knew some of his relatives, and Abraham inquired about them. Winchester told him of the Reverend Eliakim Marshall, Congregational minister, respected citizen, and long-time pedobaptist in New England. Upon hearing of him, Abraham said, "Well, if this be his character, I shall expect to baptize him before I return; for if he had a sound judgement, he will understand my arguments . . . and if he has a tender conscience, they will have an influence on his mind."[1]

Actually, when Abraham arrived at Windsor, Connecticut, he was the guest of his cousin Eliakim, and in the course of time, the subject of baptism was introduced. After long discussions from the Word of God, Eliakim was convinced of immersion, but his wife opposed his desire to be obedient in immersion. Eliakim had been raised in the Congregational denomination from the time of his birth, and he belonged to the Poquonock or Third Society in Windsor until the time of his conversion during the Awakening. Following his conversion, he found little of interest in the Congregational church and, in fact, was fined in 1746 for nonattendance at public meetings. He united with the Separate church in Wetherfield, Connecticut, and left the church of his youth. In the course of time, Eliakim was ordained as pastor of a Separate church (these were New Lights who left the Congregationalists), and he gained great respect. Eliakim was also active politically and served the state assembly from 1779 to 1783 and ran for governor in 1780.[2] Thus, Mrs. Eliakim Marshall felt it would be demeaning to repudiate such prominence with the admission of doctrinal error.

Eliakim sought Abraham's advice as to what to do. The young Marshall responded, "I will mention two passages of Scripture, which my father frequently made use of in difficult cases, which are these: 'Conferred not with flesh and blood. What thy hand findeth to do, do it with all thy might.' "[3] Abraham recorded in his diary this description of Eliakim's immersion:

> After (the) sermon Eliakim Marshall mounted the stage, and gave a clear striking and powerful account of God's work on his soul, greatly to the satisfaction of the congregation. Also he told them that he had been an advocate for infant sprinkling, in opposition to the

> primitive and apostolic mode; that he was now convinced he had no warrant for it in the Bible, and he was about to comply with the baptism of our Savior. . . . At two p.m. preached a second sermon; . . . (God) graced the assembly with His glorious and awful presence; heaven began on earth. Then we advanced . . . to a river . . . and baptized . . . Eliakim Marshall in the presence of hundreds who had never seen the ordinance administered according to the pattern and example of the great Head . . . before.[4]

The following day Abraham had the privilege of delivering the ordination sermon of Eliakim as a Baptist preacher, and from 1786 until his death in 1791, Eliakim served as pastor of the Baptist church in Windsor, Connecticut. Surely this was the highlight of Abraham's first journey to his father's homeland!

DLC

---

[1]James Donovan Mosteller, *A History of the Kiokee Baptist Church in Georgia* (Ann Arbor: Edwards Bros., 1952), p. 141.

[2]William G. McLoughlin, ed., *The Diary of Isaac Backus* (Providence: Brown University Press, 1979), 3:1320.

[3]Mosteller, p. 141.

[4]Ibid., pp. 141-42.

November 17—"My Times Are in Thy Hands"

Scripture: Psalm 90

We have briefly observed (July 9) the life of Dr. J. G. Binney, who served the Lord faithfully in Burma for twenty-six years. Our attention is now on his wife, Mrs. Juliette Pattison Binney. Mrs. Binney was born October 1, 1808. As a young lady she was baptized by her own brother, Dr. R. E. Pattison, pastor of the First Baptist Church in Providence, Rhode Island, and later home secretary of the Missionary Union. After receiving her education, Miss Pattison taught at the Charlestown Female Seminary. During that time she met her future husband. The couple married in 1833, and after several pastorates in America, they sailed for Burma on November 17, 1843. Dr. Binney's father, though saved, could not understand the "necessity of seeking a more extended field of usefulness."[1] The farewells must have been difficult to bear. However, the Reverend J. G. Binney made an early commitment to seek the will of God in his life. He wrote, "When I commenced my Christian course I resolved never to ask what I preferred . . . but what God commanded, and His will should control my steps.''[2] After one hundred and forty days on the sea, they arrived in Burma on April 6, 1844.

The life of a ''missionary wife'' was severe, and in time, Mrs. Binney's health began to fail. She was forced to return to America in April of 1850, and a letter to her brother eighteen months earlier gave rich insights into her heart and life.

> As you see by the date of this letter I have entered on my fortieth year; and yesterday was the fifteenth anniversary of my marriage; can you think of your ''little sister'' as being so very old? . . . Joseph, I can see, is a little anxious about my health. I am not. I did not expect to live many years when I came to this country, and I remember our precious mother, when I was trying to hide her grey hairs by brushing them under, used to tell me that I would never be troubled in that way. My husband said yesterday, that if on leaving his church in Savannah, he could have known that he would only live long enough to accomplish what the Lord has permitted us to do here, he would not have hesitated a moment. Do not be alarmed, lest if I grow worse, I should go home. We have not the most distant idea of ever seeing your dear face again, though I would give anything short of sacrificing conscientious convictions to do so.[3]

Her health amended in the States, and Dr. and Mrs. Binney boarded a vessel for Burma. But when her health deteriorated again in 1863, she was forced to return to the United States a second time. During her forced rest in America, Dr. Binney's health failed as well, and he returned home. However, as soon as their health allowed, the couple sailed again for Burma.

The story of their life of service cannot be fully related here, but upon the death of her dear husband at sea on November 26, 1877, Mrs. Binney continued on to Rangoon, where she spent her last years in service to the Savior. She passed away on May 18, 1884, but had ''taught her Bible-class . . . on the day before the night in which she went to her heavenly home. Her . . . training and acquisitions of mind and heart, qualified her for the great changes and heterogeneous tasks to which she was called. Her life was devoted to the welfare of the Karens, and the property which God had placed in her hands with the exception of proper provision for her relatives, was given to the cause of missions.''[4] Though anticipating an early death, Mrs. Binney lived to be almost seventy-five. Surely our lives are in His hands!

May we, who profess the name of Christ in this day, determine never to seek what we would like to do but rather what the Lord would have us do, as did Dr. and Mrs. J. G. Binney.

DLC

---

[1]Mrs. J. G. Binney, *Twenty-Six Years in Burma* (Philadelphia: American Baptist Publication Society, 1880), p. 153.

[2]Ibid., p. 31.

[3]Ibid., p. 23.

[4]A. H. Burlington, *The Story of Baptist Missions* (St. Louis: C. R. Barnes Publishing Co., 1892), p. 925.

November 18—Record Keeper For Remembrance

Scripture: Malachi 3:16-18

A baby son was born to James and Elizabeth (Cously) Cathcart in the northern county of Londonberry in Ireland on November 18, 1826. James and Elizabeth were of Scotch ancestry, and the lad, William Cathcart, was raised in the Presbyterian church, which predominated among the Scots. The boy grew up in the warmth of that heritage and was converted at an early age. However, as a young man of nineteen, William became convinced of believer's immersion and was thus baptized in January of 1846 by the Reverend R. H. Carson of Tubbermore.

As a young man, William Cathcart was impressed by the Lord that he was a chosen vessel to preach the gospel. He received his training in the University of Glasgow, Scotland, and furthered his theological studies in the Rawdon (Baptist) College in Yorkshire, England. Early in 1850, he was ordained as pastor in the Baptist church of Barnsley, near Sheffield, England, and that same year he married Eliza Caldwell. For three years Cathcart served that congregation as pastor.

The political ideas of the day and his strong aversion to the state church sentiments influenced the man of God to emigrate to America. The Cathcarts sailed for the United States in 1853 and arrived in America on November 18th of that year. The following month Cathcart accepted the call of the Third Baptist Church in Groton, on the Mystic River, Connecticut. He served that congregation until April of 1857 and then accepted a call to the Second Baptist Church of Philadelphia. His ministry in the City of Brotherly Love lasted for twenty-seven years.

William Cathcart was a man of staunch conviction and treasured the distinctives of the Baptist cause. He was no stranger to controversy, but this conflict stemmed from firmness of faith and not from a distressing disposition.

The man of God enjoyed history and began amassing biographies of Baptist preachers and compiling data. He became one of the greatest

Baptist encyclopedist/historians in the denomination. In 1873 the University of Lewisburg (Pennsylvania) honored Cathcart's efforts by conferring on him the Doctor of Divinity degree. On the retirement of Dr. Howard Malcom as president of the American Baptist Historical Society in 1876, Dr. Cathcart was chosen to succeed him, and he led the Society for eight years. "In 1875, in view of the first Centennial year of our national independence, . . . the Baptist Ministerial Union of Pennsylvania appointed Dr. Cathcart to read a paper entitled 'The Baptists in the Revolution' at their annual meeting. This paper met with such immediate approval that the Ministerial Union formed a special committee to work with Dr. Cathcart in publishing an enlarged edition of the essay. Thus it was published as a book in 1876 and entitled *The Baptists and the American Revolution.*"[1] In 1884, because of failing health, the man of God resigned his pastorate and retired. He continued to be active in Baptist interests through the remainder of his life.

The greatest literary contribution made by Dr. Cathcart has to be his two-volume set entitled *The Baptist Encyclopedia*. This monumental work first appeared in 1881 and contains invaluable information concerning many early Baptists in America as well as in England.

Following his retirement from active service, the Lord allowed Cathcart many additional years, and he passed into the presence of the Lord on July 8, 1908, at the age of eighty-one.

DLC

---

[1]Publisher's Foreword from William Cathcart, *Baptist Patriots and the American Revolution* (Grand Rapids: Guardian Press, 1976), p. vii.

November 19—Judson's First Furlough After Thirty-three Years of Service

Scripture: I Corinthians 15:57-58

It was a dark day on November 19, 1845, as the Triennial Convention met. The Baptists of the South had withdrawn, and it was apparent that a reduction in the budget would be necessary. The officers had been directed in the spring meeting to prepare a proposal to be presented at the November meeting that would make the needed recommendations for the revised commitments. The solemn report was read by Dr. Solomon Peck, foreign secretary. One of the suggestions was to abandon the Arakan mission. The Convention was being asked to sound "retreat!"

Seated that day among the messengers was Adoniram Judson. After thirty-three years of missionary service, which included unbelievable privations and imprisonment, Judson was back in America for the first time. Now the premier Baptist missionary was being forced to hear the report that would close a field comprising part of the work in Burma. It is not difficult to surmise what must have passed through his mind in those moments.

After becoming Baptists by conviction, the Judsons waited three years before being appointed as missionaries of the Triennial Convention. Judson had waited seven years before the first convert was won and on June 27, 1819, he finally baptized Moung Nau. In 1815 the little seven-month-old son of the Judsons died and was buried under Burma's sod. Mrs. Judson became ill and had to return for two years to America, and Adoniram persevered alone. The First Burman War broke out in May of 1824. In June, Judson was cast into the death prison. The sufferings were indescribable, but God's grace was sufficient. After eleven months of imprisonment in Ava, Judson endured six more months of incarceration in Oungpenla. While Adoniram was helping the Burmese to secure terms of peace with the British, Ann Judson died (October 24, 1826). Judson's little daughter Maria died six months later.

Judson became almost a recluse. He refused to accept the degree of Doctor of Divinity given him by Brown University. He fasted and prayed and even dug a grave and sat beside it brooding. His sadness was increased by the lethargy of the churches in America. How could they be so slow in their obedience to God? During the next trying years, Judson spent much time and effort in translating. He nailed his will to the cross and determined that no desire should ever be pursued unless it furthered the message of Calvary.

After eight years of loneliness, Judson married Mrs. Sarah Boardman who had been a widow for three years. They were married on April 10, 1834. His life turned now for the better, as a little daughter was born to the couple in October of 1835 and a son in 1837.

Judson's health showed the evidence of the many hardships he had endured, and he was ordered to go to Calcutta. A throat problem followed, and for almost a year he was unable to preach or teach. A third child had been born to the Judsons (little Henry), but he too had died. All of the sufferings that Judson endured cannot be catalogued but when Mrs. Judson became ill and it was apparent she must be returned to the States, Judson consented to accompany her with their children. They sailed on April 26, 1845, but Mrs. Judson died en route and was buried on the Island of St. Helena in September 1845.

Thus it was that the heavy-hearted Judson arrived back in Boston on October 15, 1845, and a month later he heard of the closing of the Arakan mission. He was unable to speak above a whisper, "but when this report was read the lion roused. Rising to his feet, Mr. Judson, in a full voice, said, 'Though forbidden of the doctors to speak in public, I must protest against the abandonment of the Arakan mission.' It was all he could say, but it was enough. The Convention unanimously resolved not to abandon any mission work."[1]

O that God would multiply the Judsons in our days of need!

DLC

[1]Albert Henry Newman, *A Century of Baptist Achievement* (Philadelphia: American Baptist Publication Society, 1901), p. 187.

November 20—From the Acorn Planted the Mighty Oak Spread Its Branches

Scripture: Psalm 68

Shubal Stearns, a native of Boston, Massachusetts, had come under the influence of the preaching of George Whitefield and the spirit of the Great Awakening in the 1740s. He labored as a minister among the "Separates," or "New Lights" as they were called, until 1751 when he embraced the principles of the Baptists. So many of the Separates became Baptists that on occasion, Whitefield even took pains to declaim against what he considered "rebaptism" of adults and argued for pedobaptism. In order to make it plain that the Baptists did not belong to his flock, he stated that many of his "chickens had become ducks."

Shubal Stearns soon took his leave of New England and halted for a short time at Opeckon, Berckley County, Virginia, where he was received kindly by a Baptist church under the pastoral care of John Garrard. There he met the man who would become his brother-in-law, Daniel Marshall, also a Separate, who had just returned from a mission among the Indians. Soon after Marshall's arrival, Stearns became a Baptist.

Little did those men realize that God was forming and preparing a nucleus for the spread of the gospel and Baptist principles throughout the South. Being restless in spirit and under pressure from Indian raids and massacres after the defeat of Braddock, Stearns and a little party of sixteen Baptists left Virginia and settled at Sandy Creek, Guilford County, North Carolina. As soon as they arrived, they built a little meetinghouse, and this small party organized into a Separate Baptist church with Shubal Stearns as pastor and Daniel Marshall and Joseph Breed as his assistants. From this small beginning a powerful and extensive work was born. It soon multiplied from sixteen to six hundred and six. Before long, as a result of the evangelistic zeal, the work of grace spread not only throughout North Carolina but over into Virginia, South Carolina, and Georgia. God raised up preachers like James Read, Samuel Harriss, and Dutton Lane who had great success in Virginia. Daniel Marshall traveled further south and planted churches in South Carolina and the Kiokee Baptist Church across the Savannah River, which was the first Baptist church in Georgia and was the mother of many other Baptist churches.[1]

Benedict states, "While Marshall was sojourneying Southward and planting churches in various places where he pitched his habitations, Harriss bent his course to the Northward, amongst his rude and insolent countrymen, the Virginians; and while his brethren were thus engaged to the North and South of him, Stearns maintained his station at Sandy Creek, where his labors were greatly blessed; he however travelled a considerable distance in the country around, to assist in organizing and regulating the churches which he and his associates were instrumental in raising up. Thus the Separate Baptists were headed by the most distinguished men; distinguished not from human acquirements, but for purity of life and godly simplicity, which they amidst the shipwrecks of many, maintained to the end; and for pious ardour and invincible boldness and perseverance in their Master's service."[2]

A span of only twenty years had passed from the time Shubal Stearns embraced Baptist principles until his death on November 20, 1771.[3] During that period, there was a great expansion westward. The spread of the gospel went forward in spite of the French and Indian War and in the face of a vast wilderness with no means of communication except by foot or horseback. Shubal Stearns left no natural children but was responsible for a vast number of spiritual offspring as a result of his faithfulness and zeal for our Lord Jesus Christ. Even today, we, as recipients of such a great spiritual heritage, should be thankful for Shubal Stearns and those who followed in his footsteps down through the years.

EWT

---

[1]George Washington Paschal, *History of North Carolina Baptists* (Raleigh: Edwards and Broughton Co., 1930), 1:271-77.

[2]David Benedict, *A General History of the Baptist Denomination in America* (Boston: Manning and Loring, 1813), 2:41-42.

[3]Paschal, p. 228.

November 21—When the Shoe Is on the Other Foot

Scripture: Psalm 94

Soon after Elisha Paine was ordained into the gospel ministry in May of 1752, he was seized by the authorities of Windham, Connecticut, on November 21, 1752, and imprisoned because he failed to pay a tax to the state church minister. In defending liberty of conscience and putting forth the necessity of maintaining neutrality between the church and the state, Baptists often had to remind the Congregationalists of the time when the "shoe was on the other foot," and their fathers suffered under papal authority and tyranny as well as from Rome's child, the Church of England. Elisha Paine provides the following eloquent reminder:

> I cannot but marvel to see how soon the children will forget the sword that drove their fathers into this land, and take hold of it as a jewel, and kill their grandchildren therewith. O, that man could see how far this is from Christ's rule! That all things which we would have others do unto us, that we should do even so unto them. I believe the same people, who put this authority into the hands of Mr. Cogswell, their minister, to put me into prison for not paying him for preaching, would think it very hard for the church I belong to, and am pastor of, if they should get the upper hand, and tax and imprison him, for what he should be so unjustly taxed at; and yet I can see no other difference, only because the power is in his hands; for I suppose he has heard me as often as I ever have him, and yet he hath taken from me by force two cows and one steer, and now my body held in prison only because the power is in his hands.[1]

He later compared the law of Connecticut with that of Rome and referred to Psalm 94:20-22—"Shall the throne of iniquity have fellowship with thee, *which frameth mischief by a law?* They gather themselves together against the soul of the righteous, and condemn the innocent blood. But the Lord is my defense; and my God is the rock of my refuge.'' He continued by saying, ''If this constitution hath its rise from that throne, then come forth to the help of the Lord against the mighty, for it is better to die for Christ than to live against Him.''[2]

Five days later Elisha Paine was released from prison. The severe winter kept him from his family, who suffered much in an unfinished house for lack of Paine's assistance. The oppression of Baptists continued in Connecticut until 1771, and through it all, the Baptists not only saw the clear principles of liberty of conscience but also fearlessly set them forth in spite of all the persecution brought to bear upon them.

May our Lord help us to set forth, clearly teach, and impress these principles on future generations, lest through lethargy and indifference the truths are lost to our posterity. The liberties we may lose today may take centuries to regain.

EWT

---

[1]Charles G. Sommers, ed., *A History of the Baptists in New England,* The Baptist Library, vol. 1 (New York: Lewis Colby and Co., n.d.), p. 152.

[2]Ibid.

November 22—A Summary of the Influence of Separate Baptists

Scripture: Psalm 68:10-11

My personal admiration for the ''Separate'' Baptists has exhibited itself on many pages of this volume, and I am forced to concur with George Washington Paschal in his statement, ''I make bold to say that these Separate Baptists have proved to be the most remarkable body of Christians America has known.''[1] I further agree with Paschal that had the Baptist cause in America continued under the domination of a strong Calvinism, such as the Particular Baptists advocated, Baptists would not have grown into such a force for God in our land.[2]

It was a memorable day indeed when the little group of Separate Baptists traveled to Sandy Creek, Guilford County, North Carolina, and constituted the church of which Shubal Stearns became pastor. There were eight families in the little company composing the sixteen-member assembly, and the flock built a meetinghouse. Shubal Stearns had two men to assist him, Daniel Marshall and Joseph Breed, for the congregation expected growth. The membership soon grew from sixteen to over six hundred! Daniel Marshall, whose life and ministry are discussed in other entries, was tireless in his efforts and soon was preaching in Virginia with tremendous results. In an early visit to Virginia, Marshall baptized Dutton Lane, and the convert soon began exhorting. As a result, revival fell. Mr. Marshall, at one time, baptized forty-two persons. Samuel Harriss, who later became the leader among the Separatist Baptists in Virginia, was baptized by Marshall. The growth of the Separatist Baptist cause in Virginia was almost breath-taking. Revival swept the area; persecution followed, and the cause of the Baptists proliferated in every direction. Morgan Edwards said, "Sandy Creek is the mother of all the Separate Baptists. From this Zion went forth the word, and great was the company of them who published it. This church in seventeen years has spread her branches westward as far as the great river Mississippi; southward as far as Georgia; eastward to the sea and Chesapeake Bay; and northward to the waters of the Potomac; it, in seventeen years, is become mother, grandmother, and great-grandmother, to forty-two churches, from which sprang 125 ministers."[3]

The genius of the work in Sandy Creek surely centered in the Reverend Shubal Stearns. He was born in Boston on January 28, 1706. Thus he was almost fifty years old when the Sandy Creek Church was constituted on November 22, 1755. He spent the remainder of his life in North Carolina and passed away on November 20, 1771. Though many of his contemporaries commented on the unique quality of Stearns's voice, his real success was not due to his pulpit ability or physical appearance. Stearns possessed talents in organizing his work. He sent out young preachers, organized churches, ordained ministers, and taught an interdependence of churches while preserving the autonomy of each. He was a motivater who learned to challenge believers to unite in doing collectively what a local church could not do individually. Stearns's system of operation was captured and incorporated into the Southern Baptist Convention, and his methods have worked to our modern day.

The rapid growth of the Separate Baptists involved enthusiastic evangelism, but one is forced to agree with Morgan Edwards when he said, "I believe a preternatural and invisible hand works in the assemblies of the Separate Baptists bearing down the human mind, as was the case in the primitive (ie. New Testament) churches."[4] In days of apathy, we do well to reflect upon such cases in history and cry out to God to turn our hearts unto Him once again in full surrender.

DLC

---

[1]George Washington Paschal, *History of North Carolina Baptists* (Raleigh: Edwards and Broughton Co., 1930), 1:240.

[2]Ibid., p. 270.

[3]Morgan Edwards, *Materials Toward a History of the Baptists* (Danielsville, Ga.: Heritage Press, 1984), 2:92.

[4]Ibid., p. 93.

November 23—Any Truth Rationalized to an Extreme Becomes a Heresy

Scripture: Matthew 15:1-14

In the early eighteenth century, many General Baptists embraced extreme liberalism in the form of Arian and Socinian views. They had been influenced by the apostasy of the state churches. Between 1715 and 1750 the General Baptists experienced a severe decline—the number of their churches fell from 146 to 65. The winds of false doctrine are dry and deadly, withering the spiritual vitality of the body.

During the same period, there were winds of change shifting among the Particular Baptists. An exaggerated emphasis on election and predestination dried up their springs of evangelism. Instead of leaders like Benjamin Keach and Hanserd Knollys, who balanced their conservative Calvinism with a warm and fervent evangelism, they embraced and propagated a hardened hyper-Calvinism that became theologically narrow, rigid in sterile orthodoxy, and a rationalistic rather than a biblical faith. Though their staunch belief in the sovereignty of God protected them from the Arian error, their rationalistic fatalism and antinomianism brought tremendous decline, and over the same period of time, 1715 to 1750, the Particular Baptist churches were reduced from 220 to 146.[1]

Dr. John Gill, who was born November 23, 1697, was an influential leader of the Particular Baptists and a highly respected scholar of this period. He, through private teachers, became a superior scholar in Latin, Greek, and logic. After many years of study, he became a profound scholar in the Rabbinical Hebrew and a master of the Targum, Talmuds, the Rabboth, and the book of Zohar, with their ancient commentaries. The preparation made him academically qualified as a biblical commentator. As a prolific writer, he produced many works, including a commentary on the entire Bible. He still is acknowledged among Baptists as one of the most profound scholars.

Armitage says of him,

> And yet, with all his ability, he was so high a supralapsarian, that it is hard to distinguish him from an antinomian. For example, he could not invite sinners to the Savior, while he declared their guilt and condemnation, their need of the new birth; and held that God would convert such as He had elected to be saved, and so man must not interfere with His purposes by inviting men to Christ. Under this preaching His church steadily declined, and after half a century's work he left but a mere handful.[2]

The decline among the Baptists of England continued until 1750, when they were impacted by the spiritual awakening that swept England and America. Men like Andrew Fuller shook off the shackles of the extreme rationalistic positions of liberalism and hyper-Calvinism and returned to the evangelical spirit of presenting the gospel to every creature. The classic statement of the renewed evangelical doctrine was "The Gospel Worthy of All Acceptation." It was Fuller who held the ropes in England, while Carey descended into the pit in India.

May we learn that any truth taken to an extreme by rationalistic processes will become a heresy that could lead to apostasy, and that is deadly.

EWT

---

[1]H. Leon McBeth, *The Baptist Heritage* (Nashville: Broadman Press, 1987), pp. 171-72.

[2]Thomas Armitage, *The History of the Baptists* (1890; reprint ed., Watertown, Wis.: Maranatha Baptist Press, 1976), 2:561.

November 24—Swallowed Up in the Will of God

Scripture: Matthew 26:37-46

Susanna Mason was born in Rehoboth, Massachusetts, in 1724 or 1725. Her great-grandfather had been a soldier in Oliver Cromwell's Roundhead Army. The families were Baptists in background. She was converted in 1745, joined the Separate church, and maintained her Baptist convictions when she married Isaac Backus. Backus, not fully persuaded of Baptist principles relating to pedobaptism at that time, was aware of her views when he asked her to marry him. Later he became "fully persuaded" and became one of the leading lights among the Baptists and exercised great influence relating to freedom of conscience in the formation of our nation.

Consider the following description of Susanna and Isaac's wedding on Wednesday, November 29, 1749:

> He [Isaac] refused to permit any of the frivolous merrymaking and frolicking which normally accompanied marriages in New England, because he considered it a solemn ordinance of God.
>
> "I have often looked with abhorrence upon the Comon Practis of most people in this Point; namely their giving way to their lusts and indulging themselves in vanity and carnality when they are about to Seek a Companion and to Enter into a Married State."
>
> Susanna agreed with him. The wedding took place in her father's house in Rehoboth and was performed by a justice of the peace in accordance with the prevailing custom. But Backus received permission of the justice to have his friends transform it into a religious ceremony:
>
> Br. Shepherd read a Psalm and we Sung; then we went to prayer and the Lord did hear and Come near to us. Then I took my dear Sister Susanna by the Hand and Spoke Something of the Sense I had of our Standing and acting in the presence of God, and also how that He had clearly pointed out to me this Person to be my Companion and an helper meet for me. And then went on and declar'd the Marriage Covenant; and She did the same to me. Then Esq. Foster Solemnly declar'd that we were Lawful Man and Wife: then Brother Shepherd went on to Wish us a blessing and gave us a Sweet Exhortation. And so did some others; then brother Paine pray'd and had freedom therein. Then I read, and we sung the 101 Psalm after that I preached a Short Sermon from Acts 13:36.[1]

Susanna was a very capable and thrifty wife to Isaac. She raised nine children with comparatively little help from her husband. Backus spent much of his time in travel, and even when he was home, he was often busy writing or fulfilling his pastoral responsibilities. Because of this, the task of maintaining the household fell heavily upon Susanna.

Backus wrote of his wife: "Her prudence and economy did much toward the support of our family . . . and her exemplary walk and conversation caused her to be highly esteemed by her acquaintances in general. In several revivals of religion among us, and in one just before her death, she most heartily rejoiced, and was much engaged."[2]

Through a painful, debilitating illness, Susanna said, "I am not so much concerned with living or dying, as to have my will swallowed up in the will of God."[3] On November 24, 1800, five days before her 51st wedding anniversary, Susanna Backus quietly departed, having had a fulfilling life as a loving wife who supported her influential husband.

Without Susanna's strong, efficient help, her husband would have had a far less productive ministry. Backus lived during America's formative years, and his understanding of the biblical principle of the separation of church and state was used of God to guide our founding fathers.

EWT

---

[1]William G. McLoughlin, ed., *Isaac Backus and the American Pietistic Tradition* (Boston: Little, Brown and Company, 1967), pp. 68-69.

[2]William G. McLoughlin, ed., *The Diary of Isaac Backus* (Providence: Brown University Press, 1979), 3:1462.

[3]McLoughlin, *Isaac Backus and the American Pietistic Tradition,* p. 229.

November 25—From One Generation to Another

Scripture: Matthew 16:16-18

Two previous entries have focused expressly on the Wightman family of England and early America. Valentine Wightman was born April 16, 1681, in Rhode Island. On February 10, 1702, he married Susannah Holmes, who was the granddaughter of the Reverend Obadiah Holmes who had been severely whipped at Lynn, Massachusetts, and the great-granddaughter of Roger Williams, the dauntless apostle of freedom of conscience. Mr. and Mrs. Valentine Wightman surely came from Baptist stock that knew what it meant to suffer for the cause of Christ!

In 1704 a company of Dissenters petitioned the " 'Hounorable Court Setting at Newhaven' signifying that we differ from you in some Poynts of Religeon but yett we desier to live Pesable and quietly with our Neighbors . . . that since it has Pleased the Almity God to putt it into the hart of our grasious Queen to grant us dissenters proclamated liberty of Conscience . . . and we understand that your laws requiers us to Petition to you for the Settling of our Meeting . . . do beseech of you that you would not deny us herein, . . . that our meeting might be stated and held at Will Starks in New London."[1]

This request was apparently ignored, and accepting silence as consent, the group of twelve dissenters called Mr. Valentine Wightman to be their pastor. The young preacher had been married only two years and did not immediately take up permanent residence in Groton, Connecticut, but on September 6, 1707, the Wightmans and two young children made the move. Wightman departed from Rhode Island, where Baptists had established freedom of religion for all, but Connecticut still had a "Standing Order" (state church), and dissenters felt the force of political and social disfavor. The following extracts taken from Court Records, New London County, November Term, 1707, and September Term, 1708 are of interest: "To the Sheriff of New London County . . . or to the Constable of Groton, Greeting: . . . Petition that Sheriff summon and give notice to the aforesaid Valentine Wightman and his said wife . . . that they appear before Richard Christopher . . . to answer the charges and be dealt with as the Law directs. 25 Nov. 1707."[2]

The case was resolved on June 4, 1708, when it was proved that Valentine Wightman was in compliance with the terms of the Act of Toleration.

From 1712 to 1714, Wightman made regular trips to New York, and his converts were formed into a Baptist church, the first in New York City. Wightman was also used of God in beginning other churches during his Groton ministry. "Through his instrumentality, and in the face of sharp opposition from the Standing Order, Baptist Churches were gathered in Waterford, Lyme, Stonington, and other places. His preaching cost him much unpleasant controversy, and not a little persecution.[3]

Valentine Wightman was considered a "General Six Principle" Baptist. That group practiced the laying on of hands at baptism and made the custom a requirement for membership and its absence a bar to communion. However, Wightman tempered his views during later years. Of highest interest is Wait Palmer's conversion to Baptist views under the ministry of Wightman.[4] Palmer pastored a Baptist church in North Stonington and itinerated widely. In 1751, Palmer immersed the famous Shubal Stearns, who became the "Father of the Separate Baptists." (See November 20 and 22.) Though we do not believe in "apostolic succession," we are pleased to trace the line of Bible truth from the martyrs to our present day. After a forty-two-year ministry in Groton, our Lord called His valiant Valentine unto Himself in glory on June 9, 1747.

DLC

---

[1]Mary Ross Whitman, *George Wightman of Quidnessett, R.I., (1632-1721/22) and Descendants* (Chicago: n.p., 1939), p. 31.

[2]Ibid., pp. 32-33.

[3]William B. Sprague, *Annals of the American Pulpit* (New York: Robert Carter and Bros., 1865), 6:27

[4]William G. McLoughlin, ed., *The Diary of Isaac Backus* (Providence: Brown University Press, 1979), 1:271.

November 26—The Word of God, the Dictates of Conscience Made Me a Baptist

Scripture: Acts 24:14-27

John Holcombe was born in 1762. When he was still a child, his family moved from Virginia to South Carolina. By eleven years of age, he completed all the education to be received from a living teacher. He had a naturally inquiring mind which desired knowledge of every kind. He especially dwelt on the vast number and grandeur of the heavenly bodies.

At the commencement of the Revolutionary War, Holcombe was quite young. However, he was impressed with a sense of wrong done to his country and felt the stirrings of patriotism. When he had scarcely emerged from boyhood, he entered the army, where he demonstrated so much courage and discretion that he quickly rose to an important post of authority. It was during this period that his mind became impressed with religious truth. Here, amidst the temptations of a camp and the intense excitement incident to the contest for liberty, he made a profession of his faith in Christ.

In conversation with his father, he was informed that he was baptized a Presbyterian in his infancy. After searching the Scriptures relating to that matter, he concluded (in his own words) that "to follow the dictates of conscience, I must be a Baptist; and not conferring with flesh and blood, I rode near twenty miles to propose myself as a candidate for admission into a Baptist church."[1]

Immediately after his baptism, Holcombe received a license to preach and commenced his work with energy and fervor. His labors were accompanied with uncommon blessing. He soon baptized twenty-six persons, among whom were his wife Frances, her brother and mother, and shortly after, seventeen more, including his father, who had endeavored to persuade Holcombe that he was a Presbyterian.

It was no small testimony of the confidence of his fellow citizens that they appointed Holcombe to represent them in the Constitutional Convention of South Carolina, held in Charleston, for ratifying the Constitution of the United States.

After preaching at his own expense in several locations in South Carolina, Holcombe moved to Savannah, where a few Baptists had undertaken to erect a house of worship. While it was yet unfinished, they had rented it to a group of Presbyterians whose building had burned. For a short period of time he attempted to pastor a Presbyterian church. He and the Baptists found this unworkable, and on November 26, 1800, they constituted a Baptist church.

Though having limited educational opportunities, Holcombe was active in writing and promoting Christian literature, establishing charitable and educational institutions and promoting humanitarian causes. His vigorous opposition to infidelity, theatrical amusements, and other things which he regarded of evil tendency, rendered him anything but a favorite with the profligate and profane. Several times his life was in jeopardy because of his open and strong stand against sin.[2]

Let us pray that God shall grant us strong, humble men of courage to stand against the evil tide of our day that they might leave memorials for future generations.

EWT

---

[1]William B. Sprague, *Annals of the American Pulpit* (New York: Robert Carter and Bros., 1865), 6:216

[2]Ibid., p. 217.

November 27—The Testament of a Godly Mother

Scripture: Isaiah 59:1-8

A godly woman named Soetgen van den Houte fell into the hands of the same persecutors that her husband had fallen into previously. She was left a widow with three children. After experiencing the fierce assaults and imprisonments described before in this volume by others who shared like sufferings and martyrdom, she witnessed to the truth she professed and sealed it with her blood and death November 27, 1560, in the city of Ghent.

Just prior to her death, Soetgen left a testament to her children:

> In the name of the Lord:
>
> Grace, peace and mercy from God the Father, and the Lord Jesus Christ, be to you, my dear children. A loving salutation to you, David, Betgen, and Tanneken, written by your mother in bonds, to put you in mind of the truth, to which I hope to testify by word and by death, by the help of the Almighty, and as an example to you. May the wisdom of the Holy Spirit instruct and strengthen you, that you may be nurtured in the ways of the Lord. Amen.
>
> Further my dear children, since it is pleasing to the Lord to take me out of the world, I will leave you a memento, not of silver or gold, for such jewels are perishable. I would fain inscribe a jewel in your heart were it possible—the word of truth. Thus I will a little teach you by the Word of the Lord, with my best wishes, according to the small ability I have received of the Lord, and in my simplicity.[1]

At this point, Soetgen began to exhort her children to fear the Lord and to yield themselves to those who would teach them godliness. She desired for them not to pursue riches and temporal things of life but to live humbly and uprightly, walking in the ways of the Lord. She warned them that the world is seductive and ''that men find much more earth of which to make earthen vessels, than gold of which to make golden vessels; and like as the great waters of the sea are more than the drops, so will they be the greater number that be condemned.''[2]

Soetgen concluded by saying, ''Oh! My dear children, I have written this with tears, admonishing you from love, praying for you with a fervent heart, that if it were possible, you may be found among that number (the redeemed). When your father was taken from me I did not spare myself, day or night, to bring you up; and my prayer and care continually was for your salvation; and being now in bonds it has always been my greatest concern that I could not, according to my anxious desire, better provide for you.''[3]

After commending the children to her family and to the Lord, Soetgen concluded her letter and was soon reunited with her husband in the presence of the Lord.

A godly mother is a priceless jewel. May we see godly Christian homes established across our nation and the world. God grant that godly mothers be multiplied who will glorify Christ in life and in death.

EWT

---

[1]T. J. Van Braght, trans., and Edward Bean Underhill, ed., *A Martyrology of the Churches of Christ Commonly Called Baptists* (London: J. Haddon and Son, 1853), 2:289-90.

[2]Ibid., p. 292.

[3]Ibid., p. 293.

November 28—Jonah's Three Days and Baker's Three Ships—Same Results

Scripture: Jonah 2

The names Elijah Baker and Philip Hughes should be emblazoned in Baptist history as outstanding pioneers of the faith. Elijah Baker was born in Lunenburg County, Virginia, in 1742. He was converted under the ministry of Jeremiah Walker and was baptized by Samuel Harriss in 1769. Soon Baker was preaching with great power as an itinerate evangelist and was used of God in the establishment of a number of churches. Philip Hughes was born in Colver County on November 28, 1750. Following his conversion, he was baptized by David Thompson on August 10, 1773, and three years later he was ordained into the ministry.

In the early days of the labors, Elijah Baker seems to have escaped the imprisonment that many early Virginia Baptists endured. However, such a fruitful ministry attracted great attention, and thus it was in Accomack County, he was imprisoned for fifty-six days. Oddly enough, Baker was incarcerated during the Revolutionary War, when the colonists were fighting for political and civil liberty. The year was 1778, and Elijah Baker would rather go to jail than surrender his liberty of conscience.[1] But as is so often the case, our Lord overrules in the adversities and trials of life. Thus Elijah Baker preached through the grates of the jail windows. One man who heard him during that period was Thomas Batston, Esq.[2] The gentleman invited Baker to his home state of Delaware. Of course, Baker was not at liberty to accept the offer immediately, but the Lord had other plans. "The rude Virginians (in order to silence him) took him out of jail and put him on board a privateer, with orders to land him on any coast out of America. Here he was compelled to work, and for his refusing and praying and preaching and singing was ill used. The privateer put him on board another ship, but the wind keeping . . . still, they began to think that it was owing to their having poor Baker in the harbor; therefore that other ship put him on board a third, and the third put him ashore."[3]

Amazingly, Elijah Baker discovered that he had landed in Delaware, and remembering the invitation from Squire Batston, he made his way to the gentleman's house. The following year (1779) Baker was joined by Philip Hughes from Virginia. "They labored together as evangelists for about twelve months, preaching at Broad Creek, Gravelly Branch and other places. Many converts were baptized on profession of faith and repentance. They . . . resolved to build churches. . . . They were not only well received but were assisted in their efforts, by ministers and laymen, in organizing churches and ordaining ministers. These men were instrumental in founding twenty-two churches in Virginia, Maryland, Delaware and spent much time in 'visiting them, as fathers do their children.' "[4]

Baker and Hughes were challenged by two Methodist preachers to debate the subject of baptism during their labors, and Philip Hughes presented the Baptist case. He debated in Fowling Creek, Maryland, in 1782, and three Methodist "class leaders" were later immersed by Hughes. Again in Virginia, in 1785 he was challenged to debate, and twenty-two of the audience were immersed the next day.

At the age of fifty-six, Elijah Baker passed into the presence of his Lord on November 6, 1798, at the home of his friend Dr. Richard Lemmon. The testimony of the doctor was this: "He retained his senses to the last minute; and seemed rather translated, than to suffer pain in his dissolution.''[5] Thank God for men such as Elijah Baker and Philip Hughes—heroes of the faith!

DLC

---

[1]Lewis Peyton Little, *Imprisoned Preachers and Religious Liberty in Virginia* (Lynchburg, Va.: J. P. Bell Co., 1938), p. 472.

[2]Morgan Edwards, *Materials Toward a History of the Baptists* (Danielsville, Ga.: Heritage Press, 1984), 2:11.

[3]Ibid.

[4]John T. Christian, *A History of the Baptists* (1922; reprint ed., Nashville: Broadman Press, 1926), p. 123.

[5]Little, p. 476.

November 29—Baptist Jailbirds You Should Know

Scripture: James 1:2

The faithful clerk of the Broadmead Church in Bristol, England, inserted this sad note: ''On ye 29th of Nov., 1685, our Pastour, Bro. Fownes, dyed in Gloucester Jail, having been kept there for Two years and about 9 months a Prisoner, unjustly and maliciously, for ye Testimony of Jesus and preaching ye Gospel. He was a man of Great Learning, of a sound Judgment, an able Preacher, having great knowledge in Divinity, Law, Physic, & c.; a bold patient Sufferer for ye Lord Jesus, and ye Gospel he preacht.''[1]

The entry for August 3 focuses on Fownes, and the April 26 entry focuses on the Broadmead Church, but as we mark the death of one of the martyr/pastors of that fine company of Baptist believers, we ought to introduce the man who initially established that witness. The Broadmead Church was founded by the celebrated John Canne.

> He was born about 1590, became eminent for his learning and piety, was well versed in the Scriptures, and zealous in the work of reformation. In his early life he was a member of the Church of England. He united with the Baptists, and became pastor of a church in Southwark, London, in 1621. This church had but recently been founded and held its meetings secretly, in private houses, for fear of persecution. Mr. Canne preached for them only a short time, when he was compelled to flee. In 1641 he returned for a short time to England when he founded the Broadmead church, at Bristol. . . . The name of John Canne has been immortalized by his being the first to prepare

> and publish the English Bible with marginal references. He proceeded on the principle, that Scripture is itself the best interpreter of Scripture. His days were ended in Amsterdam in 1667, where English tyranny had forced him to publish his first Bible with references in 1644.[2]

From the Broadmead records we discover that Pastors Thomas Ewins, Thomas Hardcastle, and George Fownes were all imprisoned unjustly for the cause of Christ. But many other Baptist ministers endured imprisonments, and some died in jail merely because of their convictions. Francis Bamfield suffered for eight years in Dorchester jail. Thomas Delaune died in Newgate prison. John Miller was a prisoner for ten years in Newgate. Henry Forty was incarcerated for twelve years at Exeter. Joseph Wright, a man of great piety and learning, pastored at Maidstone but was imprisoned in the common jail there for twenty years.

It is not generally known that so many Baptists suffered these long imprisonments, for their names are lost in history as we consider the few whose names are so well known. Most are familiar with John Bunyan's twelve-year imprisonment at Bedford. Some are aware of Thomas Helwys, who fled to Amsterdam but in time became convinced that he and the others had been wrong in fleeing from persecution. Believing it was his duty to return to England and witness of the truth, he went to London in 1611 with twelve of his followers and settled at Spitalfields. This was not the first Baptist church in England, however, for the Braintree church dates its origin from 1550.[3] Be that as it may, Helwys appealed to the king to grant liberty of conscience. He claimed, "The King is a mortall man and not God, therefore hath no power over ye immortall soules of his subjects to make lawes and ordinances for them, and to set spirituall Lords over them."

For his convictions, "Newgate Prison became his home. He died in Newgate, barely forty years of age."[4]

Again we are compelled to thank God for those who have preceded us and have stood firmly for the faith once delivered to the saints! May we stand in our generation as "torch bearers" of truth as well!

DLC

---

[1]Edward Terrill, *The Records of a Church of Christ Meeting in Broadmead, Bristol*, ed. Nathaniel Haycroft (London: J. Heaton and Son, 1865), p. 274.

[2]Richard B. Cook, *The Story of the Baptists* (Baltimore: H. M. Wharton and Co., 1886), pp. 156-57.

[3]Henry W. Clark, *History of English Nonconformity* (London: Chapman and Hall, 1911), 1:302.

[4]Ronald W. Thompson, *Heroes of the Baptist Church* (London: Carey Kingsgate Press, 1948), p. 24.

November 30—A Humble Tinker and the Grace of God

Scripture: Hebrews 2:9-18

In the midst of the struggle between the friends of Christianity and infidelity, John Bunyan was born November 30, 1628. His year of birth was honored with a signal victory gained over lawless violence by the passing of the English Bill of Rights. The sum of the act was that "no man shall be taxed without the consent of Parliament, nor be arrested, imprisoned, or executed but by due course of law." Every attempt was made by the court to recover arbitrary power. To attain this power, the court perpetrated cruelties, which rendered it still more odious. Laymen and clergymen, renowned for learning and piety for opposing the view of the court, had their ears cut off, noses slit, faces branded with red-hot irons. They were also publicly whipped on the naked body, every lash bringing away the flesh. They were then imprisoned with such cruelties that when released, they could neither hear, see, nor walk. These cruelties were followed by a desolating civil war which overwhelmed the country with demoralization and debauchery.[1]

The village of Elstow, one mile from Bedford, was the place of Bunyan's birth into a family of tinkers which Bunyan himself described as "being of that rank that is meanest and most despised of all the families in the land."[2] His father, in an age when very few of the poor were taught to read and write, was able to put John in school, where he learned both but soon forgot both almost utterly.

Having a warm, light, and frolicsome heart, Bunyan was drawn into sins, principally lying, swearing, and profaning the Sabbath. He experienced the agonies of conviction of sin over a long period of time to the extent of dreaming frightful dreams, hearing warning voices, and reading his doom in letters of fire. He had several close brushes with death. On one occasion he fell into the Bedford River and, yet again, later into a creek of the sea, nearly drowning. He also had an encounter with a poisonous snake and fell into a deep pit. He came through all these experiences unscathed. Bunyan also served in the army and fought in the battle of Leicester. He was spared any serious injury, though he tragically took on the wicked habits of his peers.

Bunyan married a very poor, but pious, woman. She encouraged him with two books in her possession, *The Plain Man's Pathway to Heaven,* and *The Practice of Piety,* and through this he regained his ability to read. Her affectionate tenderness became a blessing to him, his rugged heart was softened, and he felt alarm for the salvation of his soul. Another woman of entirely different character, whom he described as "a loose and ungodly wretch," heard his oaths and protested to him "that he swore and cursed at that most fearful rate, that she trembled to hear him," and that he would spoil the rest of the youth of the town. That experience, linked with his overhearing conversations of three poor, godly women about the new birth, alarmed him about his perilous state and brought a great struggle of mind and soul. Those dear women introduced him to their Baptist pastor, John Gifford. Under Gifford's instruction, Bunyan was driven to his Bible and experienced the quickening power of the Holy Spirit. Space does not permit relating all the struggles Bunyan endured, but when one reads his biography, it is clear that his classic volume *The Pilgrim's Progress* was drawn from his biblical insights and personal experiences.

EWT

---

[1]George Offar, "Memoir of John Bunyan," introduction to *The Pilgrim's Progress* (London: Routledge, Warne and Routledge), 1861, p. ii.

[2]John Bunyan, "The Life of John Bunyan," *The Pilgrim's Progress* (New York: J. B. Hurst Co., n.d.), p. 3.

December

December 1—The Man with the Twenty Hands

Scripture: Deuteronomy 11:16-28

It is interesting to read the biographies of well-known men and women who have been used of God. It is also thrilling to read about some of the people not so well known who have been used in a great way by our Lord. As we trace the life of John Mason Peck, we perceive the hand of God upon his life each step of the way. In the entry for July 25, we witnessed the report of his conversion, his call to the ministry, his encounter with Luther Rice, and his yielding to go to the mission field of the Missouri Territory. God used Luther Rice to challenge and direct Peck's life and to prepare him for the rigorous ministry into which God ultimately led him.

The Pecks made their way westward for 129 days by wagon, by boat, and on foot until they arrived in St. Louis on December 1, 1817. It had been a long, arduous trip, and John, sick with a fever and unable to walk, had to be carried ashore on a stretcher.[1] As soon as he was able, Peck began to preach in the area, gathered children for a school, began evangelistic work among the black population, and made excursions into surrounding areas to preach and to distribute Bibles and tracts.

Peck was a pioneer in the true sense of the word, laying foundations for the strong Baptist witness in the Midwest and establishing a way station where the thousands of settlers moving westward could hear the gospel and carry it to their final destinations. He planted the earliest Baptist churches west of the Mississippi River and pioneered in the establishment of Sunday schools and missionary societies. Although somewhat limited in his own education, he founded the first college in the West. So great was his energy and so many were his ministries, Peck was given the sobriquet, "the man with the twenty hands."[2]

The following diary entry from 1825 provides a glimpse of the magnitude of Peck's work: "I have been absent from home fifty-three days; have travelled through eighteen counties in Illinois and nine in Indiana, rode nine hundred and twenty-six miles, preached regular sermons thirty-one times, besides delivering several speeches, addresses and lectures. I have been able to revive three Bible societies . . . to establish seven new societies . . . aided in forming three Sabbath-school societies, and in opening several schools where no societies exist."[3]

Peck and his family had to live frugally, receiving only five dollars a month from the Massachusetts Baptist Mission Society. Peck eked out their living by teaching, publishing a paper, and occasionally working as a manual laborer. In answer to the often-asked ordination counsel question heard periodically in our day, "Could you do anything other than preach?" Peck would have been able to answer, "Yes!" However, the call was so clear, the dedication was so strong that our pioneering fathers found no obstacle too great, no sickness so debilitating, and no discouragement so overwhelming to cause them to turn back. When the interest of the Baptist missionary societies in the East waned, Peck never gave up. He and Jonathan Going doubled their efforts and laid the foundation for a new Baptist Mission Society in a period of strong antimission sentiment. We owe much to the persevering labors of our pioneering fathers. May we repay the debt by leaving a similar testimony to our posterity.

EWT

---

[1]H. Leon McBeth, *The Baptist Heritage* (Nashville: Broadman Press, 1987), p. 355.

[2]Ibid, p. 354.

[3]Ibid.

December 2—Preparing Great Men Through Great Hardship

Scripture: Psalm 130

Many men who have been used mightily of the Lord went through a refining time early in life, and this process prepared them for a ministry that would stand above the mediocre. Thus it was in the life of Billington McCarter Sanders, who was the eldest child of Ephriam and Nancy Sanders. Sanders was born in Columbia County, Georgia, December 2, 1789.[1] By age nine he had lost both of his parents, but the family of Mr. Ambrose Jones provided him with an excellent home.

Sanders received his early education in the Kiokee Seminary. As a student, he was eager to learn, high tempered, a little proud, quite spirited, always truthful, kindhearted, and generous. After further education in various institutions, Sanders returned to his native county, where he made his profession of faith, was baptized by Abraham Marshall, and was admitted into the first Baptist church ever planted in Georgia, the Kiokee Baptist Church of Appling. He was married to Martha Lamar, by whom he had nine children. All of his children died in infancy or childhood except two. Martha died in 1822, and Sanders then married Cynthia Holliday, who bore him thirteen children. Of the twenty-two children, only nine of them survived their father. He knew the burden and grief of standing at the side of the graves of a wife and thirteen children. Thus he was able to have great empathy toward his people, who lived in a period when infant mortality was prevalent.

Sanders represented his county in the state legislature, served as one of the judges of the Superior Court, and taught school. His pastor at one of the church conferences where Sanders was serving as clerk asked permission to submit a resolution. "It turned out to be a resolution urging Mr. Sanders forward to the work of the ministry; and, as it was read and passed, Mr. Sanders dropped his head and burst into tears. He immediately recognized it as the voice of Providence, and shortly after, commenced his career as a minister of the Gospel."[2] He prepared a room in his house and set it aside as a place of worship for the accommodation of his family, servants, and neighbors.

In 1831 the Georgia Baptist Convention determined to establish a Classical and Theological Seminary. Mr. Sanders was called upon to take charge of the enterprise. This undertaking involved great self-denial and required great effort, yet the objective lay so near to his heart that he was willing to make any sacrifice for its accomplishment. The enterprise began very primitively. The students lived "as in a camp" with the cheapest fare, no place for study but a common schoolroom, no place to retire but a garret without heat. They labored diligently three hours of each day with no complaint, and the most entire cheerfulness ran through all of their words and actions. Thus was the foundation of Mercer University laid.

Before his death at age sixty-five, Sanders was involved in many ministries which required a great amount of energy and labor. The lessons that are set forth by his life are many. Sufferings in early life are used by the Lord to conform us to the image of His Son. Also, others often recognize the gifts and calling of God in the life of another and should publicly declare such. Further, a classical and a theological education is important to every minister—the former to provide him with the tools of study and communication and the latter to ground him in the sound doctrine and eternal truths of God's Word.

EWT

---

[1]William B. Sprague, *Annals of the American Pulpit* (New York: Robert Carter and Bros., 1865), 6:740.

[2]Ibid., p. 141.

December 3—Richard Major Watered the Plants

Scripture: I Corinthians 3:1-9

During the early history of our nation, it was customary to bury the bodies of the dead in a cemetery adjacent to the church where the family were members or on the estate in the "family cemetery." Many of these cemeteries throughout our land have gone into oblivion, being overgrown with brush and forests or excavated for highways and high-rises. Fortunately, the estate of Richard Major, who was the subject of the entry of February 6, has been preserved and the brick home renovated by the contractors who developed a business park which surrounds it. We are thankful for those who are still sensitive to the value of our heritage and have gone to the expense and effort to preserve this memorial to one of our pioneer Baptist preachers.

The writer of an article relating to this house remarked:

> The significance of the Hutchison House lies in the fact that it is one of the few remaining fourth quarter, 18th century plantation houses in Western Fairfax County, (Virginia), and the only one in brick. . . . The basic form interiors and exteriors are little changed, giving one a peek into the lifestyle of the upper class in the 18th century.
>
> I believed it had a deeper significance as I stood at a grave site behind the house, and saw chiseled on a crude stone, "Richard Major, Died December 3rd, 1796."[1]

This man's name has not been recorded in history alongside others who were considered great spiritual lights and leaders. He seemed to be an able assistant and establisher of ministries that others began. I also believe that there are thousands of faithful men whose names have gone into oblivion, who are recorded in the annals of heaven because they were faithful. It is recorded by Lewis Peyton Little that

> Little River Church, in Loudon County, was a branch of Broadrun in Fauquier, and "was some of the fruits of David Thomas's ministry in

Virginia. In this work, however, he was powerfully aided by Rev. Richard Major, their first pastor; for although the first seeds were sown by Mr. Thomas, yet Mr. Major watered and nourished the plants until he brought them to perfection. So rapidly did the Gospel spread in this church, that just two years after they were constituted, they were the most numerous church in the association; having two hundred and seventy-two members. Her branches, however, extended into neighboring parts. When any of these branches became sufficiently numerous, they were constituted into new churches: by which the mother church was reduced in numbers."[2]

Eventually Richard Major started five Baptist churches in the surrounding area. As I walked through the spacious rooms of this house, I was sure that each one had some experience to tell. There was possibly the conversation of his wife and children as they anxiously awaited the return of their husband and father. Perhaps a room could tell of the joyful shouts of the family as he, returning after a long, cold, wet, and arduous journey through snow and swollen streams, was welcomed to a warm home filled with love and peace. Certainly the rooms could tell of the agonizing prayers as Major interceded for some erring brother he had to reprove and rebuke or for a family that had been touched by the chilling hand of death. The walls were saturated with Major's praise for the security he experienced at the hands of a gracious God when he was threatened and pummeled by enemies of the gospel.

May we do all we can to preserve the written record of these servants of God and the houses that stand as memorials to their faithfulness to the principles of God's truth. Whatever sacrifices we must make to do this will be worthwhile to our posterity.

EWT

---

[1]Gravestone of Richard Major, Western Fairfax County, Virginia.

[2]Lewis Peyton Little, *Imprisoned Preachers and Religious Liberty in Virginia* (Lynchburg, Va.: J. P. Bell Co., 1938), p. 89.

December 4—A Man Who Wouldn't Take "No" for an Answer

Scripture: Psalm 103:1-5

The names of Carey, Marshman, and Ward are outstanding in missionary history. We have previously considered William Carey and

William Ward, but Joshua Marshman deserves our serious contemplation as well. Born in a Baptist home in Wiltshire, England, on April 20, 1768, the lad knew early the message of saving grace. He possessed a voracious appetite for reading and perused everything available to him in his youth. When he was twenty-four, he moved to Bristol, England, to supervise a school which the Broadmead Baptist Church provided. Immediately, Mr. Marshman enrolled to take classes simultaneously at the seminary, and for five years he studied the classics, Hebrew, and Syriac.

Carey had gone to India in 1793, and the missionary reports had stirred the hearts of the Marshmans for the cause of missions. Mr. and Mrs. Marshman applied to the mission, were accepted, and sailed in May, arriving in Calcutta in October of 1799. The Marshmans opened a young ladies' boarding school which became the largest of its kind in India. This was done to supplement the support from the English brethren, and all profits accrued to the Serampore Mission. During their ministry, the Marshmans established two other such schools, and all three institutions were very successful. This work was carried on primarily by Mrs. Hannah Marshman, and she thrived in her labors and the climate. She continued on in Serampore until her death in 1847, ten years following the home going of her blessed husband.

Joshua Marshman had not been robust in his youth, and "at the time of his embarkation, his health was very poor. One day, meeting the blunt but popular Methodist preacher, 'Sinner Saved' Huntington, and remarking to him that he was about to go to Calcutta—'You go out to India!' exclaimed Huntington; 'you look as pale as if you had been kept by the parish!' " But the Lord undertook for His servant, and "hence he could in his old age boast that, after a residence of thirty-six years in India, his medicine had not cost him a single sovereign."[1]

Mr. Marshman labored in association with Mr. Carey, translating the Scripture, preaching, and performing other missionary work. In 1806 Mr. Marshman began the gargantuan work of mastering Chinese so that he might translate the Scriptures into that language. For eighteen years, he used every spare moment that he could wrest from his regular responsibilities, for it was imperative to Mr. Marshman that the teeming millions in China's empire should be able to read the Word of God. When the governor general refused to assist financially in the printing of the Chinese Bible for fear of the response of the East India Company, Mr. Marshman hit upon an idea empowering him to care for the matter himself. He printed the works of Confucius and used the profits to place God's precious Word in the hands of the disciples of Confucius.

Satan stirred up opposition in India and abroad. In preaching to the nationals, Mr. Marshman was mobbed and arrested on at least one occasion. Tragically, the worst trials were to come from abroad. With the death of the original mission society leaders, youthful ministers took control of the leadership. They knew nothing of the mission operation in India but desired to obtain control over the property. The end result was that Dr. Carey, the Marshmans, and Mr. Ward actually gave approximately £80,000 to keep the work solvent. This money had been gained through their own employment on the field.

Dr. Marshman was honored by Brown University with an honorary Doctor of Divinity degree in June of 1811. He died on December 4, 1837, and was laid to rest in "God's Acre." That plot is now consecrated by the mingled dust of generations of missionaries and converts who are awaiting the resurrection call of our Lord and Savior Jesus Christ.

DLC

---

[1]G. Winfred Hervey, *The Story of Baptist Missions in Foreign Lands* (St. Louis: C. R. Barnes Publishing Co., 1892), p. 228.

December 5—Commissioned by Christ and the United States Government

Scripture: Nehemiah 2

Joseph Smedley was born December 5, 1792, in Westmoreland County, England.[1] Little is known about his life there except that he professed Christ and became a member of a Baptist church in that area. After immigrating to the United States, he applied to the Fifth Baptist Church of Philadelphia for membership, and a committee was appointed to investigate the matter and report to the church. Upon investigation, they discovered he had been excluded by a church in England, and they would need time to correspond with that church to determine the facts of his exclusion. After seven months no reply had come; so the church decided that if no correspondence was received by the next monthly business meeting, they would consider the matter of membership. On August 23, 1834, in the absence of a letter, they decided to receive him into church membership based on the recital of his Christian experience and on his approval of the church's confession of faith and discipline. This gives us insight into the importance Baptist churches placed on church membership. It also reveals their respect for each local church's counsel relating to membership and their procedure when such correspondence failed. We would do well to proceed just as deliberately and carefully in such matters. It would enhance our integrity, avoid problems, eliminate misunderstanding, and strengthen our testimony.

The following month Smedley requested a letter of dismission in order to go west, where under the advisory counsel of the Baptist Board of Foreign Missions and the employment of the United States Government, he became a teacher and missionary among the Indians.[2] During this time, his wife, Mary Radcliff, died and left him with the care of seven children in July of 1836. In spite of this loss, he continued his ministry among the Choctaws, Creeks, and Cherokees in an area ranging some eighty miles west of Fort Smith along the Arkansas and Canadian rivers.

It is interesting to note that the relationship of the United States government was friendly and helpful toward such missionary efforts. Evidently, they broadly interpreted the Constitution, for they recognized the moral and educational value of teaching biblical Christianity. Also, the salt of Christianity had not lost its savor, and humanistic values and principles had not permeated every governmental agency. Today, however, humanistic thought prevails in government, and we now have an adversary relationship between church and state in our nation.

Smedley organized the first black Baptist church in Fort Smith in 1856. He continued his missionary work, but the Civil War greatly curtailed his ministry. After the outbreak of hostilities, he was able to make only occasional visits to his churches.

After a long and arduous ministry of over forty years, Smedley died on August 27, 1877.[3] May his dedication and hard work under severe circumstances be an example to us in these days of abundance and ease.

EWT

---

[1]Norman Wade Cox, ed., *Encyclopedia of Southern Baptists* (Nashville: Broadman Press, 1958), 2:1205.

[2]Ibid.

[3]Ibid.

December 6—Doing Collectively What a Single Church Cannot Do Alone

Scripture: II Corinthians 8:7-21

One of the features of nineteenth-century Baptist life in America was the development of associations and state conventions. It is noteworthy that what little cohesion Baptist churches experienced was formed in 1707 and "from the first . . . engaged earnestly in efforts for the proper education of its ministers and the spread of the Gospel in the world."[1] The growth of associations was very slow among the Baptist churches, for "Baptists at first were afraid of the assumption of power by associations. It was not till sixty years after the birth of the Philadelphia organization, that the Warren Association, of Rhode Island, was formed."[2] Early Baptists were intent on preserving the autonomy of each local church, and only after assurances such as that given by Edward T. Hiscox in his *Baptist Directory* (1866) did the growth of the associations proliferate. Hiscox wrote, "All such Associations, Conventions, Ministers' Meetings and the like, are entirely voluntary. No church or individual is obligated to unite with them; and if so united, can leave them when they wish."[3]

The outstanding research by Robert G. Gardner reveals that in 1780 there were approximately one thousand sixty-six Baptist churches in America.[4] Yet there were only fourteen associations at that time, representing 286 churches. Less than twenty-five per cent of the Baptist churches were members of any association. However, that was to change drastically when Luther Rice returned to America from India to report on the missionary activity of the Adoniram Judsons. With the birth of a national body for the cause of missions in 1814, the rapid development of associations and state conventions became a reality.

For all intents and purposes, on December 6, 1821, the first state convention was formed by the brethren in South Carolina. Two items of great importance were stated: "The grand objects of this Convention shall be the promotion of evangelical and useful knowledge, by means of religious education; the support of missionary service among the destitute; and the cultivation of measures promotive of the true interest of the churches of Christ in general, and of their union, love and harmony in particular." And yet again, "The Convention shall recognize the independence and liberty of the Churches of Christ, and consequently shall not in any case arbitrarily interfere with their spiritual or secular interests. But, when requested, will be considered as under obligations to afford them any assistance which may be in their power."[5]

We note with interest that denominational colleges were begun rapidly in the states as they followed the pattern of establishing state conventions. Luther Rice and others had envisioned a national Baptist college, and in May of 1818, the Baptist Board for Foreign Missions, acting for the General Convention, approved such a plan. In 1820 the General Convention ratified the project, and in 1821 the Columbian College opened in Washington, D. C. From the outset, the college was fraught with financial difficulties, but the state conventions met the challenge and established such institutions both for literary and theological purposes. In time, almost every state in the Union had a Baptist institution of higher education.

It must be pointed out that particularly in the North, some Baptist churches remained detached and maintained their totally independent stance. The state conventions, however, were born on this date in history.

DLC

---

[1]A. D. Gillette, ed., *Minutes of the Philadelphia Baptist Association from* A.D. *1707 to* A.D. *1807* (1851; reprint ed., Minneapolis: James Publishing Co., n.d.), p. 5.

[2]Richard B. Cook, *The Story of the Baptists* (Baltimore: H. M. Wharton and Co., 1886), p. 256.

[3]Edward T. Hiscox, *The Baptist Directory* (New York: Sheldon and Co., 1866), pp. 131-32.

[4]Robert G. Gardner, *Baptists of Early America* (Atlanta: Georgia Baptist Historical Society, 1983).

[5]Robert A. Baker, *A Baptist Source Book* (Nashville: Broadman Press, 1966), p. 76.

December 7—Obeying Conscience in the Light of God's Word

Scripture: John 1:19-34

Chesterfield County, Virginia, was notorious for its persecution of Baptist preachers. We are reminded of these atrocious acts by a monument to religious liberty on the courthouse square in Chesterfield, Virginia, in memory of those who courageously suffered in its behalf. Semple, in his history (1810), mentions, "It is worthy of remark, that generally the Baptist cause has flourished, most extensively where it met with the most severe opposition in the offset. In the history of Chesterfield jail, seven preachers were confined for preaching, viz. William Webber, Joseph Anthony, Augustine Easton, John Weatherford, John Tanner, Jeremiah Walker and David Tinsley. Some were whipped by individuals, several fined. They kept up their persecution after other counties had laid it aside."[1]

The first recorded instance of imprisonment for preaching the gospel in Chesterfield County occurred when two zealous young preachers from Goochland Church responded to an invitation and crossed the James River. William Webber and Joseph Anthony had great success in an area of which it was said "that at that time there was not a Baptist in the entire county."[2] "Their success led to their arrest on December 7, 1770."[3] "They were held in prison until on January 4, 1771, they were brought before the magistrates on charges of misbehaviour by Itinerant preaching in this County being of that sect of dissenters from the Church of England commonly called anabaptists, and on hearing they acknowledged that they had preached in the upper end of this County at a meeting of sundry people there."[4]

The court refused their offer to take the oath as prescribed by the so called Toleration Act, and thus for conscience' sake they remained in jail until March 7, 1771.

Incarceration enhanced their preaching activities as they preached through the grates. Their preaching was so powerful that the jailer was inclined to leave the door of their cell ajar so they could escape. Their reply was, "They have taken us openly, uncondemned, and have cast us into prison; and now, do they cast us out privily? Nay, verily, but let them come themselves and fetch us out."[5]

They had to obey the voice of conscience in the light of God's Word. Mrs. John Welch, the daughter of John Knox, the great Scottish reformer, understood conscience when her husband, imprisoned for his faith, was in the last stages of consumption. She made her way before King James and pled for his release. "I will send him home with you," said the King to her importunate pleading, "if you will persuade him to submit to the bishops." "Please, your majesty," said Mrs. Welch as she held out her apron, "I'd rather carry his head home there, than tempt him to sin against his conscience."

In our day when consciences seem to be "seared with a hot iron," may God raise up men of faith and conviction, sensitive to their consciences under the guidance of God's Word. When this takes place, our ministries will meet with the same success as our forefathers', and we will leave our posterity with many effective witnesses.

EWT

---

[1]Robert B. Semple, *A History of the Rise and Progress of the Baptists in Virginia* (Richmond: Published by the author, 1810), pp. 206-7.

[2]Lewis Peyton Little, *Imprisoned Preachers and Religious Liberty in Virginia* (Lynchburg, Va.: J. P. Bell Co., 1938), p. 209.

[3]David Benedict, *A General History of the Baptist Denomination in America* (Boston: Manning and Loring, 1813), p. 400.

[4]Little, p. 210.

[5]Ibid., p. 213.

December 8—Another Black Hero of the Faith

Scripture: Joshua 14:6-15

While sitting in a funeral director's office, waiting for a memorial service to begin, I commented on how few were in attendance. The undertaker responded facetiously, "Pastor, you must die young if you desire a large funeral." But, as we consider the "immense procession about a mile long, with fifty-eight carriages"[1] making its way from the church to the cemetery on December 14, 1856, we cannot help but wonder what dignitary is being honored. We are further shocked to find that the deceased was over one hundred years old! But let me tell you the story of the Reverend Andrew Marshall.

He was thought to have been born in 1755 in South Carolina, but no one took time to record the date of birth of the little "slave-born" son. Andrew's first "master" was John Houston, the colonial governor of Georgia. The governor died when Andrew was about twenty-one years of age. Freedom had been bequeathed to Andrew at the death of the governor, for the slave had at one time saved his master's life. "The executors, however, failed to carry out the will, and Andrew was again sold . . . becoming the property of Judge Clay."[2]

While in the service of Judge Clay, Marshall made several trips to the North, for Judge Clay had become a senator. Andrew Marshall saw General George Washington on several occasions, and when President Washington visited Savannah later, Andrew was honored by being appointed the President's "body servant" and acted as his carriage driver as well. During the Revolutionary War, Andrew Marshall had been loyal to the American cause and enjoyed recollections of General Nathaniel Green, who directed the army of the South in driving the British from Georgia and the Carolinas.

Andrew purchased his freedom about the time he was converted, and in 1785 he joined the church and was soon licensed to preach. In 1806 he became pastor of Savannah's Second Baptist Church. The church grew from one thousand to three thousand members, and it was thought best to divide the congregation. The Reverend Mr. Marshall formed a new church which took the name of the First African Baptist Church. He remained its pastor until his death on December 8, 1856. During his ministry, crowds overflowed the church building. His reputation as a pulpiteer grew, for "his voice was . . . deep, sonorous, and tender and its capacity for the expression of pathos was unsurpassed.''[3] His piety and ability were so well known that wherever he journeyed to preach, throngs both of black and white greeted him. He was honored on one occasion to address the entire body of the legislature of the state of Georgia, and his travels took him often into South Carolina and as far south as Louisiana.

Andrew Marshall took pleasure in stating publicly that he had never had any formal education, but he possessed a considerable library and majored in reading the commentaries of Dr. John Gill, predecessor of Charles H. Spurgeon in London. During his long ministry in Savannah, Marshall baptized nearly four thousand converts.

At the time of the beginning of the First African Baptist Church in Savannah, Marshall had led his people to purchase the facility of the old First Baptist Church (white). The years took their toll on the building as they did on its pastor. Thus, in the last year of his life, Marshall decided to raise funds to construct a new brick building. He determined to travel to the North with his wife to contact benefactors. He preached for Dr. Spencer H. Cone and others in New York. He raised $600, but his health failed, and he was urged to return home immediately. Reaching Richmond, Virginia, he could proceed no further. Dr. Basil Manly, Jr., president of the Richmond Female College, took him into his home and cared for him for more than a month until Marshall's entrance into his Lord's presence. Andrew Marshall's remains were conveyed to Savannah, where the Reverend Thomas Rambaut, pastor of the First Baptist Church, delivered the funeral sermon before one of the largest audiences to attend a funeral at that time in Savannah.

DLC

---

[1]William Cathcart, *The Baptist Encyclopedia,* ed. Louis H. Everts (Philadelphia: Louis H. Everts, 1881), 2:750.

[2]William B. Sprague, *Annals of the American Pulpit* (New York: Robert Carter and Bros., 1865), 6:254.

[3]Cathcart, *Baptist Encyclopedia*, 2:750.

December 9—Baptists Changing the Course of the Sun

Scripture: Joshua 10:1-15

The principles of taxation for the support of an ecclesiastical system that was repulsive to them and of taxation without representation were causing great unrest throughout the colonies. Patrick Henry, the eloquent Virginia lawyer who had upheld the rights of Baptists and other Dissenters to worship freely, had also asserted the right of the colonial states to legislate independently of the British Parliament, especially with respect to taxation.

The Baptists had approached the General Court of Massachusetts and local authorities again and again with petitions asking for redress of their grievances relating to taxes for the support of religious teachers. There is no record that any of these petitions were given any attention by the courts. The Baptists of Massachusetts had been persecuted and imprisoned for conscience' sake under these laws, and Isaac Backus their agent, with the support of his fellow Baptists, persisted with presenting their petitions for relief.[1]

Ultimately in the Massachusetts Provincial Congress, Mr. John Hancock, the president of the body

> informed the House that Mr. Backus had sent in a petition to them in behalf of the Baptists, etc; and with a smile, asked them whether it should be read, or not? One answered: no; we are no ecclesiastical court, and have no business with it. Another, another and another agreed to the same. At last, one of the members got up and said; . . . This is very extra-ordinary, that we should pay no regard to a denomination who in the place where he lived were as good members of society as any, and were equally engaged with others in defense of their civil liberties, and motioned to have it read. Upon a second it was read December 9, 1774, but essentially buried to await the General Assembly.[2]

The persistent Backus would not let the issue die. When twelve colonies responded to the call of Massachusetts for a Continental Congress, he was there in Carpenter's Hall to press for complete religious liberty. Patrick Henry met with the Massachusetts delegates, who were embarrassed and resented that the Baptists implied that their great state did not grant religious freedom. The four-hour discussion closed with John Adams saying, "Gentlemen, if you mean to try to effect change in Massachusetts laws respecting religion, you may as well attempt to change the course of the sun in the heavens." John Hancock, presiding over the Continental Congress, ordered the petition read and considered.

With this encouragement, when the General Court met at Watertown, Massachusetts, in July 1775, the members heard and pondered this vigorous memorial:

> Our real grievances are, that we, as well as our fathers, have from time to time been taxed on religious accounts where we were not represented: and when we have sued for our rights, our causes have

> been tried by interested [i.e., partial] judges . . . and for a civil legislature to impose religious taxes, is, we conceive, a power which their constituents never had to give, and is, therefore, going entirely out of the jurisdiction. . . . We beseech this honorable assembly to take these matters into their wise and serious consideration before Him who has said, "with what measure ye mete, it shall be measured to you again."[3]

May we not be counted among those "good men who do nothing," but be among the vigilant who carefully watch and do battle to preserve those principles of liberty for our posterity in the great traditions of Baptists under the leadership of men like Isaac Backus. Ultimately the "sun did change its course," and full religious liberty came to Massachusetts.

EWT

---

[1]O. K. and Marjorie Armstrong, *The Baptists in America* (New York: Doubleday and Co., 1979), p. 98.

[2]William G. McLoughlin, ed., *The Diary of Isaac Backus* (Providence: Brown University Press, 1979), 2:927-28.

[3]Armstrong and Armstrong, p. 100.

December 10—The Bird That Was Given a Sporting Chance

Scripture: Luke 12:35-48

Dutton Lane was born November 7 near Baltimore, Maryland, the same year that George Washington, "Father of Our Country," was born—1732. It is not known when, in the providence of God, Dutton's father moved the family to Virginia near the North Carolina border. Neither Dutton nor his father could anticipate the events that would launch the name Dutton Lane into the annals of Virginia Baptist history among the leading lights that established religious liberty and planted Baptist churches throughout the land.

After settling in North Carolina and establishing Sandy Creek Church, Shubal Stearns and Daniel Marshall soon entered adjacent Virginia, where they preached the gospel and baptized believers among whom was Dutton Lane. A revival followed, and Elder Marshall baptized forty-two persons at one time. It was not long until Dutton Lane began preaching, and Samuel Harriss, a man of distinction in that area, was converted. People far and wide began requesting someone to come preach to them, even as far as Culpeper and Spotsylvania Counties.[1]

In August of 1760 the first Separate Baptist church in Virginia was organized at Dan River. Dutton Lane became its pastor, and by 1772 he had established five different preaching stations with five assistants. The success of the Baptists brought the wrath of Satan down upon them. The hand of the Lord was revealed as "James Roberts was going for a warrant in 1769 against Richard Elkins (one of Lane's assistants). As Roberts and another man were traveling for the warrant in the night a strong glare of light shone about them so much that the horses squatted on the ground; and was succeeded by such thick darkness that they could not see anything. Roberts concluded it was a warning to him and thence forth ceased to be an opposer."[2]

As the Dan River Church grew, the opposition rose in great fury. "One Wm. Cocker had conceived such a malignity against the Baptists that he was wont to say, 'He had rather go to hell than heaven if going to the latter required his being a Baptist;' but coming accidentally to hear Dutton Lane this same malignant fell to the ground roaring, 'Lord have mercy upon me! I am a gone man! What shall I do to be saved?' In this manner went he on for an hour."[3] He later became a pious Baptist.

No one opposed Dutton more strongly than his father, who carried out a threat to horsewhip his own wife, Dutton's mother, because she slipped out to hear their son preach. He then pursued Dutton with a gun in order to murder him. His wife courageously challenged her husband, pointing out that he, as a sporting man, gave a bird a chance at flight before he shot it. She proposed that he should hear his son preach before shooting him. Dutton's father accepted the challenge, and he fell under the conviction of the Holy Spirit and soon was made alive in Jesus Christ. He was baptized by that same son whom he had purposed to slay.

The year 1769 was one of much fruitfulness, the establishment of local churches, and the increase of persecution. Dutton Lane actively planted churches and was instrumental in the constitution of Nottoway Baptist Church on December 10, 1769.[4] This church ultimately founded many others. Christians are to reproduce Christians, preachers are to reproduce preachers, and churches should reproduce churches because we are "born to reproduce."

EWT

---

[1]Robert B. Semple, *History of the Baptists in Virginia*, rev. ed. (Lafayette, Tenn.: Church History Research and Archives, 1976), p. 17.

[2]Lewis Peyton Little, *Imprisoned Preachers and Religious Liberty in Virginia* (Lynchburg, Va.: J. P. Bell Co., 1938), pp. 32-33.

[3]Ibid., p. 35.

[4]Ibid., p. 145.

December 11—John, the Baptist Preacher

Scripture: Jeremiah 1:4-9

The Word of God has many examples of the revealed will of God for individuals, even before their births. Often God's calling is made known to any number of individuals long before those people themselves become aware that God is preparing them for a very special ministry. Such was the experience of Dr. John R. Rice, who was born December 11, 1895, near Gainesville, Cooke County, Texas.[1]

At the time of John's birth, his father Will Rice, who was the pastor of a country church, had gone to his Bible and heavily underscored Luke 1:63, the words Zacharias had written: "His name is John." This was not merely giving a child a name; it was also an expression of hope and faith that his son John would be a great preacher "to give knowledge of salvation unto his people by the remission of their sins" (Luke 1:77).

Later in his life, John Rice discovered a letter his mother had written to his Aunt Esse. In this letter his mother distinguished him from the rest of the children by saying, "Let me tell you what my preacher boy did the other day." This was done without naming him in the letter, thus indicating that Aunt Esse knew that the "preacher boy" was John. At John's birth, his parents had prayed together that God would make him a preacher. When he was a small boy, someone would ask him his name and he would respond, "I am John, the Baptist preacher."[2]

No one can measure the value of a strong Christian home in which the father leads that family in devotions and emphasizes the importance of the ministry of the local church. Such was the home in which John Richard Rice was nurtured. No wonder he became one of America's outstanding evangelists and was used as an example to and leader of preachers.

The downward moral and spiritual trend of compromise has accelerated to proportions not even these great men of God who had outstanding insights could have imagined. Our only hope of deliverance from impending judgment upon our beloved nation is a great revival among God's people which could usher in a period of spiritual awakening throughout the land. In the early history of our country, there were periods of awful moral depravity which preceded a time of a powerful moving of the Holy Spirit in revival and quickening. Dr. Rice, in his book on revival, insists that "we can have revival now" if God's people will meet the conditions for revival. These conditions must be met in our homes by parents and grandparents who pray for and are examples to their posterity and who claim their children and grandchildren to become instruments of God's grace and great spiritual leaders committed to the principles of God's Word. May we see these leaders coming forth in our day to call future generations to repentance and faith in our Lord Jesus Christ.

EWT

---

[1]Robert L. Sumner, *Man Sent from God* (Grand Rapids: Eerdmans Publishing Co., n.d.), p. 20.

[2]Ibid., pp. 16, 20.

[3]Ibid., p. 7.

December 12—Two Scottish Brothers Whose Minds and Money Belonged to God

Scripture: Acts 4:34-37

The Baptist cause has flourished throughout the years by the conversion to the truth of immersion of many outstanding men who had been trained in other denominations. Such was the case of Robert and James Alexander Haldane of Scotland. Robert was born on February 28, 1764, in London and was trained at Dundee and Edinburgh. James Alexander Haldane was born at Dundee on July 14, 1768, and received his education in the same schools. Both men served in the British navy, and in 1786 they inherited a large estate.

Robert Haldane "became a great writer and philanthropist, giving $350,000 for charitable purposes within fifteen years, and during his life educating three hundred ministers of the Gospel at an expense of $100,000."[1]

James Alexander was converted early in life, traveled throughout Scotland as an evangelist, and was ordained in 1799 as an independent pastor in Edinburgh. Robert and James were outstanding men, and "as the Church of Scotland had no use for unauthorized preachers, they worked independently, trained men, building and endowing tabernacles, founding a Society for Propagating the Gospel at Home."[2]

The brothers were so magnanimous that when the reports of the work of Carey in India began to circulate in England, "Robert Haldane . . . devoted £35,000 to the work of the Missions"[3] even though it meant supporting Baptist work.

We have mentioned the training of ministers of the gospel, but when several of these preachers, upon study of the subject of baptism, were immersed and became Baptists, the Haldane brothers investigated the subject as well. Repudiating pedobaptism, both brothers, in time, were immersed, and in 1808 they became Baptists.

Both men were scholarly, but Robert Haldane authored meaningful volumes which have stood the test of time. Perhaps his best-known tome is *Exposition of the Epistle to the Romans,* which he wrote in 1835. This book is still reprinted in our day and is considered a classic. In 1817, Robert Haldane lectured to theological students at Geneva and Montauban, and throughout his lifetime, he continued his generous gifts for the propagation of the gospel. Mr. Robert Haldane died on December 12, 1841, in Edinburgh.[4]

James Alexander Haldane continued his preaching ministry, serving gratuitously for fifty years, and he too authored several useful items. His pamphlets had a wide circulation, and he wrote *An Exposition of the Epistle to the Galatians* in 1848. James continued faithfully in his ministry until his death on February 8, 1851.

In the days when Baptists were not allowed to function freely and were openly persecuted, formal training of men for the ministry was impossible. Thus our Baptist forebears were primarily to be found in rural areas, and the ministers, though called of God, were unschooled. Some of them were brilliant, but they were considered uncouth by society. That rather reminds us of another who was tagged "the Baptist." His attire, attitude, and approach were quite different from the professional religionists of his day. Thankfully, however, God raised up from time to time those who were able to bear the message of truth into the halls of learning and before leaders of the genteel society. Such were the Messrs. Haldane, who, early in the nineteenth century, became champions of the Baptist cause in England. Today we honor their memory on the anniversary of Robert's home going to glory.

DLC

---

[1]Thomas Armitage, *The History of the Baptists* (1890; reprint ed., Watertown, Wis.: Maranatha Baptist Press, 1976), 2:574.

[2]W. T. Whitley, *A History of British Baptists* (London: Charles Griffin and Co., 1923), p. 295.

[3]John Brown Myers, *The Centenary Volume of the Baptist Missionary Society* (London: Baptist Missionary Society, 1892), p. 60.

[4]William Gedde and J. Liddell Gedde, *Chamber's Biographical Dictionary* (London: W. R. Chambers, 1926), p. 450.

December 13—From a Free Society, to an Oppressed People, to a Vast Wilderness

Scripture: Exodus 18

In the annals of history there are people whose names are set in the forefront because of the circumstances surrounding them and the nature of their personalities. There are multitudes in the history of the Baptists whose names have gone into oblivion but who had a vital part in leading these humble people through times of crises and important eras of their history. There are also those who were known in their time but were overshadowed in the record of events by other better-known men who carried on a vital and important function.

Such was John Davis, who was born at Welsh Tract, Pencader Hundred, New Castle County, Delaware, in 1737. His father came from South Wales and was pastor of the Welsh Tract Baptist Church for over twenty years. His mother was the daughter of Elisha Thomas, who had been the second pastor of the Welsh Tract Church. He, therefore, was of good Welsh Baptist heritage.

John was educated at the College of Philadelphia and graduated in 1763. After his father's death, John served as pastor of the Welsh Tract Church, where he was ordained to the gospel ministry. In 1770 he was called to pastor the Second Baptist Church of Boston. At that time, Baptists in Massachusetts were suffering under strict laws.

The Baptists appointed Pastor Davis to the "Committee of Grievances," which heard all complaints and from which an agent was chosen to represent them to the authorities. While serving in this agency, Pastor Davis was thrust into the front ranks of the churches. Isaac Backus said that "no tongue or pen could fully describe all the evils that were perpetrated under" the Act of Assembly, passed in England in 1757, which was designed to give relief to the Baptists and Quakers.[1] The oppression was especially troubling to Davis, who had come from the full religious liberty enjoyed by all denominations in Pennsylvania and Delaware. He was in the forefront, preparing petitions for the courts and appearing before them with appeals for laws that would give relief to the Baptists. He was abused, ridiculed, and one time was referred to publicly as a "little upstart gentleman." A young gentleman he was, but he would not surrender. Dr. Benedict said of him, "His learning abilities, and zeal were adequate to any services to which his brethren might call him."[2]

When he was thirty-five, his health failed, and Davis returned to Delaware, where he hoped a milder climate would restore him to his former vigor. Hoping to recuperate, he very soon set out on a journey with David Jones, who was at that time a missionary to the Indians west of the Ohio River. The journey was strenuous and the weather severe. They did not arrive until December at the home of Dr. James McMachan on the Ohio River. Davis was in a weakened condition and soon took his departure into the presence of his Lord in fulfillment of what he had anticipated and longed for over a period of several days.

The final resting place of Davis's body is near Grave Creek, marked by a large black oak tree on which David Jones cut with his tomahawk, "John Davis, 13th Day of December, 1772." He was the first white man to die in that part of the country.[3]

From a free society to an oppressed people to a vast wilderness, Davis faithfully served the Lord.

EWT

---

[1]William B. Sprague, *Annals of the American Pulpit* (New York: Robert Carter and Bros., 1865), 6:117-18.

[2]Ibid., p. 119.

[3]Ibid.

December 14—Virginia, the Battleground for Religious Liberty

Scripture: Revelation 12

Virginia was known as the great battleground for religious liberty. The colony was founded by members of the Church of England, and no other church was tolerated. The Charter of 1606 provided that "the presidents, councils and ministers should provide that the true Word and service of God should be preached and used according to the rites and doctrines of the Church of England."[1]

The bloody military code of 1611, the first published for the government of the colony, required all men and women in the colony, and any who should afterwards arrive, to give an account of their faith and religion to the parish minister, and if not satisfactory to him, they should report often to him for instruction. If one refused to go, the governor could whip the offender for the first offense. For the second refusal, he would be whipped twice and would acknowledge his fault on the Sabbath day in the congregation, and for the third offense, he would be whipped every day until he complied. [2]

Efforts to legislate religion continued under Sir William Berkeley, who passed the following law on December 14, 1662: "Whereas many schismatical persons out of their averseness to the orthodox established religion, or out of new fangled conceits of their own heretical inventions, refused to have their children baptized. Be it therefore enacted by the authority aforesaid, that all persons that, in contempt of the divine sacrament of baptism, shall refuse when they carry their child to lawful minister in that country to have them baptized shall be amersed two thousand pounds of tobacco, half to the publique."[3]

Of course such statutes were directed at the Baptists, whose principles and convictions dictated that they baptize only believers on their confession of faith and who believed pedobaptism to be a Romish invention carried over into Protestantism by the Reformers. The Church of England increased her membership by pedobaptism, but the Baptists by evangelism and proselytizing. This difference of belief caused a head-on collision between the established religion, the Church of England, which tenaciously held to pedobaptism, and the lowly Baptists, who repudiated it and baptized all who believed and gave their testimony to their faith in Jesus Christ and His finished work on the cross for their salvation.

Hawkes, the historian of the Episcopal Church of Virginia, said, "No dissenters in Virginia experienced, for a time, harsher treatment than did the Baptists. They were beaten and imprisoned; and cruelly taxed the authorities' ingenuity to devise new modes of punishment and annoyance." [4]

Despite the persecution, the Baptists continued to increase in influence and number. The very nature of salvation by grace alone repudiates persecution of any kind and any system that endeavors to legislate its principles and doctrines of human works.

Thank God for our Baptist forefathers who clearly defined the gospel of the grace of God in the face of the persecution that a tyrannical religious system brought to bear upon them.

EWT

---

[1]John T. Christian, *A History of the Baptists* (1922; reprint ed., Nashville: Broadman Press, 1926), 1:381.

[2]Ibid.

[3]Ibid., p. 382.

[4]Ibid.

December 15—A Conversion That Shook the World

Scripture: Isaiah 45:22

According to William Cathcart, ''on December 15 [1850, Charles H. Spurgeon] happened to go into a Primitive Methodist Chapel in Colchester, and heard a sermon on the text, 'Look unto Me and be ye saved.' From that hour he rejoiced in salvation.''[1] However, in a sermon that Spurgeon himself delivered in the New Park Street Chapel on Sunday, January 6, 1856, he gave the date of his conversion as January 6, 1850. [2] Nevertheless the conversion of the fifteen-year-old boy can never be called into question, for his life was changed radically as he placed his trust in the finished work of Christ for his redemption.

It was a cold, snowy day, and the storm was so fierce that the scheduled preacher did not arrive to preach his message. Fifteen people or fewer made up the congregation. A local layman finally agreed to preach, and he chose for his text Isaiah 45:22, ''Look unto Me, and be ye saved, all the ends of the earth.'' In a brief few minutes, the speaker had exhausted the text of all he could find, and thus he emphasized the idea of looking to Christ. Seeing the guilt-ridden face of the lad under the balcony, he fixed his eyes upon Charles, and pointing with his finger he shouted, ''Young man, you're in trouble! Look to Jesus Christ! Look! Look! Look!''[3] And Spurgeon did look in faith, believing, and God brought peace and purpose to his heart and life.

Little could that layman have known that the storm in Spurgeon's heart was more severe than the storm outside the building! In his *Autobiography,* Spurgeon gives an entire chapter to the subject of his conviction. ''Moreover, in telling of it, this master of description seems almost at a loss to fix upon words severe enough to portray the agony he suffered.''[4] One cannot read the account of the spiritual battle that the young man experienced without thinking of the similar experience of John Bunyan. Spurgeon himself wrote,

> Let none despise the strivings of the Spirit in the hearts of the young; let not boyish anxieties and juvenile repentance be lightly regarded. He incurs a fearful amount of guilt who in the least promotes the aim of the evil one by trampling upon a tender conscience in a child. No one can guess at what age children become capable of conversion. I, at least, can bear my personal testimony to the fact that grace operates

> on some minds at a period almost too early for recollections. When but young in years, I felt with much sorrow the evil of sin. My bones waxed old with my roaring all the day long. Day and night God's hand was heavy upon me. I hungered for deliverance, for my soul fainted within me. I feared lest the very skies should fall upon me, and crush my guilty soul. God's law had laid hold upon me, and was showing me my sins. If I slept at night, I dreamed of the bottomless pit; and when I awoke, I seemed to feel the misery I had dreamed.[5]

How we ought to thank God for conviction for without it, there is no real conversion!

When Spurgeon experienced God's salvation by simple, saving faith in Christ's redemptive work for sin, his long-experienced sense of terrible guilt was removed. This event was the great pivotal point in his life, and he was a new creation in Christ Jesus. His conversion proved to be so intrinsic in his nature that it became foundational to his preaching. His burden caused him to present salvation as clearly as possible, and his desire that others might receive the same deliverance set him at once to the work of telling others and distributing leaflets!

In our day of confession without deep conviction or thorough conversion, we would do well to pray for the convincing work of the Holy Spirit, making the desperate need of Christ known.

DLC

---

[1]William Cathcart, *The Baptist Encyclopedia,* ed. Louis H. Everts (Philadelphia: Louis H. Everts, 1881), 2:1093.

[2]Charles H. Spurgeon, *The Autobiography of Charles H. Spurgeon* (Philadelphia: American Baptist Publication Society, n.d.), 1:108.

[3]Richard Ellsworth Day, *The Shadow of the Broad Brim* (Philadelphia: Judson Press, 1934), p. 57.

[4]Arnold Dallimore, *Spurgeon* (1984; reprint ed., Glasgow: Banner of Truth Trust, 1985), p. 15.

[5]Spurgeon, *Autobiography,* p. 79.

December 16—He Rejected the Title "Doctor" for "Brother"

Scripture: Romans 12:3

Dr. Jesse Mercer ''was the most distinguished and influential Baptist minister ever raised in the State of Georgia; and it is doubtful if any one, under the providence of God, ever exerted a more beneficial influence among the Baptists of Georgia.''[1]

Born on December 16, 1769, in Halifax County, North Carolina, Jesse was the oldest child of the Reverend Silas Mercer. Jesse's young life was circumspect in every regard, but at the age of fifteen, he saw himself as a sinner and was converted. In his seventeenth year, Jesse was baptized and united with the Phillips' Mill Church. In his nineteenth year, he was married, and before he was twenty, he was ordained into the ministry and began his fruitful work for the Lord.

For over fifty years, the man of God served as pastor, but he never limited his ministry to only one church. He traveled extensively preaching the gospel. The Reverend Jesse Mercer felt strongly that only by itinerant preaching could the gospel reach the spiritually impoverished in sparsely settled areas of his state.

Influenced strongly by the Reverend Luther Rice, Mercer became an ardent advocate of missions. He encouraged mission effort among the slaves, promoted the Sunday school movement, and led in the efforts of the temperance movement. He served as a trustee of the Columbian College in Washington, D.C., and was the benefactor of education, particularly in the training of ministerial students.

Mercer was used of God in evangelism, and though he was usually given to a pulpit ministry as a pastor, he could preach with great emotion and pathos. His life was marked with great diversity. ''Jesse Mercer was the recognized leader of the Georgia Baptist Association and in the Georgia Baptist Convention. He served as clerk of the association for twenty-one years, as moderator for twenty-three years, and as writer of its history. He was president of the Georgia Baptist Convention for nineteen years, from its founding in 1822 until 1841, when feeble health made his attendance impossible.''[2]

Mercer purchased ''The Christian Index,'' a periodical, and served for several years as editor. The paper was later given to the Georgia Baptist Convention, but Mercer continued to greatly influence his state through its pages. Soon after the turn of the nineteenth century, Mercer published *The Cluster of Spiritual Songs,* a hymnal used widely in Baptist circles through the state of Georgia.

While Mercer was returning from a meeting of the Triennial Convention where he had preached in 1826, his wife became seriously ill and passed away in South Carolina. In December of the following year, the Reverend Mr. Mercer married Nancy Simons, a wealthy widow, and together they became generous donors to the cause of Christ.

It is interesting that though Mercer was granted the Doctor of Divinity degree from Brown University in 1835, he preferred not to be called by that title. Throughout Georgia his friends and co-laborers referred to him merely as "Brother" and with the endearing term "Father."

Upon one occasion, after Mercer had been evangelizing during a time of revival, he traveled home with a heavy heart. He was leaving folks who were enthusiastic in the gospel and was returning to his own church, which was rather apathetic. He stood in his pulpit and recounted the blessings of God in his itinerate ministry, for many had called upon the Lord for salvation. Then, realizing anew the indifference of his own people, he "lifted his hands, [and] exclaimed, 'O, my congregation, I fear you are too good to be saved!' and then burst into a flood of tears."[3] Many responded; revival was experienced and spread through the association.

Jesse Mercer died on September 6, 1841. May God give us such versatile men in our day!

DLC

---

[1]William Cathcart, *The Baptist Encyclopedia,* ed. Louis H. Everts (Philadelphia: Louis H. Everts, 1881), 2:779.

[2]Norman Wade Cox, ed., *Encyclopedia of Southern Baptists* (Nashville: Broadman Press, 1958), 2:849.

[3]Charles O. Walker, *A History of the Georgia Baptist Association, 1784-1984* (Atlanta: Georgia Baptist Historical Society, 1988), pp. 69-70.

December 17—He Was Awakened by "America's Greatest Earthquake"

Scripture: Acts 16:25-31

The Philippian jailer was awakened from sleep, physically and spiritually, when the Lord sent an earthquake to liberate Paul and Silas from jail. Jacob Bower of Muhlenberg County, Kentucky, experienced a similar awakening in the early morning of December 17, 1811, as "America's Greatest Earthquake" struck.[1] The earthquake, centered in the Mississippi River, sent shock waves into Tennessee, Kentucky, Missouri, Georgia, South Carolina, Virginia, and Indiana. Mild tremors were felt as far as Boston! Jacob Bower cried out, "Lord, have mercy on us, we shall all be sunk and lost, and I am not prepared. O God, have mercy upon us all."[2]

Jacob Bower was born into a Christian family on September 26, 1786, His father led the family in morning and evening devotions and instructed the children to live moral, upright lives, but he failed to lead his children into a personal relationship with Christ. Hearing the truth read and having morality set before him as a standard, young Bower matured, trusting his own righteousness.

Upon leaving home for employment, the young man was soon influenced by a Universalist, and for five years, Bower embraced that fallacious heresy. During that period, he began drinking and fell into many vices and sins. When conviction came, he would assure himself of salvation, for Universalism taught that all men would be saved, regardless of their lifestyle.

Bower married in 1807 at the age of twenty-one, and the Lord again began to stir his heart with conviction. When he visited his father's home in 1811, his father attempted to register truth in his heart. Through the additional witness of a Baptist preacher, his heart was stirred again, and whenever he paused to consider death and eternity, his mind was greatly troubled. Throughout the fall of 1811, conviction of sin grew. Then came the devastating earthquake on that fateful morning in December. A tremendous struggle ensued in Bower's life, and in February of 1812, Jacob Bower found the peace of salvation. He made public profession on February 8th and was baptized in March into the membership of the Hazel Creek Baptist Church.

In 1814 Jacob Bower preached his first sermon. He was licensed to preach by his home church in 1816. In 1818 the family moved to Logan County, and Bower was asked to take the oversight of the church there. His ordination took place on February 27, 1819. After serving three Kentucky churches for ten years, Bower moved his family to Illinois in 1828. "A few weeks after his arrival the Winchester Baptist Church . . . was constituted. Two years afterward the Manchester Baptist Church . . . was organized. Of both these churches Elder Bower became pastor. But in 1832 by the accidental discharge of a rifle his foot was so lacerated that he was permanently lame."[3]

His work was just beginning! "In 1832 he accepted an appointment as a missionary under the Home Mission Society and for many years did valiant work, organizing new churches and forming circuits. From 1832 . . . to 1848 he traveled 40,925 miles; preached 2,931 sermons; aided in organizing 14 churches and ordained 12 ministers . . . in both Illinois and Missouri."[4]

We do not know that the Philippian jailer ever preached a sermon, but we rejoice in the faithful frontier preacher and missionary, the Reverend Jacob Bower, who responded to the gospel when God got his attention with an earthquake!

DLC

---

[1]Blake Clark, "America's Greatest Earthquake," *Reader's Digest,* April 1969, p. 110.

[2]William Warren Sweet, *Religion on the American Frontier—The Baptists* (New York: Cooper Square Publishers, 1964), p. 191.

[3]Edward P. Brand, *Illinois Baptists: A History* (Bloomington, Ill.: Pantagraph Printing Co., 1930), p. 70.

[4]Sweet, p. 185.

December 18—Fellowship with Vital Error Is Participation in Sin

Scripture: II Peter 2:1-9

The ministry of Charles Haddon Spurgeon began during a general spiritual decline in England. The evangelical churches had not escaped the tendencies of the times. The work of Whitefield and Wesley was admired, but it was little followed. The cutting edges of biblical truth had been gradually dulled. There seemed to be a prevailing feeling that a more refined and intellectual presentation of the gospel was needed in the Victorian Era.

The things that were true of the country in general were particularly true of London and of the Baptist Chapel at New Park Street, situated in a dim and dirty region close to the South bank of the Thames. This congregation had a great history stretching back into the seventeenth century. For some years it had been in a state of decline, and the large ornate building, built to seat about a thousand, was three quarters filled with empty pews. This was the scene confronting nineteen-year-old Spurgeon when he first stood in the pulpit of New Park Street Chapel on the cold, dull morning of December 18, 1853.[1] Spurgeon soon attacked this lifeless traditionalism in very direct language:

> You think that because a thing is ancient, therefore it must be venerable. You are lovers of the antique. You would not have a road mended, because your grandfather drove his wagon along the rut that is there. "Let it always be there," you say; "let it always be knee deep. Did not your grandfather go through it when it was knee deep with mud, and why should you not do the same? It was good enough for him, and it is good enough for you. You always have taken an easy seat in the chapel. You never saw revival; you do not want to see it."[2]

We have previously noted that things soon changed under the ministry of Spurgeon, and on an ordinary Sunday, 1866, at the Metropolitan Tabernacle, morning and evening the congregation exceeded ten thousand people. But may we never forget that Spurgeon never forsook those fundamental principles of the faith that the Baptists always have stood upon in order to be accepted by his peers when many in the Baptist Union were departing those ancient landmarks. He identified the source of theological errors as "a want of adequate faith in the divine inspiration of the sacred Scriptures."[3] Mischievous errors creep in where the full confidence in the Scripture is weak. In this struggle, the majority of the Baptists would not follow his leadership, even though many of them agreed with his theological position. They preferred unity above the maintenance of doctrinal purity. He attacked this position by saying, "First pure, then peaceable; if only one is attainable, choose the former. Fellowship with known and vital error is participation in sin. . . . To pursue union at the price of truth is treason to the Lord Jesus."[4]

May these principles be instilled into our consciences, and may God grant to us the character to stand on them and the ability to teach them to future generations.

EWT

---

[1]Iain H. Murray, *The Forgotten Spurgeon* (London: Banner of Truth Trust, 1966), pp. 30-31.

[2]Ibid, p. 30.

[3]L. Russ Bush, and Tom J. Nettles, *Baptists and the Bible* (Chicago: Moody Press, 1980), p. 247.

[4]Ibid., p. 249.

December 19—Another Faithful Widow

Scripture: Luke 2:36-38

In the early years of the modern missionary movement, many faithful men of God experienced the heartache of separation by death from wives and children. Devoted women often died during childbirth, and since there was very little medical help available, the children often succumbed to the terrible fevers and dysentery which were so prevalent. Many servants of God experienced this kind of testing. Thus it was with the Reverend Lovell Ingalls, whose first wife died as they served in Burma.

The Lord provided another faithful helpmeet in Mrs. Marilla B. Ingalls, who went with him as he returned to Burma to face the hostile conditions of that country as well as the disappointments of lack of support from the churches at home. Because of the separation of the Baptist churches of the North and South over the slavery issue, finances were scarce, thus affecting the ministry in Burma. Lovell Ingalls expressed the gravity of the situation in a letter to his mission: "Tell the churches that the missionaries cannot endure what they put upon them. We must come and preach, and build houses and chapels without funds, and beg money; and the churches at home are living in luxury. . . . The churches at home, and every member, and every preacher of the gospel are as much bound to give the gospel to every nation as we are. And God will hold them responsible in 'that great day.' "[1]

Shortly after writing this and after nineteen years of ministry in Burma, Lovell Ingalls died at sea between Calcutta and Rangoon. His young widow continued their faithful ministry for forty-six more years. After returning to America for a short period to bring her husband's daughter from his previous marriage for education, she returned to the small jungle village of Thongze, where there were two or three native Christians. There she began the great work of her life. She remained in Thongze and gave over fifty years of fruitful, loving ministry to Burma. F. P. Haggard reported: "Over one hundred Buddhist priests, the most difficult class in Burma to reach, have as a result of her personal labors become humble followers of the once despised 'Jesus religion.' To the sick and suffering, she has been doctor and nurse; to the wronged and oppressed, both lawyer and judge; to pastor and preacher, the faithful theological professor."[2]

Marilla Ingalls was buried on December 19, 1902. She left a strong native church, a Christian school, and Christian homes from which earnest pastors and preachers, evangelists and teachers, and happy wives and mothers went out and spread the good tidings of salvation.

In the entry for July 10, we noted that Mrs. Ingall's service in Burma was not without trials of fire and threats of death. In this day of apathy and lack of zeal for world evangelism, may the life of this devoted widow challenge us to greater commitment to our Lord Jesus Christ and His command to reach every creature in our generation with the message of the gospel of His grace.

EWT

---

[1]Maung Shwe Wa, *Burma Baptist Chronicle* (Rangoon: Burma Baptist Convention, 1963), p. 159.

[2]F. P. Haggard, ed., *Baptist Missionary Magazine,* July 1903, p. 36 (296).

December 20—A Baptist Preacher Promotes Literary Skills

Scripture: Acts 17:11-15

Samuel Green was born December 20, 1822, in Falmouth, England. We know little about his conversion to Jesus Christ and call to preach, but we do know that he was a Baptist pastor from 1844 to 1851. After that time he gave himself to education and literary work.

Education of Baptist preachers has been the subject of much debate for many years. Many outstanding Baptist preachers in England and America had been educated in the colleges and seminaries before their conversion to Christ and/or persuasion to Baptist principles. Because a part of their classical education required them to become familiar with Hebrew, Greek, and Latin, they were enabled to have a deeper understanding of the Bible, and as a result, were persuaded that Baptist principles were biblical principles.

Not only were they persuaded of those Baptist principles, but they were also persuaded of the value of an educated ministry. Certainly there were many who had the qualifications of discipline and access to literature for self-education. But there were a majority of others who felt as the Ethiopian who responded to Philip's inquiry, "Understandest thou what thou readest?" with "How can I except some man should guide me?" Being aware of this need, Samuel Green gave himself to teaching at Rowdon College from 1851 to 1863 and served as president from 1863 to 1876. Thus, his life and skills were given to others in order that they might develop and use their gifts for the glory of Jesus Christ and the salvation and edification of their fellow man.

In 1876 he entered another important ministry as editor of the Religious Tract Society in London and served in this capacity until his retirement in 1899. This was another important related facet of his ministry in reaching the minds and hearts of men and women with the gospel of Jesus Christ and providing Christians with literature that would help them understand the truths of spiritual growth and maturity. Samuel Green not only edited the works of others but also authored many books on the Bible, church history, and related subjects.[1]

As I write this one hundred years later in 1990, there are millions in the world crying out for Bibles and Christian literature that will provide them with the Bread of Life. Opportunities such as we never had before are confronting us as Baptists to feed these hungry masses the truth of God's Word. In Soviet Russia alone multiplied millions of people are pleading for Bibles and the materials to effectively teach God's Word. At least for a period of time, the doors have opened, and the enforcement of their laws have relaxed relating to evangelizing and propagating God's Word.

To our shame and horror, too often the cults and apostates quickly respond with great zeal and skill, while we hesitate and squander the tremendous opportunity afforded us. Among fundamentalist Baptists, there appears to be a dearth of scholarship dedicated to obtaining the skills of effectively communicating through writing at a time when there is such a demand throughout the world for Christian literature. May our Lord raise up others who like Samuel Green, with commitment and dedication, develop skills in writing and give their educational abilities to the training of the bright minds of youth and challenge them to go and do likewise.

EWT

---

[1]William D. Blake, *An Almanac of the Christian Church* (Minneapolis: Bethany House Publishers, 1987), p. 366.

December 21—The New Light Gathered Them with the Ducks Instead of the Chickens

Scripture: Psalm 15

The great revivals that sprang up from the preaching of George Whitefield produced the Separate Congregationalists from which God raised up some of our most effective preachers and powerful leaders. Among these were Shubal Stearns and his brother-in-law, Daniel Marshall. They were known as Separates and migrated through Virginia into North Carolina. In the process they were persuaded, as were many other Separates, of Baptist principles including believers baptism. These reversals were to the consternation of Whitefield. It has been previously pointed out that he expressed his exasperation and opposition by saying, "All my chickens have turned into ducks."

One of the chief functions of the Church of England's ministry in North Carolina, where Stearns and Marshall ultimately settled, was to oppose the growing Baptists and expose the supposed fallaciousness of believers baptism. However, this endeavor met with little success. Some among the Anglican clergy saw value in the work of these frontier Baptists and appreciated the courtesies shown them by their churches and people. Thus the Reverend Michael Smith wrote, "I find that these preachers have been of great service to me in my office, for many of the back settlers who were in a manner totally ignorant of the Christian religion and overrun with sensuality have been roused from their treacherous slumber, brought to a serious way of thinking, and from hearing enthusiastical incoherent harangues have been prepared for more solid discourses."[1]

A letter from the Reverend James Reed, a clergyman of the Church of England, dated December 21, 1764, reveals how Whitefield's preaching helped the Baptists and what his views were about believers baptism.

> In his [Whitefield's] conversation with the Parish Clerk he mentioned the particular number of small tracts which the Society had sent me, and seemed to intimate that in my letter to the Society, I had improperly called the enthusiastic sect [Baptists] in these parts by the name of Methodist, for that none were properly called by that name but the followers of himself and Mr. Wesley. Tho' with submission to Mr. Whitefield, granting they were not his immediate disciples and followers, I do affirm they were sprung from the seed which he first planted in New England and the difference of soil may perhaps have caused such an alteration in the fruit that he may be ashamed of it. However, on the whole I think his discourse has been of some service here, for he particularly condemned the rebaptizing of adults and the doctrine of the irresistible influence of the Spirit, for both which the late Methodists in these parts had strongly contended; and likewise recommended infant baptism, and declared himself a minister of the Church of England.[2]

Thus, we discover the origin of the name "Separate Baptists" and learn of their zeal and success in evangelizing as well as their strong, uncompromising stand on believers baptism to the consternation of the Episcopalians and Methodists. Whitefield was clearly a pedobaptist and a state-church preacher, even though he insisted on the new birth. When men receive the "new light" of the Holy Spirit, they are more likely to embrace believers baptism and to gather with the ducks rather than the chickens. "Birds of a feather flock together."

EWT

---

[1]George Washington Paschal, *History of North Carolina Baptists* (Raleigh: Edwards and Broughton Co., 1930), 1:310.

[2]Ibid., p. 311.

December 22—Pilgrim's Progress; "I Will Print It"

Scripture: Job 19:23-29

The time from the birth of John Bunyan on November 30, 1628, until his entrance into the ''Celestial City'' August 31, 1688, was a period of religious controversy, political unrest, and social violence. Being a man of deep religious faith and conviction, Bunyan was soon caught up in the conflagration, even though in his heart, he despised confrontation. In one of his treatises he wrote, ''Jars and divisions, wranglings and prejudices, eat out the growth, if not the life of religion. These are those waters of Marah that embitter our spirits, and quench the Spirit of God. Unity and peace is said to be like the dew of Hermon (Psalm 133:3), and as a dew that descended upon Zion, when the Lord promised His blessing.''[1]

Controversy also surrounded his writing of *Pilgrim's Progress,* which was licensed December 22, 1677.[2] For several years, it had lain in his drawer as he had numerous consultations with various associates and friends as to whether it was worthy of publication. The responses were numerous and varied. Some had a sense of impropriety, that the allegory was too trifling a way to express such a somber subject as a way of escaping from destruction. The result of these consultations was his determination, ''I will print it.'' The book's publication not only raised an imperishable monument to his memory but also brought multitudes to serious consideration of their peril as they read such a serious presentation expressed in a colloquial manner.

Pilgrim's Progress met with such popularity that the tenth edition was published by 1685. Some of these editions included illustrations and a few additions to the text. The rapidity with which these editions succeeded one another caused Bunyan to prefix the second part, *Christiana,* with; ''Some have, of late, to counterfeit My Pilgrim, to their own, my title set; Yea, others, half my name, and title too, Have stitched to their books, to make them do.'' This statement indicates that some endeavored to counterfeit his writings for personal profit.

Also, some attacked his integrity and accused him of copying the works of others. He defended himself by prefacing his *Holy War* with a verse which began,

> Some say the Pilgrim's Progress is not mine,
> Insinuating as if I would shine

In name and fame by the worth of another,
Like some made rich by robbing their brother.

He continued by declaring:

It came from mine own heart, so to my head,
And thence into my fingers trickled,
Then to my pen, from whence immediately
On Paper I did dribble it daintily.[3]

Because of some criticism relating to his motives for writing *Pilgrim's Progress* and the allegorical method he employed, he prefaced the work with *The Author's Apology for His Book.* This is not an apology in the sense of asking forgiveness for writing it, but an apology as a defense. Among other things that he wrote in this defense, he indicted,

I find that holy writ in many places,
Hath semblance with this method, where the cases
Do call for one thing to set forth another:
Use it I may, then, and yet nothing smother
Truth's golden beams: nay, by this method may
Make it cast forth its rays as light as day.

And now, before I put up my pen,
I'll show the profit of my book; and then
Commit both thee and it unto that hand
That pulls the strong down, and makes weak ones stand.[4]

Though Bunyan's library at one time consisted only of the Holy Bible and *Foxe's Book of Martyrs,* his writings, and in particular *Pilgrim's Progress,* grace private and public libraries the world over, by the thousands, and in many languages. This demonstrates what God can do with a tinker when, in a time when all circumstances seem to be against him, he yields his will to his Lord and stands firm upon the principles of God's Word.

EWT

---

[1]John Bunyan, *The Pilgrim's Progress* (New York: J. B. Hurst Co., n.d.), p. 48.

[2]Ronald W. Thompson, *Heroes of the Baptist Church* (London: Carey Kingsgate Press, 1948), pp. 50-51.

[3]Ibid., p. 57.

[4]John Bunyan, *The Pilgrim's Progress* (New York: Routledge, Warne and Routledge, 1861), pp. 6-7.

December 23—From a Profane Gambler to an Ambassador for Jesus Christ

Scripture: Isaiah 50

John Waller was born December 23, 1741, in Spotsylvania County, Virginia, and was a descendant of the honorable Wallers in England. At a very early age, he manifested a great talent for satirical wit. Thus his uncle, who had the direction of his education, determined to bring him up for the profession of law. His uncle's death, his father's limited resources, and his own unbridled inclinations to vice prevented him from finishing even his classical education. Letting himself loose to every species of wickedness and profanity, he quickly acquired for himself the infamous appellation of "Swearing Jack" Waller, by which he was distinguished from others of the same name. He also was sometimes called the "devils adjutant" to muster his troops.[1]

He was one of a grand jury who presented Lewis Craig and heard his address when he said, "I thank you, gentlemen of the grand jury, for the honor you have done me. While I was wicked and injurious, you took no notice of me; but since I have altered my course of life, and endeavored to reform my neighbors, you concern yourselves much about me. I forgive my persecuting enemies, and shall take joyfully the spoiling of my goods."[2]

When Waller heard him speak in such an humble manner, he was persuaded that Craig was possessed of something he had not seen in him before and desired to have the same experience.

Waller began to attend the Baptist meetings, and he experienced very intense conviction for seven or eight months. He relates his spiritual exercise in the following words, "I had long felt the greatest abhorrence of myself, and began to despair of the mercy of God. However, I determined in my own soul, never to rest from seeking, until it pleased God to show mercy or to cut me off. Under these impressions I was, at a certain place, sitting under preaching. On a sudden, a man exclaimed that he had found grace, and began to praise God. No mortal can describe the horror with which I was seized at that instant. I felt my heart melt, and a sweet application of the Redeemer's love to my poor soul."[3]

There were periods of struggle after this, but he took refuge in the Word of God, especially the passage, "Who is among you that feareth the Lord; . . . that walketh in darkness and hath no light; let him trust in the name of the Lord, and stay upon his God'' (Isa. 50:10).

He was ordained to the ministry June 20, 1770. His ministry was attended with great success, which also brought great opposition. Wherever he went, he was attended with a divine power, turning many to righteousness. The ungodly considered him a bold fanatic, but the Baptists looked to him for leadership. This leadership he provided except for a short period when he fell away from sound doctrine with one of Arminian persuasion. However, he could find no contentment and sorely missed the sweet fellowship of his brethren. He turned from this error and was fully reinstated in 1787, when a full union between Separates, Regulars, and Independents took place. At that time, a great revival began under his ministry and continued for several years, and his church increased to about fifteen hundred members in a short time.

Imprisonments, whippings, and other persecutions that followed Waller are recorded elsewhere in this volume. No man suffered more or experienced greater success in his ministry in Virginia and South Carolina than John Waller. His life truly demonstrates the amazing grace of God in His transformation of a profane gambler into an ambassador of the King of kings, Jesus Christ. Our God is still the same God and is able to do the same in our day!

EWT

---

[1]Robert B. Semple, *A History of the Rise and Progress of the Baptists in Virginia* (Richmond: Published by the author, 1810), pp. 403-4.

[2]David Benedict, *A General History of the Baptist Denomination in America* (Boston: Manning and Loring, 1813), p. 394.

[3]Ibid., pp. 394-95.

December 24—The Southern Baptists' Most Famous Missionary

Scripture: Matthew 28:19-20

Lottie Moon, the ''Southern Baptists' most famous missionary,''[1] served in China for nearly forty years. Born into an unusual family in Albermarle County, Virginia, on December 12, 1840, Miss Moon was given a broad educational background. She was trained in the Virginia Female Seminary and the Albermarle Female Institute. Lottie proved to be a brilliant student and was very adept in several languages. She had no interest in the things of God until her conversion in the spring of 1859 "in a meeting by John Albert Broadus, then pastor at Charlottesville, Virginia."[2]

Lottie's older sister Orianne was the first woman physician in their state, and during the Civil War, Dr. Moon served as a surgeon in Confederate hospitals. Her younger sister Edmonia served as a missionary in China under the Foreign Mission Board of the Southern Baptist Convention for four years and actually preceded Lottie to the field.

Following the completion of her academic training, Miss Lottie Moon taught at Danville, Kentucky, and Cartersville, Georgia. In February of 1873, hearing a missionary challenge from the text, "Lift up your eyes, and look on the fields; for they are white already to harvest," Miss Moon volunteered for service in China. She was appointed by the Foreign Mission Board on July 7, 1873. In 1861 she had considered marriage to Crawford H. Toy, who had been appointed to Japan the year previously, but she had broken off the engagement. Apparently Mr. Toy was "prevented from going [to Japan] by [the] Civil War, and instead had studied for two years in Berlin."[3]

Lottie possessed an indomitable spirit in her service for Christ. She began her labors in Tengchow, China, where she supervised a school for girls. Transferring to the city of Pingtu, she labored alone. As she presented Christ, she distributed gospel literature and was known to mount her rickshaw and project her voice in order to be heard. She was accused by some of "preaching," but with adamant protest she urged that complaining men should come and replace her efforts. Miss Moon stood just over four feet in height, and though she was sensitive about her size, she ministered among short people and therefore was easily accepted. She remained in China for fourteen years before taking her first furlough. During her ministry in Pingtu, she wrote the board stating, "I hope no missionary will ever be as lonely as I have been."[4]

For the second time Miss Moon rejected Crawford Toy's proposal of marriage "because she considered his doctrinal position untenable. . . . When asked by a relative in later years if she had ever been in love, she answered, 'Yes, but God had first claim on my life, and since the two conflicted, there could be no question about the result.' "[5]

Perhaps Miss Moon is best known and remembered because of her suggestion in 1887 that Southern Baptist women institute a week of prayer and sacrificial offering for foreign missions in connection with Christmas. This money was to assist in sending reinforcements for the work, and a goal was set to raise $2,000 in 1888. The Woman's Missionary Union raised $3,315.26, and the week of prayer and Christmas offering became an annual event. In 1918 the annual offering was named the "Lottie Moon Christmas Offering for Foreign Missions."

The Boxer Rebellion took a heavy toll on Lottie Moon as she sacrificed her own food for the Chinese during the time of famine. The Foreign Mission Board sent a nurse, Cynthia Miller, to escort the missionary home. Death came to the frail servant of Christ on Christmas Eve aboard ship in the harbor of Kobe, Japan. A simple monument is to be found in the cemetery of her home church near Crewe, Virginia. Thank God for the blessed memory of this faithful servant to China.

DLC

---

[1]H. Leon McBeth, *The Baptist Heritage* (Nashville: Broadman Press, 1987), p. 416.

[2]Norman Wade Cox, ed., *Encyclopedia of Southern Baptists* (Nashville: Broadman Press, 1958), 2:923.

[3]Robert A. Baker, *The Southern Baptist Convention and Its People, 1607–1972* (Nashville: Broadman Press, 1974), p. 302.

[4]Cox, 2:923.

[5]L. Russ Bush and Tom J. Nettles, *Baptists and the Bible* (Chicago: Moody Press, 1980), p. 227.

December 25—The New Testament Indigenous Policy Proved Timeless

Scripture: II Timothy 2:1-2

William Ashmore served the Lord for many years in China, and his methods of operation were greatly used of God in establishing national believers. He believed that the primary need was not for "professional missionaries," such as professors and writers, but for evangelists and church planters. He held that "mission stations" and boarding schools actually stifled the reaching of the masses, and he claimed, "Too often these mission-schools become settled camps; the army goes into the barracks and is in danger of becoming perpetually occupied with camp work, while the field work has been put off."[1]

William Ashmore was born on December 25, 1821, in Putnam, Ohio. He graduated from Granville College and took his theological training in the Covington Theological Institution in Kentucky. In 1848 he was ordained by the Baptist church in Hamilton, Ohio, and assumed the pastorate of that church.

Having applied for missionary service in China, Ashmore was appointed the following year and sailed on August 17, 1850, for the field. He arrived at Hong Kong on January 4, 1851, and at Bangkok on April 14. Applying himself to the language, he was soon able to work among the people and continued his labors there until 1858, at which time he was transferred to Hong Kong. Because his wife's health failed, she sailed for America in May of that year, tragically died en route, and was buried at sea off the Cape of Good Hope. Two years later, Ashmore's ill health compelled his return to the States. Upon recovering, the man of God returned in 1864 to China with his second wife. They went to Kak-Chie and were successful in 1870 in teaching the indigenous policy. Two national missionaries were sent out to be supported by the funds raised in the church that Dr. Ashmore led. That church, with one hundred and forty-two members, paid almost all the expenses of their own two countrymen.

Dr. and Mrs. Ashmore returned to the States again in 1875 because of the poor health of Mrs. Ashmore, but they were able to go back in 1877. They were delighted to find the church they had left in good condition with growing influence. Dr. Ashmore had translated four portions of the New Testament into the language of the common people. The continuity of the work was ensured as his son, the Reverend William Ashmore, Jr., labored with his father. In 1885, when Dr. Ashmore returned again to the United States, his son continued on in that ministry.

Mrs. Ashmore passed away in the States in 1885, and the Missionary Union asked Dr. Ashmore to remain in America to serve as the Home Secretary. He presented the work of missions in many cities and even traveled to Siam, Japan, India, and Burma on behalf of the mission, but his heart was in China. He resigned his office in 1891 and returned to the land of his choice. That same year he married a missionary widow from Japan and thus had a partner again in his labors among his adopted people. Dr. Ashmore's gifts of speech and his keen mind were greatly used of God in evangelism. He was a man of balance and surely did not deny the necessity of the tedious work of the translation of Scriptures into the vernaculars nor the requirement of education, but he never lost sight of the essential of building indigenous works that would endure when foreign missionaries would be removed. This New Testament principle is surely valid for our days as well.

DLC

---

[1]G. Winfred Hervey, *The Story of Baptists Missions in Foreign Lands* (St. Louis: C. R. Barnes Publishing Co., 1892), p. 539.

December 26—Parliament, the Baptists, and Their Principles

Scripture: Acts 21:27-39

The troubled times of the civil war gave the Baptists in England an opportunity to make real growth. Robert Baillie, one of the enemies, said, "Under the shadow of Independency, they have lifted up their heads and increased their number above all sects in the land. They have forty-six churches in and about London; they are a people very fond of religious liberty, and very unwilling to be brought under bondage of the judgement of any other."[1]

The Baptists were strongly attached to liberty, and they joined themselves in great numbers to the Parliamentary army. In the forces of Oliver Cromwell particularly, many officers were accustomed to preaching, and both commanders and privates were continually searching the Scriptures and praying in meetings. As a result of these activities, many more became Baptists. Major General Harrison, one of the army's distinguished leaders, was a Baptist. Harrison was a long-time friend of Cromwell but became alienated from him when he came to believe that Cromwell sought triumph, not as a matter of principle, but for his own personal aggrandizement. Favorable to liberty and inaccessible to flattering promises of power, Harrison became the object of suspicion to Cromwell, who, again and again, threw him in prison.

The Baptists soon recognized that the Parliamentary party was not, on the whole, a real friend of the Baptists and true liberty of conscience. The Presbyterian faction, which controlled the Parliamentary forces in the 1640s, responded favorably to petitions, sent from many sources to Parliament, which asked that severe laws be enacted against all sects who would not come into the Presbyterian establishment. An example of some of these ordinances passed was one of December 26, 1646, which stated in part,

> The commons assembled in parliament do declare, that they do dislike and will proceed against all such persons as shall take upon them to preach, or expound the Scriptures in any church or chapel, or any other public place, except they may be ordained, either here or some other reformed church, as it is already prohibited in an order of both houses of the 26th of April, 1645, and likewise against all such ministers, or others, as shall publish or maintain, by preaching, or writing,

> or any other way, anything against, or in derogation of church government which is now established by authority of both houses of parliament.[2]

The ordinance went on to describe how the authorities were to proceed in enforcing it and punishing the offenders.

The persecutions were directed mainly against the Baptists because they denied the necessity of infant baptism. Almost every prominent Baptist preacher was sooner or later committed to prison. We must fully realize that history confirms the deterioration of any marriage of church and state, no matter how noble the intent of any such union may be. The result will usually be a tyrannical, persecuting, bloody, religio-political hierarchy with a voracious appetite for absolute power and control of the entire man. Ultimately, the state church body would seek a position of power that would supersede the individual conscience. History also attests that true Baptists never have had such ambitions because they tenaciously have clung to the true principles of soul liberty, not only for themselves but for others as well.

God help us to continue in this great spiritual heritage and diligently teach its principles and our history to generations to come.

EWT

---

[1]John T. Christian, *A History of the Baptists* (1922; reprint ed., Nashville: Broadman Press, 1926), 1:330.

[2]Ibid., p. 338.

December 27—Boast Not Thyself of Tomorrow

Scripture: Proverbs 27

We often see evidence of the wonderful working of God's grace in the lives of the very young. Generally it is manifest in a home where the children are exposed to God's Word. There they are familiar with the atmosphere that is created by praying parents, and they see consistent godly living day by day. We also cannot ignore the influence of the local church, where children are exposed to the godly influence of their pastor, Sunday school teachers, missionaries, and evangelists.

God loves children and Jesus exhorted, "Suffer the little children to come unto me, and forbid them not: for of such is the kingdom of God" (Mark 10:14). God bless parents who know that Jesus can touch their children and bring their lives to maturity as His choice servants.

Thus it was with Baron Stow, who became one of the most eloquent and successful Baptist ministers in New England.

He was born a country boy on his father's farm in 1801. God uses not only the aforementioned instruments of His grace but also those quiet times alone that are vital to the spiritual growth of a sensitive young man. It was apparent that Baron, as a small child, was listening, like Samuel, to the voice of God. He began to demonstrate that he was spiritually gifted. By the roadside near his home was a boulder which, from its peculiar construction, was called ''the pulpit.'' Taking possession of this pulpit, the boy-preacher would draw around him his associates and preach the gospel.[1]

After preparation for college in Newport, New Hampshire, Stow became a member of the student body of Columbian College in Washington, D.C., in 1822, where he sat under outstanding professors. He was a good student and completed the entire course of study in a little over three years.

Following a time as editor of the Triennial Convention's periodical, *Columbian Star,* he became pastor of the Baptist church in Portsmouth, New Hampshire. Soon the church grew to such proportions that they had to build a new house of worship to accommodate the people. Stow served this church for five years and then answered the call to Baldwin Place Baptist Church in Boston. His ministry there was even more fruitful. At the close of 1837 he preached a remarkable sermon from ''Boast not thyself of tomorrow; for thou knowest not what a day may bring forth'' (Prov. 27:1). More than one hundred people referred to that sermon as the means of their awakening and conversion.[2] The year 1838 opened with a powerful revival, and during the next five years, 502 people were added to the church on profession of their faith in Jesus Christ.

Stow was concerned not only with the souls of men in Boston but also with the cause of foreign missions. He preached and wrote concerning world evangelism, endeavoring to stir up fellow Christians to respond to the mandate of their Lord.

Toward the end of his nearly forty years of ministry, ill health forced him from the pulpit several times. He ended his sojourn December 27, 1869. Dr. Stow takes his place as one of the most outstanding Baptist preachers of any generation.[3]

EWT

---

[1]William Cathcart, *The Baptist Encyclopedia,* ed. Louis H. Everts (Philadelphia: Louis H. Everts, 1881), 2:1115.

[2]Ibid., 2:1116.

[3]Ibid.

December 28—The Translator, the Doctor, and Their First Fruits

Scripture: I Corinthians 16:10-24

Often when we read or hear the name of some outstanding missionary, we think of some facet of his or her ministry that peculiarly sets him or her apart. So it is with William Carey. Carey and the translation of the Scriptures are synonymous. This painstaking task was one of great magnitude.

Dr. Thomas, Carey's companion and fellow laborer in the ministry, had carried out medical work for many years. We must never fail to remember that all this time the ultimate purpose was to reach the people of India with the gospel of Jesus Christ. They both faithfully witnessed and preached, Carey for six years and Dr. Thomas for sixteen years, before they saw the first fruits of their labors. The labor had been hard and discouraging, but they never became despondent nor gave up.

Krishna Pal, a carpenter by trade, fell and broke his arm. Dr. Thomas was called and set his arm. After his work as a surgeon was done, he most fervently preached the gospel to Krishna and his neighbors. In this discourse, Thomas set forth the folly of idolatry and proclaimed the great truths of Christianity. Krishna was deeply affected and moved to tears. He accepted the opportunity at the invitation of the missionaries to receive further instruction. Before long, he openly renounced idolatry and the caste, professing his faith in Jesus Christ. He related the gospel to his wife and daughter, and then the three offered themselves for believers immersion.

The news of Krishna's conversion stirred up the natives, "and soon Krishna was besieged by a mob of two-thousand persons, who poured out torrents of maledictions upon him, and then dragged him to the magistrate, who immediately released him and commended him for the piety of his course, and commanded the mob to disperse."[1]

The magistrate placed a guard at his house and offered armed protection to the missionaries during the baptism.

When his wife and daughter saw what a controversy their profession of Christianity had caused, they faltered, postponed their baptism, and left Krishna alone to venture forth through the great crowds of Mohammedans and Hindus who had come to see the ordinance. In the presence of the governor of India and a number of Portuguese, Dr. Carey walked down amidst the profoundest silence with his eldest son, Felix, and Krishna into the Ganges River. He explained that it was not the water of the sacred river that could wash away sin but only the blood of Jesus Christ, after which he baptized them both. All hearts were so impressed that even the governor wept. On that day, December 28, 1800, the wall of partition was broken down between Englishman and Hindu, and the Lord's Supper was celebrated in Bengali for the first time.[2]

For more than twenty years, Krishna Pal preached the gospel of God's grace among his people with great ability and success. Before his death, he composed a beautiful hymn from which the following stanzas are taken:

O Thou my soul, forget no more.
The Friend who all thy misery bore;
Let every idol be forgot,
But, O my soul, forget Him not.

Jesus for Thee a body takes;
Thy guilt assumes, thy fetters breaks,
Discharging all thy dreadful debt;
And canst thou e'er such love forget.[3]

EWT

---

[1]William Cathcart, *The Baptist Encyclopedia,* ed. Louis H. Everts (Philadelphia: Louis H. Everts, 1881), 2:667.

[2]G. Winfred Hervey, *The Story of Baptist Missions in Foreign Lands* (St. Louis: C. R. Barnes Publishing Co., 1892), p. 924.

[3]Cathcart, *Baptist Encyclopedia,* 2:667.

December 29—He Created Music with a Message

Scripture: Ephesians 5:19

The name of P. P. Bliss is inseparably linked with the musical ministry of evangelism in nineteenth-century America. Born in Rome, Pennsylvania, on July 9, 1838, in the "home of praying and singing parents, [Bliss spent] his youth . . . on a farm (and) early formal education was (very) limited."[1] "His name was originally spelled 'Phillipp,' and from this singular form he wisely altered it to Philip P. Bliss, or more commonly, P. P. Bliss—not Philip Paul, as some writers have supposed."[2]

In his twelfth year, Philip Bliss was converted and "joined the Baptist church at Tioga, Pennsylvania, upon his baptism."[3] He was familiar with camp meetings and revival services, and from 1856 to 1860, he taught several semesters of school while he studied music. In 1859 Bliss married a young woman who was a musician-poet in her own right. The following year he began teaching music professionally just at the outset of the Civil War. Toward the end of that conflict he was drafted, but after only two weeks in the military, he was discharged when the national strife concluded. In 1865 Mr. and Mrs. Bliss moved to Chicago, where Mr. Bliss became associated with a music publishing company. During the next months, he conducted musical institutes, gave concerts, and composed music for the Sunday school. "One night when he attended a revival meeting in Chicago, his marvelous voice came to the attention of the preacher, D. L. Moody, who at the close of the service hastened to speak to him. Moody related in after years, that the 'power of solo singing of Gospel songs at evangelistic meetings dated from that time.' "[4]

Mr. Moody urged Bliss to give up his business career and enter into the ministry of full-time gospel singing. In 1874 Bliss united with Major D. W. Whittle and served as soloist, song leader, and children's worker. His service in the field of music seemed very secure, and he was thrilled with the opportunity. "In writing to a friend, P. P. Bliss said, 'This singing and talking about the Good News of a present, perfect, free salvation and justification by faith is so popular and attractive, I do not believe I shall ever find time for any else. It seems to me it is needed. How much of everything else we hear preached, and how little Gospel!' "[5]

The ministry of the next two years was very rewarding for Mr. and Mrs. Bliss, and their service was very effective. At the Christmas season of 1876, the couple traveled back to Pennsylvania to spend the holidays with his mother and sister. On their return trip to Chicago on December 29, 1876, a bridge collapsed near Ashtabula, Ohio, and the Pacific Express, on which they were riding, plunged into a ravine sixty feet below. The train was crushed and began to burn. Bliss survived the fall and escaped through a window, but he returned to rescue his wife and perished with her in the flames.

His wonderful voice and music were destroyed in the fire in Bliss's thirty-eighth year, but his blessed hymns live on. He had written "Man of Sorrows! What a Name!," "Almost Persuaded," "Hold the Fort," "The Light of the World is Jesus," "Let the Lower Lights be Burning," "Wonderful Words of Life," and "Jesus Loves Even Me." Perhaps my favorite of Bliss's hymns was written after he read a spiritual treasure given him by his wife as a birthday present. Considering the believer's deliverance by the death of Christ from the curse of the law and seeing the believer's position in relation to Christ setting him entirely free from the law's dominion, he sat down and wrote the hymn "Once for All," which proclaims, "Cursed by the law and bruised by the fall, / Christ hath redeemed us, once for all!"

On this memorial of the home going of Mr. and Mrs. P. P. Bliss, we thank God for their contribution to the cause of Christ in gospel music.

DLC

---

[1]Englin S. Moyer, *Who Was Who in Church History* (Chicago: Moody Press, 1962), p. 46.

[2]Christopher Knapp, *Who Wrote Our Hymns?* (Denver: Willson Foundation, n.d.), p. 220.

[3]Carey Bonner, *Some Baptist Hymnists from the Seventeenth Century to Modern Times* (London: Carey Kingsgate Press, 1937), p. 123.

[4]Kathleen Blanchard, *Stories of Beautiful Hymns* (Grand Rapids: Zondervan Publishing House, 1952), p. 54.

[5]Ibid., p. 55.

December 30—The Lone Star Pioneer Baptist

Scripture: Hebrews 4:12-13

Baptists in Texas are fully aware of the indebtedness they owe to Zacharius Morrell. He has "the distinction of being the most daring, uncompromising and aggressive of the pioneer Baptist preachers of Texas," wrote B. F. Riley.[1] Of Morrell, J. M. Carroll said that to his credit "is due as much, or more, than to any other man, the right beginnings and right foundations of organized Baptist work in Texas." And Joseph Martin Dawson wrote, "His name is perhaps the best known and most cherished of any among the Texas Baptist fathers."[2]

Born in South Carolina on January 17, 1803, Zacharius Morrell received little formal education but was early known for his courage and fiery temperament. Although he was physically handicapped, Morrell began preaching before he was twenty and served for fourteen years in Tennessee. For a period of nine years, he averaged preaching a sermon a day! Due to lung hemorrhaging, the man of God was advised by physicians to discontinue his preaching and seek a milder climate.

With his wife and four children he moved to Mississippi in 1835, considering the possibility of living in Texas. He paused however, because he had heard of the domination of the Roman Catholic Church in that

> land and reports that a political revolution was beginning in Texas. In December, 1835, he returned from a preaching tour to find his physician and several other friends from Tennessee en route to Texas. He determined to go with them to survey the situation to see if his family could safely be taken there. Two lawyers, two Baptist deacons, the physician, and Morrell began the journey immediately. They arrived at the Falls of the Brazos, near what is now Marlin, on December 30, 1835, where a Tennessee colony was camped. On that night, with a clear voice and a stronger body than he had known for years, he preached his first sermon on Texas soil. He determined that he would bring his family to Texas and cast his lot with this turbulent empire.[3]

The antimissionary forces had made inroads into Texas but Morrell formed the first ''missionary'' Baptist church in the state at Washington on the Brazos with eight members in 1837. As a champion of missions, temperance, Sunday schools, and education, he stamped his impression upon the early labors in his adopted state. He organized churches and associations during his years of labor. Morrell was very outspoken in what he believed and had no fear in excoriating politicians or religious leaders when he felt they were to be censured. He believed that the Bible should be wielded as a sharp two-edged sword and referred to his Bible as ''old Jerusalem blade.'' Morrell counteracted much of the antimission sentiment of the ''Hard-Shells,'' and when the doctrines of Alexander Campbell penetrated the state of Texas, again Z. N. Morrell led the battle in defeating the heresy. What would one expect from a preacher who was not afraid to contend with Satan with his Bible or fight Indians with his rifle? On one such occasion, Morrell was preaching forty-five miles from home when Indians attacked and killed two of the congregation. After pursuing the Indians, he returned and buried the dead, consoled the grieving, and then by cover of night traveled home. He knew that he ''was liable to be attacked at any moment.''[4] But he persevered as the servant of God.

His frontier style of ministry fit well the rugged atmosphere of the ''Old West.'' It is estimated that in 1835, when he first arrived in Texas, there were no more than fifty Baptists of all varieties in the state, but by the time of Morrell's death in December 1883, there were more than 80,000 ''Missionary'' Baptists in sixty associations. He was buried in Kyle, Texas, but his body was reinterred in the state cemetery in Austin in 1946. His figure is represented on a bas-relief of outstanding Baptists at the Southwestern Baptist Theological Seminary in Fort Worth, Texas.

DLC

---

[1]B. F. Riley, *History of the Baptists of Texas* (Dallas: Published by the author, 1907), p. 18.

[2]L. R. Elliott, ed., *Centennial Story of Texas Baptists* (Dallas: Baptist General Convention of Texas, 1936), p. 22.

[3]Robert A. Baker, *The Blossoming Desert* (Waco, Tex.: Word Books, 1970), pp. 28-29.

[4]Elliott, p. 10.

December 31—Teach Me to Study Thy Glory in All Things

Scripture: Psalm 90

Oliver Hart was born in Bucks County, Pennsylvania, on July 5, 1723, of reputable parents. Early in life he was exposed to the preaching of Whitefield, the Episcopalian; the Presbyterian Tennents; and Edward and Abel Morgan, the Baptists. In those early years, Hart made his profession of faith in Jesus Christ. He was baptized by Elder Jenkins Jones and became a member of the Baptist church in Southampton, Pennsylvania.

After Hart's ordination on October 18, 1749, he was challenged by a call for ministers to go to Charleston, South Carolina. He departed for that city and arrived the very day that the only ordained Baptist preacher in that area, Isaac Chamber, was buried. The unexpected arrival of Oliver Hart was considered the leading of the Lord, and the people immediately asked him to assume the pastoral care of the church. He accepted this position on February 16, 1750, and continued for thirty years. He experienced seasons of joy and depression but exhibited at all times an uprightness and dignity revealed in his temperament and conduct. All of this was an outstanding testimony of his spirituality and upright character.

When the British fleet invaded Charleston in 1780, Hart desired to preserve his political liberty, which was being threatened. Thus he traveled to New Jersey, where he assumed the pastorate of the Baptist church at Hopewell. He continued there for fifteen years with a very fruitful ministry.

Hart was another example of one who did not have the privilege of a college education nor indeed much assistance from any personal instruction. However, he so applied his mind to private study that the college of Rhode Island conferred upon him the honorary degree of Master of Liberal Arts. He was interested in the training of others and involved in the laying of the groundwork upon which men like his friend Richard Furman and others built.

On the occasion of Oliver Hart's death on December 31, 1795, Dr. Richard Furman said, "From a part of his diary now in my possession, it appears that he took more than ordinary pains to walk humbly and faithfully with God; to live under the impressions of the love of Christ; to walk in the light of the divine presence; and to improve all his time and opportunities to the noblest purposes of religion and virtue."[1]

As we close the pages of this volume and of another year, let us reflect upon our great spiritual heritage. May the lives and events we have viewed momentarily of days gone by humble us and challenge our hearts. May we reflect upon what Oliver Hart wrote in his diary on August 5, 1754:

> Oh, that, for time to come, I may become more active for God! I would this morning resolve, before Thee, O God, and in Thy name and strength, to devote myself more unreservedly to Thy service than I have hitherto done: I would resolve to be a better improver of my time, than I have heretofore been; to rise earlier in the morning; to be sooner with Thee in secret devotion; and oh, that I may be more devout therein! I would be more engaged in my studies. Grant, O Lord, that I may improve more by them! And when I go abroad, enable me better to improve my visits, that I may always leave a savor of divine things behind me. When I go to Thy house to speak for Thee, may I always go full fraught with things divine, and be enabled faithfully and feelingly to dispense the Word of Life. I would begin and end each day with Thee. Teach me to study Thy glory in all I do.[2]

Amen!

EWT

---

[1]David Benedict, *A General History of the Baptist Denomination in America* (Boston: Manning and Loring, 1813), 2:326.

[2]Ibid., p. 327.

Glossary of Terms

General Baptists trace their beginnings to Holland in 1609, and the group held to the Arminian interpretation of Scripture—conditional election, general atonement, human freedom and the possibility of falling from grace. Those who hold to that position today are usually referred to as "Free Will Baptists" or by the original term of "General Baptist."

Particular Baptists were known for their emphasis on the limited (particular) atonement, and this focus characterized them as Calvinists. Today those known as "Hardshell," or "Primitive Baptists," attempt to trace their heritage to the Particular Baptists. However, in time, those holding to the Particular Baptist position became commonly known as "Regular" Baptists, and the theological position was somewhat modified. A modern rebirth of the theological system among Baptists with a re-emphasis on unconditional election has seen the rise of a group who might be described as the "Sovereign Grace" or "Reformed" Baptists.

Separate Baptists came into being as a result of the Great Awakening in the 1720s and 1730s. These brethren are also known in some Baptist histories as "New Lights." The group was mildly Calvinistic in theology, but its members were much more emotional than the Particular-Regular Baptists. They insisted on using the Bible, rather than formal confessions of faith, as the basis of their belief. The Particular-Regular Baptists were known for their "order," while the Separate Baptists were known for their "ardor." In the course of time, the Regulars and Separates merged in the state of Virginia and became known for a time as the "United" Baptists.

Seventh-Day Baptists (Sabbatarian Baptists) differed from other Baptist groups in consistently worshiping on Saturday as the Lord's Sabbath. They came to America from England in about 1664 but have never been large in number. Their theology has varied from Calvinism to Arminianism, but the Sabbath observance has always set them apart from other Baptists.

Selected Bibliography

"Annals of America." *Encyclopedia Britannica.* Chicago: Encyclopedia Britannica, 1976.

American Baptist Magazine. Vol. 15. Board of Managers of the Baptist General Convention. Published under various titles. Boston: John Putnam, 1820-1913.

Anderson, Fred. "John Roberts Moffett, Virginia Baptists' Martyr for Temperance." *Virginia Baptist Register,* no. 26:1289-1301.

Armitage, Thomas. *The History of the Baptists.* 2 vols. 1890. Reprint. Watertown, Wis.: Maranatha Baptist Press, 1976.

Armstrong, O. K., and Armstrong, Marjorie. *The Baptists in America.* New York: Doubleday and Co., 1979.

———. *Baptists Who Shaped a Nation.* Nashville: Broadman Press, 1975.

Backus, Isaac. *A History of the Baptists in New England.* Edited by Charles G. Sommers. The Baptist Library. Vol. 1. 1846. Reprint. New York: Lewis Colby and Co., n.d.

———. *Your Baptist Heritage, 1620-1804.* 1844. Reprint. Little Rock, Ark.: Challenge Press, 1976. [Originally published as *Church History of New England from 1620 to 1804.*]

Baker, Robert A. *A Baptist Source Book.* Nashville: Broadman Press, 1966.

———. *The Blossoming Dessert.* Waco, Tex.: Word Books, 1970.

———. *The Southern Baptist Convention and Its People, 1607-1972.* Nashville: Broadman Press, 1974.

Baker, Robert A., and Craven, Paul J., Jr. *Adventure in Faith.* Nashville: Broadman Press, 1982.

Baptist Quarterly of the Baptist Historical Society. Vol. 2. London: Baptist Union Publication Department, 1924-25.

Barck, Oscar Theodore, Jr., and Lefler, Hugh Talmadge. *Colonial America.* New York: Macmillan Co., 1968.

Barker, W. M. *Memoirs of Elder J. N. Hall.* Fulton, Ky.: Baptist Flag Print, 1907.

Barnes, Lemuel Call; Barnes, Mary Clark; and Stephenson, Edward M. *Pioneers of Light.* Philadelphia: American Baptist Publication Society, 1924.

Beale, David O. *In Pursuit of Purity*. Greenville, S.C.: Unusual Publications, 1986.

Benedict, David. *A General History of the Baptist Denomination in America*. Vol. 2. Boston: Manning and Loring, 1813.

———. *A General History of the Baptist Denomination in America*. New York: Lewis Colby and Co., 1848.

———. *Fifty Years Among the Baptists*. New York: Sheldon and Co., 1860.

Binney, Mrs. J. G. *Twenty-Six Years in Burma*. Philadelphia: American Baptist Publication Society, 1880.

Biographical Digest of Lulu Celestia Fleming. Valley Forge, Pa.: International Ministries of the American Baptist Churches U.S.A., n.d.

Blake, William D. *An Almanac of the Christian Church*. Minneapolis: Bethany House Publishers, 1987.

Blanchard, Kathleen. *Stories of Beautiful Hymns*. Grand Rapids: Zondervan Publishing House, 1952.

Bogard, Ben M. *Pillars of Orthodoxy; or, Defenders of the Faith*. Louisville: Baptist Book Concern, 1900.

Bonner, Carey. *Some Baptist Hymnists from the Seventeenth Century to Modern Time*. London: Carey Kingsgate Press, 1937.

Bostick, Lena Stover. *An Ambassador for Christ*. Luray, Va.: Lauch and Co., 1959.

Boyd, Jesse L. *A History of Baptists in America Prior to 1845*. New York: American Press, 1957.

Boyte, Robert, and Howell, C. *The Early Baptists of Virginia*. Philadelphia: American Baptist Publication Society, 1857.

Brackney, William Henry. *The Baptists*. New York: Greenwood Press, 1988.

———. *Dispensations of Providence*. Rochester, N.Y.: American Baptist Historical Society, 1984.

Brand, Edward P. *Illinois Baptists: A History*. Bloomington, Ill.: Pantagraph Printing Co., 1930.

Breasted, J. H., and Robinson, J. H. *History of Europe, Ancient and Medieval*. New York: Ginn and Co., 1914.

Breen, J. F. *The Baptist*. Chicago: Northern Baptist Convention, 1920.

Broadus, John A. *Memoir of James Petigru Boyce*. New York: A. C. Armstrong, 1893.

Brooks, Charles Wesley. *A Century of Missions in the Empire State*. Philadelphia: American Baptist Publication Society, 1909.

Brown, J. Newton. *Memorials of Baptist Martyrs*. Philadelphia: American Baptist Publication Society, 1854.

Brush, John Woolman. *Baptists in Massachusetts*. Valley Forge, Pa.: Judson Press, 1970.

Bunyan, John. "Life of John Bunyan." *The Pilgrim's Progress from This World to That Which Is to Come*. New York: J. B. Hurst Co., n.d.

———. *The Pilgrim's Progress*. London: Routledge, Warne and Routledge, 1861.

Burrage, Henry S. *Baptist Hymn Writers and Their Hymns*. Portland, Maine: Thurston and Co., 1883.

———. *A History of the Anabaptists in Switzerland*. Philadelphia: American Baptist Publication Society, 1882.

———. *A History of the Baptists in Maine*. Portland, Maine: Marks Printing House, 1904.

———. *A History of the Baptists in New England*. Philadelphia: American Baptist Publication Society, 1894.

Bush, L. Russ, and Nettles, Tom J. *Baptists and the Bible*. Chicago: Moody Press, 1980.

Busher, Leonard. *Religions Peace: A Plea for Liberty of Conscience*. London: John Sweeting, 1646.

Carey, Eustace. *Memoirs of William Carey*. Boston: Gould, Kendall and Lincoln, 1836.

Carey, S. Pearce. *William Carey*. London: Hodder and Stoughton, 1924.

Carlile, John C. *The Story of the English Baptists*. London: James Clarke and Co., 1905.

Carruth, Gordon, ed. *Encyclopedia of American Facts and Dates*. New York: Thomas Y. Crowell Co., 1956.

Cartledge, Tony W. "Samuel Cartledge: Colonial 'Saul of Tarsus.' " *Viewpoints—Georgia Baptist History* 8 (1982): 13-31.

Cathcart, William. *The Baptist Encyclopedia*. Edited by Louis H. Everts. 2 vols. Philadelphia: Louis H. Everts, 1881.

———. *Baptist Patriots in the American Revolution*. Grand Rapids: Guardian Press, 1976.

———. *The Baptists and the American Revolution*. Grand Rapids: Guardian Press, 1976.

Chalandeau, Alexander de. *The Christians in the USSR*. Chicago: Harper and Row, 1978.

Christian, John T. *A History of the Baptists*. 2 vols. 1922. Reprint. Nashville: Broadman Press, 1926.

Chute, Arthur C. *John Thomas, First Baptist Missionary to Bengal*. Halifax, N.S.: Baptist Book and Tract Society, 1893.

Clark, Blake. "America's Greatest Earthquake." *Reader's Digest*. April 1969. pp. 110-14.

Clark, Henry W. *History of English Nonconformity*. Vol. 1. London: Chapman and Hall, 1911.

Clearwaters, R. V. "The Passing of Dr. W. B. Riley." *Central Baptist Quarterly*. Spring 1961.

"Code of Virginia." *The Act of Religious Freedom*. Va.: n.p., n.d.

Cone, Edward W., and Cone, Spencer W. *Some Account of the Life of Spencer Houghton Cone*. New York: Livermore and Rudd, 1856.

Conwell, Russell H. *Life of Charles Haddon Spurgeon*. Philadelphia: Edgewood Publishing Co., 1892.

Cook, Richard B. *The Story of the Baptists*. Baltimore: H. M. Wharton and Co., 1886.

Cox, F. A. *History of the Baptist Missionary Society*. Vol. 1. London: T. Ward and J. Dyer, 1842.

Cox, Norman Wade, ed., *Encyclopedia of Southern Baptists*. 2 vols. Nashville: Broadman Press, 1958.

Cramp, J. M. *Baptist History from the Foundation of the Christian Church to the Present Time*. London: Elliott Stock, 1870.

Crosby, Thomas. *The History of the English Baptists*. 1738-40. Reprint. Lafayette, Tenn.: Church History Research and Archives, 1979.

Dallimore, Arnold A. *George Whitefield*. London: Banner of Truth Trust, 1970.

———. *Spurgeon*. 1984. Reprint. Glasgow: Banner of Truth Trust, 1985.

Darter, Oscar H. *The History of Fredericksburg Baptist Church*. Richmond: Garrett and Massie, 1960.

Davis, J. *History of the Welsh Baptists*. Pittsburgh: J. M. Hogan, 1835.

Dawson, Joseph Martin. *Baptists and the American Republic*. Nashville: Broadman Press, 1956.

Day, Richard Ellsworth. *Rhapsody in Black*. Valley Forge, Pa.: Judson Press, 1953.

———. *The Shadow of the Broad Brim*. Philadelphia: Judson Press, 1934.

De Blois, Austen Kennedy. *Fighters for Freedom*. Philadelphia: Judson Press, 1929.

Doane, W. Howard, and Johnson, E. H., eds. *Baptist Hymnal*. Philadelphia: American Baptist Publication Society, 1883.

Douty, Norman F. *Another Look at Seventh-Day Adventism*. Grand Rapids: Baker Book House, 1962.

Dowling, John. *The Judson Offering*. New York: Lewis Colby and Co., 1846.

Edwards, Morgan, *Materials Toward a History of the Baptists*. 2 vols. Danielsville, Ga.: Heritage Papers, 1984.

Elliott, L. R., ed. *Centennial Story of Texas Baptists*. Dallas: Baptist General Convention of Texas, 1936.

Emurian, Ernest K. *Living Stories of Famous Hymns*. Grand Rapids: Baker Book House, 1955.

Estep, William R. *The Anabaptist Story*. Nashville: Broadman Press, 1963.

Evans, Philip S. *History of the Connecticut Baptist State Convention*. Hartford: Smith-Linsley, 1909.

Fitts, Leroy. *A History of Black Baptists*. Nashville: Broadman Press, 1985.

Forbush, William Byron, ed. *Foxe's Book of Martyrs*. Philadelphia: John C. Winston Co., 1926.

Fristoe, William. *The History of the Ketocton Baptist Association, 1766-1808*. Staunton, Va.: William Gilman Lyford, 1808.

Fuller, Andrew, comp., *Memoirs of the Late Rev. Samuel Pearce*. Edited by Levi L. Hill. The Baptist Library, Vol. 3. 1846. Reprint. New York: Lewis Colby and Co., n.d.

Gammie, Alexander. *A Romance of Faith*. London: Pickering and Inglis, n.d.

Gardner, Robert G. *Baptists of Early America*. Atlanta: Georgia Baptist Historical Society, 1983.

Gaustad, Edwin S. *Baptist Piety*. Grand Rapids: Christian University Press, 1978.

Gedde, William, and Gedde, J. Liddell. *Chamber's Biographical Dictionary*. London: W. R. Chambers, 1926.

Gillette, A. D., ed. *Minutes of the Philadelphia Baptist Association from 1707 to 1807*. 1851. Reprint. Minneapolis: James Publishing Co., n.d.

Goadby, J. Jackson. *Bye-Paths in Baptist History*. New York: Bible Publishing Co., n.d.

Gordon, A. J. *In Christ*. New York: Fleming H. Revell Co., 1880.

Haldeman, I. M. *The Truth About Baptism*. Bristol, Tenn.: Evangelistic Press, n.d.

Ham, Edward E. *Fifty Years on the Battle Front with Christ*. Louisville: Old Kentucky Home Revivalist, 1950.

Hatcher, William E. *John Jasper*. New York: Fleming H. Revell Co., 1908.

Hawker, George. *The Life of George Grenfell*. London: Religious Tract Society, 1909.

Hefley, James, and Hefley, Marti. *The Secret File on John Birch*. Wheaton, Ill.: Living Books, 1981.

Hervey, G. Winfred. *The Story of Baptist Missions in Foreign Lands*. St. Louis: C. R. Barnes Publishing Co., 1892.

Higgins, T. A. *The Life of John Mockett Cramp, D.D.* Montreal: W. Drysdale and Co., 1887.

Hiscox, Edward T. *The Baptist Directory*. New York: Sheldon and Co., 1866.

Historical Records. Richmond: Commonwealth of Virginia Archives, n.d.

Hoadley, Frank T., and Browne, Benjamin P. *Baptists Who Dared*. Valley Forge, Pa.: Judson Press, 1980.

Hoover, J. Edgar. ''Why I Believe in the Sunday School.'' *United Evangelical Action* 10 (September 1951).

Indiana Baptist Annual. Indiana Baptist Convention, 1913.

Ireland, James. *The Life of the Rev. James Ireland.* Edited by Arthur C. Johnson. 1819. Reprint. Ashland, Ky.: Economy Printers, n.d.

Ivimey, Joseph. *History of the English Baptists.* London: Bruditt and Morris, 1811.

———. *Memoir of William Fox, Esq., Founder of the Sunday School Society.* Edited by George Whightman. London: n.p., 1831.

James, Charles F. *A Documentary History of the Struggle for Religious Liberty in Virginia.* 1900. Reprint. New York: Da Capo Press, 1971.

Jellema, Dirk. *The New International Dictionary of the Christian Church.* Edited by J. D. Douglas. Grand Rapids: Zondervan Publishing House, 1974.

Jewett, Milo P. *The Mode and Subjects of Baptism.* Philadelphia: American Baptist Publication and Sunday School Society, 1845.

Johnson, Elizabeth J., and Wheaton, James Lucas, IV. "The Annotated Index—Reminiscences and New Series of Rev. David Benedict." *History of Pawtucket, Rhode Island.* Pawtucket, R.I.: Spaulding House Publishing Co., 1986.

Kenworthy, James. *History of the Baptist Church at Hill Cliffe.* 1882. Reprint. Gallatin, Tenn.: Church History Research and Archives, 1987.

King, Joe M. *A History of South Carolina Baptists.* Columbia: South Carolina Baptist Convention, 1964.

Knapp, Christopher. *Who Wrote Our Hymns?* Denver: Willson Foundation, n.d.

Knowles, James D. *Memoir of Ann H. Judson.* Philadelphia: American Baptist Publication Society, 1835.

Latch, Ollie. *History of the General Baptists.* Poplar Bluff, Mo.: General Baptist Press, 1954.

Light, Alfred W. *Bunhill Fields.* London: C. J. Farncombe and Sons, 1915.

Little, Lewis Peyton. *Imprisoned Preachers and Religious Liberty in Virginia.* Lynchburg, Va.: J. P. Bell Co., 1938.

Loudon, Archibald. *A Selection of Some of the Most Interesting Narratives of Outrages Committed by the Indians in Their Wars with the White People.* Vol. 1. Carlisle, Pa.: n.p., 1808.

Lumpkin, William L. *Baptist Foundations in the South.* Nashville: Broadman Press, 1961.

March, W.H.H. *The Modern Sunday School.* Philadelphia: American Baptist Publication Society, 1874.

Marsden, George M. *Fundamentalism and American Culture.* New York: Oxford University Press, 1980.

Marshall, Jabez P. *Memoirs of the Late Rev. Abraham Marshall.* Mount Zion, Ga.: Published by the author, 1824.

Massey, Homer, ed. "The Struggle for Religious Liberty." *Forgotten Facts of Virginia's History.* Norfolk, Va.: Published by the author, n.d.

McBeth, H. Leon. *The Baptist Heritage*. Nashville: Broadman Press, 1987.

———. *The First Baptist Church of Dallas*. Grand Rapids: Zondervan Publishing House, 1968.

McInturff, J. B. *The Old Paths: They Being Dead Yet Speak*. Woodstock, Va.: W. N. Grabill, 1897.

McKibbens, Thomas R., Jr., and Smith, Kenneth L. *The Life and Works of Morgan Edwards*. New York: Arno Press, 1980.

McLoughlin, William G., ed. *The Diary of Isaac Backus*. 3 vols. Providence: Brown University Press, 1979.

———. *Isaac Backus and the American Pietistic Tradition*. Boston: Little, Brown and Co., 1967.

Metropolitan Tabernacle Pulpit. Vol. 7. Reprint. Pasadena, Texas: Pilgrim Publications, 1969.

Meyer, Joseph, ed. *Baptist Establishers of Religious Liberty*. Chicago: Privately printed, 1923.

Minutes of the Illinois Baptist Pastoral Union. Alton, Ill.: S. V. Crossman and Co., 1865.

Minutes of the Ketocton Association of Regular Baptists. Luray, Va.: n.p., 1989.

Minutes of the Twenty-Ninth Annual Meeting of the Illinois Baptist Pastoral Union. Edited by J.D.C. Aurora, Ill.: Knickerbocker and Hodder, 1874.

Mitchell, S. H. *The Indian Chief, Journeycake*. Philadelphia: American Baptist Publication Society, 1895.

Moon, Norman S. *Education for Ministry—Bristol Baptist College, 1679-1979*. Bristol, England: Bristol Baptist College, n.d.

Morris, Dan, and Morris, Inez. *Who Was Who in American Politics*. New York: Hawthorn Books, 1974.

Mosher, R. C. *The Baptist in History*. Albert Lea, Minn.: Simonson and Whitcomb, 1900.

Moss, Lemuel, ed. *The Baptists and the National Centenary*. Philadelphia: American Baptist Publication Society, 1876.

Mosteller, James Donovan. *A History of the Kiokee Baptist Church in Georgia*. Ann Arbor: Edwards Brothers, 1952.

Moyer, Englin S. *Who Was Who in Church History*. Chicago: Moody Press, 1962.

Mullins, E. Y. *Baptist Beliefs*. Philadelphia: Judson Press, 1925.

Murray, Iain H. *The Forgotten Spurgeon*. London: Banner of Truth Trust, 1966.

New Catholic Edition of the Holy Bible. New York: Catholic Book Publishing Co., 1954.

Newman, Albert Henry. *A Century of Baptist Achievement*. Philadelphia: American Baptist Publication Society, 1901.

———. *A History of the Baptist Churches in the United States*. Philadelphia: American Baptist Publication Society, 1915.

———. *A Manual of Church History*. Philadelphia: American Baptist Publication Society, 1948.

Newman, Robert C. *Baptists and the American Tradition*. Des Plaines, Ill.: Regular Baptist Press, 1976.

Northrop, Henry D. *Life and Works of Rev. Charles H. Spurgeon*. Philadelphia: Monarch Book Co., 1891.

Offar, George. ''Memoir of John Bunyan.'' Introduction to *The Pilgrim's Progress*. London: Routledge, Warne and Routledge, 1861.

Olson, Adolf. *A Centenary History*. Chicago: Baptist General Conference, n.d.

Our Most Indispensable Institution. Chicago: National Sunday School Association, n.d.

Paschal, George Washington. *History of North Carolina Baptists*. 2 vols. Raleigh: Edwards and Broughton, 1930.

Pawtucket Gazette & Chronicle. Pawtucket, R.I. 15 September 1876.

Pierson, Delavan L. *Arthur T. Pierson*. New York: Fleming H. Revell Co., 1912.

Prestridge, J. N. *Modern Baptist Heroes and Martyrs*. Louisville: World Press, 1911.

Quincy, Josiah. *The History of Harvard University*. Vol. 1. Cambridge, Mass.: John Owen, 1840.

Ramsbottom, B. A. *Samuel Medley—Preacher, Pastor, Poet*. Rushden, Northamptonshire: Fauconberg Press, 1978.

———. *Stranger Than Fiction*. Harpenden, England: Gospel Standard Trust Publications Co., 1989.

Representative Men and Old Families of Rhode Island. Chicago: J. H. Beers and Co., 1908.

Riley, B. F. *History of the Baptists of Texas*. Dallas: Published by the author, 1907.

Russell, C. Allyn. *Voices of American Fundamentalism*. Philadelphia: Westminster Press, 1976.

Rutland, Robert Allen. *The Birth of the Bill of Rights, 1776-1791*. Chapel Hill, N.C.: University of North Carolina Press, 1955.

Santayana, George. *The Life of Reason*. New York: Charles Scribner's Sons, 1953.

Sassaman, Richard. ''The Original 'Big Cheese.' '' *American History Illustrated*. January 1989, pp. 34-35.

Scarborough, L. R. *The Tears of Jesus*. New York: George H. Doran and Co., 1922.

Schaff, Philip. *History of the Christian Church*. Vol. 8. Grand Rapids: Eerdmans Publishing Co., 1958.

Scott, Anna Kay. *An Autobiography of Anna Kay Scott, M.D.* Chicago: Published by the author, 1917.

Semple, Robert Baylor. *History of the Baptists in Virginia.* Rev. ed. 1972. Reprint. Lafayette, Tenn.: Church History Research and Archives,1976.

———. *A History of the Rise and Progress of the Baptists in Virginia.* Richmond: Published by the author, 1810.

Shindler, R. *From the Usher's Desk to the Tabernacle Pulpit.* London: Passmore and Alabaster, 1892.

Wa, Maung Shwe. *Burma Baptist Chronicle.* Rangoon: Burma Baptist Convention, 1963.

Slaughter, Linda W. *Leaves from Northwestern History.* Vol. 1. Bismarck: Historical Society of North Dakota, 1906.

Smellie, Alexander. *Men of the Covenant.* Edinburgh, Scotland: Banner of Truth Trust, 1975.

Smith, Alfred B. *Al Smith's Treasury of Hymn Histories.* Greenville, S.C.: Better Music Publications, 1985.

Soderlind, Arthur E. *Colonial Connecticut.* New York: Thomas Nelson Inc., 1976.

Speeches and Letters of Abraham Lincoln, 1832-1865. New York: E. P. Dutton and Co., 1907.

Spencer, J. H. *A History of Kentucky Baptists from 1769 to 1885.* 2 vols. Cincinnati: J. R. Baumes, 1886.

Sprague, William B. *Annals of the American Pulpit.* Vol. 6. New York: Robert Carter and Bros., 1865.

Spurgeon, Charles H. *Autobiography of Charles H. Spurgeon.* 4 vols. Philadelphia: American Baptist Publication Society, n.d.

Stevens, Daniel Gurden. *The First Hundred Years of the American Baptist Publication Society.* Philadelphia: American Baptist Publication Society, n.d.

Stewart, Walter Sinclair. *Early Baptist Missionaries and Pioneers.* Philadelphia: Judson Press, 1925.

———. *Later Baptist Missionaries and Pioneers.* Philadelphia: Judson Press, 1928.

Stiansen, P. *History of the Baptists in Norway.* Chicago: Blessing Press, 1933.

Strong, Polly. *Burning Wicks.* Cleveland: Baptist Mid-Missions, 1984.

Sumner, Robert L. *Man Sent from God.* Grand Rapids: Eerdmans Publishing Co., n.d.

Sweet, William Warren. *Religion on the American Frontier—The Baptists.* New York: Cooper Square Publications, 1964.

———. *The Story of Religion in America.* 1950. Reprint. Grand Rapids: Baker Book House, 1973.

Taylor, George Braxton. *Virginia Baptist Ministers*. Third Series. Lynchburg, Va.: J. P. Bell Co., 1912.

Terrill, Edward. *The Records of a Church of Christ Meeting in Broadmead, Bristol*. Edited by Nathaniel Haycroft. London: J. Heaton and Son, 1865.

Thompson, Ronald W. *Heroes of the Baptist Church*. London: Carey Kingsgate Press, 1948.

Torbet, Robert G. *A History of the Baptists*. Philadelphia: Judson Press, 1950.

Trowbridge, M.E.D. *History of Baptists in Michigan*. N.p.: Michigan Baptist State Convention, 1909.

Underhill, Edward Bean, ed. *A Martyrology of the Churches of Christ Commonly Called Baptists*. Vol. 2. Translated by T. J. Van Braght. London: J. Haddon and Son, 1853.

Underhill, Edward Bean, ed., *Confessions of Faith and Other Documents Illustrative of the History of the Baptist Churches of England in the 17th Century*. London: Haddon Bros., 1845.

Valley Forge, Pa. American Baptists Missionary Society Archives. Missionary Register of the American Baptist Missionary Union.

Van Braght, Thieleman J., Jr. *The Bloody Theater; or, Martyrs Mirror of the Defenseless Christians*. Scottsdale, Pa.: Herald Press, 1950.

Vedder, Henry C. *A Century of Baptist Achievement*. Edited by A. H. Newman. Philadelphia: American Baptist Publication Society, 1901.

———. *A Short History of Baptist Missions*. 1907. Reprint. Philadelphia: Judson Press, 1927.

Verduin, Leonard. *The Anatomy of a Hybrid*. Grand Rapids: Eerdmans Publishing Co., 1976.

———. *The Reformers and Their Stepchildren*. Grand Rapids: Eerdmans Publishing Co., 1961.

Vojta, Vaclav. *Czechoslovak Baptists*. Minneapolis: Czechoslovak Baptist Convention, 1941.

Walker, Charles O. *A History of the Georgia Baptist Association 1874-1984*. Atlanta: Georgia Baptist Historical Society, 1988.

Wayland, Francis. *A History of the Life and Labors of the Rev. Adoniram Judson*. Vol. 1. New York: Sheldon and Co., 1860.

Webster's Biographical Dictionary. Springfield, Mass.: G. and C. Merriam Co., 1972.

Weston, David. *The Baptists and the National Centenary*. Edited by Lemuel Moss. Philadelphia: American Baptist Publication Society, 1876.

White, B. R. *A History of the English Baptists*. Vol. 1. N.p.: American Baptist Historical Society, n.d.

White, Blanche Sydnor. *First Baptist Church, Richmond—1780-1955*. Richmond: Whittet and Shepperson, 1955.

White, Charles L. *A Century of Faith*. Philadelphia: Judson Press, 1932.

Whitley, W. T. *A History of British Baptists*. London: Charles Griffin and Co., 1923.

Whitman, Mary Ross. *George Wightman of Quidnessett, R.I., (1632-1721/22) and Descendants*. Chicago: n.p., 1939.

Woolley, David Collier. *Baptist Advance*. Nashville: Broadman Press, 1964.

World Book Encyclopedia. Vol. 2. Chicago: Doubleday and Co., 1968.

The 1980 World Book Year Book. Chicago: Doubleday and Co., 1980.

Would You Cheat Your Child? Chicago: National Sunday School Association, n.d.

Wright, Louis B. *The Cultural Life of the American Colonies*. New York: Harper and Row, 1962.

Wyeth, Walter N. *Ann H. Judson*. Cincinnati: n.p., 1888.

Ypeij, Anne, and Dermount, Isaac Johannes. *Geschiedenis der Nederlandsche Hervormde Kerk*. [History of the Dutch Reformed Church]. Te Breda: W. Van Bergen en Comp., 1819.

Index